MANAGERIAL ACCOUNTING

SIXTH EDITION

CARL L. MOORE, MA, CPA

Professor of Accounting
Lehigh University

ROBERT K. JAEDICKE, PhD

William R. Kimball Professor of Accounting
Dean of Graduate School of Business
Stanford University

LANE K. ANDERSON, PhD, CPA, CMA

Professor of Accounting
Texas Tech University

Published by

A95 **SOUTH-WESTERN PUBLISHING CO.**

CINCINNATI   WEST CHICAGO, IL   DALLAS   PELHAM MANOR, NY   PALO ALTO, CA

PREFACE

The objective of this edition of *Managerial Accounting*, as it was in the earlier editions, is to explain how accounting data can be interpreted and applied by management in planning and controlling business activities. The major purpose of this book is to show how accounting can help to solve the problems that confront those who are directly responsible for the management of an enterprise. Attention is also given to the use of accounting data by investors and potential investors whenever appropriate.

The book is intended for a one-semester or a one-quarter course for students who expect to use accounting data in their future occupations. We believe that accounting majors will benefit from this material as much as those students who are studying other fields of business and economics. Professional accountants must be as familiar with the use of accounting data as they are with its collection and presentation. It is important for accountants to know the *why* as well as the *how*. Students should use this book after having had a one-semester or two-quarter course in the introductory principles of accounting. Students who need a review of introductory accounting are referred to Appendixes A and B, which deal concisely with the accounting cycle.

The textbook may be used for undergraduate courses, for MBA students, and for executive development programs. It is not an advanced level text but, instead, is intended to give the student an introductory level exposure to how accounting data can be useful in the management of a business or a not-for-profit enterprise.

While concepts and theories are discussed to some extent as an aid in understanding, the primary focus is on the pragmatic aspects. Illustrations and examples are given throughout the text to show how accounting data can be applied in the solution of management problems. It is expected that a student completing the course will have not just a theoretical background but will be able to put the concepts to work in actual situations.

Organization of Material

The basic structure of the fifth edition has been retained with chapters being arranged more closely by topics or parts.

This edition consists of an introduction and four parts:

Part		Chapters
	Introduction	1
I	Manufacturing Costs and Control	2-5
II	Cost Behavior and Profit Planning	6-8
III	Analysis and Decision Making	9-15
IV	Interfaces of Financial and Managerial Accounting	16-18

Chapter 1 serves as an introduction and makes a distinction between financial and managerial accounting. The role of the accountant in the business organization is discussed more completely than in earlier editions. The concept of a budget is introduced to show how management makes use of a budget in control and planning situations.

In Part I, cost concepts and terminology are explained and illustrated in Chapter 2. In this edition, particular attention is paid to the difference in the measurement of cost flow between merchandising organizations and manufacturing organizations. Chapter 3 deals with manufacturing costs and how they are organized in costing products and in tracing costs through the entity. The job order cost system is emphasized with process cost accounting being included in a chapter appendix. Questions, exercises, and problems are provided for both types of cost accounting systems. The concepts of standard cost accounting as applied to direct materials and direct labor are covered in Chapter 4. Coverage includes material on how data can be used to control costs. Chapter 5 discusses manufacturing overhead in a standard cost accounting system. Variances are explained and computed as an aid to improved budgeting and control. In this edition, more attention has been given to governmental and not-for-profit entities. Illustrations are given to bring out differences in points of view and to show how the general concepts of planning and control for manfacturing organizations can be adapted for governmental or not-for-profit organizations.

In Part II, cost behavior and profit planning are stressed. Chapter 6 deals with the segregation of semivariable costs into variable and fixed components.

Emphasis is placed on how more accurate cost estimation leads to better budgeting and cost control. Cost, volume, and profit relationships are discussed in Chapter 7. The various ways in which a company can use the break-even concept to improve profitability are emphasized. The concept of variable costing (direct costing) is compared with the concept of absorption costing in Chapter 8. The advantages of both approaches are discussed.

Part III shows how accounting information can be used for planning and making decisions. Chapter 9 deals with the way in which revenue and cost data can be applied in making special managerial decisions. In Chapter 10, the use of data in special decisional situations is illustrated for specific applications such as make or buy and product pricing. Chapter 11 goes into the time value of money and how this is especially important in making capital investment decisions. The various complexities of capital investment planning are discussed in Chapter 12, including the various provisions of the Economic Recovery Tax Act of 1981. In Chapter 13, attention is directed to the problems of management in a decentralized operation.

In Part IV are included topics that are important to both financial and managerial accounting. An introduction to the budget process is given in Chapter 14. Chapter 15 continues with a master budget plan, showing how all aspects of budget planning are brought together. Chapter 16 deals with the problem of changing prices and their effect on the comparability of financial data. In Chapter 17 the analysis of financial statements is covered. Chapter 18 discusses the importance of net working capital and cash flow and shows how they can be computed.

Special Highlights of the Text

Chapter 1	Managerial Accounting and the Management Process	In this introductory chapter, material has been added to explain more fully the accountant's role and position in the organization.
Chapter 5	Manufacturing Overhead Cost Control	This chapter has been expanded to provide material on how governmental and not-for-profit organizations can apply the principles of managerial accounting.
Chapters 9 and 10	Accounting Data for Managerial Decisions I and II	This subject area has been expanded with two chapters included to provide a better theoretical background for applications.

Chapters 11 and 12	Capital Investment Decisions I and II	The capital investment area has also been expanded to provide a thorough theoretical background in Chapter 11 followed by applications in Chapter 12. Provisions of the Economic Recovery Tax Act of 1981 are included, and options in selecting the investment tax credit with ACRS depreciation are also covered.
Chapter 16	The Price-Level Problem	This chapter has been completely rewritten, includes material from FASB 33, and covers both constant dollar and current cost accounting.

In addition to the revision of the chapters themselves, other features have been added. Chapter objectives have been inserted at the beginning of each chapter. A terminology review has been placed at the end of each chapter to help the student in studying important concepts that were discussed.

The end-of-chapter material has been extensively revised. The basic format is the same with questions, exercises, and problems. All the exercises and problems for each chapter have been revised and additional exercises and problems have been added. Many long problems have been retained, but attention has been placed primarily upon providing a greater variety and number of short exercises and problems. (Student check figures are available for all chapter problems.)

The test bank is completely different. The instructor can prepare a test by selecting from the variety of short problems or multiple-choice type exercises.

In this edition, for the first time, there is a student study guide. This has been added to help the student organize the material presented.

Suggestions for Sequencing Material

The chapters may be assigned in sequence, or they may be assigned in a different order, depending upon the background of the class and the objectives of the course. With students who need a review of basic accounting, it may be helpful to start with Appendixes A and B. Some instructors may prefer to discuss cost behavior (Chapter 6) immediately after Chapter 2. Other instructors may want to begin this course with Part IV, building upon the students' exposure to financial accounting. Chapter 16, for example, on price-level problems can be assigned early in the course if desired. Also, in subject areas that have been expanded into two chapters such as managerial decisions, capital investment decisions, and budgets, some instructors may want to assign both chapters as one unit. To an extent, this choice will depend upon the background of the students and the time available for the course.

The authors acknowledge with gratitude the many helpful comments received from instructors and students who have used the fifth edition. Particular recognition is given for the help received from Professors James A. Largay III, Lehigh University, who reviewed Chapter 16, and to Arthur Kagle, Central Michigan University, and I. Max Reed, Eastern Kentucky University.

In addition we are grateful to Sharon M. Ruhf who typed and edited much of the manuscript.

We are indebted for the use of materials included in the publications of the American Institute of Certified Public Accountants, the Financial Accounting Standards Board, and the National Association of Accountants.

Carl L. Moore
Robert K. Jaedicke
Lane K. Anderson

CONTENTS

INTRODUCTION

1 MANAGERIAL ACCOUNTING AND THE
   MANAGEMENT PROCESS   1
   Financial Accounting, 2: The Regulation of Accounting, 2; Organization of
   the Firm, 2; Finance, 3 ● Managerial Accounting, 4 ● Scope of Managerial
   Accounting, 5 ● The Objective of Management, 5 ● Planning and Control
   Decisions, 6: Levels of Management, 6; Classifying Decisions, 8 ● Classification of Decisions by Function and Time Element, 8 ● The Contribution of
   the Accountant, 9 ● Planning, 10: Budgets, 11; The Advantages of Budgets,
   11 ● The Scope of Budgeting, 12: Project or Product Budget, 12; Responsibility Budget, 12; Capital Investment Budget, 13; Personal Attitudes, 13 ●
   Master Budget Plan, 14 ● The Budget Period, 14 ● The Timing Concept,
   15 ● Preparation of the Budgets, 15: Specialized Decisions, 17; Differential
   Revenue and Costs, 18 ● Control, 18 ● The Use of Accounting Data, 19.

MANUFACTURING COSTS AND CONTROL

2 COST CONCEPTS AND CLASSIFICATIONS   23
   Cost Concepts, 24 ● Costs for Planning, 24: Differential Costs, 25; Sunk
   Costs, 26; Opportunity Costs, 26; An Illustration of Decision-Making Costs,

27 • Costs and Control, 28: Direct and Indirect Costs, 30; Cost Allocations, 30; Controllable and Noncontrollable Costs, 32 • **Responsibility Accounting, 33**: Cost Reports, 34; Some Difficulties with Responsibility Accounting, 36; Control Features, 37 • **Income Measurement, 39**: Merchandise Inventory Flow, 39; Manufacturing Inventory Flow, 40; Period Cost, 41; Product Cost, 41; Cost Accounting Beyond the Manufacturing Area, 41; The Cost Elements, 42; The Costing Procedure, 43; Fixed and Variable Costs, 44.

3 MANUFACTURING COSTS   60
The Job Order Cost System, 61 • **Costing Direct Materials and Direct Labor, 61**: Costing Factory Overhead, 64; Control of Factory Overhead, 67; Normal Capacity, 71 • **A Job Order Cost Illustration, 71** • **Appendix: The Process Cost System, 75**: The Departmental Production Report, 75; A Process Cost Flow, 75; The Equivalent Unit Concept, 78; The Cost Elements, 79.

4 MATERIALS AND LABOR COST CONTROL   93
The Use of Standards, 94: Advantages of Standard Cost Accounting, 95; The Quality of Standards, 96 • **Revising the Standards, 98** • **Materials Standards and Control, 99**: Materials Price Variance, 99; Materials Quantity Variance, 101; Materials Acquisition, 103; The Inventory Level, 103 • **Labor Standards and Control, 105**; Labor Rate Variance, 105: Labor Efficiency Variance, 106 • **Summary of Variances, 110** • **Appendix: Some Quantitative Methods—Materials and Labor, 111** • **Materials, 111**: Balancing Order and Storage Costs, 111; Shipping Routes, 115 • **Labor, 116**: The Learning Curve, 117.

5 MANUFACTURING OVERHEAD COST CONTROL   133
A Flexible Budget and Variances, 134 • **Overhead Variances, 135**: The Spending Variance, 135; The Efficiency Variance, 136; The Controllable Variance, 136; Capacity or Volume Variance, 137; Plant Capacity and Control, 138 • **Summary of Overhead Variances, 140** • **A Standard Cost Illustration, 141** • **Nonmanufacturing Costs, 144**: Merchandising and Service Entities, 145; Not-for-Profit and Governmental Entities, 146.

COST BEHAVIOR AND PROFIT PLANNING

2

6 COST BEHAVIOR AND ESTIMATION   165
Fixed Costs, 166 • Variable Costs, 166 • Cost Behavior Options, 167 • Cost Segregation, 167: The Visual Fit, 168; The High-Low Point Method, 170; Least Squares Method, 170 • **Control Limits, 172**: Normal Distribution, 172; Checking Some Inferences, 175 • **Correlation, 177**: The r^2 Test, 179; Multiple Regression, 183.

7 COST, VOLUME, PROFIT RELATIONSHIPS   199
Break-Even Analysis, 200: The Break-Even Chart, 201; Cost Detail on the Break-Even Chart, 201; Curvature of Revenue and Cost Lines, 204; An

Alternative Form of Break-Even Analysis, 204 • **The Profit-Volume Graph,** **206:** Sales Volume, 207; Variable Costs, 208; Price Policy, 210; Fixed Costs, 213 • **Variable or Fixed Cost Decision, 214** • Changes in the Sales Mix, 216 • **Short-Term and Long-Term Plans, 219.**

8   **VARIABLE COSTING**   **235**
Absorption Costing, 235 • Variable Costing, 237 • Absorption and Variable Costing Compared, 237 • A Balance of Sales and Production, 239 • Sales and Production out of Balance, 241 • Profits and Inventory, 244 • Emphasis on Production or Sales, 245 • The Advantages of Variable Costing, 245 • The Disadvantages of Variable Costing, 246 • Variable Costing in Planning and Decision Making, 247 • Variable Costing and Budget Variances, 248.

ANALYSIS AND DECISION MAKING

3

9   **ACCOUNTING DATA FOR MANAGERIAL DECISIONS–I**   **265**
Decision Making—an Overview, 266: The Problem, 266; The Decision Rule, 266; The Available Alternatives, 266; The Consequences of Actions, 267; Evaluating Alternatives, 267; Choosing the Best Alternative, 267; The Decision, 267 • **Identification of Alternatives, 267:** The Problem and the Alternatives, 268; Importance of Prediction, 269; Accounting Data and Prediction, 269 • **Evaluation of Alternatives, 270:** Relevant Revenues, 271; Relevant Cost, 272; Review of Other Cost Concepts Useful for Predicting Differential Costs, 274 • **The Form of the Analysis, 277:** The Use of Breakeven Analysis, 277; Total vs. Incremental Analysis, 278.

10   **ACCOUNTING DATA FOR MANAGERIAL DECISIONS–II**   **292**
Combination Decisions, 293: Process or Sell, 293; Product Combinations, 294; Make or Buy, 299; The Elimination of a Product Line, 300 • **The Pricing Decision, 301:** Price Based on Full Cost, 301; Variable Cost Pricing, 305; Outside Influences on Price, 309.

11   **CAPITAL INVESTMENT DECISIONS–I**   **322**
The Time Value of Money, 323: Future Value of Money, 324; Present Value of Money, 326; The Present Value of a Series of Future Cash Flows, 328; Comparison of the Present Value and Future Value of a Series of Cash Flows, 330 • **Present Value Analysis Applied, 331:** Financial Decision Examples, 331; Approximation of the Interest Rate, 334; A Simple Capital Investment Example, 334; Capital Investments in Not-for-Profit Organizations, 335.

12   **CAPITAL INVESTMENT DECISIONS–II**   **343**
Comparison of Capital Investment Decisions with Decisions Not Involving Capital Investment, 344 • The Capital Budgeting Process, 345: An Overview, 346; The Net Investment, 346; The Net Returns, 347; The Lowest Acceptable Rate of Return, 347 • **Rating Investment Alternatives, 347:** The Payback Method, 347; The Discounted Rate of Return Method, 348; The

Net Present Value Method, 350 • **Refining the Investment, 351:** Avoidable Costs, 351; Additional Investment in Current Assets, 352; Net Proceeds from the Sale of Other Properties, 353 • **Income Tax Effects, 354:** Depreciation, 354; Tax Advantage of Accelerated Depreciation, 356; Depreciation Deductions Under the Current Tax Law, 358; The Investment Tax Credit, 360; Immediate Expensing of Assets, 360; Tax Options, 361; Illustration— Tax Options, 361 • **Incremental Returns, 364** • **The Evaluation Process, 366:** Anticipation of Change, 367; The Post Audit, 368.

13   MANAGERIAL CONTROL AND DECISION MAKING IN DECENTRALIZED OPERATIONS   **379**
The Criteria Needed for a Control System, 380 • **The Profit Index, 382:** Division Net Profit, 383; Division Direct Profit, 384; Division Controllable Profit, 384; Division Contribution Margin, 385 • **Some Problems in Using Division Controllable Profit as an Evaluation Index, 385** • **Determining Division Investment, 387:** The Investment Base, 387; Residual Income, 388 • **The Intracompany or Transfer Pricing Problem, 389:** Market Price, 390; Negotiated or Bargained Market Price, 391; Transfer Price Based on Cost, 392; Dual Transfer Prices, 393 • **Transfer Prices for Decision Making—A System of Information and Communication, 395:** The Intermediate Market Case, 396; The No Intermediate Market Case, 400 • **The Evaluation Criterion or Standard, 400.**

14   THE BUDGET PROCESS   **417**
Sales Forecasting, 417: Wide Variety of Factors Affecting Sales, 418; Basis for Sales Forecasts, 418 • **Models for Planning, 419** • **A Sales Budget Illustration, 422** • **Sales and Production, 423** • **Inventories and Production, 424** • **The Production Budget Illustrated, 425.**

15   A MASTER BUDGET PLAN   **432**
The Manufacturing Cost Budget, 434: The District Materials Budget, 434; The Purchases Budget, 435; The Direct Labor Budget, 437; The Factory Overhead Budget, 438 • **The Selling Expense Budget, 440** • **The General and Administrative Expense Budget, 441** • **The Capital Budget, 443** • **The Cash Receipts Budget, 443** • **The Cash Payments Budget, 445** • **Financial Planning, 446** • **The Estimated Income Statement, 447** • **The Estimated Balance Sheet, 449** • **Work Sheet, 451** • **The Use of Budgets, 452.**

INTERFACES OF FINANCIAL AND MANAGERIAL ACCOUNTING

4

16   THE PRICE-LEVEL PROBLEM   **471**
The Character of Assets and Equities, 473: Monetary Items, 473; Non-Monetary Items, 474 • **More Recent Costs Matched Against Revenues, 474:** Lifo Inventory, 475; Accelerated Depreciation, 475 • **Illustration—Historical Cost/Constant Dollar Statements, 476** • **Illustration—Historical Cost/Current Cost Statements, 480** • **Illustration—Current Cost/Constant Dollar**

Statements, 482 ● Managerial Policy and Price Level, 485: Plant Asset Replacement, 485; Dividend Policy, 486; Holding Gains and Losses, 486.

17   ANALYSIS OF FINANCIAL STATEMENTS   504
Rate-of-Return Concept, 505: Rate of Return—Assets, 505; The Management of Assets, 508; Leverage, 512; Earnings and Market Value of Stock, 515 ● Comprehensive Analysis, 516 ● Some Hazards of Analysis, 516: A Mixture of Valuations, 517; Differences Between Companies, 517; Variations in Accounting Methods and Estimates, 517; An Average Concept, 517 ● Illustration of Analysis, 518: A Review of Earning Power, 519; The Management of Working Capital, 521; The Equity Relationships, 524; Net Income and Fixed Charges, 525; An Evaluation of the Company, 525.

**18   TRACING THE FLOW OF NET WORKING CAPITAL AND
       CASH   547**
Description and Evaluation of the Statements, 548 ● The Significance of Net Working Capital Flows, 549 ● Net Working Capital Flows, 549: Sources of Net Working Capital, 550; Uses of Net Working Capital, 552 ● A Comprehensive Illustration—Sources and Uses of Net Working Capital, 553: Step One—Schedule of Changes in Net Working Capital, 555; Step Two—Net Working Capital from Operations, 555; Step Three—Analysis of Noncurrent Items, 556; Statement of Sources and Uses of Net Working Capital, 558; Statement of Changes in Financial Position, 558 ● The Demand for Net Working Capital, 558 ● Cash Flow, 559: Cash and Operations, 561; Analysis of Other Current Items, 565; A Statement of Cash Flow, 565; Simplified Cash Flow from Operations, 566

**APPENDIX A ● AN OVERVIEW OF THE
ACCOUNTING PROCESS   592**

**APPENDIX B ● THE ACCOUNTING CYCLE:
PRACTICE PROBLEMS   632**

APPENDIX C ● THE PRESENT VALUE CONCEPT   640

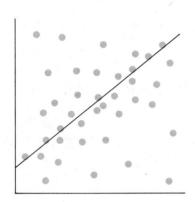

1 Introduction

MANAGERIAL ACCOUNTING AND THE MANAGEMENT PROCESS

Chapter Objectives

After studying Chapter One, you will be able to:

1. Understand the difference in the point of view between financial accounting and managerial accounting.
2. Explain how the functions of management are carried out by planning and control decisions.
3. Describe the concept of budgeting and how the feedback of information can lead to both better plans and better control.
4. Explain how attitudes toward budgets can lead to the success or failure of a budget system.
5. Describe how control can be accomplished through reports prepared on a responsibility accounting basis.

The subject of accounting may be approached from two general points of view:

1. Financial accounting.
2. Managerial accounting.

The objective in financial accounting is to organize financial information for presentation to the general public. In managerial accounting, the objective is to organize or to reorganize financial information so that it can be used by the internal management of the enterprise. In short, financial accounting concentrates on the outside user of financial data while managerial accounting concentrates on the inside user, the management. Strict lines of distinction are not necessarily observed. Often there is overlap with financial accounting data being used by internal management and managerial data being supplied to outsiders as a part of the financial accounting function.

FINANCIAL ACCOUNTING

The concepts and principles of financial accounting should be understood by the person undertaking the study of managerial accounting. Financial information is frequently collected, classified, recorded, and summarized for reports and statements, and since this information is presented to various segments of the public, it is necessary to follow certain rules and regulations.

The Regulation of Accounting

The Securities and Exchange Commission (SEC) was established in 1934 by an act of Congress for the purpose of regulating security exchanges and the marketing of securities of corporations whose stock is held by the general public. As a part of this overall function, the SEC requires that financial reports be prepared in accordance with generally accepted accounting principles. These reports must be filed with the SEC.

The SEC has, for the most part, delegated the task of establishing generally accepted accounting principles to the private sector. In 1973, the Financial Accounting Standards Board (FASB) was formed under the auspices of the American Institute of Certified Public Accountants (AICPA) and other professional accounting associations for the purpose of making special accounting studies leading to the issuance of discussion memoranda, statements, and interpretations of various accounting principles and applications in specific situations. The FASB, consisting of full-time members, replaced the Accounting Principles Board (APB). The APB was made up of part-time members who were drawn from the accounting profession. Many of the opinions issued by the APB are still in force along with the statements of the FASB.

Other regulatory bodies, such as the Federal Power Commission, the Interstate Commerce Commission, state public utility commissions, and state insurance commissions, set forth more specific reporting requirements for organizations that fall within their jurisdiction.

Without regulation and without prescribed principles of accounting and reporting standards, the public would be confused by a variety of accounting presentations and could easily be misled. Modern business is complex, and guidelines must be provided for financial reporting.

Organization of the Firm

Responsibility for the design and operation of the accounting system within an enterprise rests upon the chief financial officer and the operating staff. An abbreviated form of organization chart shows how the finance vice-president, the treasurer, and the controller fit into the organization.

The governing board that sets general policies for the entity is called the board of directors, board of trustees, board of governors, or other designation according to the type of organization and custom. Responsibility for the operation of the entity on a day-to-day basis is vested in the president, who in turn delegates authority in various functional areas to vice-presidents.

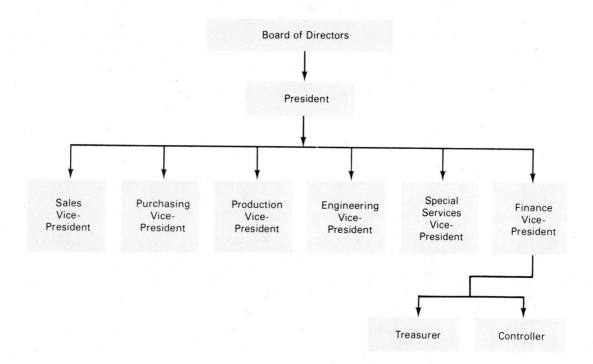

Finance

The vice-president of finance is responsible for the accounting and monetary functions of the entity. The treasurer, operating under the vice-president of finance, is responsible for granting credit, collecting and depositing money, disbursing money, and obtaining credit. Essentially, the treasurer's function is a monetary function. The controller, on the other hand, has the following responsibilities:

1. Design of the accounting system.
2. Operation of the system:
   (a) General ledger
   (b) Accounts receivable
       Accounts payable
   (c) Inventory accounting
   (d) Plant accounting
3. Tax planning and accounting

4. Budgets and budgetary control
5. Internal audit
6. Operational review

The functions of the controller may be classified or handled in various ways, depending upon company policy and differences in preference. In general, the controller is responsible for the design of the accounting system, its operation, and the preparation of financial statements and reports that meet government or regulatory requirements. In addition, the controller is responsible for budgets, an internal review of operations for accuracy and conformity to policies, and a review of operations for the purpose of finding ways to improve profitability. In some organizations, the operational review is included as a part of the internal audit function.

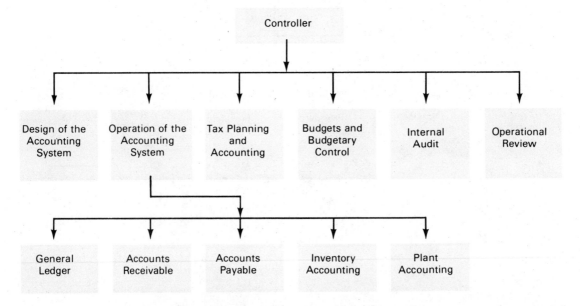

The student of accounting first learns about the operation of an accounting system in a financial accounting course. Subsequent courses expand on financial accounting and deal with specialized topics such as information systems, tax accounting, and auditing. Managerial accounting concentrates on the budgeting and operational review aspects.

MANAGERIAL ACCOUNTING

Managerial accounting, or **management accounting**, is a segment of accounting that deals specifically with how accounting data and other financial information can be used in the management of business, governmental, or not-for-profit entities. Because managerial accounting is designed to assist internal management, it is relatively free from the restrictions imposed by regulatory bodies that prescribe how accounting information should be presented to the public.

Although managerial accounting is to a large extent free from restrictions, it does rely upon broad general concepts and certain applications that are most useful to management. Specific applications in given situations, however, depend upon the needs and preferences of the individual managers who are to receive the information.

SCOPE OF MANAGERIAL ACCOUNTING

Often it is thought that managerial accounting is a variation of cost accounting and that it deals exclusively with costs and prices. Cost and price data are very important, but management cannot afford to limit itself to this area.

Management wants to consider the total situation. For example, if management decides to finance business growth with long-term debt, it may question: What effect will this decision have upon the earnings per share of stock? Will debt in the equity structure become too large in relation to the stockholders' equity? In still other situations, management may want to consider how it can guard against losses in purchasing power from rising prices or how it can plan a flow of cash receipts from operations that will be sufficient for the payment of current obligations.

Managerial accounting makes use of information that is drawn from financial accounting and may extend beyond the boundaries of accounting to draw upon economics, finance, statistics, operations research, or other disciplines as necessary.

THE OBJECTIVE OF MANAGEMENT

If managerial accounting is expected to serve management, it is necessary to consider the goals of management. It may seem that management is striving only to increase business volume or to maximize profit, but this may not be so.

Many enterprises do not even attempt to produce profit. A governmental agency may be primarily concerned with giving a needed service to the public. Individuals may also form an association for the purpose of promoting some common idea. The success of the enterprise is measured by the realization of an established common goal rather than in economic terms. However, the economic realities cannot be ignored. In any type of enterprise, management must use its resources in such a way that the desired goals will be attained in an efficient manner.

A **governmental unit**, for example, may make use of the profit concept in measuring whether or not resources have been used effectively and efficiently. Plans may be made with profit goals included and with activity conducted accordingly. Performance may then be rated by comparing the results with the resources and effort dedicated to the achievement of the objectives.

A commercial enterprise, of course, is normally interested in profit; management is judged according to its ability to earn profit from the resources entrusted to its care.

Modern management recognizes that business enterprise is also responsible to many persons who belong to diverse groups. For example, the general public expects to receive dependable products at a fair cost, and the employees depend upon the business for a means of livelihood. In addition, the business is expected to be a good neighbor in the community in which it operates. Various groups must be given recognition along with the owners and the creditors who have invested tangible resources in the enterprise. It is now generally understood that the interests of each group are best served by the harmonious reconciliation of all interests. Hence, the objective of maximizing the rate of profit must be accomplished within socially and legally accepted bounds.

PLANNING AND CONTROL DECISIONS

The decisions of management may be classified as planning and control decisions. In any type of enterprise, plans must be made to guide future operations. An enterprise must have its course charted and must be given direction in light of future expectations. A coordinated and detailed plan for the future is a budget. The various interrelated budgets of the operation are brought together and synchronized in a master or comprehensive budget. Included in the budget but extending beyond the current fiscal period are plans for the selection of new product lines, investments in new facilities or equipment, and ways of financing new investments.

Plans, of course, are not enough. There must be a follow-through. Steps must be taken to put the plans into operation and to see that they are being carried out as intended. Actual operations have to be directed and controlled if the plans are to be realized. Sometimes as operations progress it becomes necessary to revise the plans and to direct activities along a different course from that originally plotted. The decisions that pertain to the direction of actual business activity may be looked upon as decisions of control.

Levels of Management

Both planning and control decisions are made at all levels of management. Top-level management, for example, may investigate new investment opportunities and may plan for the future by accepting or rejecting certain proposals. When a course of action has been decided upon, the results should be measured and compared with the original plan. Operations should be directed so that unfavorable tendencies are eliminated or at least minimized. Whenever necessary, the initial plan should be altered to fit a change in circumstances. The illustration below indicates the process that management exercises to optimize the best course of action.

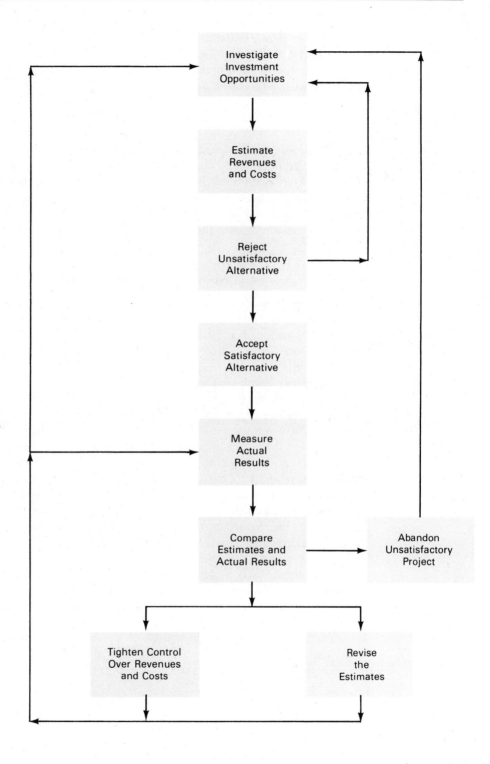

Supervisors may likewise make planning and control decisions within their own jurisdictions. It may be up to them to plan the work within their departments, to assign people to different tasks, and to guide operations in accordance with established plans.

Classifying Decisions

A firm does not have complete freedom of choice in making decisions. Limitations are imposed by conditions in the marketplace and by other outside influences. A company may find it necessary to adjust to the demand for its products, the relative scarcity of productive factors, their cost, and other conditions that prevail. Basic managerial decisions of a business enterprise have often been classified under three general headings as decisions with respect to:

1. The methods of operation.
2. The size or scale of the operation and prices to be charged.
3. The combination of products or services to be offered.

Under the methods of operation, management considers the services to be rendered or products to be sold. In operating a motel, for example, will a restaurant be included and will limousine service to the airport be furnished? Should products be manufactured or should they be purchased in completed form for resale?

Management must also consider the size of the operation. How much service will be rendered or what quantity of products will be available for sale? In order to handle a given volume of business, the firm must have adequate resources. These resources must be in balance so that there will be sufficient cash to pay creditors, an adequate quantity of goods to deliver to customers, and satisfactory facilities to support the operation. Prices and costs are examined in relation to the volume of business conducted, and decisions are made that tend to maximize the rate of return on the resources invested.

If there is more than one product line or service to be considered, management has to select the combination that appears to be the most profitable. Prices and costs are identifiable with each product or service. In a combination situation it may be better to concentrate attention on the product or service that yields the greatest profit. Further analysis may show, however, that profit can be improved by selling a combination that does not necessarily maximize the sale of the most profitable item.

These decisional classifications are mentioned for the sake of convenience. In practice, one type of decision cannot be isolated from another; they tend to blend together. A combination decision, for example, may very well influence methods of operation and the size of the operation.

CLASSIFICATION OF DECISIONS BY FUNCTION AND TIME ELEMENT

Managerial decisions may sometimes be classified under given functions such as sales, production, and finance. A decision may be spoken of as a sales decision or as a production decision. A decision to concentrate sales effort in a given area would be primarily a sales decision, whereas a decision to use a certain method in manufacturing would be primarily a production decision. The breakdown of decisions according to function and activity is possible in many cases.

However, there is some risk in the classification of decisions by function. Not all decisions can be classified. In some instances, decisions that appear to fall within a functional area will have a widespread effect upon the entire operation. It would seem, for example, that the decision to manufacture a part instead of buying it would be a production decision. Yet, the effect may extend beyond the production area. By producing parts, the company may be competing with its former suppliers. This in turn may have an effect upon sales, particularly if excess parts produced are sold on the market. It is also possible that the costs of administering the business will increase if parts are manufactured. Before going ahead with its plans, management should make certain that it has considered the total effect of these plans upon the enterprise as a unit.

It is also possible to classify decisions according to time element. Certain decisions have an effect for only a relatively short period of time, while others are so long-range as to have an impact extending many years into the future. A budget for the coming year would be a short-range plan. Likewise, an estimate of expected cash collections during the next three months would be a plan of short duration. On the other hand, a plan to construct a new plant or to lease properties would probably commit the enterprise to a course of action extending several years into the future. Decisions having an influence over a relatively long period of time are spoken of as long-range decisions.

THE CONTRIBUTION OF THE ACCOUNTANT

Management depends upon information in making decisions. Much of this information is provided within the framework of the managerial organization itself. Policies and instructions are transmitted to subordinates, who in return report to their superiors showing how well they have discharged the tasks assigned to them. Without these channels of communication, effective business management would be impossible.

The accountant is expected to furnish financial information. It is also the accountant's responsibility to maintain the financial records and to prepare the statements that present the financial position of the business, the changes in the financial position, and the results of operations. In the illustration on page 10 the accountant combines financial data in various ways in the preparation of reports that serve as a guide to management.

The accountant is not only a service arm to management but is a part of management. The controller of a company, for example, is responsible for the management of the accounting function, thus selecting ways to process

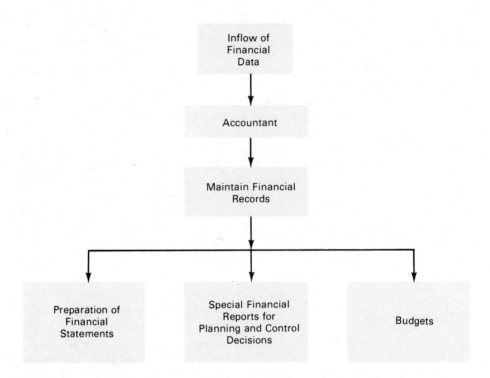

accounting data and methods of presentation. In the accounting area itself, the principles of management are applied. What combination and quantity of reports should be prepared, how should they be prepared, and what is the best method of collecting data? By the nature of the work, the accountant is drawn into the management of the business and often assists in the decision-making process.

PLANNING

Planning through the use of budgets has already been pointed out as a highly significant management function. The accountant helps to bring together budget estimates and the results of various decisions to form a comprehensive plan for the future. Throughout this text, attention is given to the decision-making process. As mentioned earlier, management may question: Should the firm continue processing a product to its finished form or sell it partially processed, and should the firm make or buy the parts used in production? These individual decisions have ramifications throughout the firm and must be considered in the preparation of a comprehensive budget for the year. After all separate decisions have been made, the results can be brought together to form a coordinated budget of total sales revenue, total cost of operation, and a projection of the financial position.

Budgets

A budget is a plan showing how resources are to be acquired and used over a specified time interval. While operations are in progress, the budget serves as a basis for comparison and facilitates the control process. The use of a budget as a means for controlling operations is called budgetary control. Also, information derived from operations is used in forming better budgets for the future.

Budgets and budgetary control operate together as essential features of a total management system. The system is set forth in the following diagram. If investigation reveals that the plan is satisfactory but that performance can be improved, steps are taken to bring future performance into line with the plan. If investigation reveals that the plan is unsatisfactory, the plan is corrected. These corrective actions are shown on the diagram as feedback loops.

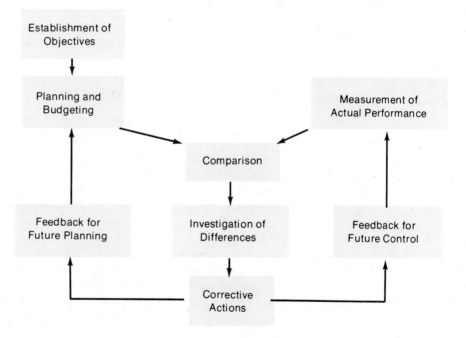

The Advantages of Budgets

Budgets are tools that are made and used by management. Benefits can be derived from the budgeting process, although budgeting is not an end in itself. By preparing a budget, management is forced to look ahead and to consider how the various functions of a business fit together. Some of the more significant advantages of budgets and budget preparation are as follows:

1. Budgeting is a means of coordinating activities with the cooperation of those who seek to achieve a common goal.

2. Budgeting helps to make the various members of management aware of the problems faced by others and the factors that interlock in running a business organization.

3. A budget is more than speculation; it is a workable pattern to be followed.

4. A budget places an obligation upon the enterprise to maintain adequate financial records that can be tied in with the budget.

5. With a budget, all people in the organization become conscious of the need to conserve business resources.

6. Efficient or inefficient use of resources is revealed by budgets intended for that purpose.

7. A budget gives management a means for self-evaluation and can be used to measure progress.

THE SCOPE OF BUDGETING

Budgeting and budgetary control are at the heart of the managerial planning and control process. Therefore, in studying managerial accounting it is appropriate to start with the concepts that underlie the overall budgeting process. In subsequent chapters, attention is directed to specialized budgets that are prepared for particular purposes. These budgets, however, also fit within the framework of the comprehensive budget for the company or entity.

Project or Product Budget

A budget for a particular segment of a business, such as a project or a product line, serves as a general guideline to the probable results of that particular activity. For example, total cost to remodel a portion of a building can be budgeted and then actual cost can be compared with the budget. Similarly, revenue and costs can be budgeted for various product lines. Fixed costs may be allocated, as a separate item, to determine whether or not the activity or product line can bear its share of total fixed cost. Budgets prepared in this way provide an overall picture of various functions and projects. However, an overall picture may not be suitable as a means of personalized control. Various persons may be responsible for individual costs of a function or project with no one person being responsible for the total operation.

Responsibility Budget

A budget that identifies revenue and costs with the individual responsible for their incurrence, a responsibility or control budget is more suitable for control purposes. In this type of budget, revenue and costs are not allocated but are identified directly with the responsible individual. A departmental supervisor, for example, has a budget for the department which includes only revenue and costs that are subject to the supervisor's control. Actual data from operations are then accumulated, and a comparison with the budget shows whether or not the supervisor achieved what was expected. A budget of this type localizes differences between the budget and actual operations, making it possible to measure individual performance. In responsibility accounting, the manager budgets the costs that he or she controls and thus has a valuable tool for evaluating his or her own performance.

Capital Investment Budget

A capital investment budget is a long-range plan for the acquisition of facilities or equipment or for an investment in an intangible item, such as a patent, that yields benefits for a relatively long period of time. A capital investment is an investment that is expected to yield benefits over a relatively long life. Capital investment planning may extend five, ten, or more years into the future with each annual segment of the plan being brought into the appropriate comprehensive budget.

Personal Attitudes

The term "budget," like the terms "restrictions" or "rationing," evokes negative emotions. A budget imposes restraint and, hence, is sometimes received with mixed emotions. The discipline of a budget, however, is necessary to attain a desired goal.

An authoritarian type of manager who overemphasizes conformity with a budget may encourage tacit compliance. Yet operations may not in fact be controlled as strictly as it would appear. Lower levels of management armed with a detailed knowledge of a particular function or operation tend to overstate cost budgets or understate revenue budgets, that is, incorporate budget slack.[1] During periods of reasonably good business, for example, a manager may budget costs higher than necessary and with a minimum of control may meet the budget. When business conditions are less favorable, cost saving programs may be introduced. The manager with slack in the budget may then give up some of the slack to receive credit for cost savings, savings that could have been obtained before.

A preoccupation with the budget as a means of rewarding or penalizing managers can have a backlash effect. Managers may tend to view the budget negatively and consider the budgeting operation a game to be played against higher levels of management. The result may be that operations are not controlled realistically and the company is not making the best use of budgeting and budgetary control.

The negative aspects of budgeting may be minimized, if not eliminated entirely, by an enlightened management. If top management does not judge a subordinate manager too closely by demanding strict adherence to a budget,

---

[1] Mohamed Onsi, "Factor Analysis of Behavioral Variables Affecting Budgetary Slack," *The Accounting Review*, Vol. XLVIII, No. 3 (July, 1973), pp. 535–548.

the budget tends to be more realistic and as a result is more valuable to the company. The person to whom the budget applies is more likely to cooperate if some latitude has been permitted in the preparation of the budget. A top management should formulate budget policy that motivates individuals to cooperate in achieving desired goals.

MASTER BUDGET PLAN

The types of budgets discussed earlier in the chapter are not separate in the sense that they are unrelated. Costs that are budgeted by project or product line can also be budgeted according to the individual responsible for incurring the costs. The costs may be collected and reported in various ways, but they are brought together in one coordinated master budget for the firm. The master budget plan will be discussed in greater detail in Chapter 15.

The computer has made it possible to rearrange costs and other data in many different ways with relatively little clerical effort. Large amounts of information can be processed to serve different purposes. For example, actual and budgeted costs can be classified (1) by product line, (2) by territory, or (3) by any other relevant basis, and can be brought together in a total budget report for the firm. The realignment of costs for different cost reports would be a formidable task if it were carried out manually, but the task is relatively easy for a computer. Furthermore, the costs can be reconciled with little risk of error.

THE BUDGET PERIOD

The length of the budget period may be a week, a month, a quarter of a year, a year, or even more than a year. There is no set interval of time. The duration depends upon how the budget is to be used. Normally, a budget is made for a year and is divided into months or quarters of a year. In any case it should be complete, tracing an activity or a project from the time it starts until it ends. The comprehensive operating budget, for example, should cover at least one cycle of operations. The cycle that begins with plans to purchase merchandise extends to a sales budget, a cash collection budget, and plans to repay any debt incurred to finance the purchase of the merchandise.

A budget for the acquisition of capital investments may be made for five or more years into the future. The plans for later years will probably be somewhat indefinite, because they are based upon long-term prospects. With the passage of time, the plans should be revised to reflect current conditions.

Generally, some provision is made for revising the budget and bringing it up to date. After a few months have elapsed, it may be quite evident that the budget for the year no longer applies. Usually at the end of the first quarter or at some other designated time, the budget is reviewed and corrections are made as necessary.

Sometimes a rolling or progressive budget is used. When a month goes by, the budget is extended one more month into the future. At the end of February, for example, a budget for the following February is added; and at the end of March, a budget for the following March is added, and so forth. Budgeting is then a continual process. There is always a budget for a year in advance; and as time passes, the budgets for future months are adjusted as circumstances warrant.

Often it is desirable to compare one month with another; but the comparison may be distorted merely because of the variations in the lengths of months. Perhaps more business may be transacted in January than in February because there are more days in January. On a comparable time basis, the business volume may be constant. Some companies eliminate these arbitrary differences by dividing their fiscal year into 13 periods of four weeks each, thereby making it possible to compare one period of the year with another.

THE TIMING CONCEPT

In business planning, time is not looked upon only as a means for measuring intervals such as months or years. Allowances must be made for the sequential flow of events and the time required for events to unfold and influence different parts of the total operation. Activities and transactions are not translated into results right away in many instances, but instead they develop and reach fruition at some later date.

Timing the logical progression of events is important in non-business situations. Heavy mountain snowfalls, for example, may result in spring floods for downstream areas; but the conditions leading to the floods precede them by several weeks. Steps may be taken to prepare for the floods, or, if possible, to prevent them.

Similarly, in business, plans are formulated so that all activities are synchronized. If a new plant is to be built, weeks or months may elapse before products can be manufactured and sold. When a new product line is to be added, it may take several months or years to develop its profit-making potential. Even in the normal course of operations, there is a natural sequence of events. If large purchases are made in certain months, some arrangement has to be made to pay the suppliers. Cash may be borrowed from the bank, or presently held cash reserves may be reduced. As cash is realized from subsequent sales, it may be applied to reduce loan balances, it may be retained, or it may be used in various ways.

PREPARATION OF THE BUDGETS

In budgeting, all functions and activities of the business are carefully interlocked. The plans for the manfuacturing division must be tied in with the plans for the sales division. If large shipments are to be made to customers during particular months, the manufacturing division should have the products ready at that time. At a still earlier date, the materials to be used in production have to be ordered, allowing enough time for their receipt from suppliers and their conversion into finished products. This concept of timing and coordinating activities applies in all areas of budgeting.

A budget is prepared by combining the efforts of many individuals. Those who are in charge of a particular function or activity make up the budget estimates. The estimates for separate departments or divisions that perform a similar function are adjusted as necessary and are summarized in one budget for that function. For instance, sales estimates may be made by regional sales managers, with the approved estimates being combined into one sales estimate for the company. At the same time, the functions such as sales, production, product engineering, purchasing, and so forth, are coordinated so that all of the budgets fit together properly.

Ordinarily individuals prepare their own budgets or, at the very least, are consulted before any budget is assigned to them. This is particularly true if the budget is to be used in controlling their activities. The self-imposed budget has certain distinct advantages, as follows:

1. A person who is in immediate contact with an activity should be able to make reliable estimates.
2. The person tends to feel recognized as a member of the team.
3. Most likely the person makes every effort to fulfill a self-imposed budget.
4. The self-imposed budget has its own peculiar control. The individual is forced to assume the blame if unable to operate within the limits.

The self-imposed budget, however, is not necessarily accepted as it stands. If too much freedom is allowed, there is a possibility that the budgets will be too easy and that they will offer no challenge. Undeserved credit may be taken for favorable budget comparisons. Before the budgets are accepted, they are reviewed by higher levels of management. If changes are to be made, they can be discussed and compromises can be reached that are acceptable to all concerned.

The person in immediate contact with any activity is in a good position to make budget estimates. However, an individual whose energy is devoted to one thing may have a narrow viewpoint or exaggerate the activity's importance, forgetting that it is only a part of a larger activity. For instance, a regional salesperson may wonder why a product line that has sold successfully has been discontinued. The top executive group, however, may have discovered that the sales in total were not sufficient to justify further production.

Top management and the lower levels of management work together to produce the budget. As a general rule, those who are in higher positions are not familiar with the details of any activity and depend upon their subordinates for underlying information. On the other hand, the top executives of the firm know more about the business as a whole, are better informed with respect to the general business outlook, and take a broader point of view. Each member of the management group, acting as an individual and cooperating with others, makes a contribution to the budget.

Specialized Decisions

Accounting data can be used selectively to fit special situations. Learning to use accounting data properly is very important in the process of mastering managerial accounting. Accounting data are like tools, and one must carefully select the appropriate accounting information to fit the specified requirement.

A plant manager, for example, may plan to introduce a new product line that can be sold for $15 per unit and has collected the following cost information:

```
Cost for each unit manufactured:
Materials ............................................... $ 5
Labor .................................................    3
*Other costs .........................................    2
Cost per unit ........................................  $10
```

*For example, supplies, lubrication, maintenance of equipment, and other costs that can be identified with this product line without allocation.

Plant facilities must be acquired; and the cost of rent, heat, light, insurance, and taxes for these facilities is estimated at $6,000. To simplify the illustration, assume that there are no selling and administrative expenses for this product line.

The plant manager believes that 6,000 units of product can normally be manufactured and sold each year. The full cost to manufacture the product is determined to see if the product line can bear its share of the cost of facilities when 6,000 units are made and sold. The full cost is the total cost to produce 6,000 units including the cost of facilities used.

Full production cost:	Total Cost (6,000 units)	Unit Cost
Materials (6,000 × $5)	$30,000	$ 5
Labor (6,000 × $3)	18,000	3
Other costs (6,000 × $2)	12,000	2
Plant facility cost (unit cost: $6,000 ÷ 6,000)	6,000	1
Total	$66,000	$11

The total profit from the sale of 6,000 units after income tax at a 40 percent tax rate is estimated at $14,400.

Estimated total revenue (6,000 × $15)	$90,000
Estimated total cost (6,000 × $11)	66,000
Profit estimated before income tax	$24,000
Income tax (40%)	9,600
Profit estimated after income tax	$14,400

This estimate is good only if 6,000 units are manufactured and sold.

In this specialized decision, the profit in relation to the investment can also be evaluated. At this point, however, it is not known how much each unit sold contributes to profit, nor is there a basis for comparing this line of product with a competing line that can be produced with the same facilities.

Differential Revenue and Costs

When two or more alternative courses of action are available, the manager should consider only the differential revenue and costs (the revenue and costs that will be changed by the decision). Suppose the facilities in the previous example can also be used to manufacture a product line that can be sold for $25 per unit and the cost to produce each unit is estimated at $17. The company can only manufacture and sell 5,000 of these units each year. Assume that if the facilities are used to produce this line, the other product line considered earlier cannot be produced.

The additional revenue expected from the alternative product line when compared with the original is $35,000. Increased cost for the alternative line is estimated at $25,000. The net advantage of the alternative line is $10,000. In the computation given below, the cost of the original product line is $10. The cost of $6,000 to use the facilities each year is disregarded in making the decision, since it will be the same in either case.

	Original Product Line	Alternative Product Line	Differences in Revenues and Costs
Revenue:			
(6,000 × $15)	$90,000		
(5,000 × $25)		$125,000	$35,000
Cost:			
(6,000 × $10)	60,000		
(5,000 × $17)		85,000	25,000
Net contribution to profits	$30,000	$ 40,000	$10,000

With the information given, the alternative line is better because it will increase profits by $10,000.

In planning, both full costs and differential revenues and costs are relevant when used for given purposes. When a decision is to be made between alternatives, the differential revenue and costs should be used, not the full costs.

CONTROL

Strictly speaking, cost control is not so much a control over costs as it is a control over the people who incur the costs. No one likes to be controlled; however, any type of control, if it is to be successful, depends upon the willingness of people to accept certain objectives and the means by which the objectives may be attained. In the control area, the relevant costs are the costs that can be identified with the individual who authorizes the costs. This approach to accountability—cost identification with the responsible person—is called responsibility accounting.

To illustrate, assume that Lisa DeBrosse has prepared a budget of costs that she expects to incur in operating her department for the month of June, 19--. Actual results for the month are compared with the budget, as shown below.

Department 5
Manager—Lisa DeBrosse
Operations Report
For the Month of June, 19--

	Budget	Actual	Actual Over	Actual Under
Materials used	$18,400	$18,350		$ 50
Labor	14,600	14,800	$200	
Indirect materials and supplies	3,200	3,350	150	
Travel and entertainment	600	800	200	
Heat and light	150	450	300	
Repairs and maintenance	850	750		100
Miscellaneous	100	150	50	
Total	$37,900	$38,650	$900	$150

Assuming that the budget fits the level of operations with which it is compared, attention is immediately called to heat and light. What has caused the relatively large variance? With a knowledge of the department costs, DeBrosse can determine the reason for the variance and can use this information to prepare a more realistic budget and to exert tighter control over the operation. In many instances a monthly report is not sufficient. Sometimes a report of weekly or even daily costs may be required so that the costs can be brought under control more quickly.

THE USE OF ACCOUNTING DATA

The focus in this discussion of the framework of managerial accounting has been on the idea that management needs data in making decisions. The remainder of this text is devoted to showing how accounting data can be used in decision making, budget preparation, and control. Accounting data are useful to both the insider and the outsider; hence, the use of data by both types of users will be considered. Problems that arise in the collection and the processing of data are not of primary concern. The important problem is the use of data by management, and this use will be emphasized.

Terminology Review

Treasurer (3)   Capital investment budget (13)
Controller (3)   Capital investment (13)
Managerial accounting (4)   Budget slack (13)
Budget (6, 11)   Rolling or progressive budget (15)
Budgetary control (11)   Full cost (17)
Responsibility or control budget (12)   Differential revenue (18)
Responsibility accounting (13, 19)   Differential costs (18)

QUESTIONS FOR REVIEW

1. What two general points of view can be taken in considering the subject of accounting?

2. Why is financial accounting subject to more strict rules and regulations than managerial accounting?

3. Distinguish between the functions of a company treasurer and a controller.

4. How can the decisions of management be classified in a broad sense?

5. What is a budget?

6. Define budgetary control.

7. How does the feedback of information contribute to improved budgeting and improved control of operations?

8. What is a responsibility budget?

9. Why are budgets considered distasteful by some people?

10. Can budgets influence behavior? Explain.

11. Explain what is meant by "budget slack."

12. What is the minimum period of time to be covered by a comprehensive operating budget?

13. What is a rolling or progressive budget?

14. Explain why timing is so important in making budget plans.

15. What are the advantages that can be derived from a self-imposed budget? disadvantages?

16. What is responsibility accounting?

17. How can it be said that cost control is more of a control over people than it is of costs?

EXERCISES

1. Budget Policy. The plant superintendent of the Mavis plant of Harding Pumps Inc. watches budget performance closely and evaluates departmental managers almost exclusively on their ability to stay within the budget limits.

    Recently the company started a cost reduction campaign. One of the department managers, who always had a good budget record, found a way to save $23,000 on a certain operation for the year and was rewarded with a bonus equal to 20% of the amount saved.

Required: Comment briefly on the advantages and disadvantages of the plant superintendent's policy. Explain how this policy may have made it possible for the department manager to receive an undeserved bonus.

2. Budget Policy. Howard DeFazio retired after many years as a plant manager at Ritchey Mills Inc. He had gained a reputation for being an astute cost-conscious manager who tolerated no budget overruns. Sarah Crowley, a department manager who had also been with the company many years, retired soon after DeFazio. She had always been able to meet her budget of about $29,000 a month for labor, supplies, repairs, maintenance and other costs over which she had control. Sometimes she had operated very close to the budget but never exceeded it. DeFazio had been very pleased with the budget results.

    The new plant manager took a more liberal point of view and permitted department managers to take an active part in budget preparation. Furthermore, the budget was only one of several criteria used to evaluate them. The new department manager prepared a budget of $21,000 for the month and in the first month of operation was $1,700 over the budget.

Required:

(1) Comment briefly on the budget policy of the two plant managers.

(2) Should the new department manager be censured for being over budget? Explain.

(3) Calculate the possible minimum slack in the retired department manager's budget.

3. Budget Timing. Caliente Heaters Inc. has just received a large government contract to supply portable heating units for military units. The heaters must be delivered by October 1. Late deliveries will activate penalties specified in the contract. Management, from previous experience, knows that a month is required before the necessary materials can be obtained after orders have been placed with suppliers. Usually one month is required for production. Because of the size of this order and the need to maintain the regular level of production, it has been estimated that three months will be needed to complete all units required by the contract. Payment on the contract can be expected one month after all of the units have been delivered. Suppliers expect to be paid one month after the materials are delivered.

Required:

(1) When must the materials be ordered to meet the delivery schedule on the contract?

(2) If money is borrowed to pay the suppliers, how long will the loan be outstanding before it can be paid out of receipts from the contract?

4. Budget Timing. The president of Olean Instrument Company has been considering an opportunity to manufacture a sensitive measuring device. The company has had no experience in this particular area but has handled similar work. Specialized equipment for this production must be ordered and can be obtained two months after it has been ordered. Employees will require three months of training for this work and can be trained with simulator equipment that can be obtained from the manufacturers within a month. The training is provided by the manufacturer as a service.

Materials must be ordered in advance, allowing 6 weeks (1½ months) for delivery. The instruments themselves can be manufactured in two months. An additional month is required to ship and deliver the instruments to customers.

On February 1, the board of directors approved the manufacturing proposal, and the project was started at that time.

Required:

(1) When should the specialized equipment be available for the beginning of production?

(2) What is the first step to be performed in activating this project?

(3) When will the first units of product be finished for delivery?

(4) At what time can the customers expect to receive the first shipments?

5. Differentials and Decisions. Professor Hogan is making plans for a conference on the problems of small business. If the conference can be held on the college campus, there will be room for only 100 participants. A hotel in the area will provide conference space for 200 persons at a cost of $500. Meals can be provided for 100 persons by the university at a cost per person of $15. The hotel will charge $25 per person if there are from 100 to 150 attendees with a $2,500 minimum. If over 150 people attend, a cost of $20 per person will be charged for each person in attendance.

The cost of speakers, travel, and advertising will be the same for either conference location. The estimated cost is $6,000.

Based upon past experience, Professor Hogan believes that 100 people will come if a conference registration fee can be established at $100 per person. With a registration fee of $120 per person, the conference should attract 200 persons with the better accommodations at the hotel.

Required:

(1) Based upon the estimates, will the conference cover more than its cost if only 100 persons attend at the university?

(2) Based upon the estimates, will the conference cover more than its cost if 200 persons attend at the hotel?

(3) Compute the difference in revenue between 100 persons at the university and 200 persons at the hotel.

(4) Compute the difference in cost between 100 persons at the university and 200 persons at the hotel.

(5) What can be expected if only 100 persons attend at the hotel?

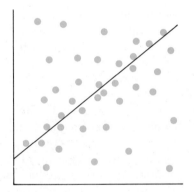

2

COST CONCEPTS AND CLASSIFICATIONS

Chapter Objectives

After studying Chapter Two, you will be able to:

1. Describe how costs are used in planning and controlling operations and in income measurement.
2. Understand differential costs, sunk costs and opportunity costs.
3. Distinguish between direct and indirect costs; controllable and noncontrollable costs.
4. Explain the concepts of responsibility accounting.
5. Distinguish between variable costs and fixed costs.

Costs are measured and used in many different ways by managers to fit the requirements of various situations. Cost data are especially important in the following areas:

1. Planning—the estimation of future costs in budget preparation and in decision making.
2. Control—the measurement of costs incurred and the comparison of those costs with budgets or standards in the process of directing and controlling the enterprise.
3. Income Measurement—the determination of the costs associated with the goods sold during the fiscal period and the costs of inventories remaining at the end of the fiscal period.

COST CONCEPTS

A cost may be very broadly defined as being the sacrifice required to obtain a given object or objective. There are many different kinds of costs, however, and it is important to understand how one concept of cost may be suitable for a given purpose while another concept is entirely unsuitable. The problem of working with costs can be simplified if one considers carefully how the costs are to be used and selectively chooses cost data that serve that purpose. Costs can be useful tools when used properly. A hammer is a useful tool for driving nails but is not a very satisfactory instrument for smoothing wood surfaces. Similarly, costs must be selected carefully to fit the need.

Management, stockholders, employees, and other groups are interested in summarized cost data. However, frequently management requires more detailed information. For example, to manage an enterprise effectively, it is necessary to know how much it costs to operate a given segment of the business such as a division or a department, how much it costs to produce and sell a given quantity of a certain product line, and how much it costs to produce and sell each unit of the various lines handled. Detailed cost information is furnished by a system of cost accounting and can be used to control business activities, plan operations, and make decisions.

COSTS FOR PLANNING

Costs for planning may be achieved through the use of a budget. In budgeting, a thorough study of operations is combined with past experience and estimates of future possiblities. Individual budgets prepared for each function, department, and product line are related to each other and are interlocked in a master budget plan. For example, the estimated production of a microcomputer company for the next fiscal year is broken down by product line. From this figure it is possible to estimate the future activity level and draw up cost budgets for the manufacturing departments. In turn, the budgets of costs for the departments, when related to the number of units of various product lines to be manufactured, yield budgeted costs per unit for each line of product. Budgets are prepared in the same way for other functions of the business, such as sales and administration.

Cost data can be combined and analyzed in the process of either budgeting or reporting costs. Some costs, such as past or historical costs, may serve as a basis for estimating what costs will be in the future; yet these costs are not accounted for in a conventional manner in decisional analysis. The costs measured in the accounting records are not necessarily costs used in decision making. If past performance is to be measured, historical costs are relevant; but if plans are to be made for the future, estimated changes in costs and revenue are more significant.

Differential Costs

Management is expected to make decisions and in doing so compares alternatives. Perhaps a choice must be made between two types of equipment that can be used to perform the same work, or the choice may involve the selection of a plant location. There are various business situations in which alternatives must be compared with one alternative being accepted to the exclusion of the others.

In making a decision, management compares the costs of the alternatives. The costs that remain the same in any case can be disregarded but the difference in cost between alternatives is relevant to decision making. A difference in cost between one course of action and another is a differential cost. If a decision results in an increased cost, the differential cost may be more specifically referred to as an incremental cost. If the cost is decreased, the differential cost may be referred to as a decremental cost.

Differential cost is a broad concept. For example, it may cost $6 to produce one unit of product and $11 to produce two units. The differential cost is $5. The additional cost of producing a unit of product over a given volume of output is ordinarily spoken of as the variable cost per unit. The variable cost can also be designated as the differential cost or the incremental cost of producing and selling one more unit. In the situations previously mentioned, the cost differentials are usually designated specifically as marginal costs or as variable costs, as the case might be.

A decision may result in changes in costs that are ordinarily fixed. Costs are said to be fixed if they are not altered by changes in output or activity. But a fixed cost may be changed by a management decision. Assume that plans are being made to change a certain production process. Some of the costs will be higher, and some will be lower. Costs that are ordinarily considered to be variable costs may change in the rate of variability, and fixed costs may be increased or decreased if the new producion process is accepted. Costs of the present process and the new process are listed as follows:

	Present Process	New Process	Differential Cost: Incremental (Decremental)
Materials and labor	$ 90,000	$ 93,000	$ 3,000
Supervision	49,000	31,000	(18,000)
Insurance	5,000	4,000	(1,000)
Property tax	11,000	11,000	—0—
Depreciation	6,500	6,500	—0—
Total	$161,500	$145,500	$(16,000)

In the example, the costs of materials and labor, supervision, and insurance are changed. They are differential costs (incremental and decremental) with respect to the decision and in this case are net decremental costs, decreasing by a net amount of $16,000, thus favoring the new process. The differential cost is the difference in cost from operating under one alternative as compared with another.

Sunk Costs

A sunk cost is a cost that has already been incurred. Therefore, a sunk cost cannot be changed by any decision made at the present time or in the future. An individual may regret having made a purchase but, after the purchase has been made, cannot avoid the cost by taking subsequent action. Perhaps the property can be sold, in which case the cost of the property is matched against the proceeds from the sale in the determination of gain or loss. Or the person may decide to keep the property, in which case the cost is matched against revenue over the time that it is used in operations. In any event, the cost has been incurred and cannot be avoided. It is a sunk cost with respect to present and future decisions.

To illustrate, assume that Lafayette Products Company purchased a filter for water purification at a cost of $750. The firm is considering using the filter as a swimming pool filter or as a filter for drinking water. Or, it may be resold to someone else for $900. The cost of $750 has already been incurred and has no effect on any decision to be made with respect to the use or disposal of the filter. The net benefit of each alternative is shown as follows:

| | Use | | Disposal |
	Swimming Pool	Drinking Water	
Revenue from use of pool	$5,000		
Revenue from sale of filtered water		$ 2,600	
Other costs of operation	(1,800)	(1,000)	
Proceeds, from sale of filter			$ 900
Cost of filter	(750)	(750)	(750)
Net benefit of alternative	$2,450	$ 850	$ 150

Note that the sunk cost (cost of filter of $750) is the same for each alternative and has no effect on the decision to be made.

Opportunity Costs

Costs are generally looked upon as being outlays or expenditures that must be made either in the present or in the future to obtain goods and services. But the concept of cost can be extended to include sacrifices that are made when incoming benefits or returns are refused. In choosing between alternatives, management tries to select the best alternative but in doing so has to give up the returns that could have been derived from the rejected alternatives. The sacrifice of a return or benefit from a rejected alternative is spoken of as being the opportunity cost of the alternative accepted. Opportunity costs are not entered in the accounting records, of course, but they are used in decision making.

Often management is confronted with alternatives, each having its advantages. For example, there may be an opportunity to make one of two different product lines, but both product lines cannot be manufactured with the present facilities. It may be estimated that Product A will contribute $16,000 a year to profits and that Product B will contribute $21,000 a year to profits. Product B should be selected, and the opportunity cost of selecting Product B is the sacrifice of the $16,000 that could be earned by Product A.

Estimated increase in annual profits from Product B	$21,000
Less opportunity cost (sacrifice of estimated annual profits from Product A)...	16,000
Advantage of Product B	$ 5,000

An Illustration of Decision-Making Costs

The distinctions that have been made between fixed and variable costs are important in product costing and are important in the control of operations. In costing products and in controlling operations, management needs to know which costs can be identified directly with a function or operation and which costs can be controlled at a certain management level. In addition, cost behavior is important. A distinction must be made between costs that are expected to vary with changes in activity or output and costs that remain fixed over a given range of changes in activity or output. These cost distinctions are important in product costing and in controlling operations and, when used properly, are most helpful in planning and in decision making.

Differential costs and opportunity costs have little or no value in costing products or in controlling costs, but these cost concepts are most valuable in decision making. Decisions influence the future course of events, and the emphasis is on what lies ahead and not on what has already taken place.

Assume that Damon and Kell, Inc., are presently using a unit of equipment to manufacture a certain line of fishing lures. The results of operations are as follows:

Sales		$170,000
Cost of fishing lures sold plus operating expense (excluding depreciation)..........................	$110,000	
Depreciation of equipment	21,000	
		131,000
Net income		$ 39,000

The present operation can be continued, or the company can use the same equipment to manufacture another line of fishing lures that should produce sales of $210,000 each year. The cost to manufacture this product and the operating expenses excluding depreciation of the equipment are estimated at $130,000. The results of operations are as follows:

Sales		$210,000
Cost of fishing lures sold plus operating expense		
(excluding depreciation)............................	$130,000	
Depreciation of equipment	21,000	
		151,000
Net income		$ 59,000

The new product line adds $40,000 to sales, and the incremental cost is $20,000. Hence, there is an advantage of $20,000 in accepting the new product line. The depreciation of the equipment is a sunk cost in each situation and can be ignored in making the decision. The differentials are the relevant factors in making the decision.

Additional revenue from new product line ($210,000 − $170,000)	$40,000
Additional costs of new product line ($130,000 − $110,000)	20,000
Net advantage of new product line............................	$20,000

The problem can be examined in still another way by using depreciation in the decision. The present operation provides $60,000 each year, as determined by adding depreciation, a sunk cost, to the net income ($21,000 + $39,000 = $60,000). Any alternative use of the equipment must provide at least $60,000 if it is to be equally acceptable. Stated in another way, the opportunity cost of any other alternative is the $60,000 that must be sacrificed if another alternative is selected.

The new product line is expected to contribute $80,000 each year as determined by adding depreciation, a sunk cost, to the net income ($21,000 + $59,000 = $80,000).

Expected contribution from new product line each year	$80,000
Less opportunity cost (the sacrifice of the contribution of the	
present product line each year).............................	60,000
Net advantage of new product line each year	$20,000

COSTS AND CONTROL

Management, in carrying out its control over operations, must rely heavily on cost data. However, the costs that are useful for control purposes are not necessarily the costs that are reported on conventional accounting statements. Much of the disagreement about how costs should be accounted for arises because of a misunderstanding of how the cost data will be used. One concept of cost will not serve all purposes.

For example, the costs to operate a given plant for a year totaled $870,000, and the costs to operate the two departments in the plant were $450,000 and $420,000 respectively. Suppose that depreciation of the plant, the plant superintendent's salary, and other costs of operating the plant as a unit were included in the departmental cost totals. This information may not be satisfactory if management wants to know how much cost is specifically incurred for the operation of each department. Assume further that these costs of overall plant operation amounted to $360,000 and that they have been allocated equally to both departments; that is, $180,000 to each department. On this basis, the costs specifically incurred to operate each department were $270,000 for the first department and $240,000 for the second department as determined by the following:

	Dept. 1	Dept. 2	Total
Total cost	$450,000	$420,000	$870,000
Less allocated cost	180,000	180,000	360,000
Specific department cost........	$270,000	$240,000	$510,000

Further assume that management wants to know how much cost can be controlled by each departmental supervisor. The salary of each departmental supervisor is included as a specific cost incurred for operation of the department, but the departmental supervisor does not set or control this salary. Also, depreciation of equipment used exclusively within a department is not controlled by the supervisor if the supervisor does not acquire the equipment; but it is included as a specific cost of the department. Assume that costs of $200,000 and $80,000 for each of the respective departments are included as specific costs of the departments but cannot be controlled by the departmental supervisors. The costs controllable at the departmental level are computed as follows:

	Dept. 1	Dept. 2	Total
Specific departmental cost	$270,000	$240,000	$510,000
Less costs not controllable at departmental level	200,000	80,000	280,000
Cost controllable at departmental level	$ 70,000	$160,000	$230,000

Note that the supervisor of Department 2 has control over a large proportion of the cost of this department while the supervisor of Department 1 controls a smaller proportion of the departmental cost. This information was not revealed by the previous cost reports.

An allocation of costs does serve a purpose in that it shows the full cost of operating a unit. But cost allocation tends to blur areas of responsibility. In the evaluation of departmental supervisors, it would be more useful to charge them with only the costs for which they are responsible. Their particular cases can be controlled more effectively by comparing the costs over which they have jurisdiction with budgets or standards prepared on the same basis.

In arriving at a decision as to whether or not operations have been conducted efficiently, management depends upon some basis of measurement, such as a budget or a cost standard. The budget or the standard serves as a point of reference. Differences between the actual costs incurred and the budgeted or standard costs can be calculated and put to use in evaluating performance. If further investigation reveals that budget differences were caused by unsatisfactory conditions, positive steps can be taken to correct the situation. In other words, budget comparisons produce information that can be used to control the business at various levels of operation.

Direct and Indirect Costs

Costs are sometimes spoken of as being direct or indirect with respect to an activity, a department, or a product. If a cost can be directly attached to the unit under consideration, it is a direct cost of that unit. If it is a cost of a unit only through allocation, it is an indirect cost. The distinction depends upon whether or not the cost can be identified with the activity or other relevant unit without allocation. A cost such as the plant superintendent's salary can be readily identified with the plant and hence is a direct cost of the plant. However, it is an indirect cost of any department within the plant or of any line of product manufactured. The plant superintendent's salary cannot be identified with any unit within the plant except by allocation. With respect to product lines, the materials and labor that are easily identified as a part of the product cost are the direct materials and the direct labor cost of the product. However, the factory overhead costs are not directly identifiable with any particular product and are thus indirect costs with respect to the product. The cost of supplies used, for example, may be identified directly as a cost of a particular department yet not be a direct cost of the products manufactured.

There is a dangerous tendency to oversimplify and to look upon direct costs as being variable costs and indirect costs as being fixed costs. This is not necessarily true. For example, a plant superintendent's salary is a fixed cost. It does not increase or decrease automatically with changes in activity or production. However, as stated earlier, it is a direct cost of the plant. It is also an indirect cost with respect to departments within the plant or with respect to the products. Supplies used may vary with the number of hours of production and be a variable cost. The cost of the supplies used may be a direct cost of a given department but an indirect cost of any particular product manufactured within that department. One must be careful not to confuse the direct and indirect distinction with the fixed and variable distinction. There is no established relationship between the two concepts.

Cost Allocations

The indirect costs, the costs that cannot be directly identified with a department or division of the company, may be allocated to the departments or divisions as indicated earlier in the chapter. The allocation is made on a judgmental basis by using a factor that can be identified with both the department or division and the cost in question. The allocation, while based on logical assumptions, cannot be viewed as a precise cost measurement for the department.

For example, assume that a building is used for four different operating departments. The costs of building occupancy, such as taxes, insurance, repairs, and depreciation, are allocated to the departments. The space in the building that is occupied by each department can be measured and can be reasonably identified with the cost of occupancy.

Craig Products Company, for example, has four operating departments in one building. Data relative to occupied space are given as follows:

	Square Meters of Space	Percentage of Total Space
Department 1	45 000	30%
Department 2	60 000	40
Department 3	15 000	10
Department 4	30 000	20
Total	150 000	100%

The total cost of building occupancy has been estimated at $120,000 for the year. The cost is allocated to the departments on the basis of the percentage of the building occupied.

	Departments				
	1	2	3	4	Total
Building occupancy	$36,000	$48,000	$12,000	$24,000	$120,000

Cost allocation is misleading if the intention is to determine the direct costs of operating a department with no support from the rest of the organization. However, cost allocation does indicate whether or not a department is producing enough revenue to cover not only its direct costs but also its share of the total costs of the organization. Some departments, for example, may cover all of their direct costs but not all of the allocated costs. Still other departments may cover all of their direct costs and their entire share of allocated costs, and show a final profit.

In the planning and control operation, it is most important to distinguish between the direct costs of a department and the allocated costs. Under normal circumstances, the cost to be allocated will not be reduced by the elimination of any one department; that is, the amount of insurance, taxes, and depreciation will continue at the same amount whether or not all building space is utilized. Therefore, the allocated cost may not be relevant in deciding whether or not to retain a department.

In the last example, assume that Department 4 is to be eliminated. The cost of building occupancy would still remain at $120,000 and could be reallocated to the other three departments as follows:

	Department			
	1	2	3	Total
Revised space occupancy (square meters)	45 000	60 000	15 000	120 000
Revised percentages............	37.5%	50%	12.5%	100%
Revised cost allocation...........	$45,000	$60,000	$15,000	$120,000

If the cost was not reallocated, the portion of cost previously assigned to Department 4 may be unassigned as a cost of the unused space. Or, if the space assigned to Department 4 was used for another purpose, the allocated cost would be assigned to the new use.

The key point is that the cost is not reduced by $24,000 if Department 4 is eliminated. The total cost remains at $120,000. The elimination of a department or function does not eliminate the allocated portion of a fixed cost.

Controllable and Noncontrollable Costs

Another important aspect of cost to be considered is the distinction between costs that can be controlled by a given person and those that cannot be controlled by that person.

This cost classification also depends upon a point of reference. Costs are incurred upon the authorization of some member of the management group. If a manager is responsible for a given cost, that cost is said to be controllable with respect to that person. If the manager does not authorize that cost, the cost is uncontrollable with respect to that person. Almost all costs are controllable at some level of management. Top management has broad authority over costs and directly or indirectly controls most of the costs of the entity. For example, top management can increase or decrease executive salaries and can initiate or abandon major projects. At intermediate or at lower management levels, such costs are beyond their authority and are uncontrollable. Costs that can be authorized at a certain managerial level are said to be controllable at that level. A departmental supervisor, for example, may have control over the supplies used by the department but have no control over the plant asset acquisitions that result in the depreciation allocated to the department.

Direct costs and controllable costs are not necessarily the same. A cost may be a direct cost of a given department but may not be controlled by the departmental supervisor. For example, the salary of a departmental supervisor, which is a direct cost of the department, is controlled at a higher level of management rather than by the supervisor.

In addition, a cost cannot be looked upon as being uncontrollable because it is a fixed cost. Often there is a tendency to view a cost as either controllable or uncontrollable because it is either variable or fixed. It is as incorrect, however, to confuse cost behavior characteristics with controllability as it is to confuse cost behavior characteristics with the direct and indirect concept.

While a fixed cost such as property insurance may be uncontrollable at a given managerial level, it is nevertheless subject to control by a manager who has the authority to obtain insurance coverage for the firm.

Time also plays a part in controllability. For example, a manager may have authority to purchase materials. The manager controls the cost. If the manager purchases materials at different times in relatively small quantities, the quantity ordered and the unit cost are controlled at each order point. However, if a binding contract is signed for a large quantity at a set unit cost, the manager has control only when the contract is negotiated. During the period that the contract is in force, the manager cannot change the terms or control the cost until the contract is fulfilled. True, the manager is responsible for the cost in either case, but the long-term nature of a contract commitment removes flexibility or control in the short run.

RESPONSIBILITY ACCOUNTING

A system of responsibility accounting relies heavily upon the distinction between controllable and noncontrollable costs and is designed to fit the requirements of the persons within the firm. It is a people-oriented system of accounting. In responsibility accounting, costs are identified with the persons responsible for their incurrence. With responsibility localized, it is possible to rate individual managers on a cost basis by comparing the controllable costs of the department or division with a budget prepared on the same basis.

Managers are expected to prepare budgets of the costs that they control, and they are expected to operate within the limits of their budgets. Periodic cost reports prepared on this basis of cost responsibility are compared with the budgets and are used by each manager as a basis for self-evaluation. Managers at higher levels may rate subordinate managers by using this information.

The frequency of reporting, the type of information reported, and the detail depend upon the attitudes of the recipients. The success of responsibility accounting depends in large part upon the sensitivity of top-level management and the accountants to the needs and preferences of the individuals within the organization. The accountant is a supplier of financial and other business data. The information must be presented so that it can be understood by the recipient and must be communicated in a way that best helps users carry out their functions.

Some individuals want reports at frequent intervals so that they can control an operation while it is in progress. Others, who may feel that frequent reporting is not necessary and that it may even become a nuisance, prefer that reports be furnished over longer intervals of time.

The kind of information required varies according to the type of operation and the desires of the recipient. Some managers, for example, are responsible for several projects and may tend to favor a form of cost report that shows the controllable costs for each project, the direct costs, and the allocated costs. Other managers may have no projects but may have continuous functions. For them reports on controllable costs broken down by natural classification, such as telephone, rent, and insurance, may be sufficient.

By nature, some individuals like to receive a large amount of statistical detail, and these individuals want detailed reports. On the other hand, there are those who are annoyed with detail and want condensed reports that give them a summary of the areas requiring attention. The accountant working with management seeks the form of report that best serves the purposes of the responsible manager and the firm.

Cost Reports

Joan Leddon is the plant manager of the Bremerton Plant of Kuchar Fabrics Inc. She is responsible for the costs that she authorizes for plant administration and for the costs authorized by the various departmental supervisors in the plant. Each month she will receive a report showing in summary form the costs incurred by her and by the departmental supervisors. The following is a report for the month of June.

Kuchar Fabrics Inc.
Cost Report—Departmental Costs
Bremerton Plant
For the Month of June, 1985

Plant Manager
Joan Leddon

	Year to Date			June, 1981		
	Budget	Actual	Variance Over (Under)	Budget	Actual	Variance Over (Under)
Plant administration.....	$ 72,760	$ 75,790	$ 3,030	$ 11,950	$ 12,620	$ 670
Department 1..........	386,420	385,280	(1,140)	68,210	68,970	760
Department 2..........	263,140	278,230	15,090	46,300	49,500	3,200
Department 3.........	143,810	143,670	(140)	23,970	23,920	(50)
Total...............	$866,130	$882,970	$16,840	$150,430	$155,010	$ 4,580

All costs that are controllable at the plant level may also be reported to the plant manager by natural classification as shown at the top of page 35.

If Joan Leddon believes that a cost incurred in a certain department is excessive, she can obtain a cost report for that department with the costs broken down by natural classification. For example, the cost of materials and supplies may appear to be too large in Department 3, in which case she and the supervisor of Department 3 can work together to find reasons why the actual costs were in excess of budgeted costs.

Each supervisor receives reports like Joan Leddon receives, showing costs that are controlled, including costs controlled by his or her subordinates. The costs are also reported by natural cost classification. Each supervisor also receives a report on the costs that he or she controls personally. A network of

Kuchar Fabrics Inc.
Cost Report—Natural Classification
Bremerton Plant
For the Month of June, 1985

Plant Manager
Joan Leddon

	Year to Date			June, 1985		
	Budget	*Actual*	*Variance Over (Under)*	*Budget*	*Actual*	*Variance Over (Under)*
Materials and supplies ..	$391,650	$393,890	$ 2,240	$ 70,600	$ 72,000	$ 1,400
Wages and payroll taxes	380,180	390,660	10,480	64,520	67,060	2,540
Labor fringe benefits ...	76,220	80,320	4,100	12,380	13,180	800
Travel and entertainment	4,970	5,110	140	750	680	(70)
Insurance..............	6,000	6,000	—0—	1,000	1,000	—0—
Telephone	4,280	4,340	60	670	710	40
Miscellaneous	2,830	2,650	(180)	510	380	(130)
Total	$866,130	$882,970	$16,840	$150,430	$155,010	$ 4,580

reports showing a comparison of controllable costs with budgets extends all the way from the president's office to the lowest level of management.

Joan Leddon personally controls the costs of plant administration and receives a report classified by natural classification. The following is a report of the costs of plant administration.

Kuchar Fabrics Inc.
Cost Report—Plant Administration
Plant Manager—Bremerton Plant
For the Month of June, 1985

Plant Manager
Joan Leddon

	Year to Date			June, 1985		
	Budget	*Actual*	*Variance Over (Under)*	*Budget*	*Actual*	*Variance Over (Under)*
Materials and supplies ..	$10,870	$10,880	$ 10	$ 1,760	$ 1,710	$ (50)
Wages and payroll taxes	47,550	49,320	1,770	7,830	8,460	630
Labor fringe benefits ...	8,450	10,100	1,650	1,410	1,700	290
Travel and entertainment	2,680	2,290	(390)	430	320	(110)
Insurance..............	1,500	1,500	—0—	250	250	—0—
Telephone	1,140	1,110	(30)	170	180	10
Miscellaneous	570	590	20	100	—0—	(100)
Total	$ 72,760	$ 75,790	$ 3,030	$ 11,950	$ 12,620	$ 670

This report can help Leddon to control the costs that she is responsible for in the administration of the plant. Costs that are substantially over budget may be given closer attention. In this report, for example, both labor and fringe benefit costs are well over the budgeted amounts. Perhaps this increased cost has become necessary because of changes in the type or volume of work done since the budget was prepared. The information derived from the report may be useful both as a tool for control and as a basis for budget revision or for the preparation of future budgets.

If more detail is needed, supplemental reports may be issued. For example, a report may be furnished to show the voucher numbers and the names of payees for individual items of cost under each natural cost classification. Before computers were commonly used, management hesitated to request detailed information since the cost of the information in both hours of work and in dollars might well have exceeded its value. Detailed reports in many cases would have taken too long to prepare and could have taken office personnel away from regularly assigned duties. Now management must be careful to select what is necessary or run the risk of being confused by unnecessary detail. If information is included in coded form on input media, it is relatively easy to design computer programs that reclassify and accumulate information in various ways to serve the needs of management. In this example, suppose that the plant manager wants to know the composition of the wages and payroll taxes for the month of June. A report prepared by computer can show the payroll detail for the month and provide basic information on charges to this classification.

Some Difficulties with Responsibility Accounting

It may seem that costs can be budgeted and reported quite easily on the basis of controllability, but such is not the case. Costs may be authorized by one responsible individual, and in that sense are controlled by that person; but other persons within the organization may influence the amount of the cost. Thus, control by one individual is not absolute.

For example, it may be more economical to have one service contract for repair and maintenance for the entire plant than to have several separate contracts negotiated by each of the departmental supervisors. One of the departmental supervisors may be given the authority to obtain the contract for all departments. This is similar to a personal situation in which one person plans a dinner party at a restaurant for several persons. The person who has the authority to execute the plans has control in one sense but in another sense does not. The participants will probably demand some exceptions, and a compromise may increase costs. As a result, the budget may be exceeded; and the fault cannot be placed entirely with the person making the plans. On the other hand, an allocation of the costs is a violation of the responsibility accounting concept because individuals are being held accountable for costs that they did not personally incur.

Service departments can also create problems in a responsibility accounting system. For example, a plant engineering department may prepare blueprints and templates for the production departments. The supervisor of the plant engineering department is responsible for the costs incurred, but these costs in turn are influenced by the actions of other departments. If one department requests rush service, the service department may incur overtime and go over the budget. While other departments may have no direct control over the costs of the service department, they influence the costs and in that sense are responsible.

Sometimes the problem is solved by allocating the service department costs to other departments on the basis of (1) the investment in machinery and equipment in other departments or (2) hours of service given. In making allocations, however, the basic principle of responsibility accounting is violated; that is, an individual should only be held accountable for the costs that are personally incurred. The allocation procedure may also be unsatisfactory because the service department may not control its costs properly and may pass these higher costs to other departments by allocation. Also, an increase in the service department costs because of a request by one department for rush service should not be considered a responsibility of the service department nor should it be allocated to other departments.

One solution is to establish for the service department an hourly billing rate based on a normal service department budget. Each department is billed as if it were an outside customer, thus absorbing the penalty cost for rush work. Charging the managers only for the costs that they control directly may cause them to operate more efficiently and may also minimize friction over cost responsibility between the service department and the other departments of the company.

In some cases it is believed that costs should be allocated even though they are not controlled directly by the departments receiving the service. The argument for cost allocation is that all managers should be conscious of the full cost of operating their departments and as a result will be more careful in requesting services. This is a departure from pure responsibility accounting. Whether or not it produces results depends upon the attitudes of the individuals within the organization. Responsibility accounting, at the very least, is an attempt to identify costs with individuals and in some circumstances may have to be modified to receive acceptance by the various individuals that comprise management.

Control Features

The responsibility cost reports provide a basis for control. They identify specific responsibility centers and costs within the centers that may require further attention. An identification of trouble areas, however, is only the beginning of the control process. Questions must be asked. Is the difference between the budgeted cost and the actual cost material enough to justify further investigation? What caused the variation? Is it likely that a variation from the budget will be repeated in the future if action isn't taken? It may be found that measures can be taken that reduce variations in the future or that the variation was a normal variation from the average and didn't warrant investigation. In some cases it is found that the budget was unrealistic and should be revised. The responsibility reports are somewhat like switchboards that flash warning lights when there is trouble. They furnish the initial information that serves as a basis for corrections.

Responsibility of Costs and Charges

A responsibility cost system can be a subtle means of enforcing company policy. Decisions are made at the top management level which compel cost control at the lower management levels. At all levels of management, supervisory personnel are especially careful when costs are charged against them. Top management does not have to spell out policy in a directive; lower levels of management will be guided according to how the costs are charged to their responsibility areas.

Costs that would normally be included in the reports of subordinates may be excluded if top management believes that the company will benefit from a more liberal policy. On the other hand, costs that are to be controlled more rigorously are given more attention if they are authorized by and charged to the area manager.

For example, a company may provide a copying service to expedite the duplication of forms and reports. The services may be given to all departments with no charge, thus encouraging the departmental supervisors to make use of this service with no cost appearing on their cost reports. However, if top management believes that the service is being drawn upon too freely, a charge may be made to the departments for this service. Managers, knowing that they will be charged for the service, tend to use the service more sparingly.

Human Elements of Costs

The successful operation of a responsibility accounting system depends to a large extent upon the attitudes of company personnel. Some research has been done in the area of human behavior within organizations, but there is still much to be done. The central objective is to assign cost responsibility in such a way that the individuals affected are motivated to act in the best interests of the company to achieve the established goals. A policy that may work in one organization may not necessarily work in another because of the differences in the attitudes and behavior of the personnel.

Often it is believed that the only goal of business enterprise is to maximize profits. This is not necessarily true. Ordinarily there is a combination of goals. In addition to profits, the company may seek to provide a superior product or service and may be concerned with the welfare of the employees and community at large.

The various goals of the organization should be coordinated. If one goal is inconsistent with another, management will be confused and will need direction as to how much attention is to be given to one objective as compared with another. For example, a company may seek to train employees on the job in an effort to develop skilled personnel. However, this can interfere with efficient performance and may reduce profits. Guidelines should be established that spell out how much cost and supervisory effort is to be expended on job training, and a balance must be struck that is clearly understood by the personnel affected.

INCOME MEASUREMENT

Cost accounting for an enterprise that buys merchandise and distributes it through sales to customers is relatively simple when compared with the cost accounting problems of a manufacturer. The manufacturer does not buy products in order to sell them in their present state. Instead, the manufacturer buys materials that must be converted to a product for sale. The cost of the product includes not only the cost of the materials used but also includes the manufacturing costs of converting the materials to a product that can be sold.

Merchandise Inventory Flow

The flow of costs for an enterprise that buys and sells merchandise is as follows:

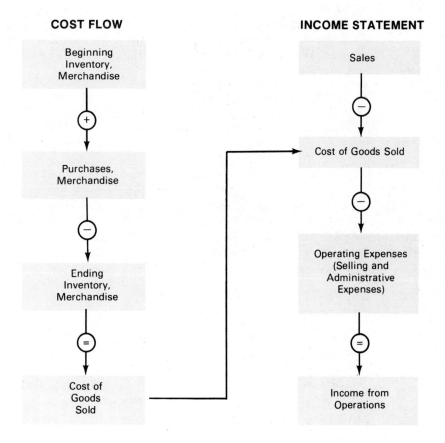

In short, the cost of goods sold is equal to the cost of the beginning inventory and the purchases made during the year less the cost of the inventory on hand at the end of the year.

In financial accounting, you learned that inventory may be assigned older costs, more recent costs, or an average cost. If older costs are assigned to the inventory on hand at the end of the year, the more recent costs become cost of goods sold. This is the last-in, first-out inventory method (lifo) Conversely, if more recent costs are assigned to the inventory on hand at the end of the year, then the older costs become cost of goods sold. This is the first-in, first-out method (fifo). Sometimes the inventory costs are an average of the costs with the average being computed in various ways.

Manufacturing Inventory Flow

In a manufacturing operation, assets used in production are transformed and become a part of the inventory of products to be sold. An asset may lose its original identity in the transformation process, but its status as an asset is retained until the products are sold. When the products are sold, the cost of the various assets that have been transformed into product cost is released as expense.

The transformation process is illustrated by using a simple example. Gasoline is purchased to give power to a saw used in Operation 3 to trim lumber. The saw is employed to make the products. The following table shows the process of transformation.

Transaction	Asset Conversion	Account	Type of Account
1. Purchase of gasoline	Acquisition of potential energy	Gasoline Inventory	Asset
2. Consumption of fuel by saw in Operation 3	Potential energy becomes active energy	Manufacturing Cost in Operation 3	Asset
3. Cost of Operation 3 applied to products	Active energy identified with products	Work in Process	Asset
4. Products completed and transferred to finished stock	Products are completely manufactured	Finished Goods	Asset
5. Products removed from finished stock and sold	Products sold	Cost of Goods Sold	Expense

The use of the gasoline does not constitute expense. The gasoline has merely changed form and has been converted to energy. The cost of the energy used (gasoline used) becomes a part of the cost of the products that have been manufactured. The fuel cost becomes expense when the products leave the business as a result of sales transactions. Gasoline cost, along with other costs, then becomes a part of the cost of goods sold.

Period Cost

The cost that is referred to as period cost is identified with measured time intervals and not with goods or services. Insurance protection, for example, may be furnished at a cost of $1,200 per year or at a rate of $100 a month. Each month the insurance cost is $100 regardless of the amount of business transacted. The cost is matched against revenue as expense according to the time interval that has elapsed. An income statement for the year will show insurance expense of $1,200.

Cost is usually recorded by natural classification to identify the type of service received, such as telephone, electric, repairs, and rent. A designation such as wages is a natural classification for the cost of labor service. Cost may also be classified by function, that is, according to the type of work performed—manufacturing, selling, or administrative. The cost of labor service, for example, is under the natural classification of wages and, if used to manufacture products, is classified by function as a manufacturing cost.

Product Cost

Cost cannot always be properly matched against revenue on a period-of-time basis. For example, insurance on a factory building for a certain year should not be charged to insurance expense for that year if the products that were manufactured are not sold until the next year. The insurance cost should follow the products and should be matched against the revenue from their sale as expense. In the income determination process, costs incurred to produce revenue should be offset as expenses against the resulting revenue. The period in which the benefit is received is the period in which the cost should be deducted as expenses. The cost incurred to manufacture products should become a part of the product cost and should become expense only when the products to which they are attached are sold. Usually manufacturing cost is treated as a product cost and not as a period cost. Factory insurance accrues on a time basis, but even so it is not treated as a period cost. Instead it is a manufacturing cost and is generally considered to be a part of the cost of the goods produced. If the goods produced during a year are the only goods sold in that year with no inventory remaining at the end of the year, the resulting net income will be the same under either a period basis or a product basis of accountability. But if completed or partially completed goods are on hand at the end of the fiscal year, some of the insurance cost will be inventoried and treated as a product cost.

Cost Accounting Beyond the Manufacturing Area

The principles of cost accounting do not have to be restricted to manufacturing operations. In recent years, much attention has been given to the determination of costs by units in service industries. For example, automobile insurance companies have calculated the cost of servicing customers by age classification, marital status, accident record, location, etc. Banks also make use of cost analysis in arriving at service charges and amounts to be charged for handling special checking accounts.

Even in a manufacturing enterprise, the principles of cost accounting can be extended to include the selling and administrative areas. Usually the formal accounting records show selling and administrative cost as a period cost and not as a part of product cost. But for managerial purposes, supplemental analysis may be made to show what it costs to serve certain customers, or what its costs to sell certain product lines, or the cost to sell in particular geographical areas. This breakdown of cost provides a means for control over sales and administration in much the same way as manufacturing cost accounting provides a means for control over production.

The Cost Elements

The manufactured cost of any product consists of three elements:

1. **Direct materials.**
2. **Direct labor.**
3. **Factory overhead.**

Direct materials cost is the cost of materials incorporated in the product. For example, the steel used in manufacturing socket wrenches would be a part of the product, and its cost could be measured as direct materials cost. The cost per unit may be too insignificant to measure as direct materials cost and may be classified under factory overhead as an indirect materials cost. For example a galvanizing solution used to coat the tools, while a part of the product, may not be easy to measure as a cost of any particular unit processed. Similarly, the cost of other materials that are not even a part of the product, such as abrasives and polishes, are classified as indirect materials.

Direct labor cost is the labor cost directly traceable to the creation of the products. Some workers, frequently designated as production workers, spend most of their time in turning out products. The labor cost attached to this time is called the direct labor cost. Labor cost that cannot be traced to the products is included as a part of factory overhead under the general heading of indirect labor. For example the idle time of the production workers, which is not related to any group of products under production, may be wasted, or may be used in cleaning the factory and repairing the equipment, or may be put to use in some other way. The wages or salaries of the factory supervisors, engineers, maintenance crew, and others who do not work on the product itself but who assist in the manufacturing operation are likewise classified as indirect labor.

Factory overhead cost consists of all manufacturing costs with the exception of direct materials and direct labor. Included under the heading of factory overhead are the costs of indirect materials, indirect supplies used, repairs and maintenance, heat and light, taxes, insurance, depreciation, and other costs to operate the manufacturing division. The factory overhead cost cannot be readily identified with individual products and thus is allocated to the products by a procedure discussed later in this chapter.

The Costing Procedure

The costs of manufacturing, regardless of their various characteristics, are recorded in an inventory account designated as Work in Process. This asset account is a focal account into which all product costs are funneled. After the products have been completed and placed in finished stock, the cost is transferred to another asset account, Finished Goods. When the products are sold, the cost is transferred from Finished Goods to Cost of Goods Sold.

Two basic systems of cost accounting are employed in the assignment of cost to products or service units. The system used depends upon the type of manufacturing operation.

1. The job order cost system—production by identifiable order or to customer specifications.
2. The process cost system—production through a process or an operation. Costs are averaged over the units produced.

A diagram of the cost flow in a job order cost system is as follows:

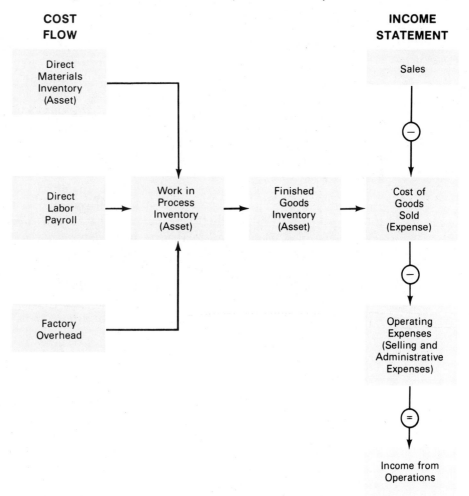

Fixed and Variable Costs

If costs are to be identified with some relevant unit, such as a department, product line, or given amount of service, it is necessary to determine how costs can be expected to behave under different conditions. For example, which costs can be expected to remain constant when there are increases or decreases in the amount of work done? Also, which costs increase as more work is performed and decrease when less work is performed? If costs are to be estimated and controlled properly, it is necessary to know whether or not the cost can be expected to change under given conditions and, if so, by what amount.

In accounting, fixed costs refer to the costs that do not change in total amount with changes in volume of output or activity over an established or relevant range. Such items as salary of a plant superintendent, depreciation, insurance, taxes, and rent usually remain the same regardless of whether the plant is above or below its normal operating capacity. However, a fixed cost, like any cost, is subject to certain variations. Rent may increase or insurance rates go up, but these changes are caused by factors independent of the firm's operating level.

Fixed costs are sometimes classified as being either committed costs or programmed costs. Management, in making long-range decisions, may commit a company to a cost pattern that extends several years into the future. For example, when a building is acquired, future years have to absorb the depreciation cost and the related property tax, insurance, repairs, and maintenance. These fixed costs are committed costs. Programmed costs, also referred to as **managed costs** or **discretionary costs**, are determined as a part of general management policy. A budget for product research and development, for example, may be established each year; or supervisory salaries are set each year by management decision. These costs are established at a certain fixed amount, but the amount is determined by management.

 Variable costs, in the strict sense, are costs that vary in direct proportion, or in a one-to-one relationship, to changes in productive output or activity. For example, direct materials cost is usually a variable cost with each unit manufactured requiring a certain quantity of material. Thus, the materials cost changes in direct proportion to the number of units manufactured.

Many costs are semivariable, i.e., they may change, but not in direct proportion to the changes in output. Often semivariable costs, which have the attributes of both variable and fixed costs, are falsely designated as variable costs. Repairs, for example, are not fixed in amount but probably increase as hours of activity increase. Among costs that are semivariable are indirect materials, supplies, indirect labor, fuel, and payroll taxes. Semivariable costs may be broken down into fixed and variable components, thus making it easier to budget and control costs and to apply cost data for decision-making purposes.

The Troublesome Fixed Costs

Fixed costs are often responsible for difficulties in accounting for costs. By definition, the total fixed cost remains constant over a specified range of activity or output, which means that the fixed cost per unit of product will vary. When a greater number of units are produced, the fixed cost per unit decreases. Conversely, when a smaller number of units are produced, the fixed cost per unit increases. This variability with respect to unit costs creates problems in product costing. The cost per unit depends upon the number of units being manufactured.

This problem of product costing is illustrated by assuming that variable factory overhead costs vary at a rate of $8 per unit of product manufactured and that the total fixed factory overhead amounts to $600,000 for the year. Cost budgets show the following:

Number of units of product manufactured..................	30,000	40,000	50,000
Variable factory overhead	$240,000	$320,000	$ 400,000
Fixed factory overhead...................................	600,000	600,000	600,000
Total factory overhead	$840,000	$920,000	$1,000,000
Unit factory overhead cost:			
Variable	$ 8	$ 8	$ 8
Fixed...	20	15	12
Total	$28	$23	$20

Note that the total variable cost increases with increases in the number of units produced but remains the same per unit of product. On the other hand, the total fixed cost, by definition, does not change with changes in output; it remains at $600,000. As more units are manufactured, however, the cost per unit decreases. For example, the fixed cost per unit is $20 when 30,000 units are produced but is only $12 when 50,000 units are produced.

Thus, the fixed costs create a problem in cost accounting. The unit cost of a manufactured product depends upon the number of units produced during the year. However, the products must be assigned a cost before the number of units produced during the year is determined. Ordinarily this problem is resolved by assigning a fixed factory overhead cost to each unit of product from a budget of costs and units to be manufactured at a defined normal level of operation.

For example, assume that the company in the illustration is normally expected to manufacture and sell 40,000 units a year with its present facilities. In this case, each unit of product would bear $15 of fixed factory overhead. At the end of the year, it may be found that only 30,000 units were actually manufactured. Therefore, only $450,000 of the total fixed factory overhead of $600,000 has been costed to the products by using a rate of $15 per unit (30,000 units × $15). The remaining $150,000 that was *unabsorbed* can be measured in the accounts as a capacity variance. It is the *variance*, or in other words the difference, that was caused by not using the manufacturing facilities according to the plan incorporated in the normal budget of operations. This type of problem is quite common in cost accounting and is discussed at greater length in later chapters.

Terminology Review

Cost (24)
Differential cost (25)
Incremental cost (25)
Decremental cost (25)
Variable cost per unit (25)
Fixed cost (25, 44)
Sunk cost (26)
Opportunity cost (27)
Cost standard (29)
Direct cost (30)
Indirect cost (30)
Controllable cost (32)
Uncontrollable cost (32)
Responsibility accounting (33)
Cost responsibility (33)

Lifo inventory method (40)
Fifo inventory method (40)
Period cost (41)
Natural classification (41)
Function (41)
Product cost (41)
Direct materials (42)
Indirect materials (42)
Direct labor (42)
Indirect labor (42)
Factory overhead (42)
Committed costs (44)
Programmed costs (44)
Variable costs (44)
Semivariable costs (44)

QUESTIONS FOR REVIEW

1. Explain, in general, how costs are used in budget preparation?

2. What are differential costs?

3. Can a fixed cost be a differential cost? How?

4. What is a sunk cost?

5. Why are sunk costs not relevant in decision making?

6. What are opportunity costs? Are opportunity costs important in decision making? Explain.

7. Distinguish between direct and indirect costs.

8. Can a direct cost be an indirect cost in some other situation?

9. Are direct costs always variable costs? Explain.

10. Explain how cost allocation can help management decide whether or not a department is able to carry its share of total supporting costs.

11. Will an allocated cost be reduced by the elimination of a department? Explain.

12. If a department is eliminated, how is the cost handled that was previously allocated to that department?

13. An advertising budget has been established at $600,000 a year and is allocated to divisions on the basis of sales revenue. A division to which $100,000 of the advertising was allocated, has been eliminated. Does this mean that the advertising cost of $600,000 will be reduced? Explain.

14. Referring to Question 13, are there circumstances under which the $600,000 of advertising could be reduced by elimination of a division?

15. Distinguish between controllable and noncontrollable costs.

16. Are fixed costs uncontrollable? Explain.

17. Does time have any effect upon the controllability of cost? Explain.

18. What is responsibility accounting?

19. How does a responsibility accounting system serve as a subtle means of enforcing company policy?

20. How do period costs differ from product costs?

21. Name the three cost elements. Can all three cost elements be identified directly with the product? Explain.

22. Distinguish between fixed costs and variable costs.

23. Why are fixed costs considered to be troublesome?

EXERCISES

1. Cost Decision. Weyman Construction Company has equipment that can be rented to another contractor for $5,000 a month under an agreement whereby Weyman pays the operating costs estimated at $1,500 a month. This equipment can be used by Weyman to earn $8,000 a month with operating costs estimated at $1,500 a month.

Required:

(1) Identify the sunk cost in this decisional situation.

(2) What is the opportunity cost?

(3) Compute the profit advantage from the better alternative.

2. Cost Decision. Grove Metals Company purchased soaking vats last month at a cost of $38,000. The superintendent of production finds that the vats are not large enough to be used as intended and can be used only for a relatively minor part of production.

The office manager informs the superintendent that a company has been located that will buy the vats at a price of $22,000.

The superintendent states that the company cannot afford to take a loss by selling the vats. With $38,000 invested, the company must continue to use the vats the best way that it can over the next several years until the cost is recovered.

Required: Comment on the positions taken by the office manager and the superintendent.

3. Opportunity Cost and Sunk Cost. Benjamin Kessel is planning to retire early from a position that pays him a salary of $50,000 a year. If he retires early, he plans to pursue his hobby of making and selling porcelain figures but will enlarge his operations into a part-time business. During the past years while he has been working, he has earned $4,000 a year before income tax from this hobby and can reasonably expect the same return each year in the future.

If he were to operate on a larger scale as a part-time business, he estimates total revenues and costs would be as follows:

Revenue		$56,000
Cost of figures made and sold	$21,000	
Wages for helper	10,000	
Rent	2,400	
Utilities	1,500	
Miscellaneous	800	35,700
Income before income tax		$20,300

Kessel also will receive $25,000 a year from an annuity that he purchased. The annuity will be received when he retires.

Required:

(1) If Kessel decides to retire, what is the minimum value that he places on the pursuit of the hobby?

(2) What is the opportunity cost of retirement?

(3) What is the sunk cost in this decisional situation?

4. Product Line Decision. Any one of three different product lines can be produced by Van Ness Parts Company with the present equipment in one of the divisions. The annual depreciation of the equipment is $7,200, and the annual cost to operate the equipment, regardless of product line manufactured, is $6,100.

Product A is expected to yield sales revenue of $87,000 a year with increased costs of production amounting to $51,000. Product B should yield sales revenue of

$58,000 a year with increased costs of $17,000. Product C should yield sales revenue of $156,000 with increased costs of $122,000.

Required:

(1) Which of the three product lines seems to offer the best profit potential based on the information given? Show computations.
(2) Identify the sunk costs.
(3) What is the opportunity cost of selecting only the best product line?

5. Opportunity Cost and Sunk Cost. Angela Powell is considering the possibility of obtaining an advanced degree from State University. She already has credits toward the degree and estimates that she can obtain the degree in one year.

In order to do this, however, she must give up her job that pays a salary of $24,000 per year. Living costs, whether she goes on for the degree or not, are estimated at $15,000 for the year. However, the cost of tuition and books at the university will amount to $4,800.

Required:

(1) What is the opportunity cost if Powell decides to return to school?
(2) What is the sunk cost in this decision?
(3) Identify the differential cost in the decision.

6. Cost Classifications. Tina Rozelle is the manager of Department 7 and has the authority to buy supplies, hire labor, and incur telephone and postage charges for the department. Various costs for the month of March, 1985, are as follows:

Plant superintendent's salary	$ 8,000
Factory heat and light	3,200
Maintenance and repairs—Dept. 7	2,600
Telephone and postage—Dept. 7	1,100
Plant maintenance and repairs	1,700
Supplies used—Dept. 7	1,400
Salary—Tina Rozelle	2,500
Labor cost—Dept. 7	14,600
Plant depreciation	3,000
Equipment depreciation—Dept. 7	2,300
Total	$40,400

Required:

(1) List the costs that can be controlled by Tina Rozelle.
(2) List the costs that can be directly identified with Department 7.
(3) List the costs that can be directly Identified with the plant.
(4) To determine the full cost to operate Department 7, which costs were allocated?

7. Controllable and Noncontrollable Costs. The manager of Department 3 of Billings Tool Company is responsible for the acquisition and use of materials and supplies in the department, maintenance and repair of equipment, telephone, postage, and travel. The manager also hires personnel and sets wage rates. The superintendent of the division, however, acquires equipment used in the departments and is responsible for building occupancy costs such as depreciation of the building, heat and light, taxes, and insurance.

A budget report for Department 3 for the month of March, 1985, follows. Costs of building occupancy have been allocated to the departments.

	Budget	Actual	Variance Over (Under) Budget
Materials and supplies	$ 7,300	$ 7,420	$ 120
Salary of department manager	3,000	3,000	—
Wages	19,500	19,300	(200)
Maintenance and repairs of equipment	1,700	1,740	40
Building maintenance	2,600	2,950	350
Depreciation—equipment	1,200	1,200	—
Depreciation—building	2,300	2,300	—
Taxes and insurance—building	850	850	—
Heat and light	1,400	1,870	470
Telephone	380	350	(30)
Postage	220	210	(10)
Travel	450	430	(20)
Total	$40,900	$41,620	$ 720

Required:

(1) List the direct cost classifications of Department 3.

(2) Prepare a cost report that shows only the costs controlled by the department manager.

8. Elimination of a Department. The president of Holland Company notes that Department 2 has been operating at a loss. The president believes that profits would be increased by $18,000 if this department were to be eliminated, inasmuch as the costs of this department are in excess of revenue by this amount as shown on the following table:

	Departments					
	1	2	3	4	5	Total
Revenue	$214,000	$173,000	$217,000	$136,000	$115,000	$855,000
Direct costs of department	$113,000	$146,000	$107,000	$ 82,000	$ 62,000	$510,000
Allocated company costs	58,000	45,000	61,000	41,000	32,000	237,000
Total cost	$171,000	$191,000	$168,000	$123,000	$ 94,000	$747,000
Net income (loss)	$ 43,000	$(18,000)	$ 49,000	$ 13,000	$ 21,000	$108,000

Required: Is the president correct? Prepare an analysis to indicate what the results would be if Department 2 were eliminated.

9. Full Cost of Departmental Operation. The superintendent of a division of Abbott Wiring Inc. is responsible for the operation of three departments that are located in one building. Department A occupies 60% of the space, and the remaining two departments share the rest of the space equally. Total building occupancy cost amounts to $90,000 for the year. The superintendent's salary for the year is $75,000. There are 30 employees in Department A, 30 in Department B, and 40 in Department C.

The direct costs of departmental operation for the year are as follows:

| | Departments | | | |
	A	B	C	Total
Direct costs......................................	$47,000	$54,000	$61,000	$162,000

Required: Prepare a report showing the total cost to operate each department.

10. *Direct and Indirect Cost.* Teller Fine Foods Inc. operates with three divisions: A, B, and C. Division A produces revenue of $1,500,000 for the year; Division B produces revenue of $900,000; and Division C produces $750,000. The total cost for the year for each division is given below.

| | Divisions | | | |
	A	B	C	Total
Materials, labor, and other direct costs	$ 720,000	$435,000	$521,000	$1,676,000
Allocated company costs	300,000	300,000	300,000	900,000
Total cost..............................	$1,020,000	$735,000	$821,000	$2,576,000

Required:

(1) List by division the costs that can be directly attributed to that division.
(2) Do all three divisions provide an amount over their direct costs to the total operation? Identify any division that does not.
(3) Is there any division that covers direct costs but does not bear its full share of costs of the total operation? Identify that division, if any.
(4) Which division(s) can bear all of its share of the allocated cost?

11. *Unit Fixed Costs.* Nestor Fixtures Company has budgeted fixed costs for the year at $120,000. It is estimated that no less than 40,000 units of product are to be manufactured next year. In a relatively poor year, 50,000 units would be made. If the company were to operate at an average or normal level, it could make 60,000 units. With very good conditions, it would be possible to make 80,000 units.

Required:

(1) Determine the fixed cost per unit under each of the assumptions stated.
(2) Which unit cost would you be inclined to use in determining product cost in the long run? Explain.

12. *Unit Product Cost.* You were told that materials costing $21 for each unit of product are needed to produce a certain product line. Three units of product can be manufactured in each hour with a labor cost of $15 per hour. Total fixed cost of manufacturing amounts to $300,000 per year. No other costs are incurred in manufacturing.

Required:

(1) Why are you unable to determine the total unit cost to manufacture the product?
(2) If 60,000 units are to be manufactured each year, what would be the unit product cost?

13. *Income and Flow of Merchandise.* Allen Stores had an inventory of merchandise at the beginning of the year consisting of 25,000 units at a cost of $5 per unit. During the year, 150,000 units of this line of merchandise were purchased at a cost of $7 per unit. The company sold 160,000 units during the year for a total of $1,600,000.

Required:

(1) Determine the cost of goods sold by the first-in, first-out (fifo) method.

(2) Determine the cost of goods sold by the last-in, first-out (lifo) method.

(3) Compute the excess of revenue over cost of goods sold (that is, the gross margin) under both inventory methods.

14. Income Measurement in Manufacturing. Bolling Manufacturing Company used materials costing $180,000 in the production of 10,000 units of product. No materials were on hand at the beginning or at the end of the year. Labor costing $50,000 was used in producing the units. Other costs of manufacturing, such as factory superintendence, heat and light, taxes, and insurance, are all fixed costs and amounted to $100,000 for the year. Normal production for the year is considered to be 10,000 units. There was no finished goods inventory at the beginning of the year, and 8,000 units of product were sold during the year.

Required:

(1) Compute the unit cost of manufacturing the product. Show the unit cost broken down by cost element, that is, direct materials, direct labor, and factory overhead.

(2) Determine the cost of the goods sold and the cost of the finished goods inventory at the end of the year.

PROBLEMS

2-1. Cost Classification. The various costs of production for the Bellevue Plant are as follows:

Materials—used only for the manufacture of Product 17 in Department 8
Production wages in Department 8
Plant taxes and insurance
Lubrication of equipment, Department 8
Supplies used, Department 8
Plant heat and light
Plant supervision
Depreciation of equipment, Department 8
Salary, supervisor of Department 8
Plant depreciation

Required:

(1) Identify the costs that are direct or indirect with respect to Department 8.
(2) Identify the costs that are controllable by the supervisor of Department 8. (Give your reason for classification in situations that are uncertain.)
(3) Identify the costs that are fixed or variable. (Give your reason for classification in situations that are uncertain.)

2-2. Identification of Controllable Costs. The departmental supervisors at Reed-McAlister Inc. are authorized to purchase the materials needed in production, to hire and assign the production workers, and to incur various costs for their departments. The equipment used in the department is acquired at a higher management level, but supervisors are responsible for proper care and maintenance. The salaries of the supervisors are shown under the cost of supervision.

Sometimes labor is loaned to another department. Company policy is to charge the supervisor who loans the workers with the labor cost. However, the cost of this labor is not included as a cost of the products of the lending department.

During the year, Department 7 manufactured 40,000 units as budgeted. Budgeted and actual costs for Department 7 are:

	Budget	Actual
Materials	$210,000	$208,600
Labor	119,000	121,300
Labor loaned to Department 11	17,000	16,500
Department costs:		
Supervision	21,000	21,000
Indirect materials	14,300	14,700
Repairs and maintenance	2,100	2,200
Equipment operating cost	3,400	3,300
Depreciation—equipment	4,000	4,000
Allocated plant costs:		
Superintendence	19,500	21,000
Heat, light, and power	3,700	3,900
Taxes and insurance	5,400	6,100
Other plant occupancy cost	5,000	6,700
Depreciation—plant	7,000	7,000
Total cost	$431,400	$436,300

Required:

(1) Compute the budgeted unit cost of the product and the actual unit cost following the established company policy.
(2) Prepare a cost report that will show only the costs that can be controlled by the supervisor. Show cost variations from the budget.
(3) Does it appear that the supervisor was responsible for a large part of the variation between budgeted and actual costs?
(4) Why should a supervisor be held accountable for the labor cost of workers loaned to other departments?

2-3. Types of Cost and Product Cost. A small metal cutter is manufactured at the Hartsville plant of Welden Products Inc. Normal production is 200,000 units, and fixed costs are applied to the products on the basis of 200,000 units produced per year.

The cost report for last year is as follows:

Direct materials	$ 700,000
Direct labor	400,000
Supervision	50,000
Supplies used	10,000
Maintenance and repairs	40,000
Telephone	30,000
Postage	10,000
Depreciation	20,000
Heat and light	80,000
Insurance	5,000
Property taxes	6,000
Rent	4,000
Allocated home office costs	15,000
Total	$1,370,000

Direct materials, supplies used, and direct labor are the only costs that vary with production. The costs of plant occupancy (heat and light, insurance, property taxes, and rent) are allocated to the metal cutter division on the basis of the space occupied by that division.

Required:

(1) Determine the variable and the fixed costs per unit of product.
(2) Determine the total and unit direct costs for the product line center.
(3) Determine the total unit cost of the product.
(4) If the metal cutter is sold for $5 per unit, will the product contribute anything above the variable costs to the recovery of the fixed costs?
(5) If the cutter is sold for $6.50 per unit, will all of the direct costs be covered?
(6) If the cutter is sold for $7.50 per unit, will all of the costs be covered?
(7) Assume that next year only 150,000 units will be manufactured but that the fixed costs will be assigned to production on the basis of a normal production of 200,000 units. How much of the fixed overhead will not be costed to the products? What term is used to designate the unabsorbed fixed overhead?
(8) What would the total unit cost be if 150,000 units a year is designated as normal capacity?

2-4. Product Costs and Control. Heavy metal pails used as containers for roofing, asphalt, aluminum paint, and various heavy industrial materials are manufactured by RB Containers Company. The cost of the materials for each of these containers is $6.50; the labor cost per container is $4. Various supplies used in production cost $1 per container.

The costs to operate the department in which these containers are made are fixed and have been estimated for the year as follows:

Supervision	$73,000
Equipment and operating costs	6,000
Repairs and maintenance of equipment	3,500
Depreciation	1,500
Total	$84,000

The supervisor of this department can control all of these costs with the exception of depreciation of equipment at $1,500 and the supervisor's own salary of $45,000 that is included in the total cost of departmental supervision.

Costs for the overall plant have been estimated for the year as follows:

Plant superintendence	$130,000
Indirect labor	61,000
Plant occupancy cost	23,000
Depreciation—factory	26,000
Total	$240,000

Factory overhead is allocated to the various departments on the basis of a factor that combines space occupied with the number of employees. The department in which these containers are produced is expected to absorb 25% of the total plant cost of $240,000. This department produces this type of container exclusively.

Required:

(1) What is the variable cost per container? Does the answer depend upon the number of containers produced?

(2) Identify the indirect costs of the department. Identify the costs that can be controlled by the department supervisor.

(3) What is the total cost per container if the production of 120,000 units per year is considered normal? What would the answer be if a production of 150,000 units was considered normal?

(4) Assume that there was no finished goods inventory at the beginning of the year and that 120,000 units were produced according to normal expectations. During the year, 90,000 units were sold. Compute the cost of goods sold and the cost of the inventory of finished goods at the end of the year.

2-5. Cost Control and Emergencies. Wayne Alpert states that he does not have control over some of the costs charged to him. For example, his supervisor may at times accept orders that must be completed in a very short time, making it necessary for Alpert to engage additional casual labor at a cost of $6 per hour. Also, materials and supplies may have to be obtained under emergency conditions at unfavorable terms. The budgeting process is very difficult, he states, because of the many uncertainties.

Last year Alpert estimated the cost of materials and supplies at a cost of $116,000. Repairs and maintenance are his responsibility, as well as telephone, office supplies, and postage. The estimate for telephone last year was $4,600; for office supplies, $17,300; and for postage, $14,400. Repairs and maintenance costs were budgeted at $21,600. Included in the budget was Alpert's salary of $30,000. Regular labor cost was budgeted at $153,000. Casual labor was budgeted at 800 hours for a cost of $4,800. General factory overhead allocated to the department was budgeted at $72,000. Machinery and equipment are the responsibility of plant management. Depreciation is not charged to the departments.

Actual costs charged to Alpert's department are:

Materials and supplies	$127,000
Salary (Alpert)	30,000
Wages, regular	153,000
Wages, casual labor	16,800
Telephone	5,300
Office supplies	17,200
Postage	14,600
Repairs and maintenance	23,700
Allocated factory overhead	78,000
Total	$465,600

Required:

(1) Comment on the merits of Alpert's argument with respect to cost control.

(2) Compare actual and budgeted costs for the year, showing variances.

(3) Are there costs included in the budget over which Alpert has no control? Identify these costs.

2-6. Responsibility Cost Report. Joseph Manzek is responsible for the operation of the finishing department at Weber Mills Inc. A budget for the department for the month of June is as follows:

Materials and supplies	$ 9,640
Labor	7,320
Supervision	3,000
Fuel	1,680
Telephone	430
Postage	260
Taxes and insurance	1,750
Heat and light	1,540
Repairs and maintenance	1,870
Depreciation—equipment	900
Other allocated plant costs	3,400
Total	$31,790

The actual cost of materials and supplies for the month was $9,570, fuel, $1,710. Telephone amounted to $480. Repairs and maintenance cost was $1,850. Heat and light cost was $1,600, and the other allocated plant costs were $5,700. All other costs were in agreement with the budget.

The taxes and insurance, heat and light, depreciation of equipment, and other allocated plant costs are controlled by upper levels of management. All other costs with the exception of supervision are approved by Manzek.

Required:

(1) Prepare a responsibility cost report showing a comparison of the budget and actual costs for June.

(2) Compare the total cost for the department with the total budget. Does it appear that Manzek was responsible for a large part of the unfavorable cost variation?

2-7. Preparation of Responsibility Cost Budget. Hayes Boyd has just been appointed supervisor of a production department of Koplin Industries. This department manufactures small parts used by other departments. To a large extent, costs are influenced by the demands of other departments.

In preparing the budget, Boyd reviews the production budgets of those other departments that have requested hours of service from his department as follows:

Requesting Department	Hours Requested
8	5,200
11	7,500
14	5,800
19	6,500

Boyd has discussed the budget estimates with his superior, Lisa Cummings. She advises him that the supervisor of Department 11 tends to overestimate requirements and that the budget will be more realistic if reduced by 20% of the hours requested.

Conversely, the supervisor of Department 19 is likely to underestimate and to come in with last minute requests that will probably add as much as 500 hours to the budget.

All workers in the department are to receive a wage rate of $10 per hour, and each will be expected to work 1,600 hours per year. Boyd has the authority to hire an assistant at a salary of $24,000 per year, and his own salary has been established by Cummings at $37,000.

Materials required for the year are estimated to cost $323,000. Other costs related to departmental operation have been budgeted as follows:

Supplies	$39,000
Fuel	7,000
Repairs and maintenance	4,500
Plant occupancy cost allocated	14,000
Total	$64,500

Cummings states that top management does not like to see much overtime but recognizes that some of it may be unavoidable. She advises that 700 hours of overtime pay at time and a half be added to the budget.

Required: From the information given, prepare a responsibility cost budget for Boyd's department. Estimate the number of employees needed for production.

2-8. Responsibility Cost Report. A cost report for the month of March for Department A of Foster Metals Company is given below.

	Budget	Actual	Variance (Under) Over
Materials and supplies	$17,280	$17,250	$ (30)
Wages	23,400	23,400	—
Payroll taxes	1,800	1,800	—
Employee benefits	2,400	2,400	—
Taxes and insurance	3,300	3,700	400
Travel	450	1,240	790
Postage	220	230	10
Heat and light	1,580	1,540	(40)
Repairs	800	2,670	1,870
Maintenance	200	150	(50)
Lubrication	500	400	(100)
Fuel	1,320	1,350	30
Supervision	6,000	6,000	—
Depreciation—equipment	700	700	—
Other plant costs allocated	3,400	3,700	300
Total	$63,350	$66,530	$3,180

The department supervisor states that the breakdown of a major unit of equipment during the month made it necessary to have the work done on an emergency basis at an abnormally high cost.

Another unrelated problem with an equipment breakdown caused travel cost to be high. An emergency trip was made to obtain an essential part for replacement on a machine that suddenly broke down in operation.

The supervisor has no authority over taxes and insurance, heat and light, supervision, or other plant costs allocated.

Required:

(1) Prepare a revised cost report showing only the costs controlled by the supervisor.

(2) Do you accept the reasoning given for the relatively large cost variances in repairs and in travel expense? Comment.

2-9. Cost Decision. Benedict Stamp Company uses one area of its plant for record storage. The plant superintendent complains that this is a waste of valuable space that could be put to productive use or at least rented out to some other company. The records could be microfilmed and stored in a much smaller area at an estimated cost of $16,000. The space released can be rented to Western Truck Lines at an annual rental of $21,000.

A new line of product can be manufactured in this space. Marketing studies and cost estimates show that the new product can be expected to produce the following results each year:

Net sales	$258,000
Materials	$ 83,000
Labor	31,200
Other additional costs	17,800
Allocated costs of the plant (relative space occupied):	
Heat and light	12,000
Repairs and maintenance	11,500
Taxes and insurance	19,000
Superintendence*	50,000
Depreciation	25,000
	$249,500
Income before income tax	$ 8,500

*Allocated on the basis of employees in each work area.

The superintendent is disappointed to learn that the new product will contribute relatively little to the total operation and is inclined to rent the space to Western Truck Lines.

Required:

(1) How much will the new product line contribute to the total operation? (Exclude allocated costs.)
(2) What is the *net* contribution of the new product line, assuming that the estimates are accurate and considering alternatives?
(3) Identify the sunk costs in this decision.
(4) Identify the opportunity cost in this decision.

2-10. Cost Allocations. Cambria Public Library has four divisions, classified by type of books and reading materials. The four divisions are Technical, Historical, General, and Children. Direct costs of operation of each division for the year are as follows:

	Technical	Historical	General	Children
Salaries	$58,000	$31,000	$34,000	$28,000
Books	11,400	8,900	12,600	3,200
Periodicals	3,300	3,100	3,700	2,300
Supplies	2,900	3,200	2,800	2,600

Other data with respect to library operation are:

	Percentage of Space Occupied	Number of Employees	Number of Orders Processed
Technical	25%	40	40
Historical	35	30	20
General................................	20	20	30
Children	20	10	10
Total	100%	100	100

The costs of operating the library as a total entity follow.

Building occupancy and utilities.......................	$40,000
Library administration	75,000
Order department	50,000

Required: Prepare a cost report showing the total direct cost for each library division, the total allocated cost, and the total cost for each division.

2-11. Cost Flow—Merchandise and Manufacturing. Boston Company manufactures a type of tubular steel furniture. The tubing that is used to produce the furniture is purchased from Donatelli Distributors. Donatelli Distributors is not a manufacturer. Donatelli buys the tubes of steel and resells to customers without doing any work to convert the tubes to other forms.

Donatelli had no inventory on hand at the beginning of the year. During the year, the distributor purchased tubing at a cost of $380,000. The costs per unit remained the same throughout the year. Tubing with a cost of $310,000 was sold during the year. Operating costs of sales and office salaries, advertising, taxes and insurance, rent, heat and light, and telephone in aggregate amounted to $65,000 and were period costs for the year. Sales revenue was $435,000.

Boston Company had no inventory of materials at the beginning of the year. Tubing having a cost of $175,000 was purchased from Donatelli Distributors. Other materials costing $275,000 were also purchased. At the end of the year, Boston Company counted materials inventory and assigned a cost of $50,000 to this inventory.

During the year, Boston operated at a normal capacity of 80,000 product units. Labor cost of manufacturing was $240,000. Various other costs of manufacturing such as plant supervision, factory taxes and insurance, factory heat and light, and factory telephone amounted to $120,000.

Boston Company also incurred selling and administrative expenses for the period, such as sales and office salaries, advertising, rent, taxes and insurance, and telephone. These operating expenses for the year amounted to $130,000. During the year 75,000 units of furniture were sold for $900,000. There was no inventory of partially completed or completed furniture on hand at the beginning of the year.

Required:

(1) Prepare a summary income statement for the year for Donatelli Distributors showing revenue, cost of goods sold, and operating expenses.

(2) Compute the cost for Boston Company to produce a unit of this furniture. Determine the unit cost by cost element: direct materials, direct labor, and manufacturing overhead.

(3) Prepare a summary income statement for the year for Boston Company showing revenue, cost of goods sold, and operating expenses.

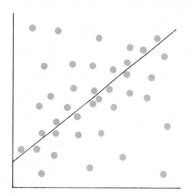

3

MANUFACTURING COSTS

Chapter Objectives

This chapter should enable you to:

1. Explain when a job order cost accounting system is used.
2. Describe how direct materials, direct labor, and factory overhead are costed to products in job order costing.
3. Determine factory overhead rates.
4. Explain why a saving in direct labor time may result in both labor and overhead savings.
5. Explain what is meant by normal capacity.

In addition to knowing how costs can be used for planning and control, management needs to know how costs can be used to determine the cost of manufacturing a product line or a unit of a given product line. In cost accounting, one of the objectives is to determine the cost of the products manufactured. These costs are a major factor in the determination of net income and in the determination of the inventory value on the balance sheet. Product costs can also be applied, at least to some extent, in planning and control.

A manager of a production function may estimate that it will cost a given amount to manufacture a specified quantity of product for a customer. Hence, the manager will watch the progress of the job and will control costs as the job moves toward completion. In other manufacturing situations, it may not be possible to exercise control on a project or product order basis because of the nature of the manufacturing operation.

In a not-for-profit organization, the cost of manufacturing a product line or the cost to operate a department may not be relevant. The cost objective may, instead, be the estimation, measurement, and control of the cost to conduct a special program to educate better mathematics and science teachers as a part of the function of a university. Or, a museum may want to determine the cost of having a particular exhibit for a season. In any situation, there will be direct costs that can be readily identified with the objective; and there will be indirect costs that may be allocated by using some reasonable basis for allocation. The principles used in accounting for the costs of a manufacturer can often be adapted for a wide variety of applications and will be discussed in this chapter.

As stated in Chapter 2, manufacturing costs are accumulated and assigned to the products through the use of one of two basic cost accounting systems:

1. The job order cost system.
2. The process cost system.

This chapter will concentrate on the job order cost system with process cost accounting being covered in an appendix at the end of the chapter.

THE JOB ORDER COST SYSTEM

The job order cost system is used when the products are manufactured in identifiable lots or groups or when the products are manufactured according to customer specifications. A printer, for example, may receive an order to print 5,000 copies of a summer school bulletin. This bulletin is prepared as directed by the school, and it differs in form and content from the printing work done for other customers. The printer's cost is accumulated by customer order. Manufacturers and contractors, like the printer, may work on a project or order basis and identify cost by project or order.

In a job order cost system, the cost is assigned to the jobs passing through the plant and accumulated on forms referred to as job or production orders. A separate production order is kept for each job going through the plant. Each order is usually divided into three basic sections—materials, labor, and overhead; thus, the three cost elements are accounted for separately. An additional section is usually provided in which a summary of the cost is shown and a unit cost is determined. This section is completed when the job is finished. The file of production orders in process constitutes a subsidiary ledger in support of the work in process account in the general ledger. A production order is shown at the top of page 62.

COSTING DIRECT MATERIALS AND DIRECT LABOR

Direct materials and direct labor are the materials and labor that can be identified with the products without allocation. These costs are measured and assigned directly to the production orders. When materials are purchased on

PRODUCTION ORDER

Customer _____   Job Order _____

Description _____   Date Started _____

Quantity _____   Date Completed _____

Materials			Labor			Overhead	
Date	Code	Amount	Date	Hours	Amount		
						Direct Labor Hours	_____
						Overhead Rate	_____
						Applied Overhead	_____
						Summary	
						Direct Materials	
						Direct Labor	
						Factory Overhead	_____
						Total Cost	_____
						Unit Cost	_____

account for $75,000, an entry is made to debit Materials and to credit Accounts Payable as follows:

Materials	75,000	
Accounts Payable		75,000
Purchase of materials to be used in production.		

As direct materials are used in production, requisition tickets are prepared showing the cost of materials used on specific production orders. If requisition tickets indicate that direct materials costing $60,000 have been transferred from the materials inventory to production, the journal entry appears as follows:

Work in Process	60,000	
Materials		60,000
Direct materials requisitioned for production.		

Factory payroll is recorded by a debit to Payroll with offsetting credits to Employees Income Tax Payable, FICA Tax Payable, other liability accounts for payroll deductions, and Wages Payable as follows:

Payroll	100,000	
Employees Income Tax Payable...........................		18,000
FICA Tax Payable..		7,000
Union Dues Payable.....................................		1,000
Wages Payable		74,000
To record factory payroll for the month.		

In this example, for the sake of simplicity, it has been assumed that all labor is direct labor. In practice, there will be some idle time and set-up time for production workers. Hence, a portion of the payroll, even a payroll for all production workers, will consist of pay for some hours that cannot be charged to any production order. This cost will be a part of factory overhead along with the cost of hospitalization, sick pay, or other benefits that cannot be identified with orders of production.

The entry for distribution of the above direct labor payroll to the various production orders, assuming that direct labor time tickets showing 10,000 hours of labor at $10 an hour were used in producing various orders, is:

Work in Process	100,000	
Payroll		100,000
Direct labor costed to production.		

Assume that included in the total materials is $21,000 for Order #1017 and $20,000 for Order #1018. Also assume that $20,000 of labor applies to Order #1018. Entries are also made on the individual production orders supporting the work in process account.

Production supervisors, in planning their operations, may estimate the direct materials and direct labor cost for each of the orders for which they are responsible. They subsequently measure the actual cost and compare it with the estimates, taking into account the stage of completion for each order.

For example, a report on production may be prepared as given. The variance column shows the differences between estimated and actual amounts. The total estimates for each order have been adjusted by the percentage completed so that a valid comparison can be made with the actual amounts. The total direct materials cost of Order #1019 was estimated to be $20,000. The order is 50 percent complete as to materials. Hence, the estimated cost at 50 percent is $10,000 (50% of $20,000).

For example, the production schedule may be prepared as follows:

Direct Materials

Order Number	Estimate	Actual	Dollar Variance Over (Under)	Percentage of Completion
1017	$22,000	$21,000	$(1,000)	100%
1018	19,500	20,000	500	100
*1019	10,000	14,000	4,000	50
*1020	5,000	5,000	-0-	25
Total	$56,500	$60,000	$3,500	

*Estimates adjusted to percentage of completion basis.

A report that compares actual direct labor hours with the estimated hours can reveal whether or not more hours were used on an order than expected. Again, the estimates are made comparable with the actual results by determining the percentage of work completed and applying that percentage to the total estimate. For example, Order #1020 is only 10 percent complete with respect to direct labor. The total estimate on that order for direct labor hours must have been 4,500 hours if 450 hours is 10 percent of the total estimate.

Direct Labor Hours

Order Number*	Estimate	Actual	Direct Labor Hour Variance Over (Under)	Percentage of Completion
1017	4,450	4,000	(450)	80%
1018	1,800	2,000	200	50
1019	3,300	3,500	200	50
1020	450	500	50	10
Total	10,000	10,000	-0-	

*Estimates adjusted to percentage of completion basis.

The report on direct labor hours can be converted to a direct labor cost report by multiplying the direct labor hours by the direct labor hour rate (in this case, $10) as shown below.

Direct Labor Cost

Order Number*	Estimate	Actual	Direct Labor Dollar Variance Over (Under)	Percentage of Completion
1017	$44,500	$40,000	$(4,500)	80%
1018	18,000	20,000	2,000	50
1019	33,000	35,000	2,000	50
1020	4,500	5,000	500	10
Total	$100,000	$100,000	-0-	

*Estimates adjusted to percentage of completion.

Supervisors are able to use such cost information as they follow each order from its inception to completion. As a cost overrun (unfavorable variation from estimate) develops, they can take corrective measures. The preceding example shows that Order Number 1019 is 50 percent completed with respect to both materials and labor and that more materials and more hours were used than anticipated. Knowing what caused the overrun may enable the supervisor to find ways to reduce cost. Or, it may be found that the estimate was unrealistically low; in which case, budgets are revised.

COSTING FACTORY OVERHEAD

Factory overhead, unlike direct materials and direct labor, cannot be requisitioned or measured directly as a cost of any particular production order.

Factory overhead consists of a variety of costs, such as indirect materials, indirect labor, insurance, and taxes, all of which are indirectly related to the products.

Factory overhead is attached to the products indirectly by means of a factor that can be directly related to the products. This factor serves as a bridge between factory overhead and the products. Often the factor chosen for overhead allocation is direct labor hours, machine hours, or direct labor cost. Factory overhead is budgeted for the year, and the factor selected is also budgeted. The budgeted factor is then divided into the budgeted overhead to obtain an overhead rate. Products then are assigned overhead cost by mutliplying the actual quantities of the factor by the rate calculated.

The factor chosen as a basis for overhead allocation should be related logically to both the overhead and the product. If machinery plays an important role in the manufacturing operation, the overhead cost likely consists largely of power cost, lubrication, maintenance, repairs, depreciation, and other costs closely related to machine operation. This cost is necessary in the manufacturing process and assists in the creation of the products. The benefits received by the products can probably be best measured by the machine hours used in their production. Therefore, overhead cost should be allocated to the products on a machine hour basis. For other departments in the plant that are more "labor intensive" than "capital intensive," direct labor cost, direct labor hours, or some other basis may be more appropriate for overhead allocation.

Computing the Overhead Rate

The calculation of an overhead rate is illustrated by assuming that several factory overhead budgets have been prepared for various levels of operating activity. A series of budgets for various levels of operating activity is called a flexible budget, as illustrated at the top of the following page.

In this example, budgeted direct labor hours have been selected as the factor for obtaining a product costing rate. Note that the variable cost is $3 per hour at any level of operation, whereas the fixed rate depends upon the number of direct labor hours used in the computation. The total rate of $8 per hour used for this illustration has been computed at 10,000 direct labor hours.

$$\frac{\text{Budgeted factory overhead}}{\text{Budgeted direct labor hours}} = \frac{\$80,000}{10,000} = \$8 \text{ per direct labor hour}$$

During the year, the products passing through the plant were charged with budgeted factory overhead. Assume that 10,000 hours of direct labor were used during the year. While the manufacturing operation was going on, various entries were made to cost the products. In aggregate, it would be as if one summary entry were made as follows:

Work in Process	80,000	
Applied Factory Overhead		80,000
Allocation of factory overhead cost to the orders, 10,000 hours at $8 each.		

Budgeted direct labor hours	6,000	8,000	10,000*	12,000
Budgeted factory overhead:				
Variable:				
Indirect materials	$ 7,500	$10,000	$12,500	$15,000
Repairs and maintenance	5,700	7,600	9,500	11,400
Power and light	4,800	6,400	8,000	9,600
Total	$18,000	$24,000	$30,000	$36,000
Fixed:				
Indirect labor and supervision	$18,000	$18,000	$18,000	$18,000
Repairs and maintenance	6,500	6,500	6,500	6,500
Power and light	5,500	5,500	5,500	5,500
Factory rent	8,000	8,000	8,000	8,000
Depreciation of equipment	12,000	12,000	12,000	12,000
Total	$50,000	$50,000	$50,000	$50,000
Total budgeted overhead	$68,000	$74,000	$80,000	$86,000
Rate per direct labor hour:				
Variable	$ 3.000	$ 3.000	$ 3.000	$ 3.000
Fixed	8.333	6.250	5.000	4.167
Total	$11.333	$ 9.250	$ 8.000	$ 7.167

*Level selected for rate to cost the products.

Each order is charged with a portion of the overhead as it goes through production at the rate of $8 for each direct labor hour charged to the order.

The cost shown for Order Number 1018 may now be summarized at this stage of its production as follows:

Direct materials	$20,000
Direct labor (2,000 hours at $5 each)	10,000
Factory overhead (2,000 hours at $8 each)	16,000
Total cost	$46,000

Cost for direct labor and overhead is accumulated for orders until they are completed. At completion, the cost of the orders is transferred out of work in process and into finished goods.

Why does the accountant go to so much trouble in assigning factory overhead cost to the products, instead of waiting until the end of the year when all of the actual factory overhead has been collected, the actual direct labor hours of operation have been determined, an actual overhead rate has been calculated, and actual cost has been allocated to the orders that were manufactured during the year? Why bother with a budget and a budget rate?

When a budget rate is used, product costs can be determined quickly. There is no need to wait until the end of a month or other fiscal period to determine the cost of making a certain order or batch of product units. The cost is available while production is in process, thus making it easier to control operations as they occur.

Also, product cost does not fluctuate as it would if actual overhead rates were used in computing monthly cost. Seasonal variations throughout the year would cause the overhead cost per unit to be higher or lower depending upon the volume produced. Interim financial reports might show various unit product cost, total cost, and profit depending upon seasonal operations. These variations can be leveled out by using a budget rate.

Control of Factory Overhead

Returning to the illustration, assume that the actual factory overhead for the year amounted to $81,500. The total of $81,500 is recorded as a debit to the control account, Factory Overhead. Supporting the control account is a subsidiary ledger in which the detailed costs of factory overhead are accumulated.

The actual factory overhead cost is compared with the budgeted cost as shown below.

Comparison—Budget With Actual Factory Overhead

	Budget	Actual	Variance Over (Under)
Variable:			
Indirect materials	$12,500	$13,400	$ 900
Repairs and maintenance...........................	9,500	9,300	(200)
Power and light	8,000	8,800	800
Total	$30,000	$31,500	$1,500
Fixed:			
Indirect labor and supervision	$18,000	$18,000	—0—
Repairs and maintenance...........................	6,500	6,500	—0—
Power and light	5,500	5,500	—0—
Factory rent	8,000	8,000	—0—
Depreciation of equipment	12,000	12,000	—0—
Total	$50,000	$50,000	—0—
Total factory overhead.............................	$80,000	$81,500	$1,500

Each of the overhead classifications, such as indirect materials and repairs and maintenance, is controlled by management. In this example, questions may arise as to why indirect materials cost $900 more than budgeted. If the $900 variation is within a tolerable limit of variation, then no further action is necessary.

Overhead by its very nature is not directly related to production orders or projects. Hence, control is exercised to a large extent over each individual overhead classification. However, the aggregate variable overhead can be controlled to an extent on a production order basis if the overhead varies with a factor that can be brought under control.

If variable overhead, for example, varies with direct labor hours, the supervisor should recognize that the variable overhead will be higher if more direct labor hours are used on an order than budgeted. Both the direct labor cost and the variable overhead cost will depend upon the efficient use of production hours.

In the example, variable overhead varies at the rate of $3 per hour. The following is an estimate of the difference in variable overhead cost attributable to a difference between the actual and estimated hours.

Order Number	Variance In Hours*	Variable Overhead Difference (Variance × $3)
1017	(450)	$(1,350)
1018	200	600
1019	200	600
1020	50	150

*This is the same as the variance for direct labor hours.

Not all of the costs of production can be controlled on a project or production order basis. Direct materials and direct labor cost, however, may be budgeted and controlled by specific order. Variable overhead, to an extent, may be controlled by controlling the factor related to the job.

If the company can find a way to reduce the time used in production or any factor related to variable overhead, there is a saving in the cost of the factor and in variable overhead. For example, suppose that variable overhead varies at a rate of $3 for every direct labor hour. Further assume the direct labor cost per hour is $10. If only one direct labor hour can be saved, there is a saving of $10 in labor cost plus an additional saving of $3 in variable overhead for a total saving of $13.

Cost Estimates of Production Order

In the following example, the total cost estimated for a production order was $29,000. Direct labor cost amounts to $10 per hour and variable overhead cost is at the rate of $3 per hour. There is no fixed overhead to be assigned to the product in this example. It was estimated that 1,000 direct labor hours should be used to produce this order. However, a careful review of operations with revisions in the production process reveals that the order can be made in 950 direct labor hours.

Original Estimate 1,000 Direct Labor Hours		Revised Estimate 950 Direct Labor Hours	
Direct materials	$16,000	Direct materials	$16,000
Direct labor (1,000 × $10)	10,000	Direct labor (950 × $10)	9,500
Variable overhead (1,000 × $3)	3,000	Variable overhead (950 × $3)	2,850
Total	$29,000	Total	$28,350

By saving 50 hours of direct labor, the company can reduce the cost of this order by $650. Management recognizes that substantial savings in cost are possible by finding ways to reduce labor time or other factors related to variable overhead. One very important function of management is to review operations closely with the objective of reducing production time and cost.

Small savings in time can be translated into substantial cost savings when volume of production is considered.

Costing Fixed Overhead

Assume now that the full cost of the order is to be computed with an apportioned share of the fixed overhead included. The fixed overhead cannot be controlled by job or project. It is allocated to the orders by the use of an hourly costing rate. The budget for fixed overhead in this example is $50,000, and the company is generally expected to operate at 10,000 direct labor hours a year. The fixed overhead rate per direct labor hour is then $5.

$$\frac{\$50,000 \text{ fixed overhead}}{10,000 \text{ direct labor hours}} = \$5, \quad \begin{array}{l} \text{fixed overhead rate} \\ \text{per direct labor hour} \end{array}$$

The full cost estimate of the production order is given

Original Estimate 1,000 direct labor hours		Revised Estimate 950 direct labor hours	
Direct materials	$16,000	Direct materials	$16,000
Direct labor (1,000 × $10)	10,000	Direct labor (950 × $10)	9,500
Variable overhead (1,000 × $3)...	3,000	Variable overhead (950 × $3)	2,850
Fixed overhead (1,000 × $5)	5,000	Fixed overhead (950 × $5)	4,750
Total	$34,000	Total	$33,100

If the company actually operated at 10,000 direct hours during the year, all of the fixed overhead of $50,000 would be apportioned to the orders using a rate of $5 per hour. Suppose, however, that there were only 8,000 hours of operation. Then, only 40,000 of the fixed overhead would be costed to the products by using the fixed overhead rate of $5 an hour established for 10,000 hours.

$$8,000 \text{ actual hours} \times \$5 \text{ fixed overhead} = \$40,000 \text{ fixed overhead} \atop \text{rate per hour} \qquad \text{costed to products}$$

Budgeted fixed overhead	$50,000
Fixed overhead costed to products	40,000
Capacity variance	$10,000

The difference between the budgeted fixed overhead and the fixed overhead costed to products by the use of the predetermined fixed overhead rate is designated as a capacity variance, or **volume variance**. Capacity variance is discussed further in Chapter 5.

Disposition of the Overhead Variance

While the products were being costed with budgeted factory overhead, actual overhead costs were being incurred and recorded as debits to Factory

Overhead. At the end of the year, after all adjusting entries have been made, the factory overhead accounts would have balances as follows:

FACTORY OVERHEAD	APPLIED FACTORY OVERHEAD
81,500	80,000

Not all of the actual factory overhead was charged to products by means of the budget. There was a difference, or variance, of $1,500. This difference can be closed to Cost of Goods Sold at the end of the year or, if desired, can be allocated to Cost of Goods Sold, Finished Goods, and Work in Process on the basis of relative cost. If too little overhead has been costed to the products, the variance is called an underapplied, underabsorbed, or unfavorable variance. On the other hand, if too much overhead has been costed to the products, the variance is called an overapplied, overabsorbed, or favorable variance. The entry to close out the actual overhead, the applied overhead, and the variance is given below:

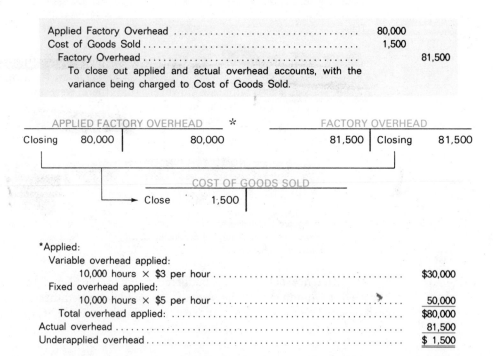

Applied Factory Overhead	80,000	
Cost of Goods Sold..	1,500	
Factory Overhead		81,500

To close out applied and actual overhead accounts, with the variance being charged to Cost of Goods Sold.

APPLIED FACTORY OVERHEAD *	FACTORY OVERHEAD
Closing 80,000	80,000	81,500	Closing 81,500

COST OF GOODS SOLD
Close   1,500

*Applied:

Variable overhead applied:	
10,000 hours × $3 per hour	$30,000
Fixed overhead applied:	
10,000 hours × $5 per hour	50,000
Total overhead applied:	$80,000
Actual overhead	81,500
Underapplied overhead...	$ 1,500

If the overhead had been overapplied in the example given, the variance would have been credited to Cost of Goods Sold.

Normal Capacity

Products are usually costed by using an overhead rate calculated at the level of normal capacity or normal activity. The reason for having to choose a certain level of capacity is that the fixed cost per unit depends on the number of units produced. This practice of assigning fixed overhead cost to units is necessary as long as full cost is to be used in the income determination process. Hence, the prime emphasis on the costing procedure comes from the need for data to calculate profit.

Normal capacity is not easy to define. The term has been used in many different ways, partly because there is no real agreement as to what is meant by "normal." In a good many cases, normal capacity is looked upon as an average use of facilities over a sufficiently long period of time so that minor variations in production cost due to seasonal and cyclical influences can be evened out. Sometimes plant capacity is considered to be a theoretical maximum capacity without regard for sales demand and for delays and inefficiencies in production. This concept of maximum output may be useful in evaluating what the plant could conceivably produce, but it cannot be considered a normal condition. Practical capacity may be a more useful concept in costing products for profit determination. Certain interruptions and inefficiencies in production can be expected. Perfection cannot be achieved. For example, production may be slowed down or stopped at times because of breakdowns, shortages of labor and materials, or retooling. These possibilities should be taken into account in arriving at practical plant capacity. Sales demand is also a factor. If there is insufficient demand for the product, then there is little point in striving to produce at practical plant capacity. Normal capacity is often a compromise between practical plant capacity and sales demand over the long run.

Seemingly, a normal overhead rate should not be used if the company does not plan to operate at normal capacity during the next year. For profit reporting, if all the overhead is to be attached to the products, it would appear that the costing rate should be calculated from a budget at the expected level of operation. However, if this were done, the product cost would increase or decrease each year because of differences in the volume of production. Also, management would not have a measurement of the extent of plant utilization. The capacity variance is a measurement of the underutilization or overutilization of the plant and should be brought to the attention of management.

A JOB ORDER COST ILLUSTRATION

Summarized cost data for the year ended April 30, 1985, are presented at the bottom of page 72 for Gable Machine Company to illustrate job order cost procedures using historical cost.

Historical cost is the actual cost that has been incurred, and in this chapter it will be assumed that the actual or historical cost is to be assigned to the products to the extent that this is possible. In Chapters 4 and 5, a standard cost accounting system will be discussed. Standards of cost and performance will be established, and standard cost will be identified with the products. Actual cost is measured and compared with the standard. The difference is identified and serves as a basis for better control and for better planning.

It should be borne in mind that the entries given are in composite form and that in practice there are many repetitious entries to record individual transactions that take place during the fiscal year.

The sequential order of the cost transactions should also be understood. For example, the budget of factory overhead and the overhead rate calculation were made before the beginning of the fiscal year. The overhead rate must be calculated from a budget of factory overhead so that the products being manufactured during the year can be assigned the proper overhead cost, as nearly as it can be determined. Only at the end of the year did the company know that 220,000 direct labor hours were used and that the actual factory overhead cost was $1,336,200. Throughout the year, the manufacturer purchased materials and incurred labor and factory overhead costs as products were continually being worked on, completed, and sold. At the same time, costs were being attached to the products and released as expenses when deliveries were made against sales.

Gable Machine Company
Transactional Data
For the Year Ended April 30, 1985

1. Materials were purchased during the fiscal year at a cost of $840,000.
2. Direct materials requisitioned for production cost $631,400. Included in this amount is the materials cost for Job 216 of $3,480. Indirect materials costing $47,200 were also requisitioned.
3. Factory payrolls in total amounted to $1,874,000. The income taxes withheld from the employees' wages totaled $393,400, and the deduction for FICA taxes withheld amounted to $106,600.
4. A distribution of the factory labor cost of $1,874,000 shows that $1,760,000 was direct labor while the remaining $114,000 was indirect labor. The portion of the direct labor cost that pertained to Job 216 was $1,600.
5. Factory overhead at the normal operating level of 250,000 direct labor hours has been calculated at $6 an hour. During the year, 220,000 direct labor hours were used.
6. The factory overhead, in addition to the indirect materials and the indirect labor previously referred to amounted to $1,175,000. Included in this amount was depreciation of $120,000. The balance of the overhead was acquired through accounts payable. Job 216 was completed with 200 direct labor hours. The production order for Job 216 is shown on page 73.
7. Jobs costing $2,945,200 were completed and transferred to stock during the year.
8. The cost of orders sold during the year was $2,320,000.
9. Applied Factory Overhead and Factory Overhead were closed out at the end of the fiscal year with the variance being closed to Cost of Goods Sold.

PRODUCTION ORDER

Customer_____ Del Ray Supply Co. _____   Job Order_____ 216 _____

Description_____ Welded Parts Code #735 _____   Date Started_____ 1/19/85 _____

Quantity_____ 1,000 _____   Date Completed _____ 1/27/85 _____

Materials			Labor			Overhead		
Date	Code	Amount	Date	Hours	Amount	Direct Labor Hours			200
Jan. 19	52	$3,130	Jan. 19 to 23	140	$1,120	Overhead Rate			$6.00
						Applied Overhead			$1,200
23	68	350	Jan. 26 to 27	60	480				
							Summary		
						Direct Materials			$3,480
						Direct Labor			1,600
						Factory Overhead			1,200
						Total Cost			$6,280
						Unit Cost			$6.28
	Total	$3,480	Total	200	$1,600				

The transactions were entered in the accounts as follows:

1. Materials purchased:
   Materials   840,000
      Accounts Payable.   840,000
        Purchase of materials.
        (The cost of each type of material was also entered on
        the appropriate materials inventory ledger cards.)

2. Materials requisitioned:
   Work in Process   631,400
   Factory Overhead   47,200
      Materials   678,600
        Materials issued to production.
        (Requisition forms were the basis for entries reducing the
        materials inventory ledger and for posting direct materials
        costs to each job order and the indirect materials costs to
        the factory overhead subsidiary ledger.)

3. Factory payrolls:
   Payroll.. 1,874,000
       Employees Income Tax Payable   393,400
       FICA Tax Payable   106,600
       Wages Payable......................................   1,374,000
       Aggregate factory payrolls.

4. Distribution of labor cost:
   Work in Process 1,760,000
   Factory Overhead   114,000
       Payroll... 1,874,000
       Payroll distribution for the year.
       (A classification of labor time by jobs as shown by labor
       time tickets was a basis for distribution of direct labor
       cost to individual job orders and for posting indirect labor
       cost to the factory overhead subsidiary ledger.)

5. Factory overhead applied:
   Work in Process 1,320,000
       Applied Factory Overhead 1,320,000
       Factory overhead applied to products on direct labor
       hour basis. 220,000 hours x $6 rate = $1,320,000.

6. Actual factory overhead (in addition to indirect materials and indirect labor):
   Factory Overhead 1,175,000
       Accumulated Depreciation   120,000
       Accounts Payable...................................   1,055,000
       Actual factory overhead recorded.
       (Entries were made to record costs in the factory
       overhead ledger.)

7. Work completed during the year and transferred to stock:
   Finished Goods.................................... 2,945,200
       Work in Process 2,945,200
       Transfer of cost of completed orders to Finished
       Goods.
       (Completed job orders were removed from the file of job
       orders in process and held as a subsidiary ledger
       supporting the finished goods inventory. Separate ledger
       cards may be kept for the finished goods inventory if
       sales are not made on a strict order basis.)

8. The cost of products sold:
   Cost of Goods Sold 2,320,000
       Finished Goods.................................... 2,320,000
       To record the cost of products sold to the customers.
       (Deductions were recorded in the finished goods
       inventory ledger cards. Entries were also made to bill the
       customers for the sales.)

9. Applied Factory Overhead and Factory Overhead closed:
   Applied Factory Overhead.......................... 1,320,000
   Cost of Goods Sold   16,200
       Factory Overhead 1,336,200
       To close factory overhead accounts.
       (Actual overhead not absorbed during the year as a part
       of the product cost is closed to Cost of Goods Sold.)

APPENDIX
THE PROCESS COST SYSTEM

In many cases specific costs cannot be identified readily with a specific unit. For example, in the candy industry all chocolate of a given type will be the same. When all of the units of product are similar, a process cost system can be used. The cost is directly or indirectly assigned for an interval of time to the departments in which the products are made, rather than identified by product groups or orders. Unit cost is computed by dividing the departmental cost by the number of units completed in the department.

The unit cost is applied to the number of units transferred in the manufacturing process and ultimately identified with the units completed and sold. Before a product is completed, it may be transferred from one department to another in a series of processing operations. Each unit of product carries the cost that has been charged to it from the various departments in which it is processed.

The Departmental Production Report

Both the number of units manufactured and the cost are accounted for on a departmental basis. Monthly production reports are prepared for each producing department showing the quantities of product, the total cost, and the unit cost. The production report is the focal point in process cost accounting, whereas in job order costing it is the production order. The production report may provide departmental cost and quantity data either separately or combined in one report with each section showing (1) what responsibility is charged to the department and (2) how that responsibility is discharged.

The number of units accounted for is always equal to the number of units charged to the department. Lost units must be accounted for as such. Cost is similiarly charged to a department and must be accounted for.

A production report for both quantities and costs is given at the bottom of page 76.

A Process Cost Flow

Often the units of product go through several manufacturing operations (departments) before they are completed. In the first operation, for example, impurities may be removed from the basic raw materials. In subsequent operations, the materials may be refined and treated in various ways before the product units are completed.

A flow of cost through two departments is illustrated using the following cost data. Work in process in Department I at the beginning of the month amounted to $3,000, but there was no work in process in either department at the end of the month. All units of product were sold during the month.

	Departments	
	I	*II*
Work in process, beginning of month	$ 3,000	—0—
Materials	18,000	—0—
Labor	14,000	$ 8,000
Factory overhead	9,000	3,000
Total cost	$44,000	$11,000
Number of units produced	22,000	22,000
Unit cost (department)	$2.00	$.50
Accumulated unit cost:		
Dept. I	$2.00	
Dept. II	.50	
Total unit cost	$2.50	

The 22,000 units completed with respect to Department I each had a unit cost in that department of $2. These units were transferred to Department II and accumulated an additional unit cost of 50 cents. The total unit cost was $2.50.

The cost elements for each department were entered in the respective work in process accounts. As the units moved through the departments, the related cost was transferred to the next departmental work in process account and was combined with the cost of that department. Eventually the goods were completed and transferred to the finished goods inventory. When the units were sold, the cost was transferred to the cost of goods sold account and the customers were billed for the sales.

Departmental Production Report
Department 1
For the Month of August, 1985

Quantities:	
Charged to the department:	
In process, beginning	2,000 units
Transferred in	20,000
Total units charged to department	22,000
Units accounted for:	
Transferred out	22,000 units
In process, ending	—0—
Total units accounted for	22,000

Costs:	
Charged to the department:	
In process, beginning	$ 3,000
During the period	41,000
Total cost charged to department	$44,000
Cost accounted for:	
Transferred out	$44,000
In process, ending	—0—
Total cost accounted for	$44,000

The following is a diagram of the cost flow:

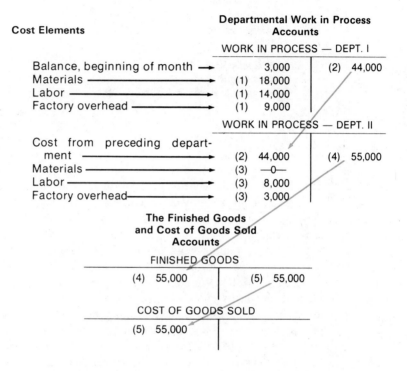

Cost Elements	Departmental Work in Process Accounts		
	WORK IN PROCESS — DEPT. I		
Balance, beginning of month →		3,000	(2) 44,000
Materials	(1)	18,000	
Labor	(1)	14,000	
Factory overhead	(1)	9,000	
	WORK IN PROCESS — DEPT. II		
Cost from preceding department	(2)	44,000	(4) 55,000
Materials	(3)	—0—	
Labor	(3)	8,000	
Factory overhead	(3)	3,000	

The Finished Goods and Cost of Goods Sold Accounts

FINISHED GOODS

(4) 55,000	(5) 55,000

COST OF GOODS SOLD

(5) 55,000	

Journal entries to record the flow of costs follow:

1.

Work in Process—Department I	41,000	
Materials		18,000
Payroll		14,000
Applied Factory Overhead		9,000
Cost of manufacturing during the current month for Department I.		

2.

Work in Process—Department II	44,000	
Work in Process—Department I		44,000
Transfer of cost from Department I to Department II.		

3.

Work in Process—Department II	11,000	
Factory Labor		8,000
Applied Factory Overhead		3,000
Manufacturing cost of Department II.		

4.

Finished Goods	55,000	
Work in Process—Department II		55,000
Transfer of cost from Department II to Finished Goods (22,000 × $2.50).		

5.

Cost of Goods Sold	55,000	
Finished Goods		55,000
Cost of goods sold during the month.		

The Equivalent Unit Concept

In the preceding illustration all of the work was completed in each department, and the entire production for the month was sold. In most cases, however, not all of the work is completed and sold within the month. Usually there are units and cost remaining in process and in finished goods at the end of the month. Cost is attached to the units transferred out of a department and to the remaining work in process by means of a unit cost.

In process cost accounting, the problem of determining unit cost is resolved by using equivalent units. Equivalent units, as defined under the average cost method, are units completed during the month, regardless of when the work was begun, plus the equivalent units of work done on the ending work in process inventory. The objective of this computation of equivalent units is to obtain an average cost by adding the cost of work done in previous months to the cost of work done during the current month.

Assume that equivalent units and unit cost are to be computed for Department A. Quantity and cost data follow:

	Number of Product Units	Total Cost
Charged to department:		
Inventory in process at the beginning of the month	2,000	$ 3,000
Placed in production during the month	26,000	37,000
Total units and cost charged to department	28,000	$40,000

	Number of Product Units	Total Cost
Accountability:		
Completed and transferred to Department B	16,000	?
Inventory in process at the end of the month (1/3 completed)	12,000	?
Total units accounted for	28,000	

At this point, the costs to be assigned to the units transferred to Department B and to the ending inventory of work in process have not been determined. However, they can be computed as follows:

Equivalent Units Computation

Units completed during the month	16,000
Equivalent units of work done on the ending work in process (12,000 units × 1/3)	4,000
Equivalent units	20,000

Average Unit Cost Computation

$$\text{Average unit cost} = \frac{\text{Costs of Dept. A}}{\text{Equivalent units}} = \frac{\$40,000}{20,000} = \$2$$

Accountability—Costs of Department A

Cost of units completed and transferred to Department B (16,000 units × $2 average unit cost)	$32,000
Cost of work in process at the end of the month (4,000 units × $2)	8,000
Total costs accounted for	$40,000

The Cost Elements

In a process cost accounting system, no distinction is made between direct materials and indirect materials with respect to the product. The materials are not requisitioned for particular orders. Instead, both the direct materials and the indirect materials are identified only with the department in which they are used. A measurement is taken of the materials consumption in a department over a stated interval of time, but the requisition forms do not show how much material was used in the manufacture of any particular group of products.

Labor cost is also accumulated by department with no distinction being made between direct and indirect labor. The wages of the workers are identified by department rather than by order.

The various factory overhead costs are assigned to departments directly or by allocation. If factory overhead cost is evenly distributed throughout the year and production is at a fairly uniform level, this method may result in reasonably accurate product cost. However, if production is seasonal or if overhead cost is unequally distributed throughout the year, a more accurate product cost can be obtained by using a predetermined annual overhead rate calculated from a budget. Departmental overhead rates can be computed in the same way as they are in job order cost accounting. When a predetermined overhead rate is used, all products processed during the year bear their share of the overhead cost.

Terminology Review

Job order cost system (61)
Job or production order (61)
Direct materials, direct labor (61)
Cost overrun (64)
Factory overhead (65)
Overhead rate (65)
Flexible budget (65)
Capacity variance (69)
Underapplied, underabsorbed, or
    unfavorable variance (70)

Overapplied, overabsorbed, or favorable
    variance (70)
Normal capacity (71)
Practical capacity (71)
Historical cost (71)
Process cost system (75)
Departmental production report (75)
Equivalent units (78)

QUESTIONS FOR REVIEW

1. Are costs of production charged to expense when incurred?

2. Name the three cost elements. Can all three cost elements be identified directly with the product? Explain.

3. What are the two basic cost accounting systems?

4. Describe briefly how costs flow through the accounts in job order costing.

5. What are the characteristics of a manufacturing operation when a job order cost system is used? When a process cost system is used?

6. In a job order cost system, how is the cost of direct materials and direct labor identified with the production orders?

7. Why is it difficult to identify factory overhead with the products manufactured?

8. Explain why a budget is used in costing factory overhead and why actual overhead cost is not assigned to the products after the end of the year.

9. What is the basis for selecting a factor to be used in costing factory overhead?

10. If variable overhead varies on the basis of direct labor hours, explain how a saving in direct labor hours can result in a saving of cost on more than one cost element.

11. What is the total cost saving if 80 direct labor hours can be saved when direct labor cost per hour is $7 and variable overhead that varies on a direct labor hour basis is $5 per hour?

12. What account is credited when factory overhead cost is assigned to work in process?

13. How is the difference between the actual factory overhead and the overhead assigned to the products handled at the end of the year?

14. What is normal capacity?

15. If the company does not expect to operate at normal capacity during the next year, why should the products be costed by using an overhead rate determined at normal capacity?

EXERCISES

1. **Cost Flows.** Metal blanks to be used in the production of medals awarded for scholastic and athletic achievement were purchased by Victory Productions at a cost of $131,000. Metal blanks costing $100,000 were placed in production. During the fiscal period, 20,000 direct labor hours at a cost of $8 an hour were used in production. Factory overhead is applied to production at the rate of $6 per direct labor hour. Eighty percent of the production orders were completed during the fiscal period, and 70% of the completed orders were sold and delivered to customers. Costs on all orders are uniform, and there were no inventories on hand at the beginning of the fiscal period.

   Required: Estimate the total cost in each of the following accounts at the end of the fiscal period before making any adjustment for over- or underabsorbed overhead.

   (1) Work in Process
   (2) Finished Goods
   (3) Cost of Goods Sold

2. **Cost Control of Project.** Juan Morales is responsible for the completion of a project that has been estimated to require a total of $165,000 in direct materials and 6,000 direct labor hours to be paid at a rate of $10 per hour. Variable overhead generally varies at the rate of $8 per direct labor hour. He estimates that all materials cost has already been incurred, and the actual cost of materials was $163,700. Labor is approximately 80% completed, and 4,650 hours have been used at the rate indicated. Variable overhead amounted to $37,900.

   Required: Compare the actual cost with the estimates and determine the variances. How would the labor hour variance affect variable overhead?

3. **Cost Control of Orders.** Ruff Printing Company started work on two production orders in October, Order 126 and Order 127. The total materials cost for both orders has been estimated at $40,000 with 60% of the cost applying to Order 126 and the balance to Order 127. At the end of October, three quarters of the total materials to be used cost $45,000 and were placed in production in the proportions indicated. Total direct labor hours were estimated at 700 for Order 126 and at 400 for Order 127. The labor rate amounts to $9 per hour. Variable overhead varies at the rate of $5 per hour. By the end of October, each order was 50% completed with respect to labor and overhead. Labor hours were charged as follows during October: 360 hours to Order 126 and 180 to Order 127. Variable overhead followed the hourly rate given.

   Required: Compare the actual cost with the estimate for each order and determine variances. What effect would the labor hour variance have on variable overhead?

4. **Tracing the Flow of Job Order Cost.** Nelson Tool Company purchased $138,000 in direct materials during the fiscal year and used direct materials costing $87,000 in production. Factory payrolls amounted to $190,000 in direct labor and $56,000 in indirect labor. Factory overhead for the fiscal year in addition to indirect labor was $41,000. Factory overhead is applied to the production orders at 50% of direct labor cost. The cost of production orders completed during the fiscal year was $323,000. The cost of goods sold was $280,000, and sales revenue was $410,000. No inventories were on hand at the beginning of the fiscal year.

Required:

(1) Prepare T-accounts as follows:

Materials	Applied Factory Overhead
Payroll	Accounts Payable
Work in Process	Wages Payable
Finished Goods	Accounts Receivable
Cost of Goods Sold	Sales
Factory Overhead	

Enter the transactions directly in the T-accounts. Close the factory overhead variance directly into Cost of Goods Sold.

(2) Prepare a summary statement showing sales revenue, cost of goods sold, and gross margin for the fiscal year.

5. Factory Overhead Rates. Folsum Marine Supply Company normally operates at 250,000 direct labor hours a year. At this level of operation, variable overhead has been budgeted at $625,000 and fixed overhead has been budgeted at $1,250,000.

Required:

(1) Compute the total factory overhead rate per direct labor hour at normal capacity.
(2) Determine the variable portion of the overhead rate at normal capacity. What would the variable overhead rate be if normal capacity had been established at 200,000 direct labor hours, assuming no changes in rate of variability per hour?
(3) Determine the fixed portion of the overhead rate at normal capacity. What would the fixed overhead rate be if 200,000 direct labor hours were considered to be normal capacity? Explain why the rate differs depending upon the level set as normal capacity.

6. Factory Overhead Rates. Martinez Electric Products has prepared a flexible budget of factory overhead for the year. The budget is summarized as follows:

	100,000	120,000	150,000
Budgeted machine hours	100,000	120,000	150,000
Variable overhead	$600,000	$ 720,000	$ 900,000
Fixed overhead	300,000	300,000	300,000
Total overhead	$900,000	$1,020,000	$1,200,000

Required:

(1) If 120,000 machine hours are considered to be a normal level of operation, determine the factory overhead costing rate. Give the variable and fixed portions of the rate.
(2) Assume that the company operated at an actual level of 100,000 machine hours. How much of the variable overhead would be apportioned to the products by using the rate determined at 120,000 machine hours? Would all of the variable overhead budgeted for 100,000 machine hours be absorbed?
(3) Assuming again that the company operated at 100,000 machine hours, how much of the fixed overhead would be apportioned to the products by using the rate determined at 120,000 machine hours?
(4) Explain why all of the budgeted fixed overhead would not be absorbed at 100,000 machine hours. What name is given to the difference between the budgeted fixed overhead and the fixed overhead absorbed by the products?

7. Factory Overhead Costing. Jessel Patterns Inc. has estimated that variable factory overhead varies at the rate of $7 per machine hour. Fixed factory overhead has been budgeted at $800,000 for the year.

Normal capacity has been determined to be 100,000 machine hours for the year. The company actually operated at 90,000 machine hours for the year. Variable overhead for the year was $630,000, exactly the amount that would be budgeted for 90,000 machine hours. Actual fixed overhead was $800,000 as budgeted.

Required:

(1) Compute the factory overhead costing rate, breaking it into a variable and a fixed rate.

(2) Determine the balance of actual overhead in the factory overhead control account before closing.

(3) Determine the balance of Applied Factory Overhead before closing.

(4) Was there a factory overhead variance for the year? Explain why there was a variance and determine the amount of the variance.

8. Factory Overhead Costing. The following is a summary flexible budget of factory overhead for the year for Mesarona Products Company.

Budgeted direct labor hours	50,000	60,000	70,000
Variable overhead	$200,000	$240,000	$280,000
Fixed overhead.....................................	360,000	360,000	360,000
Total overhead	$560,000	$600,000	$640,000

The factory overhead rate has been computed at a normal operating capacity of 60,000 direct labor hours for the year.

During the next year, the company operated at 50,000 direct labor hours. The actual variable overhead amounted to $212,000, and the actual fixed overhead was $360,000.

Required:

(1) Prepare a journal entry to record the application of factory overhead to the job orders.

(2) Prepare a journal entry to record the actual factory overhead for the year. (Credit Accounts Payable.)

(3) Close the actual and applied factory overhead, closing the variance directly to Cost of Goods Sold.

(4) How much of the total variance was caused by operating at below normal capacity?

9. Journal Entries for Flow of Job Order Cost. During 1984, Coburn Supplies Company purchased materials at a cost of $316,000. Direct materials costing $283,000 were requisitioned for the various job orders. Factory payrolls for the year totaled $420,000. Income tax of $86,000, FICA tax of $28,000, and union dues of $9,000 were withheld from wages. Assume that all of the factory payroll was direct labor for the job orders. Factory overhead was applied to production at the rate of $8 per machine hour. During the year, the company operated at 55,000 machine hours. Actual factory overhead for the year was $458,000. Credit the actual factory overhead to Accounts Payable.

Required: Prepare journal entries to record the information given. Close the factory overhead variance to Cost of Goods Sold.

10. Journal Entries for Flow of Job Order Cost. The Delta Parts Company purchased materials in 1984 at a cost of $216,000. Direct materials costing $163,000 were requisitioned for various job orders. Other indirect materials costing $41,000 were requisitioned for general factory use. (Charge Factory Overhead.) The factory payroll for the year amounted to $237,000. Income tax of $48,000 and FICA tax of $15,000 were withheld from wages. The direct labor portion of the payroll amounting to $193,000 has been identified with the job orders. The balance of the factory payroll consisting of indirect labor should be charged to Factory Overhead. Factory overhead is applied to the job orders at the rate of $5 per machine hour. During the year, the company operated at 38,000 machine hours. Actual factory overhead, in addition to the indirect materials and indirect labor already referred to, amounted to $132,000. This portion of the overhead should be credited to Accounts Payable.

Required: Prepare journal entries to record the information given. Close the factory overhead variance to Cost of Goods Sold.

11. Equivalent Units (Appendix). In each of the following situations, determine the equivalent units produced by the average cost method in a process cost system. Each situation is independent of the others.

(1) The company completed 18,000 units with respect to Department A during the month and performed 30% of the work on 9,000 units remaining in inventory at the end of the month.

(2) Department 7 had an inventory of 4,000 units in process at the beginning of the month. During the month 20,000 units were received from Department 6. Work performed on these units during the month resulted in 22,000 units that were completed in that department and transferred to Department 8. The units on hand at the end of the month were 50% completed in Department 7.

(3) Department C had an inventory of 12,000 units in process, 40% completed with respect to Department C, at the beginning of the month. The department received 60,000 units from Department B and completed a total of 52,000 units that were transferred to Department D. Units on hand at the end of the month were 30% completed with respect to work in Department C.

12. Equivalent Units and Unit Costs (Appendix). Fast Molds Inc. places all materials in process at the beginning of operations in Department I. The inventory in process at the beginning of January consisted of 2,000 units with a total cost of materials of $5,000 and labor and overhead of $1,000. In January, 10,000 units were started in process with a materials cost of $25,000. Labor and overhead in January cost $14,000. An inventory, complete with respect to materials but only 60% completed with respect to labor and overhead, was on hand at the end of January. The ending inventory consisted of 5,000 units.

Required:

(1) Compute the equivalent units of material and the unit cost of materials.

(2) Compute the equivalent units of labor and overhead and the unit cost of labor and overhead.

(3) Determine the total cost of the work in process inventory at the end of January.

13. Tracing Process Costs (Appendix). Bender Mixes has two processing operations: Operation 1 and Operation 2. All materials are added at the beginning of Operation 1. At the beginning and at the end of March, there was no inventory in process in either of the operations. During March, materials costing $70,000 were started in Operation 1. Labor cost was $25,000 and applied overhead was $15,000. All units were transferred to Operation 2 where the labor cost was $15,000 and applied overhead was $10,000. During the month, a total of 20,000 units were completed and transferred to finished goods, and 15,000 of these units were sold.

Required: Prepare journal entries to record the flow of processing costs for March.

14. Production Report (Appendix). Andrews Tile Company had an inventory of 6,000 units in process on May 1 with a materials cost of $12,000 and a labor and overhead cost of $6,000. During the month, 30,000 units were started. Materials cost during May was $96,000 and labor and overhead cost was $18,000. The equivalent units of materials for May were 36,000, and the equivalent units of labor and overhead were 30,000. At the end of the month, 10,000 units of product were left in work in process inventory.

Required:

(1) Compute the unit cost of materials.
(2) Compute the unit cost of labor and overhead.
(3) Determine the total cost of goods completed in May and the cost of work in process inventory at May 31.

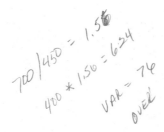

PROBLEMS

3-1. Factory Overhead Rates. Corben Mills Inc. manufactures a product line that has a direct materials cost of $10 per unit and a direct labor cost of $6 per unit. Factory overhead is applied to production on the basis of machine hours with one unit produced each machine hour. Under normal conditions, the company operates at 350,000 machine hours each year and produces 350,000 units of product.

The following is a summarized flexible budget:

Machine hours	300,000	350,000	400,000
Variable overhead	$ 900,000	$1,050,000	$1,200,000
Fixed overhead	700,000	700,000	700,000
Total overhead	$1,600,000	$1,750,000	$1,900,000

175/350

Required:

(1) Compute the overhead rate at the normal operating capacity. 5
(2) If 300,000 machine hours is considered to be normal capacity, what would the overhead rate be? 5.333   160/300
(3) Determine the total unit cost of the product at a normal operating capacity of 350,000 machine hours. 2\6   10+4
(4) If the company operated at 400,000 machine hours during the year and made 450,000 product units, what would the capacity variance be? Would the fixed overhead be overapplied or underapplied to the products? (Use 350,000 machine hours as normal.)

3-2. Factory Overhead Rates. Mellon Parts Company apportions factory overhead to products on a machine hour basis. The machine hour rate is computed from a budget of factory overhead at normal operating capacity. The company operated at 180,000 machine hours in 1984.

Budgeted factory overhead at a normal capacity of 200,000 machine hours a year is as follows:

Variable overhead:	
Indirect materials	$ 326,500
Supplies	147,000
Lubrication	71,500
Repairs and maintenance	35,000
Total variable overhead	$ 580,000
Fixed overhead:	
Supervision	$ 150,000
Indirect labor	426,000
Repairs and maintenance	78,500
Rent	24,000
Heat and light	16,500
Taxes and insurance	12,500
Depreciation	192,500
Total fixed overhead	$ 900,000
Total overhead	$1,480,000

In 1984, the fixed overhead cost was in agreement with the budget. Variable factory overhead in 1984 is listed below.

Indirect materials	$331,500
Supplies	148,000
Lubrication	69,500
Repairs and maintenance	36,000
Total variable overhead	$585,000

Required:

(1) Determine the machine hour rate for costing variable overhead and the machine hour rate for costing fixed overhead.
(2) Compute the overabsorbed or underabsorbed factory overhead.
(3) How much of the total variance was caused by operating at below the normal operating capacity?

3-3. Factory Overhead Rates. Under normal operating conditions, Ellsworth Systems Inc. operates at 300,000 machine hours. One type of product line is manufactured with direct materials of $5 per unit of product and direct labor of $2 per unit of product.

A budget of factory overhead in summary form for 300,000 machine hours is given below.

Variable overhead	$240,000
Fixed overhead	360,000
Total budgeted overhead	$600,000

The product is priced at 150% of full cost. Two units of product are manufactured each machine hour.

Next year the company anticipates a sharp drop in sales and expects to operate at only 200,000 machine hours.

The president of the company states that the overhead rate should be recomputed at the 200,000 expected machine hours of operation and that the products be priced at 150% of the revised cost.

The vice president of production disagrees, stating that the product will be overpriced on the market if the price is based on a cost for the expected machine hours of operation. Furthermore, the vice president believes that a failure to operate at normal capacity should be revealed as a capacity variance and not buried in product cost.

Required:

(1) Compute the variable and the fixed overhead rates at normal operating capacity.
(2) Determine the selling price of the product by using the cost determined for 300,000 machine hours.
(3) Determine the selling price of the product by using the cost determined for 200,000 machine hours.
(4) Evaluate the arguments of the president and the vice-president.

3-4. Labor Hours and Variable Overhead. The Vine Color Company ordinarily uses 80,000 labor hours to manufacture 240,000 units of product. Labor cost is at the rate of $9 per labor hour. At a normal capacity of 80,000 labor hours, the budget of factory overhead is as follows:

Variable overhead	$240,000 — 3
Fixed overhead	200,000
Total overhead budget	$440,000

The production manager has found a way to reduce the labor time so that 4 units can be manufactured per hour instead of 3. "This will not only help to reduce labor cost," the manager says, "but it will also reduce overhead."

The superintendent of the plant agrees that this reduction in labor cost will mean a lot, but the superintendent says that overhead cost is a fixed item and cannot be reduced by saving labor time.

Required:

(1) Do you agree with the production manager or the superintendent? Give your reasons.
(2) What is the total labor and overhead cost when 80,000 labor hours are used?
(3) What is the total labor and overhead cost if 60,000 labor hours are used?

3-5. Fixed Overhead and Product Cost. There is some disagreement at the Maplewood Plant of Dunbar Tool Company with respect to how the fixed overhead cost should be identified with the products.

The manager of purchasing believes that fixed overhead should be assigned to the products on the basis of a normal capacity of 300,000 machine hours per year. The cost accountant states that 300,000 machine hours is not normal and that 200,000 machine hours is a better measurement of normal capacity.

Another point of view expressed is that it will make little difference which number of hours is designated as normal. The cost per unit of product will be the same in any event. Furthermore, the major portion of the product cost is the cost of direct materials.

Cost data for three typical orders are:

	Orders		
	1	*2*	*3*
Direct materials cost per unit of product	$21	$16	$12
Variable overhead cost per unit of product	$ 1	$ 1	$ 1
Product units manufactured each machine hour	5	2	4
Number of units on order..	2,000	2,400	1,800

Direct labor cost is $8 per machine hour, and one hour of direct labor is equivalent to two machine hours. In addition to the variable overhead per unit of product, there is a variable overhead of $6 per machine hour.

Fixed overhead for the year has been budgeted at $2,400,000.

The company has followed the practice of billing customers at 140% of the total cost of the order.

Required:

(1) Determine the total and unit costs for each of the three orders under both assumptions as to normal operating capacity.

(2) What price would be billed to the customers for each of the three orders under both assumptions as to normal operating capacity?

(3) Comment on the statement, "It will make little difference which number of hours is designated as normal. The cost per unit of product will be the same in any event."

3-6. Job Order Cost Transactions. A summary of manufacturing cost transactions for Uhler Motors Inc. for 1984 follows:

(a) Materials costing $917,000 were purchased from suppliers on account.

(b) Materials were requisitioned during the year as follows:

Direct materials	$828,000
Indirect materials (factory overhead)	84,000

Included among the requisitions were requisitions for $11,000 of direct materials for Order 86.

(c) The factory payroll for the year amounted to $340,000. FICA taxes withheld amounted to $22,600, income tax withheld amounted to $71,000, and the net amount paid to the employees was $246,400.

(d) The factory labor was utilized as follows:

Direct labor	$262,000
Indirect labor (factory overhead)................................	78,000

Direct labor costing $9,000, included in the direct labor cost, was identified by labor time tickets with Order 86.

(e) Factory overhead was applied to production at 150% of the direct labor cost.

(f) Factory overhead cost during the year, in addition to the cost of indirect materials and indirect labor previously referred to, amounts to $238,000. Included in this amount is depreciation of $46,000. Credit the balance of the cost to Accounts Payable.

(g) Orders costing $1,150,000 were completed during the year. Order 86 is included among the completed orders.

(h) Goods costing $960,000 were sold to customers on credit terms for $1,593,000.

Required:

(1) Journalize the transactions and close the factory overhead variance to Cost of Goods Sold.

(2) Compute the cost of Order 86 and the cost per unit, assuming that 5,000 units were produced on that order.

3-7. Factory Overhead Cost Control. Cynthia Jenkins is the supervisor of Department 8 in the Liberty plant of Jordan Wire Company. She is responsible for the cost of direct materials, direct labor, and variable overhead costs incurred in this department. The fixed overhead cost is not under her jurisdiction.

During the month of April, factory overhead costs for Department 8 were as follows:

Variable overhead:	
Indirect materials	$19,600
Supplies	18,200
Telephone	600
Heat and light	1,600
Power	4,700
Repairs and maintenance	2,200
Total variable overhead	$46,900
Fixed overhead:	
Indirect labor	$ 32,000
Supervision	15,000
Heat and light	4,000
Repairs and maintenance	7,000
Depreciation	17,000
Total fixed overhead	$ 75,000
Total overhead	$121,900

The department operated at 20,000 direct labor hours during the month of April. A budget of factory overhead for 20,000 direct labor hours appears on page 90.

Required:

(1) How much overhead was costed to the products in April?

(2) Compute the total factory overhead variance for April.

(3) How much of the total overhead variance can be attributed to operating below the normal capacity?

(4) Prepare a cost report for Jenkins that will compare the actual overhead cost with the budgeted overhead cost. Indicate variances over or under the budget for each item of overhead under her jurisdiction.

(5) List any items of overhead that are over the budgeted amount by more than 10%. List any variances over 10% that are material in amount.

Variable overhead:

Indirect materials	$ 17,200
Supplies	19,100
Telephone	500
Heat and light	1,500
Power	3,600
Repairs and maintenance	2,100
Total variable overhead	$ 44,000

Fixed overhead:

Indirect labor	$ 32,000
Supervision	15,000
Heat and light	4,000
Repairs and maintenance	7,000
Depreciation	17,000
Total fixed overhead	$ 75,000
Total overhead	$119,000

Variable overhead is costed to the products at the rate of $2.20 per direct labor hour, and fixed overhead is costed to the products at the rate of $3 per direct labor hour.

3-8. Costs of Individual Orders. During the month of June, Jacobs Company started Orders 37, 38, and 39. Order 36 was in process at the beginning of the month with direct materials cost of $26,000, direct labor cost of $8,000, and applied factory overhead of $4,000.

(a) Direct materials were requisitioned during the month as follows:

Order No.	
37	$38,000
38	47,000
39	23,000

(b) Direct labor was identified with the orders as follows:

Order No.	
36	$16,000
37	38,000
38	24,000
39	6,000

Factory overhead is applied to the orders at 50% of direct labor cost.

Orders 36, 37, and 38 were completed and sold in June. Order 39 was incomplete on June 30.

Required:

(1) Determine the cost of each order by cost element.

(2) What was the total cost of materials requisitioned in June and charged to Work in Process?

(3) Determine the cost of goods sold in June.

(4) What was the Work in Process balance on June 30?

3-9. Process Cost Transactions (Appendix). A sun tan lotion is manufactured by South Coast Products Inc. in three processing operations. During the month of April, 150,000 units were started in process in Operation 1. There were no units in process at the beginning or at the end of the month in any operation. The materials are all added at the beginning of Operation 1, and the cost of the materials used in April was $255,000.

Labor and overhead costs for the three operations for the month of April are summarized below.

	Operations		
	1	2	3
Labor	$75,000	$270,000	$45,000
Overhead	60,000	135,000	15,000

Required:

(1) Journalize the flow of cost to each of the three operations and to finished goods inventory.

(2) Determine the unit cost of the three operations and the total unit cost of the product.

3-10. Process Cost and Production Report (Appendix). At the beginning of July, Kemmerer Parts Company had 40,000 units of product in process in Department 1. These units were 60% completed with respect to work in Department 1.

During the month of July, 200,000 units of product were started in Department 1. At the end of July, 25,000 units remained in work in process that were 80% completed as to materials, labor, and overhead.

The cost of the 40,000 units in process at July 1 was $68,000. Production cost in Department 1 during July amounted to $496,000.

Required:

(1) Compute the equivalent units of production for the month of July and the unit cost.

(2) Prepare a production report for Department 1 for the month of July.

3-11. Process Cost and Production Report (Appendix). Ondrechen Candy Company produces a mint-flavored breath freshner in two processing operations.

Units in process at the beginning of the month	8,000
Units started in process during February	260,000
Units transferred from Operation 1 to Operation 2 during February	248,000
Units in work in process at the end of the month..........................	20,000
Cost of beginning work in process on February 1	$ 2,000
February production cost	$ 87,600

The work in process at the end of the month was 40% completed in Operation 1.

Required:

(1) Compute the number of equivalent units of production.

(2) Determine the unit cost for the month of February.

(3) Prepare a production report for the month of February.

3-12. Process Cost and Production Report (Appendix). The costs of processing at Crystal Chemicals Inc. have been increasing during the past few months in Operation 3. Data for the last month are summarized below.

Operation 3:

Work in process, beginning of the month (60% completed, Operation 3) .	20,000 units
Transferred in from Operation 2	250,000 units
Work in process, end of the month (40% completed, Operation 3)	50,000 units

Costs:

Work in process, beginning of the month:

Prior operations	$	50,000
Operation 3		55,200
Transferred in:		
Prior operations		625,000
Operation 3		1,048,800

A change in the processing procedure in Operation 3 is expected to reduce the total cost of that operation by 20% effective at the beginning of next month. The processing costs in Operation 3 are fixed costs. The manager of Operation 3 expects to receive 300,000 units from prior operations next month. There will likely be 50,000 units in process at the end of the next month, 40% completed with respect to Operation 3.

Required:

(1) Prepare a cost of production report for Operation 3 for the last month.

(2) By how much will the planned saving in production cost reduce the average unit cost of work performed in Operation 3 next month? (Do not include costs from the last month.)

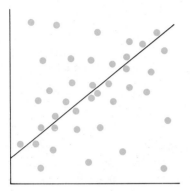

4

MATERIALS AND LABOR COST CONTROL

Chapter Objectives

This chapter should enable you to:

1. Understand the concept of standards.

2. Recognize the advantages of a standard cost accounting system.

3. Distinguish between tight standards and lax standards and to know which type is more appropriate in a given situation.

4. Compute the materials price and quantity variances and to understand what they mean.

5. Compute labor rate and efficiency variances and to understand what they mean.

6. Recognize that incentive systems used to encourage increased labor productivity can lead to increased profits for the firm.

In exercising control over any activity, there is usually some basis for comparison. When one states that a job was exceptionally well done, it means that the performance was better than usual or better than some standard established as acceptable. Likewise, control over costs can be exercised by comparing actual performance and costs with standards. Variations from the standards are a basis for either tighter control over the operation or a revision of the standards. During this process, efforts are made to protect the company from waste or loss and to determine the most economical way to acquire and use goods and services.

Inasmuch as the cost of materials and labor is often substantial, a great deal of effort is made to control their cost. Even a very small saving on a unit basis or on an operation performed can add many dollars to profit. Although this chapter will consider materials and labor as direct costs, many of the control measures apply to both direct and indirect materials and labor.

THE USE OF STANDARDS

A standard may be used as a basis for control by service industries, retailers, manufacturers, or governmental and not-for-profit entities. Wherever it is possible to establish a criterion for cost of a material or service and to set standards of performance, standards can be used as a basis for control. For example, the driver of a delivery truck is expected to handle a certain number of deliveries in a normal day. The number of expected or normal deliveries serves as a standard for the measurement of performance.

Standards such as budgets tend to be viewed by employees with suspicion. A standard has a restricting or inhibiting effect upon a person and in that sense interferes with individual expression. With increased automation and the demands of a large society, a person may feel lost in the crowd and merely an appendage of some gigantic production system.

While it is not possible to return to a simple craft economy, it may be possible to reduce some of the tedium of repetitive chores by permitting changes in assignments and by breaking down the work so that it can be handled by small closely knit groups. Some steps have already been taken in this direction by large companies.

Along with changes in work patterns, there may be more participation by workers and lower levels of management in the setting of standards. Values and attitudes of individuals differ, and this may be reflected in setting standards. Better results may be obtained by grouping together workers who share common values and attitudes and giving them a right to participate in setting reasonable standards of performance.

Work measurement techniques are usually employed in setting standards. A thorough study is made of plant operations, general economic conditions, and the effect of economic conditions on the cost that must be incurred for materials and services. Engineers measure the length of time required to complete various manufacturing operations and establish standards of performance. Cost standards are also set and, when related to performance standards, may be referred to as the standard costs of the operations to which they apply.

Often a standard cost is expressed on a unit basis. There is a standard price for a unit of materials and a standard quantity of materials to be used for a unit of product, and there is a standard labor rate and a standard length of time to perform a certain amount of work. The standards remain unchanged as long as there is no change in the method of operation or in the unit prices of materials or services.

Advantages of Standard Cost Accounting

Standards are particularly useful in accounting as a basis for evaluating various operations. Within a standard cost accounting system, there are checkpoints at which variations from the standards can be detected and brought under control. While operations are in progress, comparisons of actual results with the standards can be made and unfavorable conditions can be corrected before losses accumulate.

Management by Exception

Standard cost accounting follows the principle of management by exception. Actual results that correspond with the standards require little attention. The exceptions, however, are emphasized. In actual or historical cost accounting, it is sometimes difficult to separate the exceptions from the flow of data being processed. Furthermore, many of the measurements may not be made until after it is too late to take corrective action.

The management by exception principle can be desirable in that it calls attention to weak areas that require control and saves management the task of going over data that require no attention. When applied to persons, however, the management by exception principle has some drawbacks. If a worker is ignored when operating according to the standard and is noticed only when something is wrong, the worker may become resentful and perform less satisfactorily. While it may be argued by some that the worker is being paid to operate at standard, the human factor cannot be ignored. Without recognition, the worker becomes discontented, and this discontent may spread throughout the organization with a loss of both morale and productivity.

When reasonable standards are used, there is normally a desirable secondary effect. Often employees become cost conscious, watching the standards and seeking ways to improve their work. This tendency can, of course, be encouraged by having an incentive system that is tied in with the standards.

Variations and Control of Standard Costs

For purposes of income determination as well, a standard cost system may be more economical and less complicated than a historical cost accounting system. Standard cost cards are set up for each job or process showing what quantities of materials, labor, and overhead should be used according to the standards. These cards are printed in advance, with the standard quantities and costs being listed. When a job is started in production, the standard cost card shows the complete costs that should apply to it. Materials, for example, are issued on a standard requisition according to the standard quantities required for the order. If more materials are needed than are called for by the standard, a supplemental requisition having a distinctive color may be prepared to call attention to a quantity variance on the order. Many of the transactions follow the preestablished standard pattern. Any variations from the standards receive extra attention.

When operations are automated, standard conditions can be built into the computer program that controls the manufacturing process. Any deviation from the standards can be detected immediately, and corrections can be made while the work is being performed. Losses can be reduced or eliminated entirely in a system that provides for an immediate reaction to any tendency to stray from a predetermined standard. Automatic control devices are used to redirect space vehicles in mid-flight when the vehicle strays off the prescribed course. Similarly, a manufacturing operation can be controlled automatically by an on-line, real-time system. An on-line, real-time system is a system that provides immediate feedback of actual conditions so that corrections can be made at the time the event itself is taking place.

In an automated production system, management is not as concerned with the problem of controlling the actual operations as it is with the planning of controls. Considerable attention should be given to the development of standards and to the development of programs that provide checkpoints to keep the operation in line with the standards. Variations from the standards may measure, in part, inadequacies of the program, unreliability of the equipment, or conditions that were not provided for in the program of instructions. Control by means of standards and a comparison of results with standards is employed in any case and is applied by management to fit the circumstances.

The Quality of Standards

The term "standard" has no meaning unless it is known what type of standard is being used. A standard may be very strict, or it may be very loose. Standards may be broadly classified as follows:

1. Strict or tight standards.
2. Attainable standards.
3. Loose or lax standards.

There is no easy solution to the problem of how standards should be set. The objective, of course, is to obtain the best possible results at the lowest possible cost. Often this problem involves human behavior. A very high standard may motivate the employees and may produce the best results. On the other hand, it may discourage them to such an extent that they will not even meet fairly modest standards of achievement. In setting a level of standards, management must consider the employees, their abilities, their aspirations, and their degree of control over the results of operations.

Strict Standards

The strict standards are set at a maximum level of efficiency, representing conditions that can seldom if ever be attained. They ignore normal materials spoilage and idle labor time due to such factors as machine breakdowns. This type of standard is more a standard of perfection than a standard for the measurement of practical or attainable efficiency. Idealistically it would appear that high standards should be set. As a practical matter, however, a standard that is virtually unattainable will not necessarily motivate employees to do their best. An employee is more likely to put forth increased effort when feeling successful. Stated in another way, a person increases aspirations with success while the aspiration level is lowered with failure. In addition, with strict standards the variance accounts have little significance for control purposes. Large unfavorable variations from strict standards not only measure shortcomings from good performance but also measure expected variations from the ideal.

Attainable Standards

The attainable standards can be achieved with reasonable effort. Perhaps the standards should be somewhat lower than what can be achieved by earnest effort. With success the employees gain confidence and tend to be more productive. It is not easy to generalize. For a more experienced group of workers, an exacting standard may serve as a challenge and may be a strong motivating factor. With less experienced workers, standards may have to be set at a lower level at first. As learning takes place, the standards may be raised. Increases in standards should be made with caution and should be accepted by the employees as being fair.

Loose Standards

Loose standards are not likely to motivate employees to perform at their best; also, if workers are paid bonuses for exceeding the standard, they may receive a bonus for performance that deserves no additional reward. If the standards are too loose, certain variations from efficiency are not revealed but, instead, are incorporated as a part of the standards. As a result, management does not receive the most useful information for the control of operations.

The variations from the standards will be relatively large or small depending upon how the standards are set. Suppose, for example, that the standard cost to manufacture a unit of a certain product has been calculated in three ways as shown below:

Cost Elements	Types of Standards		
	Strict	Attainable	Loose
Materials	$10.00	$10.00	$10.00
Labor	2.00	2.50	3.00
Overhead	1.00	1.25	1.50
Total unit cost	$13.00	$13.75	$14.50

During the year, this product was manufactured at a total unit cost of $14.30, as shown in the following comparative summary:

Cost Elements	Actual Cost	Types of Standards			Actual Over (Under)		
		Strict	Attainable	Loose	Strict	Attainable	Loose
Materials	$10.00	$10.00	$10.00	$10.00	-0-	-0-	-0-
Labor	2.80	2.00	2.50	3.00	$ .80	$.30	$(.20)
Overhead	1.50	1.00	1.25	1.50	.50	.25	-0-
Total	$14.30	$13.00	$13.75	$14.50	$1.30	$.55	$(.20)

Materials prices and quantities were in agreement with the standards, which provide in each case for a unit materials cost of $10. The labor and the overhead variances are relatively high when the strict standard is used. But this total variance of $1.30 per unit is not necessarily a measurement of excessive costs or of poor performance. A portion of the variance may be looked upon as a normal deviation from perfection and hence not controllable. The more significant difference, which management has the ability to control, is not revealed but instead is buried within the total variation of $1.30. At the other extreme, when comparison is made with expected operations, it appears that the company has done very well in trimming 20 cents off the standard unit labor cost. This also may be misleading. The budget standards may be too lax. Assuming that the normal or attainable standards are reasonably tight and are realistic, the controllable variance of 55 cents will be more useful in evaluating costs and performance.

REVISING THE STANDARDS

Standards may be set with the intention that they will be retained over long periods of time, barring any substantial changes in the methods of production. Standards of this type are often called bulletin standards, **basic standards,** or **bogies.** When conditions change so that the standard is out of date, an adjustment is made by using index numbers in much the same way that index numbers are used in making adjustments for the effect of price-level changes. Often the standards are not entered in the accounting records but are used as statistical supplements in arriving at information for control purposes. On the other hand, both the actual data and the standard cost data may be entered in the accounts by dual recording.

In many cases standards are established for relatively short periods of time with revisions being made whenever necessary. For example, a standard price for a material may be relevant for a certain period of time but has no meaning after there has been an increase in the price level of that material. A variation of the actual price from the standard price does not measure purchasing department inefficiency if an outdated standard price is used for the measurement. Therefore, standards have to be changed from time to time so that they correspond to current conditions. Similarly, labor standards have to be revised if the rate structure is changed or if changes have been made in the methods of production.

MATERIALS STANDARDS AND CONTROL

Standards may be established for the cost of obtaining materials and for the quantities to be used in production. Actual costs can be compared against these standards, and variances can be measured. Basically there are two types of variances: (1) price and (2) quantity. Several different variances may be developed for specialized purposes, but they can always be classified as being variations in the price of materials, the quantities used, or a combination of price and quantity. If the actual cost is greater than the standard cost used in comparison, the variance is unfavorable; if actual cost is less than the standard cost, the variance is favorable.

Materials Price Variance

A materials price variance measures the difference between the prices at which materials were purchased and the prices at which they should have been obtained according to the established standards. Production management is responsible for how materials are used, but it may have no control over the prices that are paid. A factory may be operated efficiently; but if materials are not purchased at reasonable prices, potential profits will be lost before the manufacturing operation begins.

A standard price is set for each class of material to be purchased. If the purchasing function is being carried out properly, the standard price should be attainable. When lower prices are paid, a favorable materials price variance is recorded, indicating that the purchasing department was under the standard; whereas, higher prices are reflected in an unfavorable materials price variance, showing that the purchasing department did not meet the standard. Quality standards have to be watched, of course; otherwise the purchasing department in its zeal to surpass the standard may acquire poor quality materials that will be costly on the production floor.

Periodic reports show how actual prices compare with standard prices for the various types of materials purchased. The total cost effect is equal to the quantities purchased multiplied by the price differentials. Reports on price variances may be made monthly to the purchasing agent and to the executive who is responsible for the purchasing function. They reveal which materials, if any, are responsible for a large part of any total price variation and can help the purchasing department in its search for more economical sources of supply.

Standard costs are not always incorporated in the accounting records. The price variance, for example, can be measured even though both the materials and the liability to the supplier are accounted for on an actual cost basis. In this chapter, however, the operation of a standard cost system is illustrated by tracing the standard costs through the accounting records. At different points in the accounting operation, variations can be measured in the accounts quite easily; and a knowledge of the flow of actual and standard costs helps in understanding how the variances are determined.

Accounting for Materials Price Variance

A materials price variance can be isolated at the time materials are purchased. The actual quantity of materials purchased can be recorded in the materials inventory at standard prices, but the liability to the supplier must be recorded by using actual quantities and actual prices. The difference between the debit to Materials and the credit to Accounts Payable is caused by the difference in price and is recorded as a price variance.

To illustrate, assume that the purchasing department bought 1,000 units of a certain material at a price of 70 cents each when the standard price was 80 cents each. This is recorded by a journal entry as follows:

Materials	800	
Materials Price Variance		100
Accounts Payable		700
Purchases at below standard price, favorable variance.		

The principle of isolating the materials price variance from the previous example can be expressed in abbreviated form as shown below.

$$1.\ AQP \times AP = AC \qquad 1000 \times \$.70 = 700$$
$$2.\ AQP \times SP = MC \qquad 1000 \times \$.80 = 800$$
$$AC - MC = PV \qquad 700 - 800 = 100$$

AQP = actual quantity purchased
AP = actual price
AC = actual cost
SP = standard price
MC = mixed cost (actual quantity purchased multiplied by standard price)
PV = price variance (materials)

Note that the quantities (actual) are the same in Equations (1) and (2). Only the prices differ, and the variation is designated as a price variance. The variance can be computed more directly by multiplying the actual quantity by the difference in the prices.

$$AQP \times (SP - AP) = PV$$

The materials price variance for the previous example is computed as follows:

$$AQP \times (SP - AP) = PV$$
$$1,000 \times (\$.80 - \$.70) = PV$$
$$1,000 \times \$.10 = PV$$
$$\$100 = PV\ (favorable)$$

A materials price variance can be either **favorable** or **unfavorable** when actual costs are compared with standard costs. In this illustration, the material price variance is favorable because the materials were purchased at a cost below the established standard.

Materials Quantity Variance

Materials are withdrawn and used in production, but more or less materials may be used than specified by the standards. The variations in the use of materials are called materials quantity or **materials usage variances**. The differences can be calculated by comparing the record of materials withdrawn with consumption standards, or the differences may be directly recorded in a materials quantity variance account at the time materials are transferred into production.

Understanding Materials Usage

Reports on the quantities of materials used are made to responsible production personnel. A production supervisor, for example, may receive daily or weekly summaries showing how the quantities used in the department compared with the standards. At the operating level, the use of materials can be controlled directly. The supervisors should have daily or weekly reports on their operations so that corrections can be made before losses become too great. Summary reports of actual and standard materials consumption given in dollars, with variances and percentages of variances to the standards, can be presented to the general supervisor or to the plant superintendent on a monthly basis. If the variances in any department are too large, this is revealed so that the superintendent can localize the differences and take steps to reduce them in future months. During the month, of course, the operating supervisors are expected to watch materials use; and if they have been doing their jobs properly, the accumulated variances for the month should be relatively small.

Ordinarily, materials quantity variances are chargeable to the production departments. They often arise as a result of wasteful practices in working with materials, or they arise because of products that must be scrapped through faulty production. For example, it should be possible to get a certain number of stamped parts from a metal sheet of a given size. But if the stamping operation is not performed properly, more sheets will be used in getting the desired number of parts. Or some part may be machined improperly, with the result that the part has to be discarded.

Not all excessive materials consumption can be charged to inefficient factory operation. The purchasing department may have to share the blame. Perhaps poor quality materials were acquired in order to obtain a price saving. An inferior grade of material may contribute to losses that are detected in the factory. Any measured variance reveals a condition, but it does not tell why that condition exists. Management is given the basic information, which it can apply in looking for the underlying causes. For example, the purchase of an inferior grade of materials may be an acceptable condition if the anticipated favorable purchase price variance is expected to outweigh the unfavorable quantity variance resulting from the use of such materials.

Accounting for Quantity Variance

To account for materials used, the materials account is decreased and the work in process account is increased. Returning to the last example, assume that 600 units of materials are withdrawn from the inventory for use in the factory. The standard calls for only 500 units. The 100-unit difference between actual and standard use is multiplied by the standard unit cost of 80 cents to arrive at an unfavorable quantity variance of $80. If standard costs are recorded in the accounts, Work in Process is charged with standard quantities priced at standard unit costs. In other words, the work in process inventory is carried at standard cost. The materials inventory, however, is credited with actual quantities used as multiplied by the standard unit costs. The journal entry is shown below.

Work in Process	400	
Materials Quantity Variance	80	
Materials		480
Materials charged to production at standard cost.		

The materials quantity variance can be computed from equations as shown in the following:

$$
\begin{array}{lll}
1. & \text{AQU} \times \text{SP} = \text{MC} & 600 \times \$.80 = 480 \\
2. & \text{SQ} \times \text{SP} = \text{SC} & 500 \times \$.80 = 400 \\
& \text{MC} - \text{SC} = \text{QV} & 480 - 400 = 80
\end{array}
$$

AQU = actual quantity used
SP = standard price
MC = mixed cost (actual quantity used multiplied by standard price)
SQ = standard quantity
SC = standard cost
QV = quantity variance (materials)

In Equations (1) and (2) the unit prices are the same, standard. Only the quantities differ, and the variation is designated as a quantity variance. The variance can be computed more directly by multiplying the standard price by the difference in quantities:

$$\text{SP} \times (\text{AQU} - \text{SQ}) = \text{QV}$$

The materials quantity variance shown in the previous journal entry is unfavorable because the amount of materials used is greater than the amount called for by the standard. The amount of the variance is computed as follows:

$$
\begin{array}{rcl}
\text{SP} \times (\text{AQU} - \text{SQ}) &=& \text{QV} \\
\$.80 \times (600 - 500) &=& \text{QV} \\
\$.80 \times 100 &=& \text{QV} \\
\$80 &=& \text{QV (unfavorable)}
\end{array}
$$

Indirect materials are those materials that are used for other than the manufacture of a product. When indirect materials are used by the maintenance department, the actual quantities are recorded at standard prices as factory overhead. No variances are measured at this point. Assuming that 50 units of materials are transferred to the factory for use as indirect materials, the following entry is made:

```
Factory Overhead . . . . . . . . . . . . . . . . . . . . . . . . . . . . . . . . . . . . . . . . . . . . . . . . .    40
    Materials . . . . . . . . . . . . . . . . . . . . . . . . . . . . . . . . . . . . . . . . . . . . . . . . . . . . . . .        40
        Withdrawal of 50 units of materials having a standard unit cost of 80
        cents for indirect use in factory operations.
```

Materials Acquisition

Control over materials begins with procurement. The purchasing department will seek a reliable supplier whose materials meet the quality standard in the desired quantity at the lowest price. After receiving a purchase requisition from individual departments, the purchasing department places the order for the materials. When the materials are received, they are counted, inspected, and turned over to the storekeeper.

Invoices received by the accounting department for materials purchased are compared against purchase orders and receiving reports to determine whether or not the company was properly billed for materials ordered and received. Arithmetic computations on the invoices are checked, and the verified invoices are filed by the dates when payments must be made.

The storekeeper is the only person with access to the physical materials, which are stored in an enclosed area to prevent theft or loss. An accounting record of the quantities of materials received and withdrawn is maintained by a stores ledger clerk. Incoming items are entered from receiving reports on inventory cards or a computer terminal to reflect the inventory subsidiary ledger. The requisition forms for materials to be withdrawn for production, support the entries for inventory withdrawals. The physical inventory kept by the storekeeper should be in substantial agreement with the book record revealed by independent counts. The separation of the duties acts as a check on both the storekeeper, who realizes that a book record of the inventory is being maintained, and the stores ledger clerk, who has no access to the physical inventory and thus no reason to falsify the record. This separation of physical custodianship of property and the responsibility for accountability follows a general principle of internal control: that one person should control the physical asset while another person maintains the accounting record. This is true not only in inventory accounting but also in accounting for cash, securities, and other business properties.

The Inventory Level

Included as a very important part of materials control is control over inventory balances. Excessive amounts should not be kept on hand, nor should the inventories be allowed to become dangerously low. With insufficient inventories, there is the risk that production may be disrupted by the depletion of some critical item and that a customer may not receive an order on time. The tendency may be to overstock rather than to risk a *stock out*. However, there is a cost of maintaining excessive inventory balances. Resources that should be used more productively may be needlessly tied up in inventory. The rate of return sacrificed by holding resources idle is an implicit cost to the business. Hence, if the company has too much invested in inventory, it has sacrificed a return that could be earned by an alternative employment of resources. This return is an opportunity cost attached to inventory investment. There is also the cost of storing inventories, the cost of insurance, and the risk of loss through spoilage or obsolescence.

Insofar as possible, the company should plan to hold a minimum balance that will take care of its needs during a procurement period (the time elapsed from when materials are ordered until they are received). There is no perfect solution to the problem, but it may be possible to develop guidelines from past experience.

Assume, for example, that a procurement period is defined as one month. Forecast use and actual use of units for past months are given in the following table:

Month	Forecast Use	Actual Use	Variations	Variations Squared
January	510	520	10	100
February	500	500	–0–	–0–
March	480	490	10	100
April	520	515	5	25
May	540	530	10	100
June	540	535	5	25
July	520	525	5	25
August	500	520	20	400
September	500	480	20	400
October	480	490	10	100
Total				1,275

An estimated standard deviation is computed below.

$$\sqrt{\frac{1,275}{10-1}} = 11.9 \text{ estimated standard deviation, or 12 units}$$

Assume a forecast use for November of 500 units. If the company wants to guard against stock depletion with a 95 percent probability of being covered, it will order 524 units. The forecast is increased by two standard deviations or by 2×12. (There is roughly a 95 percent probability that data are plus or minus two standard deviations from the mean.) This is admittedly an approximate guide, but improvements can be made as more data are collected.

LABOR STANDARDS AND CONTROL

Standards are established for direct labor, and variances from the standards can be measured in much the same way as they were measured for materials. Following the same general principle used for materials, there are two types of variances: (1) price and (2) quantity. Often, in working with labor, the price variance is called a rate variance; and the quantity variance is called an efficiency variance.

Labor Rate Variance

The labor rate variance measures the difference between the actual hours worked multiplied by the actual labor rates (actual labor cost) and the actual hours worked multiplied by the standard labor rates.

Labor rate variances are often created by transferring workers with high pay rates to jobs that call for low standard rates or by authorizing overtime work at premium pay. These labor cost differences are caused by rate differences rather than by changes in performance. The cost effect of unfavorable transfers or of premium pay for overtime should be called to management's attention as a price variance.

Assume, for example, that a payroll for direct production workers shows a gross wage cost of $130,000 for a pay period. Workers were paid $5 an hour for 20,000 hours and $7.50 an hour for 4,000 hours. The standard labor rate is $5 an hour. This can be expressed in an abbreviated form as follows:

$$
\begin{array}{lllll}
\text{1. AH} \times \text{AR} & = \text{AC} & 20{,}000 \times & \$5 & = \$100{,}000 \\
 & & 4{,}000 \times & \$7.50 & = 30{,}000 \\
 & & & & \overline{\$130{,}000} \\
\text{2. AH} \times \text{SR} & = \text{MC} & 24{,}000 \times & \$5 & = \$120{,}000 \\
\text{AC} - \text{MC} & = \text{RV} & \$130{,}000 - \$120{,}000 & & = \$10{,}000
\end{array}
$$

AH   = actual labor hours
AR   = actual labor rate
AC   = actual labor cost
SR   = standard labor rate
MC   = mixed cost (actual hours multiplied by standard rates)
RV   = rate variance (labor)

The hours are the same in Equations (1) and (2), but the rates differ. Hence, the labor rate variance can be obtained directly by multiplying the actual labor hours by the difference in the rates:

$$
\begin{array}{rcl}
\text{AH} \times (\text{AR} - \text{SR}) & = & \text{RV} \\
4{,}000 \times (\$7.50 - \$5) & = & \text{RV} \\
4{,}000 \times \$2.50 & = & \text{RV} \\
\$10{,}000 & = & \text{RV (unfavorable)}
\end{array}
$$

In this case 4000 hours were paid at $2.50 per hour in excess of standard. Hence, the variance is unfavorable because the work was performed at a cost greater than the standard rate.

Labor Efficiency Variance

Labor productivity is also measured. When labor is used more efficiently, not only is the labor cost per unit of product lower, but the overhead per unit of product may also be lower. This is true if variable overhead varies with labor hours. However, if variable overhead varies on a unit-of-product basis or is related to some other factor, labor hours have no effect on the cost. Because overhead often varies on a labor hour basis, it is easy to understand why management tries to increase the productivity of its labor force by introducing better work methods and more modern equipment. There can be a double advantage in that both labor and overhead cost per unit can be reduced.

Labor performance, or labor efficiency as it is sometimes called, is compared by department and by job with established standards. Daily or weekly reports to the supervisor and the plant superintendent help to locate and solve difficulties on a particular job or in a department. The vice-president in charge of production or the plant superintendent receives a report relating labor efficiency to labor cost on a weekly or monthly basis. Differences between jobs and departments may show that a job cannot be handled at the standard labor cost or that a department is not being managed properly.

The labor efficiency variance is the difference between the actual and required time for production multiplied by the standard labor rate. Using the data from the preceding example, suppose that the 24,000 direct labor hours were used to complete work that should have been done in 25,000 hours. In this case, there is a favorable variance because the work was done in less than the standard time. A labor efficiency variance can be computed by equation as shown:

$$
\begin{array}{lll}
1.\ AH \times SR = MC & 20{,}000 \times & \$5 = \$100{,}000 \\
 & 4{,}000 \times & \$5 = \underline{20{,}000} \\
 & & \$120{,}000 \\
2.\ SH \times SR = SC & 25{,}000 \times & \$5 = \$125{,}000 \\
MC - SC = EV & 120{,}000 - & 125{,}000 = \$\ \ 5{,}000
\end{array}
$$

$$
\begin{array}{ll}
AH & = \text{actual hours} \\
SR & = \text{standard rate} \\
MC & = \text{mixed cost (actual hours multiplied by standard rates)} \\
SH & = \text{standard hours} \\
SC & = \text{standard cost} \\
EV & = \text{efficiency variance (labor)}
\end{array}
$$

Because the rates are the same in Equations (1) and (2), standard, the variance can be computed as follows:

$$
\begin{array}{ll}
SR \times (SH - AH) = EV \\
\$5 \times (25{,}000 - 24{,}000) = EV \\
\$5 \times 1{,}000 = EV \\
\$5{,}000 = EV \text{ (favorable)}
\end{array}
$$

Payroll Accounting Procedures

In labor accounting, the payrolls are accounted for in the usual manner, with gross wages earned being recorded in a payroll account pending distribution to the production account. A journal entry to record the payroll follows:

```
Payroll ......................................................  130,000
    Employees Income Tax Payable............................          28,500
    FICA Tax Payable........................................           7,500
    Wages Payable ..........................................          94,000
        To record direct labor payroll for the payroll period.
```

When the payroll is distributed to product cost, an entry is made to charge Work in Process with the standard cost of $125,000 (25,000 × $5), obtained by multiplying standard hours by standard labor rates.

```
Work in Process ............................................  125,000
Labor Rate Variance.........................................   10,000
    Labor Efficiency Variance ..............................           5,000
    Payroll ................................................         130,000
        Transfer of factory labor cost to the products.
```

Sometimes the direct labor rate and efficiency variances are isolated in the accounts in two steps. An account labeled Direct Labor may be used as an intermediate account. Direct Labor is charged with actual hours multiplied by the standard labor rates. Payroll is credited for the actual hours multiplied by the actual rates, and the labor rate variance is isolated.

```
Direct Labor:
    Actual hours × Standard rate
            24,000 × $5          = $120,000

Payroll:
    Actual hours × Actual rates
            20,000 × $5          = $100,000
             4,000 × $7.50       =    30,000
                                   $130,000
    Labor Rate Variance (unfavorable)  $ 10,000
```

The journal entry is given below.

```
Direct Labor................................................  120,000
Labor Rate Variance.........................................   10,000
    Payroll ................................................         130,000
        To transfer payroll to intermediate account, Direct Labor.
```

The direct labor is then distributed to work in process. Work in Process is charged with standard hours multiplied by standard rates, and the labor efficiency variance is isolated.

Work in Process:
Standard hours × Standard rate
            25,000 × $5   = $125,000

Direct Labor:
Actual hours × Standard rate
            24,000 × $5   = 120,000
Labor Efficiency Variance
(favorable) $ 5,000

The journal entry is given below.

Work in Process 125,000
    Labor Efficiency Variance   5,000
    Direct Labor..   120,000
        To distribute direct labor to work in process.

A payroll for indirect labor may be recorded directly in Factory Overhead. Even a direct labor payroll will likely include some indirect labor in the form of idle time, and this cost can be transferred out of Payroll to Factory Overhead when information is available for a distribution of the labor cost.

Additions to Labor Cost

There are additional related costs in connection with labor much the same as there are related costs in connection with materials. An employee, in addition to being paid a straight hourly rate, may receive bonuses, vacation payments, sick leave payments, supplemental unemployment benefits, pensions, overtime pay, and shift differential adjustments. The extras are often referred to as fringe benefits.

The proper accounting for these costs in the income determination process can be rather complicated. The estimated cost of providing pensions, for example, may be broken down by years and related to the active work force. A supplemental hourly rate can then be calculated and added to the regular hourly rate in attaching the cost to the products. Similarly, the vacation pay for the year can be reduced to an hourly rate basis for costing products. In many cases, however, the extra pay is charged to Factory Overhead and is apportioned to all jobs accordingly. If factory overhead is allocated on a direct labor hour basis, the results will be the same under either method. Additional or premium pay for overtime work or for work on a less desirable shift may be charged to Factory Overhead and allocated to all jobs. A job should not be penalized with extra cost because it happened to be worked on during an overtime period due to random production scheduling. On the other hand, a special job that causes overtime work should be charged with the additional cost.

Incentives

Additional pay may also be given for superior work performance. When employees produce more units of product in a given time period, the company gains advantages. There is increased revenue from the sale of the additional units produced, and there is an increase in the variable cost of production. But the increase in revenue should be greater than the increase in the variable cost of production resulting in increased profit.

To increase productivity, a company may install superior machinery and equipment, search for better work methods, and reward the employees for superior work performance. There are a variety of incentive pay plans that may be used to encourage employees to increase production. Employees may be given bonus pay for the time saved in production or may receive higher rates of pay when they exceed standard rates of production for sustained periods of time.

The advantage of increased labor productivity is illustrated by the following example:

(1) Arbuckle Company employs five persons, each working 1,800 hours per year at a standard labor rate of $8 per hour.

(2) The standard labor cost per unit of product is 80 cents. In short, each employee is expected to produce 10 units each hour.

(3) An employee who can exceed this standard receives a bonus equal to one half of the pay for the time saved.

(4) During the year, all employees produced at the constant rate of 15 units per hour per employee.

(5) Each unit of product was sold for $8. The direct materials cost per unit was $3, and the variable overhead cost per unit was $1. The fixed factory overhead for the year was $67,500.

Any worker who can increase productivity from 10 units an hour to 15 units an hour saves 30 minutes on the standard. The worker produces in 1 hour what would normally be produced in 1 hour and 30 minutes. The bonus is equal to 50 percent of the pay for 30 minutes or (50% of 1/2 hour × $8 hourly rate). The total pay per hour including the bonus is $10.

With five workers producing at a rate of 15 units per hour, a total of 135,000 units (15 units per hour × 5 workers × 1,800 hours per year) would be produced during the year instead of 90,000 units at the standard rate.

The comparative income statement on page 110 shows the actual results and the standard results expected.

Note that the direct labor cost per unit is lower even with the bonus. The workers received pay for only 50 percent of the time saved.

The increase in manufacturing margin is explained below the comparative income statement.

Arbuckle Company
Comparative Income Statement
For the Year Ended December 31, 1981

	Standard 90,000 units		Actual 135,000 units	
	Per Unit	*Total*	*Per Unit*	*Total*
Sales.	$8.00	$720,000	$8.00	$1,080,000
Cost of goods sold:				
Direct materials	$3.00	$270,000	$3.00	$ 405,000
Direct labor	.80	72,000	.67*	90,000
Variable overhead	1.00	90,000	1.00	135,000
Fixed overhead	.75	67,500	.50	67,500
Total	$5.55	$499,500	$5.17	$ 697,500
Manufacturing margin	$2.45	$220,500	$2.83	$ 382,500

*Rounded

Additional revenue from the sale of 45,000 more units of product (45,000 × $8).	$360,000
Additional variable costs for the production of 45,000 more units of product:	
Direct materials (45,000 × $3)	$135,000
*Direct labor bonus (45,000 × $.40)	18,000
Variable overhead (45,000 × $1)	45,000
	$198,000
Additional manufacturing margin	$162,000

*Bonus per hour (50% of 1/2 hour × $8.00)	$ 2.00
Bonus for each additional unit ($2 ÷ 5 additional units per hour)	$ .40

SUMMARY OF VARIANCES

In this chapter, a great deal of attention has been devoted to the concept of standards and the measurement of variances with respect to materials and labor. The variances provide information to guide management. Perhaps the prices paid for materials were excessive; or the employees were scheduled improperly, resulting in higher labor rates than required for certain productive functions; or the quantity of materials used or labor time was excessive for the amount of work performed.

The procedure used in isolating the price and quantity variances was described by journal entry presentations and by means of short equations. These variances can also be segregated quite easily by tracing the cost flows. This approach is summarized in the following diagram:

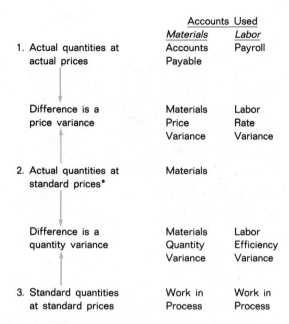

	Accounts Used	
	Materials	*Labor*
1. Actual quantities at actual prices	Accounts Payable	Payroll
Difference is a price variance	Materials Price Variance	Labor Rate Variance
2. Actual quantities at standard prices*	Materials	
Difference is a quantity variance	Materials Quantity Variance	Labor Efficiency Variance
3. Standard quantities at standard prices	Work in Process	Work in Process

*The actual quantities of materials purchased during a fiscal period are not necessarily equal to the actual quantities withdrawn for use in production.

APPENDIX

SOME QUANTITATIVE METHODS — MATERIALS AND LABOR

MATERIALS

Many different quantitative methods have been developed for use in planning inventory levels, timing the cycle for reorders, and estimating optimum order sizes. Computer programs have been designed to account for and handle the flow of inventory information.

Balancing Order and Storage Costs

One frequently used quantitative application deals with the problem of obtaining the lowest possible cost of ordering and storing materials. There is a cost to order materials, and there is a cost to store materials. When materials are stored, the company has to use space that has a rental value, there may be higher insurance costs, and the funds that are invested in inventories are committed so that they are not available for other purposes. In some industries the cost to order may be trivial; hence, there is no problem of balancing order and storage costs.

However, in industries that deal with bulky materials, the costs of receiving and handling a shipment may be substantial. For example, it may be necessary sometimes to authorize overtime pay for persons who must be available when a shipment arrives. Also, by placing frequent orders, the company may be losing quantity discounts that could be obtained by purchasing in bulk. Perhaps the saving to be obtained from placing large orders more than compensates for the increased storage costs.

Various factors must be considered, and these factors should be quantified, if possible. The cost to order and store materials is minimized in many cases when the cost of storage is equal to the cost of ordering. Normally the cost of ordering increases as orders are placed more frequently, but the cost of storage decreases; the total cost may be at a minimum when the two costs are approximately equal.

Calculating Order and Storage Costs

The order and storage costs can be tabulated under different assumptions as to the number of orders placed and the inventory investment. Assume that a company predicts that 3,000 units of a certain material are needed next year. Each unit costs $6. Past experience indicates that the storage costs are approximately equal to 10 percent of the inventory investment. The cost to place an order amounts to $9. If only one order were placed for the year, it would be for 3,000 units, and the average number of units held in the inventory during the year would be 1,500 (3,000 ÷ 2) assuming a uniform rate of withdrawal. With two orders, 1,500 units would be purchased on each order, and the average inventory would be only 750 units. The cost to order and store the inventory is computed and set forth in the table at the top of the next page. It is computed under different assumptions as to the number of orders and the investment in inventory. The company should place ten orders each for 300 units. The storage cost of $90 is equal to the total ordering cost at this point, and the combined costs are at a minimum.

This same result can be computed by use of the formula at the top of page 113.[1]

---

[1]Formula was derived as follows:

$$\text{Cost to order} = \frac{\text{Annual demand}}{\text{Optimum quantity per order}} \times \frac{\text{Cost per}}{\text{order}} \text{ or } \frac{DO}{Q}$$

$$\text{Cost to store} = \frac{\dfrac{\text{Optimum quantity per order}}{2^*}}{} \times \text{Storage cost or } \frac{QS}{2^*}$$

*Divide by 2 to get an average

$$\frac{DO}{Q} = \frac{QS}{2}$$

$$DO = \frac{Q^2S}{2}$$

$$Q^2S = 2\,DO$$

$$Q^2 = \frac{2\,DO}{S}$$

$$Q = \sqrt{\frac{2\,DO}{S}}$$

$$Q = \sqrt{\frac{2\ DO}{S}}$$

When Q = optimum quantity per order (unknown)
　　　D = annual demand for materials expressed in units of
　　　　　material — 3,000 units
　　　O = cost per order placed — \$9
　　　S = storage cost per unit — 60¢ (10% of material
　　　　　cost, \$6)

Number of Orders	Number of Units per Order	Average Inventory	Storage Cost Cost of Average Inventory	10% Storage Cost	Order Cost (\$9 Each Order)
1	3,000	1,500	\$9,000	\$900	\$ 9
2	1,500	750	4,500	450	18
3	1,000	500	3,000	300	27
4	750	375	2,250	225	36
5	600	300	1,800	180	45
6	500	250	1,500	150	54
7	429	215	1,290	129	63
8	375	188	1,128	113	72
9	333	167	1,002	100	81
10	300	150	900	90	90
11	273	137	822	82	99
12	250	125	750	75	108

The optimum order quantity can be computed directly from the formula by inserting the inventory data developed.

$$Q = \sqrt{\frac{2 \times 3,000 \times \$9}{.60}}$$

$$Q = \sqrt{\frac{54,000}{.6}}$$

$$Q = \sqrt{90,000}$$

$$Q = 300 \text{ units}$$

The annual requirement of 3,000 units purchased on the basis of 300 units per order would require the placing of ten (3,000 units ÷ 300 units) orders.

Time to Order

Forecasting the most probable quantity of inventory to be used during a period of time, as already stated, is most important along with a decision as to the most economic quantity to be ordered. As a control measure, some flexibility must be allowed in case a larger quantity is used than was forecast. An excessive investment in inventory is certainly not desirable, but some buffer stock should be held to guard against a stock out in case actual use is over the estimated use.

When an order is placed, recognition must be given to the time that will elapse between the placement of the order and the actual receipt of the quantity ordered. This is called lead time. Sufficient quantities of inventory must be on hand to provide for operations during this interval of time.

Some companies will physically segregate the inventory estimated for the lead time in a special part of the bin or shelf; it may be marked and placed in a separate box within the bin or shelf. When the supply reaches the point where this portion of the inventory is to be used, an order must be placed. If estimates have been made correctly, the materials will be received before the special stock is exhausted. Or a computer program may trigger orders when the records show that the supply on hand is down to an order point.

The concept of timing the orders is illustrated as follows:

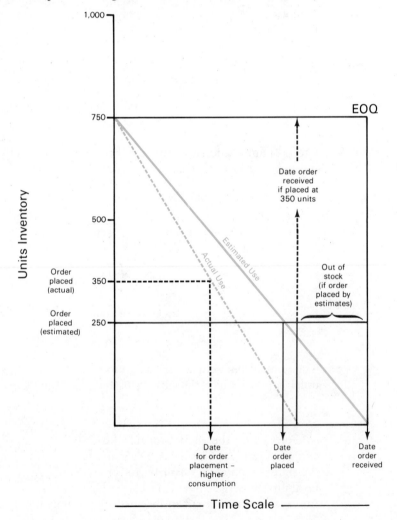

The quantity to be ordered, based upon the economic order quantity, is 750 units. When the expected use reaches the 250 units of minimum stock for the lead time, an order should be placed for 750 units. The units should be received when the lead time expires, thus bringing the inventory to its expected maximum level of 750 units.

The dotted line shows that the actual use was more than expected. If an order is placed when the inventory is expected to reach 250 units, there will be a period of stock out. The inventory is being depleted more rapidly than expected, and the order is placed too late. The inventory situation should be monitored, and an order should be placed at 350 units in this case to allow time for delivery with more rapid consumption. Furthermore, if it is perceived that the actual use will continue to be more than expected, the minimum inventory level and the economic order quantity will have to be recomputed.

Shipping Routes

Often a problem arises when materials or merchandise can be obtained from various sources for shipment to various locations. With proper planning, a program can be designed that minimizes the total cost of shipping. Routes are chosen so that all units can be delivered as scheduled with the least total cost. For example, assume that 3 units of a material are required at Destination 1 and that 3 units of this material are also required at Destination 2. There are 2 units available at Warehouse I and 4 units available at Warehouse II. The cost to ship each unit from each warehouse to each destination is shown in the matrix given as follows:

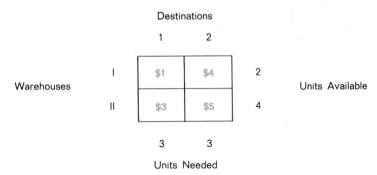

At present, the units are being shipped along the following routes at a total cost of $21.

No. Units	From Warehouse	To Destination	Unit Cost	Total Cost
1	I	1	$1	$ 1
2	II	1	3	6
1	I	2	4	4
2	II	2	5	10
Total shipping cost..				$21

By changing the route structure, the total shipping cost can be reduced to $20. Ship one more unit from Warehouse I to Destination 1 and one less unit from Warehouse II to Destination 1. The total effect on cost in this example is trivial; but in actual practice with many units and various shipping costs, the total cost may be substantial.

Cost Effect Of Route Change For Destination 1

Reduced cost: 1 less unit from Warehouse II...........................	$3
Added cost: 1 more unit from Warehouse I	1
Net advantage of this change..	$2

However, this route change makes it necessary to ship one less unit from Warehouse I to Destination 2 and to ship one more unit from Warehouse II to Destination 2.

Cost Effect Of Route Change For Destination 2

Added cost: 1 more unit from Warehouse II...........................	$5
Reduced cost: 1 less unit from Warehouse I	4
Net disadvantage of this change	$1

The net effect of the entire change is a net reduction in total cost of $1 as shown on the revised route schedule.

No. Units	From Warehouse	To Destination	Unit Cost	Total Cost
2	I	1	$1	$ 2
1	II	1	3	3
3	II	2	5	15
Total shipping cost...				$20

An optimum shipping schedule is obtained when no further cost reductions can be made by shifting the routes. The preceding schedule is the optimum schedule.

In linear programming, this type of problem is called the transportation model. With many points of origin and destination, the problem becomes more complicated; and a computer may be used in testing for route changes that result in the lowest possible cost. The principle, however, remains the same. Each change in the route structure is tested for its effect on the total cost. The opportunity cost of shipping by other routes is compared with the cost of the present plan, and the lowest cost routes are chosen until no further cost reductions can be made.

LABOR

In many industries, labor is a substantial part of the cost of production. Quantitative methods have been applied in attempting to find out how much labor time should be used in carrying out certain production functions. Time and motion studies, that take into account human limitations, can help to determine how much labor time is required for an operation.

The Learning Curve

Management can obtain additional profit from increased productivity. With more units manufactured in a given time period, there is a greater manufacturing margin even after sharing the benefits of increased productivity with the employees. Efforts are constantly being made to upgrade the skills of employees and to increase their efficiency through education and motivation.

Learning Phase and Static Phase

A study can be made of the rate of learning a new task with the resulting productivity plotted on a graph as a learning curve. As experience is gained in production, the average time to manufacture a unit will decrease. This condition is known as the learning phase. Assume, for example, that the first batch of 100 units to be manufactured is produced in 500 labor hours. After this experience, the workers can produce the next 100-unit batch in less time. Perhaps the second 100-unit batch can be produced in 300 hours. An additional batch of 200 units may be produced with an additional 480 hours. When an optimum point is reached at some stage, no further increases in productivity can be expected and productivity is known to be at the static phase.

The example just given illustrates what is called an 80 percent learning curve. It is so designated because when production doubles, the cumulative average time per unit decreases to 80 percent of the previous cumulative average time.

Units Per Batch	Cumulative Number Of Units	Hours Per Batch	Cumulative Hours	Cumulative Average Hours Per Unit*
100	100	500	500	5.0
100	200	300	800	4.0*
200	400	480	1,280	3.2*

*Cumulative average is 80 percent of previous cumulative average.

The learning rate may be such that when the production is doubled, the cumulative average time per unit is 70 percent, 60 percent, or any other percentage of the previous cumulative average time per unit. At some point, learning stage is completed and further increases in productivity cannot be expected. Experience with the learning rates for certain types of functions may be used in predicting expected results.

The data given for the 80 percent learning curve are plotted on a graph as follows:

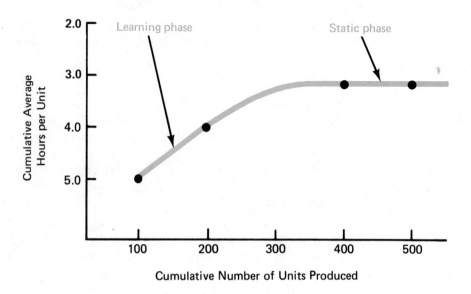

Sometimes data are plotted on log-log graph paper so that the learning curve
will be a straight line and somewhat easier to read.

Terminology Review

Standard (93)
Variations (93)
Standard costs (94)
Management by exception (95)
On-line, real-time system (96)
Strict standards (96)
Attainable standards (97)
Loose standards (97)
Bulletin standards (98)
Materials price variance (99)
Materials quantity variance (99, 101)

Unfavorable variance (99)
Favorable variance (99)
Procurement period (104)
Labor rate variance (105)
Labor efficiency variance (105, 106)
Fringe benefits (108)
Lead time (114)
Transportation model (116)
Learning curve (117)
Learning phase (117)
Static phase (117)

QUESTIONS FOR REVIEW

1. Why are budgets and standards generally considered to be unpleasant?

2. What is meant by management by exception?

3. Point out advantages and disadvantages of following the principle of management by exception.

4. What are some of the aspects of human behavior that must be considered in setting standards?

5. Explain why it may be necessary to revise standards from time to time.

6. During the month of April, Hess Products purchased 50,000 units of a material to be used in production at a price of 40 cents per unit. The standard price for this material was 36 cents per unit. What was the materials price variance?

7. During the month of May, Pasco Company used 30,000 units of a certain material in production. Standards indicate that only 27,000 units should have been used. The standard price per unit was $3.00. What was the materials quantity variance?

8. Explain how the purchase of materials at less than the standard price may have an adverse effect upon the use of materials in production.

9. An examination of the cost records of Judson Machine Company reveals that the materials price variance is favorable but that the materials quantity variance is unfavorable by a relatively large amount. What might this indicate?

10. What is meant by procurement period?

11. How can the concept of standard deviation be used in predicting order requirements?

12. How are labor rate variances and labor efficiency variances computed?

13. The departmental supervisor assigned 3 persons with a labor rate per person of $6 an hour to a project with a standard labor rate of $5 an hour. Each person spent 70 hours on this project. What effect will this have on the labor rate variance?

14. A job calling for 350 hours of direct labor time was completed in 330 hours. The standard labor rate per hour is $5.50. What was the labor efficiency variance?

15. Does the increased productivity of labor have any relationship to factory overhead? Explain.

16. D'Ambrosio Products, Inc., incurs direct labor cost of $8 per unit to manufacture a unit of product that can be produced in one hour and fifteen minutes. Factory overhead varies at the rate of $12 an hour. If the labor time can be reduced to one hour, what will be the total expected cost saving per unit of product?

17. Describe briefly the way in which the variances are isolated in standard cost accounting.

EXERCISES

1. *Materials Price Variance.* An electric circuit component used in the production of an electronic game has a standard cost of $8 per unit. During the last month, Havfun

Games purchased 70,000 components at the standard unit cost, 12,000 at a cost of $8.50 each, and 10,000 at a cost of $9 each.

Required: Determine the materials price variance.

2. Materials Price Variance. Three types of materials, designated as A15, B28, and C46, are used by Eppes Machine Company in production. Data with respect to June purchases are as follows:

Materials Code	Number of Units Purchased	Standard Unit Cost	Actual Unit Cost
A15	7,200	$8	$9
B28	4,400	5	4
C46	3,600	3	4

Required:

(1) Determine the total materials price variance for the month of June.

(2) Do you believe that sufficient information is provided by the total materials price variance? Explain.

3. Materials Quantity Variance. During the month of July, 51,000 units of materials having a standard cost of 80 cents a unit were requisitioned for the production of 12,000 units of a product line. Standards reveal that 4 units of this material should be used for each unit of product manufactured.

Required: Prepare a journal entry to cost materials to production and to set up the materials quantity variance.

4. Materials Variances. A wheelbarrow is manufactured by Wheel Horse Inc. Standard quantities and costs of the parts used are as follows:

Per Product Unit	Description	Cost per Unit of Part
1	steel pan	$4.00
4	steel tubes	.40
2	rubber handles	.10
4	bolts-1/4"	.05
1	bolt-1/2"	.10
1	wheel	2.00

In 1985, the company assembled 40,000 wheelbarrows. No materials were on hand either at the beginning or at the end of the year. The quantities purchased and used in production are at actual costs, as follows:

Number of Parts Used	Description	Actual Cost
40,000	steel pan	$240,000
162,000	steel tubes	72,900
115,000	rubber handles	11,500
161,000	bolts—1/4"	8,050
40,200	bolts—1/2"	4,020
40,000	wheels	84,000

Required:

(1) Compute (a) the materials price variance and (b) the quantity variance by individual components.

(2) Determine (a) the total materials price variance and (b) the total materials quantity variance.

(3) Identify components with relatively large price variances and components with relatively large quantity variances.

5. **Labor Rate Variances.** During the month of September, Sanchez Machine Company started and completed three projects. Data with respect to actual and standard hours for the project along with actual and standard labor rates, are as follows:

| Project Number | Standards | | Actual | |
	Hours	Labor Rate per Hour	Hours	Labor Rate per Hour
32	450	$ 7	400	$ 7
	300	8	350	8
33	520	8	460	10
	430	10	490	10
34	260	12	240	12
	300	14	320	14

Required:

(1) Compute the labor rate variance in total and for each project.

(2) Compute the labor efficiency variance in total and for each project.

(3) Prepare a journal entry to distribute factory payroll and to record the labor rate and the labor efficiency variance.

6. **Selection of Standards.** An analysis of operations shows that a very skilled employee can do the welding on 30 units of product per hour. This rate of production has been established as a standard for all employees. Before the new standard was set, the workers each produced an average of 20 units per hour. During the week, after the new standard was established, the four workers in the department, by working a 35-hour week, completed the welding on 3,920 units. However, materials scrap cost increased by $2,700 over the normal level that week; and 800 units were rejected in inspection and must be done over. The standard labor rate per hour is $15.

Required:

(1) What was the labor cost per unit when 20 units per employee were made each hour?

(2) What would the labor cost per unit have been when 3,920 units were made, assuming no losses?

(3) What was the actual labor cost per unit when 3,920 units were made with all losses included in the computation of unit cost?

(4) Comment on the new labor standard and possible reasons for the losses.

7. **Labor Efficiency Variance.** Fries and Mackey Inc. has established a labor production standard of 5 units per hour for a certain product line. During October, the company made 18,400 units in 4,600 direct labor hours. The standard labor rate is $12 per hour.

Required:

(1) Prepare a journal entry to distribute the labor cost to work in process and to set up the labor efficiency variance.

(2) Determine the labor cost per unit at the standard rate of production.

(3) Determine the actual labor cost per unit for the month of October.

8. Labor Efficiency Variance. During June 18,000 units of product were made in 6,000 direct labor hours. At the end of June the superintendent of the Wayne Company believed that productivity could be improved by setting labor standards. It was determined that 4 units of product were to be the standard production each direct labor hour. During July the company made 25,000 units of product in 6,000 direct labor hours. The standard labor rate is $10 per hour.

Required:

(1) Compute the direct labor cost per unit (a) when 18,000 units are made in 6,000 direct labor hours and (b) when 25,000 units are made.

(2) Does it appear that the superintendent was correct in that productivity was lower than it should be?

9. Labor Variances. The payroll for Ulmer Parts Company for the month of November amounted to $423,000. Income taxes of $85,000 and FICA taxes of $29,000 were withheld, and union dues of $7,000 were deducted. The net amount paid to the employees was $302,000.

Included in the total payroll was indirect labor of $65,000 (not on an hourly basis). The standard labor rate of $10 per hour was paid for 25,000 hours, and $12 per hour was paid for 9,000 hours.

The company made 175,000 units of product during the month. Standards show that 5 units of product should be manufactured each hour.

Required: Journalize the payroll for the month of November and prepare whatever other journal entries are needed to cost production and to isolate the labor rate and efficiency variances.

10. Labor Variances. The direct labor payroll for Anders Supply Company in May consisted of 24,000 direct labor hours. The standard rate of $9 per hour was paid for 21,000 hours, $10 per hour was paid for 2,000 hours, and $12 per hour was paid for 1,000 hours.

Standards show that 36,000 units of product should be produced in 24,000 direct labor hours. In May, 30,000 units were manufactured.

Required:

(1) What was the actual direct labor cost for May?

(2) Compute the result of multiplying the actual hours by the standard labor rate.

(3) Determine the labor rate variance.

(4) Compute the standard labor cost of the 30,000 units made.

(5) Determine the labor efficiency variance.

11. Materials and Labor Variances. The Knight Company purchased 80,000 units of direct materials in April at a cost of $12 per unit. The standard cost per unit is $10.

During April, 60,000 units of this material were requisitioned for production. According to the standards, only 55,000 units of material should have been used.

The direct labor payroll for April consisted of 6,000 hours at $9 per hour and 2,000 hours at $10 per hour. The standard labor rate was $9 per hour, and 7,500 hours should have been used, according to the standards, for the production in April.

Required:

(1) Determine the variances from standard cost for direct materials and direct labor.
(2) Determine the standard direct materials and direct labor cost for the production in April.

12. Shipping Route Costs (Appendix). Kahl Tires Inc. has two plants: one located at Memphis and the other at Denver. Shipments are made from both plants to three regional warehouses. Next month the Memphis plant is expected to produce 10 units. The Denver plant is expected to produce 8 units. Unit shipping costs from each plant to each warehouse are:

	Warehouses		
Plants	A	B	C
Memphis	$ 4	$6	$10
Denver	10	2	8

Warehouse demand is as follows:

	Units
Warehouse	Needed
A	5
B	8
C	5

Required:

(1) Prepare a shipping plan for the next month that will minimize shipping cost.
(2) Determine the minimum shipping cost according to your plan.

PROBLEMS

4-1. Materials Variances. The Benes Company has established a standard cost of $6 per unit for Material A and $8 per unit for Material B. In February, the company purchased 25,000 units of Material A and 10,000 units of Material B. With the exception of 2,000 units, Material A was purchased at standard cost. The 2,000 units had a unit cost of $7. The company purchased 9,000 units of Material B at standard cost and 1,000 units at a unit cost of $12.

According to the standards, four units of Material A and two units of Material B should be used to manufacture each unit of product WIZ. In February, 3,000 units of WIZ were manufactured, and 12,100 units of Material A were used and 8,000 units of Material B were used.

Required:

(1) Compute the materials price and the materials quantity variance for each of the two types of materials.
(2) Identify the material with a price variance that seems to be the most out of line with the standard.
(3) Does either material reveal an abnormally high consumption rate?
(4) Prepare journal entries to record the acquisition of materials and their use in production. Isolate the variances in the entries.

4-2. Materials Variances. The manager of the purchasing department of Deibert Supplies Inc. is pleased that he was able to buy 40,000 units of a material at a bargain price of $56,000. The standard price for this item is $1.60 per unit.

During the following month, 28,000 of these units were used to make 5,000 units of product. Standard use in production has been established at 4 units of material per product unit.

Required:

(1) Compute the materials price variance and the materials quantity variance.
(2) Assume that the materials quantity variance resulted from the purchase of inferior materials. Determine the net advantage or disadvantage of the bargain purchase.

4-3. Labor Variances. During November, Department 7 of Harkins Metals Inc. had to operate at overtime to meet production deadlines. A total of 2,000 hours of overtime at a total hourly rate of $15 was authorized. Regular hours of labor, 10,000 hours, were at the standard labor rate of $10 per hour.

The department made 22,000 units of product in the time that is allowed for 24,000 units.

Required:

(1) Prepare journal entries to record the payroll and the distribution of labor to Work in Process.
(2) Determine, from the information given, a possible reason for the relatively large unfavorable efficiency variance.

4-4. Labor and Overhead Savings. Standard costs have been established for Liebig and Hassler Inc. for the production of a machine part. The production workers are paid $9.60 an hour and are expected to make 8 units of this part each hour. The standard direct materials cost per unit of product is $7. Variable factory overhead, consisting of indirect materials, varies at the rate of $4 per unit of product. Other variable factory overhead varies at the rate of $6.40 per direct labor hour. By revising the production process slightly, management expects to increase output to a level of 10 units of product per hour.

Required:

  (1) Determine the standard unit variable cost of the product at the present time.

  (2) Determine the standard unit variable cost of the product under the revised production plan.

4-5. Labor Savings and Bonus. The management at Jeffrey Novelty Company has a policy of encouraging productivity by sharing savings in labor cost with the employees. A bonus equal to 75% of the regular pay for the time saved is granted for exceeding the standard rate of production of 10 units per hour. The standard labor rate is $10 per hour. Variable factory overhead is estimated to vary at the rate of $6 per direct labor hour. Direct materials cost per unit is $2. During 1985, the company manufactured and sold 780,000 units of product in 65,000 direct labor hours. The product is sold for $6 per unit. All costs in 1985 conformed with the standards with the exception of the differences caused by increased labor efficiency.

Required:

  (1) Compute the manufacturing margin (profit) by unit and in total for 1985.

  (2) Compute the total net cost benefit to the company by rewarding the employees for the saving in labor time.

4-6. Forecasting Inventory Level. José Amarillo has been following a company policy of keeping inventories to a minimum level in order to minimize the cost of storing inventories. Each month he has estimated consumption for the next month and has placed orders accordingly. The procurement period is one month. For example, if he estimates on March 1 that 500 units will be needed in April, he will order that quantity and will receive the order in time to make deliveries on April sales.

    Last year he found that there were times when the inventory was insufficient to meet customer demand. If possible, he would like to improve the estimating technique and have 95% assurance that his decision will not result in stock depletion before the new order arrives. The company agrees that it would be better to have some extra inventory storage cost and minimize the risk of inventory shortages.

    A record of estimates and consumption for the past year is as follows:

Month	Forecast Use	Actual Use
January	450	420
February	380	360
March	350	380
April	400	400
May	420	410
June	520	500
July	540	530
August	580	550
September	460	480
October	450	440
November	440	420
December	420	420

The estimate for September of the current year is 450 units.

Required:

(1) From the record of past estimates and consumption, set up a plan that may help Amarillo avoid stock depletion and yet hold excessive inventory balances down.

(2) How many units should he order in August for September sales?

4-7. Materials and Labor Cost Flows. Standard costs have been determined for the direct materials and direct labor used in the production of a small storage tank that is manufactured at the Monterrey plant of Castillo Industries Inc. The standard costs per tank are:

Direct materials:	
3 units of Material 88	$ 8.70
4 units of Material 93	24.00
6 units of Material 112	30.00
Standard materials cost...........................	$62.70
Direct labor:	
3 hours each at $8.00	24.00
Total standard materials and labor	$86.70

In August, 15,000 of these tanks were manufactured in 44,000 direct labor hours. The direct labor payroll for the month was $354,000.

The plant used 45,500 units of Material 88, 61,000 units of Material 93, and 90,000 units of Material 112.

During the month, all materials were purchased and used at the standard price except for 8,000 units of Material 88 that were purchased at a unit cost of $3.

Required:

(1) Prepare journal entries to trace direct materials and direct labor through the accounts to Finished Goods, isolating the materials and labor variances.

(2) Did the employees meet the productivity standards?

4-8. Materials and Labor Variances. The Vulcan Chemical Company has a standard cost accounting system. Recently the prices of raw materials have increased substantially, and management is concerned about increasing product costs because of the intense competition in the market.

Data with respect to standard costs for one of the product lines are:

	Standard Cost per Pound	Standard Use per Product Unit	
Material A.................	$ .20	5 lbs.	1.00
Material B.................	1.40	3 lbs.	4.20
Material C.................	.80	2 lbs.	1.4

The standard labor rate is $8 per hour, and 4 units of product (a unit defined as an 8-pound package) are processed each labor hour. The standard variable overhead amounts to $6.40 per labor hour.

Actual cost data for the last month are:

Purchases of materials:
Material A .... 28,000 pounds at a price of $ .70 per pound
Material B .... 14,500 pounds at a price of $1.75 per pound
Material C .... 9,500 pounds at a price of $1.10 per pound

Materials used in production to manufacture 4,600 packages:

Material A .... 27,600/.70 .... 39,428.57 .... 5570 ..... 27,600 lbs.
Material B .... 14,000/1.75 ...... 8000 .... 4,644.6 .. 14,000 lbs.
Material C .... 9,300/1.10 ...... 8454.54 .... 4650 .... 9,300 lbs.

30,900/32 = 1590.6

The 4,600 product units were produced in 980 labor hours. The labor rate and the variable overhead rate per hour remained at the standard.

1590.6 × 6.40 (10,179.84) VARIABLE overhead

147,200 LBS

Required:

(1) Determine the total materials price variance for the last month. Also determine the materials use variance and the labor efficiency variance.
(2) Determine the total variable costs of production last month. Also determine the actual variable cost per unit of product.

30,900/32 = $1590.60

4-9. Materials Price and Production Charges. Atwell Products Company assembles various appliances and tools that are sold to hardware dealers. Included among the various products is a small unit that can be used in spraying fruit trees and shrubs.

The costs of the materials used in the production of the sprayer are as follows:

1 cannister..	$ 8.00
1 plunger assembly	8.30
1 plastic hose, 3 ft..	.55
2 nozzle attachments @ $.40 each	.80
2 metal clamps @ $.10 each..........................	.20
3 washers @ $.05 each	.15
Materials cost, sprayer	$18.00

The materials cost per sprayer is equal to 60% of the selling price to the hardware dealer. With this relationship, management has found that labor and overhead costs can be recovered along with the selling and administrative costs and allow a modest margin for profit. Materials cost is the largest item of cost, being more than the labor and overhead costs combined.

Prices have increased substantially, and the costs of materials next year are expected to be as follows:

1 cannister	$11.25
1 plunger assembly	10.00
1 plastic hose, 3 ft.	.75
2 nozzle attachments @ $.50 each	1.00
2 metal clamps @ $.15 each	.30
3 washers @ $.10 each	.30
Materials cost, sprayer	$23.60

The sales manager is concerned that the higher costs will result in higher selling prices to the dealers. As a result, dealers may not continue to buy the sprayer.

A conference with the production personnel has resulted in a proposal for a new type of sprayer that can be manufactured with other materials at a somewhat lower cost. The materials costs to make this type of sprayer are:

1 cannister	$ 7.00
1' plunger assembly	10.00
1 plastic hose, 3 ft.	.60
2 nozzle attachments @ $.50 each	1.00
2 metal clamps @ $.15 each	.30
3 washers @ $.10 each	.30
Materials cost, sprayer	$19.20

At the present price to the dealer, it is estimated that 80,000 sprayers can be sold next year, about the same volume as last year. However, the sales department estimates that sales volume will be only 50,000 units if the price to the dealer is increased by more than 10%.

The labor and variable overhead cost per unit is expected to remain at the same amount as before, $5.

Required:

(1) Compute the selling price to the dealer under the present cost structure.
(2) Compute the selling price to the dealer, using the present materials at increased costs.
(3) Compute the selling price to the dealer, using the substitute materials.
(4) What was the total manufacturing profit from the sprayer last year?
(5) What profit can be expected next year from manufacturing if the company continues to use the original materials?
(6) What profit can be expected next year from manufacturing if the company uses different materials?
(7) Comment on the general policy of substituting cheaper materials in manufacturing.

4-10. Labor Bonus Plan. The management of DeAngelo Products Company has a bonus plan in effect that pays employees 75% of the time saved in production when production exceeds the standard level. It is recognized that an employee could exceed the standard for a short period of time and produce below standard at other times, thus collecting a bonus inconsistently. In order to encourage a more consistent performance, the bonus is computed on the basis of production for a four-week period.

Each employee works 37 hours per week. The standard production per hour has been established at 3 units of product. Each employee is paid at the rate of $7.50 per hour.

Production data for four weeks in September are as follows:

Production in Units	Employees			
	Bob	Gary	Harriet	Jennifer
1st week	107	123	124	111
2d week	100	120	121	110
3d week	110	119	122	115
4th week	108	124	125	114
Total	425	486	492	450

Production in Units	Employees			
	Jim	Joan	Paul	Ron
1st week	108	104	108	115
2d week	112	110	112	116
3d week	115	115	112	114
4th week	112	115	133	117
Total	447	444	465	462

Required:

(1) Compute the labor bonus for each employee for September.

(2) Determine the labor cost (including bonus) for each employee.

(3) Identify any employee who may not be working consistently up to his or her capacity.

4-11. Labor Productivity and Cost Effect. The Oliver Machine Company manufactures a spring clasp at one of its plants. Under standard operating conditions, the plant should produce 10 of these clasps per hour.

There are 20 employees who work exclusively in making these clasps. Each employee is paid at the rate of $9 per hour and works approximately 160 hours per month. Each month 32,000 of these clasps are produced and are transferred to another section of the plant where they are used in the assembly of metal chests.

A study of the operation shows that, with some modifications in production procedure, it is possible to produce at the rate of 12 clasps per hour.

The manager of product production suggests that the 32,000 clasps required by the assembly section can be supplied by retaining 17 of the employees in this area and transferring the other 3 to an operation where there is a labor shortage. The manager further states that the higher productivity goal can be attained by using the old standard as a basis for bonus computations. Employees would be paid the full labor rate of $9 an hour for time saved in production by making 12 units an hour instead of 10.

The variable overhead varies at the rate of $15 per hour in this type of work.

The plant superintendent believes that the labor cost will be higher under the bonus arrangement with 17 employees than under the former straight hourly pay arrangement with 20 employees. The superintendent concedes that the full bonus may be needed as an incentive for the employees but states that the cost will be somewhat higher.

Required: Determine the labor and variable overhead cost under both the old and the new arrangements. Will the new bonus plan be more expensive? Explain. (Give both the unit and total costs.)

4-12. Standards and Productivity. The superintendent of Rausch Fixture Company believes that tighter standards will lead to increased productivity. The assistant superintendent argues that the work force in Department 5 is relatively inexperienced and would lose confidence if standards were any tighter than they are now.

"Nonsense," replies the superintendent. "The new people should learn what we expect from them from the very beginning."

At present, the workers in Department 5 are expected to produce 30,000 units of product a month and use 90,000 units of materials at a standard cost of $.50 per unit of material. For the past few months, somewhat over 90,000 units of material were used each month. The output of 30,000 product units should be manufactured in 5,000 direct labor hours. This standard was being met. A few months ago, it was necessary to hire extra help that increased the total direct labor hours to 5,400 a month.

The new standards set by the superintendent require that materials waste be reduced by using 100,000 units of material to meet the new production quota of 40,000 product units per month. The 40,000 units are to be made in 5,000 direct labor hours with no additional help hired. The standard labor rate remains at $8 per hour.

During the first month under the new standard, 35,000 product units were made in 5,000 direct labor hours and 160,000 units of material were used.

Required:

(1) Determine the direct materials quantity variance for the first month under the new standard.

(2) Determine the direct labor efficiency variance for the first month under the new standard.

(3) Comment on the advantages and disadvantages in the positions taken with respect to the standards by the superintendent and the assistant superintendent.

4-13. Standards and Productivity. A review of standards is being conducted by the management of Derringer Home Products. In one department, unfavorable variances were identified as follows:

Materials price variance	$300,000
Materials quantity variance	210,000
Labor rate variance	39,600
Labor efficiency variance	137,200

The variances were viewed by management as being much too large, indicating that drastic control measures are needed. Further information with respect to direct materials and direct labor cost per unit of product is as follows:

Direct materials (4 units each at $5)	$20.00
Direct labor (1/2 hour, hourly rate, $7)	3.50
Standard cost—materials and labor	$23.50

The materials used in production can no longer be obtained at the old price of $5 per unit. Last month the company bought 80,000 units at the standard cost, before prices increased. After the price increases, under the best terms available, the company bought 150,000 units this month at a cost of $7 per unit.

During the month, 40,000 units of product were started and completed. The department used 202,000 units of material. No allowance was made for normal shrinkage of materials in production. Experience reveals that 5 units of material are needed to obtain the equivalent of 4 units of material for each unit of product.

A new union wage scale has increased the hourly wage rate to $8. The old rate for production of 2 units per hour was set before the product was redesigned. With a more complex product line, it now takes an average of one hour to complete each unit of product. Last month 39,600 hours were used in production and paid at the rate of $8 per hour.

Required:

(1) Show how the variances were computed.

(2) Set up a more realistic schedule of standard unit costs for direct materials and direct labor.

(3) Recompute the variances measured from the revised standards.

(4) Explain how outdated standards can mislead management.

4-14. Balancing Order and Storage Costs (Appendix). At a recent meeting of purchasing executives, Don Ryan stated that in his line of business the economic order quantity has little significance. The cost to place an order is nominal, and the cost of receiving and handling the material is a fixed cost for the year. Hence, it did not matter whether or not he ordered at frequent intervals.

One of the other members, Holly Spahr, stated that her situation is different. In her company, basic raw materials are bulky and must be handled promptly with the use of heavy equipment. When a shipment arrives, all effort must be made to unload the trucks promptly. Persons who do not ordinarily work in receiving are released from their regular assignments and are given extra pay for this work.

Ordering data for Spahr's company are given below:

Estimated annual demand . . . . . . 8,000 units
Cost per unit $8
Cost per order placed $5

Storage costs are estimated at 25% of the inventory investment.

Required: How many orders should be placed to minimize the combined costs of placing orders and the costs of storage? Show computations and prove your answer by showing the combined costs for 35 orders, 40 orders, and 45 orders.

4-15. The Learning Curve (Appendix). The employees at Hammond Engine Company are working on a new type of product that shows a future market potential. The employees are all experienced, and it is estimated that productivity will improve as they become more familiar with the new production techniques.

The first lot of 1,000 units was completed in 4,000 labor hours. Past studies of learning experiences indicate that these employees can be expected to produce another 1,000 units in 2,000 additional hours. The next 2,000 units should be produced in an additional 3,000 hours.

In order to encourage increases in productivity, the management has authorized a bonus of 25% of the base pay per hour after the first 2,000 units are produced as expected in a total of 6,000 labor hours. The bonus for the next 3,000 hours will be paid if 2,000 more units are made in that time. The base pay per hour is $8.

The workers met the challenge and received the bonus by producing 2,000 units in 3,000 hours.

Required:

(1) Compute the labor cost of the last batch of 2,000 units including the bonus.

(2) What was the labor cost per unit of product on the 2,000-unit batch. (Include bonus.)

(3) Determine the rate of learning predicted by management. Show computations.

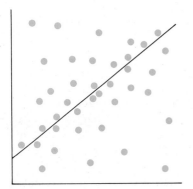

5

P140

MANUFACTURING OVERHEAD COST CONTROL

Chapter Objectives

This chapter should enable you to:

1. Distinguish between a spending variance, an efficiency variance, and a capacity variance.
2. Describe why the spending variance and the efficiency variance are called controllable variances.
3. Understand that an overhead spending variance is to overhead what a combination of the price variance and quantity variance is to direct materials and direct labor.
4. Explain why the efficiency variance is related only to variable overhead.
5. Explain why the capacity variance is related only to fixed overhead.
6. Understand that a capacity variance, in some cases, may be controllable.
7. Describe how the principles of standard costs and variances can be applied by nonmanufacturing entities.

The manufacturing overhead costs are also controlled by making use of information developed through a standard cost accounting system. The overhead costs are accumulated by departments or other identifiable units of the company. The actual costs are then compared with a budget prepared for various levels of output. The comparison shows whether the prices paid for and the quantities used of indirect materials, indirect labor, and other overhead were too high or too low in relation to the budget.

For example, Department 15 used supplies costing $3,200 for 5,000 hours of operation during the month of June. A budget for supplies at 5,000 hours of operation shows that the cost should have been $2,500. The unfavorable variance of $700 is used as a basis for investigating underlying causes. It may be found that supplies were used excessively or that the prices of the supplies were too high. Perhaps steps can be taken to correct this condition before cost becomes more excessive.

A FLEXIBLE BUDGET AND VARIANCES

As explained in Chapter 3 overhead is applied to the products by means of an overhead rate that is calculated by dividing a budgeted factor such as machine hours into budgeted overhead at normal capacity. As an aid in the control process, a series of budgets, known as a flexible budget, is prepared for different levels of activity.

Standards are established for the time required to make a given quantity of product as well as for the level of activity expected at normal capacity. Hence, the standard overhead cost per unit of product can be determined for the normal capacity level.

Assume that Ellis Parts Company has a normal operating capacity of 100,000 machine hours, and standards indicate that 4 units of product should be manufactured each hour. The total overhead at normal operating capacity has been budgeted at $600,000.

In 1985, it is assumed that the company (1) produced 280,000 units of product, (2) used 80,000 machine hours, and (3) incurred total overhead cost of $529,000. The fixed overhead included in the total amounted to $203,000. A flexible budget for the company is summarized below. Details with respect to individual items such as indirect materials, repairs, and heat and light are omitted in the interest of brevity.

Ellis Parts Company
Summarized Flexible Budget (Standard Cost)

	Overhead Budgets (at various hours of operation)				
Machine hours of operation	110,000	100,000	90,000	80,000	70,000
Standard production (product units) .	440,000	400,000	360,000	320,000	280,000
Variable overhead	$440,000	$400,000	$360,000	$320,000	$280,000
Fixed overhead	200,000	200,000	200,000	200,000	200,000
Total overhead	$640,000	$600,000	$560,000	$520,000	$480,000

Overhead rate per hour:
　Variable $4.00
　Fixed 2.00
　　Total rate $6.00

Overhead rate per unit of product:
　Variable $1.00
　Fixed .... .50
　　Total rate $1.50

*Normal operating capacity

Note that the overhead rate has been computed at the normal capacity and that it can be expressed either as a rate per hour or as a rate per unit of product. Cost computations can be made using either the hourly rate or the unit-of-product rate. To avoid error, it is necessary to be consistent; that is, use hours with the hourly rate and units of product with the unit-of-product rate.

OVERHEAD VARIANCES

Each unit of product has a standard overhead cost of $1.50. The standard overhead cost of the 280,000 units manufactured was $420,000 (280,000 units × $1.50 rate per unit of product).

The total overhead variance is the difference between the actual overhead and the standard overhead assigned to the products.

	Variable	Fixed	Total
Actual overhead	$326,000	$203,000	$529,000
Standard overhead for 280,000 units produced . .	280,000	140,000	420,000
Total unfavorable overhead variance	$ 46,000	$ 63,000	$109,000

The total variance can be analyzed in three portions and used as a tool for planning and control. The three variances are:

1. Spending variance.
2. Efficiency variance.
3. Capacity (or volume) variance.

The first two of these variances, the spending variance and the efficiency variance, are often called the controllable variance. These two variances are called controllable because production management should be able to minimize any unfavorable variances of this type by economic and efficient operation.

The Spending Variance

The difference between the actual overhead cost and the budgeted cost for the actual hours of operation is called a spending variance. Note that this variance is to overhead what the price and quantity variances are to direct materials and direct labor. It is the combination of the price and quantity variances for overhead. The other variances developed for overhead do not pertain to overhead itself but rather to the relationship of overhead to the level of activity expressed as machine hours, direct labor hours, and direct labor cost.

To summarize the concept of a spending variance, note that actual overhead cost is $529,000 and that the budget for the level of machine hours operated is $520,000. The spending variance is computed as follows:

	Variable	Fixed	Total
Actual overhead	$326,000	$203,000	$529,000
Budget of overhead for actual hours of operation			
(80,000 hours)...................................	320,000	200,000	520,000
Unfavorable spending variance	$ 6,000	$ 3,000	$ 9,000

The company either used more overhead materials and services or paid higher prices than anticipated by the budget. The spending variance has been computed by comparing the actual overhead costs with a budget for the actual time used.

The Efficiency Variance

The efficiency variance reveals the difference in variable overhead cost as a result of using more or fewer hours than planned for the manufacture of the products. It does not result from the saving or improper use of overhead or favorable or unfavorable overhead prices. Instead, it measures the difference in variable overhead that arises by efficient or inefficient use of the factor used in costing overhead to the products.

The efficiency variance, in this illustration, is computed as the difference between the budget for the actual hours used and budget for the hours that should have been used to obtain the quantity of product produced. The efficiency variance is computed below.

	Variable	Fixed	Total
Budget of factory overhead for 80,000 machine			
hours (actual)	$320,000	$200,000	$520,000
Budget of factory overhead for 70,000 machine			
hours (standard hours allowed to manufacture			
280,000 units)	280,000	200,000	480,000
Unfavorable efficiency variance	$ 40,000	–0–	$40,000

The variance can also be computed simply by multiplying the difference between the actual hours used and the budgeted hours allowed by the variable overhead rate per hour: (80,000 actual hours − 70,000 standard hours) × $4 variable rate per hour = $40,000 unfavorable efficiency variance.

The efficiency variance includes only the variable cost. Fixed cost by definition remains the same over the relevant range of hours and is not affected by the efficient or inefficient use of machine time or labor time.

The Controllable Variance

As stated earlier, the spending variance and the efficiency variance together constitute the controllable variance. The earlier results are summarized at the top of the next page in a computation of the controllable variance, which is unfavorable by $49,000. It is equal to the unfavorable spending variance of $9,000 plus the unfavorable efficiency variance of $40,000. It may also be

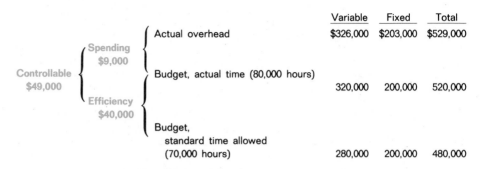

			Variable	Fixed	Total
		Actual overhead	$326,000	$203,000	$529,000
Controllable $49,000	Spending $9,000	Budget, actual time (80,000 hours)	320,000	200,000	520,000
	Efficiency $40,000	Budget, standard time allowed (70,000 hours)	280,000	200,000	480,000

computed as the difference between the actual overhead of $529,000 and the budget of $480,000 for the standard time allowed to complete 280,000 units.

Production management is expected to obtain overhead materials and services at the budgeted prices and to use such materials and services efficiently. There can be a spending variance for either variable or fixed overhead. For example, a budget for property insurance for the year (fixed cost) may have no allowance for an increase in the premium. Hence, there will be a difference between the actual insurance cost and the budgeted amount. Although the insurance cost in itself cannot be controlled on a day-to-day basis, management should be careful to revise budgets as necessary and to consider how much insurance service is required relative to its cost.

Production management is also expected to control the time used for production. As stated in the previous chapter, both labor cost and variable overhead are affected by the efficient or inefficient use of labor time. A saving in labor or machine time not only saves labor cost but also saves variable overhead cost.

Capacity or Volume Variance

The third variance developed in connection with overhead is the capacity or volume variance. Overhead is costed to the products using a rate computed at a defined normal capacity. If the company does not operate at normal capacity, the fixed overhead will be either overabsorbed or underabsorbed. The over- or underabsorption of fixed overhead reveals that the company did not operate at normal capacity. This is the capacity, or **volume**, variance. In this text, the term "capacity" variance will be used.

In the illustration given, the company operated at 70 percent of normal capacity. It produced an output of 280,000 units but was expected to produce 400,000 units at normal capacity. Hence, it produced at 70 percent of the normal capacity (280,000 ÷ 400,000 = 70%). This percentage can also be computed by using hours of operation. The output of 280,000 units should have been completed in 70,000 machine hours. Normal capacity is 100,000 machine hours. The company operated at 70 percent of normal capacity (70,000 ÷ 100,000 = 70%).

By operating at only 70 percent of normal capacity, only 70 percent of the fixed overhead was absorbed by the products. The absorbed fixed overhead was $140,000 (70% × $200,000). The balance of the fixed overhead amounting to $60,000 was unabsorbed ($200,000 − $140,000). The capacity variance was an unfavorable $60,000, the amount of capacity available but unused.

The capacity variance can be computed in still another way as follows:

	Variable	Fixed	Total
Budget of factory overhead for 280,000 units or 70,000 hours of standard time allowed	$280,000	$200,000	$480,000
Standard overhead costed to 280,000 units of product (280,000 units × $1.50 product rate or 70,000 hours × $6 hourly rate)	280,000	140,000	420,000
Unfavorable capacity variance	−0−	$ 60,000	$ 60,000

The variable overhead is not relevant in the computation of a capacity variance, because the variable overhead cost varies with the level of production. The computation could be simplified by considering only the fixed overhead.

	Fixed Overhead
Budget of factory overhead for 280,000 units or 70,000 hours of standard time allowed	$200,000
Standard fixed overhead costed to products at a rate of 50 cents for each of 280,000 units	140,000
Unfavorable capacity variance	$ 60,000

One may argue that the company used 80,000 machine hours and should have produced 320,000 units of product when manufacturing at the rate of 4 units per hour, reasoning that the company operated at 80 percent of normal capacity and that the capacity variance was only 20 percent or was equal to $40,000 (20% × $200,000). It is true that the company did use 80,000 machine hours, but 10,000 of these hours were wasted. The company produced 280,000 units, and these units should have been made in 70,000 machine hours. Hence, only 70 percent of the normal capacity was used effectively. It is also true that 320,000 units should have been made in 80,000 hours, but they were not. Standard overhead cost can be applied only to the tangible units that are available, the 280,000 units produced.

Plant Capacity and Control

In general, the capacity variance is not considered to be controllable by plant management. The plant produces what is needed to meet sales requirements, and plant management cannot be blamed if the sales demand is unable to absorb production at a normal level of plant operation. Moreover, factors such as excessive machine downtime, lack of rapidity in completing tasks due to unskilled workers, and inefficient production scheduling may all contribute to not producing at capacity.

In attempting to place responsibility for idle capacity, it is better to measure in terms of units of product rather than dollars. Also, different concepts of capacity should be considered.

In the preceding example, normal capacity was defined at 100,000 machine hours or 400,000 units of product. Normal capacity, as defined in Chapter 3, is an average concept representing the average level of plant operation over the years considering variations from year to year.

Practical plant capacity, on the other hand, is the level at which the plant can operate if all facilities are used to the full extent. Some allowance must be made for expected delays because of changes in machine setups, necessary maintenance time, and other interruptions. Hence, practical capacity is less than theoretical maximum capacity that could be obtained only under ideal conditions.

A comparison of the actual output with the output for practical plant capacity broadly measures the failure of the plant to operate at the level for which the plant was designed. Assume, for example, that Ellis Parts Company has a plant that can reasonably be expected to produce 500,000 units a year. Yet only 280,000 units were produced.

Practical capacity	500,000 units
Actual production	280,000
Total idle capacity	220,000 units

The idle capacity, as expressed in product units, can be analyzed further to determine why the plant was not used as intended. Assume that the sales budget shows that 400,000 units were to be sold during the year but that orders for only 350,000 units were received.

Practical capacity	500,000		
		100,000	(1)
Sales budget	400,000		
		50,000	(2)
Sales orders received	350,000		
		70,000	(3)
Actual production	280,000		

(1) **Practical capacity minus sales budget**
The difference between the practical plant capacity and the sales budget for the year requires further investigation. Perhaps the company was overly optimisitic and provided too much plant capacity. Or the sales department may not be obtaining potential available sales. Additional analysis may reveal the true nature of the problem and provide a foundation for improvements.

(2) **Sales budget minus sales orders received**
The difference between the sales budget for the year and the sales orders received is a measurement of the inability of the sales department to meet the budget quota. Perhaps the sales quota was too high, or the sales department was not sufficiently aggressive.

(3) **Sales orders received minus actual production**
The difference between the sales orders received and actual production reflects

a mixture of idle capacity and inefficiency. Ellis Parts Company used enough machine time to produce 320,000 units of product but only produced 280,000 units. Hence, 40,000 units included under idle capacity really indicate wastefulness rather than nonutilization. The difference between the sales orders received and the expected production for the time used (350,000 − 320,000) is a measurement of idle capacity. The idle capacity may be chargeable to poor production scheduling or to some other lapse in production management that caused production to fall below scheduled customer deliveries.

In the example given for Ellis Parts Company, no allowance was made for inventories at either the beginning or the end of the period in order to simplify the example. In practice, adjustments must be made for units carried over into the year as inventory or for units remaining on hand at the end of the year.

The significance of the variances may be emphasized by considering the dollar effect. If the sales department fails to meet the sales quota, there is an opportunity cost of lost profit that should be realized. For example, assume that 50,000 units of product may be expected to bring in $750,000 in revenue. Additional cost to manufacture and deliver these units is estimated at $500,000. The $500,000 consists of the direct materials, direct labor, and variable overhead costs as well as the cost to deliver the units. The opportunity cost of not meeting the sales budget (sales budget of 400,000 units minus sales orders received of 350,000 units = 50,000 units) is then estimated at $250,000. At best this is an approximation. Arguments can be made that the additional units could only be sold by reducing prices or that the cost estimates are not entirely accurate. Nevertheless, this approach to the problem can be helpful in that it points out how dollars of profit may be sacrificed by not using the facilities as intended.

SUMMARY OF OVERHEAD VARIANCES

The overhead variances that were discussed in this chapter are now summarized. The following diagram indicates how the total overhead variance can be subdivided into three segments when the system is used for both product costing and control.

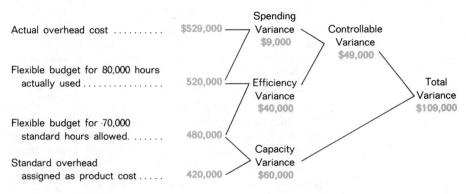

Actual overhead cost .... $529,000 — Spending Variance $9,000 — Controllable Variance $49,000

Flexible budget for 80,000 hours actually used .... 520,000 — Efficiency Variance $40,000

Flexible budget for 70,000 standard hours allowed. 480,000

Standard overhead assigned as product cost ..... 420,000 — Capacity Variance $60,000

Total Variance $109,000

A STANDARD COST ILLUSTRATION

Cost transactions for Dantzer Mills Inc. are traced through the records for the year in summary form. Only one product line is manufactured, with a standard unit cost shown on the standard cost card which appears as follows:

Dantzer Mills, Inc.
Standard Cost — Product A

Materials: 5 units of material × $2 standard price	$10
Labor: 6 hours × $6 standard labor rate	36
Overhead: 6 hours × $8 standard overhead rate	48
Standard production cost per unit	$94

The total factory overhead at normal operating capacity has been budgeted at $960,000, and 120,000 direct labor hours have been budgeted at normal capacity. The overhead rate per direct labor hour is $8.

Summary transactions and cost data pertaining to the year are as follows:

1. Materials purchases, 100,000 units at a unit cost of $2.40.
2. Direct materials issued to production, 93,000 units. The standards required only 90,000 units of materials.
3. Factory payrolls, $814,000; employees income tax withheld, $178,000; FICA tax withheld, $48,000.
4. Labor distribution:
   Direct labor, 90,000 hours @ $6
                 6,000 hours @ 9
   Indirect labor, $220,000
5. Factory overhead other than indirect labor:

Indirect materials	$258,000
Reduction of prepaid insurance	4,000
Accrued expenses	219,000
Depreciation	172,000

6. There were no units in process at either the beginning or the end of the year. During the year, 18,000 units of product were manufactured; and 17,000 units were sold on account for $200 apiece.
7. A portion of the flexible factory overhead budget is given in summary form as follows:

	Percentage of Normal Operating Capacity			
	70%	80%	90%	100%
Standard production in units of product . . .	14,000	16,000	18,000	20,000
Variable overhead	$350,000	$400,000	$450,000	$500,000
Fixed overhead . . . . ⸴	460,000	460,000	460,000	460,000
Total overhead	$810,000	$860,000	$910,000	$960,000
Budgeted direct labor hours	84,000	96,000	108,000	120,000
Overhead rate per hour				$8.00

The flow of the transactional data through the accounts is shown in summary journal entry form as follows:

1. Materials purchased during the year:

Materials	200,000	
Materials Price Variance	40,000	
Accounts Payable		240,000
Acquisition of materials. (Standard: 100,000 units × $2 = $200,000; actual: 100,000 units × $2.40 = $240,000.)		

2. Direct materials issued to production at various times:
   On standard requisitions:

Work in Process	180,000	
Materials		180,000
Standard quantities issued. (5 material units × 18,000 product units = 90,000 standard units of materials × $2 standard unit cost = $180,000.)		

   On supplemental requisition:

Materials Quantity Variance	6,000	
Materials		6,000
Requisition of 3,000 (93,000 issued minus 90,000 standard) units in excess of standard at $2 standard unit cost.		

3. Factory payrolls for the year:

Payroll	814,000	
Employees Income Tax Payable		178,000
FICA Tax Payable		48,000
Wages Payable		588,000
Summary of factory payrolls.		

4. Labor distribution for the year:

Work in Process	648,000	
Factory Overhead	220,000	
Labor Rate Variance	18,000	
Labor Efficiency Variance		72,000
Payroll		814,000
Distribution of payroll. Standard hours per unit of product of 6 × 18,000 product units = 108,000 standard hours × $6 standard rate = $648,000 product cost.		

Rate variance = $3 per hour ($9 actual minus $6 standard) × 6,000 hours = $18,000. Efficiency variance = 12,000 hrs. (108,000 standard minus 96,000 actual) × $6 standard rate.

5. Actual factory overhead for the year, excluding indirect labor:

Factory Overhead	653,000	
Accounts Payable		258,000
Prepaid Insurance		4,000
Accrued Expenses Payable...............................		219,000
Accumulated Depreciation		172,000

      Summary of factory overhead including result of adjusting entries made at end of year. (In this example, it is assumed that indirect materials have been expensed as acquired with no adjustment necessary.)

6. Factory overhead applied to production during the year:

Work in Process	864,000	
Applied Factory Overhead		864,000

      Standard hours allowed for production: 6 standard hours per unit × 18,000 units = 108,000 total standard hours. 108,000 standard hours × $8 rate = $864,000 standard overhead cost.

Completed units transferred to finished goods inventory:

Finished Goods	1,692,000	
Work in Process		1,692,000

      Transfer of 18,000 units to stock at a standard cost of $94 apiece.

Total sales of 17,000 units:

Accounts Receivable	3,400,000	
Sales		3,400,000
Sale of 17,000 units at $200 per unit.		
Cost of Goods Sold......................................	1,598,000	
Finished Goods		1,598,000

      The standard cost of 17,000 units is charged to Cost of Goods Sold (17,000 units × $94 per unit).

7. Actual and applied factory overhead accounts closed and variance recorded:

Applied Factory Overhead	864,000	
Factory Overhead Variance	9,000	
Factory Overhead		873,000

      To close actual and applied overhead accounts. The unfavorable variance is recorded. (Indirect labor, $220,000 + other factory overhead, $653,000 = $873,000.)

Analysis of Factory Overhead Variance

Spending:

Actual overhead incurred	$873,000	
Flexible budget for 96,000 hours of operation.....	860,000	
Spending variance (unfavorable)		$13,000

Efficiency:

Flexible budget for 96,000 hours of operation...	$860,000	
Flexible budget for 108,000 standard hours allowed	910,000	
Efficiency variance (favorable)		(50,000)

Capacity variance:

Flexible budget for 108,000 standard hours allowed	$910,000	
Standard overhead applied (108,000 standard hours × $8 rate).........................	864,000	
Capacity variance (unfavorable)		46,000
Total variance (unfavorable)		$ 9,000

Variances closed to Cost of Goods Sold at the end of the year:

Cost of Goods Sold....................................	1,000	
Labor Efficiency Variance	72,000	
Materials Price Variance		40,000
Materials Quantity Variance		6,000
Labor Rate Variance...................................		18,000
Factory Overhead Variance		9,000
To close out all variances for the year.		

NONMANUFACTURING COSTS

The use of a standard cost as a basis for cost control is most frequently illustrated by a manufacturing operation. A manufacturing operation is relatively complex, and by concentrating on cost control in this area, it is possible to understand the general principles and to apply them to other situations.

The manufacturing company, itself, incurs costs that lie outside of the manufacturing area. There are costs to sell the manufactured products, and there are costs of administration. Standards may be developed for selling and administrative costs. As a general rule standards for selling and administrative costs are not incorporated in the accounting records, but are used outside of the formal system for the evaluation of performance and for the preparation of budgets.

Merchandising and Service Entities

Many business concerns do not manufacture products. Instead, they may purchase completed products for distribution to customers, or render services instead of a tangible good. The cost to sell a product in a given territory, for example, can be accumulated in the same manner that manufacturing costs can be accumulated. Direct materials and labor costs of the selling function can be identified with the selling operation, and indirect or overhead costs can be applied by using a predetermined rate.

Organizations such as banks, insurance companies, and finance companies that sell services instead of products can determine how much it should cost to render their services under different conditions to various customer groups. Work measurement techniques can be used to measure the standard output expected in a unit of time from a given activity or function. The time standards are then combined with cost standards to establish a standard cost for a service.

Assume that two hours are required to process an insurance claim. The standard variable cost per hour is $5. The fixed cost of operating the claims division is budgeted at $4,000 a month. Normally, 400 claims are processed each month. The standard cost to process a claim is:

Variable cost (2 hours × $5)	$10.00
Fixed cost ($4,000 ÷ 400 claims)	10.00
Standard cost per claim	$20.00

In a given month, assume that 360 claims were processed in 750 hours with actual fixed cost as budgeted and actual variable cost of $3,840. Variations from the standards can be identified for control purposes by the following analysis:

Actual variable cost	$3,840	
Budget of variable cost for 750 actual hours (750 hours × $5 rate)	3,750	
Unfavorable spending variance		$ 90
Budget of variable cost for 750 actual hours	$3,750	
Budget of variable cost for 720 standard hours allowed (360 claims × 2 hours per claim = 720 standard hours. 720 standard hours × $5 rate)	3,600	
Unfavorable efficiency variance		150
Fixed overhead	$4,000	
Overhead absorbed (360 claims × $10 rate)	3,600	
Unfavorable capacity variance		400
Unfavorable total variance		$640

For any function or activity that can be performed in a measured unit of time, a standard cost can be developed. The general principles of variance analysis can be employed as an aid in cost control.

Not-for-Profit and Governmental Entities

A large number of organizations in our society are not expected to earn profits. Instead, the objective of these organizations is to provide a useful service or good to the general public or to a segment of the general public. Hospitals, public libraries, universities, and municipalities, for example, are expected to provide services and to recover costs but not earn profits.

Cost accumulation is the same for this type of organization as it is for a business entity that is expected to earn a profit. The direct costs of maintaining a hospital bed, for example, can be estimated. The actual costs can then be compared with the estimates. Indirect costs, such as heat and light, can be allocated on the basis of space occupied in the hospital. Other indirect costs can be apportioned by using a relevant factor for apportionment.

Recently, much attention has been given to cost-benefit analysis. In cost-benefit analysis, the objective is to provide a given amount of benefit at a defined quality level at the lowest possible cost. How much additional cost is justified, for example, to provide either more service or a better quality of service?

Often, the real problem is to place a value on the benefit. In commercial operations, the customer decides whether or not to purchase a service or product at a given price. The business organization, seeking the most profitable course of action, will provide the goods or service according to what the market will pay.

A governmental entity, however, is faced with a more difficult problem involving its many different citizens with different sets of values. The citizen must pay taxes that may or may not be used for purposes desired by that particular taxpayer. Hence, there is not a true market choice as is the case in commercial situations. A city, for example, may have estimated the additional costs required to support the following activities during the coming year.

Library fund	$300,000
Street repairs	800,000
City parks	200,000

These costs can be adjusted up or down to reflect different amounts of service or qualities of service.

With the public highly conscious of tax rates, there is a problem of allocating the tax revenues. Not everything can be done in a way that will suit all persons.

Suppose that the cost estimates for the above services are converted to a millage basis. The owner of a home assessed at $10,000, would have to pay additional taxes as follows:

Function	Estimated Cost	Tax Increase, Mills	*Additional Tax on $10,000 Assessment
Library fund	$300,000	.3	$3
Street repairs	800,000	.8	8
City parks	200,000	.2	2

*Computations are based on the assumption that property taxes are to bear the cost, and that properties in the city have a total assessed value of $100,000,000.

Some taxpayers may favor accepting all alternatives, while others favor holding the line on taxes with no projects accepted. Others may favor street repairs as essential and accept increases there but not for the other functions. Still others will view the library or city parks as being more essential. In the budgeting process, compromises are frequently made.

Assume, for example, that the library board agrees to eliminate a lecture series and the acquisition of a rare book collection. As a result, the increase in costs can be held to $200,000. The department of public works agrees to postpone some street repairs and to make minimal repairs where some work is essential. Cost increases will then be $500,000. The parks and recreation department agrees to reduce the summer concert series and to increase charges for the use of the golf course and swimming pools. As a result, cost increases will be $100,000 instead of $200,000.

The revised budget, while probably not entirely satisfactory from the point of view of any group, will retain certain benefits at a more acceptable tax cost.

Function	Estimated Cost	Tax Increases, Mills	Additional Tax on $10,000 Assessment
Library fund	$200,000	.2	$2
Street repairs	500,000	.5	5
City parks	100,000	.1	1

In this situation, it can be pointed out to the citizens that for every $100,000 increase in a city expenditure, there will be a $1 increase in property taxes for every $10,000 of assessed property value.

The main point is that there is no pricing mechanism where individuals can choose what they want to buy on an open market. The best that can be done is to explain how the cost of benefits will affect the tax rate. The citizens must vote according to how they view the benefits in relation to the effect on their taxes.

Terminology Review

Overhead variance (135)   Capacity variance (137)
Controllable variance (135)   Normal capacity (139)
Spending variance (135)   Practical plant capacity (139)
Efficiency variance (136)   Cost-benefit analysis (146)

QUESTIONS FOR REVIEW

1. How can management use an overhead spending variance in controlling the cost of overhead?

2. Explain how an overhead spending variance is similar to price and quantity variances for direct materials and rate and efficiency variances for direct labor.

3. What is a flexible budget?

4. At what level of capacity is a factory overhead rate computed?

5. Explain how a standard overhead cost per unit of product can be determined.

6. With increases in production, variable cost in total will increase; but the variable cost per unit will tend to remain the same. Explain.

7. Explain why the fixed overhead cost per unit depends upon the level of production that is selected for computing the rate.

8. Name three factory overhead variances that are often developed in standard cost accounting.

9. Which two of the three variances are called the controllable variance?

10. How does an overhead efficiency variance help management in the control of overhead?

11. Is fixed overhead cost included in an overhead efficiency variance? Why or why not?

12. Does an overhead efficiency variance measure efficiency in the use of overhead? Explain.

13. What is a capacity, or volume, variance?

14. Should the standard overhead be applied to the products actually manufactured or to the products that should have been manufactured in the time used? Explain.

15. How can variances be used to control operations?

16. Can a capacity variance be controlled?

17. How are the variances handled at the end of the year?

18. Explain briefly how the total factory overhead variance can be analyzed into a spending variance, an efficiency variance, and a capacity variance.

19. Can the principles of standard cost accounting be applied by nonmanufacturing companies? Explain.

EXERCISES

1. **Spending Variance.** In 1984, Flynn Systems Inc. operated at 250,000 direct labor hours and incurred total factory overhead cost of $2,382,000. A budget of overhead shows that

variable overhead should vary at the rate of $7 per hour and that fixed overhead should amount to $600,000.

Required: Compute the total overhead spending variance.

2. Spending Variance. Leonard Sparks states that his department generally uses indirect materials with a cost of $18,000 when operating at 4,000 direct labor hours. This cost increases to $22,500 for 5,000 direct labor hours and to $27,000 for 6,000 direct labor hours. During February, the department operated at 5,000 hours with an indirect materials cost of $23,200. In January, the department operated at 6,000 hours with an indirect materials cost of $26,800.

Required:

(1) Compute the overhead spending variance for indirect materials in January. In February.

(2) Does the variance show that the price paid for the indirect materials was over or under the standard price? Or, does the variance mean that more or less indirect materials were used than budgeted?

3. Spending Variance. A department of the Lanterman Finishing Company incurred the following overhead costs during the month while operating at 50,000 direct labor hours.

Indirect materials	$43,400
Indirect labor	25,600
Heat and light	6,300
Repairs and maintenance	5,800
Taxes and insurance	3,500
Depreciation	8,000
Total	$92,600

A budget for 50,000 direct labor hours shows indirect materials cost of $40,800, heat and light of $5,400, and repairs and maintenance of $6,000. All other budgeted costs agreed with the actual costs.

Required:

(1) Compute the overhead spending variance by item and in total.

(2) Identify any unfavorable variances that are over $1,000.

(3) Identify any unfavorable variances that are more than 10% over budget.

4. Efficiency Variance. Eppes Fabricating Company made 114,000 units of product in the time allowed for the production of 120,000 units. Manufacturing overhead varies at the rate of $6 per hour. Fixed overhead has been budgeted at $200,000 for the year. Standards show that 3 units of product should be manufactured each hour.

Required: Compute the manufacturing overhead efficiency variance.

5. Efficiency Variance. Mesa Verde Inc. has determined normal capacity of 450,000 machine hours. The standard rate of production is 5 units of product per hour. The standard variable overhead rate is $10 per machine hour, and the fixed overhead rate of $5 per hour. In 1985, the company made 2,150,000 units of product in 450,000 machine hours. Calculations made by the superintendent show that there was no efficiency variance. The company operated at 450,000 machine hours, according to the superintendent, and normal capacity is 450,000 machine hours—hence, no variance.

Required:

(1) Do you agree with the reasoning of the superintendent? Explain.

(2) Compute the manufacturing overhead efficiency variance.

6. Efficiency Variance. Welden Parts Inc. has set a standard of producing 6 units of product for each direct labor hour. The variable overhead varies at $12 per direct labor hour, and fixed overhead has been budgeted at $9 per hour at a normal operating level of 300,000 direct labor hours per year. Last year the company manufactured 1,500,000 units of product in 230,000 direct labor hours. The vice-president of production is pleased with the productivity of labor and the savings in labor cost.

Required:

(1) Compute the manufacturing overhead efficiency variance.

(2) Does the vice-president have other reasons to be pleased? Explain.

7. Spending and Efficiency Variances. During 1985, Rosedale Optical Company operated at 50,000 machine hours in one department and incurred $147,500 in variable manufacturing overhead cost and $300,000 in fixed overhead. In the 50,000 machine hours, production was equal to 165,000 units, the production set for a standard of 55,000 machine hours. The variable overhead budgeted for the actual time used in production was $150,000, and the fixed overhead budget was $300,000.

Required:

(1) Compute the overhead spending variance.

(2) Compute the overhead efficiency variance.

8. Controllable Variance. One of the departments of Uhler Devices Inc. operated at 73,000 direct labor hours and incurred variable overhead of $446,000 during the month of July. The department produced what should have been produced in 70,000 hours. The variable factory overhead is budgeted at $438,000 for 73,000 direct labor hours and at $420,000 for 70,000 direct labor hours.

Required:

(1) Compute the controllable overhead variance.

(2) Split the controllable variance into a spending variance and an efficiency variance.

(3) From the information given, determine the variable overhead rate per hour.

9. Flexible Budget. Overhead budget data for two manufacturing departments of Troy Appliances Inc. are as follows:

Dept. 1

Factory overhead varies at the rate of $7 per machine hour, and the fixed overhead is budgeted for the year at $500,000. At normal capacity, the department should operate at 200,000 machine hours.

Dept. 2

The department is expected to incur variable overhead of $240,000 when operating at 60,000 direct labor hours and is expected to incur $280,000 in variable overhead at 70,000 direct labor hours. The fixed overhead rate is $3 per hour at a normal capacity of 80,000 direct labor hours.

Required: Prepare in summary form a flexible budget for each department showing costs at normal capacity and at 90%, 80%, and 70% of normal capacity. Determine the overhead rate per hour at normal capacity for each department.

10. Capacity Variance. From the records of Holden Company, you have derived the following information:

Actual variable overhead for the year	$600,000
Budget of fixed overhead for the year	$432,000
Actual hours of operation during the year.........................	55,000
Standard hours allowed to manufacture the 300,000 units made during the year	60,000
Normal hours of operation for a year..............................	90,000

Required: Compute the capacity variance for the year.

11. Overhead Variances. Information taken from cost reports and flexible budgets of Cotters Company are as follows:

Budget of factory overhead at 85,000 machine hours.................	$405,000
Budget of factory overhead at 90,000 machine hours.................	$420,000
Budget of factory overhead at 100,000 machine hours defined as normal capacity	$450,000
Actual machine hours of operation	85,000
Machine hours required for units of product made	90,000
Actual factory overhead	$421,000

Required:

(1) Determine the factory overhead spending variance.
(2) Compute the factory overhead efficiency variance.
(3) Compute the factory overhead capacity variance.

12. Efficiency and Capacity Variances. The Wilder Company has allowed a standard time of 20 minutes for the production of a certain product unit. During the year, the company made 150,000 units of product in 60,000 machine hours. Normal capacity has been defined as 80,000 machine hours with variable overhead budgeted at that level at $240,000. The fixed overhead has been budgeted at $120,000. The actual variable overhead for the year was $180,000, and actual fixed overhead was in agreement with the budget.

Required:

(1) Compute the overhead efficiency variance. Does fixed overhead enter into your computation? Explain.
(2) Compute the overhead capacity variance. Does variable overhead enter into your computation? Explain.

13. Overhead Variances. Santa Ana Cable Company has prepared a flexible budget of factory overhead for the year. A summarized portion of the budget follows:

| | Percentages of Normal Capacity | | |
	80%	90%	100%
Variable overhead	$168,000	$189,000	$210,000
Fixed overhead	90,000	90,000	90,000
Total overhead	$258,000	$279,000	$300,000

The company has budgeted 30,000 machine hours at the normal capacity level. Four units of product should be manufactured each machine hour. The company actually produced 96,000 units of product in 27,000 machine hours. Actual variable overhead for the year was $188,000, and actual fixed overhead was $95,000.

Required:

(1) Compute the overhead spending variance.
(2) Determine the overhead efficiency variance.
(3) How much of the budgeted fixed overhead was costed to the products?
(4) Compute the capacity variance.

14. Variances in a Service Enterprise. Jersey Delivery Service delivers packages and messages in a large city and hires drivers to make deliveries. An average standard time has been established to make a delivery. According to the standards, it should be possible to make a delivery in an hour. The office is centrally located, and it takes about as much time to deliver to one location as it does to another. Fixed costs have been budgeted at $120,000 for the year. Under normal conditions, the company expects to make 40,000 deliveries a year. The variable cost has been budgeted at $15 per hour. Last year the company made 30,000 deliveries in 35,000 hours and incurred a total cost of $648,000 including the fixed cost as budgeted.

Required:

(1) Compute the standard cost of making a delivery.
(2) Determine the spending variance and the efficiency variance.
(3) How much of the total variance can be considered to be a capacity variance?

15. Labor and Overhead Variances. At a normal operating capacity, Claymore Fixtures Inc. operates at 400,000 direct labor hours with a standard labor rate of $10. Variable factory overhead is applied at the rate of $6 per direct labor hour, and fixed overhead is applied at the rate of $5 per direct labor hour. Four units of product should be manufactured in an hour. Last year 900,000 units of product were manufactured in 200,000 direct labor hours. All labor hours were paid at the standard rate. Actual factory overhead for the year was as follows:

Variable	$1,246,000
Fixed	2,000,000

Required:

(1) How much labor cost was saved by producing at more than the standard rate?
(2) What was the saving in variable overhead cost by using less than the standard direct labor hours?

(3) Compute the overhead spending variance, the efficiency variance, and the capacity variance.

PROBLEMS

5-1. Overhead Variances. A flexible budget of factory overhead for Markezin Parts Company is summarized below.

	Percentages of Normal Capacity			
	80%	90%	100%	110%
Variable overhead	$320,000	$360,000	$400,000	$440,000
Fixed overhead	200,000	200,000	200,000	200,000
Total overhead	$520,000	$560,000	$600,000	$640,000

Standard cost is used to measure managerial performance. According to the standards established, 3 hours are required to produce 1 unit of product. When operating at a normal capacity of 150,000 machine hours, 50,000 units of product should be manufactured. Last year the company made 45,000 units of product in 150,000 machine hours. The total variable overhead for the year was $427,000, and the fixed overhead amounted to $207,000.

Required:

(1) Compute the overhead variance for the year. Analyze the variance, determining a spending variance, an efficiency variance, and a capacity variance.
(2) Last year the company actually used 150,000 machine hours, the hours selected as normal capacity. If this is true, how could there be a capacity variance?

5-2. Standard Product Cost. Cost standards are being established for a division of Knob Products. According to the standards, 5 units of a material costing $2 per unit are required for each product unit. The standard labor rate is $12 per hour, and 4 units of product should be produced each hour. Standard variable overhead is $5 per direct labor hour, and the standard fixed overhead rate established at normal capacity, defined as 80,000 direct labor hours, is $6 per direct labor hour. During the first year under the standards, the company made 260,000 units of product in 70,000 direct labor hours. The actual manufacturing overhead was $837,000.

Required:

(1) Determine the standard unit cost of the product by cost elements.

(2) What was the total standard cost of production in the first year?

(3) Compute the overhead variances for the first year: spending, efficiency, and capacity.

5-3. Variances in a Service Enterprise. Swift Typing Service types manuscripts for students, professors, and the general public. A standard of 6 pages an hour has been established for straight copy that involves no equations or tabulations. The variable cost of operation has been estimated at $6 an hour. The fixed cost to rent an office and to rent typewriters has been estimated at $900 per month. In a normal month, the manager estimates that the business should operate at 500 hours. During May, 2,880 pages were typed in 480 hours. Actual variable cost was $3,530, and the fixed cost was in agreement with the budget.

Required:

(1) Determine the total standard cost for the 2,880 pages typed in May.

(2) Compute the total variance from standard cost and analyze the variance into a spending variance, an efficiency variance, and a capacity variance.

5-4. All Standard Cost Variances. Summarized manufacturing cost data from the records of Hamilton Windings Inc. are as follows:

(a) Direct materials—Purchased 90,000 units of materials at an actual cost of $282,000. Standard cost is $3 per unit of materials. Used 84,000 units of direct materials in production. Only 82,000 units should have been used.

(b) Direct labor—The standard rate is $9 per hour. The company operated at 75,000 direct labor hours but produced a quantity of product that should have been produced in 80,000 direct labor hours. All but 600 of the direct labor hours were paid for at the standard rate, and the 600 hours were paid for at the rate of $12 per hour.

(c) Overhead—The factory overhead budget for a normal capacity of 90,000 direct labor hours was $360,000. Actual overhead was $312,000.

Budget—75,000 hours—$315,000
Budget—80,000 hours— 330,000

Required: Compute all the variances determinable from the data given.

5-5. Overhead Variances. King Company estimates that it will operate its manufacturing facilities at the normal capacity of 800,000 direct labor hours for the year. The budgeted overhead at normal capacity is $2,000,000. The standard variable overhead rate is estimated to be $2 per direct labor hour or $6 per unit. The actual data for the year are presented as follows:

Actual finished units	250,000
Actual direct labor hours	764,000
Actual variable overhead	$1,610,000
Actual fixed overhead	$ 392,000

Required:

(1) Compute the variable overhead spending variance.
(2) Compute the variable overhead efficiency variance.
(3) Compute the fixed overhead spending variance.
(4) Compute the fixed overhead capacity variance.

(CMA adapted)

5-6. Preparation of Overhead Budget and Variance Analysis. Ross Damon Company has a standard cost accounting system and is expected to operate at a normal capacity of 5,000 machine hours per month and produce 20,000 units of product.

The company does not have a flexible budget. The overhead budgets were prepared from the following data:

Supplies, $4.00 per product unit.
Electricity, $2.00 each hour.
Power, $5.00 each hour.
Repairs, $4,000 plus $1.00 each hour.
Maintenance, $5,500 plus $.50 each hour.
Indirect labor, $46,000.
Property taxes, $6,500.
Insurance, $3,200 plus $.50 per product unit.
Telephone, $1,000.
Depreciation, $4,800.

Product demand was down for the month of May, and only 18,000 units of product were manufactured. The company operated at 4,200 machine hours during May with overhead costs as follows:

Supplies	$ 77,400
Electricity	8,700
Power	22,300
Repairs	7,900
Maintenance	7,300
Indirect labor	46,000
Property taxes	6,500
Insurance	11,500
Telephone	1,200
Depreciation	4,800
	$193,600

Required:

(1) Prepare the portions of a flexible overhead budget that can be applied in variance analysis.
(2) Determine the total overhead variance.
(3) Analyze the variance into (a) a spending variance, (b) an efficiency variance, and (c) a capacity variance. Show the detail of overhead in determining the spending variance.
(4) Did the company spend more time than it should have in producing 18,000 units of product? Does it appear that there may have been waste in the use of overhead materials and services?

5-7. Incomplete Data. Kearsage Fixtures Inc. has a standard cost accounting system. You were recently hired as a manager in the production area and have been given data for the month of October. In looking over the data, you discover that various items of information are missing but find that you can reconstruct the data that you need. The information that you have is given as follows:

Materials purchased at standard unit costs.	$782,000
Actual quantity of materials placed in production at standard unit costs	723,700
Units of product manufactured in October	220,000
Standard direct labor rate	$8.00
Labor efficiency variance, favorable	$20,000
Standard direct labor cost for 220,000 product units	$440,000
Materials quantity variance, unfavorable..................................	$9,700
Materials price variance, unfavorable	$6,800
Labor rate variance, unfavorable	$14,000
Standard variable overhead per direct labor hour	$5.00
Variable overhead spending variance, unfavorable.........................	$17,500
Fixed overhead, spending variance	-0-
Fixed overhead absorbed by the product units manufactured (direct labor hour basis)..	$264,000
Capacity variance, unfavorable	$24,000

Required: Develop the following information:

(1) Actual cost of materials purchased.
(2) Standard cost of materials used to manufacture 220,000 product units.
(3) Actual direct labor cost.
(4) Cost of actual direct labor hours at standard labor rate.
(5) Standard variable overhead cost of 220,000 units.
(6) Actual variable overhead cost.
(7) Budget of fixed overhead for the month.
(8) Fixed overhead rate per direct labor hour.
(9) Direct labor hours at normal capacity for the month.
(10) Actual direct labor hours for the month.
(11) Standard direct labor hours for 220,000 product units.
(12) Standard cost per unit of product by cost element.

5-8. Journal Entries for Flow of Costs. Whiteman Products Inc. has established standard costs for a unit of product manufactured as follows:

Materials (4 kilograms @ $2.00)...............................	$ 8.00
Labor (1/2 hour @ $12).......................................	6.00
Variable overhead ($5 per labor hour)	2.50
Fixed overhead ($8 per labor hour)............................	4.00
Total standard unit cost	$20.50

At normal operating capacity, 200,000 units of product should be manufactured in a year.

Cost data pertaining to the operations for the year are summarized as follows:

Materials purchased (750,000 kilograms)	$1,536,000
Materials used in production	735 000 kilograms
Labor hours	96,000
Labor rate	$11 per hour
Factory overhead:	
Variable	$ 476,000
Fixed	$ 800,000

During the year, 180,000 units of product were put into production and were completed. There were no units in process at the beginning or at the end of the year.

Required: Prepare journal entries to record the flow of cost data from the time the materials were purchased until the products were completed. (Ignore withholdings from the wages of employees and credit Accounts Payable for all factory overhead costs incurred). Variances from the standard costs are to be segregated in the accounts.

5-9. Incomplete Data. The Simpson Iron Company is in the process of relocating some of the plant offices at the Kansas City plant. Much of the data with respect to standard cost and variances for the past month were sent by the planning office to Brussels, Belgium, by mistake and were lost en route.

However, you do have some information and hope that you can reconstruct data that will be helpful in cost control.

Standard costs for each unit of the product line produced at the Kansas City plant are:

Direct materials (5 units of materials for each product unit)	$31.50
Direct labor (1/4 hour, each unit)	2.00
Factory overhead:	
Variable	3.00
Fixed	5.00
Total standard cost, each unit..	$41.50

The plant operates at a normal rate of 50,000 product units each month and applies factory overhead to the products on the basis of direct labor hours.

Last month 300,000 units of direct materials were purchased at a cost of $1,950,000. The inventories of direct materials increased by 55,000 units. All units were bought at the same price.

During the month, 48,000 units of product were produced. The total direct labor payroll for the month consisted of 12,500 labor hours at a total cost of $106,000.

The factory overhead spending variance was unfavorable by $14,000. The fixed overhead for the month was in agreement with the budget.

Required:

(1) Determine the direct materials quantity variance.
(2) Determine the direct materials price variance on the basis of materials purchased.
(3) Compute the labor rate variance.
(4) Determine the labor efficiency variance.
(5) What were the budgeted and the actual fixed overhead amounts for the month?
(6) How much fixed factory overhead was costed to the products during the month?
(7) Determine the capacity variance.
(8) Determine the factory overhead efficiency variance.
(9) How many direct labor hours should have been used for the production for the month?

5-10. Incomplete Data. Blaine Curry, a financial analyst for Pride Industries Inc. has been given information with respect to standard cost variances for one of the plants. These variances are as follows:

Materials quantity variance	$ 8,000 (unfavorable)
Labor rate variance	2,000 (unfavorable)
Labor efficiency variance	9,000 favorable
Factory overhead spending variance	3,000 (unfavorable)
Factory overhead efficiency variance	6,000 favorable
Factory overhead capacity variance	100,000 (unfavorable)

He has determined that the company has manufactured 60,000 units of product with standard costs as follows:

Direct materials	$ 420,000
Direct labor*	180,000
Variable factory overhead	120,000
Fixed factory overhead	300,000
Total standard cost	$1,020,000

*Standard labor time per product unit is 20 minutes.

The fixed factory overhead was in agreement with the budgeted fixed factory overhead. Curry would like to use the variances to develop some of the cost data for the fiscal period.

Required:

(1) How many units of product should be manufactured at normal operating capacity?
(2) Determine the total fixed factory overhead.
(3) How many direct labor hours should have been used to manufacture 60,000 units of product?
(4) How many direct labor hours were used?
(5) What was the actual variable factory overhead cost?
(6) What was the budget of variable factory overhead for the actual time used to manufacture the 60,000 units of product?
(7) What was the budget of variable factory overhead for the required time to manufacture the 60,000 units of product?
(8) What was the actual direct labor cost?
(9) What was the standard cost of the direct materials that were actually used in production?
(10) Determine the standard unit cost of the product by cost element, dividing the factory overhead into a variable portion and a fixed portion.

5-11. Variance Analysis. Last year, Morello Parts Inc. manufactured 2,200,000 spring assemblies at a unit cost of $3.70 each, which is more than the standard unit cost of $3.50 per unit. The company operates in a highly competitive industry and must make every effort to keep costs down.

Actual manufacturing costs for last year are given below.

Direct materials used	$3,600,000
Direct labor	2,290,000
Factory overhead	2,410,000
Total actual cost	$8,300,000

The direct materials were all acquired at the standard cost of $.30 per unit of materials. Five units of materials are required for each unit of product.

All direct labor hours were at the standard rate of $10 per hour with the exception of 8,000 hours at a rate of $15 per hour. The standard rate of production is 10 units of product per direct labor hour.

Normal capacity has been established at 240,000 direct labor hours per year. Last year the company operated at 225,000 direct labor hours. The fixed overhead is applied to the products at the rate of $.50 per unit of product, and the fixed overhead for the year was in agreement with the budgeted fixed overhead. The variable overhead for the year was 10% over the standard variable overhead cost.

Required:

(1) Determine the standard cost per unit of product. Show separate costs for direct materials, direct labor, variable overhead, and fixed overhead.

(2) Determine variances from total standard cost, showing price and quantity variances for direct materials, and rate and efficiency variances for direct labor.

(3) Analyze the overhead variance into a spending variance, an efficiency variance, and a capacity variance.

(4) Identify the unfavorable variances that were primarily responsible for the actual cost being in excess of standard.

5-12. Variance Analysis. Quier Products Company made 80,000 units of product during the month of May, 1985.

Three units of materials, each having a standard cost of $5, are required for each unit of product. The company purchased 300,000 units of materials at a cost of $1,680,000. During the month, 265,000 units of materials were used to produce the 80,000 units of product.

According to the standards, 80,000 units of product should be manufactured in 40,000 labor hours at a standard labor rate of $10 per hour. The actual labor time was 38,000 hours, and 34,000 of these hours were paid at the standard rate. The remaining hours were paid at the rate of $15 per hour.

The company has a normal operating capacity of 50,000 labor hours per month. The variable overhead cost is budgeted at $6 per labor hour, and the fixed overhead is budgeted at $150,000 for the month.

Actual overhead for the month amounted to $380,000. The fixed overhead was in agreement with the budget.

Required: Calculate price and quantity variances for direct materials and rate and efficiency variances for direct labor. Divide the factory overhead variance into a spending variance, an efficiency variance, and a capacity variance.

5-13. Fixed Overhead Cost Budgets and Rates. With a decline in sales volume, the superintendent of Bostwick Mills Inc. has been searching for ways to reduce both variable and fixed overhead costs. At the present time, the company has been operating at a normal capacity of 800,000 machine hours each year with a fixed overhead budget as follows:

Plant superintendence	$ 720,000
Indirect labor	546,000
Taxes and insurance	161,000
Repairs and maintenance	92,000
Depreciation	81,000
Total fixed overhead	$1,600,000

The normal level of capacity is to be reduced to 600,000 machine hours next year. Plant superintendence cost is to be reduced to $680,000 a year, indirect labor is to be reduced to $486,000, and all other fixed costs are expected to remain the same.

Standards at the present time show that 2 units of product should be manufactured per hour. With improved production scheduling, it is estimated that 3 units of product should be made per hour during the next year.

Required:

(1) At the present time, what is the fixed overhead rate per machine hour? per unit of product?

(2) How much saving is expected by reducing fixed overhead?

(3) Is this saving dependent upon the quantity of products made? Explain.

(4) What is the expected fixed overhead rate per machine hour next year? per unit of product?

5-14. Efficiency or Capacity Variance. Connors Electrical Fixtures Inc. manufactures various electric switches and insulators at the Milvale plant. A standard cost accounting system is used. When operating at a normal capacity of 500,000 machine hours, the plant should produce 2,500,000 units of a certain type of insulating and switching device.

In the past few years, the company has been able to sell only 2,000,000 units of this product line each year. Management is aware of the relatively high fixed overhead costs budgeted at $4,000,000 for the year and is conscious of the need to operate as closely to normal capacity as possible.

The variable overhead varies at the rate of $2 per unit of product, and another category of variable overhead varies at the rate of $5 per machine hour.

Last year the plant operated at 450,000 machine hours and produced 2,000,000 units of this product line with $4,000,000 in fixed overhead.

One of the production supervisors, Harry Dalton, has stated that some improvement has been made in solving the problem of operating at below normal capacity. "By operating at 450,000 machine hours, the plant is up to 90% of normal capacity. If the plant had operated at only 400,000 machine hours, as it did last year, we would have absorbed only 80% of the fixed overhead. This year, by operating at 90% of normal capacity, we had only $400,000 as an unfavorable capacity variance."

The supervisor of another department, Debra Ettinger, disagreed and replied, "The capacity variance can't be eliminated by using more hours. I wonder if we aren't confusing the concept of a capacity variance with an efficiency variance."

Harry Dalton answered by saying, "An efficiency variance involves only the variable overhead and has nothing to do with what we are discussing, the absorption of fixed overhead."

Required:

(1) Which of the two supervisors is correct? Explain.

(2) Compute both the overhead efficiency variance and the capacity variance for the past year.

(3) Compute the standard unit overhead cost of the product.

(4) Compute the actual unit cost based on operations for the last year. Show the addition to unit cost for the efficiency variance and the capacity variance as separate items.

5-15. Efficiency Variance or Capacity Variance. The Van Horn Company produces various household tools. One of the divisions manufactures a line of product that is sold for $80 per unit.

A standard cost accounting system is used. The standard direct materials cost per unit of product is $30, and the standard direct labor cost per unit of product is $5. There are seldom any variances in direct materials cost. The only direct labor variance is ordinarily a favorable efficiency variance, inasmuch as the employees generally are highly skilled and are motivated to produce at better than the standard rate. The employees are paid a bonus equal to the time saved in production. As a result, the direct labor cost per unit of product remains at $5.

In 1984, the division operated at a normal capacity of 600,000 direct labor hours and made 2,000,000 units of product. At a standard rate of production, 1,800,000 units should be produced in 600,000 direct labor hours. The company operated in 1984 with no direct materials variances, labor rate variances, or overhead spending variances.

Competition in the industry made it necessary to reduce the selling price to $75 per unit for 1985. Also, sales volume and production for the year were budgeted at 1,500,000 units. There were no variations from standard cost other than the production of 1,500,000 units in 400,000 direct labor hours.

A summary budget for factory overhead for normal operating capacity is given as follows:

Variable overhead (varies with direct labor hours)	$ 7,200,000
Fixed overhead	12,000,000
Total budgeted factory overhead	$19,200,000

The president of the division believes that the favorable overhead efficiency variance will overcome to a large extent the effect of the unfavorable capacity variance.

Required:

(1) What is the standard unit cost for the product line?

(2) Compute the actual unit cost for 1984, including the variances in the computation.

(Continued)

(3) Compute the actual unit cost for 1985, including the variances in the computation.

(4) Show the extent to which the favorable overhead efficiency variance compensated for the unfavorable overhead capacity variance.

5-16. Capacity Variance and Net Income. Lisa Gibson estimated that Osgood Prints Inc. would report a gross margin of $7,500,000 for the year if production standards were met and if 500,000 units of product were sold during the year. Standard costs per unit are as follows:

Direct materials	$16
Direct labor (1/2 hour at $10 per hour)	5
Variable overhead (rate of $8 per hour)	4
Fixed overhead (at normal capacity of 500,000 units of product)	8
Standard unit cost	$33

During the year, the company manufactured and sold 400,000 units of product at the estimated selling price of $48 per unit. Direct materials cost amounted to $6,400,000. The actual labor rate was in agreement with the standard rate, and the company operated at 200,000 direct labor hours. Fixed overhead was in agreement with the amount budgeted, and variable overhead was in agreement with the amount budgeted for 200,000 direct labor hours.

Required:

(1) Prepare a partial income statement for Osgood Prints according to Gibson's estimates.

(2) Prepare a partial income statement for the year according to actual operations.

(3) Explain why the expected results were not realized.

5-17. Manufacturing Income Statement With Variance Analysis. A standard cost accounting system is used by Hartford Tool Company in a plant where parts are manufactured for furnaces and heating units. At normal operating capacity, the plant should manufacture 1,200,000 units of a given part with fixed factory overhead of $4,200,000.

During 1985, the company purchased 1,300,000 units of materials at a price of $.80 a unit. The standard price per unit has been established at $.60 per unit, and one unit of materials is required for each unit of product. In 1985, the plant used 1,080,000 units of materials to manufacture 1,000,000 units of product.

The standard labor rate is $8 per hour, and 4 units of product should be manufactured each direct labor hour. During 1985, the company recorded 262,000 hours of direct labor. The standard rate was paid for 258,000 hours, and the balance of hours were paid for at the rate of $10 per hour.

Variable factory overhead varies at the rate of $5 per direct labor hour. The variable factory overhead for the year amounted to $1,296,000, and the fixed overhead was in agreement with the budgeted amount.

At the beginning of the year, there were 50,000 units of product in finished goods inventory at standard cost. At the end of the year, there were 10,000 units of product in finished goods inventory at standard cost. Each unit of product was sold for $11.

Required: Prepare an income statement for the manufacturing division for 1985 using standard costs. Show variances at the end of the statement.

5-18. Changes in the Standards. The general manager of Boroski Fittings Inc. believes that some improvements in operation can be incorporated in the standards and are necessary if the company is to maintain its position in the market.

The following are the existing standards for one of the major product lines given on a unit-of-product basis.

Direct materials	$32
Direct labor (2 hours each at $10)	20
Variable overhead:	
Per unit of product	2
Per hour (2 hours each at $3)	6
Fixed overhead (at a normal capacity of 100,000 units of product per year) .	12
Total unit standard cost	$72

The company has followed the practice of selling this product at 150% of standard manufactured cost.

Improvements in production have reduced the direct labor time per unit of product from 2 hours to 1 hour. Furthermore, the variable overhead per direct labor hour can be reduced to $2. The total fixed overhead can be reduced to $900,000 for the year.

The company has a market for all the units that can be produced at normal capacity provided that the selling price is competitive at no more than $100 per unit.

Required:

(1) Compute the selling price per unit under existing conditions.

(2) Prepare a new standard cost schedule per unit of product.

(3) Determine the new selling price at 150% of standard manufactured cost.

(4) With the new standard, how much profit should be earned for a year from the production and sale of 100,000 units of product?

5-19. Variances and Decrease in Profits. The president of Avery Plastic Company is disappointed to find that the profit for one division was lower than expected in 1985.

The product manufactured by this division sells for $75 per unit, and 240,000 units were produced and sold as anticipated. The standard unit cost of the product is given below:

Direct materials	$26
Direct labor (10 minutes of labor at $12 per hour)	2
Variable overhead (10 minutes at $24 per hour)	4
Fixed overhead (based on normal production of 240,000 units per year)	6
Unit standard cost	$38

During the year, the actual use of materials at standard cost amounted to $6,266,000. To produce these products, the company operated at 58,000 direct labor hours. The variable overhead cost was $1,392,000. The fixed overhead was in agreement with the budgeted amount.

The president recognizes that the profit may deviate to some extent from the standard manufacturing profit expected of $8,880,000, but in this case, the deviation is too much.

Required:

    (1) Compute the actual income from operations for 1985.
    (2) Compute the variances.
    (3) Explain to the president what caused the profit to be lower than expected.

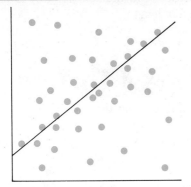

PART TWO | Cost Behavior and Profit Planning

6

COST BEHAVIOR AND ESTIMATION

Chapter Objectives

This chapter should enable you to:

1. Explain the difference between fixed and variable costs.
2. Determine whether a cost shall be fixed or variable.
3. Identify semivariable costs and to separate them into fixed and variable components by visual inspection, the high-low point method, or by the line of regression method.
4. Describe how the standard deviation principle can be applied in cost control.
5. Determine whether or not there is a good correlation between costs and the independent variable selected for estimation of cost behavior.
6. Explain the r^2 computation and the logical basis for its use in correlation measurement.

In cost control and planning, management must understand how the various costs behave under different conditions. With an understanding of cost behavior, management can prepare better budgets and develop more accurate plans for the future. Also, by knowing what costs should be, management can control costs better by comparing actual costs against budgets and taking measures to change conditions when variations are unfavorable.

Certain costs, variable costs, will increase in proportion to changes in hours worked, units of product manufactured, or in relation to some particular factor. Certain other costs, fixed costs, will remain at a set amount regardless of changes in level of activity or output. Also, many costs are neither entirely variable nor entirely fixed. These semivariable costs must be examined closely to determine the variable portion and the fixed portion.

In Chapter 2, both fixed and variable costs were defined. At this point, both types of costs will be examined at greater length.

FIXED COSTS

Fixed costs do not change with changes in level of output or activity. A fixed cost appears as a horizontal line on the following graph, which shows hours of activity on the horizontal or X axis and costs on the vertical or Y axis.

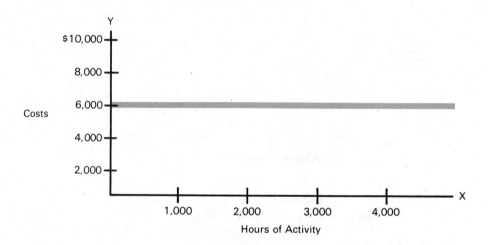

The total fixed cost remains at the same amount, $6,000, for any number of hours of activity. However, the unit cost (the cost per hour) changes. At 1,000 hours, for example, the cost per hour is $6 ($6,000 ÷ 1,000 hours); and at 2,000 hours, the cost per hour is $3 ($6,000 ÷ 2,000 hours).

VARIABLE COSTS

Variable costs change proportionately with changes in some factor such as hours of operation or units of product. A variable cost, as shown in the graph on page 167, appears as a line rising at the rate of variability per hour. The total variable cost changes with changes in hours of activity, but the unit cost is the same over the relevant range. In this example, variable cost varies at the rate of $2 per hour. The total variable cost for 1,000 hours is $2,000 and for 2,000 hours is $4,000.

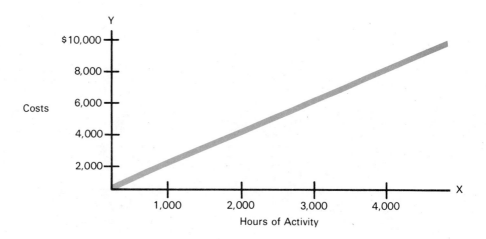

COST BEHAVIOR OPTIONS

In general, costs such as the salary of a plant superintendent or insurance on a building are considered to be fixed costs. These costs are set for the year and will not go up or down with changes in some factor such as hours of operation. Of course, the level of the fixed cost may be changed by management decision, but the cost is still a fixed cost.

A cost such as materials cost is usually a variable cost. The cost for each unit of material is the same, and the total cost increases in proportion to increases in the quantity of materials used.

However, there are circumstances in which management may be able to decide whether a cost is to be variable or fixed. For example, an outside repair and maintenance service firm may provide repair and maintenance on the basis of a flat charge per call. Hence, the service is a variable cost that varies on the basis of the number of calls made. On the other hand, a contract may state that repair and maintenance service will be provided at a flat cost per year. In this case, the cost is a fixed cost. Where this option is available, management will have to judge whether or not the quality and cost of service is better under a variable charge per unit of service or a fixed cost for the year.

COST SEGREGATION

Semivariable costs, that is, the costs that have characteristics of both variable and fixed costs, are the costs that require especially close analysis in the evaluation process. A semivariable cost may appear as shown on the following graph.

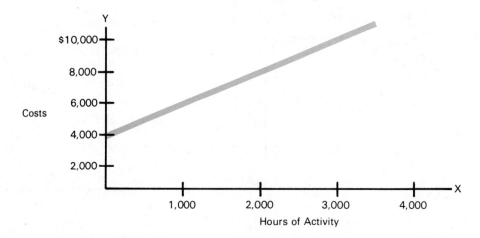

The cost increases at the rate of $2 per hour after starting at a cost of $4,000. The $4,000 is the fixed portion of the cost, and the $2 per hour is the variable rate. This is a fairly simple example. Sometimes the costs will rise at an increasing or a decreasing rate and form a curved line on a graph.

Three general methods are often employed in cost segregation:

1. The visual fit.
2. The high-low point.
3. The line of regression.

The Visual Fit

Costs for various hours of operation may be plotted on a graph, and a line of average may be drawn on the graph by visual approximation. The line is drawn, insofar as it is possible by visual judgment, so that the distances of the observations above the line are equal to the distances of the observations below the line. The line represents the data as a line of conditional expected values and is called the line of regression. The variable cost per hour is indicated by the slope of the line, and the fixed cost is measured where the line begins at zero hours of activity.

For purposes of illustration, it is assumed that a record of maintenance cost has been kept for various hours of operation as follows:

Hours X	Maintenance Cost Y
50	$120
30	110
10	60
50	150
40	100
30	80
20	70
60	150
40	110
20	50

The maintenance costs have been plotted on the following graph, and a line of regression has been fitted to the data. The line is drawn so that the sum of the distances from the line to all points above the line is equal to the sum of the distances from the line to all points below it. The average (defined as an arithmetic mean) is the point at which the sum of the deviations above that point is equal to the sum of the deviations below that point. The line of regression represents a continuous series of average points and thus is a line of averages.

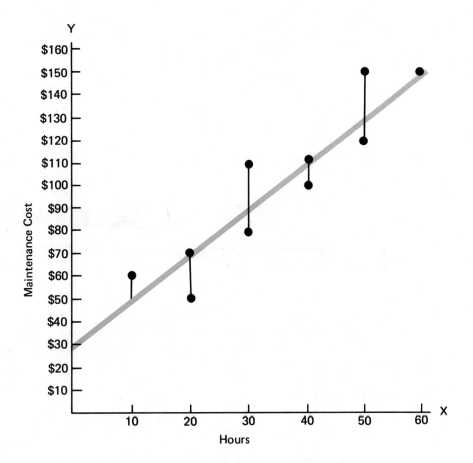

The line of regression illustrated begins at $30 and rises $20 for each increase of 10 hours. Therefore the estimated fixed cost is $30, and the variable cost is an average rate of $2 per hour ($20 ÷ 10 hours).

The High-Low Point Method

In the high-low point method, the observed costs for various hours of activity are listed in order from the highest number of hours in the range to the lowest. The difference in hours between the highest level and the lowest is divided into the difference in cost for the corresponding hours to arrive at a rate of variable cost per hour. For example, the costs of a certain supply for various hours of operation have been incurred in the past as follows:

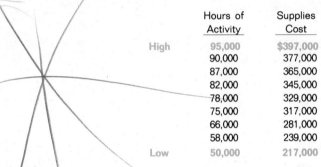

	Hours of Activity	Supplies Cost
High	95,000	$397,000
	90,000	377,000
	87,000	365,000
	82,000	345,000
	78,000	329,000
	75,000	317,000
	66,000	281,000
	58,000	239,000
Low	50,000	217,000

The difference in hours is 45,000 (95,000 − 50,000), and the difference in cost is $180,000 ($397,000 − $217,000). The variable supplies cost is computed below:

$$\frac{\text{Difference in cost}}{\text{Difference in hours}} = \frac{\$180,000}{45,000} = \$4 \text{ variable cost per hour}$$

The fixed cost can be estimated at any level (assuming a uniform or constant variable cost) by subtracting the variable cost portion from the total cost. At 95,000 hours, for example, the total cost is $397,000; and the total variable cost is $380,000 (95,000 hours × $4 variable cost per hour). Hence, the fixed cost is $17,000 ($397,000 − $380,000). In this example, it is assumed that uniform variability applies over the entire range. In some cases, however, the rate of variability may change, and this must be considered in cost analysis.

Least Squares Method

A line of regression can be fitted to a large quantity of data more precisely by the least squares method. Using the high-low point method, an average is computed from data taken only at the high and low points of the range, but the line of regression or least squares method includes all data within the range. The line of regression is determined so that the algebraic sum of the squared deviations from that line is at a minimum. The line of regression is derived by solving two simultaneous equations which are based on the condition that the sum of deviations above the line equals the sum of deviations below the line.

The equation for the determination of a straight line is given below:

$$Y = a + bX$$

This equation states that the value of Y is equal to a point (a) plus a percentage of variability applied to X. In the last example, a was the $30 of fixed cost. The percentage (b) was the change in Y in relation to the change in X. In the example, Y increased by $20 for each increase of 10 hours. Hence, the percentage of change was 200 percent (20/10).

$$Y = \$30 + 200\%X$$

If X is assigned a value of 10, Y is equal to 50.

$$Y = \$30 + 2(10)$$
$$Y = \$50$$

By substituting various values for X, a line is formed on a graph.

As another illustration, assume that supplies costs for various hours of operation have been recorded and that computations have been made as shown in the following table:

Hours X	Supplies Cost Y	X²	XY
30	$ 500	900	$ 15,000
50	650	2,500	32,500
20	300	400	6,000
10	300	100	3,000
60	900	3,600	54,000
50	750	2,500	37,500
40	650	1,600	26,000
60	700	3,600	42,000
30	450	900	13,500
10	350	100	3,500
40	600	1,600	24,000
20	450	400	9,000
$\Sigma X = 420$	$\Sigma Y = \$6,600$	$\Sigma X^2 = 18,200$	$\Sigma XY = \$266,000$

The first step in obtaining a line of regression is to set up an equation for a line that will represent all of the data.

Equation (1) $\Sigma Y = Na + b\Sigma X$

Another equation [Equation (2)] is formed by multiplying each point that constitutes Equation (1) by ΣX. Note that Equation (1) is not merely multiplied by ΣX. Instead, each point ($Y = a + bX$) is multiplied by ΣX.

Equation (2) $\Sigma XY = \Sigma Xa + b\Sigma X^2$

Referring to the preceding data listed, substitute values and by simultaneous equations solve for either *a* or *b*.

$$\text{Equation (1)} \quad \$6,600 = 12a + 420b$$
$$\text{Equation (2)} \quad \$266,000 = 420a + 18,200b$$

To solve for *b*, multiply Equation (1) by 35 (420 ÷ 12):

$$\text{Equation (3)} \quad \$231,000 = 420a + 14,700b$$

Subtract Equation (3) from Equation (2); the *a* values will cancel out to yield:

$$\$35,000 = 3,500b$$
$$b = \$10 \text{ the rate of variable supply cost per hour}$$

Substitute the value of *b* in Equation (1) and solve for *a*.

$$\$6,600 = 12a + 4,200$$
$$12a = \$2,400$$
$$a = \$200 \text{ estimated fixed supply cost}$$

A line of regression for the data given is shown on page 173.

CONTROL LIMITS

From the data given in the preceding example, it has been estimated that the fixed supply cost should amount to $200 and that the variable supply cost should vary at the rate of $10 per hour. For 30 hours of operation the total cost is estimated to be approximately $500. This is an average cost, however, and it is unlikely that the actual cost will be precisely $500.

Because some variation in cost can be expected, management should establish an acceptable range of tolerance. Costs that lie within the limits of variation can be accepted. Costs beyond the limits, however, are identified and may be investigated.

Normal Distribution

In dealing with cost variances, or variances in any type of data, it is necessary to consider the way that the data are distributed. Statistical data may form a pattern of distribution designated as a normal distribution. In a normal distribution, data can be plotted on a smooth, continuous, symmetrical bell-shaped curve with a single peak in the center of distribution. Surveys have revealed, for example, that the height of persons in a given society or the length of steel bars manufactured in a production process can be described by a normal distribution.

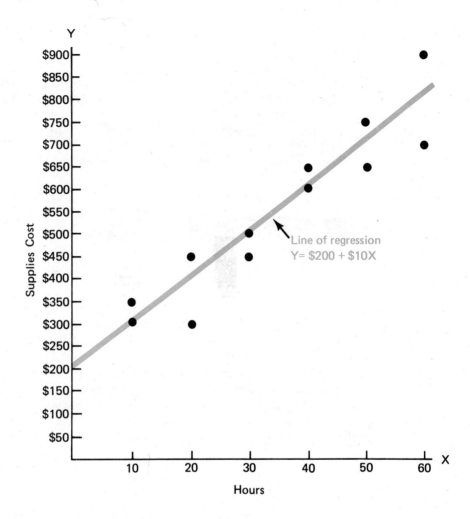

Management may find that cost data are normally distributed for a given level of operation and, in deciding upon an acceptable range of cost variability, may employ the concept of standard deviation that is commonly used in statistics. The standard deviation measures the extent of variation that may be expected in a distribution of data, and in this chapter it will be assumed that cost data are normally distributed for each relevant level of operation. Published tables show what proportion of the data may be expected to lie within plus and minus a given number of standard deviations from the mean (average).

In the example, an estimated conditional standard deviation is computed. It is conditional because it is dependent upon the number of hours of operation. Also, it is an estimated conditional standard deviation inasmuch as it has been derived from a sample. The estimated conditional standard deviation is conceptually the same as the standard deviation, except that it is based upon a sample rather than upon the universe of data. Also, it is subject to changes in hours of operation or some other independent variable. In this illustration, the sample size has been kept small in order to simplify the computations. Ordinarily in practical applications many more cost observations would be included.

The equation for the computation of an estimated conditional standard deviation is given as follows:

$$\text{Estimated conditional standard deviation} = \sqrt{\frac{\Sigma(Y - \overline{Y})^2}{N - 2}}$$

Y = actual supplies cost
$\overline{Y}$ = line of regression supplies cost
N = number of items of data

Expressed in words, the estimated conditional standard deviation is equal to the square root of the sum of the squares of the deviations from the line of regression, divided by the number of items reduced by two. The sample size (N) is reduced by two because both the fixed cost and the variability by hours had to be estimated from the sample.

An estimated conditional standard deviation is computed from the twelve items of data given in the supplies cost illustration. This computation is as follows:

Hours	Actual Cost Y	*Conditional Expected Average Cost $\overline{Y}$	Deviations $(Y - \overline{Y})$	Deviations Squared $(Y - \overline{Y})^2$
30	$500	$500	-0-	-0-
50	650	700	$ 50	$ 2,500
20	300	400	100	10,000
10	300	300	-0-	-0-
60	900	800	100	10,000
50	750	700	50	2,500
40	650	600	50	2,500
60	700	800	100	10,000
30	450	500	50	2,500
10	350	300	50	2,500
40	600	600	-0-	-0-
20	450	400	50	2,500
			$\Sigma(Y - \overline{Y})^2 =$	$45,000

*Line of regression values (hours multiplied by $10 plus $200).

The estimated conditional standard deviation is calculated as follows:

$$\text{Estimated conditional standard deviation} = \sqrt{\frac{\$45,000}{12 - 2}} = \$67.08$$

A table of probabilities for a normal distribution shows that approximately two thirds of the data (more precisely, 68.27%) lie within plus and minus one standard deviation from the mean. In this example, then, approximately two thirds of the cost observations should lie within plus and minus one estimated conditional standard deviation from the line of regression, or lie between $67.08 above the line of regression and $67.08 below it.

At 40 hours of operation, for example, the cost can be expected to lie between $532.92 and $667.08 about two thirds of the time.

	Estimated Conditional Standard Deviation	
	Plus One	*Minus One*
Line of regression cost..........................	$600.00	$600.00
Estimated conditional standard deviation	+67.08	−67.08
	$667.08	$532.92

If more confidence is desired in the prediction that a cost is within the limits of tolerance, the limit of variation may be extended. For example, there is a 95 percent probability that a cost in a normal distribution will lie within plus and minus 1.96 standard deviations. From the data given, there is a 95 percent probability that the cost will be between $468.52 and $731.48 at 40 hours of operation ($600 plus and minus $131.48 [1.96 × $67.08]). Management must make a decision by balancing two alternatives:

1. A relatively narrow range of cost variation with a relatively low probability of a cost being within the zone.
2. A relatively wide range of cost variation with a relatively high probability of a cost being within the zone.

Checking Some Inferences

Before making use of a sample of cost data for cost estimation and control, one must have assurance that inferences with respect to cost behavior are correct. Otherwise the cost data may be misleading.

In this chapter, the illustrations show that the cost data are represented by a straight line (line of regression) and not by a curve. In some situations, the linear relationship may not be appropriate. Costs, for example, may not increase at a constant rate but instead increase at an increasing or a decreasing rate with increases in the independent variable. Hence, the cost data would be represented by a curve rather than a straight line. The shape of the line can be revealed by plotting a sufficient amount of data for various hours of operation.

Also, the data may not be uniformly dispersed along the line of regression. At the extremes, for example, the data may be more widely dispersed than at the middle portion of the range. As a result, lines drawn for plus and minus one estimated conditional standard deviation may not be parallel. This is illustrated on the graph as follows:

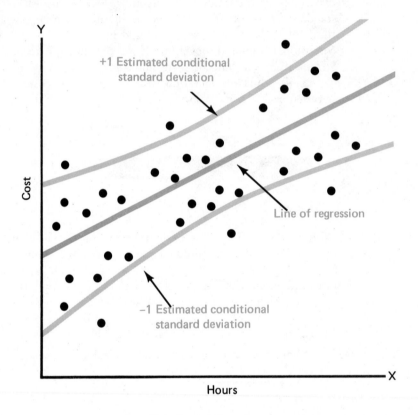

Wide Dispersion at Extremes

In each situation, the data should be plotted and inspected as a part of the total evaluation. As more data are collected, the cost estimation process can be refined. In general, there is more risk in making predictions at the extremes of the range, that is, when the costs are further from the average (total cost divided by the total hours).

In the graph which follows, it is assumed that the lines for the estimated conditional standard deviation are parallel to the line of regression over the relevant range depicted. A value for the estimated conditional standard deviation may then be helpful in the identification of costs that should be investigated over this range of activity. In situations where the degree of dispersion varies

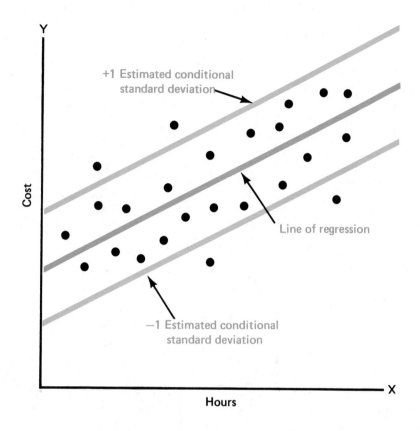

Uniform Dispersion

over the range, it will be necessary to determine the estimated conditional standard deviation for each position in the range.

CORRELATION

In the process of estimating and controlling costs, management must determine whether or not the factor selected for estimating cost behavior is suitable for that purpose. Costs may or may not vary with changes in hours of operation or with changes in the factor selected for cost analysis. In making a study of cost behavior, management is constantly looking for relationships between costs and various factors in the operation, such as pounds of materials used, hours of operation, or labor cost.

Sometimes it may be found that the costs are randomly distributed and are not at all related to the factor selected, as illustrated in the following graph:

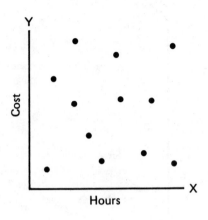

No Correlation

At the other extreme, the relationship may be so close that the data can almost be plotted on a line, as shown in the following graph:

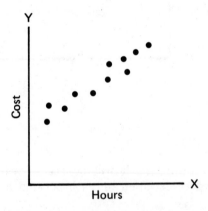

Positive Correlation

Between these extremes the correlation may not be so evident. A high degree of correlation exists when the estimated conditional standard deviation from the line of regression is relatively small when compared with the standard deviation from the average determined without respect to changes in the factor selected.

Assume, for example, a situation with all data lying relatively close to a line of regression for costs related to hours of operation. Cost data are plotted on the following graph.

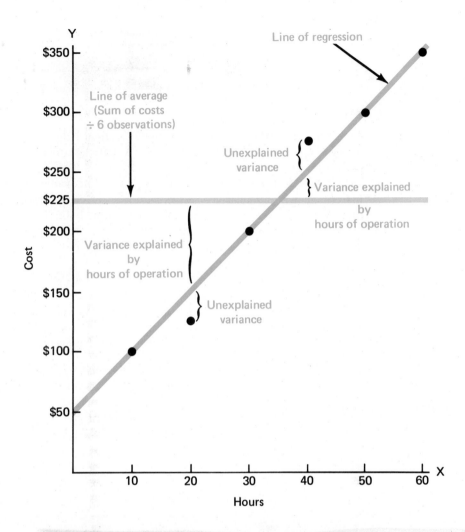

The average is computed in the conventional way by adding the costs and dividing by the number of items. In this case, the average is $225. Any variance between the line of regression and the average can be explained by hours of operation. The unexplained variances are the variances between the actual costs and the line of regression. In the example given, a large part of the variance from the average can be explained by hours of operation; only a small amount is unexplained. Hence, there is a good correlation between cost and hours.

The r^2 Test

The degree of correlation is measured by the coefficient of determination, most frequently designated as r^2. The equation is given as follows:

$$r^2 = 1 - \frac{(\text{Estimated conditional standard deviation measured from the line of regression})^2}{(\text{Standard deviation measured from the average of all data})^2}$$

If the squared estimated conditional standard deviation from the line of regression is small in proportion to the squared standard deviation measured from the average, the value of the fraction in the equation will be small. When this fraction is subtracted from one, the value of r^2 expressed as a percentage will be relatively large and the correlation will be good. On the other hand, a large squared estimated conditional standard deviation from the line of regression in relation to the squared standard deviation from the average results in a low r^2. Hence, the costs do not closely follow the factor selected and the correlation is poor.

A value for r^2 is computed using data from the earlier supplies cost example. The estimated conditional standard deviation from the line of regression has already been computed at \$67.08. The average for the data is computed by dividing the sum of costs by the number of items (\$6,600 ÷ 12). The average is \$550. The variations from this average are computed, squared, and totaled.

Supplies Cost	Average	Variations	Variations Squared
\$ 500	\$550	\$ 50	\$ 2,500
650	550	100	10,000
300	550	250	62,500
300	550	250	62,500
900	550	350	122,500
750	550	200	40,000
650	550	100	10,000
700	550	150	22,500
450	550	100	10,000
350	550	200	40,000
600	550	50	2,500
450	550	100	10,000
\$6,600			\$395,000

The standard deviation to be used in the r^2 application is equal to the square root of the sum of the squared variations divided by 10 (N −2, or 12 −2).

$$\text{Standard deviation} = \sqrt{\frac{\$395,000}{10}} = \$198.75$$

The r^2 is computed by substituting values in the equation:

$$r^2 = 1 - \frac{(\$67.08)^2}{(\$198.75)^2}$$

$$r^2 = 1 - \frac{\$4,500}{\$39,502}$$

$$r^2 = 1 - .1139$$

$$r^2 = .8861 \text{ or } 88.61\%$$

In the illustration given, there is apparently a high degree of correlation between hours of operation and supplies cost.

The logic underlying why a high value for r^2 indicates a good correlation can be demonstrated by graph. On the graph which follows, a range bounded by plus or minus one estimated conditional standard deviation is shown. Note that the band or range is narrow, indicating relatively good correlation.

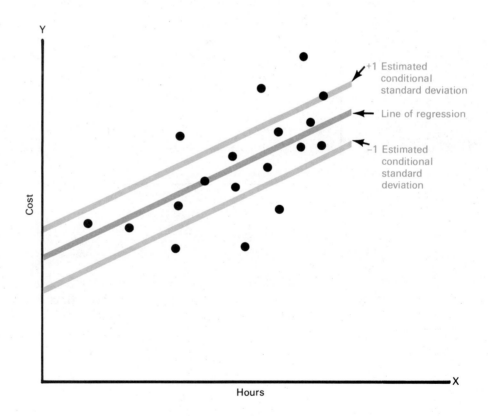

Estimated Conditional Standard
Deviations Around Line of Regression

The standard deviation around the general average, computed without regard to hours when placed on the graph, shows a wide range.

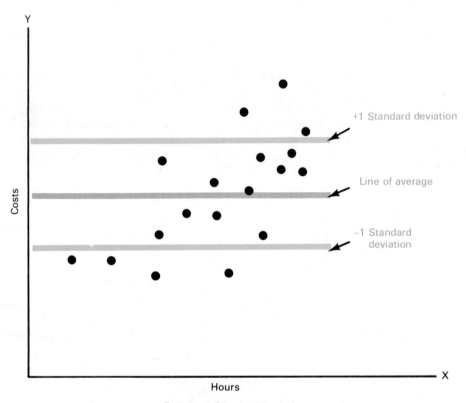

Estimated Standard Deviation
Around Line of Average

In a given circumstance, assume that the proportion of the estimated conditional standard deviation squared to the estimated standard deviation squared forms a small fraction such as 1/10. The r^2 value is then .9 or 90%.

$$r^2 = 1 - \frac{1}{10}$$
$$r^2 = .9 \text{ or } 90\%$$

In a relatively poor correlation, the zone formed by a line representing one estimated conditional standard deviation is wide relative to a similar zone formed around the general average, as shown in the illustrations on pages 183 and 184.

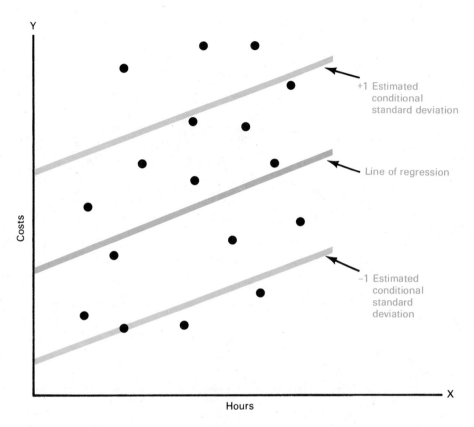

Estimated Conditional Standard Deviations
Around Line of Regression

Assume that a fraction formed by the proportion of the estimated conditional standard deviation squared to the estimated standard deviation squared is 3/4. Then r^2 is small, and correlation is relatively poor.

$$r^2 = 1 - 3/4$$
$$r^2 = .25 \text{ or } 25\%.$$

Multiple Regression

Usually it will be found that more than one factor will be related to cost behavior. Hours of operation, for example, may not be the only factor to be considered. A certain cost may vary not only with changes in the hours of operation but also with the weight of product produced, temperature changes, or other factors. In simple regression only one factor is considered, but in multiple regression several factors are considered in combination. Insofar as

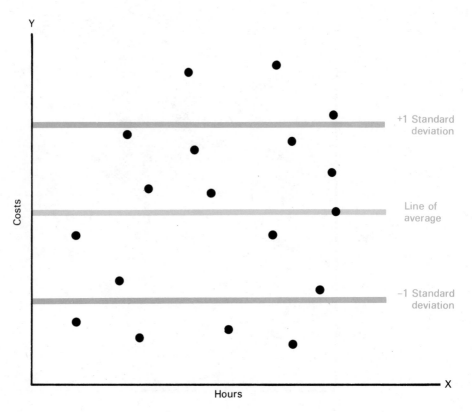

Estimated Standard Deviation Around
Line of Average

possible, all factors that are related to cost behavior should be brought into the analysis. With a penetrating analysis, costs can be predicted and controlled more effectively.

The equation for simple regression can be expanded to include more than one variable factor. Two variable factors are given in the following equation:

$$Y = a + bX + cZ$$

The b is the average change in Y resulting from a one unit change in X, and c is the average change in Y resulting from a one unit change in Z. The cost relationship can no longer be depicted on a two-dimensional graph. The value of Y (cost), however, can be determined by using simultaneous equations. The arithmetic computations become more complex as other factors are introduced, but the principle is the same as it is in simple regression. However, with the use of computer library programs, the complexity of the computations is reduced insofar as the numerical manipulations are concerned.

Terminology Review

Fixed costs (166)
Variable costs (166)
Semivariable costs (167)
Line of regression (168)
Average (169)
High-low point method (170)
Least squares method (170)
Normal distribution (172)

Standard deviation (173)
Estimated conditional standard
  deviation (173)
Correlation (178)
Coefficient of determination or,
  r^2 (179)
Multiple regression (183)

QUESTIONS FOR REVIEW

1. Why is cost estimation so important?

2. When costs are plotted on a graph, it is possible to draw a line to represent the variability of costs with hours of operation. What is this line called?

3. How can the average rate of cost variability be determined from the line?

4. Describe the high-low point method of cost segregation.

5. How can a standard deviation measurement be used in cost control?

6. In a normal distribution of data, what proportion of the data should lie within plus and minus one standard deviation?

7. At the high point of the relevant range, hours were 15,000 and cost was $35,000. At the low point of the relevant range, hours were 5,000 and cost was $15,000. What is the estimated variable cost per hour? the fixed cost?

8. You have computed a line of regression value of $6,000 for 5,000 hours of operation. One estimated conditional standard deviation has been computed at $800. If you are willing to accept costs that have a 95% probability of being within your zone of acceptability, what is the maximum cost that you would accept for this cost at 5,000 hours of operation?

9. If the cost of repairs is expected to vary at the rate of $6 per hour with fixed cost estimated at $2,400, what is the average repair cost that can be expected at 1,500 hours of operation?

10. The cost of lubrication for the month was $5,800. The line of regression value for the hours worked was $4,500. One estimated conditional standard deviation amounts to $600, and costs are to be investigated if they are more than one estimated conditional standard deviation from the line of regression. Should this cost be investigated according to the rule?

11. Assume that an average cost was $6,000 and that the actual cost was $9,000. With a standard deviation of $3,000, determine the number of standard deviations above the mean for $9,000. What is the probability of a cost being this number of standard deviations from the average?

12. Is it possible to predict costs beyond the range of X values used in the sample? Explain.

EXERCISES

1. Cost Segregation by High-Low Point Method. The maintenance costs of Department 6 have been recorded for various hours of operation as follows:

Hours	Cost
21,600	$141,600
19,800	130,800
24,200	157,200
23,700	154,200
20,600	135,600
21,500	141,000
19,200	127,200
21,900	143,400
23,300	151,800
22,400	146,400

Required: Determine the average rate of cost variablity per hour and the fixed cost.

2. Cost Segregation by High-Low Point Method. The costs to lubricate equipment in Department 4 have been recorded for various hours of operation as follows:

Hours	Cost	Hours	Cost
6,720.	$36,160	6,560	$35,680
7,140.	37,420	7,220	37,660
5,860.	33,580	8,460	41,380
7,190.	37,570	8,210	40,630
8,070.	40,210	5,930	33,790

Required: Determine the average rate of cost variablity per hour and the fixed cost.

3. Cost Segregation by Least Squares. Joan Deibert wants to estimate the variability of the cost of supplies used with hours of operation. With this information, she hopes to be able to prepare a more accurate budget and have better control over costs for which she is responsible.

Hours of operation and costs have been recorded each month for 20 months. The hours have been totaled at 9,000, and the costs have been totaled at $350,000. The hours and costs for each observation have been multiplied together, and the sum of the products is 165,000,000. The summation of the hours squared is 8,500,000.

Required:

(1) From the data collected by Joan Deibert, compute the expected variable cost per hour. (Round to the nearest cent.)

(2) Compute the fixed cost per month. (Round to the nearest cent.)

4. Cost Segregation by Least Squares. The manager of the cutting department of Renfrew Metal Plate Company has collected the following data on indirect materials cost for the department for each month.

Number of observations	10
Sum of the hours (ΣX).	4,000
Sum of the costs (ΣY)	46,000
Sum of the hours multiplied by the costs (ΣXY)	21,800,000
Sum of the hours squared (ΣX^2)	2,400,000

Required:

(1) From the data given, compute the variable cost per hour for the cutting department. (Round to nearest cent.)

(2) Compute the fixed cost per month. (Round to nearest cent.)

5. Fixed or Variable Cost Option. A new piece of drill equipment with certain automatic features was purchased by Stetler Parts Company. The equipment manufacturer offers a maintenance and repair service contract at a fixed cost of $4,600 per year. Without the service contract, the cost for a service call is $200 plus a charge of $50 an hour for the time spent on the maintenance and repairs. The company has had some experience on similar equipment and has found that on the average, 10 service calls are made in a year with average time for service being 3 hours.

Required: Assuming that the quality of service is the same in each case, which option has a lower cost potential? Approximately how many service calls must be made to make the cost about equal to the cost of a service contract? Show computations.

6. The r² Test. You are trying to find out if there is a good correlation between the quantity of direct materials used and the cost of indirect materials used in production. According to your study, the indirect materials cost can be expected to increase by $20 for each increase of 100 pounds in direct material used. The fixed cost of indirect materials for the month was estimated at $1,200.

After making several observations, you computed a line of regression and determined an estimated conditional standard deviation from the line of regression of $50. An average of all data was computed, and a standard deviation from this average was computed at $200.

Required:

(1) Compute the r^2. Does the correlation appear to be good?
(2) What would the r^2 have been if the standard deviation from the general average were $100 instead of $200? Would the correlation be better or worse than the correlation computed in (1)? Explain why this would be true.

7. The r² Test. The cost of a lubricant used in a machining process is to be estimated at various hours of operation. Management wants to know whether or not there is a good correlation between the cost and the hours of operation. A sample of 12 items was selected, and you computed the sum of the deviations from the line of regression values squared at $5,760. You also determined that the sum of the deviations from the general average squared is equal to $10,240. The general average was computed without regard to hours of operation.

Required:

(1) Compute the r^2.
(2) Is there a high correlation between the cost of materials and hours of operation?

8. Control Limits. The controller of Conover Fabrics Inc. has been investigating variances from budgeted cost that are more than 1.96 estimated conditional standard deviations from the line of regression. Inasmuch as there is a 95% probability that costs will lie within plus and minus 1.96 estimated conditional standard deviations, the controller believes that costs that are beyond the upper limit warrant investigation. One estimated conditional standard deviation for an indirect material was computed at $200. Line of regression values for various hours of operation are given below:

Hours	Cost	Hours	Cost
400	$1,600	600	$2,200
450	1,750	650	2,350
500	1,900	700	2,500
550	2,050	750	2,650

The controller is concerned that the rule for investigating cost variances may be too liberal and that better control could be exerted by investigating variances that are more than one estimated conditional standard deviation from the line of regression.

Required:

(1) For each of the observations given, determine the acceptable range of cost variance according to the established rule.

(2) Is the risk of overlooking costs that should be controlled greater when a limit of 1.96 estimated conditional standard deviations is established than when a limit of 1.00 estimated conditional standard deviation is set?

(3) If the actual cost is $2,670 at 650 hours, would the cost be investigated under the present rule? Would the cost be investigated if the limit were set at one estimated conditional standard deviation?

9. Control Limits. A good correlation has been established between the cost of fuel consumed and the weight of metal charged in the furnaces at New Kensington Metals Company. A line of regression has been computed for various weights of the metal, and an estimated conditional standard deviation has been computed at $180. Weights and costs from the line of regression are given for the range of input weights.

Weight (tons)	Fuel Cost
50	$ 600
60	690
70	780
80	870
90	960
100	1,050
110	1,140
120	1,230

Required:

(1) From the information given, what is the rate of cost variability for each ton of metal heated?

(2) Determine the cost for each weight at plus and minus one estimated conditional standard deviation from the line of regression.

(3) Assume that a rule was established to investigate any variation in cost that is in excess of or below one estimated conditional standard deviation from the line of regression. On one occasion, the cost for 110 tons was $1,360. According to the rule, should this cost be investigated?

10. Estimating Costs from a Sample. Data with respect to the cost of a certain polishing material have been collected for various hours of operation:

Hours	Cost	Hours	Cost
2,700	$23,600	2,600	$22,700
3,500	30,000	2,400	21,200
2,900	25,200	3,000	26,000
2,600	22,800	2,800	24,500
3,200	27,500	2,500	21,900
3,100	26,800	2,800	24,400

The plant controller notes that the costs have followed a certain pattern and that they should be relatively easy to estimate. Next month, the company plans to operate at 3,300 hours. In the month after that, plans were made to increase the hours of operation to 4,200 hours.

Required:

(1) By the high-low point method, estimate the variable cost per hour and the fixed cost.

(2) Estimate the cost of the polishing materials next month for 3,300 hours.

(3) Estimate the costs for the month after next for 4,200 hours.

(4) Do you have more confidence in your estimate under (2) or (3)? Explain.

PROBLEMS

6-1. Variable or Fixed Cost. George Grassic and Gary Wagner both work in the cost department at the Butler plant of Arlington Metals Inc. and were discussing the behavior of costs over lunch one day.

"One thing you can be sure of," Gary said, "materials costs are always variable costs. One more unit of product is produced, and the cost of materials goes up at a certain amount."

"I wouldn't be too sure of that," George replied. "Suppose that a large sheet of steel were purchased at a given price. The cost per unit of a part stamped out depends upon the skill in cutting and the number of parts that can be obtained from the sheet."

Required:

(1) Prepare an example to show that direct materials cost fits the definition of a variable cost.

(2) Prepare an example to show that direct materials cost may fit the definition of a fixed cost.

6-2. Cost Segregation and Cost Budget. The manager of the division for Acorn Dye and Bleach Company expects to operate at 85,000 hours next year and is making very tentative budget plans.

Past experience shows that the cost of indirect materials and supplies tends to vary at $3 per hour. Indirect labor is a fixed cost at $37,000. Heat and light varies at $4 per hour with a fixed cost of $7,000. Lubrication varies at $1 per hour plus a fixed cost of $2,000. The company has not had much experience with repairs and maintenance cost for a new type of equipment. However, these data have been developed.

Hours	Cost
76,000	$690,000
88,000	798,000
90,000	816,000
74,000	672,000

Required:

(1) Based on the information given, prepare a budget of costs next year for the manager of the mixing division.

(2) What is the rate of variability per hour for repairs and maintenance cost? What is the fixed cost?

(3) Do you feel comfortable with your estimate for repairs and maintenance? Explain.

6-3. Change in the Estimates. For a number of months, Jay Hefner found that he could make reasonably good estimates of the cost of indirect materials by using a variable rate of $4 per hour plus a fixed cost of $3,000 per month. Data drawn from past records are as follows:

Hours	Cost	Hours	Cost
4,700	$21,800	3,600	$17,400
4,200	19,800	4,000	19,000
3,800	18,000	4,500	21,200
4,600	21,400	4,300	20,200
4,100	19,500	4,400	20,600

In more recent months, he has found that his estimates have been incorrect. Data for each of the past 6 months are given in the following table:

Hours	Cost	Hours	Cost
4,800	$27,000	5,800	$32,000
5,000	28,000	6,000	33,000
5,600	31,000	5,900	32,500

Required:

(1) Was Jay Hefner justified in using a $4 variable rate and a fixed cost of $3,000 in the past? In looking over the past records, were there any months when the costs did not follow this $4 per hour pattern plus $3,000 fixed cost?

(2) Why has Jay Hefner been incorrect in recent months? Can you suggest a new basis for estimation?

6-4. Least Squares and Cost Segregation. The cost of equipment maintenance at Stedry Plains Company is to be broken down into variable and fixed cost components. Sally Maginess supervises this operation and has kept cost records for various production levels as follows:

Hours	Cost	Hours	Cost
200	$1,400	400	$2,600
300	2,000	500	3,200
500	3,300	200	1,400
400	2,500	400	2,600
300	2,100	500	3,100

Required: Compute the estimated variable cost per hour and the amount of the fixed cost by the least squares method. (Round answers to nearest cent.)

6-5. Comparison: High-Low Point and Least Squares. Harry Hopper has collected data with respect to maintenance cost in his department of Central Fuel Company. The data are as follows:

Hours	Cost	Hours	Cost
100	$ 500	500	$900
200	600	400	800
600	1,000	200	700
400	900	300	600
300	700	400	800

He has estimated the costs in the past by the high-low point method. A recent graduate from State University has recommended that the least squares method be used in cost estimation.

Harry grumbles that these young college kids don't have the experience and try to bring in fancy ways of doing things that he has been doing for years with very simple calculations.

Required:
(1) Compute the variable maintenance cost per hour and the fixed cost by the high-low point method.
(2) Compute the variable maintenance cost per hour and the fixed cost by the least squares method.
(3) Which of the two methods should give better results?
(4) Criticize the position taken by Harry Hopper.
(5) Defend the position taken by Harry Hopper.

6-6. Comparison of Cost Segregation Methods. The management at Quentin Glass Company is trying to predict production costs at a new plant. Some data from past experience have been collected, and cost data for equipment maintenance in one of the departments are as follows:

Hours of Operation	Cost	Hours of Operation	Cost
300	$ 900	700	$1,700
800	1,900	600	1,500
600	1,500	400	1,000
700	1,600	500	1,200
400	1,200	400	1,400
500	1,300	500	1,300

The manager of the department suggests that the variable and fixed portions of the cost be estimated by the high-low point method.

An assistant in the plant controller's office objects to this method, stating that it only considers the extremes of the relevant range but ignores the other data. As an alternative, it has been suggested that costs be segregated by the least squares method. Computations for the least squares method have been processed as follows:

Sum of the hours.....................................	6,400
Sum of the costs	16,500
Sum of the hours multiplied by the costs	9,240,000
Sum of the hours squared...........................	3,660,000

Required:

(1) Determine the variable cost per hour and the fixed cost by the high-low point method.

(2) Determine the variable cost per hour and the fixed cost by the least squares method. (Round to the nearest cent.)

(3) Comment as to why the results differ between the two methods and whether or not one method is better than the other.

6-7. Reexamination of Costs and Controls. Marion Tellarico started a hobby of making decorative earthenware bowls and plates. The hobby developed into a part-time business, and during the past two years she has hired some outside help and produces and sells various items of this type at craft shows and to gift shops.

You have taken a course in managerial accounting at a university in the area, and she has asked you to try to find a way to estimate costs in advance and to suggest a basis for cost control. Last month she had costs of $3,600 for 500 hours of operation. At one time she had roughly estimated that costs amounted to $4 per hour and that the fixed costs per month were $800. Last month she was surprised to find that the costs were $800 more than she expected. This large variation, she believes, may have been caused either by not paying proper attention to cost control or by using an out-of-date basis for estimating costs.

Complete cost data are available for the past year and are presented as follows:

Months	Hours	Costs
July	300	$2,400
August	200	2,200
September	500	3,400
October	600	4,300
November	500	3,600
December	400	3,000
January	800	4,800
February	700	4,500
March	600	3,900
April	700	4,600
May	400	3,000
June	300	2,500

Required:

(1) Based upon the past year, estimate the variable cost per hour and the fixed cost by the high-low point method.

(2) Estimate the variable cost per hour and the fixed cost by the least squares method.

(3) Why do your answers for variable cost and fixed cost differ between the high-low point method and the least squares method?

(4) What simple control method can you suggest to determine whether or not costs are within a range of acceptability? As an illustration for Marion Tellarico, prepare a table showing the ranges of acceptability for the various hours of operation (based on hours from the last year).

(5) Does the cost of $3,600 for December fall within the range of acceptability? Explain.

6-8. Correlation and Cost Estimation. The plant controller of Faust Products Inc. would like to find a way to estimate the cost of a lubricating compound used in machine operation based upon the hours of machine running time.

A sample of 12 observations has been made as a preliminary step in estimating future cost behavior. Information from the sample is given in the following:

Sum of the hours......................................	300
Sum of the costs......................................$	6,000
Sum of the hours multiplied by the costs	3,000,000
Sum of the hours squared..............................	100,000
Square of the estimated conditional standard deviation	1,000
Square of the standard deviation from the general average	8,000

Required:

(1) Compute the estimated variable cost per hour and the fixed cost.

(2) Determine the r^2.

(3) Does there appear to be a good correlation fit?

6-9. Control Limits. For several years, Hatfield and McCoy Inc. has used the least squares method in the segregation of semivariable costs into variable and fixed components. Also, correlation studies have been made to determine whether or not the relationship established between the independent variable and the dependent variable (hours and cost in this case) appears to be valid.

The two principal owners, however, are not in agreement as to the criterion used for cost control. Larry Hatfield believes that all costs should be investigated if they lie outside the zone bounded by plus and minus one estimated conditional standard deviation from the line of regression. Marshall McCoy, however, is of the opinion that this would involve needless cost investigation and prefers to investigate only if the cost is more than plus or minus 1.96 estimated conditional standard deviations from the line of regression. He states that only about two thirds of the data can be expected to lie within plus and minus one estimated conditional standard deviation from the line of regression but that 95% of the data can be expected to lie within plus and minus 1.96 estimated conditional standard deviations from the line of regression.

The company incurs an equipment maintenance cost that has been estimated at $12 per hour of operation with a fixed cost per month of $4,000. The estimated conditional standard deviation from the line of regression is $500.

Required:

(1) Evaluate the position taken by each of the principal owners. Which position is better?

(2) What should the equipment maintenance cost be at 1,700 hours of operation?

(3) What is the range of tolerance before the cost is investigated at 1,700 hours with limits set at plus and minus one estimated conditional standard deviation from the line of regression?

(4) What is the range of tolerance before the cost is investigated at 1,700 hours with limits set at plus and minus 1.96 estimated conditional standard deviations from the line of regression?

6-10. Control Limits. Repair and maintenance costs for Plata Pura Company are given for various hours of operation during the past year. Conditional expected average costs are also given. Miguel Martinez has found that the costs to investigate a variance from the expected average cost is relatively high, and he is reluctant to investigate unless there is a strong probability that the cost variance is not attributable to random factors. Hence, he has determined that the cost must be more than 1.96 estimated conditional standard deviations from the line of regression before it will be investigated. There is a 95% probability that a cost will lie within plus and minus 1.96 estimated conditional standard deviations from the line of regression.

Hours of Operation	Conditional Expected Average Cost	Actual Cost
800	$4,200	$4,200
1,000	5,000	5,200
1,500	7,000	6,700
1,200	5,800	5,900
900	4,600	4,600
1,800	8,200	8,400
2,000	9,000	9,000
1,400	6,600	6,600
1,700	7,800	7,700
1,600	7,400	7,400
1,300	6,200	6,300
1,100	5,400	5,500

Required:

(1) Compute the estimated conditional standard deviation from the line of regression. (Round to nearest dollar.)

(2) During the next month, the repairs and maintenance cost for 1,600 hours of operation was $8,000. According to the rule established, should the cost be investigated?

(3) Comment on the control limit established by Martinez.

6-11. Cost Segregation and Control. The overhead costs for the Palmdale plant of Greenspan Industries Inc. are being reviewed by the plant manager, Helen Vero. Budgets of average overhead costs for various hours of operation are as follows (in thousands of dollars):

Hours of operation	50,000	60,000	70,000	80,000
Indirect materials	$ 410	$ 492	$ 574	$ 656
Supplies	315	361	407	453
Payroll taxes	100	120	140	160
Maintenance	155	178	201	224
Repairs	110	127	144	161
Heat	82	96	110	124
Light	30	36	42	48
Indirect labor	264	264	264	264
Supervision	92	92	92	92
Fringe benefits	210	210	210	210
Insurance	51	51	51	51
Property taxes	26	26	26	26
Depreciation—equipment	68	68	68	68
Total	$ 1,913	$ 2,121	$ 2,329	$ 2,537

During the last year, the plant operated at 75,000 hours and incurred the following overhead costs. An estimated conditional standard deviation has been computed from a line of regression for each of the variable costs and the variable portion of the semivariable costs and is also given.

	Actual Overhead	One Estimated Conditional Standard Deviation
Indirect materials	$ 627,000	$ 8,000
Supplies	446,000	10,000
Payroll taxes	154,000	7,000
Maintenance	210,000	5,000
Repairs	151,000	9,000
Heat	118,500	3,000
Light	45,500	1,000
Indirect labor	264,000	—
Supervision	92,000	—
Fringe benefits	210,000	—
Insurance	51,000	—
Property taxes	26,000	—
Depreciation—equipment	68,000	—
Total	$2,463,000	

Helen Vero has established a policy of investigating cost variances that are more or less than one estimated conditional standard deviation from the average.

Required:

(1) Determine the average costs at the operating level of 75,000 hours.

(2) Compare the actual costs with the average costs and compute the variances.

(3) Which costs, if any, would be investigated according to the established rule?

(4) Comment on whether or not you believe the rule for cost investigation is appropriate.

6-12. Decision on Correlation. The cost of indirect materials and supplies is a relatively important part of the overhead cost of Department 6 in the Wendell Falls plant of Tecumseh Inc.

In estimating and controlling the indirect materials and supplies cost, the departmental supervisor believes that there is a correlation between machine hours of operation and the cost. The assistant to the supervisor, however, disagrees and states that the cost is correlated more with the variations in the mix and quantities of direct materials used in production.

Data have been collected for the past 20 months on the costs and quantities for each month. Line of regression values have been computed using both machine hours and quantities of materials. The sum of the squared deviations from the line of regression calculated for machine hours is 480. The sum of the squared deviations for machine hours calculated from the general average is 5,300. The sum of the squared deviations from the line of regression calculated for material quantity specifications is 850. The sum of the squared deviations for material quantity specifications calculated from the general average is 980.

Required:

(1) Based upon the information available, compute a coefficient of determination for both machine hours and materials quantities.

(2) Which of the two factors, machine hours or materials quantities, appears to be more suitable in estimating indirect materials and supplies cost?

(3) Comment on your findings and suggest possible steps to be taken.

6-13. Cost Segregation and Production Decision. Howell and Marts manufacture a small tool kit consisting of small wrenches and screwdrivers at their plant located in East Ridge. Cost estimates for different levels of plant operation with standard quantities of production established at each level are as follows:

	Machine Hours		
	50,000	75,000	100,000
Direct materials	$ 80,000	$ 120,000	$ 160,000
Direct labor	400,000	600,000	800,000
Supplies used	180,000	255,000	330,000
Indirect labor	50,000	50,000	50,000
Rent	18,000	18,000	18,000
Heat and light	35,000	50,000	65,000
Building maintenance	15,000	15,000	15,000
Insurance	22,000	27,000	32,000
Equipment maintenance	48,000	68,000	88,000
Equipment repairs	30,000	40,000	50,000
Depreciation	12,000	12,000	12,000
Total	$890,000	$1,255,000	$1,620,000

The company can operate at a level of 120,000 machine hours, if necessary, but has never had any experience at this level of operation. At 120,000 hours, the building maintenance cost is expected to increase to $21,000, insurance to increase to $40,000, and indirect labor to increase to $65,000.

Orders for regular business are expected to absorb 100,000 machine hours next year. In addition, the company has an opportunity to sell additional units for export with additional revenue of $425,000. The export order, however, will make it necessary for the plant to operate at 120,000 machine hours.

Required:

(1) Determine the variable and fixed costs for 50,000 hours, 75,000 hours, 100,000 hours, and 120,000 hours.

(2) Point out why the estimate at 120,000 hours may be unreliable.

(3) Does it appear that the company should accept the order for export?

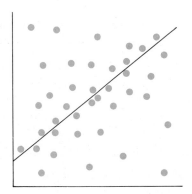

7

COST, VOLUME, PROFIT RELATIONSHIPS

Chapter Objectives

This chapter should enable you to:

1. Explain break-even analysis.
2. Describe both a break-even chart and a profit-volume graph.
3. Explain the effect of fixed costs on profits.
4. Describe the effect of substituting a variable cost for a fixed cost or vice versa.
5. Compute a break-even point when several product lines are sold in combination.

Profit planning is fundamental to the overall management function of a business. The profit plan is an essential part of the total budgeting process. Before a detailed budget can be prepared for the various segments of the total operation, there must be a profit plan. Management establishes profit goals and prepares budget plans that will lead to the realization of these goals.

In order to plan profit, management must have knowledge of cost behavior. Under given conditions, does a cost vary and if so by how much? Also what costs can be expected to remain fixed over a range of different amounts of activity or volume of production? In the preceding chapter, much attention was paid to the important problem of segregating costs into variable and fixed components. In this chapter, discussion will focus on the application of the differences in cost behavior to the specific problems of planning future profits.

The difference between sales revenue and the variable cost is called the contribution margin. Stated in another way, the contribution margin is the balance remaining after deducting total variable cost from revenue. This balance contributes to the recovery of the fixed cost and to the realization of profit. The concept of the contribution margin is essential to the process of planning profit.

Several factors affect profit. They are:

1. Selling prices.
2. Volume of sales.
3. Unit variable cost.
4. Total fixed cost.
5. Combinations in which the various product lines are sold.

All of these factors must be considered in profit planning. Fundamental to profit planning is the relationship of the contribution margin per unit of product, the volume of sales, the mix of product lines in sales, and the total fixed cost.

BREAK-EVEN ANALYSIS

Break-even analysis, sometimes called cost-volume-profit analysis, stresses the relationship of the factors affecting profit. The break-even point, the point at which there is no profit or loss, serves as a base indicating how many units of product must be sold if a company is to operate without a loss.

Each unit of product sold is expected to yield revenue in excess of its variable cost and thus contribute to fixed cost and profit. At the break-even point, the profit is zero; that is, the contribution margin is equal to the fixed cost. If the actual volume of sales is higher than the break-even volume, there will be profit.

Assume that a company manufactures and sells a single product line as follows:

Unit selling price	$ 20
Unit variable cost.	10
Unit contribution margin	$ 10
Total fixed cost.	$100,000

Each unit of product sold contributes $10 to cover fixed cost and profit. Based on these data, the company must sell 10,000 units of product to break even. The break-even volume is calculated by dividing the total fixed cost by the contribution per unit as shown below:

$$\frac{\$100,000 \text{ fixed cost}}{\$10 \text{ unit contribution margin}} = 10,000 \text{ units break-even volume}$$

If the company can sell more than 10,000 units, it earns a profit. If less than 10,000 units are sold, a loss is incurred. The profit is equal to the number of units sold in excess of 10,000 multiplied by the unit contribution margin.

For example, if 22,000 units are sold, the company is operating at 12,000 units above its break-even point and can earn a profit of $120,000 (12,000 units over break-even point × $10 unit contribution margin).

Sales (22,000 units @ $20)	$440,000
Less variable cost (22,000 units @ $10).........................	220,000
Contribution margin	$220,000
Less fixed cost...	100,000
Income before income tax	$120,000

The Break-Even Chart

Total revenue and total cost at different sales volumes can be estimated and plotted on a break-even chart. The information shown on the break-even chart can also be given in conventional reports, but it is sometimes easier to grasp the fundamental facts when they are presented in graphic or pictorial form. Dollars are shown on the vertical scale of the chart, and the units of product sold (or produced) are shown on the horizontal scale. The total costs are plotted for the various quantities to be sold and are connected by a line. Total revenues are similarly entered on the chart. The break-even point lies at the intersection of the total revenue and the total cost line. Losses are measured to the left of the break-even point, the amount of the loss at any point being equal to the dollar difference between the total cost line and the total revenue line. Profit is measured to the right of the break-even point and at any point is equal to the dollar difference between the total revenue line and the total cost line.

The data from the last example are presented on the break-even chart shown on page 202.

The data provided from an analysis of the chart are presented in the following table.

Units of product sold	5,000	10,000	15,000	20,000	25,000	30,000
Total revenue	$ 100,000	$200,000	$300,000	$400,000	$500,000	$600,000
Total cost:						
Variable	$ 50,000	$100,000	$150,000	$200,000	$250,000	$300,000
Fixed..........................	100,000	100,000	100,000	100,000	100,000	100,000
Total cost......................	$ 150,000	$200,000	$250,000	$300,000	$350,000	$400,000
Profit (loss)	$ (50,000)	–0–	$ 50,000	$100,000	$150,000	$200,000

It is assumed, of course, that the selling price remains at $20 and that the variable cost per unit remains at $10 over the range of units sold. With only one product, there is no problem of sales mix. The sales mix or product combination problem will be discussed later.

Cost Detail on the Break-Even Chart

Additional information is sometimes shown on the break-even chart by drawing separate lines for the different cost classifications. A desired profit

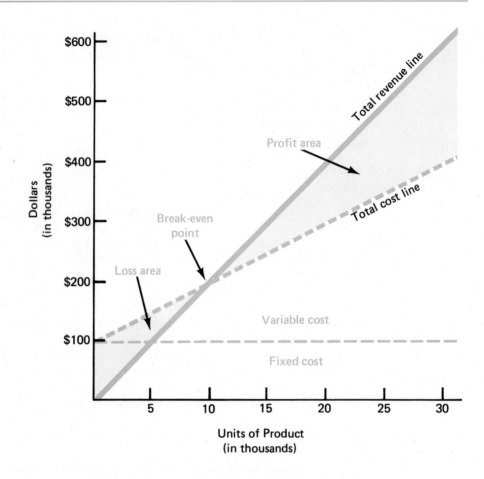

before tax can also be added as if it were a fixed cost. Then, both the break-even point and the point of desired profit are revealed on the chart. Using the same data as before, assume that the costs are broken down as follows:

```
Unit variable costs:
    Direct materials ..............................................  $      4
    Direct labor ...................................................         2
    Variable factory overhead ....................................         2
    Variable selling and administrative expense.................         2
        Total unit variable cost ..................................  $     10
    Fixed factory overhead........................................  $ 80,000
    Fixed selling and administrative expense ....................    20,000
        Total fixed expense ......................................  $100,000
```

The desired profit before income tax is $100,000. The company must sell 10,000 units to recover the $100,000 in fixed cost (to break even) and must sell another 10,000 units to earn a $100,000 profit before tax. In other words, the company must sell 20,000 units if it expects to earn a profit of $100,000 before income tax. The following break-even chart shows cost and profit details.

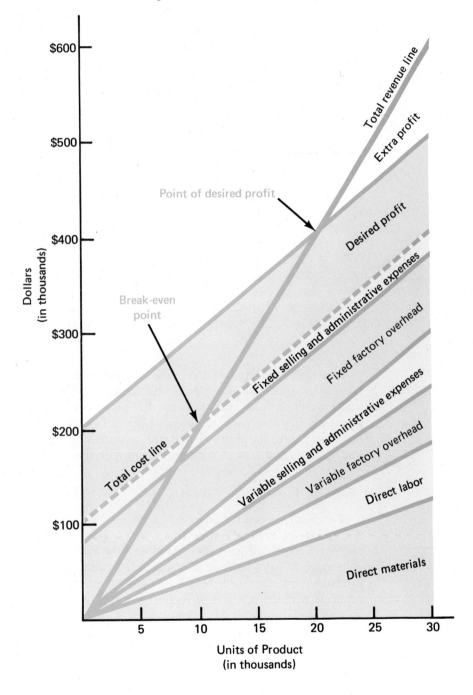

Curvature of Revenue and Cost Lines

In some cases, revenue and cost cannot be represented by straight lines. If more units are to be sold, selling prices may have to be reduced. Under these conditions, the revenue function may be a curve rather than a line. Cost on the other hand, may also be nonlinear. The curve may rise slowly at the start but may rise more steeply as volume is expanded. As more units are manufactured, the variable cost per unit may become higher. Therefore, it may be possible to have two break-even points as shown in the following chart.

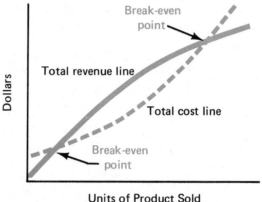

Units of Product Sold

In many cases, however, revenue and cost can be represented by straight lines. Any given company probably operates within certain volume ranges where revenue and cost can usually be plotted without any noticeable curvature. If the revenue and the cost curves begin to converge, the company is not maximizing its profit. Total cost is increasing faster than total revenue; that is, each unit sold is adding more to cost than to revenue.

An Alternative Form of Break-Even Analysis

Frequently a break-even point is calculated in terms of the sales revenue that must be realized in order to break even. A break-even point is not necessarily expressed in units of product. The variable cost may be stated as a percentage of sales revenue and subtracted from 100 percent to arrive at the percentage of the contribution margin to sales revenue. For example, a company may sell one line of product for $15 a unit with unit variable cost of $9 and total fixed cost for a year of $60,000.

		Percentage
Unit selling price	$15	100%
Unit variable cost	9	60
Unit contribution margin	$ 6	40%

The break-even point can be calculated at 10,000 units by dividing the total fixed cost of $60,000 by the unit contribution margin of $6. But the break-even point can also be computed in dollars of sales. As shown above, 60 percent of the revenue is needed to cover the variable cost. This means that 40 percent of the sales revenue remains for the recovery of the fixed cost and for profit. When 40 percent of the sales revenue is equal to the fixed cost of $60,000, the company will break even. Therefore, divide $60,000 by 40 percent to arrive at a break-even revenue of $150,000. Hence, a break-even point in terms of sales dollars can be computed by using the following equation:

$$\frac{\text{Fixed cost}}{\substack{\text{Contribution margin expressed} \\ \text{as a percentage of sales} \\ \text{revenue}}} = \text{Sales revenue required to break even}$$

$$\frac{\$60,000}{40\%} = \$150,000 \text{ sales revenue required to break even}$$

	Amount	Percentage
Sales revenue	$150,000	100%
Variable cost	90,000	60
Contribution margin	$ 60,000	40%
Fixed cost	60,000	
Profit or (loss)	–0–	

By extending the break-even concept further, it is possible to set a profit goal and to calculate the required sales revenue necessary to produce a given or desired profit. This can be seen in the following equation:

$$\frac{\text{Fixed cost} + \text{Desired profit}}{\substack{\text{Contribution margin expressed as} \\ \text{a percentage of sales revenue}}} = \substack{\text{Sales revenue required to earn} \\ \text{a desired profit}}$$

Using the data from the last example, assume that an income before income tax of $72,000 is budgeted. The sales revenue must then be $330,000, computed as follows:

$$\frac{\$60,000 + \$72,000}{40\%} = \$330,000 \text{ sales revenue required to earn a profit of \$72,000}$$

In many cases, the profit objective may be stated as a net income after income tax, in which case an additional computation must be made to solve for the income before income tax. Assume that the company wants a net income after income tax of $60,000 and that the income tax rate is 40 percent. If the income tax is 40 percent of the income before tax, then the net income after tax is 60 percent of the income before tax.

Income before income tax 100%
Less income tax 40
Net income after income tax........................... 60%

To compute the income before tax, divide the after-tax net income by 60 percent; that is, by the complement of the tax rate or, in other words, by (1 − tax rate). The break-even equation is as follows:

$$\frac{\text{Fixed cost} + \dfrac{\text{Desired after-tax profit}}{1 - \text{Tax rate}}}{\text{Contribution margin percentage}} = \begin{array}{l}\text{Sales revenue required to earn} \\ \text{a desired profit after tax}\end{array}$$

$$\frac{\$60,000 + \dfrac{\$60,000}{1 - 40\%}}{40\%} = \frac{\$60,000 + \$100,000}{40\%}$$

$$= \$400,000$$

A proof of the computation follows:

Sales revenue $400,000
Variable cost (60% of revenue) 240,000
Contribution margin (40% of revenue)........... $160,000
Fixed cost 60,000
Income before income tax $100,000
Income tax (40%) 40,000
Net income after income tax .... $ 60,000

THE PROFIT-VOLUME GRAPH

A profit-volume graph, or P/V graph, is sometimes used in place of or along with a break-even chart. Profit and loss are given on the vertical scale; and units of product, sales revenue, or percentages of activity are given on the horizontal scale. A horizontal line is drawn on the graph to separate profit from loss. The profit and loss at various sales levels are plotted and connected by the profit line. The break-even point is measured at the point where the profit line intersects the horizontal line. Dollars of profit are measured on a vertical scale above the line, and dollars of loss are measured below the line. The P/V graph may be preferred to the break-even chart because profit and loss at any point can be read directly from the vertical scale; but the P/V graph does not clearly show how cost varies with activity. Break-even charts and P/V graphs are often used together, thus obtaining the advantages that can be derived from each form of presentation.

Data used in the earlier illustration of a break-even chart given on pages 200 to 202 have also been used in preparing the following P/V graph.

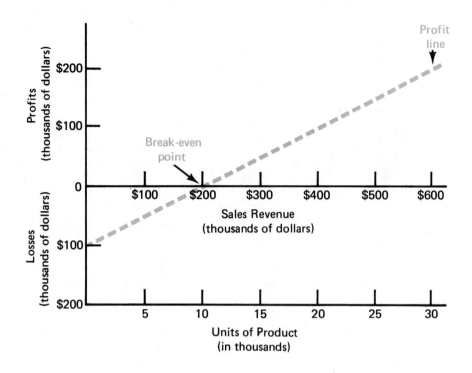

The profit-volume graph is a convenient device to show how profit is affected by changes in the factors that affect profit. For example, if unit selling price, unit variable cost, and total fixed cost remain constant, how many more units must be sold in order to realize a greater profit? Or if the unit variable cost can be reduced, what additional profit can be expected at any given volume of sales? The effect of changes in sales volume, unit variable cost, unit selling price, total fixed cost, and sales mix are discussed in the following paragraphs.

Sales Volume

In some industries profit depends upon high sales volume. If each unit of product is sold at a relatively low contribution margin, profit can be made only by selling in large quantities. This will be all the more true when the fixed cost is high. For instance, a company may handle one product line that sells for $1 a unit. Assume that the variable cost per unit is 70 cents and that the fixed cost per year amounts to $180,000. Each unit sold contributes 30 cents in excess of its variable cost to fixed cost and profit. Before any profit can be made, enough units must be sold at a 30-cent contribution per unit to recover the fixed cost. Therefore, 600,000 units must be sold just to break even. For every unit sold in excess of 600,000, there will be a 30-cent profit before tax. In such a situation, the company must be certain that it can sell substantially more than 600,000 units to earn a reasonable profit on the investment.

Selling price	$1.00
Variable cost...	.70
Contribution margin	$ .30

Fixed cost ÷ Contribution margin = Break-even point
$180,000 ÷ $.30 = 600,000 units

When the products sell for relatively high prices, the contribution margin per unit is often higher even though the rate of contribution may be fairly small. The fixed cost is recaptured with the sale of fewer units, and a profit can be made on a relatively low sales volume. Suppose that each unit of product sells for $1,000 and that the variable cost per unit is $900. The fixed cost for the year is $180,000. The percentage of contribution margin is only 10 percent, but the company receives a contribution of $100 from each unit sold for fixed cost and profit. The break-even point will be reached when 1,800 units are sold. The physical quantity handled is much lower than it was in the preceding example, but the same principle applies. More than 1,800 units must be sold if the company is to produce a profit.

Variable Costs

The relationship between the selling price of a product and its variable cost is important in any line of business. Even small savings in the variable cost can add significantly to profit. A reduction of a fraction of a dollar in the unit cost becomes a contribution to fixed cost and profit. If 50,000 units are sold in a year, a 10-cent decrease in the unit cost becomes a $5,000 increase in profit. Conversely, a 10-cent increase in unit cost decreases profit by $5,000.

Management is continuously searching for opportunities to make even small cost savings. What appears to be a trivial saving may turn out to be the difference between profit or loss for the year. In manufacturing, it may be possible to save on materials cost by using a cheaper material that is just as satisfactory. Savings can also come from buying more economically or by using materials more effectively. With improved methods of production, labor and overhead costs per unit can be decreased.

A small saving in unit cost can give a company a competitive advantage. If prices must be reduced, the low-cost producer will usually suffer less. At any given price and fixed cost structure, the low-cost producer will become profitable faster as sales volume increases.

The comparison of the operating results of three companies given in the following table shows how profit is influenced by changes in the variable cost pattern. Each of the three companies sells 100,000 units of one product line at a price of $5 per unit and has an annual fixed cost of $150,000. Company A can manufacture and sell each unit at a variable cost of $2.50. Company B has found ways to save cost and can produce each unit for a variable cost of $2, while Company C has allowed its unit variable cost to rise to $3.

	Company A	Company B	Company C
Number of units sold	100,000	100,000	100,000
Unit selling price	$5.00	$5.00	$5.00
Unit variable cost	$2.50	$2.00	$3.00
Unit contribution margin	$2.50	$3.00	$2.00
Percent of contribution margin	50%	60%	40%
Total sales revenue	$500,000	$500,000	$500,000
Total variable cost	250,000	200,000	300,000
Total contribution margin	$250,000	$300,000	$200,000
Fixed cost	150,000	150,000	150,000
Income before income tax	$100,000	$150,000	$ 50,000

A difference of 50 cents in unit variable cost between Company A and Company B or between Company A and Company C adds up to a $50,000 difference in profit when 100,000 units are sold. The low-cost producer has a $1 per unit profit advantage over the high-cost producer. If sales volume should fall to 60,000 units per company, Company B would have a profit of $30,000, Company A would break even, and Company C would suffer a loss of $30,000.

The profit picture at different operating levels for the three companies is shown on the following P/V graph.

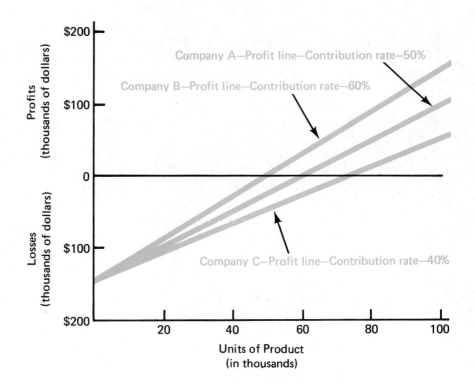

The profit line for each company starts at $150,000, the amount of the fixed cost. When 40,000 units are sold, there is a difference of $20,000 between each profit line. The lines diverge as greater quantities are sold, and at the 100,000-unit level the difference is $50,000. Company B can make a profit by selling any quantity in excess of 50,000 units, but Company C must sell 75,000 units to break even. With its present cost structure, Company C will have to sell in greater volume if it is to earn a profit equal to those earned by Company A or Company B. Company C is the inefficient producer in the group and as such operates at a disadvantage. When there is enough business for everyone, Company C will earn a profit but will most likely earn less than the others. When business conditions are poor, Company C will be more vulnerable.

Price Policy

One of the ways to improve profit is to get more sales volume; and to stimulate sales volume, management may decide to reduce prices. But results may not work out as anticipated. It does not necessarily follow that sales volume will be increased by reducing prices. If the demand for the product is perfectly inelastic, volume will not respond to change in price. The price reduction will result only in lower profits.

Suppose, however, that greater quantities can be sold at a lower price. The advantage, if there is one, is soon eliminated if competitors retaliate by lowering their prices also. Eventually the market will be shared as it was before, and possibly with lower profits for all. Even assuming that competitors will not react to price reductions, there is still no guarantee that profit can be increased by increasing sales. In fact, profit may decline in the face of increased sales. It may turn out that more effort is being put forth to get a smaller return.

While sales volume may increase with reductions in price, it may not increase enough to overcome the handicap of selling at a lower price. This point is often overlooked by the optimistic business person who believes that a small increase in volume can compensate for a slight decrease in price.

Price cuts, like an increase in the variable unit cost, decrease the contribution margin. On a unit basis, price decreases may appear to be insignificant; but when the unit differential is multiplied by thousands of units, the total effect may be tremendous. Perhaps many more units must be sold to make up for the difference.

Company A, for example, hopes to increase profit by selling more units; and to sell more, it plans to reduce the unit price by 10 percent. The present price and cost structure and one contemplated are as shown at the top of the next page.

At present, one half of each dollar in revenue can be applied to fixed cost and profit. When sales are twice the fixed cost, Company A will break even.

	Present Price and Cost	Contemplated Price and Cost
Selling price	$5.00	$4.50
Variable cost	2.50	2.50
Contribution margin	$2.50	$2.00
Percentage of contribution margin	50%	44.4%

This means that 60,000 units yielding a revenue of $300,000 must be sold if fixed cost is $150,000. But when the price is reduced, less than half of each dollar can be applied to fixed cost and profit. To recover $150,000 in fixed cost, sales revenue must amount to $337,500. Not only must the revenue be higher but, with a lower price per unit, more units must be sold to obtain that revenue. It will no longer be possible to get $337,500 in revenue by selling 67,500 units ($337,500 ÷ $5). Instead, 75,000 units must be sold just to break even.

To overcome the effect of the cut in price, sales volume in physical units must be increased by 25 percent:

75,000 units to be sold at lower price to break even
60,000 units to be sold at present price to break even
15,000 increase in number of units

$$\frac{15,000}{60,000} = \frac{1}{4} \text{ or } 25\%$$

Sales revenue must be increased by 12½ percent:

$337,500 sales revenue at new break-even point
 300,000 sales revenue at present break-even point
$ 37,500 increase in sales revenue

$$\frac{\$37,500}{\$300,000} = \frac{1}{8} \text{ or } 12\frac{1}{2}\%$$

The present income before income tax of $100,000 can still be earned by selling 125,000 units for a total revenue of $562,500, as shown in the following:

	Present Operation	Contemplated Operation
Number of units sold	100,000	125,000
Sales	$500,000	$562,500
Cost of goods sold	250,000	312,500
Contribution margin	$250,000	$250,000
Fixed cost	150,000	150,000
Income before income tax	$100,000	$100,000

After 125,000 units are sold, the company can improve its profit, but at a slower rate than when it operated with a price of $5. For every $4,500 increase in revenue, profit increases by $2,000. At present, a $4,500 increase in revenue beyond the break-even point yields $2,250 in profit.

The effect of the price reduction on profit can be depicted on a P/V graph as follows:

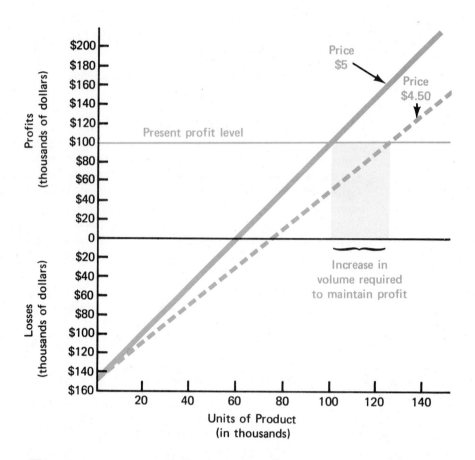

The increase in sales volume required to overcome the effect of a price reduction is proportionately greater when the rate of contribution margin is relatively low at the start. If each unit of product makes only a modest contribution, then a reduction in price makes it all the more difficult to recover the fixed cost and to earn a profit.

Seemingly, the price should not be reduced. The handicap imposed by the decrease in price appears to be overwhelming; yet, in many circumstances, profit can be increased by lowering prices. A saving in variable cost, for example, can be passed along to the customer. The contribution margin remains the same; and if more units can be sold, profit can be increased. Even with no change in variable cost, increased profit may be realized by lowering prices, provided that sales volume can be increased by more than enough to make up for the effect of the decrease in price.

The policy with respect to price will depend upon the long-range and short-range objectives of management. In any event, it is important to know what will probably happen if a certain course of action is adopted. Prices may be cut with full knowledge that immediate profit will be reduced. The company accepts this disadvantage in the hope that it will be able to establish itself as a volume producer in the market. Another company, whose management is not informed with respect to cost-volume relationships, may cut prices in an attempt to gain immediate profit; then when the profit does not materialize, the management will be unpleasantly surprised. Price policy will be discussed more fully in Chapter 10.

Fixed Costs

A change in fixed cost has no effect on the contribution margin. Each unit yields the same margin as before. Increases in fixed cost are recovered when the contribution margin from additional units sold is equal to the increase in fixed cost. On a P/V graph, the slope of the profit line is unaffected by changes in fixed cost. The new profit line is drawn parallel to the original line, and the distance between the two lines at any point on the horizontal scale is equal to the increase or the decrease in cost.

In the following P/V graph, fixed cost has increased from $600,000 to $700,000. The product sells for $5 per unit, variable cost is $3 per unit, and the contribution per unit to fixed cost and profit is $2. Under the new fixed cost structure, the profit line has shifted to the right and at any point is $100,000 lower than it was originally. To maintain the same profit as before, 50,000 more units must be sold.

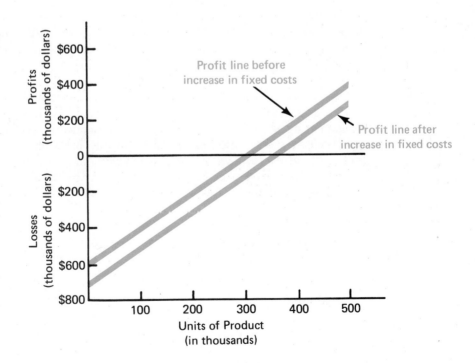

Increases in planned profit have the same effect as increases in fixed cost. For example, suppose that the fixed cost is to remain at $600,000 but that profit is to be increased from $200,000 to $300,000. Once again, 50,000 more units would have to be sold to provide $100,000, which in this case would be applied to increase profit.

Decreases in fixed cost will cause the profit line to shift to the left. The contribution to fixed cost and profit can be reduced by the amount of the decrease in cost without affecting profit. The decrease in sales volume can be calculated by dividing the unit contribution into the decrease in fixed cost. The new profit line is parallel to the original line at a distance equal to the decrease in fixed cost.

The fixed cost, like variable cost, is reduced whenever possible. Often it is necessary to handle a large volume of business merely to recover fixed cost. In some industries, fixed cost is relatively high. When expensive machinery and equipment are used in manufacturing, the fixed cost, of necessity, is large. This makes it all the more imperative to look for ways of keeping the cost down. Fixed cost has a habit of creeping upward; and before long a company is confronted with a high fixed cost structure, the result being that a large volume must be sold even though the contribution margin per unit is adequate.

VARIABLE OR FIXED COST DECISION

Management, in attempting to reduce one type of cost, may have to accept an increase in another type. For example, it may be possible to reduce a variable cost but to do so an increase in a fixed cost must be accepted. Or moving in the other direction, it may be possible to reduce a fixed cost by accepting an increase in a variable cost.

Assume that a company has found a way to decrease the direct labor cost and indirect materials cost per unit of product by $3 a unit by leasing certain equipment at an annual cost of $100,000, including the cost of operating the equipment. At the present time, the company has been able to sell 50,000 units each year at a price of $30 per unit with variable costs of $24 per unit. The fixed costs have averaged $200,000 each year. Data with respect to the present operation are as follows:

Sales (50,000 units × $30)	$1,500,000
Variable costs (50,000 units × $24)	1,200,000
Contribution margin	$ 300,000
Fixed costs	200,000
Income before income tax	$ 100,000

Break-even point:

$$\frac{\$200,000 \text{ fixed costs}}{\$6 \text{ unit contribution margin}} = 33,333 \text{ units}$$

Under the proposed arrangement with leased equipment and reduced variable costs, the results would be as follows:

Sales (50,000 units × $30)	$1,500,000
Variable costs (50,000 units × $21)	1,050,000
Contribution margin	$ 450,000
Fixed costs ($200,000 + $100,000)	300,000
Income before income tax	$ 150,000

In this illustration, the reduction in variable costs more than justifies the relatively small increase in fixed costs.

Assuming that all estimates are accurate and that product quality is maintained, the decision can be viewed as a form of general break-even analysis. A point of indifference is reached when the saving in variable cost is equal to the increase in fixed cost.

$$\text{Saving in variable cost} = \text{Increase in fixed cost}$$

In the illustration given, a break-even computation would be made as follows:

$$\begin{array}{ccc} \text{Number of} \\ \text{units sold} \end{array} \times \begin{array}{c} \text{Reduction in} \\ \text{unit variable} \\ \text{cost} \end{array} = \begin{array}{c} \text{Increase in} \\ \text{fixed cost} \end{array}$$

$$50,000 \times X = \$100,000$$
$$X = \frac{\$100,000}{50,000}$$
$$X = \$2$$

With a $2 reduction in variable cost per unit, the company recovers the $100,000 increase in fixed cost by selling 50,000 units. There is no advantage or disadvantage. This is shown in the following table:

Sales (50,000 × $30)	$1,500,000
Variable costs (50,000 × $22)	1,100,000
Contribution margin	$ 400,000
Fixed costs ($200,000 + $100,000)	300,000
Income before income tax	$ 100,000

The result is the same as when no changes are made.

In an attempt to hold down costs or to save either variable or fixed costs, management must be careful not to sacrifice the quality of the product. If the customers perceive that quality has been reduced, they will not continue to buy. Hence, anticipated savings will not materialize because of reduced sales volume.

Changes in the Sales Mix

Usually more than one type of product is sold. Several different product lines may be handled, each of which makes a different contribution to fixed cost recovery and profit. The total profit depends to some extent upon the proportions in which the products are sold. If the more profitable products make up a relatively large part of the sales mix, the profit is greater than it would be if more of the low-margin contributors were sold instead.

For any assumed mix of product sales, a break-even point can be computed. For example, assume that unit sales budget data are as shown in the following. In addition, the fixed cost for the year has been estimated at $500,000.

Product Line	Sales Volume (Units)	Unit Selling Price	Unit Variable Cost	Unit Contribution Margin
A	20,000	$50	$20	$30
B	10,000	50	30	20
C	10,000	50	40	10

The weighted contribution margin is $90, computed as follows. Each combined unit consisting of 2 units of Product A and 1 unit each of Products B and C will contribute $90 to the recovery of fixed cost and profit. The company will break even when 5,555 combined units are sold. The combined units are converted to product-line units by multiplying the combined units by the sales mix proportions.

Product Line	Sales Mix Proportions	Unit Contribution Margin	Weighted Contribution Margin
A	2	$30	$60
B	1	20	20
C	1	10	10
Total weighted contribution margin			$90

$$\frac{\$500,000 \text{ fixed cost}}{\$90 \text{ weighted contribution margin}} = 5,555 \text{ combined units}$$

Product Line	Sales Mix Proportions	Combined Units	Budgeted Units Each Line	Unit Contribution Margin	Total Contribution Margin
A	2	5,555	11,110	$30	$333,300
B	1	5,555	5,555	20	111,100
C	1	5,555	5,555	10	55,550
			Budgeted contribution margin		$499,950*

*Approximately equal to fixed cost of $500,000. Difference is due to rounding.

The total sales revenue at the break-even point is computed as follows:

Product Line	Sales Volume (Units)	Unit Selling Price	Sales Revenue
A	11,110	$50	$ 555,500
B	5,555	50	277,750
C	5,555	50	277,750
		Total sales revenue	$1,111,000

Sometimes management concentrates on total sales volume, unit selling prices, unit variable cost, and total fixed cost but overlooks the importance of the sales mix. The total revenue, unit selling prices, unit variable cost, and total fixed cost may be in agreement with the budget; but the profit may be lower. A lower profit can result from a shift in the sales mix. For example, larger quantities of the less profitable product lines may be sold with a corresponding decrease in the sales of the more profitable product lines.

The effect of a change in the sales mix is illustrated by assuming a budget plan for sales of the three product lines in a ratio of 2:1:1.

Product Line	Quantity	Unit Selling Price	Unit Variable Cost	Unit Contribution Margin	Total Contribution Margin	Sales Revenue	Contribution Margin Percentage
A	20,000	$50	$20	$30	$600,000	$1,000,000	60%
B	10,000	50	30	20	200,000	500,000	40
C	10,000	50	40	10	100,000	500,000	20
	Total......				$900,000	$2,000,000	
	Less fixed cost				500,000		
	Budgeted income before income tax.........				$400,000		

During the next year, the company operated at the capacity budgeted with fixed cost of $500,000. The unit selling prices and unit variable cost were in agreement with the budget. The results were as follows:

Product Line	Quantity Sold	Unit Contribution Margin	Total Contribution Margin	Sales Revenue
A	5,000	$30	$150,000	$ 250,000
B	20,000	20	400,000	1,000,000
C	15,000	10	150,000	750,000
	Total		$700,000	$2,000,000
	Less fixed cost		500,000	
	Actual income before income tax		$200,000	

Instead of earning $400,000 before income tax, the company earned only $200,000. Sales of Products B and C, the less profitable lines, were much better than expected. At the same time, sales of the best product line, Product A, were less than expected.

When more than one product line is handled, profit data for all products combined may be shown on one line of a P/V graph, the sales mix being assumed; or a separate graph may be made for each product line. Sometimes the effect of each product as well as total products on profit is depicted by plotting several lines on one P/V graph. A solid line is drawn to represent the net income or loss for total products. Next a broken line is drawn to the point of net income or loss contributed by one product, and then the line is extended to the point of net income or loss contribution of two products combined and continued until all of the products and the net income or loss are accounted for. The broken line is drawn so that the most profitable product is depicted first and so on until all of the products are included. The products sell in a fixed proportion, and the broken line does not indicate that the most profitable product is sold first with a certain profit or loss and that the total profit or loss is increased or decreased by a certain amount as other product lines are sold. Instead, the broken line shows the sales volume for each product in the mix; and the relative profitability of each product is revealed by the changes in the slope of the profit line. The total company profit for any combined sales volume must be read from the solid line. To illustrate, the budget data from the preceding example are entered on the following P/V graph, and the actual results are entered on the graph on page 219.

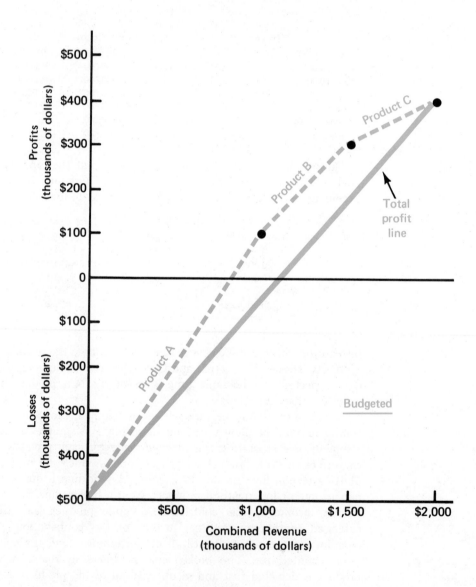

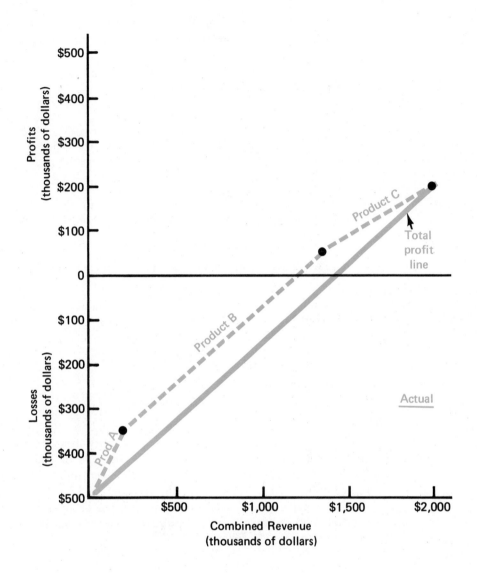

SHORT-TERM AND LONG-TERM PLANS

It is possible to earn additional profit by reducing the selling price of a product below the total unit cost, provided that the selling price is in excess of the unit variable cost. A policy of price cutting to increase sales volume and to increase profit, however, may be shortsighted. The company is expected to earn an adequate return on invested resources and may be overlooking the best use of resources in the long run by paying too much attention to short-run advantages. The contribution to profit in itself is not enough. The company should strive to obtain the best return possible on invested resources.

With existing facilities and productive resources, management should seek the best contribution margin per unit of the limiting or scarce factor. The scarce factor, in some cases, may be hours of labor time; or it may be space used for production. For example, assume that three product lines can be produced and sold as follows:

Product Line	Unit Contribution Margin	÷	Production Hours Per Unit of Product*	=	Contribution Margin Per Hour
A	$10		5		$2
B	6		2		3
C	4		1		4

*Fixed cost of $6,000 for the year is allocated on the basis of hours of production.

A profit budget for the year is given below.

Product Line	Number of Units	Unit Contribution Margin	Total Contribution Margin
A	1,000	$10	$10,000
B	1,000	6	6,000
C	1,000	4	4,000
		Total	$20,000
		Less fixed cost	6,000
		Estimated profit	$14,000

The company has 2,500 hours of idle capacity. Further study reveals that a government contract can be obtained for the sale of 500 additional units of Product A if the price is reduced by $5 per unit. This will reduce the contribution margin per unit on the contract to $5. At a production rate of five hours per unit, 500 units of Product A can be manufactured in the 2,500 additional hours available. Total profit for the firm will be increased by $2,500 (500 units × $5), as follows:

Product Line	Number of Units	Unit Contribution Margin	Total Contribution Margin
A	1,000	$10	$10,000
	500	5	2,500
B	1,000	6	6,000
C	1,000	4	4,000
		Total	$22,500
		Less fixed cost	6,000
		*Estimated profit	$16,500

*Increased profit: $16,500 with contract - $14,000 without contract = $2,500.

While profit is increased by accepting the government contract, it can be even better if the 2,500 hours are used to manufacture 2,500 additional units of Product C. Product C can be manufactured at the rate of one unit of product per hour. It is assumed that a market can be developed for the sale of a total of 3,500 units of Product C.

Additional contribution margin from sale of 2,500 more units of Product C (2,500 × $4 unit contribution margin).. $10,000
Less contribution margin from sale of 500 units of Product A on contract..... 2,500
Additional contribution margin, net.. $ 7,500

In making plans, the short-term expediency of obtaining more sales volume by price cutting may not be the best in the long run. The objective is to obtain the best possible return from resources used. The problem of optimizing the profit from available resources is discussed more fully and in a somewhat different manner in a later chapter.

Terminology Review

Contribution margin (199)
Break-even analysis (200)
Cost-volume-profit analysis (200)
Break-even point (200)

Break-even chart (201)
Profit-volume graph (206)
Point of indifference (215)

QUESTIONS FOR REVIEW

1. What is meant by the term contribution margin?

2. What factors are interrelated in profit planning?

3. What is meant by break-even point?

4. When the total contribution margin is equal to the total fixed cost, is the company operating at a profit or at a loss?

5. If the total fixed cost and the contribution margin per unit of product are given, is it possible to compute the number of units that must be sold in order to break even? Explain.

6. How is a break-even chart prepared?

7. If the total fixed cost and the percentage of the contribution margin to sales revenue are given, is it possible to compute the sales revenue at the break-even point? Explain.

8. If the total fixed cost and the percentage of the variable cost to sales revenue are given, is it possible to compute the sales revenue at the break-even point? Explain.

9. Can there be two break-even points? If there are two break-even points, how would the revenue and cost lines be drawn on the break-even chart?

10. In conventional practice, there is only one break-even point. Why?

11. Is it possible to compute the number of units that must be sold to earn a certain amount of income *before* income tax? Explain.

12. Is it possible to compute the number of units that must be sold to earn a certain amount of income *after* income tax? Explain.

13. (a) How does a P/V graph differ from a break-even chart?
    (b) Which form of presentation is superior?

14. When the contribution margin is high in relation to sales revenue, is the slope of the profit line on the P/V graph relatively steep or flat?

15. If there is an increase in the variable cost per unit of product, is there any effect on the profit line on the P/V graph? Explain the effect.

16. If there is a decrease in the selling price per unit of product, is there any effect on the profit line on the P/V graph? Explain the effect.

17. A 10% decrease in the selling price of a product has the same effect on profits as a 10% increase in the unit variable cost of the product. Is this true? Explain.

18. Does the slope of the profit line on the P/V graph change when the total fixed cost is increased or decreased? How is the profit line affected by changes in the total fixed cost?

19. Explain how an advantage can be obtained by accepting an increase in fixed costs in exchange for a reduction in the unit variable cost.

20. What is meant by sales mix?

21. If more than one line of product is sold, can a P/V graph be prepared for the combined operation? How?

22. Is it possible to earn a profit while selling a product at a price that is less than the total unit cost? Explain.

23. In planning profit, the important point is to maximize the sales volume of the product lines with the highest contribution margin per unit of product. Is this entirely true? Explain.

24. Point out differences between short-term and long-term planning.

EXERCISES

1. **Contribution Margin.** Various office supplies are sold by White Horse Stationery Inc. Susan Bevis, the manager of the store, states that a notebook purchased by many of the college students sells in sufficient volume to cover almost all of the fixed cost of operating the store. During a typical year, she says that the store sells 40,000 of these notebooks at a price of $8.50 per unit. The books cost the store $4 per unit. Fixed costs of the store amount to $135,000 for the year.

Required:
   (1) Compute the total contribution margin from sale of the notebook.
   (2) Is Susan Bevis correct? Does the sale of the notebook cover the fixed costs?

2. **Break-Even Point.** The Fitzpatrick Company incurs fixed manufacturing costs of $265,000 each year. The variable cost to manufacture a unit of product is $12. Each unit of product is sold for $17.

Required: Determine the number of units that must be sold in order to break even.

3. **Break-Even Revenue.** Harrison Company sells a product line at a unit price of $45. The contribution margin amounts to $15 per unit. Fixed manufacturing cost for the year amounts to $135,000.

Required: How much revenue must be obtained from the sale of this product line in order to break even?

4. **Break-Even Computations.** Compute the number of units of product that must be sold if the company is to break even in each of the following independent situations.
   (a) The variable cost is equal to 65% of sales revenue. Each unit of product is sold for $40. The fixed cost amounts to $182,000.

(b) A variable cost of $7 per unit of product is equal to 70% of the selling price. The fixed cost for the year amounts to $141,000.

(c) Contribution margin is equal to 24% of the revenue. Each unit of product sells for $50. The fixed cost is $432,000.

(d) The fixed cost is $270,000 a year. Each unit sold contributes $4 to the recovery of fixed cost and to profit.

(e) Each unit of product sold contributes 25% of its revenue to the recovery of fixed cost and to profit. The fixed cost is $380,000 and each unit of product is sold at a price of $16.

5. Effect of Variable Cost Charges. The manager of a department of Lowell Blending Company is searching for ways to improve the profit margin of a product line selling for $35 per unit. The materials required for each unit of product cost $26, and this is the lowest possible cost at which the materials can be obtained. Labor and other variable costs to produce the product amount to $24 per hour. Under current operating conditions, 6 units of product can be manufactured each hour. The manager has found a way to produce 8 units of product per hour. The fixed cost for the year has been budgeted at $135,000.

Required:

(1) Compute the number of units that must be sold under the current operating conditions in order to break even.

(2) Compute the number of units that must be sold under the manager's plan in order to break even.

6. Effect of Price Change. Jenner Company sells a certain product line at an established price of $42 per unit. The variable cost per unit is $36. The fixed cost for the year amounts to $540,000. Next year the selling price is to be increased to $45 per unit.

Required:

(1) How many units had to be sold at the old established price each year in order to break even?

(2) How many units would have to be sold at the new price each year in order to break even?

7. A Change in Fixed Costs. Wayne McMann is concerned about the increase in fixed costs. Last year the fixed costs of McMann and Son Inc. were $180,000. It is estimated that the fixed costs will amount to $260,000 in the current year. Last year, the company sold 80,000 units of product at a price of $20 per unit. The variable cost per unit was $15. Sales volume, the selling price, and variable costs will be the same for the current year.

Required:

(1) What was the income before income tax last year?

(2) Determine the estimated income before income tax this year.

(3) Compute the break-even point in units for last year.

(4) Compute the estimated break-even point in units for this year.

8. Solving for Sales Revenue. The Griffin Company earned an income before income tax last year of $525,000. The fixed cost of operation amounted to $450,000. The variable cost to produce and sell the line amounted to $35 per unit. The selling price per unit was $50.

Required: Compute the sales revenue for last year.

9. *Setting a Profit Goal.* The president of Bolan Forge Company has set a profit objective of $340,000 before income tax for a major product line. This product sells for $60 per unit. The variable cost to produce and sell the product line amounts to $48 per unit. The fixed cost of this operation amounts to $428,000.

Required: How many units of product must be sold in order to achieve the profit objective?

10. *Planning Profit After Taxes.* The manager of the hardware department of Plainfield Stores Inc. has estimated that the department should earn $216,000 after income tax. The fixed cost of the operation amounts to $420,000 each year. The variable cost of the product line sold is equal to 80% of the selling price per unit of $30. Income tax is computed at 40% of income before income tax.

Required: How many units of product must be sold in order to achieve the profit objective?

11. *Planning Profit After Taxes.* The president of Soto Metals Company should earn an income after income tax of $348,000. The fixed cost of operation amounts to $128,000 each year. The variable cost is equal to 70% of sales revenue. Income tax is computed at 40% of income before income tax.

Required: Compute the sales revenue required to realize the profit objective.

12. *Profit and Variable Cost Changes.* Alton Products Inc. and Flannigan Supply Company are in competition with a product line selling for $160 a unit. Both companies can produce this product at a variable cost of $140 per unit. Flannigan Supply Company has found a way to reduce the variable cost to $130 per unit and shares part of the cost saving with the customers by reducing the selling price to $155 per unit. Alton Products Inc. is unable to reduce its variable cost but must meet the selling price of Flannigan Supply Company to remain competitive. Each company sells 10,000 units of product each year.

Required:
   (1) What effect does this change have on the profit of Flannigan Supply Company?
   (2) What effect does this change have on the profit of Alton Products Inc.

13. *Shift the Variable Cost to Fixed Cost.* The production manager for Baden Products Inc. believes that profits can be improved if the variable cost per unit can be reduced from $18 to $15 by accepting an additional annual fixed cost of $72,000. The annual fixed cost is now $336,000. Each unit of product is sold for $30, and it is anticipated that the present sales volume of 75,000 units per year will be maintained.

Required: How much profit increase or decrease can be expected after the change when 75,000 units are sold?

14. *Sales Mix.* In past years, Henry Foods Company has sold 4 units of Product A for every unit of Product B that is sold. The fixed cost per year has remained at $336,000. The contribution margin per unit for Product A is $8 and for Product B is $10. The sales mix is expected to change so that 5 units of Product A will be sold for every 2 units of Product B that are sold.

Required:
   (1) In order to break even, how many units of Product A and B must be sold when 4 units of A are sold for every unit of B?

(2) In order to break even, how many units of Products A and B must be sold when 5 units of Product A are sold for every 2 units of Product B?

15. Graphic Representations. Balling and Biddle Inc. produce and sell frames used for the production of trail bikes. Each unit is sold for $120. The variable cost to make and sell each frame is $110. The fixed cost is $30,000 each year.

With improved production methods, the variable cost can be reduced to $100 per unit.

Required: Prepare a profit-volume graph showing a profit line to reflect conditions before the improved production methods. Draw another profit line on the same chart to reflect conditions after the improved production methods become operational. Show intervals for cost of $20,000 from zero to $100,000. Show intervals of 1,000 for units extending from 1,000 to 5,000.

PROBLEMS

7-1. Sales Volume and Break-Even. The sales manager at Stapleton Supply Company asks you to compute the sales volume required each year in order to break even if the selling price is $21 per unit and if the selling price is $18. The variable cost in each case is to be $16 per unit. The fixed cost for the year is $60,000.

Required: Make the break-even computations requested by the sales manager.

7-2. Break-Even and Price and Variable Cost Changes. The superintendent of Vandergrift Glass Company hopes to lower the break-even point by reducing variable costs. At the same time, it is recognized that price concessions must be made. Last year the product line sold for $60 per unit with unit variable costs of $50. A redesigned product can be sold for $55 with variable costs reduced to $48 per unit. The fixed costs per year are expected to remain at $560,000.

Required:

(1) Compute the units required to break even under each condition outlined.
(2) Was the superintendent able to lower the break-even point? Explain.

7-3. Sales Promotion and Profits. The manager of Hobart Shoe Store at Marysville Mall has recently purchased 1,000 uncirculated Indian head pennies of common dates for $2,000. These pennies will be used for sales promotion with one penny being given to each purchaser of a pair of shoes selling for $40. The promotion will be continued until the supply of pennies is exhausted. Costs of advertising the promotion have been estimated at $800.

The variable cost of each pair of shoes is $36.75, and no additional variable cost is expected in connection with the promotion.

The fixed costs of operating the store for one week under normal circumstances amount to $1,500 per week. In a normal week, the store sells 600 pairs of shoes.

The manager estimates that the promotion will last a week and that during that week 1,800 pairs of shoes can be sold. The assistant manager is skeptical and believes that only 1,000 pairs will be sold.

Required:
(1) What is the expected profit from the store in a normal week?
(2) What will the expected profit be if the manager is correct?
(3) What will the expected profit be if the assistant manager is correct?

7-4. Sales Volume and Prices. The Williams Company regularly sells two lines of products with the following selling prices and variable costs:

Product Line	Unit Selling Price	Unit Variable Cost
A	$90	$60
B	70	50

The sales revenue from Product A was $2,700,000 last year and the sales revenue from Product B was $1,400,000. The fixed cost for the year of $900,000 was allocated to each product line on the basis of the number of units sold.

For next year, plans have been made to sell 10,000 additional units of Product B on the export market at a price of $65 per unit. Sales volume in the regular market will be the same as it was last year.

The vice-president of production argues that the export contract will reduce profits. At a price of $65 per unit, Product B will be selling below the unit cost computed at $68. Hence, the vice-president strongly recommends that the export opportunity be rejected.

Required:
(1) Compute the contribution margin for each product line in total.
(2) Determine the expected income before income taxes without the export contract.
(3) Determine the expected income before income taxes with the export contract.
(4) Evaluate the position of the vice-president.

7-5. Rebates and Sales Volume. The manager of new car sales at Downtown Motors, Kay Douglas, hopes to increase sales volume by giving $500 cash rebates to car buyers who purchase new Whiz cars with accessories. The car without accessories is sold for $8,700 and at $9,500 with accessories. The cost of the car to the dealer is $7,600 and the cost of the accessories is $250.

Recently new car sales have been flat, averaging only 500 cars a month without accessories and 200 a month with accessories. Douglas believes that with the rebate, sales of cars without accessories will decrease to 400 cars a month. However, sales of cars with accessories should increase to 500 cars a month. It is her belief that not only will profits be increased but that customers will become better satisfied with the luxury Whiz car with accessories. Fixed costs of the sales promotion have been estimated at $2,000 per month.

Required:

(1) Compute the contribution margin per month without the rebate policy.

(2) Assuming that Douglas' estimate of sales volume is correct, does it appear that profits can be increased by the rebates?

(3) Compute the estimated contribution to total profits per month with the rebate policy.

7–6. Additional Sales and Lower Price. The manager of a division of Saturn Company is concerned about the low volume of sales. In order to increase sales volume and profits, the manager states that prices should be reduced by 10%. The assistant manager, expresses concern that the price reductions on low contribution margin items may not result in sufficient increases in sales to increase the profits.

Given below are the selling prices and variable costs per unit, along with sales volume and contribution margins for last year.

Product Line	Number of Units Sold	Selling Price	Variable Cost	Unit Contribution Margin	Total Contribution Margin
A	30,000	$20.00	$16.00	$ 4.00	$120,000
B	15,000	30.00	15.00	15.00	225,000
C	40,000	10.00	8.00	2.00	80,000
D	20,000	20.00	10.00	10.00	200,000
		Total contribution margin				$625,000

The sales manager estimates that with the reduced selling prices, sales volume for next year will be as follows:

Product Line	Number of Units Sold
A	40,000
B	25,000
C	80,000
D	30,000

Required:

(1) Compute the total expected contribution margin by product lines for the next year.

(2) Identify product lines that can be expected to show increased total contribution margins next year.

7–7. Profit Targets and Cost Changes. Grady Hamlin, the president of Hamlin Programs Inc., notes that variable costs are likely to increase substantially next year with little opportunity, if any, to increase selling prices. In anticipation of the increases, management plans to decrease the fixed costs from $7,000,000 a year to $5,800,000.

Last year the company produced and sold 150,000 units of product at a selling price of $300 per unit. The variable cost per unit was $200, and the fixed costs amounted to $7,000,000.

Next year the variable cost per unit will probably be 20% higher than it was last year.

Income taxes are at the rate of 40% of income before tax.

Required:

(1) Determine the income after income tax last year.

(2) How many units of product must be sold next year in order to earn the same income after tax that was earned last year?

(3) If fixed costs cannot be reduced, how many units would have to be sold next year in order to earn the income after tax that was earned last year?

(4) Assuming that fixed costs can be reduced, how many units must be sold next year in order to break even?

7–8. Fixed and Variable Cost Alternatives. Willard Mallory is responsible for a production operation in which a large unit of equipment is used in the production of a product line. This unit of equipment is leased from the equipment manufacturer at an annual cost of $400,000. The lease is due for renewal, and the equipment manufacturer plans to discontinue the fixed annual payment arrangement and substitute a plan for the payment of a $3 royalty for each unit of product manufactured by this equipment.

Mallory is searching for an alternative that will be less costly. Another manufacturer of similar equipment offers an agreement for the annual payment of $150,000 plus a payment of $1 for each unit produced.

The fixed costs of production have amounted to $1,600,000 each year, excluding the annual lease payment of $400,000. Fixed costs, aside from the lease payment, are expected to remain unchanged. The variable costs to produce each unit of product, aside from any royalty payment, have amounted to $4 per unit, and no change is estimated.

The product is sold at a price of $12 per unit.

Required:

(1) How many units of product had to be sold under the original lease agreement in order to break even?

(2) How many units of product would have to be sold under a new agreement with the original manufacturer in order to break even?

(3) How many units of product would have to be sold under an agreement with the other manufacturer in order to break even?

(4) If the company plans to manufacture and sell 300,000 units of product each year, which of the two available plans will yield more profit? (Show computations.)

7–9. Sales Volume and Capacity Limits. The vice-president of sales of Baylor Equipment Company is excited about the prospects for selling twice as many units of equipment next year as were sold last year. Last year 6,000 units of equipment were sold at a price of $4,000 a unit. The variable cost per unit amounted to $3,000, and the fixed costs were $2,000,000.

The vice-president of production states that the company has the capacity to manufacture only 10,000 units a year. Furthermore, the production vice-president points out that the vice-president of sales has not said much about obtaining the increased sales volume by reducing the selling price to $3,500 per unit.

"The increased sales volume will more than compensate for price concessions," the vice-president of sales replies. "If you get moving on production, we'll sell them," the vice-president continues.

Required: Which vice-president is correct, assuming that the basic facts are stated correctly? Compute the contribution margin and income before income tax to show whether or not increased sales volume with reduced prices will improve profits.

7–10. Sales Mix and Profit Planning. Tarzia Industries produces three lines of product. Data with respect to these lines are as follows:

Product	Unit Contribution Margin	Percentage of Total Sales Volume
A	$30	10
B	10	60
C	40	30
		100

The total fixed cost for the year has been budgeted at $3,150,000. Management has set a profit goal of $1,575,000 after income tax. Income taxes are at the rate of 40% of income before tax.

Required:

(1) How many units of each product line must be sold merely to break even at the sales mix given?

(2) How many units of each product line must be sold to earn the desired profit at the sales mix given?

7–11. Selling Price to Break Even. Joe Keenan and his sister, Barbara, have heard many people in the area tell about how heavy winter snows have broken and bent valuable shrubs. They believe that they can construct protective wooden shelters for the shrubs and can sell each one for less than the commercial price of $85.

The production and sale of the shelters is a temporary hobby type of project, but each of the Keenans hopes to realize a profit of $1,000 that will help meet personal expenses during the next year while they are at the university.

Estimates of the cost to make and sell each protection unit are as follows:

Lumber and other materials...................... $17
*Labor $12
Commission to stores selling the units .... 10% of selling price.

*Joe and Barbara charge their own labor time as the sacrifice of wages that they could earn at summer jobs.

Radio and direct mail advertising have been estimated at a total cost of $3,000. In order to make deliveries, they will have to rent a pick-up truck at a cost of $1,000. Joe estimates that they can make and sell 500 units during the summer. Barbara believes that Joe is somewhat cautious in his estimates and believes that 600 units can be made and sold.

Required:

(1) Compute a selling price to break even with the desired profit if 500 units are sold.

(2) Compute a selling price to break even with the desired profit if 600 units are sold.

(3) Assume that the selling price is based upon the sale of 500 units but that 600 units are actually sold. How much additional profit does each of the Keenans make?

7–12. Costs and Profit Planning. Wesley Conner has a part-time business refinishing and repairing antique tables. In order to remain competitive, he must sell a refinished table for no more than $300.

Variable costs have been estimated as follows:

Cost of finishing materials	$30
Labor	60
Incidental supplies	10

The fixed costs, consisting of rent, insurance, depreciation of tools, heat and light, etc., amount to $4,000 a year. Conner can refinish and sell 400 tables a year. The tables in unfinished condition can be purchased at auctions and sales.

Required: From the information given, what is the maximum price that he can pay for an unfinished table and earn an income of $20,000 a year from this part-time business?

7–13. Planning Profit Improvement. The management of Crestview Appliances Inc. is considering alternatives to improve profit from the three lines of appliances that are manufactured.

Cost data pertaining to the three product lines are as follows:

	Products		
	A	**B**	**C**
Selling price per unit	$85	$120	$70
Variable cost per unit	29	66	38
Contribution margin per unit	$56	$54	$32
Time required to make each unit	4 hrs.	3 hrs.	2 hrs.

The fixed overhead has been at $2,200,000 per year.

Last year sales were as follows:

Product A	30,000 units
Product B	20,000 units
Product C	50,000 units

A suggestion has been made that sales volume could be increased by granting a $10 refund for each unit sold. With a refund policy, the sales department estimates that sales for the next year would be as follows:

Product A	40,000 units
Product B	40,000 units
Product C	60,000 units

The production department further recommends that a new product line, Product D, be added. It would take 1 hour to produce each unit of the new product line with a unit variable cost of $25. With the new product line, fixed overhead would be increased to $2,400,000 for the year. No refund is to be granted on sales of Product D.

The sales department estimates that with Product D, the sales volume of Product C would be reduced to 50,000 units even with the refund provision for Products A, B, and C. Sales of Product D would be 20,000 units at a unit selling price of $45.

Required:

(1) Prepare a summary income statement showing the contribution margin for each product line and the income before income tax for the last year.

(2) Prepare an estimated summary income statement for the next year using the same model as (1) and assuming that the refund policy is accepted.

(3) Prepare an estimated summary income statement for the next year using the same model as (1) and assuming the refund policy and the addition of Product D.

(4) If there is a limitation on hours available for production, which of the four product lines should be favored assuming that the market can absorb the production.

7–14. Effect of Changes on Profits. The management of Logan Plastics Inc. is in the process of preparing a budget for the next year. The company manufactures car mats, dishware and figures that can be used as decorations or as toys for children. Some changes in prices and costs are expected along with changes in sales volume.

Data from operations for the past last year are as follows:

	Figures	Mats	Dishware
Units sold	550,000	1,200,000	350,000
Unit selling price...............................	$12.00	$8.00	$40.00
Variable costs per unit:			
Materials	$3.00	$3.00	$12.00
Indirect materials and supplies..................	.40	.40	1.00
Labor	1.50	1.50	6.00
Packing and shipping	.60	.60	1.50
Utilities	.50	.50	.50
Fixed costs:			
Supervision			$ 230,000
Employee benefits			765,000
Postage and telephone			73,000
Property taxes and insurance			126,000
Heat and light...			192,000
Repairs and maintenance			94,000
Depreciation			86,000
Advertising...			549,000
Travel and entertainment			162,000
Sales office, other			236,000
Office, and administration			372,000
			$2,885,000

Sales volume of figures next year is expected to be only 80% of the volume for the past year. The sales volume of mats is expected to remain constant. The volume of dishware sales should increase by 10% if the advertising budget is increased by $170,000. The selling price of figures is to be reduced to $10 per unit, and the selling price of mats is to be increased to $9 per unit.

Materials prices next year per unit of product have been estimated as follows:

Figures	$ 3.50
Mats	3.50
Dishware	14.00

Labor cost for next year is estimated at $2 per unit for both figures and mats. For dishware, labor is estimated at $7 per unit. The utility costs are estimated at $1 next year for each unit of each product line. Fixed costs, with the exception of advertising referred to, will probably increase by 10%. Income taxes are at 40% of income before income tax.

Required:

   (1) Compute the contribution margin and percentage of contribution margin per unit of product for the past year.

   (2) Compute the contribution margin and percentage of contribution margin per unit of product according to the estimates for the next year.

   (3) Determine the net income for the past year by product lines.

   (4) Determine the expected net income next year by product lines.

   (5) Will the expected volume increase in dishware sales more than compensate for the expected cost increases in dishware? Show computations.

7–15. Alternate Profit Plans. The board of directors of Daubert and Herman Inc. is considering three independent plans for profit improvement. One or more of the alternatives may be approved if the estimates appear to be favorable.

1. New product line

A new type of plastic sealer can be produced, and it is estimated that 80,000 units can be sold at a unit price of $15. Costs have been estimated as follows:

	Per Unit
Materials	$7.00
Labor	2.00
Variable overhead	1.00
Variable selling expenses	2.00

Fixed costs are expected to increase by $216,000 if the new product line is added. The sales division made a survey of the market potential and estimates that 150,000 units can be sold if the selling price is reduced to $12 per unit. Furthermore, with the increase in volume, unit materials cost can be reduced to $5.

2. Restructure a product line

One of the present lines can be redesigned, and it is estimated that the sales volume will remain unchanged at 15,000 units per year. Unit price and cost estimates are as follows:

	Present Data	**Estimated Data**
Selling price	$30	$38
Materials cost	12	20
Labor	6	4
Variable overhead	3	2

Fixed overhead is expected to remain the same.

3. Expand sales volume

In one of the divisions, sales volume of a product line can be increased by 50,000 units per year with the increased production being sold at a price of $18 per unit. Two units of product are manufactured each machine hour. Overhead varies at the rate of $10 per machine hour. The materials cost per unit is $3, and the labor cost is $4 per unit. Fixed overhead costs are expected to increase by $175,000 per year if volume is increased.

Required:

(1) Determine the profit advantage or disadvantage of each alternative.

(2) If only one alternative can be selected, which alternative appears to be better?

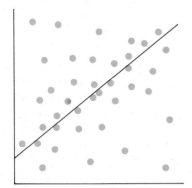

8
VARIABLE COSTING

This chapter should enable you to:

1. Understand the principle of costing under either absorption costing or variable costing.
2. Explain how variable costing can be more useful as a profit planning tool.
3. Understand how fixed costs can be carried over from one year to another as a part of inventory cost.
4 Explain how profits can be increased or decreased under absorption costing by decisions with respect to inventory balances.

Fixed costs are troublesome in product costing because they tend to remain the same in total dollar amount within various ranges of productive output. This creates a problem in determining the cost to manufacture a unit of product. The unit cost depends upon how many units are manufactured in the same fiscal period.

ABSORPTION COSTING

According to generally accepted cost accounting theory underlying income determination, all manufacturing costs are allocated to the products either directly or indirectly. Accordingly, the cost of any manufactured article includes the cost of the direct materials, the cost of the direct labor, and an apportioned share of the other manufacturing costs. These other manufacturing costs, collectively referred to as factory overhead, differ greatly from each other. Some of the costs, such as the salary of the plant manager, depreciation, and insurance on the plant, tend to remain fixed within various ranges of output; other costs, such as the cost of supplies used, fuel, and electric power, may increase or decrease with changes in output. All of these costs, however, are to be identified with the manufactured products. This conventional theory of product costing is sometimes called an absorption costing or a full costing method, the terms being derived from the fact that the full or total manufacturing cost is to be absorbed by the products.

Each product line and each unit of product should bear its share of the total cost. However, some product lines may not be able to carry their full share of the total cost but may be able to contribute to the overall profitability of the firm. For example, a product line may be sold at a price which is sufficient to recover more than the variable cost required to produce it but which is not sufficient to recover all of its share of the fixed cost. By contrast, other product lines are able to bear their share of the total cost and produce a return on the total supporting investment. Management needs to know whether or not a product line can produce an adequate return on investment after absorbing its share of the overall cost. In the long run, both variable and fixed costs must be recovered with a remaining profit that is satisfactory in relation to the invested resources.

One of the more difficult problems in cost accounting centers around the allocation of cost to the various products. The cost that cannot be directly identified with any particular department, function, or product may be apportioned; but then there is always some doubt about the validity of the product cost. Because some costs cannot be directly identified with the product lines, they are apportioned on the basis of some measurable factor such as machine hours, labor hours, or the relative amount of space used in production. It is not easy to prove that costs should be traced to the products by some method of apportionment. In fact, it may even be said that the costs should not be apportioned at all.

The total fixed cost, for example, is not affected to any extent by differences in the volume of productive output that fall within an established range. Therefore, when only a few units of product are made, the fixed cost per unit is high. The unit cost decreases as more units are produced. This in turn means that the profit for the year is influenced not only by the volume of sales, the sales price, and the cost of production but also by the quantity of units manufactured during the year.

As explained in the earlier chapters, factory overhead is applied to the products by using a predetermined rate. The fixed factory overhead, for example, is budgeted along with the hours of operation at a normal level of production. The budgeted cost is divided by the budgeted hours to obtain a rate per hour that can be used in costing the products. The products then are assigned a normal or a standard charge for fixed overhead. Variable factory overhead cost is, of course, assigned to the products in the same way. If the plant operates above or below its normal capacity, the fixed overhead will be over- or underabsorbed. The over- or underabsorbed overhead is designated as the capacity variance and is written off to operations for the year.

VARIABLE COSTING

In cost accounting there will always be the problem of cost apportionment. The real issue is whether or not certain costs should be assigned to the products. According to the **variable costing** concept, only the variable manufacturing costs should be assigned to the products. The fixed manufacturing costs should be written off each year as period costs. An investment in facilities and other productive factors is required before any products can be manufactured. There are fixed costs, such as depreciation, insurance, taxes, heat and light, and salaries of plant management, that must be incurred each year. Hence, the fixed cost of manufacturing is not a product cost but is the annual cost incurred in operating a plant. The fixed manufacturing cost, like the selling and administrative cost, is too remotely related to the product to be assigned as a part of its cost. Following this theory, the fixed cost of manufacturing should be expensed each year and not included as a part of the cost of an inventory of product.

Variable costing is more widely known as direct costing. This is unfortunate. It is not correct to say that the direct cost is attached to the products; rather, the variable cost is assigned. A direct cost can be identified readily with a department, a function, a unit of product, or some other relevant unit. Factory overhead cost is an indirect cost with respect to the products, yet the variable factory overhead is included in product cost when the direct costing method is used. Direct costs can be either fixed or variable. For example, a machine operator's salary may be a direct cost and may be fixed under a guaranteed annual wage agreement. The salary is a fixed cost; and although it may be directly identified with a product line, it is not considered a part of the product cost in direct costing. A variable cost that may or may not be directly identified with the product becomes part of the product cost in direct costing; hence, direct costing is more appropriately called variable costing. Both terms should be recognized, but the term "variable costing" is a more accurate designation.

ABSORPTION AND VARIABLE COSTING COMPARED

The differences between the two costing concepts can be emphasized by showing how an income statement prepared by the absorption costing method compares with an income statement prepared by the variable costing method.

To illustrate, a comparative income statement is presented on page 239 for Platt Supply Company, using the following data.

	Per Unit of Product
Selling price	$80
Variable manufacturing cost	10
Variable selling and administrative expense	5

	Total Cost
Fixed manufacturing cost for the year	$2,000,000
Fixed selling and administrative expense for the year	500,000

When products are costed by the absorption costing method, the fixed manufacturing cost is allocated to the products. Assume that the company produced 50,000 units of product at its normal capacity. The fixed manufacturing cost per unit is $40 ($2,000,000 ÷ 50,000 units). The total manufacturing cost per unit of product is $50.

Variable manufacturing cost per unit	$10
Fixed manufacturing cost per unit	40
Total manufacturing cost per unit	$50

If the variable costing method is used, however, only the variable manufacturing cost of $10 a unit will be assigned to the products.

Assume that 50,000 units of product were manufactured and sold in 1984 and that there were no units in inventory at the beginning or at the end of the year. The income statement is illustrated using both the absorption costing method and the variable costing method.

The net income, in this case, is the same under either costing method. All of the fixed cost for the year has been matched against revenue in both methods. Due to the absence of inventories, the fixed manufacturing cost has not been carried over from an earlier year as a part of beginning inventory cost, nor has it been included in inventory at the end of the year. In the absorption costing column, the fixed manufacturing cost is deducted as a part of the cost of goods sold. In the variable costing column, the fixed manufacturing cost is deducted as a period cost.

The excess of the revenue over the variable manufacturing cost of goods sold is designated as manufacturing margin. It is the amount contributed to the recovery of fixed manufacturing cost, operating expense, and profit. The difference between the revenue and all variable costs is the contribution margin. It is equal to the revenue minus all variable costs and is the net contribution to fixed cost and profit. The contribution margin concept is most important and can be applied by management in planning profit and in making certain types of decisions. The contribution margin concept and applications are discussed later in this chapter.

Platt Supply Company
Comparative Income Statement
For the Year Ended December 31, 1984

	Absorption Costing	Variable Costing
Number of units manufactured and sold	50,000	50,000
Sales (50,000 units @ $80)	$4,000,000	$4,000,000
Cost of goods manufactured and sold:		
Variable manufacturing cost (50,000 units @ $10)	$ 500,000	$ 500,000
Fixed manufacturing cost (50,000 units @ $40)	2,000,000	–0–
Cost of goods manufactured and sold	$2,500,000	$ 500,000
Gross margin	$1,500,000	
Manufacturing margin		$3,500,000
Selling and administrative expenses:		
Variable selling and administrative expense (50,000 units @ $5) .	$ 250,000	250,000
Fixed selling and administrative expense	500,000	–0–
Total selling and administrative expense....................	$ 750,000	
Contribution margin		$3,250,000
Fixed costs:		
Manufacturing		$2,000,000
Selling and administrative..................................		500,000
Total fixed cost.......................................		$2,500,000
Income before income tax	$ 750,000	$ 750,000
Income tax (40%)	300,000	300,000
Net income	$ 450,000	$ 450,000

A BALANCE OF SALES AND PRODUCTION

When sales and production are in balance at any level of operation, the results tend to be the same under either absorption or variable costing. If standard costs are assigned to the products, each unit of product bears the same amount of cost. Therefore, when sales and production are in balance, the number of units in the beginning inventory is equal to the number of units in the ending inventory, and the costs of the beginning and ending inventories are the same. As a result, fixed manufacturing cost equal in amount to the fixed manufacturing cost for the year is deducted from revenue by either costing method. If the absorption costing method is used, the fixed manufacturing cost is deducted as cost of goods sold. If the variable costing method is used, the fixed manufacturing cost is deducted as an expense of the fiscal period.

For example, assume that Platt Supply Company had an inventory of 10,000 units of product on hand at the beginning of a certain year and that 50,000 units were manufactured and sold during the year. The selling price and cost data are the same for beginning inventory and current production. A partial income statement showing results of the manufacturing operation by the two costing methods is given as follows:

Platt Supply Company
Partial Comparative Income Statement
(Manufacturing Operation)
For the Year Ended December 31, 19--

	Absorption Costing	Variable Costing
Number of units manufactured and sold	50,000	50,000
Sales (50,000 units @ $80)	$4,000,000	$4,000,000
Cost of goods sold:		
Inventory, beginning of year:		
[10,000 units @ ($10 + $40)]..........................	$ 500,000	
(10,000 units @ $10)...................................		$ 100,000
Cost of production:		
[50,000 units @ ($10 + $40)]..........................	2,500,000	
(50,000 units @ $10)...................................		500,000
Cost of merchandise available for sale......................	$3,000,000	$ 600,000
Less inventory, end of year:		
[10,000 units @ ($10 + $40)]..........................	500,000	
(10,000 units @ $10)...................................		100,000
Cost of goods sold	$2,500,000	$ 500,000
Gross margin	$1,500,000	
Manufacturing margin		$3,500,000
Less fixed manufacturing cost		2,000,000
Income from manufacturing	$1,500,000	$1,500,000

Fixed cost of $2,000,000 has been deducted in both columns. The cost of production (the cost of goods manufactured in this case) is equal to the cost of goods sold; and in the absorption costing column, the fixed cost of $2,000,000 has been deducted (included in $2,500,000) as cost of goods sold. In the variable costing column, the same amount has been deducted as a period cost.

If the company operates above or below its normal operating capacity, part of the fixed manufacturing cost is deducted as product cost under the absorption costing method, and the balance of the fixed manufacturing cost is shown as a capacity variance. An amount equal to the fixed manufacturing cost for the year is deducted from revenue assuming a standard cost system and assuming that inventories are not increased or decreased during the year.

In another year, assume that Platt Supply Company began the year with no inventory, operated at 90 percent of its normal capacity, and manufactured and sold 45,000 units of product. There were no changes in the selling price or the cost. An income statement prepared by the absorption costing method and the variable costing method is illustrated at the top of page 241.

Again, note that the net income as reported by both costing methods is the same. This is true whether or not the company operates at normal capacity as long as there is a balance between sales and production.

Platt Supply Company
Comparative Income Statement
For the Year Ended December 31, 19--

	Absorption Costing	Variable Costing
Number of units manufactured and sold	45,000	45,000
Sale (45,000 units @ $80)	$3,600,000	$3,600,000
Cost of goods manufactured and sold:		
Variable manufacturing cost (45,000 units @ $10)	$ 450,000	$ 450,000
Fixed manufacturing cost (45,000 units @ $40)	1,800,000	–0–
Cost of goods manufactured and sold (standard cost)	$2,250,000	$ 450,000
Capacity variance (5,000 units @ $40)	200,000	
Total	$2,450,000	
Gross margin	$1,150,000	
Manufacturing margin		$3,150,000
Selling and administrative expenses:		
Variable selling and administrative expense (45,000 units @ $5)	$ 225,000	225,000
Fixed selling and administrative expense	500,000	–0–
Total selling and administrative expense	$ 725,000	
Contribution margin		$2,925,000
Fixed Costs:		
Manufacturing		$2,000,000
Selling and administrative		500,000
Total fixed cost		$2,500,000
Income before income tax	$ 425,000	$ 425,000
Income tax (40%)	170,000	170,000
Net income	$ 255,000	$ 255,000

SALES AND PRODUCTION OUT OF BALANCE

Differences in net income reported under the two costing methods appear when the sales for the year are more or less than the production. When absorption costing is employed, the fixed manufacturing cost is shifted from one year to another as a part of the inventory cost. If a company produces more than it sells in a given year, not all of the current fixed manufacturing cost is deducted against revenue; part of it is held as inventory. This fixed cost will be released as part of the cost of goods sold in a later year, perhaps in a year when sales are in excess of production.

Hence, profit does not necessarily increase with increases in sales revenue. In fact, profit decreases if the effect of shifting the fixed cost from one year to another as a part of inventory cost is more than the increased contribution margin to be derived from the increased sales.

Management may find it difficult to understand how profit can decrease with increased sales volume and no change in selling price and cost. Seemingly, profit should increase when sales revenue increases. The shift of fixed manufacturing cost from one year to another must be recognized when an absorption costing system is used.

The peculiarity in profit behavior is illustrated by income statement data for 1984 and 1985. The selling price and cost data remain the same. Sales and production data follow:

1984 — Produced	....	50,000 units
Sold	....	45,000 units
1985 — Produced	....	45,000 units
Sold	....	50,000 units

A comparative income statement prepared by the absorption costing method for 1984 and 1985 is illustrated as follows:

Platt Supply Company
Comparative Income Statement
(Absorption Costing)
For the Years Ended December 31, 1985 and 1984

	1985	1984
Number of units manufactured	45,000	50,000
Number of units sold	50,000	45,000
Sales	$4,000,000	$3,600,000
Cost of goods sold:		
Inventory, beginning of year	$ 250,000	—0—
Current production costs:		
Variable cost	450,000	$ 500,000
Fixed cost	1,800,000	2,000,000
Cost of merchandise available for sale	$2,500,000	$2,500,000
Less inventory, end of year	—0—	250,000
Cost of goods sold (standard cost)	$2,500,000	$2,250,000
Capacity variance	200,000	—0—
Total	$2,700,000	$2,250,000
Gross margin	$1,300,000	$1,350,000
Selling and administrative expenses:		
Variable cost	$ 250,000	$ 225,000
Fixed cost	500,000	500,000
Total selling and administrative expense	$ 750,000	$ 725,000
Income before income tax	$ 550,000	$ 625,000
Income tax (40%)	220,000	250,000
Net income	$ 330,000	$ 375,000

The income statement shows that Platt Supply Company earned less in 1985 than it did in 1984, and yet more units were sold in 1985 with no change in the selling price or the cost structure. Ordinarily profit is expected to increase with increases in sales volume.

The income statement prepared by the absorption costing method tends to conceal the fact that fixed manufacturing cost from 1984 in the amount of $200,000 (5,000 × $40) has been shifted to 1985 as a part of the inventory carry-over to 1985. The reduction in income before income tax of $75,000 can be explained as follows:

Increased revenue (5,000 more units @ $80)		$400,000
Increased variable costs:		
Manufacturing (5,000 more units @ $10)	$ 50,000	
Selling and administrative (5,000 more units @ $5)	25,000	75,000
Increased contribution margin		$325,000
Less fixed cost included in inventory (5,000 units @ $40 = $200,000):		
Shift of fixed cost out of 1984 by inventory carry-over	$200,000	
Shift of fixed cost into 1985 by inventory carry-over	200,000	400,000
Decrease in income before income tax		$ 75,000

An income statement on a variable costing basis shows that the final contribution margin has increased in 1985 as a result of selling 5,000 more units of product. The fixed manufacturing cost is not transferred from one year to another as part of the inventory cost. A comparative income statement on a variable costing basis for 1984 and 1985 is given as follows:

Platt Supply Company
Comparative Income Statement
(Variable Costing)
For the Years Ended December 31, 1985 and 1984

	1985	1984
Number of units manufactured	45,000	50,000
Number of units sold	50,000	45,000
Sales	$4,000,000	$3,600,000
Cost of goods sold:		
Inventory, beginning of year	$ 50,000	—0—
Current production cost, variable	450,000	$ 500,000
Cost of merchandise available for sale	$ 500,000	$ 500,000
Less inventory, end of year	—0—	50,000
Cost of goods sold	$ 500,000	$ 450,000
Manufacturing margin	$3,500,000	$3,150,000
Less variable selling and administrative expense	250,000	225,000
Contribution margin	$3,250,000	$2,925,000
Less fixed costs:		
Manufacturing	$2,000,000	$2,000,000
Selling and administrative	500,000	500,000
Total fixed cost	$2,500,000	$2,500,000
Income before income tax	$ 750,000	$ 425,000
Income tax (40%)	300,000	170,000
Net income	$ 450,000	$ 255,000

The income statement as prepared by the variable costing method shows that the net income was greater in 1985 when more units were sold. The income before income tax in 1985 was $325,000 greater than it was in 1984. This would be expected, considering that 5,000 more units were sold with each unit making a contribution of $65 to fixed cost and profit (selling price of $80 minus variable unit manufacturing cost of $10 and variable selling and administrative expense of $5). The profit tends to vary with sales volume when the variable costing method is used. However, differences attributable to a lack of balance between sales and production are not revealed by variable costing. Sales may be overemphasized at the expense of production. In reality, profit depends upon both sales and production.

PROFITS AND INVENTORY

With a standard absorption costing system, profit can be shifted from one year to another with increases or decreases in inventory. Management should be aware of this effect in evaluating operations. For example, assume that Platt Supply Company, in preparing a budget for the next year, estimates sales of 40,000 units with price and cost data remaining the same. There is no inventory at the beginning of the year. With sales of 40,000 units expected, the company may plan to produce 40,000 units. However, the profit for the year can be increased by producing 50,000 units and selling 40,000 units, as shown in the following table.

	50,000 Units Produced	40,000 Units Produced
Sales (40,000 units @ $80)	$3,200,000	$3,200,000
Cost of goods sold:		
Cost of production:		
(40,000 units @ $50)		$2,000,000
(50,000 units @ $50)	$2,500,000	
Cost of merchandise available for sale	$2,500,000	$2,000,000
Less inventory, end of year	500,000	–0–
	$2,000,000	$2,000,000
*Capacity variance	–0–	400,000
Cost of goods sold	$2,000,000	$2,400,000
Income from manufacturing	$1,200,000	$ 800,000

*Production at 40,000 units is 80 percent of the normal capacity of 50,000 units. Hence, 20 percent of the fixed manufacturing cost of $2,000,000 was not absorbed by the products.

Income has been increased merely by building up the inventory. In both examples, the total fixed manufacturing cost for the year has been matched against revenue. With production at 80 percent of normal capacity, 80 percent of the fixed manufacturing cost is charged to the products produced and sold. The remaining 20 percent is deducted as a capacity variance. At normal capacity, the products bear all of the fixed manufacturing cost; but the portion of the fixed manufacturing cost attached to the ending inventory is not deducted as a part of the cost of goods sold but is carried over as a cost to the next year. As a result, the income is increased by the amount of fixed manufacturing cost included in the inventory at the end of the year.

EMPHASIS ON PRODUCTION OR SALES

In absorption costing, the effects of sales and production are combined. Particular emphasis is placed upon plant utilization. The cost of idle facilities either is added to product cost or is shown separately as a capacity variance.

In variable costing, the emphasis is placed on sales. The cost of each unit of product manufactured is not affected because of changes in the level of activity. Unit variable cost is assumed to remain the same over certain ranges of output. Of course, both unit variable cost and total fixed cost may change in certain production levels. However, the data used for variable costing apply to a range of output at which unit variable cost and total fixed cost are relatively constant. Variable costing serves a useful purpose in bringing out the relationships between prices, costs, and volume.

But if management relies too heavily on variable cost analysis, it may be deluded into thinking that the company can operate profitably at low contribution margin rates only to find that volume does not come up to expectations. Selling at less than normal prices may be helpful in short-term situations, but in the long run this policy may result in margins that are not adequate in relation to invested resources. Short-term expediency should be recognized for what it is and should not be allowed to become a part of long-term strategy. Both costing methods can be useful when applied in appropriate circumstances.

THE ADVANTAGES OF VARIABLE COSTING

Variable costing is particularly useful to management in applications where the relative profitability of product lines is to be determined or where the effect of changes in volume, prices, or costs is to be calculated. When fixed cost is allocated to the products, analysis by product line becomes more difficult.

The following advantages to be derived from variable costing are summarized in NA(C)A Bulletin, Research Series No. 23:

1. Cost-volume-profit relationship data wanted for profit planning purposes is readily obtained from the regular accounting statements. Hence management does not have to work with two separate sets of data to relate one to the other.

2. The profit for a period is not affected by changes in absorption of fixed expenses resulting from building or reducing inventory. Other things remaining equal (e.g., selling prices, costs, sales mix), profits move in the same direction as sales when direct costing is in use.

3. Manufacturing cost and income statements in the direct cost form follow management's thinking more closely than does the absorption cost form for these statements. For this reason, management finds it easier to understand and to use direct cost reports.

4. The impact of fixed costs on profit is emphasized because the total amount of such cost for the period appears in the income statement.

5. Marginal income figures facilitate relative appraisal of products, territories, classes of customers, and other segments of the business without having the results obscured by allocation of joint fixed costs.

6. Direct costing ties in with such effective plans for cost control as standard costs and flexible budgets. In fact, the flexible budget is an aspect of direct costing and many companies thus use direct costing methods for this purpose without recognizing them as such.

7. Direct cost constitutes a concept of inventory cost which corresponds closely with the current out-of-pocket expenditure necessary to manufacture the goods.[1]

The data produced by variable costing are easily understood by management. By considering the troublesome fixed costs as period costs rather than product costs, sales revenue can be directly related to the variable costs. The difference between the sales revenue and the variable cost is the contribution of the products to the recovery of fixed cost and to profit.

THE DISADVANTAGES OF VARIABLE COSTING

Variable costing may encourage a shortsighted approach to profit planning at the expense of the long-run situation. Over a short period of time, there may be an advantage in selling products at prices that are below the total unit cost. Profit is made so long as the fixed cost is covered by the sales from regular operations and so long as the selling price is in excess of the unit variable cost. Or in other cases, the fixed cost that would not be covered otherwise may be recovered through making sales at a price below the total unit cost. Products may also be sold in another market at less than the full cost to absorb idle plant capacity. This approach should be recognized, however, for what it is, a short-term expediency.

In the final analysis, all costs must be recovered along with an adequate return on investment. The product lines that cannot carry their share of the fixed cost are reducing the overall profit. A low-profit line may be carried to round out the other product lines or as a customer service. But unless there is some compelling reason for continuing with low-profit products, these products should be replaced with more profitable items.

---

[1] *NA(C)A Bulletin, Research Series No. 23,* "Direct Costing" (New York: National Association of Cost Accountants, 1953), p. 1127.

Variable costing tends to give the impression that variable cost is recovered first, that fixed cost is recovered later, and that finally profit is realized. Actually the revenue from the sale of each unit of product contains a portion of variable cost, fixed cost, and profit. No one cost has priority over another, and each unit of product earns a share of the profit.

The nonacceptability of variable costing for general reporting purposes and for income tax is not a valid argument against the use of the method in reporting to management. There are various cost concepts and techniques like variable costing that are useful to management but that are not acceptable in reporting to outsiders. If they can be utilized by management, they should not be discarded.

VARIABLE COSTING IN PLANNING AND DECISION MAKING

The concept of variable costing may be applied in the measurement of income, but it is most important in planning and decision making. For example, a certain line of product selling for $10 a unit with a variable cost of $7 contributes $3 per unit to the fixed cost and profit. If the fixed cost amounts to $300,000 a year, the company must sell 100,000 units to break even ($300,000 fixed cost ÷ $3 unit contribution margin). As defined in Chapter 7, the break-even point is the point at which there is neither profit nor loss.

In this example, management knows that at least 100,000 units must be sold if there is to be no loss. In addition, management plans profit on the basis of the expected contribution margin. Suppose that income before income tax is budgeted at $120,000. The contribution margin must then be equal to the fixed cost of $300,000 plus the budgeted profit of $120,000, or $420,000. The company must sell 140,000 units of a product yielding a $3 contribution margin a unit to cover the fixed cost of $300,000 and to earn income before income tax of $120,000.

Management may also plan to sell a product at a regular price in one market and to sell the same product at a reduced price in another market. It is presumed, of course, that the additional sales can be made without disturbing the regular market or without violating any price discrimination laws. The fixed cost does not have to be considered. The additional profit that can be obtained from selling at a lower price in another market can be calculated easily from variable cost information.

Kelly Forms Inc. manufactures and sells 150,000 units of a product that sells for $20 a unit. The variable manufacturing cost amounts to $12 per unit, and the fixed manufacturing cost amounts to $600,000. The results of the manufacturing operation appear as follows:

Sales (150,000 units @ $20)	$3,000,000
Cost of goods sold (150,000 units @ $12 unit variable cost)	1,800,000
Contribution margin	$1,200,000
Fixed cost	600,000
Income from manufacturing	$ 600,000

An opportunity presents itself to sell 50,000 additional units at a price of $14 per unit. Apparently the opportunity should be rejected because the manufacturing cost is $16 per unit according to conventional or absorption costing with normal capacity defined at 150,000 units of product. There is a unit variable cost of $12 and a unit fixed cost of $4 ($600,000 ÷ 150,000 units). Even when 200,000 units are produced, the unit fixed cost would still seem too high at $3 a unit ($600,000 ÷ 200,000 units) to permit the sale of products at $14 per unit. Yet variable costing shows that Kelly Forms Inc. can earn an additional profit of $100,000 by accepting this opportunity. The profit computation is shown below:

	Total	Regular Operations	Additional Sales
Sales	$3,700,000	$3,000,000	$700,000
Cost of goods sold	2,400,000	1,800,000	600,000
Contribution margin	$1,300,000	$1,200,000	$100,000
Fixed cost	600,000		
Income from manufacturing	$ 700,000		

The sale of the additional units has no effect upon the fixed cost. In making this type of decision, only the additional revenue and the additional cost are important.

The distinction between the variable cost and the fixed cost can be helpful in planning profit and in making decisions with respect to the pricing and sale of the various product lines. For managerial purposes, it is not essential that variable costing be used for income measurement. But the data processing system should furnish information on variable cost and fixed cost for use in planning operations and in making decisions.

VARIABLE COSTING AND BUDGET VARIANCES

For cost control purposes, however, a distinction between variable and fixed costs may not be too important; nor will it make much difference whether products are costed with the variable manufacturing cost or total manufacturing cost when the objective is to control the total cost of the manufacturing operation.

For example, assume that Maguire Tool Company budgeted sales and manufacturing costs for 1984 as follows:

Estimated production	200,000 product units
Estimated sales	180,000 product units

	Per Unit of Product	Total
Sales revenue (180,000 units sold)	$5	$900,000
Variable cost (200,000 units produced)	2	400,000
Fixed cost (normal production of 200,000 product units)	1	200,000

There was no inventory on hand at the beginning of the year.

During the year, the company sold 180,000 units at $5 apiece and incurred a variable manufacturing cost of $412,000 and a fixed manufacturing cost of $208,000. The actual variable cost was $12,000 more than budgeted for the production of 200,000 units, and the actual fixed cost was $8,000 more than budgeted resulting in a total unfavorable variance for the year of $20,000.

It must be remembered that fixed costs are fixed only in the sense that they do not vary with changes in productive output or activity. They are not fixed in the sense that they cannot be changed. An outside influence, such as an increase in property tax rates or a change in management policy with respect to discretionary cost, can result in a change in the fixed cost.

A comparison of the budgeted income statement with the actual income statement is given on a variable costing basis, and on an absorption costing basis, in the following statements.

Maguire Tool Company
Income Statement (Variable Costing)
Budget and Actual Comparison
For the Year Ended December 31, 1984

	Budget	Actual	Variance Over (Under) Budget
Sales	$900,000	$900,000	—0—
Cost of goods sold:			
Variable manufacturing cost	$400,000	$412,000	$ 12,000
Less inventory, end of year (20,000 units @ $2)	40,000	40,000	—0—
Cost of goods sold	$360,000	$372,000	$ 12,000
Manufacturing margin	$540,000	$528,000	$(12,000)
Less fixed manufacturing cost	200,000	208,000	8,000
Income from manufacturing	$340,000	$320,000	$(20,000)

Maguire Tool Company
Income Statement (Absorption Costing)
Budget and Actual Comparison
For the Year Ended December 31, 1984

	Budget	Actual	Variance Over (Under) Budget
Sales	$900,000	$900,000	—0—
Cost of goods sold:			
Variable manufacturing cost	$400,000	$412,000	$ 12,000
Fixed manufacturing cost	200,000	208,000	8,000
Total manufacturing cost	$600,000	$620,000	$ 20,000
Less inventory, end of year (20,000 units @ $3 standard unit cost)	60,000	60,000	—0—
Cost of goods sold	$540,000	$560,000	$ 20,000
Income from manufacturing	$360,000	$340,000	$(20,000)

A review of the statements shows that the income reported by absorption costing is $20,000 more than the income reported by variable costing. The budgeted statements show the same difference. This difference arises because the fixed cost of $20,000 is included in the ending inventory and will be carried over to 1985 under the absorption costing method, whereas it is expensed as a period cost under the variable costing method. The budget variance is $20,000 in both cases.

The budgeted and actual cost comparison is not affected by the costing method selected. The cost comparison is based on the total cost that is incurred and used in production. The method used to match costs against revenue is important in measuring income but is of little importance when the objective is to control costs.

Terminology Review

Absorption costing or full
   costing (236)
Capacity variance (237)
Direct costing (237)
Direct cost (237)

Variable costing (237)
Manufacturing margin (238)
Contribution margin (238)
Break-even point (247)

QUESTIONS FOR REVIEW

1. Why do fixed costs create difficulties in product costing?

2. In conventional cost accounting practice, how is the fixed factory overhead cost applied to the products?

3. How is a fixed manufacturing cost shifted from one year to another in absorption costing?

4. When the variable costing concept is employed, how is the fixed factory overhead cost applied to the products?

5. How does absorption costing differ from variable costing?

6. The fixed manufacturing cost should be treated as a period cost. Give arguments to support this statement. Give arguments against it.

7. Why is there no capacity variance under variable costing?

8. What is the contribution margin?

9. Why is the concept of a contribution margin important to management?

10. When a company sells the same number of units that it produces, the profit as reported by absorption costing and by variable costing tends to be the same. Explain.

11. If a company sells more units than it produces, would the profit reported by absorption costing tend to be higher or lower than the profit reported by variable costing? Why?

12. Explain why profit may be higher with a standard absorption cost system when production volume exceeds sales volume.

13. Assume that a company is operating at a profit. Can the profit be increased by selling additional units at a price that is only slightly higher than the variable cost per unit?

14. Why might variable costing be looked upon as a shortsighted approach to profit planning?

15. Should management make use of techniques that may not be accepted for use in the preparation of financial statements for the public? Explain.

EXERCISES

1. Contribution Margin. Valley Stores Inc. reported sales of $2,320,000 during 1985. The variable costs were 70% of sales revenue. The fixed cost was $370,000 for 1985.

Required: Prepare a summary income statement that shows contribution margin and income before income tax.

2. Contribution Margin. Dustin Manufacturing Company sold 130,000 units of a product line at a price of $8 per unit in 1985. The variable manufacturing cost for the year was $340,000. The fixed manufacturing cost was $160,000. Selling and administrative costs were $2 per unit sold. The fixed selling and administrative expenses were $80,000.

Required: Prepare a summary income statement showing the manufacturing margin, the contribution margin, and the income before income tax.

3. Variable Costing. Isaac Supply Company had an inventory of 25,000 units of product on hand at the beginning of the year, each unit having a cost of $6. During the year, 200,000 units were manufactured at a unit variable cost of $7. The company uses the fifo inventory method. During the year, the company sold 210,000 units for $2,520,000. Fixed costs of manufacturing were $650,000.

Required: Prepare an income statement for the manufacturing operation on a variable costing basis.

4. Variable and Absorption Costing. During 1985, Wilcox Company operated at 80% of normal capacity and manufactured 240,000 units of product. There was no inventory at the beginning of the year. The company sold 200,000 units during the year at a price of $40 per unit. The variable manufacturing cost was $25 per unit, and the total actual and budgeted fixed manufacturing cost were in agreement at $615,000.

Required: Prepare a summary income statement for the manufacturing operation:
(1) Using the variable costing method.
(2) Using the absorption costing method

5. Variable and Absorption Costing. In 1985 Castor Products Inc. operated at normal capacity and made 600,000 units of product. The variable manufacturing cost for 600,000 units was equal to 75% of the sales revenue of $3,000,000 derived from the sale of 500,000 units. The total fixed manufacturing cost for the year was $270,000. There was no inventory at the beginning of the year.

Required:
(1) Prepare a summary income statement for the manufacturing operation using the absorption costing method.
(2) Prepare a summary income statement for the manufacturing operation using the variable costing method.

6. Sales and Production Out of Balance. Production and cost data are given below for Oak Valley Parts Inc.

	1985	1984
Number of units produced	60,000	75,000
Number of units sold	75,000	60,000
Unit selling price	$25	$25
Unit variable manufacturing cost	$8	$8
Total fixed manufacturing cost	$750,000	$750,000

In 1984, the company operated at a normal level of capacity. There was no inventory on hand at the beginning of 1984.

Required:

    (1) Prepare a comparative income statement for the manufacturing operation for the 2 years on a standard absorption costing basis.

    (2) Explain the difference in income from the manufacturing operation, pointing out why the income for 1985 was higher or lower than it was in 1984.

7. Balanced Sales and Production. Production and cost data are given for Ashton Company.

	1985	1984
Number of units produced......................	90,000	120,000
Number of units sold	90,000	120,000
Unit selling price	$50	$50
Unit variable manufacturing cost	30	30
Unit fixed manufacturing cost....................	10	10

There was no inventory of finished product on hand at the beginning of 1984, and the company manufactures 120,000 units of product when operating at normal capacity.

Required:

    (1) Prepare a comparative income statement for the manufacturing operation for the 2 years on a standard absorption costing basis.

    (2) Prepare a comparative income statement for the manufacturing operation for the 2 years on a variable costing basis.

    (3) Explain why there are differences or why there are no differences in income from manufacturing when different costing methods are used.

8. Variable Costing and Income Differences. The president of Coastal Electric has been examining past income statement data in an attempt to estimate income expected for the next year. Past data are given in the table below.

Year	Number of Units Sold	Selling Price per Unit	Variable Cost per Unit	Fixed Cost
1982	8,000	$120	80	$15
1983	10,000	120	80	15
1984	7,000	120	80	15

The fixed cost per unit was computed at a normal operating level of 10,000 units to be produced each year. Actual fixed cost has remained at the same level over the years. The president estimates that 9,000 units will be sold in 1985 with no other changes expected.

Required:

    (1) Compute the contribution margin for 1982, 1983, and 1984 and the income from manufacturing by the variable costing method.

    (2) Estimate the contribution margin for 1985 and the income from manufacturing by the variable cost method.

9. Production and Profit. Clifford McMunn, the president of Hadden Industries, has observed that the sales volume in 1985 will probably be down from 140,000 units in 1984 to 110,000 units. To keep the profit from decreasing, he decides to build up inventories at the end of the year by producing 150,000 units. Some of the fixed cost will then be held over as part of the ending inventory. The normal capacity is 150,000 units per year with a fixed overhead cost per unit of $12.

In 1984, the company had an inventory of 10,000 units at both the beginning and at the end of the year. The company made and sold 140,000 units at a price of $60 per unit. The variable cost per unit was $40. The selling price and the cost structure are expected to be the same in 1985.

Required:

(1) Prepare a comparative income statement for the manufacturing operation for both 1984 and 1985 by the absorption costing method.

(2) Comment upon the position taken by McMunn.

10. Variable Costing and Pricing Policy. Harold Rainey has found that variable costing concepts have helped him in pricing products. He knows that he can reduce prices to a point where his store will recover more than the variable cost and that profit will increase when he gets more sales volume as a result of underselling the competitors. Data for 1984 and 1985 are as follows.

Years	Sales Volume	Selling Price per Unit	Variable Cost per Unit	Total Fixed Cost
1983	50,000	$25	$15	$300,000
1984	80,000	20	15	300,000

In 1985, he plans to sell 120,000 units for $18 per unit. The cost structure is not expected to change.

Required:

(1) How much income before income tax was realized in 1983 and 1984?

(2) How much income before income tax can be expected in 1985?

(3) Comment on the policy established by Rainey.

11. Unexplained Profit Decrease. The president of Titus Fittings Inc. exclaims:

> This income statement for 1984 is a lot of nonsense. Our sales volume increased from 160,000 units in 1983 to 170,000 units in 1984, and yet this silly statement says that earnings declined with no change in the selling price or the cost structure.

In both 1983 and 1984, the selling price was $50. The variable cost for both years was $32, and the total fixed overhead in each year was $1,600,000. In 1983, the company manufactured 180,000 units, and in 1984 the company manufactured 160,000 units. There were no units on hand at the beginning of 1983. The fixed overhead cost per unit was $8, computed from a normal capacity of 200,000 units.

Required:

(1) Prepare income statements for 1983 and 1984 by the absorption costing method.

(2) Prepare income statements for 1983 and 1984 by the variable costing method.

(3) Explain to the president why the profit was less than expected for 1984.

12. Fixed Costs and Inventories. Debra Shaw, the president of Danny Products Inc. asks you to show how fixed manufacturing cost was shifted from one year to another as a part of inventory cost. The fixed manufacturing cost for each year was $300,000. At normal capacity, 60,000 units of product should be manufactured. Capacity variances are charged or credited to the year in which the company operated over or below normal capacity. There was no inventory at the beginning of 1982.

Years	Production in Units	Sales in Units	Inventory in Units End of Year
1982	60,000	50,000	10,000
1983	50,000	40,000	20,000
1984	50,000	55,000	15,000

Required: For each year determine the following data:
  (1) Fixed cost included in cost of goods sold
  (2) Fixed cost included in inventory at the end of the year.
  (3) Capacity variance for each year.

PROBLEMS

8-1 Variable Costing with Volume Changes. DuChamps Supply Company sold 160,000 units of product last year at a price of $6 per unit. The variable cost per unit was $4. Fixed costs for the year were $145,000.

In the current year, the sales manager estimates that with improvements in the general economy sales volume will increase to 270,000 units. Selling price, unit variable cost, and fixed costs will remain the same.

Required:
  (1) Prepare income statements for each of the two years by the variable costing method.
  (2) Can you relate the increase in profit to the increase in volume? Explain.

8-2. Variable Costing with Volume and Price Changes. The president of Hamburg Fabricating Company anticipates that sales volume in 1985 will be 600,000 units, an increase of 150,000 units over 1984. Furthermore the selling price per unit in 1985 will be $7 per unit in contrast with the price of $6 for 1984.

    The fixed cost for each year is expected to remain at $560,000 and the unit variable cost will remain at $4 per unit.

Required:

(1) Prepare income statements for each of the two years by the variable costing method.

(2) Explain the profit increase by showing the effect of the volume increase at the old price and the effect of the price increase spread over the total volume.

8-3. Profit Effect of Inventory Reduction. The Cumberland Line Company reported a record profit in 1984. It appears, however, that profit may be lower in 1985 even with a higher volume of sales. The inventory at the beginning of 1984 consisted of 45,000 units. Costs of this inventory are given below.

Variable cost......................	$ 135,000
Fixed cost	900,000
Total inventory cost...............	$1,035,000

    In 1985, the company is scheduled to make 250,000 units, as it did in 1984, and will operate at normal capacity. The fixed cost is applied at a rate computed at normal capacity. The selling price, variable cost per unit, and total fixed cost will be the same as in 1984.

    The selling price per unit is $24. The company plans to sell 275,000 units in 1985, a 10% increase in volume over 1984.

Required:

(1) Prepare a partial income statement for 1984 and 1985 by the absorption costing method.

(2) Explain why the income before income tax may be lower in 1985 than in 1984.

(3) Prepare a partial income statement for 1984 and 1985 by the variable costing method.

(4) Explain why the results are different when variable costing is used instead of absorption costing.

8-4. Profit Effect of Inventory Increase. Green Hill Company has increased inventory in anticipation of future increases in sales volume. The inventory at the beginning of 1984 consisted of 25,000 units at a unit variable cost of $4 and a unit fixed cost of $20. The unit fixed cost is computed at a normal operating capacity of 200,000 units per year.

    During 1984, the company made 200,000 units and sold 175,000 units at a price of $40 per unit. There were no changes in the cost structure during 1984.

Required:

(1) Prepare an income statement for the manufacturing operation for 1984 by the absorption costing method.

(2) Would your answer have been different if the company had made and sold 175,000 units in 1984? Explain.

8-5. Income Determination by Variable Costing. Data from the records of Gilbert Town Company are as follows:

Years	Units Sold	Units Produced	Unit variable Cost	Total Fixed Cost
1981	130,000	140,000	$5	$300,000
1982	150,000	140,000	5	300,000
1983	125,000	140,000	5	300,000
1984	160,000	170,000	5	300,000

Each unit of product was sold for $12 in each year. The normal operating capacity has been defined at 150,000 units.

Required:

(1) For each year, compute the income from manufacturing by the variable costing method.
(2) With the variable costing method, is there a capacity variance for any year in which production is above or below the normal level? Explain.
(3) With variable costing, explain why profit tends to increase or decrease with increases or decreases in sales volume.

8-6. Income Determination by Variable Costing. Several estimates of sales volume and production have been made by the management of Purity Products for the fiscal year ending June 30, 1985. These estimates are given as follows:

Estimates	Units of Sales	Units of Production
1	30,000	40,000
2	50,000	50,000
3	50,000	60,000
4	60,000	70,000

There was no inventory of product on hand at the beginning of the fiscal year.

The selling price per unit is $25, and the variable manufacturing cost per unit is $16. Fixed manufacturing cost for the fiscal year has been estimated at $300,000, or $6 per unit at a normal operating level of 50,000 units per year.

The president of the company requests an estimate of income from manufacturing for each of the four alternatives. Variable costing concepts are to be used in making the computations. The president expresses concern that the company may have a loss under alternative 1.

The production superintendent states that the production level must be considered inasmuch as the fixed cost should be included as a part of product cost. Furthermore, the superintendent argues that if the accounting is handled properly, there will be no loss under Alternative 1.

Required:

(1) Provide the information requested by the president.

(2) Is the production superintendent correct? Explain.

8-7. Market Decision. The president of Happy Snacks Inc. believes that too large a proportion of the sales volume is being sold to large grocery outlets at discount prices. While this is a relatively dependable market, the few large customers tend to exercise too much control over prices. In the president's opinion it would be better to drop Country Days Inc. as a customer at a price of $15 per case and spend $100,000 on promotion that would increase sales to individual stores by 100,000 cases.

The market was divided last year as follows:

	Sales Volume (number of cases)	Selling Price per Case
Walnut Creek Stores Inc.	200,000	$18.00
Country Days Inc.	150,000	15.00
Life Products Inc.	350,000	16.00
Various individual stores	200,000	23.00

The cost to produce and sell a case last year was $16.50. The variable costs were $12.50 per case. Total fixed costs were $3,200,000 with 800,000 cases being considered to be normal volume. It appears that the costs will remain at this level for the next year.

Required:

(1) Prepare an income statement for last year by the variable costing method.

(2) Does it appear that profits can be improved by following the president's suggestion? Show computations.

(3) Presuming that there is sufficient capacity, would it be better to retain Country Stores, Inc. as a customer and increase the sales volume to individual stores according to the president's plan?

8-8. Inventories and Absorption Costing. The president of Timba Creations Inc. finds it hard to understand why profits have varied so much during the past two years.

"It seems that we make less when sales volume is up and we make more when volume is down," she states. "Something is wrong somewhere. Perhaps, we would really do well if sales went to zero," she adds with a puzzled smile.

Production and sales data are as follows for 1982, 1983, and 1984. The selling price and the cost structure were the same for all three years.

Unit selling price $75
Unit variable cost..................................45
Unit fixed cost 20

Total fixed cost per year...$8,000,000
Inventory at January 1, 1982...50,000 units.

	Number of Units Produced	Sold
1982.........................	400,000	400,000
1983.........................	500,000	350,000
1984.........................	300,000	450,000

Required:

(1) Prepare income statements in summary form for each of the three years by the absorption costing method.

(2) Explain to the president why profits increased when sales volume went down and why they decreased when sales volume went up.

(3) Prepare income statements in summary form for each of the 3 years by the variable costing method. (Assume that the inventory at the beginning of 1982 is already on a variable costing basis.)

8-9. Variable Costing Statements. For the past 3 years Fetherlin Electric Products Inc. has had wide fluctuations in production and sales. Sales volume has increased, and the variable cost of production has also increased with no compensating increase in the selling price for the product. Unit cost data follow:

	1984	1983	1982
Direct materials	$3.60	$3.00	$2.40
Direct labor.....................................	3.00	2.50	2.00
Variable factory overhead	1.40	1.00	1.00

In each of the 3 years, the product was sold for $10 per unit.

The fixed manufacturing cost amounted to $140,000 each year. Each year the selling and administrative expense amounted to $.50 per unit with fixed selling and administrative expense each year amounting to $60,000. Income tax is estimated at 40% of income before taxes.

Sales data for the 3 years are given as follows:

	Number of Units Sold
1982.............	250,000
1983.............	220,000
1984.............	240,000

The president of the company recognizes that the company cannot continue to hold the prices steady in light of the increases in variable costs. In fact, in 1985 it is essential that fixed manufacturing costs be increased to $180,000 per year. Materials cost per unit will increase to $4.00 per unit in 1985, but the other variable costs are expected to remain at the 1984 levels. He proposes that the selling price per unit be increased to $12 per unit in 1985. Competitors are also expected to increase prices, and he estimates that 240,000 units should be sold.

Required:

    (1) Prepare a comparative set of income statements for the 3 past years by the variable costing method.

    (2) Prepare an estimated income statement for 1985, based upon the president's estimates.

    (3) Explain how the profit will increase or decrease in 1985 relative to 1984.

8-10. Production Levels and Variable Costing. Emil Johansen, the production manager of Weiss Products, states that the sales volume remained at 450,000 units in 1984 and in 1985 but that production increased from 450,000 units in 1984 to 500,000 units in 1985. The selling price per unit was $6 in both years, and the unit variable cost was $4 per unit.

    The fixed cost at a normal production of 500,000 units is $300,000. Fixed cost was at the same amount each year.

    He believes that the profit should be higher in 1985 because of the production at normal capacity.

Required:

    (1) Prepare income statements for the manufacturing operation each year by the variable costing method.

    (2) Explain to Emil Johansen why the profit did not increase in 1985.

8-11. Comparison of Absorption and Variable Costing. Karen Bennington, the president of Barr and Wood Inc. would like to see a comparison of the absorption costing method with the variable costing method. Operations for the past 3 years are to be used as a basis for comparison. Sales and production data are given as follows:

	1984	1983	1982
Number of units manufactured	350,000	500,000	500,000
Number of units sold	450,000	350,000	400,000
Units selling price	$25	$25	$25
Standard variable cost of good produced	$5,600,000	$8,000,000	$8,000,000
Total fixed cost (manufacturing)	2,000,000	2,000,000	$2,000,000

Production was at normal operating capacity in 1982 and 1983, and there was no inventory on hand at January 1, 1982. Inventories are maintained on a first-in, first-out basis.

    Selling and administrative expense varied at the rate of $.50 per unit sold. The fixed selling and administrative expense for each year amounted to $200,000. Income tax is estimated at 40% of income before tax.

Required:

    (1) Prepare a comparative income statement for the three years by the absorption costing method.

    (2) Prepare a comparative income statement for the three years by the variable costing method.

8-12. Comparison, Absorption and Variable Costing. The sales manager of Dolly Home Products Inc. objects to the accounting procedure in costing the manufactured products. She states that sales were lost from a failure to grant price concessions to customers. By including fixed overhead as a part of product cost, the costs are, of course, higher than they would be under variable costing. As a result, the president is reluctant to authorize sales at a price below the full cost. At any price above the unit variable cost, the sales manager states that the company can earn additional profits. Furthermore, she believes that the income statements give a false picture by shifting fixed costs from one year to another as a part of inventory cost.

The financial vice-president defends the accounting policy. The objective, she says, is to maintain prices and gain a reputation for quality products at an established price. Too many companies, she continues, have been short-sighted and have spoiled their markets at an established price by granting price concessions merely to get sales volume. Profits are not earned until after all costs are covered, and each unit of product should bear a share of the fixed overhead.

Cost and sales data are given for the past 3 years.

	Units Manufactured	Units Sold
1983.	160,000	140,000
1984.	180,000	150,000
1985.	200,000	220,000

There was no inventory on hand at the beginning of 1983. The company increased inventories in anticipation of increased sales volume, and the sales volume finally did increase in 1985.

Cost to manufacture (each year):

	Per Unit
Materials	$ .80
Labor	.50
Variable overhead	.30
	$1.60

The fixed overhead for each year was $720,000. The fixed overhead has been applied to the production units on a pre-determined basis of normal production and amounts to $3 per unit.

Each unit of product for each year has been sold for $7 per unit.

Required:

(1) Answer the arguments of both the sales manager and the financial vice-president and give your opinion.

(2) Prepare income statements for the manufacturing operation by both the absorption costing method and the variable costing method.

(3) Using the absorption costing statements, explain the difference in profit between 1984 and 1983 and between 1985 and 1984.

8-13. Explanation of Profit Decline. Daniel Crowley, the vice-president of Master Key Products Inc. has just received the financial statements for the second quarter of 1985 and is disturbed by the results.

"With an increase in sales volume in the second quarter and with no change in prices or the cost structure, we make less money? No way," he exclaims.

He asks you to see where the mistake has been made and to give him corrected statements.

The income statements, as presented for the first and second quarters of 1984, are as follows:

Master Key Products Inc.
Comparative Income Statements
For the First Two Quarters of 1984

	Second Quarter	First Quarter
Number of units sold	50,000	40,000
Sales	$600,000	$480,000
Cost of goods sold:		
Inventory, beginning of quarter	$160,000	$ 80,000
Current production cost	320,000	400,000
Cost of merchandise available for sale	$480,000	$480,000
Less inventory, end of quarter	80,000	160,000
Cost of goods sold	$400,000	$320,000
Capacity variance	50,000	–0–
Total	$450,000	$320,000
Gross margin	$150,000	$160,000
Selling and administrative expense	50,000	40,000
Income before income tax	$100,000	$120,000
Income tax (40%)	40,000	48,000
Net income	$ 60,000	$ 72,000

The company operated at normal capacity and made 50,000 units of product during the first quarter and 40,000 units of product during the second quarter. All selling and administrative expense is variable and varies at $1 per unit of product sold.

Required:

(1) Explain to Crowley that no mistake was made and show him how the income before income taxes decreased in spite of increased sales volume.
(2) Revise the statement for each of the two quarters, to show the results on a variable costing basis.

8-14. Variable Costing and Profit Planning. The Cruz family has had experience in the production of optical equipment and plans to start a business of their own. Preliminary estimates of the market and production costs have been made.

Three lines of product can be manufactured and sold at the prices and costs given in the following table along with the time required to make each unit.

Product Lines	Unit Selling Price	Unit Variable Cost	Unit Contribution Margin	Hours Required to Make a Unit
1.	$16	$12	$4	1/2 hour
2.	12	7	5	1 hour
3.	6	3	3	1/3 hour

Only 60,000 hours are available for production. The fixed costs of manufacturing have been estimated at $185,000 per year, and the fixed costs of selling and administration have been estimated at $30,000 per year.

Market studies show that the company can sell 45,000 units of Product 1, 50,000 units of Product 2, and 60,000 units of Product 3 each year. The costs to deliver each unit will amount to $.25.

A younger member of the family who is currently taking a course in accounting at a local college states that, in order to obtain the full unit cost of the product, the fixed manufacturing costs must be allocated to the units manufactured at a predetermined normal level of operation.

An older member of the family states that this won't be necessary for profit planning and that for this purpose, it is more important to know how much each unit can contribute to the operation with the fixed costs deducted in total.

Required:

(1) How do you think the fixed costs should be handled in this situation?

(2) Prepare an estimate of expected maximum profit from the data given.

8-15. Inventory Liquidation and Profits. Matt Bovard is concerned that the inventory is excessive. He states that with too much inventory, the company, Redfern Metals Inc., is wasting resources that could be put to other uses.

An income statement is given in summary form for the past year.

Redfern Metals Inc.
Income Statement
For the Past Year

Net sales (700,000 units @ $14)	$9,800,000
Cost of goods sold:	
Inventory, beginning of year (350,000 units @ $8)	$2,800,000
Current production (800,000 units @ $8)	6,400,000
	$9,200,000
Less inventory, end of year (450,000 units @ $8)	3,600,000
	$5,600,000
Capacity variance, unfavorable	1,000,000
Total cost of goods sold	$6,600,000
Gross margin	$3,200,000
Operating expenses	1,500,000
Income before income taxes	$1,700,000
Income taxes, 40%	680,000
Net income	$1,020,000

Next year it is estimated that the company will sell 800,000 units of product with no change in the selling price or cost structure. Last year the company produced at 80% of normal capacity. Total fixed manufacturing overhead for the year amounted to $5,000,000 with $4,000,000 of that amount absorbed by production.

Matt Bovard, the president of the company, plans to produce at 60 percent of normal capacity next year and, by doing so, reduce the inventory to 250,000 units by the end of the year.

The controller points out that by operating at a lower capacity and reducing the inventory, a smaller profit can be expected next year.

Bovard states that the improvement in sales volume should help to overcome the disadvantage of reduced production and reduced inventories.

Required:

(1) Prepare an estimated income statement for the next year.
(2) Show how the profit next year will be more or less than the profit last year.
(3) Recast the income statements for the two years to show how they would appear if variable costing had been used.

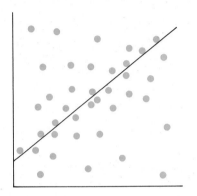

PART THREE | Analysis and Decision Making

9

ACCOUNTING DATA FOR MANAGERIAL DECISIONS – I

Chapter Objectives

This chapter will enable you to:

1. Explain the seven elements of the decision-making process.
2. Identify the difficulties in evaluating alternatives and explain the importance of simplification.
3. Define relevant revenue and relevant cost.
4. Explain the importance to decision making of the following concepts: variable-fixed cost classification, sunk cost, avoidable cost, and opportunity cost.
5. Evaluate alternatives in a decision situation using both total and incremental analysis.

The focus throughout this book has been that accounting data, concepts, and procedures are useful and supportive of the management process. A specific part of that process, and one that deserves considerable attention, is the decision-making process. For purposes of the discussion, the decision-making process begins when a problem or need arises and follows through the steps of identifying, evaluating, and choosing among future alternative courses of action. The main question of interest, then, is what accounting data, concepts, and procedures are helpful in supporting and facilitating this process? This is the subject matter of this and the next chapter. The complexities arising from capital investment and income tax effects will be discussed in Chapters 11 and 12.

DECISION MAKING – AN OVERVIEW

Decision making uses a basic framework consisting of several elements. These elements are usually thought of as defining the problem, establishing a decision rule, identifying the alternative courses of action, determining the consequences or outcomes of those actions, evaluating each alternative, choosing the best alternative, and making the decision.

The Problem

A problem exists when a manager has a need to seek alternative actions. This need, whether real or imaginary in the manager's mind, stimulates the manager to do something. Recognition of the need, identifying the components of the need, and possessing a desire to attain a certain goal are essential if the manager is to satisfy the need. The manager should develop several actions that can be taken, some of which will be more effective than others. It is also necessary to assess the consequences of these actions. Without these conditions, movement to the steps of the decision-making process is meaningless.

The Decision Rule

A decision rule, sometimes called an effectiveness measure, is a criterion selected by the decision maker that measures attainment of the goal. Some examples of criteria managers frequently apply are: maximize profits, minimize cost, maximize revenues, maximize efficiency, and maximize units of production. Managers determine the criterion appropriate for specific situations, whether it be one of the foregoing or some other one.

The Available Alternatives

The manager must identify the relevant alternatives available for a given set of circumstances. For example, a traveler going from Houston to Los Angeles must know the various modes of travel possible in order to select the most convenient way to travel. A student deciding on what courses to take must know which courses are offered.

The Consequences of Actions

A manager must be able to predict the relevant revenues and costs associated with each alternative action. In a few cases, a manager will know what the outcomes will be. Generally, however, the manager will predict the consequences by assessing the probabilities associated with the outcomes. For example, if you flip a coin, you know that the probability of heads is 50 percent. On any given flip of the coin, you don't know in advance whether the outcome will be heads, but you know the probability of that outcome.

Evaluating Alternatives

Given the decision rule, available actions, and the predictions associated with the actions, the next step is to evaluate the alternative actions. This requires selecting a form of analysis and the appropriate relevant accounting data. Each problem situation is unique and requires the form of analysis appropriate to the problem and the decision maker.

Choosing the Best Alternative

Once the foregoing steps have been accomplished, the manager chooses the best action to take from among the alternatives. The best action is the one that satisfies the decision rule.

The Decision

Choosing one alternative from among many does not automatically mean a decision has been made. So far, we have looked only at the quantitative side of the analysis. There are qualitative factors that influence the ultimate decision. For example, the political or economic environment may outweigh the quantitative-based alternative. In some cases, the qualitative factors relate to the whims, biases, and imperfect judgments of the manager.

IDENTIFICATION OF ALTERNATIVES

For purposes of illustration, assume that a firm is currently producing and selling a single product (Product A) and that the income statement for the current year just completed is as follows:

Income Statement

Sales (100,000 units × $10)		$1,000,000
Cost of sales:		
Raw materials (100,000 units × $2)	$ 200,000	
Direct labor (100,000 units × $1)	100,000	
Production supervision	50,000	
Factory rent	30,000	380,000
Gross profit		$ 620,000
Selling cost (15% × sales)	$ 150,000	
Administrative salaries	60,000	210,000
Net income before income tax		$ 410,000

Assume that the firm is operating at 80 percent of capacity in both the production and sales functions of its operation. The manager (decision maker) is seeking ways to increase the net income before income tax by using the additional capacity. The decision problem then is to select that alternative which will give the greatest increase in profit.

The Problem and the Alternatives

It is difficult to identify available alternatives at this point, because the problem is not clearly defined — it is too broad. The alternatives to a broadly stated problem may be so numerous that an exhaustive list would be almost impossible to evaluate. However, if the problem is defined too narrowly, some profitable alternatives will be overlooked. To illustrate the importance of not defining the problem too narrowly, consider the following example. If the manager views the problem as one of finding the best use of the idle capacity, he may consider only those new but like products that can be handled with the 20 percent idle capacity. Alternatively, if the problem is one of finding the most profitable use of the existing production and sales facilities, the manager may want to consider other (unlike) products that would result in completely replacing the existing product and thereby change the entire nature of the business. So, one of the key determinations is whether the problem is to find the best use of the currently unutilized capacity or, possibly, to move the firm into completely new lines of business. The second problem is likely to be much more complex than the first.

As a first step, assume that the manager decides to view the problem as one of finding the best use of the unutilized capacity. Even with this simplifying assumption, there may be a large number of alternatives to be considered. However, in order to make the problem even more manageable, suppose the decision maker chooses to evaluate three alternatives in addition to selling 100,000 units of Product A, the "status quo." (The status quo is always a possible alternative to be considered.)

Alternative 1: Expand sales of Product A, which might be done by lowering the current selling price.

Alternative 2: Expand sales of Product A, which might be done by holding the selling price at $10 per unit but increasing the sales commission.

Alternative 3: Expand the product line by adding Product B, which can be produced and sold with the current production facility and sales force.

As is apparent, it is likely that many simplifying assumptions must be made in order to make a decision in a timely manner. Even by constraining the number of alternatives under consideration, the manager may still be left with a fairly complex problem. For example, with greater production of Product A the company may be eligible for quantity discounts on raw materials purchased. If there are different discounts for different quantity levels, the alternative selected is influenced by the most profitable combination of revenue from sales and savings from quantity discounts.

In addition to noting how important it is to carefully state the problem, also note that simple assumptions may be necessary in order to proceed in a practical way. However, caution should be exercised so that more alternatives than the obvious ones are considered. A manager does not want to overlook important alternatives, either through the simplifying process or by not pursuing alternatives beyond the most obvious ones.

Importance of Prediction

In the evaluation of alternatives, the necessity and importance of prediction are probably quite apparent. It is clear that a fundamental characteristic of making decisions is that decisions affect the future; the past cannot be changed. Hence, it is the future consequences of the alternatives that are important.

In evaluating the alternatives in the example, note the types of predictions that must be made. It is necessary to make a prediction not only about the future relationship between market price charged and volume sold but also whether the historical relationships (such as cost relationships) will hold in the future. That is, how will the costs of production and selling change if additional units are added? Will there be influences that will affect the cost levels other than the change in volume? For example, will the landlord raise the rent on the physical facility? Many of the predictions may be very difficult to make but a decision maker has little choice, since predictions are so fundamental to the process of selecting the best alternative.

Accounting Data and Prediction

The accounting data given are for an accounting period just completed. In that sense, they are historical. It is important to recognize, then, that the historical data are useful in decision making only if they can serve as a good basis for predicting the future. In considering the three alternatives, it is also necessary to evaluate the status quo. That is, if the decision maker does nothing except repeat the status quo, will the firm still earn $410,000 (before tax) as it did in the period just completed? The answer is likely to be "yes" only if all the historical relationships hold for another future period. That, of course, depends on how many units are sold, the price, and the various cost relationships and the amount of the costs. The accounting data will most likely be very helpful in making a prediction about the status quo and future periods, but note that it is the prediction that is important and not the historical data per se. At the extreme, it is doubtful that any historical data are useful unless they furnish some basis for predicting what will happen in the future. The use of history to make predictions tends to be second nature when one considers decision making, but it is important to be specific on this point since it highlights the real, and probably only, value of accounting data.

To summarize, then, we note that decision making is concerned with the future choice among alternatives. In practice, several simplifications typically must be made, since in many instances the possible alternatives could be almost endless. On the other hand, the decision maker should be careful not to oversimplify, since a highly profitable alternative could be overlooked. Predictions are fundamental to the process of evaluating alternative courses of action and it is here that one finds the real value of accounting data.

EVALUATION OF ALTERNATIVES

Relevant typically means "related to the matter at hand." In the case of decisions, relevant data are data which are related to the various alternatives being considered, that is, relevant data are important because they are pertinent to the decision problem. In accounting, the relevant data are those data which are different across alternatives. It is the differences across the alternatives which need to be identified and evaluated. If the decision maker wants to select the most profitable alternative, the differences across alternatives in costs and revenues must be identified so as to identify the differences in profit. In reality, since we assume that the owners of the firm wish to maximize the future value of the firm, it is really the difference in future cash flows that we wish to identify. We use the concepts of revenue and cost predictions as a way to identify the difference in the future cash flows. Since the emphasis is on future cash flows, it is important to exclude from the analysis those costs which will not result in future cash flows. The depreciation cost on an existing machine is an excellent example. The cash flow takes place at the time of purchase or resale; the process of depreciation is a process of allocating the original machine cost to time periods and cash flows are not affected.

Relevant Revenues

Revenue predictions are almost always associated with predictions about the marketplace. Ideally, we would like to have a prediction about the market demand curve, or **market demand function**. That is, how many units of a product can be sold (would be demanded) at each price? With reference to the example, the firm is currently selling 100,000 units of Product A at $10. The demand curve, if it can be predicted, would specify how many units of Product A could be sold at prices higher and lower than $10. The $10 price and 100,000 units sold is simply a point on the demand curve. If we could predict the demand curve, we would have a basis for saying what the price would have to be for all units in order to sell 120,000 units and, thus, fill the capacity of the facility. If the prediction is that 120,000 units could be sold at $9, then the firm would enjoy revenue of $1,080,000, whereas it enjoys revenue of $1,000,000 under the status quo. If the status quo can be sustained, the relevant revenues are $1,080,000 for Alternative 1 and $1,000,000 for the status quo. We can also identify the relevant revenue as the $80,000 difference between the two alternatives, since it is this difference that makes the revenue a relevant piece of information. Whether we concentrate on the difference or the two totals for analytical purposes depends largely on the form of the analysis which will be discussed later.

In predicting the relevant revenues, accounting data may be of limited usefulness. The historical accounting report tells us that 100,000 units were sold at $10, so it gives us a basis for predicting one point on the demand curve. However, making a prediction of how many units will be sold at other prices (such as $9) may require market research rather than basing such a prediction on historical accounting data.

In summary, then, the concept of relevance is closely tied to the differences among alternatives. If the amount of revenue will differ among alternatives, then there are revenue considerations, and it is the revenue differences that are relevant. In the above example, the relevance is in the $80,000 additional revenue under Alternative 1 as compared with the status quo.

In some decision problems, there are no relevant revenue considerations; however, there are relevant cost differences. These are usually referred to as least-cost decisions. The characteristic of such decisions is that they are concerned with finding the most cost-efficient method of production and the amount of revenue is the same across all alternatives. The make-or-buy decision problem is an example. In the typical make-or-buy decision, the firm is deciding whether to make (manufacture) a certain part used in the production of the product or to buy the part from an outside vendor. If the decision is a true least-cost decision, the revenue level will be the same whether the part is manufactured by the firm or purchased from an outside vendor. In such decisions there are no relevant revenue considerations because the revenue is not different across the alternatives. The decision can be made by identifying and evaluating the differences in cost.

Relevant Cost

The concept of relevant cost is also fundamental to managerial accounting as a support for decision making. The ideas here are much the same as previously discussed. In evaluating alternatives, the key question is which costs will be different across the alternatives. The differential costs are the relevant costs. Those costs which will not change, and are therefore not differential, are not relevant to the choice among alternatives.

In evaluating the three alternatives in the example, there are both relevant revenue and relevant cost considerations. Alternative 2 suggests that the sales of the existing product might be increased if the sales commission is increased. Assume, for example, that Product A is sold through sales representatives who may also handle products of other firms. An increase in the commission above the current level of 15 percent can increase the profits of the sales representatives and may cause them to put in more selling effort on Product A. Let us suppose that management predicts that increasing the sales commission to 20 percent on all sales will result in sales of 120,000 units at $10 and will thereby fill up capacity. The relevant, differential revenue (of Alternative 2 as compared with the status quo) is 20,000 units at $10, or $200,000. That is, status quo revenue is $1,000,000 and Alternative 2 revenue would be $1,200,000. But, there are also cost considerations.

If volume is increased from 100,000 to 120,000 units of Product A, how will costs change? The differential costs are the relevant costs. Historical accounting data are normally helpful in the prediction of how costs will change. The relevant costs are usually said to be the variable costs, that is, those costs that change when volume changes.

In reviewing the income statement on page 268, let us suppose that raw materials, direct labor, and selling costs are variable with volume but that management predicts no change in the production supervision, factory rent, or administrative salaries. The costs which will not change due to the volume change are fixed costs and are not relevant costs for this decision. It is important to recognize that the "fixed" in fixed cost does not mean that such a cost never changes. The factory rent may increase because the landlord raises the rental rate. However, if such an increase is not caused by the volume change, the cost is fixed with respect to the volume change and is therefore not relevant in evaluating the alternatives in the immediate decision problem. The rent could be a variable cost, and therefore a relevant cost, if it is based on a percentage of sales, for example. However, if the rental amount is independent of volume, it is fixed. Let us assume that is the case in the example.

If the variable costs are raw materials, direct labor, and selling costs, then we can determine the differential revenue and cost for Alternatives 1 and 2 as compared with the status quo. Remember that Alternative 1 involves cost changes just like Alternative 2. This is done as follows:

	Alternative 1 As Compared With Status Quo	Alternative 2 As Compared With Status Quo
Additional revenue:		
120,000 units @ $9 − 100,000 units @ $10 ..	$80,000	
20,000 units @ $10		$200,000
Additional cost:		
Raw materials—20,000 units @ $2	$40,000	$ 40,000
Direct labor—20,000 @ $1	20,000	20,000
Selling cost—$80,000 × 15%	12,000	
1,200,000 × 20% − 1,000,000 × 15%		90,000
Total additional cost.....................	$72,000	$150,000
Additional profit	$ 8,000	$ 50,000

As can be seen, the total differential, relevant costs are $72,000 for Alternative 1 and $150,000 for Alternative 2 as compared with the status quo. Deducting these costs from the relevant revenue for each alternative shows that Alternative 2 is considerably more attractive than either Alternative 1 or the status quo. But, what about Alternative 3?

If Product B is added to the product line, the key predictions are again the relevant revenue and costs. Suppose that Product B is expected to use the same production time per unit as the existing product, so that 20,000 units can be produced at a variable cost of $1 per unit for direct labor, but that a different raw material will be required which will give a variable cost of $5 per unit. In order to sell 20,000 units of Product B, assume that management predicts that the selling price should be $15 per unit. Also assume that the normal sales commission of 15 percent will have to be paid. Given these data, the following differential revenues and costs can be calculated for Alternative 3.

Alternative 3 Compared with Status Quo

Additional revenue:		
20,000 units @ $15		$300,000
Additional costs:		
Raw materials—20,000 units @ $5	$100,000	
Direct labor—20,000 units @ $1	20,000	
Selling costs—$300,000 × 15%	45,000	165,000
Additional profit		$135,000

In comparing the alternatives, the most attractive is Alternative 3 since it produces the greatest increase in profit, which is the decision rule. The introduction of Product B will give the greatest return ($135,000) on the use of the currently available idle capacity. The differential revenues and costs shown are the relevant revenues and costs for evaluating Alternative 3.

Review of Other Cost Concepts Useful for Predicting Differential Costs

As we have seen, the differential costs are the relevant costs for decision making and the evaluation of alternatives. Elsewhere in the text, other cost concepts have been defined. Let us review some of these important concepts to show how they relate to the concept of differential costs.

The variable-fixed cost classification is fundamental to decision making because those concepts may be used as a basis for measuring the differential costs. Variable costs were defined as those costs which change in direct proportion to changes in volume. Hence, variable costs are usually considered to be constant per unit over the relevant range of volume changes. Fixed costs, on the other hand, are those costs which do not change in amount when volume changes. Fixed costs are defined over some relevant range of capacity. If that capacity range is exceeded, it is possible for the fixed costs to change, and that change would be relevant to the decision. In the problem at hand, the fixed costs do not change if volume is increased to 120,000 units. However, if the decision problem was to find ways to increase volume to 150,000 units, it is possible that a second production shift might have to be added. This may not increase the rent, but a second production supervisor might have to be added, which might cost an additional $50,000. In such a problem, the increase in fixed cost of $50,000 would be relevant to the decision problem since it is a differential cost. However, as noted earlier, the fixed costs in the decision situation being considered do not change and are, therefore, not differential or relevant costs.

Let us return now to a consideration of the variable costs and ask under what conditions the variable costs serve as a factor in estimating the differential costs. If the differential costs across the alternatives are constant per unit or change in proportion to volume changes, then variable costs will be a good estimating factor of differential costs. In order to demonstrate, refer to Alternative 3 in the example. In that alternative, the variable costs of Product B are constant per unit and amount to $8.25 as shown in the following table:

	Variable Cost per Unit for Product B
Raw materials	$5.00
Direct labor	1.00
Selling costs	
15% × $15	2.25
	$8.25

Hence, a good estimating factor of the differential cost of Alternative 3 as compared with the status quo is the variable cost per unit times the units to be produced and sold—$8.25 × 20,000 units, or $165,000. As pointed out earlier, the other costs—production supervision, factory rent, and administrative salaries—are fixed and, therefore, not differential and not relevant to the decision.

Likewise, the differential cost in Alternative 1, as compared with the status quo, is also constant per unit at $4.50 (i.e., raw materials, $2; direct labor, $1; and selling costs, $1.50). Hence, the variable cost per unit will be a good estimating factor of the differential costs for Alternative 1: $4.50 × 20,000 units, or $90,000.

However, in Alternative 2, there are some problems in using variable cost per unit unless this is done with care. In this alternative, part of the differential cost is the increased sales commissions on the current units sold, and this element of cost ordinarily will not be captured by the variable cost of the additional units. That is, a straightforward estimate of the variable cost of the additional 20,000 units is $5 per unit, shown as follows:

Raw materials cost	$2.00
Direct labor cost	1.00
Selling cost—20% × 10	2.00
	$5.00

The estimate of differential cost using the $5 variable cost per unit would be $100,000, whereas the real differential cost is $150,000. The difference of $50,000 is the increase in the selling commission cost of $.50 per unit on the 100,000 currently being sold, which is caused by increasing the sales commission from 15 percent to 20 percent on all units. In a sense, the variable costs (defined as those costs which change in direct proportion to changes in volume) are always relevant to the decision, but they may not capture all of the differential costs involved. In decision analysis, one must be careful not to incorrectly estimate differential cost by using variable costs which are typically assumed by definition to be constant per unit.

Another cost concept introduced earlier is sunk cost. This is a cost that has already been incurred. An example would be the cost of a machine. Sunk costs are not relevant to decisions because they are not differential. If the machine could be sold for scrap value, the scrap value selling price would be differential and therefore relevant. However, the original sunk cost would not be relevant.

Avoidable costs, as opposed to unavoidable costs, are typically differential and will normally be relevant costs. In the modernization of a production process, for example, the variable maintenance repair cost of an old machine that would be scrapped or retired may be avoidable and, therefore, differential. The depreciation cost, which is based on the original (now sunk) cost of the old machine, would be unavoidable and, therefore, not relevant because it is not a differential cost. Hence, in some problems, the concept of avoidable cost may be a good estimating factor of the differential costs across the alternatives under consideration.

Opportunity cost was defined in Chapter 2 as the return or benefit associated with a rejected alternative. As such, opportunity costs are relevant to decisions. It is not unusual to find differential costs which are in the form of a sacrificed benefit or return. In such cases, the benefit should be included either in the relevant revenues of the alternatives producing such benefits or as costs associated with the alternative which, if chosen, will cause the benefits to be sacrificed. Either way, the concept of opportunity cost can be an effective way of helping to identify differential cost. Let us consider some examples.

In the discussion on avoidable cost, we used the example of the variable cost of machine maintenance and repair that could be avoided if the old machine was replaced. Such a cost is also an opportunity cost of keeping the old machine. It represents the sacrifice of a benefit, through cost reduction, of not replacing the machine. This cost could be included as part of the cost of the alternative of not replacing or as part of the benefits of replacing.

As another illustration, let us refer back to the example given on pages 267-269 regarding the use of idle capacity. Suppose that the idle production capacity could have been returned to the landlord and the factory rental cost of $30,000 would thereby be reduced by $6,000. In that case, the entire rental cost would not be fixed, as was assumed earlier. The $6,000 cost reduction would be an opportunity cost of selecting any of the three alternatives associated with expanding sales of Product A or introducing Product B. By selecting any of the three alternatives, the manager would be sacrificing a cost-reduction benefit of $6,000, which is an opportunity cost of using the idle capacity. The $6,000 could be counted as a benefit associated with the status quo or as a cost of all three alternatives.

As a third example, suppose that a person, currently employed at an annual salary of $30,000, is trying to decide whether to keep working or return to school for one year to complete a master's degree program. In addition to the incremental cost of tuition, books, etc., associated with the alternative of returning to school, the person would incur an opportunity cost of $30,000 by giving up a salary. This sacrificed benefit should be included as part of the cost of returning to school or as a benefit of the alternative of not returning to school.

The concept of opportunity cost is also useful in selecting the best alternative once all alternatives have been evaluated. In the early example on the use of currently idle capacity, there were three alternatives plus the status quo. The differences in net income before taxes of each alternative compared with that of the status quo is shown as follows (see page 279 for income statements of each alternative):

	Alternatives		
	1	*2*	*3*
Net income before income tax	$418,000	$460,000	$545,000
Net income for status quo	410,000	410,000	410,000
Differences	$ 8,000	$ 50,000	$135,000

The introduction of Product B (Alternative 3) would increase profit by $135,000. The decision maker, by selecting this alternative gives up the opportunity to increase profits by $50,000 through selection of Alternative 2. This increase in profit associated with the next best alternative (Alternative 2 in the foregoing case) is an opportunity cost of $50,000. Therefore, Alternative 3 represents an incremental profit of $85,000 ($135,000 less the opportunity cost of $50,000) over the next best alternative.

Furthermore, the decision maker may want to consider whether any feasible alternatives have been overlooked. In considering this question, possible excluded alternatives would have to yield a profit increase of greater than $135,000, since this would be the opportunity cost of not accepting Alternative 3.

In summary, we have pointed out that the differential costs are the relevant costs for decision making. However, the cost concepts or cost classifications of variable vs. fixed cost, avoidable vs. unavoidable cost, and opportunity cost are all helpful in identifying and predicting the amount of the differential cost. In any given decision problem, all of these cost concepts may be important in facilitating the process of differential cost prediction.

THE FORM OF THE ANALYSIS

Having discussed several of the important accounting concepts and procedures which are useful in decision making, let us discuss the form of the analyses that might be done in support of managerial decisions. First, we ought to recognize that the managerial accounting analysis will be supportive and helpful in decisions but it will rarely do the entire job. Such an analysis may have to be supplemented with economic forecasts of the economy and the industry, and market research may have to be done to predict the market demand curve (the relationship between price and quantity sold). Furthermore, in any complex decision, there may be factors which are difficult or impossible to quantify so that the manager will have to exercise judgment based on his or her experience. An example given earlier was that the political risk involved in an overseas investment could be an important factor. The nationalization of an offshore oil production facility or subsidiary company may be a distinct possibility. In the final analysis, the decision maker may rely in part on accounting and marketing estimates of increased cash flow and profitability, but the final decision may rest on the decision maker's analysis and judgment of the future political environment in the offshore location. It is probably in only the simplest of decisions that accounting analysis even comes close to giving complete answers to what should be done.

The Use of Breakeven Analysis

In many decisions, there is likely to be uncertainty regarding sales and/or cost. In those cases where sales volume is uncertain, the analyst should not overlook the potential usefulness of cost-profit-volume (or breakeven) analysis as discussed in Chapter 7. To illustrate, assume that a firm is considering a new product with a variable cost estimated at $5 per unit and incremental annual cost for production and sales supervision estimated at $500,000. Assume that the annual cost is incremental but the amount does not vary with the volume sold. Further assume that the analyst is quite certain of the cost estimates but has considerable uncertainty as to the quantity that can be sold. The decision maker may feel that the proper price is in the $8 to $11 range because of the prices on currently available competing products, but has little basis for predicting quantity sold. In such a problem, breakeven analysis may be very helpful as a form of analysis.

The quantities required to break even on the incremental annual costs, at various prices, can be calculated as follows:

Price	Variable Cost	Contribution per Unit	Incremental Annual Cost	Units to Break Even
$11	$5	$6	$500,000	83,334
10	5	5	500,000	100,000
9	5	4	500,000	125,000
8	5	3	500,000	166,667

Such an analysis certainly does not provide the complete basis for a decision, but it may be very helpful in identifying sales levels required to justify going ahead with the new product. It may also provide the basis for market research to determine whether the likely sales will be greater than the amounts shown in the last column of the table.

This form of analysis could be modified and possibly improved by including a profit objective. That is, suppose that the manager is willing to introduce the new product if it will increase profit by $250,000 per year. The volume of required sales at $10 per unit would then be:

$$\frac{\$500,000 + 250,000}{(\$10 - \$5)} = 150,000 \text{ units}$$

Such an analysis may be helpful to a market researcher because it simplifies the question to be answered. That is, it may be easier for a market researcher to answer the question, Will sales at $10 per unit be greater than 150,000 units? than the question, What will the sales be at $10 per unit? The analysis gives a bench mark figure on volume which may be very helpful.

Total vs. Incremental Analysis

In evaluating alternatives, the analyst can also choose between an incremental and a total analysis as two different forms. In the example used earlier on the possible use of idle capacity, an incremental analysis was used, that is, the additional profit (cash flow) associated with each of the three alternatives was calculated by relating each alternative to the status quo. The same problem could have been analyzed using total analysis which has the advantage of showing the total profit associated with each alternative rather than just the change in profit. A form of total analysis is as follows:

Income Statements for All Alternatives

	Status Quo	Alternative 1	Alternative 2	Alternative 3
				(100,000 units @ $10 and 20,000 units of Product B
			(120,000 units @ $10 with commission at	
	(100,000 units @ $10)	*(120,000 units @ $9)*	*20%)*	*@ $15)*
Sales	$1,000,000	$1,080,000	$1,200,000	$1,300,000
Variable costs:				
Raw materials . . .	$ 200,000	$ 240,000	$ 240,000	$ 300,000
Direct labor	100,000	120,000	120,000	120,000
Selling cost	150,000	162,000	240,000	195,000
	$ 450,000	$ 522,000	$ 600,000	$ 615,000
Contribution	$ 550,000	$ 558,000	$ 600,000	$ 685,000
Fixed costs:				
Production supervision	$ 50,000	$ 50,000	$ 50,000	$ 50,000
Factory rent	30,000	30,000	30,000	30,000
Administrative salaries	60,000	60,000	60,000	60,000
	$ 140,000	$ 140,000	$ 140,000	$ 140,000
Net income before income tax	$ 410,000	$ 418,000	$ 460,000	$ 545,000

As is apparent, the profit differences calculated in the incremental analysis can be calculated from the total analysis as well by using either contribution or net income before income tax. This is shown as follows:

	Contribution	Net Income Before Income Tax	Difference of Each Alternative Compared with Status Quo
Status quo	$550,000	$410,000	
Alternative 1	558,000	418,000	+ $ 8,000
Alternative 2	600,000	460,000	+ $ 50,000
Alternative 3	685,000	545,000	+ $135,000

The form of total analysis may have the following advantages over the incremental analysis:

1. The total analysis shows the total profit levels, whereas the incremental analysis shows only the change in profit. This may make the analysis easier for the decision maker to understand.

2. The total analysis demonstrates why the fixed costs are not really relevant to the analysis. Since fixed costs do not change, they have no effect on the profit increase which is the important factor to isolate. However, by including the fixed cost in all alternatives, the total analysis may help to reassure the manager that the fixed costs have not been overlooked.

3. By showing the fixed costs, the decision maker and the analyst have one more opportunity to review the prediction that such costs are, in fact, fixed. It can be important to review that prediction. If the additional volume should cause an increase in production supervision for example, this increment is relevant to the analysis, since it is a differential cost. Continual review of fixed costs for such possible outcomes may be important.

The final judgment on the form of the analysis should depend on how costly the analysis is compared with the prospective benefits to the user of the analysis—the manager or decision maker. Hence, the form should be considered.

Having discussed several important concepts and procedures that can be used to provide managerial accounting support for decision making, the next chapter will extend these concepts and also apply them to several different decision problems. The discussion will continue in Chapters 11 and 12 where capital investment and income tax considerations are discussed.

Terminology Review

Problem (266)
Decision rule (266)
Alternatives available (266)
Consequences (267)
Evaluate the alternatives (267)
Best action (267)
Decision (267)
Relevant data (270)
Market demand curve (271)

Least-cost decisions (271)
Relevant cost (272)
Differential costs (272)
Sunk cost (275)
Avoidable costs (275)
Opportunity cost (275)
Incremental analysis (278)
Total analysis (278)

QUESTIONS FOR REVIEW

1. What is meant by the term "decision making"?

2. Why is so much emphasis placed on the future in decision making? Does the past have any significance in decision making?

3. Why is identifying the alternatives one of the most important steps in the decision making process?

4. What is the relationship between the concept of relevance and differential costs and revenues?

5. Are variable costs always relevant costs and fixed costs irrelevant costs?

6. How can opportunity costs be used in deciding whether a product should be sold in a partially completed state or finished and sold as a completed product?

7. Distinguish between an avoidable and an unavoidable cost.

8. Sunk costs are a fixed cost associated with a decision. Briefly explain this statement.

9. The president of Daly Company said, "The accounting data are useful for predicting the results of various alternatives, but in my company the final selection of an alternative often depends on other factors." Explain the meaning of this statement.

10. Jim Beers of Ready-Built says he prefers the incremental form of analysis. Jan Gilchrist of Commerce Manufacturing prefers the total form of analysis. Explain the difference between incremental analysis and total analysis as a format for decision making.

EXERCISES

1. Opportunity Cost. The Parkview Country Club was asked to host a golf tournament for the Century Company. The tournament would require the club to be closed to normal business for one day. This would be feasible since the tournament would be on a Monday and the course is not heavily used on Mondays. The Century Company has offered a flat fee of $5,000. Additional expenses for the day are estimated by the club manager to be $200, the cost of hiring some additional casual labor to help clean up after the post-tournament picnic. The manager has estimated that the loss of fees due to closing the club to normal business would be about $2,000. There would be some cost savings (estimated at $500) because several hourly-paid employees would not work that day. The manager feels that there would be no loss of future business as a result of closing for one Monday.

Required:

(1) What is the opportunity cost of closing the club to normal business?

(2) Calculate the additional profit or loss from hosting the tournament.

2. Relevant Costs. Lavin Corporation manufactures subassembly MC-101 for use in its major product. The costs per unit for 10,000 units of MC-101 are as follows:

Direct materials	$ 3
Direct labor	14
Variable overhead applied	7
Fixed overhead applied	10
Total unit cost	$34

Power Parts Inc. has offered to manufacture 10,000 units of MC-101 for Lavin Corporation at a unit cost of $30. If Lavin accepts the offer, it could eliminate $6 per unit of the fixed overhead cost. In addition, Lavin could use the space in the production of another subassembly and thereby save $50,000 in costs for that subassembly.

Required:

(1) Identify the two alternatives for this decision and the relevant costs associated with each alternative.

(2) What decision should Lavin Corporation make?

3. Opportunity Cost. The East Bend Company has 2,000 obsolete aluminum pans that are carried in inventory at $30,000. The pans can be reworked at a cost of $6,000 and sold for $10,000. Otherwise, the company can sell the pans as scrap for $3,000, less cost to dispose of $500.

Required: What is the opportunity cost of this decision?

4. Relevant Costs for EOQ. The Gilley Company is considering adopting an EOQ approach (economic order quantity) for one of its basic raw materials. The critical factors to consider in EOQ is the total annual cost of placing orders and the interest cost of maintaining the average inventory. The controller has estimated the following data for consideration:

Optimal units per order	500
Average inventory in units	250
Unit cost of raw material	$ 5
Interest cost on investment in average inventory	15%
Number of orders placed per year for optimal number of units	15
Cost of placing each order	$12.50

Required: Determine the total annual relevant costs for the EOQ approach.

5. Break-Even Analysis. The Means Company is planning to sell 100,000 units of its new E.T. coffee mug for $6 per unit. Variable cost amounts to $2.40 per unit. The company wants to earn a minimum profit of $200,000 if it starts production. The company is not certain what level of fixed cost will be incurred to support production of the mug.

Required: What is the maximum amount the company can pay for fixed cost?

6. Incremental vs. Total Analysis. Juniper Company currently produces 5,000 units per month of its major product. Financial data for a recent month are as follows:

Sales	$200,000
Variable costs	120,000
Fixed costs	55,000
Net income	25,000

The company would like to expand its operations to 6,000 units per month. Fixed costs would increase $16,000 for the expansion.

Required:

(1) Prepare a total analysis for the decision.

(2) Prepare an incremental analysis for the decision.

7. Relevant Unit Costs. Jessie Products sells 2,000 units of its major product each month. Manufacturing costs total $75,000 (two-thirds variable and one-third fixed). Selling and administrative expenses are $50,000 (60% variable and 40% fixed). Kelner Company would like to buy 500 units of this product at $27 per unit. If accepted, the order would not incur any selling and administrative expenses.

Required: What are the relevant unit costs for this decision?

8. Relevant Costs of Additional Processing. Black Wealth Refining produces naphtha, jet fuel, and fuel oil from a joint process costing $90,000. One thousand barrels of naphtha have been allocated $30,000 of the joint costs. They can be sold at the split-off point for $40 per barrel, or they can be further processed and sold at $65 per barrel. The processing cost for further refining 1,000 barrels of naphtha is $24,000.

Required: Determine whether the 1,000 barrels of naphtha should be sold now or after additional processing.

9. Eliminate an Operation. Treasure Shoes owns and operates several retail outlets. Management is now considering the possibility of terminating operations in one store and leasing the facilities to another retailer. The monthly results of operations are as follows:

Sales	$ 95,000
Operating expenses directly identifiable with the outlet:	
Cost of goods sold, etc.	89,000
Depreciation	8,000

Treasure Shoes can lease the facilities for $5,000 a month to a noncompeting business.

Required: Determine whether the company should continue operations or lease the facilities.

10. Least-Cost Decision. Because of a temporary economic slowdown, Palor Industries is looking for ways to reduce its administrative expenses. The personnel department has identified three feasible alternatives:

Alternative 1: Have 200 administrative personnel reduce their workweek from 40 hours to 32 hours and reduce monthly salaries by an equal proportion. This should save the company about $70,000 per month.

Alternative 2: Layoff 20% of the 200 administrative personnel. The average annual salary of each person in the 20% layoff is $20,000.

Alternative 3: Ask the 200 administrative personnel to take a 10% pay cut, which would save the company approximately $700,000 annually. The personnel department feels that either Alternative 1 or 3 would be preferred because employees would still retain their jobs. Alternative 2 creates morale problems among the employees.

Required: Which alternative results in the greatest reduction in administrative expenses, represented by salaries? Make your analysis on an annual basis.

PROBLEMS

9-1. Relevant Costs of an Automobile. Carol Bates is a sales representative in west Texas for Triple A Printing Equipment. The company has asked her to expand her territory to cover El Paso in southwest Texas. This expansion will increase Carol's mileage by 5,000 miles per year. To see whether this proposal is worthwhile to the company, Carol's supervisor asked her to estimate the additional costs expected per year.

Carol travels an average of 40,000 miles per year without expanding her sales territory. She keeps good records of her travel expenses, and her records show the following automobile expenses for 40,000 miles:

Gasoline	$ 2,400
Oil and lubrication	320
Tires (40,000 miles per set)	400
Maintenance and repairs	640
Insurance	960
Licenses and taxes	150
Depreciation based upon straightline depreciation	4,000
Total expenses	$ 8,870

Required:

(1) Indicate which of the automobile costs will change by expanding the territory to include an additional 5,000 miles per year.

(2) Prepare an analysis of differential costs between the status quo alternative and the alternative to expand the territory.

9-2. Determining Least-Cost Alternative. Ajax Construction Inc. plans to erect a new building. It will use part of the space for its own offices and lease the balance of the space to tenants. The company has two alternatives: (1) do its own construction work, or (2) use an independent contractor.

Cost estimates have been prepared showing the costs of operation for the coming year during which the new building will be constructed. The costs of constructing the building, if done by Ajax, are included in that set of estimates.

If the company does its own construction work, it will not be able to handle outside construction contracts that would contribute $500,000 to net income. The costs attributable to these outside contracts are excluded from the estimated costs of operation shown as follows:

	Estimated Costs to Operate — Construction by Independent Contractors	Estimated Costs to Operate (Including Construction) — Construction by Ajax Company
Materials	$6,000,000	$7,000,000
Labor	3,000,000	4,800,000
Indirect materials and supplies	315,000	400,000
Supervision	650,000	780,000
Taxes and insurance	50,000	55,000
Heat and light....................	47,000	47,000
Maintenance and repairs	106,000	106,000
Truck and equipment operation	91,000	91,000
Depreciation	60,000	60,000
Travel	40,000	43,000
Telephone........................	10,000	10,000
Other utilities	50,000	50,000
Miscellaneous	10,000	10,000

The independent company has bid $4,000,000 for the job.

Required: Which of the two alternatives should be selected to obtain the lowest construction cost? Show calculations. (Ignore income tax.)

9-3. Expanding Production. The president of Mount Timp Manufacturing has asked your assistance in arriving at a decision to expand production of a specialized electronics component. The company currently manufactures and sells 9,000 units per year. The market appears to have sufficient demand to absorb another 3,000 units of the company's production.

Each component currently sells for $30. Following are the total costs during this past year when 9,000 components were produced.

Direct materials	$54,000
Direct labor	45,000
Variable factory overhead	45,000
Fixed factory overhead....................................	70,000
Variable selling expense...................................	9,000
Fixed selling expense	20,000

The company maintains no inventory, since it can sell the products as fast as they come off the production line.

The president notes that costs have increased in some areas and that the selling price will be increased to $32 to help cover those cost increases. Direct materials will increase 5%; the other variable costs will increase 10%; and fixed factory overhead and fixed selling expenses will each increase by $1,000.

Production can be expanded 1,000 units (for a total of 10,000 units) without incurring any new fixed factory overhead cost. However, producing a total of 12,000 units will require new equipment that will add $34,000 to the fixed factory overhead cost, but this equipment would allow the company to expand to a total of 15,000 units without adding more equipment.

Required:

(1) What are the relevant revenues and costs that should be considered?

(2) Prepare an income statement showing the net income before taxes of selling 9,000 units, 10,000 units, and 12,000 units.

(3) What would you advise the president to do in this case?

9-4. Cost-Volume-Profit Analysis. The Gingerbread Lady has a part-time business for producing and selling gingerbread houses for Christmas. Production starts about the first week in November and runs to the beginning of December. In order to meet health codes, she rents a kitchen at a nearby preschool at a cost of $150. There she bakes and decorates the houses. The maximum number of houses she can do in the time allotted is 800 houses. Materials and labor costs amount to $2.50 per house. The houses are sold at various bazaars throughout the community. This has allowed her to charge what she felt the market would bear at each bazaar.

There are four bazaars this year, varying in length from one day to three days. Each bazaar, expressed as an alternative, is shown below with the anticipated selling price and its specific costs.

Alternative A: A private country club with an elite membership sponsors this two-day bazaar. It charges a flat fee of $25 per day for each seller. The Gingerbread Lady feels a selling price of $6.50 per house is appropriate. From past experience, she knows she can sell 150 houses with follow-up orders of 100 houses.

Alternative B: A one-day neighborhood bazaar in the lower-middle income part of the city. She can charge $5.75 per house and must pay a flat fee of $15 per day. She can sell, at most, 200 houses.

Alternative C: This two-day bazaar is held in a community center in another lower-middle income section of the city. Here the price is a bit lower at $5.25. The center charges $10 per day for each seller participating in the bazaar. Based on last year's records, the Gingerbread Lady can sell 300 houses in two days.

Alternative D: The local university sponsors a three-day bazaar and charges each seller 10% of the gross revenue from sales as a fee. Because of the student population, the Gingerbread Lady will only charge $4.70 per house. She can sell, at most, 500 houses during the three days.

For some reason, all of the bazaars this year are being held during the same week, thus forcing the Gingerbread Lady to choose which bazaar she will attend. She has already determined it is not worthwhile to do a bazaar unless she can make a minimum profit of $1 per house.

Required:

(1) Prepare an analysis showing which bazaar the Gingerbread Lady should attend this year.

(2) If the Gingerbread Lady could hire someone to handle a bazaar for her, what is the maximum amount she could pay and be no worse off than doing the one bazaar by herself?

9-5. Alternative Uses of Idle Capacity. Barrera Equipment Manufacturing built a new facility in 1980 but has only been able to use 60% of the capacity in manufacturing its major machine products. Management would like to use the excess capacity and has three possibilities. Only one of the three may be selected.

(a) The company could produce an additional 6,000 units per year of its most popular machine and develop a foreign market. Management estimates that additional freight costs would amount to $200 per machine and fixed factory overhead would increase by $60,000. To cover the additional cost, the selling price per machine would be increased by $300 per machine.

(b) The company could produce and market a new laser lathe. The capacity could be used to produce 2,000 units per year that would sell for $1,800 each. Management has estimated the following unit variable costs:

Direct materials	$ 600
Direct labor	300
Variable overhead	450
Variable selling	50
	$1,400

The new lathe would require additional fixed costs: $200,000 in fixed overhead and $80,000 in fixed selling.

(c) The Paco-Pole Company has offered to lease the facilities at $30,000 per month plus 10% of the net revenues generated by the facilities. Net revenues are estimated at $1,500,000 per year.

Required:

(1) Which of the three alternatives should management select?

(2) What is the opportunity cost of the decision?

9-6. Relevant Costs of an Inventory Decision. Recker Corporation manufactures a major component for an avionics subsystem used in commercial aircraft. With a slowdown in commercial airplane production, Recker Corporation has a number of units in inventory. On a first-in, first out (fifo) basis, the inventory is valued at $100,000. At last-in, first-our (lifo), it carries a cost of $70,000.

The federal government is willing to purchase the items for use in military airplanes but requires Recker Corporation to make some modifications at a cost of $40,000. Shipping costs will total $5,000. The government will pay $75,000 for the components.

Management of Recker Corporation also sees an option in scrapping the components for $20,000. Transportation cost and other costs to dispose will amount to $2,500. Additionally, the company could hold the items in inventory for 12 months when the market will improve. The carrying cost for the inventory is 15% of the inventory cost per year. If the market returns, management estimates revenues of $120,000.

Required:

(1) Explain the role of the inventory values under fifo and lifo in this decision situation.

(2) Which of the several alternatives should Recker Corporation select?

(3) Prepare an income statement for each of the alternatives. Use fifo costs for the inventory.

9-7. Expansion and Elimination of a Division Decision. AGRI Corporation is a corporate farmer with operations in the Pacific Northwest, Iowa, and Texas. Due to weather conditions and a downturn in the market, the Texas operations have produced marginal results for several years. Management has decided to sell its operations in Texas. However, the company must still meet current contractual commitments to provide certain commodities to processors.

Management has provided the following projection of operations for the upcoming year (000 omitted):

	Total	Northwest	Iowa	Texas
Sales	$6,600	$3,300	$2,100	$1,200
Variable cost	$ 570	$ 310	$ 220	$ 40
Fixed costs:				
Operations	2,170	995	635	540
Administrative	1,650	840	420	390
Home office—allocated	750	375	240	135
	$5,140	$2,520	$1,515	$1,105
Net income	$1,460	$ 780	$ 585	$ 95

Management believes it has three alternatives to evaluate. First, close operations and sell the assets, realizing an after-tax gain on the sale of $125,000. Second, enter into an agreement with a competitor to fill the contractual commitments. Under this agreement, AGRI Corporation would receive 15% of the net sales from these commitments, and net sales are estimated at $800,000. The third option is to expand in Iowa by using space presently idle. The move would result in several changes in Iowa as follows:

	Increase over Current Operations
Total sales	40%
Total variable cost	50%
Fixed operations cost	40%
Fixed administrative cost	20%
New transportation cost	$24,000

Under all of the alternatives, the home office expenses will remain the same in total. If the Texas operations are eliminated, the home office expenses will be allocated only to the Northwest and Iowa operations.

Required: Should AGRI Corporation close its Texas operations? If so, how should it satisfy its contractual commitments?

9-8. Crude Oil Exchange. West Tex Exploration has a contract to supply 2,000 barrels of crude oil at $30 per barrel to a refinery in New Mexico. To do so, the company must incur transportation costs averaging $6 per barrel. Management would like to see if another company, closer to the refinery, would agree to exchange crude oils with no cash changing hands.

Taos E & P Company produces a similar quality crude oil that it sells under contract to a small refinery in southern Colorado at $29 per barrel, with transportation costs running about $3 per barrel. However, if it diverts 2,000 barrels to New Mexico, Taos cannot meet its contract.

Panhandle Oil Exploration has a crude oil acceptable to the Colorado refinery, but that refinery will only pay $28 per barrel if Panhandle is an alternate supplier. The transportation cost would run about $1 per barrel. Panhandle has commitments to sell its crude oil to two refineries in Amarillo, Texas, at $27 per barrel and transportation cost of $.50 per barrel.

The management of West Tex feels it could work out a three-way exchange agreement with the other two companies. West Tex would ship its crude oil to Amarillo at $2 per barrel in transportation costs; Panhandle would ship crude oil to Colorado; and Taos would ship its crude to the New Mexico refinery. In each case, the company delivering the crude oil would receive the revenue from the refinery it delivered to.

Required:
   (1) Would the three-way exchange benefit all three companies?
   (2) If any company would not benefit, how much would West Tex need to pay to make that company no worse off than before the exchange?

9-9. **Relevant Costs of Expanding Sales.** John Prindle is a salesman with the Ramirez Company in its Kansas City office. The district manager has given John a management objective of increasing dollar sales by 20% during the coming year. Since Prindle's pay depends on the net income computed for his sales rather than the gross margin of his sales, he is concerned about generating profitable sales. Last year's records show Prindle with the following net income:

Net sales	$500,000
Cost of sales	400,000
Gross margin	$100,000
Prindle's direct selling cost	$ 50,000
Prindle's share of administrative cost, based on percent of sales	25,000
	$ 75,000
Net income before income tax	$ 25,000

One means of increasing sales is to travel more and entertain more lavishly to improve relations with the more difficult customers (stiff competition). Because Prindle would have to offer some discounts, his gross margin percentage would drop 1% of sales, but the administrative cost percentage will remain the same. Direct selling cost would increase to 12% of sales.

Another approach is to court the smaller accounts and to extend more liberal credit terms in order to penetrate deeper into the available market. This approach would retain the gross margin percentage, the direct selling cost percentage, and the administrative cost percentage. The smaller accounts will require an extra clerk to handle volume at a cost of $12,000 and extra shipping cost of $5,000. In addition, accounts receivable will increase $25,000, which increases interest costs for the year by $3,000.

Required: Which of the two approaches, if either one is appropriate, should Prindle employ during the coming year to increase sales by 20%?

9-10. **Profitability of Second Shift.** Sewell Manufacturing operates one plant in Missoula, Montana, for the production of a special wooden molding used in typewriter desktops. The company operates one shift and produces 150,000 units annually that sell for $12 each to specialty producers. The product has a derived demand sufficient to warrant considering the doubling of production. Information on current production is as follows:

Direct material cost	$6.25 per unit
Direct labor cost at 50,000 hours	$6.00 per unit
Other variable production and selling costs	$101,250
Fixed production and selling costs	$385,750

In order to increase sales to 300,000 units per year, the company would go to a second shift. Direct materials cost would remain the same per unit. Because labor efficiency is expected to be higher than on existing production, it is estimated that only 42,000 direct labor hours will be needed on the second shift. The labor rate, including shift premium, would average $7.50 per hour. Other variable production and selling costs will remain at $2.025 per direct labor hour. There will be additional fixed cost of $100,000 per year.

Required:

(1) Is there an incremental profit from the second shift?

(2) What profit will be earned by the factory as a whole if the second shift is implemented?

9-11. Make or Buy. The vice-president of production at Bracey Products Inc., Paul Cotter, complains that the quality of a certain important component used in manufacturing one of the product lines is poor. He states that this material costs $24 per unit but that 20% of the materials are broken in the production process. This part was once made of good metal, but it is now made of a cheap metal reinforced with plastic. As a result, it snaps apart easily. A search for other suppliers has not been helpful. All suppliers state that the parts aren't made in the old way—too costly.

Ann Gregory, the controller, states that there is idle capacity and suggests that the company can make its own parts at a better quality level. Gregory believes that the suppliers are unwilling to reduce their profits and are cheapening their product lines instead of absorbing higher materials costs.

The company needs 50,000 units of these parts each year and, with quality materials, would have few if any defective parts. A study reveals that Bracey Products would incur the following additional costs if 50,000 units of this part were made:

Direct materials (high quality)	$950,000
Direct labor (15,000 labor hours)	150,000
Variable overhead (15,000 labor hours)	75,000

Paul Cotter is not convinced that the components can be made at a lower cost than the cost to purchase them. Cotter believes that the cost of quality materials is too high. Furthermore, the plant has substantial fixed overhead that must be absorbed at a rate of $5 per direct labor hour. In Cotter's opinion, any existing capacity that is available should be put to better use.

Required:

(1) Based upon the data given, should the components be purchased or made? Show computations.

(2) Evaluate the argument of Paul Cotter. Does he make a valid point?

(3) If there were a slight economic advantage in buying the component, can you see any reason to reject the purchase option and make the part?

9-12. Extension of Manufacturing Operation. Little Folks Inc. manufactures the components used in the production of swing sets, sand boxes, play pens, etc. These components are not painted or processed further. Instead, they are sold to other manufacturers for completion or are sold to distributors for sale as unfinished items requiring further work.

The play pen components, for example, are sold to other manufacturers or to stores for $32 per set. Approximately 40,000 of these sets are sold each year.

The president of the company, Marge Richardson, believes that the company can do the finishing work and can then sell the completed play pens to distributors at a price of $48 per unit.

The controller of the company has provided the following cost data for use in analysis.

Cost to manufacture unfinished play pens (40,000 units):

Direct materials	$ 320,000
Direct labor	480,000
Manufacturing overhead applied at the rate of $4 per direct labor hour	160,000
Total production cost	$ 960,000

Estimated cost to finish 40,000 units:

Additional direct materials	$ 40,000
Additional direct labor cost	240,000
Additional variable overhead	20,000
Annual salary of supervisor hired for finishing operation	30,000
Other additional fixed costs	60,000
Total additional cost	$ 390,000

Required:

(1) Using the data given, compute the economic advantage or disadvantage of the finishing operation.

(2) Identify the costs that are sunk costs with respect to this decision, that is, irrelevant in making the decision.

(3) Identify the opportunity cost in a decision to finish.

(4) If the market declines so that only 20,000 finished units can be sold each year, compute the advantage or disadvantage in the finishing operation.

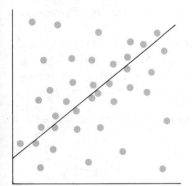

10

ACCOUNTING DATA FOR MANAGERIAL DECISIONS–II

Chapter Objectives

This chapter, will enable you to:

1. Explain the nature of combination decisions.
2. Decide upon the appropriate course of action for decisions of process or sell, make or buy, and elimination of a product line.
3. Evaluate alternatives for a two-product combination decision when there are no constraints, one constraint, and several constraints.
4. Discuss the fixed cost problem as it exists in full cost based pricing.
5. Evaluate variable cost pricing opportunities for special-order decisions and regular product pricing.

The preceding chapter discussed some important ideas and concepts which are fundamental to managerial accounting analyses in support of management decisions. It was pointed out that the emphasis was on measuring the relevant costs and revenues, and that this involved predicting the differential costs and revenues. The focus is on identifying future cash flows, which in turn will lead to future increases in profitability for the firm.

In predicting future differential costs, it was found that the cost concepts of variable versus fixed cost, avoidable versus unavoidable cost, and opportunity cost are all useful. This chapter will discuss several different decision situations which develop more completely the underlying concepts and demonstrate the use of the variable cost concepts in identifying the relevant, differential costs.

The chapter is organized into two major sections. The first section discusses what is called combination decisions. For example, such decisions involve finding the most profitable combination of products to produce and sell or the most profitable combination of departments and product lines for a department store. Firms can also face combinations on the production side. For example, what is the least-cost method of production? How should production factors be combined? This problem is illustrated by the make or buy decision.

The second section of the chapter is devoted to a discussion of the pricing decision. What role does cost play in pricing? What accounting concepts and procedures are available to help the manager set a price for the products? As in the preceding chapter, the complexities associated with capital investment and income tax considerations are not discussed. These complexities are the subject matter of Chapters 11 and 12.

COMBINATION DECISIONS

Management is constantly faced with decisions involving the best use of available facilities and how to combine productive resources to minimize cost. Combination decisions, several examples of which follow, have received a great deal of attention recently because of the increased availability of computers that can be used to solve complex decision problems having many variables.

Process or Sell

This is an example of the opportunity cost concept applied to a combination decision. Assume that a certain intermediate product can be produced and sold or can be processed further and sold as a completely processed product. In deciding which course of action to follow, the company compares the contribution margin from the sale of the partially processed product with the contribution margin from the sale of the completely processed product. The revenue to be derived from the sale of the partially processed product is the opportunity cost attached to the decision of further processing.

Assume, for example, that a partially processed product selling for $9 per unit is manufactured at a cost of $6. Further processing at a variable cost of $3 a unit will yield a product that can be sold at a unit price of $15. The firm can produce 10,000 units. The analysis is as follows:

Decision Analysis

Revenue from sale of final product (10,000 units @ $15)......		$150,000
Less:		
Additional processing cost (10,000 units @ $3)	$30,000	
Revenue from sale of intermediate product (10,000 units @ $9)...	90,000	120,000
Net advantage in further processing		$ 30,000

There is a net advantage of $30,000 in further processing the product. Note that the market value of the partially processed product is considered to be the opportunity cost of further processing, and that the partial processing cost of $6 is not included in the analysis because it is incurred under either alternative. Assuming that the company continues its processing operation and realizes profit as planned, the revenue and the cost will be accounted for in the usual manner:

Accountability

Revenue from sale of final product.........................		$150,000
Less:		
Additional processing cost	$30,000	
Cost to process intermediate product....................	60,000	90,000
Profit..		$ 60,000

Product Combinations

The product combination decision arises when several product lines are manufactured and sold. A decision must be reached as to which product combination is most profitable. Oil refineries, for example, plan refinery production to meet the varying needs of the market. During certain months, larger quantities of heating oils are produced, while in other months larger quantities of gasoline are produced. In other industries, similar problems are encountered that involve a selection of the best combination of productive factors to meet the limitations that are imposed by internal or external conditions. An increase in the production and sale of one product line often means that the production and sale of another line has to be curtailed. There is only so much that can be done with a given set of productive factors. The product lines should be manufactured and sold in the most profitable combination.

Two Products, No Constraints

Assume that a firm produces two products, A and B, whose costs and selling prices are as follows:

	Product A	Product B
Selling price per unit	$10	$8
Variable cost per unit	5	6
Contribution margin per unit	$ 5	$2
Fixed cost per year	$50,000	

One of the decisions faced by management is what combination of Products A and B should be produced. The decision rule to be followed is to choose the combination of products that maximizes contribution margin. If fixed cost remains unaffected, net income will also be maximized. The decision rule might be implemented by choosing the product that has the highest contribution margin per unit. If there are no constraints with respect to either production capacity or sales capacity, this method could give the desired result. However, this is a very unlikely situation. In most cases, the firm has a given plant facility; and it may not be possible to shift all production from Product B to Product A. Also, it is not unusual to find various market constraints that arise because the market will absorb only a limited number of units of a particular product. In these cases, the break-even or cost-volume-profit information given above is useful but insufficient to arrive at a product-combination decision. In addition, management must have information on the amount of scarce resources used up in producing each product.

Two Products, One Constraint

Assume that the market for each product is unlimited and that the firm can therefore sell all units that it produces. However, assume that the production facilities are limited to 200,000 labor hours. In this case the scarce production factor or limiting factor is the firm's labor force. Further assume that the labor requirement for each product is as follows:

	Product A	Product B
Labor hours required	10 hours	2 hours

Given the production constraint of 200,000 hours, it is possible to produce 20,000 units of Product A (200,000 hours ÷ 10 hours) or 100,000 units of Product B (200,000 hours ÷ 2 hours). Note that the firm can produce Products A and B in any combination by giving up five units of Product B for one unit of Product A.

Given this constraint, the firm should produce all Product B because it provides the greatest contribution margin per limiting factor. The alternatives are summarized as follows:

Statements of Profit

	If All A Is Produced	If All B Is Produced
Sales: (20,000 units @ $10	$200,000	
(100,000 units @ $8)		$800,000
Variable cost: (20,000 units @ $5)	100,000	
(100,000 units @ $6).................		600,000
Contribution margin	$100,000	$200,000
Fixed cost	50,000	50,000
Profit..	$ 50,000	$150,000

As can be seen, with one production constraint and two products, the solution to the product-combination problem is fairly simple. An alternate solution is to calculate a contribution margin per hour of production time and to choose the product with the highest rate. The calculation is as follows:

	Product A	Product B
Selling price	$10	$8
Variable cost	5	6
Contribution margin	$5	$2
Hour requirement	10 hours	2 hours
Contribution margin per hour	$5 ÷ 10 hrs. = $.50 per hr.	$2 ÷ 2 hrs. = $1 per hr.

Since Product B returns $1 per hour in contrast with 50 cents per hour for Product A, Product B is the preferred product. As a matter of fact, the firm will continue to be a one-product firm producing all B and no A as long as there is no market limitation on Product B. It is the market limitation which creates a product combination. If the firm can sell its most profitable product (in this case, Product B) in an unlimited market, there is no reason to produce any of Product A. However, as will be shown later, some of Product A will be produced if the market for Product B is limited to fewer units than can be produced.

This example forms the basis for a linear programming problem. The firm is maximizing contribution margin subject to a single production constraint. The solution is simple since there are only two products and one constraint. In such a simple case, the concept of a rate of return per the scarce factor is a useful and effective concept. However, as the number of products and the number of constraints increase, linear programming becomes necessary for the more complex cases.

Two Products, Many Constraints

In the previous example, it was assumed that there were no market constraints. Assume that market conditions are of such a nature that only 80,000 units of Product B can be sold but that the market for Product A is unlimited. It would be possible to solve the problem by trial and error, but a more systematic solution and one that will generalize for the many-constraints case is a graphic linear programming solution.

The previous example, involving only one production constraint, the limitation of production facilities to 200,000 labor hours, has been plotted on the graph shown at the top of page 297.

The production constraint can be given by the line $10A + 2B = 200,000$. The set of possible solutions is given by the area $0, A_1, B_1$; that is, only 200,000 hours are available, so all possible solutions must use some number of hours less than or equal to 200,000. In symbols:

$$(1) \quad 10A + 2B \leq 200,000$$

This inequality states in symbol form the production constraint. If only Product B is produced, 100,000 units are possible; and if only Product A is produced, 20,000 units are possible. Other combinations that use all of the

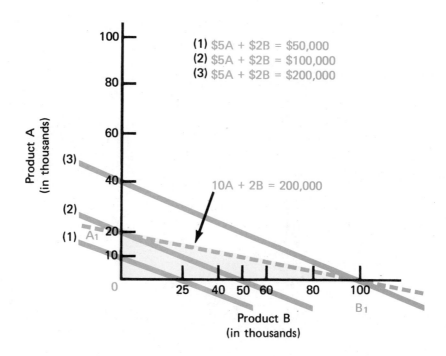

capacity (for example, 10,000 A and 50,000 B) fall on the line $10A + 2B = 200,000$. The other possible solutions fall somewhere in the area 0, A_1, B_1, but these solutions do not use 100 percent of the hour capacity. These solutions are feasible or possible but not optimal. An optimal solution is somewhere on the boundary of the area 0, A_1, B_1.

The problem is to maximize contribution margin subject to a single production constraint. In equation form:

(2) CM = $5A + $2B, where CM = contribution margin

That is, for every unit of Product A that is sold, CM increases by $5, and for every unit of Product B, CM increases by $2. In the diagram on this page, three lines have been plotted showing contribution margins at three different levels, $50,000, $100,000, and $200,000. These lines are "equal contribution" lines in that they show different combinations of Products A and B that give the same contribution margin. Since the objective is to maximize contribution margin, the CM lines should be moved upward and to the right until the CM line is at the boundary given by the production constraint equation. This occurs at the point A = 0 and B = 100,000. Higher levels of contribution margin are not feasible because of the hour constraint. This solution agrees with the one given earlier in the chapter.

The same example with the addition of the market constraint that only 80,000 units of product B can be sold has been plotted on the diagram as follows:

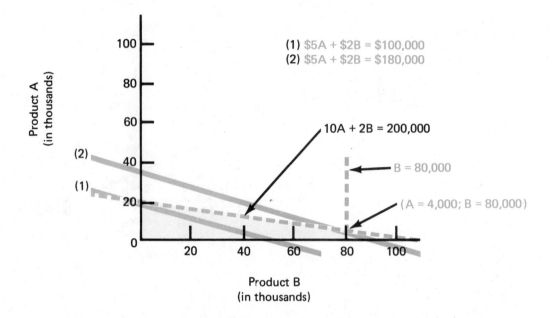

In this diagram, the previous production constraint of 200,000 labor hours has been plotted. In addition, the line $B = 80,000$ establishes the constraint that the market will absorb a maximum of only 80,000 units of Product B. In inequality form, this constraint is:

$$(2) \quad B \leq 80,000$$

The set of possible or feasible solutions is therefore given by the shaded area. The objective function or contribution margin equation can be moved upward and to the right until the point $A = 4,000$, $B = 80,000$ is reached. At this point, the contribution margin is maximized at $180,000.

As can be seen in the graphic linear programming solution, the various production and marketing constraints can be plotted and, taken together, define the set of possible or feasible solutions. The objective function or contribution margin line is then determined, and a solution giving the maximum contribution margin can be found by moving the contribution margin line to higher and higher levels until the boundary formed by the constraint equations is reached. Note that this graphic technique handles almost any number of constraints but only two products. If many products are involved, the graph becomes multidimensional and impossible to work with.

Computer methods of solving linear programming problems are readily available. Solution routines for more complex problems are beyond the scope of this text but are dealt with at length in most texts on mathematical programming. For our purposes, it is sufficient to point out that the concepts discussed are directly relevant to more complex problems; what is needed (and supplied through computer methods) is a more powerful solution technique than the graphic method.

Make or Buy

Another important type of combination decision is whether to make or buy component parts. For example, assume that a company can make a part that it has been purchasing at a unit cost of $3. The company can buy materials at a cost of $1.25 per part, direct labor cost has been estimated at 80 cents for each part, and variable factory overhead has been estimated at 50 cents for each part. The company has been operating at 75 percent of normal capacity, and in the foreseeable future no use for the excess capacity is contemplated except for the possible production of the part. Production of this part will enable the company to operate at its normal capacity and will provide all parts needed for subsequent manufacturing operations. Fixed factory overhead cost amounts to $170,000 a year, whether the plant operates at 75 or 100 percent of capacity.

The incremental cost to manufacture 50,000 units of the needed part and the make or buy decision are determined as follows:

	Unit Cost	Total Cost
Direct materials	$1.25	$ 62,500
Direct labor	.80	40,000
Variable factory overhead	.50	25,000
Total incremental cost	$2.55	$127,500
Cost to purchase part	3.00	150,000
Net advantage in parts production	$ .45	$ 22,500

If there is no better alternative for the use of the idle facilities, the part should be manufactured and not purchased.

Note that an incorrect decision would have been made if a ratable portion of the fixed overhead cost had been included in the cost to manufacture the 50,000 parts. The allocated fixed cost would have been $42,500 (25% of $170,000) or $.85 per unit, resulting in a total unit cost of $3.40 ($2.55 + $.85). This unit cost exceeds the purchase price of $3 per part and would cause the decision-maker to reject the proposal to manufacture. Total fixed overhead cost is obviously not affected by the production of the 50,000 parts, thus the preceding analysis is incorrect. Only the costs that are increased or decreased as a result of making the part are relevant to the decision.

The Elimination of a Product Line

Choosing the proper combination of products may also involve the elimination of a product line. The income statement for Harris Department Store has been prepared for a typical year, and the data have been rearranged to show which product lines should be retained or discontinued:

Harris Department Store
Income Statement
Average Year

	Product Line				
	1	2	3	4	Total
Net sales..................................	$86,200	$93,700	$81,200	$87,400	$348,500
Direct costs:					
Variable costs:					
Cost of goods sold....................	$51,800	$55,100	$68,700	$57,900	$233,500
Supplies..............................	3,300	2,800	3,900	3,800	13,800
Transportation	1,100	1,400	1,900	2,100	6,500
Total variable cost	$56,200	$59,300	$74,500	$63,800	$253,800
Contribution margin	$30,000	$34,400	$ 6,700	$23,600	$ 94,700
Fixed costs for the product line:					
Salaries	$ 6,000	$11,000	$10,000	$ 8,000	$ 35,000
Advertising	3,000	4,500	4,500	4,200	16,200
Total fixed cost for product line	$ 9,000	$15,500	$14,500	$12,200	$ 51,200
Margin over direct costs...................	$21,000	$18,900	$(7,800)	$11,400	$ 43,500
Fixed costs of the total operation:					
Salaries					$ 16,000
Rent					5,000
Taxes					2,700
Insurance............................					1,600
Heat and light					1,700
Total fixed cost of operation					$ 27,000
Income before income tax..................					$ 16,500

The variable cost identified with each product line and the fixed costs that are specifically incurred for each product line are subtracted from sales to determine whether or not the product line can cover its own costs. Note that the analysis in this case does not depend entirely upon the variable costs. It is not a question of profit planning by planning selling prices, variable costs, or sales volume. Instead, the problem is extended further. The sales volume, the unit selling price, and the variable cost per unit are assumed. The direct costs include the variable costs and the fixed costs that are incurred for each particular product line. These costs are the avoidable costs. They can be avoided if a product line is discontinued. The fixed costs for the total store should not be allocated. They are the unavoidable costs, the costs that are incurred in any event.

Product 3 should be eliminated, unless it can be proved that the line helps to increase the sales of the profitable lines. It cannot cover its own costs. Without Product 3, the income before income tax would amount to $24,300:

Profit Effect of Elimination of Product 3

Costs avoided by the elimination of Product 3:		
Variable cost..	$74,500	
Fixed cost for the product line which can be eliminated	14,500	
Total cost eliminated		$89,000
Less revenue contributed by Product 3............................		81,200
Net advantage of elimination of Product 3		$ 7,800
Income before income tax, including Product 3		16,500
Income before income tax, without Product 3.......................		$24,300

In this example, certain costs were identified with the product lines; but it cannot be assumed that these particular costs are avoidable or unavoidable in all cases. Each situation should be evaluated on its own. The important point is that a distinction should be made between the costs that can be avoided and the costs that cannot be avoided by the decision. In this example, if the $14,500 fixed cost cannot be eliminated with Product 3, then Product 3 should be retained.

THE PRICING DECISION

One of the most difficult decisions faced by the manager is the pricing decision. In some situations, there is no pricing decision. For example, a prevailing market condition may be such that a higher price is not acceptable and there may be no incentive for charging a lower price. For example, the major decision with agricultural products is determining what quantity to produce. However, in situations where the decision-maker does have some control over the price to be charged, there is a need for information on the demand for the product. The cost side of the pricing decision is emphasized in this discussion; demand is considered, but there is no systematic discussion of the determination of product demand at various prices.

Price Based on Full Cost

The markup pricing method is widely used in business. To arrive at the price, a cost per unit is computed and then a markup, stated as a percentage of cost, is added. The purpose of the markup is to provide for a profit. The term "cost" as used in this method is ambiguous until carefully defined. Two definitions are possible: (1) variable cost, or, (2) full cost. Full cost pricing will be discussed first.

The most widely used form of markup pricing is to base the markup on full cost; that is, the full cost of the unit is considered to be made up of the variable cost plus some allocated share of the fixed cost. The full cost is then used as the basis for setting price, usually by adding a percentage markup.

The Fixed Cost Problem

The proper treatment of fixed cost presents a problem in full cost pricing. Assume that a firm produces only one product and that the cost structure is as follows:

Variable materials cost	$5
Variable direct labor cost..	3
Total variable cost	$8
Fixed annual overhead and other expenses......................	$100,000

In order to determine the full cost of a unit, it is necessary to select a specific number of units over which to allocate the fixed cost. The relationship between unit fixed cost and volume is plotted as follows:

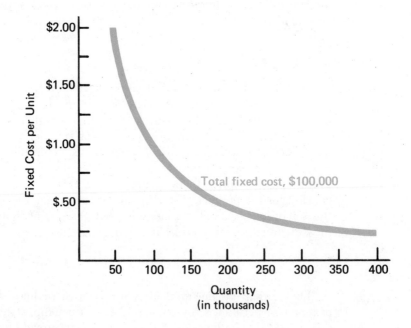

As can be seen, the fixed cost per unit decreases as the number of units increases. In an earlier discussion of job order and process cost accounting, it was indicated that the number of units at normal volume is typically used as a basis for allocating the fixed cost. If the firm has a price policy of marking up

10 percent based on full cost, the prices shown in the following table are possible, depending on the decision as to volume.

	Number of Units (In Thousands)					
	50	*100*	*150*	*200*	*250*	*300*
Variable cost.......................	$ 8.00	$8.00	$8.00	$8.00	$8.00	$8.00
Fixed cost per unit	2.00	1.00	.67	.50	.40	.33
Total full cost	$10.00	$9.00	$8.67	$8.50	$8.40	$8.33
10% markup	1.00	.90	.87	.85	.84	.83
Selling price	$11.00	$9.90	$9.54	$9.35	$9.24	$9.16

If 200,000 units are selected as the number of units over which to spread the fixed cost, the profit (markup) per unit is stated to be 85 cents. However, the profit will not be 85 cents per unit and it will not be $170,000 for the year (200,000 units × 85 cents) if some number of units other than 200,000 units is actually sold. For example, if only 100,000 units are sold, the profit will be only $35,000, as follows:

Revenue (100,000 units × $9.35)..........................		$935,000
Variable cost (100,000 units × $8)	$800,000	
Fixed cost	100,000	900,000
Profit...		$ 35,000

The difference in the profit per unit between 85 cents and 35 cents ($35,000 ÷ 100,000 units) is due to the fact that the fixed cost per unit based on 100,000 units is $1 and not 50 cents as stated for 200,000 units.

It may be argued that the demand situation can be considered in choosing the number of units over which to spread the fixed cost. Although a possibility, such a policy may be in conflict with the selection of normal volume as it is used in job order and process cost accounting. Note that normal volume and expected volume for next year are not necessarily the same. Normal volume is usually considered an average volume based on several years. If normal volume is used, the result should be a very stable price almost without regard for changes in the business cycle. Perhaps this is desirable, but there is less chance that the price will be adapted to changes in business conditions.

Another difficulty with trying to use either expected volume or normal volume for spreading fixed cost is that the number of units to be sold depends on the price, and it is the price that is being determined. Hence, any attempt to consider the demand situation in establishing the full cost of the product is likely to involve circular reasoning. The demand situation must be considered in setting the price, but the fact remains that full cost pricing does not offer a good means for considering this variable. In any particular situation, however, it may be that no other pricing method gives any better result than full cost pricing. It is usually easier to criticize a pricing method than to recommend a better one.

The Allocation Problem

When two or more products are produced, the problem of how to allocate the common cost is encountered in full cost pricing. Although the allocation problem has been discussed in previous chapters, it is reviewed here with respect to full cost pricing. The earlier discussions were primarily concerned with the cost allocation problem as it affects cost accounting systems where the data are used primarily for inventory valuation and income determination. However, the problem is much the same as that encountered in pricing. The reason for this is that the full cost data developed in cost accounting are generally the same data used in full cost pricing. At the very least, the cost accounting data provide a starting point in calculating a full cost figure for pricing purposes.

Assume that the firm produces two products, A and B, and that the cost structure is as follows:

	Product A	Product B
Variable labor cost.....................................	$7	$3
Variable materials cost	2	3
Overhead and other indirect annual expenses	$200,000	

The $200,000 common cost consists of several different individual types of costs such as machine depreciation, indirect labor, insurance, and various selling and administrative expenses. In allocating these costs to the two products, the first step should be to separate and regroup those costs that are fairly homogeneous. For example, all indirect costs related to machine operations, such as machine depreciation and repairs, should be totaled. However, even after this type of regrouping, the individual cost items in any particular group are still not entirely homogeneous and hence any method of allocation chosen is likely to be a compromise and open to criticism. Assume, for example, that the $200,000 indirect cost in the example is the cost incurred to operate the factory manager's office. Should this cost be allocated on the basis of direct labor hours, direct labor cost, materials cost, or some other base that might be chosen from a long list of allocation methods? The full cost and, therefore, the price are affected by the allocation base chosen. For simplicity, assume that the volume of each product is equal. If labor cost is chosen, $140,000 (7/10 × $200,000) of the indirect cost will be assigned to Product A; whereas if materials cost is to be the base, only $80,000 (2/5 × $200,000) will be assigned to Product A. In addition to the problem of how to allocate the indirect costs, note that the allocation process itself can involve a high clerical cost in instances where the cost and product structure is a complicated one.

The Basis of Allocation

In choosing the basis of allocation for inventory costing and income determination, it is possible to use the criterion of "benefit" received by the product; that is, the problem of allocating overhead cost to products is essentially the same as allocating depreciation or any long-term asset cost to time periods. In general, accountants try to allocate these common costs according to the benefit received by the unit of costing (in this case the products) from the incurrence of the cost. The argument is frequently made that a machine-related overhead cost should be assigned to the product on the basis of machine time but that labor-related overhead should be assigned on the basis of labor hours. The justification is that the basis of allocation chosen in this manner provides a fairly good means of allocating cost according to the benefit received by the various products. A product that uses more labor hours bears a greater portion of the labor-related overhead, while a product that uses more machine time bears a greater portion of the machine-related overhead.

The question arises, however, as to whether or not the benefit criterion provides a good basis of allocation if the cost data are to be used in setting prices. This is not an easy question to answer. It is sometimes argued that full cost pricing should give a fair price that assures the firm of social approval of the pricing scheme. If this argument is valid, perhaps the allocation of common costs according to the benefit criterion is an acceptable basis for determining full cost and thus price. It would seem that the manager could publicly defend such a price, if required. However, in seeking a price that provides the greatest positive difference between revenue and cost, it is difficult to see how the dual problems of cost allocation and choosing the volume over which to spread the fixed cost can be satisfactorily solved.

Variable Cost Pricing

Another approach to cost-plus-a-markup pricing is to use the variable cost rather than the full cost as the cost base. One major advantage of this approach is that some of the difficult problems of indirect cost allocation and the spreading of fixed cost can be avoided. In order to exploit the advantages of the variable cost approach, however, it is necessary to have a reasonably accurate estimate of product demand. If such an estimate is available and if the variable cost approach is used, it may be possible to arrive at a price that approaches a maximum profit position. At the very least, such a procedure may consider more of the pertinent factors of a price decision than does the full cost approach.

Distress and Special-Order Pricing

The argument has frequently been made that variable cost pricing should be used only in pricing a special order at a special price or in a distress situation. For example, assume that a firm has excess capacity and has the opportunity to sell additional units of product in a foreign market or in an isolated sector of a domestic market. Any price above the variable cost of these additional units yields a contribution to fixed cost and hence increases total profit.

The special-order or dumping situation can be illustrated as follows. Assume that the company, whose capacity is 100,000 units, is currently producing and selling only 90,000 units of product each year in the regular market at a price of $1 per unit. If the variable cost per unit is 50 cents and the annual fixed cost is $30,000, the profit calculation is as follows:

Sales (90,000 units @ $1)		$90,000
Cost: Variable cost (90,000 units @ 50¢)	$45,000	
Fixed cost	30,000	75,000
Profit		$15,000

The full cost of the units is 83.3 cents each ($75,000 ÷ 90,000 units). A foreign buyer approaches the company with an order for 10,000 units at 60 cents each. If sales in the foreign market will not affect the regular market, the company can add to total profit by accepting the special order even though the price is 23.3 cents below the full cost (83.3 cents − 60 cents). At a price of 60 cents, the order will contribute 10 cents per unit toward fixed cost, and profit will increase by $1,000 (10,000 units × 10 cents). In such a case, the variable cost of 50 cents may provide a better guide to action than the full cost. This same result can be seen through the comparative profit calculations shown in the following:

	Profit Calculation Based On 90,000 Units	Profit Calculation Based On 100,000 Units
Sales: (90,000 units @ $1)	$90,000	$90,000
(10,000 units @ 60¢)		6,000
	$90,000	$96,000
Cost:		
Variable cost @ 50¢ per unit	$45,000	$50,000
Fixed cost	30,000	30,000
	$75,000	$80,000
Profit	$15,000	$16,000

This example illustrates why some firms make price concessions in periods of excess capacity. However, the policy of accepting special orders at special prices is generally a good policy only when the special market can be kept separate from the regular market, and this is a marketing, not a cost, problem. For example, in the preceding illustration, assume that the foreign (special) market begins to affect the domestic market to the extent that the price in the domestic market drops from $1 per unit to 60 cents per unit. In this case, the firm's profit calculation for the next period would appear as follows:

Sales (100,000 units @ 60¢)		$60,000
Cost: Variable cost (100,000 units @ 50¢)	$50,000	
Fixed cost.....................................	30,000	80,000
Loss		$(20,000)

As can be seen, if the special market price takes over the domestic market, the profit decreases from $15,000 to a loss of $20,000 rather than increasing to $16,000. If the line of demarcation between the foreign and the domestic market cannot be maintained, then the lower price is bound to dominate; and the special order pricing policy would be a poor policy for the firm to follow. This type of example has served as a criticism of the use of variable costing as a basis for establishing prices. Of course, any pricing policy can lead to poor results if the decision maker fails to properly assess the market considerations. The problem lies not in the fact that variable costing instead of full cost was used, but that the market conditions were not properly assessed.

Sometimes variable cost pricing is felt to be more appropriate when sales are beyond the break-even point than when sales are below the break-even point. For example, assume, as in the previous illustration, that the selling price of the product is $1 per unit, the variable cost is 50 cents, the fixed cost is $30,000, and the capacity is 100,000 units. The break-even point is 60,000 units. It might be fallaciously contended that it is appropriate to use special order or variable cost pricing only after a sales volume of 60,000 units has been reached. Special-order pricing is not wise unless there is unused capacity, because there is no reason to lower the price while operating at full capacity. Assuming excess capacity does exist, the firm is $1,000 better off by accepting 10,000 units of additional business at 60 cents per unit if current sales are 50,000 units (below the break-even point) just as it is if current sales are 90,000 units (above the break-even point). In the former case, the loss is reduced from $5,000 to $4,000, while in the latter case profit is increased from $15,000 to $16,000. Of course, if the special market price takes over the regular market, the firm suffers a decrease in profit (or an increase in loss) regardless of what current volume is in relation to the break-even point. The appropriateness of variable cost pricing depends not so much on the volume position with respect to the break-even point, but rather on whether the regular market and the special market can be kept separate.

Even if the special market can be isolated from the regular market, and even if the special order is the most profitable use of the firm's excess capacity, there is an important legal consideration to be taken into account. From a legal standpoint, the company must be careful not to violate the Robinson-Patman Act, a federal antitrust law that relates to price discrimination between customers. This law makes it essential that the firm be able to justify a discriminatory price between customers if the effect is to lessen competition. If these above-mentioned legal and economic conditions can be satisfied, then variable cost pricing is probably appropriate in a special-order or dumping situation.

Regular Products

It is possible to build a pricing procedure for regular products using variable cost as a base. It is usually argued that variable cost is not appropriate in this situation. The use of variable cost pricing is frequently associated with a crisis situation. The presumed crisis in most cases is chronic overcapacity. Such an association is unfortunate, because a careful study of variable cost pricing gives additional insights into the pricing problem. The variable cost method is not a cure-all; but although not widely accepted in business circles, it has many features that should be considered in setting prices.

If variable cost is used, the markup that is added must be large enough to cover all fixed cost and to provide for a profit. There is always danger that the variable cost may, in time, come to be looked upon as the full cost; and in such instances the results would be disastrous. This fear is probably the main reason for the low acceptance of variable cost pricing in modern-day business. The problem, however, should not arise if operating management properly understands the kind of data it is working with. The misuse of cost data that stems from a lack of understanding is a problem throughout accounting and is not unique with variable cost pricing. Education in the proper use of cost data can do much to overcome such a defect.

Another reason why variable cost pricing is not widely accepted has to do with the inability of many conventional accounting systems to measure variable cost properly. Most systems are not geared for this type of measurement, and a careful review of job order and process costing provides convincing evidence of this. The historical reason for this situation is the overwhelming influence that inventory costing and income determination have had on cost systems. Full cost has been considered the most acceptable base for income determination due to the accounting postulate that requires revenue to be recognized only when it is realized. The realization postulate implies inventory valuation at cost. The benefit principle also reinforces the valuation of inventory at full cost. In past decades, perhaps it was clerically impossible to measure both full cost and variable cost; the measurement of variable or incremental cost presented some real difficulties. However, sophisticated computers now make it possible to measure almost any incremental quantity that is of use to management; thus, variable cost pricing is now more operational.

One of the important advantages to be gained from a detailed investigation of variable cost pricing (for regular products) is a deeper knowledge of the relationship between the markup percentage and the market demand function. In pricing policy, even if cost (whether it be a full or variable cost) can be determined, it is still necessary to add the markup in order to establish a price. If the markup is too high, the price is too high and the firm may price itself out of the market. If the markup is too low, the firm charges too low a price and foregoes profit. Hence, the proper markup is related to the market situation.

Outside Influences on Price

Throughout this discussion, the general assumption was made that the company had some control over its prices and that the object was to maximize profit. Frequently a company is virtually forced to accept prices already established by its competitors or finds it necessary to adjust its prices because of the action of others. In some cases the price is not set so that short-run profit is maximized. It may be better strategy in the long run to accept more modest profit and not attract attention that may result in the entry of others into the field. Such a strategy is an attempt to maximize long-run rather than short-run profit. Additionally, social considerations, such as environmental protection and affirmative action employment policies, may take precedence over short-run profit maximization.

By making a study of its costs and the factors that influence the demand for its products, a company can establish prices more intelligently than if either of these factors is ignored. Outside forces may make it difficult to set prices that tend to result in maximum profit; but with a knowledge of its price objectives, a company should be better prepared to take advantage of changing conditions.

Terminology Review

Opportunity cost (293)
Product combination decision (294)
Decision rule (294)
Rate of return per the scarce
    factor (296)
Avoidable costs (300)

Unavoidable costs (300)
Markup pricing method (301)
Full cost (301)
Normal volume (303)
Dumping (306)

QUESTIONS FOR REVIEW

1. What is meant by the term *combination decisions*?

2. How can a manager determine whether to sell an intermediate product or to process it further and sell as a completely processed product?

3. If a company has two products and no constraints, what is the decision rule to choose the combination of products?

4. Pepper Company produces two products. Product X has a contribution margin of $15. Product Y has a contribution margin of $10. Explain why the company might be more profitable by producing Product Y, assuming it could sell all of either product it produces.

5. What requirements must be met before the linear programming method can be used?

6. What is meant by the combination decision whether to *make or buy*?

7. Why might a company decide to produce a subassembly internally at a higher cost than to buy the same subassembly from an outside supplier?

8. How can a manager determine whether or not a product line is making a contribution to the total operation?

9. Should fixed costs be considered in deciding whether a product line should be discontinued?

10. What is meant by the term *markup pricing method*?

11. In markup pricing, what elements must be covered by the markup when full costs are used? When variable costs are used?

12. The proper treatment of fixed costs presents a problem in full cost pricing. Briefly explain this statement.

13. Describe the allocation problem encountered in full cost pricing.

14. Assuming the decision maker uses an accurate measure of cost (both fixed and variable), would pricing still be a difficult problem? Explain.

15. What are the major considerations in deciding whether variable cost pricing is a good pricing procedure to use for special orders?

16. Although a special order contributed $60,000 to profits and excess capacity was available, management rejected the order. What are possible reasons for management's action?

EXERCISES

1. New Product Decision. The Elliot Company currently produces and sells 210,000 units of Product A. The product sells for $10 per unit and has a variable cost per unit of $6. The company is considering whether to introduce a new product. Product B, the new product, will have variable costs per unit of $8. Since Product B is similar to several

products now on the market which sell for slightly more than $15, the manager will set the selling price of Product B at $15.

If Product A is produced, the manager is certain that the current sales level of 210,000 units will be maintained; and this product will use all available capacity. However, the manager is uncertain about the demand for Product B.

Required: Assuming that there will be no costs incurred other than those given and that the available capacity can be used to produce either product—A or B—calculate how many units of Product B would have to be sold to equal the contribution margin that could be earned by selling Product A.

2. Product Combination Decision. Data concerning four product lines are as follows:

	Product Line			
	A	B	C	D
Selling price per unit	$30	$25	$10	$8
Variable cost per unit	25	10	5	4
Hours required for each unit..........................	5 hrs.	10 hrs.	4 hrs.	1 hr.
Market limit (units)	None	None	8,000	4,000

Total fixed cost— $100,000
Total hours available—   96,000 hours

Required:

(1) Based on these data, choose the best product combination.

(2) How would the answer change if there are no market limitations on any of the products? How much greater is the profit from this combination of products than the profit associated with the combination chosen in (1)?

3. Process or Sell Decision. The Smokie Meat Company produces a meat product which can be sold after slaughtering without additional processing, or it can be processed (smoked) and then sold. For the next month the company has scheduled production of 25,000 units of the product which, if sold unprocessed, would bring a selling price of $11 per unit. The variable cost associated with producing the unprocessed product is $7 per unit, and the fixed cost of the facilities used for producing the unprocessed product is $50,000 for the month. If 25,000 units of the unprocessed product are produced, the entire capacity of that part of the plant will be used. However, there will be unused capacity in the part of the plant used for the smoking process. If the 25,000 units are smoked, this capacity, which would otherwise be idle, will be entirely used.

The additional variable cost, mainly for heat and smoking ingredients, is estimated to be $4 per unit; and the selling price of the processed product is $14.50 per unit. The monthly fixed cost depreciation on the portion of the facility used for additional processing amounts to $15,000. This cost is fixed regardless of whether or not the product is processed further.

Required: Prepare an analysis to help the manager decide whether the 25,000 units should be sold processed or unprocessed.

4. Make or Buy Decision—Graphic Solution. A firm needs two component parts, A and B, which can be manufactured or purchased. The economic information on each part is given as follows:

	Parts	
	A	*B*
Number of units required.....................................	1,000	3,000
Variable cost per unit	$15	$30
Outside price	$21	$38
Hours required per unit	1 hr.	3 hrs.
Total fixed cost..	$100,000	
Total hours available	3,000 hrs.	

Any portion of the requirement can be manufactured or purchased. Define the contribution margin as the difference between the outside purchase price and the variable cost.

Required:

(1) Prepare a graph with Part A on one axis and Part B on the other. Plot the constraints.

(2) Calculate the contribution margin and the number of units of A and B associated with each corner point on the graph.

(3) Choose the best solution.

5. Elimination of a Product Line. The Country General Store currently operates three departments. Over the past several months, sales and profit have declined, although the situation is now considered stable. As a result of the sales and profit decline, Department 2 has begun to show a loss and the vice-president has recommended that it be discontinued. The space could be rented to a grocery chain store which would pay a flat fee of $6,000 a month to Country General Store.

The following is an income statement for last month, considered to be typical. Costs of goods sold are variable costs. Sales salaries are fixed but directly identifiable with each department and would be eliminated if the department were eliminated. The fixed administrative costs (allocated equally to all departments) would not change in total if the department were eliminated.

	Department			
	1	*2*	*3*	*Total*
Sales......................................	$125,000	$ 60,000	$115,000	$300,000
Costs: Cost of goods sold	$ 75,000	$ 48,000	$ 57,500	$180,500
Sales salaries	5,000	1,500	4,000	10,500
Fixed administrative cost	25,000	25,000	25,000	75,000
Total cost...................................	$105,000	$ 74,500	$ 86,500	$266,000
Income before income tax	$ 20,000	$(14,500)	$ 28,500	$ 34,000

Required: Prepare an analysis and advise the vice-president whether the department should be discontinued and the space rented.

6. Full Cost Pricing. The A-1 Company follows the policy of calculating a selling price by adding a 15% markup to full cost. The variable cost is $50 per unit, and the total fixed cost is $1,500,000.

Required: Calculate the selling price per unit for 50,000 units, 60,000 units, and 75,000 units, assuming that fixed cost is allocated to units based on the number produced.

7. Full and Variable Cost Pricing. The Carriage Company produces two products, A and B. Data on cost and production are as follows:

	Product A	Product B
Materials cost per unit—variable...................	$25	$15
Labor hours required per unit.....................	2 hrs.	1 hr.
Hourly labor rate	$9	$7
Planned production	30,000 units	40,000 units
Annual overhead—fixed..........................	$900,000	

Required:

(1) Assuming the manager wants to set a price with a 10% markup based on full cost, prepare an analysis showing what the selling price for each product would be if the overhead cost were allocated on the basis of labor hours.

(2) Assuming that labor cost is variable, show the manager what the markup, stated as a percentage of unit variable cost, would have to be to give prices equal to those calculated in (1).

8. Special Order Pricing. The Peso Company is selling 80,000 units of a product at $10 per unit. The variable cost is $6 per unit, and the annual fixed cost is $120,000. A discount house has offered to buy 10,000 additional units of the product which would be slightly modified, but the modifications would not affect production cost. The discount house will pay $8 per unit.

Required: If the two markets can be distinguished, should the order be accepted (assuming capacity exists and has no other use)? Would your decision be affected if the manager felt that the two markets could not be distinguished and that the lower price would likely take over the main market as well as the special market?

9. Explaining Profit Differences. The Packer Company sells for $25 per unit a product which has a variable cost of $15 per unit. The planned sales for the coming year are 100,000 units. With annual fixed cost of $600,000, the controller estimates the following profit per unit:

Selling price per unit		$25.00
Variable cost per unit	$15.00	
Fixed cost per unit ($600,000 ÷ 100,000 units)	6.00	21.00
Profit per unit..		$ 4.00

During the year, the company actually produced and sold 90,000 units; and the president, based on the controller's calculations, estimated the profit to be $360,000. When the statements were prepared, the profit was $300,000 even though all of the actual costs were as estimated.

Required: Prepare an analysis to show why the profit was $60,000 lower than had been estimated.

PROBLEMS

10-1. Product Combination Decision. The Marlin Company sells three products which can be sold in any combination so long as no more than 210,000 machine hours are used. All costs are variable (labor and materials) except for the rental cost of the production facility, which is $480,000 per year. The economic data for each product are as follows:

	Product L	Product M	Product N
Selling price per unit	$20	$15	$10
Variable cost	11	9	6
Machine hours per unit	3 hours	4 hours	1 hour

Required:

(1) In the absence of any market constraints, what is the most profitable combination of products, and what is the profit?

(2) If the market for Product N is limited to 90,000 units with no market limitation on the other products, how does this change the best product combination and the profit?

(3) What is the best product combination (and the profit) if a shortage of materials for Product L limits the production of that product to 30,000 units, and there is still a market limit of 90,000 units of Product N?

10-2. Product Combination Decision. The Keller Company produces two products, using a single production process in which the main constraint is machine hours. The economic data are as follows:

	Product X	Product Y
Selling price per unit	$25	$12
Variable cost per unit	$18	$6
Machine hours per unit	2 hrs.	3 hrs.
Market limitation	60,000 units	25,000 units
Total machine hours available	180,000 hrs.	
Total fixed cost	$180,000	

Required:

(1) Find the best combination of products.

(2) If demand will hold up, should the company rent additional machines for $7,000 per year which will provide 6,000 additional capacity hours per machine? How many machines should be ordered?

10-3. Make or Buy Decision. The Peach Company produces a part used in the final assembly of its main product. Two manufacturing operations are required to produce the part. Typical annual production of the part is 160,000 units. The estimated current costs are as follows:

Operation 1:

Materials	$128,000
Direct labor	96,000
Variable overhead	64,000
General overhead	80,000
Total cost, Operation 1	$368,000

Operation 2:

Direct labor	$ 90,000
Variable overhead	50,000
General overhead	30,000
Total cost, Operation 2	$170,000

The general overhead is fixed. The other costs are variable.

Operation 1 can be eliminated if these parts are purchased from an outside vendor. The vendor will supply 160,000 units a year at $2.25 per unit. These parts would still have to be processed through Operation 2. The Peach Company would have to pay freight of $7,500 per year on the purchased parts. If Operation 1 is eliminated, the space can be rented for $12,000 per year.

Required: Prepare an analysis to help the company decide whether to purchase the parts or to continue to manufacture them in Operation 1.

10-4. Make or Buy Decision. The Anderson Division manufactures two components for a subassembly used in its primary product. Cost and production data are as follows:

Unit Cost	Component A	Component B
Direct materials	$ 7.00	$ 0.90
Direct labor	5.00	2.00
Variable overhead	1.25	.50
Fixed overhead	3.00	1.20
Total unit cost	$16.25	$ 4.60
Machine hours per unit	5	2
Units required	4,000	12,000

Although the division has manufactured its own components, the introduction of a new product will limit the available time for producing components to 25,000 hours this year. Therefore, the division must purchase some of its requirements from outside vendors. It must still incur the fixed overhead costs if the units are purchased.

Parts Galore is willing to supply any of the needed components at a cost per unit of $14 for Component A and $4 for Component B.

Required: Prepare an analysis that shows the number of units of each component Anderson Division should make.

10-5. Make or Buy Decision. The Bracken Company produces a line of iron and steel building products. Several subassemblies and parts enter into the line of products, and many of these parts and components can be either produced by Bracken or purchased from outside suppliers. Several of these parts are listed in the following table with related cost and production data.

	Iron Frames 10	Steel Frames 11	Steel Housing 12	Assembly Unit 13
Materials cost per unit	$2.00	$1.00	$ 8.00	$2.00
Variable labor cost per unit..............	1.50	1.00	5.00	3.00
Overhead cost per unit (100% of labor cost)	1.50	1.00	5.00	3.00
Total cost per unit	$5.00	$3.00	$18.00	$8.00
Hours required per unit	1 hr.	4 hrs.	5 hrs.	2 hrs.

These four parts can be produced or purchased. The plant facility is flexible in that the particular department involved can produce these parts in any combination. However, the main product in this department is a steel shaft that cannot be purchased outside. This shaft is used in most of the company's products and consequently has first priority on capacity.

The materials and the labor are considered to be variable costs, but the overhead cost in total is fixed. The overhead is assigned to products at the rate of 100% of direct labor cost. This rate is a predetermined rate established from the factory overhead budget.

The capacity of the producing department is 800,000 machine hours, and 70% of the capacity is to be used for producing shafts. The forecast requirements and outside price quotations on the parts for the coming period are as follows:

Part Number	Units Required	Outside Prices
10	80,000	$ 3.25
11	40,000	2.80
12	15,000	20.00
13	100,000	4.30

Consider the contribution margin to be the difference between the outside purchase price and the appropriate cost of manufacturing.

Required: Using contribution margin analysis, show the manager how much of each product to manufacture and how much of each to purchase. What is the dollar contribution associated with your solution? Assume that a portion of the requirement for each product can be purchased.

10-6. Elimination of Product. The Dean Company currently sells three products whose quantities, selling prices, and variable costs are as follows:

Product	Quantity	Selling Price	Variable Cost
110	10,000	$20	$14
111	15,000	10	7
112	20,000	25	16

The fixed cost for the operation is $225,000, and it is allocated on the basis of the total units produced. The plant is currently at capacity, and each unit requires the same production time. The following cost report for Product 111 shows that this product is not profitable.

Selling price per unit		$10
Variable cost per unit	$ 7	
Fixed cost per unit	5	12
Loss per unit.....................................		$(2)

The fixed cost per unit is calculated by dividing the total fixed cost, $225,000, by the units produced, 45,000.

The above report causes the sales manager to argue that Product 111 should be dropped from the product line, stating that it is difficult to make up on volume what is lost on the individual unit.

Required:

(1) If no alternative exists for the use of capacity, should Product 111 be dropped?

(2) If more of Product 110 can be sold at $20 per unit, should Product 111 be dropped?

(3) How much would the selling price of Product 111 have to be increased to make it as desirable as Product 110?

10-7. Elimination of Product Line. Assume the same situation as in Problem 10-6. However, if Product 111 is dropped, no additional units of Product 110 or Product 112 can be sold.

The sales manager finds another product, 113, which can be sold for $15 and has a variable cost of $13.50. In addition, it takes only one half the time to produce Product 113 as it takes to produce Product 111.

The sales manager argues that Product 113 should be added and Product 111 should be dropped, saying, "It is true that the contribution margin per unit is $1.50 less on Product 113 than on Product 111 ($1.50 compared with $3); but since more units of Product 113 can be produced, the fixed cost per unit will also go down. As a matter of fact, the fixed cost per unit on all units will drop by $1.25—from $5 ($225,000 ÷ 45,000) to $3.75 ($225,000 ÷ 60,000)—if we switch to Product 113."

Required: Is the sales manager right? How much would the price on Product 113 have to be increased before it would be as profitable as Product 111? Explain the error in the sales manager's reasoning.

10-8. Pricing Decision. The Howard Company is currently producing and selling two products, X and Y. The data on costs, selling prices, and volume are given as follows:

	Product X	Product Y
Selling price per unit	$16	$25
Variable cost per unit—labor and materials	11	15
Fixed overhead cost per unit allocated to products	5	5
Units sold	10,000	40,000

The total fixed overhead is $250,000 per year and is allocated equally since each product requires equal production time. Product Y requires a higher-priced material, which explains why the variable cost of this product is higher than for Product X.

A major company in the industry is looked on as a price leader. Most of the smaller companies follow its actions on price setting. Recently this company reduced the price on Product X to $14. The sales manager and the president of Howard Company are attempting to determine what to do in response to this action. The sales manager estimates that if the price on Product X is held at $16, sales will probably decline to 8,000 units. If the company follows the price decrease and reduces the price of Product X to $14, it is estimated that volume can be maintained at 10,000 units. However, the sales manager notes that Product X is already incurring zero profit at the selling price of $16 and suggests to the president that the product be dropped entirely. Such an action would provide unused capacity, since no more units of Y can be sold and there is no substitute product immediately available. Whatever is done, argues the sales manager, the price on Product X should not be reduced to $14, since the action will result in a loss per unit of $2.

Required: Advise the president on the proper course to follow. Show your calculations.

10-9. Special Order Pricing. The Dell Company produces a limited line of plastic containers that are used to store and ship certain chemical compounds. The capacity of the plant is 500,000 labor hours, and it takes an average of four hours to produce one container. For the last few years, the company has been producing about 115,000 containers per year; but the prospects for the coming year look very bright. Several new industrial plants have recently located in the area, and the company management believes that the excess capacity can now be used. The average price of the standard container is $220 per unit, and the cost structure is as follows:

	Cost per Unit
Materials	$130
Labor	50
Overhead	16
Total	$196

The materials and labor are considered to be variable costs. The total overhead is fixed and is allocated to the product on the basis of hours. The rate calculation is as follows:

$$\frac{\text{Estimated overhead}}{\text{Hours of capacity}} = \frac{\$2,000,000}{500,000} = \$4 \text{ per hour}$$

The price of $220 per standard container is now fairly well established within the industry. The company set this price by adding to the full cost a profit of $24 per unit.

The company has been approached by a contracting officer for the government to build 10,000 special containers. The materials cost has been estimated to be $25 less per unit than on standard containers, and the labor time will be about the same. The sales manager has calculated the price for the contracting officer as follows:

	Cost per Unit
Materials	$105
Labor	50
Overhead	16
	$171
Markup (4 hours @ $6)	24
Price	$195

The contracting officer, in reviewing the calculation, notices that the markup based on cost for the special container ($24 ÷ $171 = 14% approximately) is higher than for the standard container ($24 ÷ $196 = 12.2% approximately). The officer argues that the price on the special container should be reduced so as to make the special container no more profitable than the standard container.

Required: Assuming that the company wants to set the special container price to make it no more profitable than the standard container, is the $195 price appropriate? If so, explain why the contracting officer's reasoning with respect to the markup percentage is incorrect. What price should be charged?

10-10. Process or Sell Decision. The Brian Company manufactures a type of raw sheet metal that can be sold at this stage or processed more and sold as a type of alloy used in manufacturing high-grade control systems of various types. The raw sheet metal market is such that the entire output can be sold at the market price, which at the present time is $200 per ton. The processed selling price has been about $400 per ton for several years, but recently the market has been weak and the price has dropped as low as $270 on several occasions. This has caused the sales manager to suggest that the alloy is no longer profitable and should be dropped and that the entire capacity should be used to produce the raw metal. This is feasible since the production facility is interchangeable. That is, the production facility used now to produce the alloy could be devoted to producing more raw sheet metal on a ton-for-ton basis. The sales manager's suggestion is prompted by the data shown below.

	Cost per Ton of Raw Sheet Metal	Cost per Ton of Alloy
Materials	$100	
Direct labor	20	
Overhead	60	
Cost per ton	$180	$180
Selling price	200	
Profit...........................	$ 20	
Processing cost:		
Additional materials		40
Direct labor		20
Overhead		60
Cost per ton of alloy		$300
Selling price of alloy		270
Loss		$(30)

The sales manager argues that, because of a $30 loss per unit on the alloy, the product should be dropped any time the price per ton falls below $300.

In the cost calculations, materials and labor costs are variable. The overhead rate per unit is calculated by estimating the total overhead for the coming year and dividing this total by the total hours of capacity available. Since the raw metal and the alloy require the same producing time, the rate per unit is the same. The total overhead is, for the most part, a fixed cost.

Required:

(1) Should the alloy be dropped and the entire production facility be used to produce raw metal if the price per ton of alloy for the coming year is estimated to be $300? Support your conclusion with an appropriate analysis.

(2) Prepare an analysis to aid the sales manager in determining the lowest alloy price that would be acceptable to the company.

10-11. Allocation of Production Between Manufacturing Plants. The Eagle Company has two plants producing an equivalent grade of inexpensive alloy from a material which is a waste product in the manufacture of steel. One plant is located in Michigan and the other in Indiana. The Michigan plant has been operating at 75% of capacity producing 2,700 tons of alloy per period, and the Indiana plant has been operating at 80% of capacity producing 3,600 tons per period. For each ton of alloy, it requires a ton of materials—the waste metal. The price of the materials is $20 per ton at either plant with no limitation on the supply.

The cost and production data for a typical period are as follows:

	Michigan Plant	Indiana Plant
Materials: (2,700 tons used)	$ 54,000	
(3,600 tons used)		$ 72,000
Fixed cost per period	70,000	180,000
Variable cost (estimated to be constant per ton of		
output)	129,600	158,400
Total cost.....................................	$253,600	$410,400
Production	2,700 tons	3,600 tons
Cost per ton	$93.93	$114.00

The production manager would like to shift production to the Michigan plant to take advantage of the lower cost per ton. This plant is the older of the two plants and the fixed cost of operation is low.

Required: Prepare an analysis to show the production manager how the production should be scheduled. Assume that the present output of 6,300 tons will be continued (disregard any marketing costs and assume that the total fixed cost will not change). As part of your analysis, show the cost savings that will result from your recommendation.

10-12. Make or Buy with Complications. The management of Quinn Products Inc. has been operating at below normal capacity, and there does not appear to be an opportunity to add a new product line that will increase profit.

The production manager suggests that a component, presently being purchased from Patrick Supply Company, can be produced by the company. Normally 150,000 units of this component are needed each year. The cost to manufacture 150,000 units has been estimated as follows:

Direct materials	$1,125,000
Direct labor	675,000
Variable overhead	225,000
Additional fixed overhead if components are made	90,000
Allocated fixed overhead (100% of direct labor)	675,000
Total cost..	$2,790,000

This component can be purchased from Patrick Supply Company at a price of $14.60 per unit.

The sales manager objects to this plan, stating that Patrick Supply Company is also a customer and that the company sells 30,000 units of a finished product to the supplier and that these units add $30,000 to profit each year. This market will be lost if purchases are not made from the supplier. Furthermore, only 120,000 units of the component will be needed if the sales are lost, inasmuch as 30,000 units of this component are used to make the product sold to Patrick Supply Company.

Required: Based upon the information given, should Quinn Products Inc. make the component or purchase it from Patrick Supply Company?

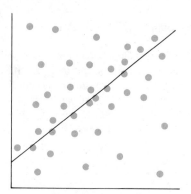

11

CAPITAL INVESTMENT DECISIONS—I

Chapter Objectives

This chapter will enable you to:

1. Define the future and present value of money.
2. Compute the present value and future value for a series of future cash flows.
3. Compute the premium or discount associated with a bond issue.
4. Determine the approximate interest rate in a decision situation.
5. Evaluate alternatives in a simple capital investment situation where a minimum interest rate is specified.

Several of the preceding chapters have discussed the use of accounting data in management decisions. In this chapter and the next, the emphasis is on capital investment decisions. The questions naturally arise, What is a capital investment decision and why is a capital investment decision different from those decisions discussed in the preceding chapter? The fundamental distinction between a capital investment decision and a noncapital investment decision is the timing difference between the cash outflows and the cash inflows associated with the project under consideration. The typical capital investment decision is one in which capital (cash) must be spent at the beginning of a project in anticipation of greater cash inflows or reduced cash outflows in future time periods. For example, a firm may be contemplating the purchase of a machine for $10,000 (the capital investment or investment outlay), which will make it possible to produce and sell a new product for the next five years (the economic life of the project). Assume that annual sales of

1,000 units are expected with a cash sales price of $7 per unit and a raw materials cost per unit of $4. Assume further that the materials can be purchased as needed so that the timing of the cash outflow for materials is exactly the same as the cash inflow from the sale of the new product. A diagram of this capital investment project is as follows:

Time in years	0	1	2	3	4	5
Cash out for machine	$(10,000)					
Cash in from sales (1,000 units × $7)		$7,000	$7,000	$7,000	$7,000	$7,000
Cash out for materials (1,000 units × $4)		(4,000)	(4,000)	(4,000)	(4,000)	(4,000)
Net annual cash inflows	$(10,000)	$3,000	$3,000	$3,000	$3,000	$3,000

In examining this example, note that the timing of the capital investment in the machine is different from the timing of the net cash inflows from the sale of the product. Thus, the decision to be made is whether the firm is willing to invest $10,000 now (year zero) in order to receive a net cash inflow of $3,000 per year for five years. In order to be precise on the timing and amount of the cash inflows and outflows, assume:

1. The investment for the machine must be made at the beginning of Year 1 (designated year zero);
2. The cash inflow from the sales of the 1,000 units of product and the cash payment to the suppliers of the materials take place at the end of each year.
3. There are no other incremental cash inflows or outflows associated with the decision. Specifically, assume there are no income tax considerations.
4. The firm is able to predict the future with certainty. Hence, there is no uncertainty about the future cash sales or cash purchases of materials.

The new element in the decision, as compared with the discussions in previous chapters, is the time value of money. How can the decision maker analyze the question of whether to invest $10,000 now in order to receive $3,000 each year for the next five years. As we will see, money has a time value. This is, the initial investment, $10,000, and the last net inflow, $3,000, five years hence, do not have the same value.

In this chapter, we will concentrate on:

1. The time value of money, which involves a discussion of present value analysis.
2. The application of present value analysis to simple capital investment examples, including the motivating example just given.

THE TIME VALUE OF MONEY

As we have observed, an amount of money to be received in the future is not equivalent to the same amount of money to be received now. When confronted with a choice, anyone would rather have $100 today, for example, than $100 two years from now. The $100 that is available today can be invested to return more than $100 two years from now. The time value of money can be compared with the visual perspective of distance as shown in the following illustration:

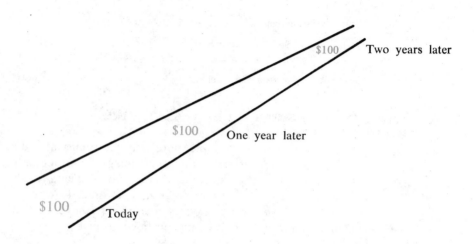

Future Value of Money

With physical objects at a distance, the objects appear to be smaller but are in reality as large as similar objects that are close at hand. In the case of money, however, it is no illusion.

A future sum of money is of less value than the same amount of money today. This is because money today will grow to a larger sum through investment. For example, $100 invested at 10 percent compound interest per year will grow to $121 at the end of two years.

$100 initial investment × 1.10 = $110, amount at the end of Year 1
$110 amount at the end of Year 1 × 1.10 = $121, amount at the end of Year 2

The $100 received today grows to $121 by the end of two years and thus is larger than $100 to be received at the end of two years.

The investment plus compound interest is called the compound amount. The compound amount of $100 in two years with interest compounded at the rate of 10 percent annually is $121. The formula for the compound amount of $1 follows:

$$\text{Compound amount} = (1 + i)^n$$
$$i = \text{interest rate}$$
$$n = \text{number of years}$$

In the example given, the compound amount could be computed as follows:

Compound amount of $1 $= (1.10)^2$

Compound amount of $1 $= (1.10) \times (1.10)$

Compound amount of $1   = \$1.21$

Compound amount of $100 $= 100 \times \$1.21$, or $121

A person who can earn 10 percent compound interest looks upon the receipt of $121 in two years as being equivalent to $100 today, assuming no uncertainty. Such a person is indifferent as to whether he or she has $100 today or $121 in two years.

By way of comparison, imagine a situation where the interest rate is zero. If this were the case, then a person would be indifferent between $100 now and $100 two years from now, assuming no uncertainty. That is, when the interest rate is zero $(1 + i)^2 = (1)^2 = 1$. However, at any positive interest rate, the right to receive $1 today will always be worth more than the right to receive $1 a few years from now. The magnitude of the interest rate is a measure of the strength of that preference, and it becomes a means of establishing the point of indifference between an amount of money to be received now as compared with an amount to be received in the future.

Obviously, many business decisions involve the investment of dollars with the expectation that more dollars will be received at some future time. The future cash inflows (returns) are compared with the investment outlay in making the investment decision. The returns and the investment, however, are not on the same time basis. Before a comparison can be made, the present and future dollars must be stated on an equivalent time basis.[1] Present dollars may be placed on a future dollar basis; that is, the compound amount of a present investment may be computed. If a person has $100 available for investment and believes that a 10 percent return with interest compounded annually can be earned, he or she will expect to receive $121 at the end of two years from a present investment of $100. Hence, an investment opportunity that is expected to yield $115 in two years from a present investment of $100 is unacceptable if $121 can normally be expected from a $100 investment. In short, the potential investor does not believe that $115 in two years is equivalent to $100 today if he or she can expect to receive $121 from other investment opportunities.

Let us consider some additional observations on the example just given. In a situation in which $100 can be invested to return $121 in two years, the return on investment is 10 percent compounded annually. So the compound rate of interest, 10 percent, is a measure of return on investment (ROI), or the rate of return as it is sometimes called. Also, note that if a decision maker has

---

[1]The adjustments to place monetary amounts on an equivalent time basis should not be confused with price-level adjustments. The adjustments are made for different purposes. Adjustments for differences in time are required even if the price level remains the same.

a choice of investments for the $100, he or she will prefer the investment with the highest ROI (other things equal—such as the degree of uncertainty). The reason, of course, is that the investment opportunity with the highest ROI will give the largest future amount. It is assumed that investors wish to maximize future wealth and the highest return on investment opportunity will lead to this outcome. Consider, for example, an alternative investment which will earn 15 percent interest. Assuming certainty, the compound amount of the $100 at 15 percent for two years is:

$$\$100 \ (1.15)^2 = \$100 \ (1.3225) = \$132.25$$

Since $132.25 is larger than $121 (the compound amount of $100 in two years in the 10 percent investment) the project earning 15 percent is preferred to the project earning 10 percent.

Present Value of Money

It is also possible to calculate the present value of an amount of money to be received at some point in the future. Although capital investment decisions can be analyzed using future value analysis as discussed, it is conventional and typically easier to use present value analysis.

In order to motivate the discussion of present value analysis consider the question of how much money must be invested today in order to receive a certain amount of money in the future? A debtor may look at the situation from a different point of view. How much money must be paid now to settle a debt that will become due in the future? In business, a choice must often be made between having a given amount of money now or the prospect of receiving a monetary return in the future. Does the expected future return justify the investment? This can be determined by computing the present value of the future return and comparing it with the amount invested.

The present value of a future amount of money (compound amount) can be computed by multiplying the future amount by the present value of $1. The formula for the present value of $1 follows:

$$\text{Present value of } \$1 \ = \ \frac{1}{(1 \ + \ i)^n}$$

$$i \ = \ \text{interest rate}$$
$$n \ = \ \text{number of years}$$

Assume, for example, that $121 is to be received two years from now and the compound annual rate of interest is 10 percent. How much money must be invested today to get $121 at the end of two years?

Solve for the present value of $1 in two years with interest compounded annually at 10 percent.

Present value of $1, 2 years, 10% interest $= \dfrac{1}{(1.10)^2}$

Present value of $1, 2 years, 10% interest $= \$.826446$

Present value of $121, 2 years, 10% interest $= \dfrac{\$121 \times \$.826446}{\text{or } \$100}$

The computation could also be made as follows:

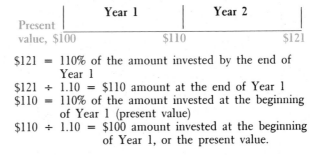

$121 = 110\%$ of the amount invested by the end of Year 1

$121 \div 1.10 = \$110$ amount at the end of Year 1

$110 = 110\%$ of the amount invested at the beginning of Year 1 (present value)

$110 \div 1.10 = \$100$ amount invested at the beginning of Year 1, or the present value.

This is summarized below:

$$\frac{\$121 \div 1.10}{1.10} \text{ is equivalent to } \frac{\$121}{(1.10)^2}$$

or

$$\frac{1}{(1.10)^2} \times \$121 = \$100 \text{ present value}$$

In comparing the (future) compound amount with the present value, it can be seen that the difference is the interest earned on the investment. The dollar amount of interest, of course, depends on the interest rate. At 10 percent, the total dollar interest for two years is $21 and the following is true:

Present value ($100) = Compound amount ($121) − $21 (the dollar interest at 10%)

The process of reducing a (future) compound amount to a present value is called discounting. The present value is sometimes called the discounted value. The dollar interest is called the dollar discount, and the rate of interest is called the discount rate.

It is seldom necessary to calculate either compound amounts or present values as shown here, because published tables giving both present values and future values are available. Since it is conventional to analyze capital investment problems using present value analysis, the tables in Appendix C give present value factors for various discount (interest) rates for various time periods expressed in years. Tabe I (Appendix C) gives the present value of $1 to be received at the end of the various time periods at interest or discount rates shown across the top row of the table. Thus, it is a tabulation in decimal form of the factor $\dfrac{1}{(1+i)^n}$ where n is the number of years and i is the interest or discount rate. The factor for two years at 10 percent is .826, and the present value (PV) of $121 to be received in two years can be calculated as follows:

$$PV = \$121 \times (.826)$$
$$PV = \$100 \text{ rounded}$$

The factors appearing in both tables are rounded to the third digit, which is sufficient precision for most capital investment problems. As is apparent, the availability of tables makes the calculation of present values much simpler than the methods used in the preceding discussion.

The Present Value of a Series of Future Cash Flows

In the motivating example given at the beginning of this chapter, the machine investment of $10,000 produced a stream of cash inflows of $3,000 each year. Annual cash inflows are a characteristic of the typical investment project rather than the one-time cash inflow as illustrated in the preceding section. How can the present value of a series of annual cash flows be calculated?

The present value of a series of annual returns is nothing more than the sum of the present values of the individual returns. Assume that $1,000 is to be received at the end of each year for five years. What is the present value of these five annual receipts of $1,000 at a discount (interest) rate of 10 percent? The present value can be computed as follows:

End of Year	Returns	Computation		
1	$1,000	$1,000 \times \dfrac{1}{1.10}$	= $ 909	present value of $1,000 received at end of Year 1
2	1,000	$1,000 \times \dfrac{1}{(1.10)^2}$	= 826	present value of $1,000 received at end of Year 2
3	1,000	$1,000 \times \dfrac{1}{(1.10)^3}$	= 751	present value of $1,000 received at end of Year 3
4	1,000	$1,000 \times \dfrac{1}{(1.10)^4}$	= 683	present value of $1,000 received at end of Year 4
5	1,000	$1,000 \times \dfrac{1}{(1.10)^5}$	= 621	present value of $1,000 received at end of Year 5

Present value of $1,000 received at the end of each year for 5 years.........................$3,790

The same result can also be computed as follows:

$$\$1,000 \left(\frac{1}{1.10} + \frac{1}{(1.10)^2} + \frac{1}{(1.10)^3} + \frac{1}{(1.10)^4} + \frac{1}{(1.10)^5} \right) = \$3,790$$

The decimal equivalents of the fractions in the equation can be found in the table of present values of $1 (Table I):

$$(.909 + .826 + .751 + .683 + .621)$$

The sum of the present values is 3.79, and the present value of $1,000 received each year for five years at 10 percent interest compounded annually is $3,790:

$$\$1,000 (3.79) = \$3,790$$

Note that the factor, 3.79, can be read from Table II in Appendix C, using the 10%-rate and the 5-year columns. The difference between this amount and the amount appearing in the table is due to rounding. The factors in Table II, (Present Value of $1 Received Annually for N Years), are the sum of the present value factors given in Table I. The following calculations using interest rates of 6 percent, 8 percent, and 10 percent for 5 years illustrate this point.

**Present Value of $1 Received
Annually for 5 Years at:**

	6%		8%		10%	
Years	Table I	Table II	Table I	Table II	Table I	Table II
1	.943		.926		.909	
2	.890		.857		.826	
3	.840		.794		.751	
4	.792		.735		.683	
5	.747		.681		.621	
Total	4.212	4.212	3.993	3.993	3.790*	3.791*

*Difference due to rounding.

When calculating the present value of a stream of equal annual cash flows, it is easier to add the yearly factors and make one multiplication than it is to make several multiplications and then add. This explains the great convenience of having Table II for evaluating a series of equal annual cash flows.

If each of the annual cash flows are not equal, then it is necessary to use Table I. For example, to calculate the present value of a series of unequal annual amounts to be received at the end of each year, the following calculation using Table I is necessary (assume a 10 percent discount rate is to be used):

Year	(1) Amount To Be Received at the End of Each Year	(2) Table I Present Value Factor at 10%	Column (1) Times Column (2)
1	$1,000	.909	$909.00
2	800	.826	660.80
3	700	.751	525.70
4	600	.683	409.80
5	200	.621	124.20
Total: Present value of the series of cash flows at 10%			$2,629.50

Comparison of the Present Value and Future Value of a Series of Cash Flows

An earlier discussion illustrated the relationship between the present value and future value (compound amount) of a single amount to be received two years hence. Using a 10 percent interest (discount) rate, the present value of $121 received at the end of two years was $100. Under certainty, a person would be indifferent between $100 now and $121 two years from now at a 10 percent interest rate because $100 would grow to $121 in two years at 10 percent compound interest.

A similar relationship exists between a present value of a stream of payments and the stream of payments. For example, the present value of $100 received at the end of each year for five years at 10 percent is $379.10 (i.e., $100 × 3.791, see Table II) as calculated earlier. Under certainty, the decision maker would be indifferent between $379.10 now or $100 to be received at the end of each year for five years because either the 379.10 or the $100 at the end of each year for five years would grow to the same future (compound) amount at the end of 5 years. This is shown by the following calculations:

Year	Amount of Investment at the Beginning of Each Year	Interest at 10%	Amount of Investment at End of Each Year
1	$379.10	$37.91	$417.01
2	417.01	41.70	458.71
3	458.71	45.87	504.58
4	504.58	50.46	555.04
5	555.04	55.50	610.54*

Year	Amount Invested at the Beginning of Each Year	Interest at 10%	Additional Investment at End of Each Year	Total Amount of Investment at End of Year
1	-0-	-0-	$100.00	$100.00
2	100.00	10.00	100.00	210.00
3	210.00	21.00	100.00	331.00
4	331.00	33.10	100.00	464.10
5	464.10	46.41	100.00	610.51*

*Difference of 3 cents due to rounding.

Hence, if 10 percent correctly expresses the decision maker's time value of money, he or she would be indifferent (assuming certainty) between $379.10

now and $100 at the end of each year for five years since both amounts would grow to the same future value at the end of five years if invested at 10 percent. As can be seen, then, either present value or future value analysis could be used to analyze the time value of money aspect of a capital investment decision even when a series of annual cash flows are involved. As stated previously, it is usually easier to use present value analysis. It should be kept in mind, however, that the assumed objective in capital investment decisions is to maximize future wealth, and present value analysis is a method of analysis for accomplishing that result.

PRESENT VALUE ANALYSIS APPLIED

In the concluding section of this chapter, several simple applications of present value analysis will be discussed. The primary focus of the discussion will be on some examples that consider the time value of money. One such area is that of capital budgeting. Capital budgeting is the term used to describe the process of evaluating, selecting, controlling, and financing capital investments. Capital budgeting involves considerations other than just the time value of money. The next chapter discusses the capital budgeting process except for the financing of capital investments, which is beyond the scope of this book. The ideas and concepts developed in this chapter will be used in the subsequent discussion of evaluating, selecting, and controlling capital investment projects.

Financial Decision Examples

Let us consider the time value of money aspects of some financial decisions. One possible example is that of bond financing. When bonds are issued, a discount or premium is sometimes involved. How does the discount or premium arise? To illustrate, assume that a company issues a 10-year bond of $100,000 par value with a coupon or bond rate of interest of 10 percent. To simplify, assume that the interest is paid at the end of each year rather than quarterly, which is normally the case. A bond contract of this type would call for the following schedule of cash payments:

Year	Interest at 10% of Par Value	Repayment of Principle	Total Cash Flow
1	$10,000		$10,000
2	10,000		10,000
3	10,000		10,000
4	10,000		10,000
5	10,000		10,000
6	10,000		10,000
7	10,000		10,000
8	10,000		10,000
9	10,000		10,000
10	10,000	$100,000	110,000

If the bond is sold (issued) at par value, the interest cost to the issuer is 10 percent, and the rate of interest return to the investor, or buyer of the bond, is also 10 percent. This is because the present value of the future cash payments specified by the bond contract is $100,000 at a 10 percent discount rate. This is illustrated as follows:

Present value = $10,000 × present value of $1 received each year for 10 years at 10% — Table II

+

$100,000 × present value of $1 received at the end of 10 years at 10% — Table I

= [$10,000 × 6.145 (Table II)] + [$100,000 × .386 (Table I)]

= $61,450 + $38,600

= $100,050 (difference due to rounding in present value factors)

As can be seen, to the investor or buyer of the bond, the present value of the $10,000 interest payments at the end of each year for 10 years is $61,450 and the present value of the principal repayment at the end of 10 years is $38,600, for a total present value of $100,000, the par value (allowing for rounding error).

However, suppose that the current market rate of interest for bonds of this particular type (i.e., given the 10-year life of the bond and the particular risk) is 12 percent. In that case, an investor would not be willing to buy the bond at par value, because he or she could earn 12 percent by investing in bonds selling in the current market. In order to sell the bond, the company would presumably have to increase the bond rate of interest or sell the bond at a discount from par value. If the bond is sold at a discount, the amount of the discount would be the difference between the par value of $100,000 and the present value of the cash flow discounted at 12 percent, the market rate of interest.

Present value at 12% = ($10,000 × 5.650—Table II) + ($100,000 × .322—Table I)

= $56,560 + $32,200

= $88,760

Bond discount = $100,000 − $88,760

= $11,240

If an investor purchased the bond at $88,760 (a discount of $11,240) he or she would earn 12 percent interest on the $88,760 invested. The 12 percent earned is usually called the yield or the effective rate of interest.

Likewise, if the current market rate of interest, or market yield, is 8 percent, an investor would be willing to pay a premium for a bond with a 10 percent bond or coupon interest rate. The amount to be paid would be the present value of the future cash flows at 8 percent, and the premium would be the difference between the present value at 8 percent, and the par value (which is the present value of the cash flow at 10 percent as shown earlier).

$$\text{Present value at } 8\% = (\$10,000 \times 6.710\text{--Table II}) + (\$100,000 \times .463\text{--Table I})$$
$$= \$67,100 + \$46,300$$
$$= \$113,400$$
$$\text{Bond premium} = \$13,400$$

As another example, consider a situation in which a bank is willing to loan you money for five years at 10 percent, but instead of paying annual interest, you repay the loan and the interest in one payment at the end of five years. If you need $100,000 now, how much would you have to repay in five years? The amount to be repaid in five years would have to be an amount whose present value now (10%, 5 years) is $100,000 (the amount you need).

$$\$100,000 = \text{Amount to be repaid in 5 years} \times \text{Present value of}$$
$$\$1 \text{ at the end of 5 years at } 10\%$$
$$\$100,000 = \text{Amount to be repaid in 5 years} \times .621 - \text{Table I}$$
$$\frac{\text{Amount to be}}{\text{repaid in 5 years}} = \frac{\$100,000}{.621} = \$161,031 \text{ (rounded)}$$

As is probably apparent, future value analysis could have been used to calculate the repayment at the end of five years, but since present value tables are available, present value analysis can also be used.

It may seem a little surprising that a 10% loan now would require a $61,031 interest payment at the end of five years (i.e., $161,031 repaid − $100,000 borrowed). Compound interest gives some rather deceptive results. Compound interest of 10 percent will more than double an amount in eight years! This can be seen by the 10%-Column in Table I, finding the year when the present value factor drops to .5. This occurs between Year 7 and Year 8 (.513 at the end of Year 7 and .467 in Year 8). If you had borrowed $100,000 for eight years, you would have to repay $214,133 ($100,000 ÷ .467 − rounded). As can be seen from Table I, even 6 percent compound interest will more than double in twelve years.

As yet another example of present value analysis, consider a loan which is paid off in equal annual payments at the end of each year. For example, suppose that you need to borrow $100,000 to buy a home and the lending institutions require 15 percent interest and equal annual payments at the end of each year for the next twenty years. What will be the amount of the annual payments? The present value of the series of twenty payments would have to be $100,000 when discounted at 15 percent.

$$\$100,000 = \text{annual payment x present value of } \$1 \text{ received}$$
$$\text{annually for 20 years at } 15\%$$
$$100,000 = \text{annual payment} \times 6.259 - \text{Table II}$$
$$\text{Annual payment} = \$100,000 \div 6.259 = \$15,977 \text{ (rounded)}$$

This may seem rather high, because over the twenty years, you would repay a total of $319,540 (20 years × $15,977) for the $100,000 loan. The total interest would be more than twice the amount of the loan. Keep in mind that we observed earlier that a 10 percent compound rate more than doubles an amount in eight years. In this example we are dealing with a loan of twenty years and an interest rate of 15 percent.

Approximation of the Interest Rate

In all of the examples given the interest rate (or discount rate) was specified. Suppose that a potential investment is proposed and we wish to find the approximate interest rate of return on the investment. Such a rate is called the internal rate of return on investment of the project. It is that discount rate which will equate the present value of the future cash inflows with the amount of the initial capital investment outlay.

Assume that a friend is interested in borrowing $100 and wants to repay the loan in equal annual installments of $30 at the end of each year for five years. If you make the loan (investment), what is the interest rate or rate of return that you will earn? To approximate the rate, we can find the internal rate of return, which is the rate that will equate the present value of $30 received at the end of each year for five years with the $100 investment or loan outlay at the beginning of year 1.

$100 = $30 × (present value of $1 received annually for 5 years at i% interest)

The amount shown in parentheses is a Table II factor corresponding to the 5 year row and an interest or discount rate which would be the internal rate of return. Using algebra, then, the Table II factor is:

$$(\text{Table II 5-year factor}) = \frac{\$100}{\$30} = 3.33$$

To approximate the interest rate of return, we need to find the factor 3.33 in the 5-year row in Table II. The 15%, 5-year factor is 3.352 and the 16%, 5-year factor is 3.274. Hence, the internal rate of return is between 15 percent and 16 percent. If a return on investment of slightly in excess of 15 percent is acceptable to you, the loan should be made. For most capital investment problems, an approximation of the rate of return is sufficient.

A Simple Capital Investment Example

Let us now reconsider the simple capital investment problem used as a motivating example at the beginning of this chapter. In that situation, the firm could invest $10,000 in a machine that would produce 1,000 units of product each year for five years. The product can be sold for $7 per unit and $4 per unit of raw materials cost would be required. It was assumed that the collection of the cash sales and the cash payment for raw materials could be made at the end of each year so that the net cash inflow would be $3,000 each year for five years (i.e., 1,000 units at $7 less 1,000 units at $4).

In order to aid the decision maker, the internal rate of return can be calculated as follows:

$$\$10,000 = \$ 3,000 \times \text{(Table II factor, 5-year, } i\%\text{)}$$
$$\text{Table II factor} = \frac{\$10,000}{\$ 3,000} = 3.33$$

Referring to Table II, the factor 3.33 corresponds to an internal rate of return of slightly more than 15 percent based on the life of the project being five years. Hence, if a return of 15 percent is acceptable to the decision maker, the investment should be made; if a return of 15 percent is not acceptable, the investment should be rejected. There are other criteria that might be used to select capital investment projects, and some of them will be discussed in the next chapter.

Capital Investments in Not-For-Profit Organizations

Unlike the company organized for profits, the not-for-profit entity ordinarily has no expected monetary return from its capital investments. In the case of a city government, for example, an investment may be made for the general welfare of the citizens.

The benefit, or return, is often not measurable in monetary terms and may have to be estimated on somewhat subjective terms. The city will attempt to obtain benefits for the citizens at the lowest possible cost. For example, neighborhood playgrounds may be formed in various sections of the city. The benefits for the children and young people of the city are evident, but how can they be measured? The problem can be approached by considering the most reasonable cost to accomplish the objective and by considering how this will affect the tax rate. In a broad sense, the acceptance by the citizens of a somewhat higher tax rate is an indication of whether or not the benefits from a proposed capital project are perceived as being sufficient in light of the cost.

Terminology Review

Capital investment decision (322)
Noncapital investment decision (322)
Time value of money (323)
Compound amount (324)
Present value (326)
Discounting (327)
Dollar discount (327)

Discount rate (327)
Present value of a series of annual returns (328)
Capital budgeting (331)
Yield (332)
Internal rate of return (334)
Not-for-profit entity (335)

QUESTIONS FOR REVIEW

1. Why is *timing* important in a capital investment decision?

2. What is meant by the term *time value of money*?

3. What is the significance of the terms *compound amount* and *compound rate of interest*?

4. What is meant by the term *present value*, and why is it important to a manager?

5. In comparing a present value and a future value, what is the basic difference between the two?

6. An annuity is a series of periodic cash flows. How can the present value of a series of annual cash flows be calculated?

7. Assuming an interest rate of 10%, explain the relationship between Table I and Table II.

8. What is the *internal rate of return*? How would you approximate such a rate?

9. If an interest rate is 12% compounded quarterly, what impact does the quarterly compounding have on computations of present values or of future values?

10. Two annual rates of interest with different compounding periods are called equivalent if they yield the same compound amount at the end of one year. The stated rate compounded on whatever basis is called the nominal rate; the rate of interest actually earned in one year is called the effective rate. What is the effective rate equivalent to the nominal rate of 4% compounded quarterly?

11. Kelli Ann wants to have $1,000 in her savings account one year from now and she must decide how much to deposit now (the present value of $1,000). She has the choice of a 5% or a 6% account. Which of the two interest rates gives the lower present value? Why?

EXERCISES

1. Future Amount. Bob Mellor has a thirteen-year-old daughter who plans to enter college in 5 years. Mellor needs to save money between now and then to pay some of her educational expenses.

Required: If Mellor deposits $1,000 now and every year hereafter (for a total of 6 deposits, the last one immediately before his daughter enters school) into a savings account earning 10% interest, how much will be in the savings account when his daughter enters college?

2. Effective Interest Rate. Joel Minar has a savings account in a local credit union that pays 6% interest compounded quarterly.

Required: What is the effective interest rate earned by this account? (Effective interest is the equivalent annual interest rate.)

3. Determining an Interest Rate. Jake Hobson has invested $20,000 in a business he manages in his spare time. He hopes to withdraw $5,825 out of the business at the end of each year for 5 years, at which time his equity in the business will be zero.

Required: What rate of return must he earn to realize the annual $5,825?

4. Determining the Length of an Investment. The manager of Macho Men's Wear is contemplating building a new retail outlet at a cost of $800,000. Annual after-tax cash flows are expected to run about $100,000.

Required: If the manager requires a 12% after-tax rate of return on investment, how many years must the new outlet generate $100,000?

5. Unpaid Principal. Patty Wagner purchased a car on time for $6,000. She agreed to make quarterly payments of $639.32 at the end of each quarter for 3 years.

Required: If interest is 16% compounded quarterly, what is the unpaid principal on the loan immediately after the 8th payment of $639.32? (Hint: the unpaid principal is the present value of the remaining payments.)

6. Interest Included in Payment. The Barley Company has just negotiated a 10-year loan with its banker. The $500,000 loan is for 12% and calls for payments of $88,500 at the end of each year until the loan is paid off.

Required: In the first payment one year from now, how much is interest and how much is principal?

7. Selecting Between Two Investments. The town of Earth has $50,000 of surplus cash in its treasury that will not be used for one year. The town treasurer has two investment possibilities available: (1) invest in 12% treasury bills for 6 months and then reinvest the proceeds in a high-grade 16% corporate bond for the remaining 6 months; or (2) invest now in a 16% corporate bond maturing in 3 months, reinvest the proceeds in 12% treasury bills for 6 months, and hold the proceeds in the town's non-interest-bearing checking account for the remaining 3 months.

Required: Which alternative allows the town to have the higher amount at the end of one year?

8. Investments With Uneven Cash Flows. Cogam Minerals has the data on two $100,000 investment opportunities. With only $100,000 in cash available, the owners must decide the better opportunity. The controller has gathered the following data:

Alternative 1: $20,000 of cash inflow for each of the first three years and $80,000 for each of the last three years.

Alternative 2: $40,000 of cash inflow in the first year, $60,000 in the next four years, and $20,000 in the sixth year.

Required: If the company has a 14% minimum rate of return, which investment opportunity would the company prefer?

9. Determining the Required Investment. The Corley Company would like to initiate an advertising campaign to increase its annual sales volume. Data show that the proposed advertising will add $60,000 to the annual cash flow each of the next two years, plus $30,000 in the third year.

Required: What is the maximum amount that Corley would invest in this campaign at the present time if the company sets a minimum-rate-of-return objective of 20%?

10. Selection of Payment Alternative. Mae Richards has won the grand prize in a supermarket bingo game. She has the option of receiving $25,000 immediately, $5,000 each year for 10 years, or $10,000 now and $3,000 each year for 10 years.

Required: If Richards can invest money at 12%, which option should she accept?

11. Pay Cash or Borrow. Roland Greer needs a new car that he could purchase now for $9,000. Although he has the cash available, Greer would rather keep as much cash as possible for investments where there is the potential for a 20% rate of return. He can pay for the car on time with a $1,000 downpayment and $800 a quarter for 4 years.

Required: Should Greer pay for the car on time? (Hint: Compare the interest rate paid on time with the potential returns from investment.)

12. Equivalence of Present Value and Future Value. Margaret Lopez wants $5,000 in her savings account at the end of four years. She could deposit $3,675 now at 8% and let it accumulate to $5,000, or she can make $1,110 annual deposits at the end of each year.

Required: Show that either approach Lopez selects will accumulate to $5,000.

13. Market Interest Rate on Bonds. On July 1, the Nevtah Corporation has a 9%, 10-year bond trading at 96.15 in the bond market. Interest on the bond is paid semiannually on June 30 and December 31. There are five years remaining to maturity. Jens Olsen is willing to purchase $20,000 of the bonds at the current market price.

Required: If Olsen purchases the bonds, what is his market rate of interest?

PROBLEMS

11-1. The Amount of an Investment in Bonds. The Stinson Corporation is issuing $10,000,000 of 10%, 10-year bonds dated October 1, with interest payment dates of September 30 and March 31. Karen Walters is interested in purchasing $100,000 worth of the bonds on October 1. Currently, Walters can earn 12% compounded semiannually on investments.

Required:

(1) Determine the semiannual cash flow Walters will receive from her investment if she holds the bonds to maturity.

(2) How much is Walters willing to invest in $100,000 face value of Stinson Corporation bonds?

(3) What is the discount or premium Walters is demanding before she will invest her money in the bonds?

11-2. Equivalence of Present Value and Future Value. Dwight Peters has 10 years before retirement. On the date of retirement, Peters would like to have $50,000 in his personal retirement fund. The local bank has a special retirement account that guarantees 12% interest per year. Peters has the option of making one deposit now into the fund or making annual deposits at the end of each year for 10 years, with deposits starting one year from now.

Required:

(1) What amount deposited now will accumulate to $50,000 in 10 years?

(2) What is the annual contribution if Peters decides to make annual payments?

(3) Show that the annual contributions will accumulate to $50,000 by the end of 10 years.

11-3. Sinking Fund Contributions. The Tiner Company is authorized to issue $5,000,000 of 8-year unsecured bonds. These bonds have a stated interest of 13%. The bond indenture requires Tiner Company to make semiannual contributions to a sinking fund each time the company makes an interest payment on the bonds. The sinking fund will grow to $5,000,000 in time to redeem the bonds at maturity. The sinking fund trustee can invest the semiannual contributions to earn 16% compounded semiannually.

Required: Determine the semiannual contribution that Tiner Company should make to the sinking fund. (Hint: find the present value of the $5,000,000 at 16% compounded semiannually and then use Table II to determine the semiannual contribution.)

11-4. Issuance of Bonds. The Carson Corporation is authorized to issue $20,000,000 of 10-year debenture bonds. The stated interest rate is 14% payable semiannually on June 30 and December 31. The bonds are scheduled for sale on July 1. Prior to the sale date, the market interest rate for long-term bonds dropped to 12% compounded semiannually (this is the rate of interest demanded by investors).

Required:

(1) What is the amount investors are willing to pay for the $20,000,000 bond issue?

(2) What is the discount or premium the company must recognize for accounting purposes?

11-5. Deficiency in Pension Fund. Five years ago Mojo Valley Manufacturing Company adopted a pension plan for its salaried employees, the first of whom retires in 18 years. The pension fund has consistently earned 8% over the last 5 years but is expected to average 10% in the future. Contributions for the past 5 years are listed as follows:

Five years ago	—	$25,000
Four years ago	—	30,000
Three years ago	—	30,000
Two years ago	—	35,000
One year ago	—	35,000

The benefits of the pension plan currently call for $2,000,000 as the balance in the pension fund on the date the first employee retires. Although the pension plan calls for a specified annual contribution, the amounts actually contributed depend upon the available cash at the end of each year, subject to a minimum payment of $25,000. Therefore, the pension fund probably does not have a sufficient balance now.

Required:

(1) Determine the current balance of the pension fund when contributions have earned 8%.

(2) Calculate the current deficiency in the pension fund.

11-6. Amortization Schedule for Loan. Ramsey Gage has $29,910 he is willing to loan to a friend for a second mortgage on a new home. The friend will repay the loan at $10,000 at the end of each year for 5 years. Ramsey set up the annual payments to yield a 20% return on his $29,910 investment. For purposes of determining the annual interest income from this loan, Ramsey needs a loan amortization schedule showing how much of each annual payment is interest and how much reduces the principal.

Required: Prepare an amortization schedule that shows the outstanding balance of the loan at the beginning of each year, the annual payment, the interest in the payment, and the reduction in principal.

11-7. Present Value of Note Receivable. On March 31, Bolding Construction Company completed a construction project for a client and negotiated a promissory note with a face value of $560,000, a stated interest rate of 4% payable at the end of each year from date of the note, and a due date 5 years from now. The controller of Bolding is concerned about how to record this transaction in the financial records, since the value of the construction work is different from the $560,000 and the 4% interest rate is low compared to other interest rates.

Under generally accepted accounting principles ["Interest on Receivables and Payables," *Opinions of the Accounting Principles Board No. 21* (New York: AICPA, 1971)], the note receivable must be recorded at its present value. The present value of a note is usually the fair value of the property, goods, or services exchanged, which is not determinable in this case. Therefore, an effective interest rate is necessary to calculate the present value. After considering the maker's credit rating, the absence of collateral, the prime interest rate on March 31, and the prevailing interest rate on the maker's outstanding debt, the controller concludes that an effective interest rate of 10% is appropriate.

If the present value is less than $560,000, generally accepted accounting principles require the difference to be computed; that is, the difference between the interest received (4% of $560,000) and the effective interest earned (10% of the present value at the beginning of each year). The amount amortized will be added to the interest income for the year.

Required:

(1) Compute the present value of the note receivable now and at the end of each year for its life. Use the 10% effective interest rate.

(2) Prepare a schedule that shows interest received each year at 4%, the effective interest at 10%, and the difference between the two.

11-8. Selection of Depreciation Methods. Bob Stem, controller of Bridges Manufacturing, is trying to assess the cash flow implications of three depreciation policies for a new machining facility the company is installing in its B-1 Division. The facility will cost $450,000 and will be technologically obsolete at the end of 8 years, at which time it will have a salvage value of $90,000. The depreciation cash flow implications are measured by the savings in income tax because of the depreciation's tax deductibility. Tax savings are measured by the annual depreciation expense times the company's income tax rate of 40%.

Stem is considering the sum-of-the-years-digits method (SYD), the straight-line method, and the units-of-production method. The vice-president of production estimates production for each of the 8 years as follows:

Year	Units
1	360,000
2	504,000
3	720,000
4	720,000
5	648,000
6	360,000
7	180,000
8	108,000

Required:

  (1) Calculate the savings in income tax resulting from each of the three depreciation methods.

  (2) Which depreciation method yields the highest present value of tax savings, assuming the company uses a 15% interest rate?

11-9. Early Retirement Decision. Terri Dunn has just finished 20 years of service with Tricore Corporation. At 55 years of age, Dunn is considering retiring now instead of waiting 7 more years. Dunn currently earns $100,000 a year and anticipates pay increases of 7% a year until retirement. The retirement benefits are:

	Salary Plus 7%	Annual Benefit	
Age	Increase	Start Drawing at 62	Collect Right Away
--	$100,000	$42,300	$30,400
56	107,000	47,200	35,900
57	114,490	52,600	42,100
58	122,504	58,200	49,100
59	131,080	65,000	57,200
60	140,255	72,000	66,400
61	150,073	80,000	76,700

All annual benefits terminate at age 80. Even if Dunn doesn't live to 80, the estate will receive the benefits until the termination date.

DSQ Inc. needs a person with Dunn's skills and experience but can only afford to offer $90,000 a year with no pension benefits. However, at the end of each year, Dunn can expect 10% pay increases as follows:

Age	Salary
56	$ 99,000
57	108,900
58	119,790
59	131,769
60	144,946
61	159,441

If Dunn retires now, he can start withdrawing $30,400 from the Tricore pension fund. The $30,400 will continue for 25 years.

Required: Assuming Dunn views money to be worth 12%, should Dunn retire now and work for DSQ Inc. or continue with Tricore until age 62?

11-10. Redemption of Bonds. Two years ago, the Minnick Company issued $2,000,000 of 8-year bonds with 16% interest payable semiannually. The company has the right to call the bonds at any time, but the call price is specified at 120. The call feature was added in the event market interest rates dropped and the company wanted to redeem the bonds early.

The long-awaited drop in long-term interest rates occurred this year, bringing high-quality industrial bonds from 16% down to 12% compounded semiannually. Minnick's treasurer believes the interest rate will drop to 10% in another year, and the company should redeem the bonds next year. The controller does not believe the interest rate will move lower but, instead, will turn around and rise. He recommends redeeming the bonds now.

The treasurer reminds him that the call price of 120 will require $2,400,000 now to redeem the bonds. This price assumes an interest rate of about 11%. She points out further that the present value of the outstanding bonds at the 12% interest rate is currently lower than the $2,400,000. If the interest rate drops to 10%, the present value of the bonds will rise above the call value.

Required: Should the company redeem the bonds now, in one year, or wait until sometime later?

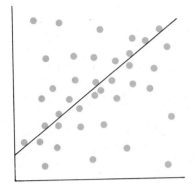

12

CAPITAL
INVESTMENT
DECISIONS—II

Chapter Objectives

This chapter will enable you to:

1. Explain the nature of capital investment decisions.
2. Evaluate alternatives in a product combination situation using the concept of "highest return per unit of the scarce factor."
3. Determine relevant cash inflows and outflows in applying discounted cash flow methods.
4. Evaluate investments using the payback method, the discounted rate of return method, and the net present value method.
5. Evaluate investments using the discounted cash flow methods, assuming the use of incremental returns.

The preceding chapter introduced the topic of capital investment decisions. It pointed out that a distinguishing characteristic of capital investment decisions is differences in the timing of the cash inflows and outflows. Usually, an initial capital outlay is made in anticipation of future incremental cash inflows or reduced future cash outflows. An example of the former situation is the purchase of a machine in anticipation of increased future sales. An example of the latter situation is the purchase of a machine in anticipation of reduced future cash labor costs. In these types of situations, the time value of money becomes a consideration, because the timing of the cash flows differ.

COMPARISON OF CAPITAL INVESTMENT DECISIONS WITH DECISIONS NOT INVOLVING CAPITAL INVESTMENT

Before discussing the factors involved in capital investment problems in addition to the time value of money, let us compare in more detail, decisions involving capital investment with those that do not involve capital investment. This discussion will help to show the relationship of the capital investment decision process, to be developed in this chapter, with the decision process discussed previously.

A typical decision problem illustrated in the previous chapter was the product combination problem. For example, suppose that a firm has a production process already in place and that unutilized capacity of 100,000 production hours exists. Assume that the two possible uses of this capacity are to produce Product A or Product B and that the selling price, variable costs, etc., are as follows:

	Product A	Product B
Selling price per unit	$10	$7
Variable cost per unit for labor and raw materials	5	5
Contribution per unit	$ 5	$2
Production hours per unit	5 hours	1 hour

In earlier discussions, it was emphasized that such a decision problem could be solved by using the contribution per hour as the criterion for making a choice. Assuming no market constraint that would limit sales, Product B would return $2 per production hour ($2 per unit ÷ 1 hour) and Product A would return $1 per production hour ($5 per unit ÷ 5 hours per unit). With no other incremental costs, Product B should be chosen, since it has the highest return per unit of the scarce factor. There are no capital investment considerations in this problem. That is, the timing of the cash flows from sales is assumed to be the same, or approximately the same, as the cash outflows for materials and labor. There is no capital investment required for a new machine, and it is assumed that no additional inventory is required. Further, the problem does not consider whether to sell the entire production facility. If this alternative is considered, capital investment might be involved.

The basic problem is how to use existing, unutilized productive capacity. Hence, the scarce factor is production (time measured in production hours), and the contribution per production hour is an appropriate rate of return measure to use in making the decision. The possible intrayear timing of the cash inflows and outflows could be slightly different, but it is not likely that such a timing difference, if it exists, will be material enough to be taken into account.

Let us now change the decision situation to bring in capital investment considerations. Suppose that no excess capacity exists but that a machine can be purchased for $300,000 which will produce 20,000 units of Product A. The selling price and other variable costs are as previously given (i.e., $10 selling price and $5 variable cost, for a contribution on net cash inflow per unit of $5 per unit). Also assume that the machine will last for five years. As can be seen, the timing of the relevant cash flows change, as does the relevant time period. The question becomes whether the firm should invest $300,000 now for expected cash inflows of $100,000 per year for five years (i.e., $5 per unit times 20,000 units per year). Since current excess capacity is no longer in the picture, a rate of return on production time is not an adequate decision criterion. Capital is now the assumed scarce factor, so it is necessary to use a rate of return based on capital instead of a return on unutilized production hours. The idea of using a rate of return on the scarce factor as the decision criterion is still the same, but the scarce factor has changed. In order to calculate a return on the scarce factor, capital, it is necessary to consider the time value of money. One way of doing this is to use the method illustrated in the previous chapter as follows:

$$\frac{\$300,000 \text{ investment}}{\$100,000 \text{ annual cash inflow}} = 3.0 \text{ (The factor corresponding to the present value of}$$
$1 received annually for 5 years at 1%, Table II)

Refer to Table II, 5 year row: Factor 3.0 corresponds to a return on capital of more than 18% and less than 20%.

Hence, if a return on capital of approximately 19% is acceptable, the investment should be made; otherwise, it should be rejected.

As can be seen, then, the concept of return on the scarce factor is a relevant concept in capital investment problems, but the time value of money becomes important in implementing and using such a concept.

Capital investment decisions are usually of special importance, and top management usually assumes direct responsibility for the authorization of substantial expenditures. Capital investment decisions deserve the attention of top management because:

1. Substantial sums of money are usually invested in capital projects.
2. The resources that are invested in a project are often committed for a long period of time.
3. It may be difficult to reverse the effects of a poor decision.
4. The success or failure of the company may depend upon a single or relatively few investment decisions.
5. Plans typically must be made well into an uncertain future.

THE CAPITAL BUDGETING PROCESS

As discussed in the previous chapter, capital budgeting is the process through which management evaluates, makes decisions about, and monitors capital investment projects. It is a long-term planning process.

An Overview

One way to describe the capital budgeting process is to identify its important parts:

1. Possible investment projects must be identified, and the factors for consideration must be evaluated. This includes the prediction of the net amount of the investment required, the amounts of the other annual cash inflows and cash outflows, and the economic life of the project.
2. It is necessary to choose a model as a method for making investment decisions. In this chapter, we will emphasize the discounted cash flow model. Since this model explicitly considers the time value of money, it is felt to be the best method for making capital investment decisions.
3. If the discounted cash flow model is used, it is necessary to predict the lowest acceptable rate of return on investment.
4. The financing of the capital budget is an important part of the capital budgeting process. Chapter 18 discusses net working capital and cash flow analysis, and these topics are related to the financing of firm activities, including the capital budget. However, the reader is referred to books on finance and financial management for a detailed discussion of financing decisions.
5. The impact of income taxes is also a consideration in capital budgeting.
6. Finally, the use of a post audit of the investment projects is one means of monitoring capital investments.

Before discussing the discounted cash flow model, let us begin with an initial consideration of the investment, the returns, and the lowest acceptable rate of return.

The Net Investment

For decision-making purposes, the net investment is not necessarily the cost that would be entered in the accounting records. Differential costs, as defined in Chapter 9, are also important to the capital investment decision. In many cases the investment is the net additional outlay of cash that is required to obtain future returns. The net investment for decision purposes is generally the net outflow of cash to support a capital investment project.

In some cases, however, the net investment is the sacrifice of an inflow of cash, that is, the opportunity cost that arises when a benefit is rejected. Assume, for example, that a building can be sold for $800,000. Should the building be sold or should it be held for use in future operations? This is an investment decision. If the building is sold, the cost of the building and the accumulated depreciation are removed from the accounting records. The proceeds from the sale are recorded along with any gain or loss on the transaction. If management refuses the sales offer and elects to use the building in operations, it has invested $800,000 in the future operation of the building. Apparently, management has decided that the future returns justify the sacrifice of an immediate return of $800,000. Obviously, no cost is recorded in the accounting records as a result of this decision. The company continues to operate as it has before. The opportunity cost is relevant only when deciding whether or not to continue operations.

The Net Returns

The net return from an investment, as defined for decision-making purposes, is not necessarily the accounting profit. Instead, the net return is the inflow of cash expected from a project, reduced by the cash cost that can be directly attributed to the project. Some projects, however, are not expected to produce an inflow of cash, but they will yield returns in the form of cash savings. For example, a new type of machine may be operated at a lower labor cost, and there may be lower costs of machine maintenance and repairs. The annual cash saving, adjusted for income tax, is the annual return on the investment.

The Lowest Acceptable Rate of Return

Relative to opportunities, funds are usually scarce and can be obtained only at a cost. There is an interest charge for the use of borrowed funds. The interest cost for the use of resources is present even when the funds are furnished by the owners, either as paid-in capital or as retained earnings. The owners expect to receive a return on their investment—interest, dividends, or rent, as the case may be. Normally an investment is not made unless the present value of the returns is expected to exceed the cost of the capital invested.

The cost of capital may be thought of as an opportunity cost. It is the rate of return expected in the future from the set of average investment opportunities normally available to the firm given its usual line of business. For example, if a company can receive a 10 percent average return from certain investments, it would not accept less than 10 percent from alternative investments in the same risk category.

RATING INVESTMENT ALTERNATIVES

As has been discussed, capital investment projects might be evaluated or rated by using a discounted cash flow model based on either a discounted rate-of-return method or a net present value method. However, a payback method (not a discounted cash flow method) might also be used, so let us lead into a discussion of the discounted cash flow method by discussing the payback method first.

The Payback Method

Investment alternatives are sometimes evaluated by relating the returns to the cost of the investment to determine how many years it will take to recover the investment. This method is simple to apply and in many cases gives answers approximately equivalent to those given by more sophisticated methods of analysis that are described later. However, this method is reliable only if the returns are evenly distributed over the years and if the investments to be compared are equal in amount and have the same life estimates with little or no salvage values.

Assume that an investment of $20,000 is expected to produce annual returns of $5,000 for ten years. No salvage recovery is expected from the investment at the end of the ten years. The investment is recovered in four years, calculated as follows:

$$\frac{\$20,000 \text{ investment}}{\$5,000 \text{ annual return}} = 4\text{-year payback period}$$

The ratio of the investment to the annual return is 4 to 1. Expressed in another way, the *unadjusted* rate of return is 25 percent, as follows:

$$\frac{\$5,000 \text{ annual return}}{\$20,000 \text{ investment}} = 25\% \text{ unadjusted rate of return}$$

The alternative with the shortest payback period or the highest unadjusted rate of return is the most acceptable, provided it meets the minimum standard that has been established. If a payback period of four years satisfies the minimum standard that has been established and if no other alternative in this investment category has a shorter payback period, the investment would be accepted.

The Discounted Rate of Return Method

As shown earlier, a rate of return can be computed on an investment by discounting the estimated future returns at an interest (discount) rate that equates the present value of the returns with the investment. This rate of return is the discounted rate of return on the investment. To be acceptable, the discounted rate of return on an investment alternative must be at least equal to the minimum-rate-of-return requirement. Ordinarily, the most acceptable investment alternative is the one that is expected to produce the highest discounted rate of return.

The discounted rate of return can be calculated by trial and error. If the annual inflows are an equal amount for each year, the ratio of the investment to the annual return is calculated just as it is in the payback method. This ratio is then compared with the present values of annuities for the same number of years given in published tables. The discount rate for the present value of an annuity that most nearly corresponds with the ratio is selected as the rate of return.

In the last example, it was assumed that a $20,000 investment would yield returns of $5,000 each year with no salvage value. The discounted rate of return is computed as follows:

1. Determine the payback period (the ratio of the investment to the annual return).

$$\frac{\$20,000 \text{ investment}}{\$5,000 \text{ annual return}} = 4\text{-year payback period}$$

2. Find the factor on the appropriate year line of a table of present values of $1 received annually that comes closest to the payback period.

   The factor 3.923, appearing in the 22% column, is closest to 4 on the 10-year line. (See Table II.) The investment is expected to have a 10-year life in this example. Therefore, the present value factor is taken from the 10-year line of the table.

3. Use the interest rate identified with this factor to discount the future annual returns.

$$\underset{\text{return}}{\$5,000 \text{ annual}} \times \underset{\substack{\text{of } \$1 \text{ received} \\ \text{annually for} \\ 10 \text{ years at } 22\%}}{3.923 \text{ present value}} = \underset{\text{of returns}}{\$19,615 \text{ present value}}$$

If the present value of the returns is approximately equal to the present value of the investment, the discounted rate of return has been determined. In the example, the present value of the returns amounting to $19,615 is not quite equal to the investment of $20,000. The investment earns somewhat less than 22 percent. If the minimum rate-of-return requirement is 18 percent, this investment alternative would more than meet the minimum standard and would be selected provided that no competing alternative promised an even better rate of return.

The returns for each year are not always equal in amount. Returns for the early years may be relatively large when compared with returns for the later years. Conversely, a project may develop slowly with returns increasing in the later years. A discounted rate of return may have to be computed by trial and error when annual returns are unequal. An average annual return may be calculated and used to find the ratio between the investment and the annual return. This ratio is compared with the present value factors in the table for the appropriate number of years. If the returns for the early years are comparatively large, the first trial may be made by selecting a rate higher than the rate found in the table. If the returns for the early years are relatively low, a lower rate may be selected for the first trial. Using the discount rate selected, the present value for each year is computed. The present values are then added and their sum compared with the present value of the investment. An example of this procedure follows.

Assume that a firm can invest in a machine that will cost $100,000 and the expected reduction in cash labor cost each year for the next five years is estimated as follows:

Year	Expected Cash Labor Cost Savings
1	$ 20,000
2	30,000
3	40,000
4	40,000
5	40,000
Total	$170,000

The savings in labor cost is expected to grow as experience is gained, but the savings will peak out after the third year. A possible starting point in approximating the rate of return is to observe that the average annual saving is $34,000 per year ($170,000 ÷ 5 years). The ratio of investment to average annual savings is about 2.94 (i.e., $100,000 ÷ $34,000). Using Table II, this five-year factor gives a rate of return of slightly higher than 20 percent. Since the savings in future years are greater than earlier years, it is reasonable to expect that the rate of return is less than that based on the average annual cash savings, so try discounting the individual cash savings at 18 percent and 20 percent using individual annual factors from Table I.

Year	Annual Savings	P.V. at 18% Factor	P.V. at 18% $	P.V. at 20% Factor	P.V. at 20% $
1	$20,000	.847	$ 16,940	.833	$16,660
2	30,000	.718	21,540	.694	20,820
3	40,000	.609	24,360	.579	23,160
4	40,000	.516	20,640	.482	19,280
5	40,000	.437	17,480	.402	16,080
			$100,960		$96,000

As can be seen, the discounted rate of return based on a present value of the $100,000 investment outlay is slightly higher than 18 percent. If this is an acceptable rate of return, the project should be undertaken.

The process of calculating a rate of return when cash flows are not uniform looks complicated. However, simple computer programs are readily available. In practice, the process is simpler than it would appear from the illustration just given.

The Net Present Value Method

Investment alternatives can also be evaluated without solving for the discounted rate of return. Using the net present value method, future dollar amounts can be discounted at the lowest acceptable rate of return and the present value of the returns compared with the present value of the investment. The alternative that produces the greatest excess of returns over the investment (on a present-value basis) is the most acceptable. If the present value of the returns is less than the present value of the investment, the investment alternative does not meet the rate-of-return requirement and should be rejected.

In a previous example, the minimum rate-of-return requirement was 18 percent. The $5,000 annual returns that are expected for ten years are discounted at 18 percent and are compared with the investment of $20,000.

$5,000 annual × 4.494 present value of $1 = $22,470 present value
     return   received each year   of returns
                for 10 years at 18%

The excess present value or net present value of the returns is $2,470.

Present value of returns $22,470
Investment   20,000
Excess present value of returns .... $ 2,470

Assume that another investment alternative is being contemplated. The net investment is $24,000 with estimated annual returns of $6,000 to be received over a period of eight years. The returns are discounted at 18 percent and are compared with the investment of $24,000.

$6,000 annual × 4.078 present value of $1 = $24,468 present value
return   received each year   of returns
                   for 8 years at 18%

The excess present value of the returns is $468.

Present value of returns $24,468
Investment   24,000
Excess present value of returns .... $ 468

Although both alternatives exceed the minimum rate-of-return objective, the excess present value of $2,470 from the first alternative is more than the excess present value of $468 from the second alternative. Assuming that available capital limits the firm to choosing only one of the projects, the alternative with the higher excess present value should be selected.

Note that the decision is not influenced by the amount of the investment or the length of time involved. The computation in either case provides for the recovery of the investment itself plus the desired rate of return. The assumption is that returns can be reinvested at this desired rate. Hence, the alternative that produces a greater excess present value adds more to total wealth as returns are reinvested over time.

REFINING THE INVESTMENT

For decision-making purposes an investment is a net outflow of cash, a commitment of cash, or the sacrifice of an inflow of cash. Sometimes adjustments must be made to determine the net investment. Three typical investment adjustments are discussed at this point:

1. The avoidable costs.
2. Additional investment in current assets.
3. The net proceeds from the sale of properties to be retired as a result of the investment.

Avoidable Costs

By making an investment, a company may be able to avoid some other cost. A cost that would otherwise be incurred will not be incurred if the investment is made.

For example, a company may be considering the purchase of new equipment costing $130,000. If this equipment is not purchased, extensive repairs will have to be made to the equipment now in service. The cost of the repairs is estimated at $15,000, and this cost is deductible in computing income tax that is estimated at 40 percent of income before income tax. The tax deduction of $15,000 for repairs cost will reduce income tax by $6,000 (40 percent of $15,000). The net cost of the repairs after income tax is $9,000. The company receives a tax benefit of $6,000 from the deduction for repairs cost. Without the deduction, income tax of $6,000 would have to be paid. Hence, if an investment is made in new equipment, the company will avoid the repair cost net of income tax or will avoid a cost of $9,000 ($15,000 − $6,000). The net investment is computed as follows:

Investment in new equipment		$130,000
Less avoidable cost:		
Repairs cost to keep old equipment in operation...........	$15,000	
Less income tax saving of 40% on repairs deduction	6,000	
Net avoidable cost.....................................		9,000
Net investment...		$121,000

The net investment of $121,000 is compared with the estimated future returns discounted at the lowest acceptable rate of return (net present value method) in making a decision. Or the estimated future returns may be discounted at a rate that equates the present value of the returns with the investment (discounted rate-of-return method) to determine if the investment meets the minimum rate of return requirement.

Additional Investment in Current Assets

Investment situations often involve the introduction of a new product line or the expansion of facilities. If the project is to be undertaken, it may have to be supported by an additional investment in current assets. For example, a new line of product may be introduced. As a result, the investment in inventory will be higher, accounts receivable will increase and the cash balance must be increased to provide for the additional operating cost. The required increment in current assets is part of the investment in the project because they must be held to support the project. When the project is eliminated, the related current assets are released.

Assume that a new project requires an investment of $500,000 in new equipment and additional current assets of $96,000 consisting of cash, accounts receivable, and inventory as shown in the following computation of the net investment.

New equipment for project		$500,000
Add additional current assets:		
Cash	$18,000	
Accounts receivable..................................	33,000	
Inventory	45,000	
Total additional current assets		96,000
Net investment...		$596,000

The investment in the current assets, as well as the salvage value of the equipment, will be recovered at the termination of the project. The present value of the current assets released and of the net salvage value recovered can be included as a return from the investment in the last year of the project's life.

It is estimated that the project will yield annual returns of $120,000 after income tax for ten years and that the equipment will have a salvage value (net of income tax) of $60,000 at the end of the project. In addition, the current assets of $96,000 that were required for operations will be released. The annual returns for the first nine years are then $120,000, but the return for the tenth year is $276,000 ($120,000 return from operation of the project plus $60,000 net salvage recovery plus $96,000 release of current assets). The returns are discounted to present values and are compared with the investment according to the procedures discussed earlier in the chapter.

Net Proceeds from the Sale of Other Properties

Properties may be retired as a result of an investment decision. If new equipment is obtained, for example, the equipment currently in operation may be sold. The proceeds from the sale of the old equipment, as adjusted for the income tax on any recognized gain or loss, are deducted from the cost of the new equipment to arrive at the net investment. To illustrate, assume that equipment costing $100,000 is to be acquired. If this equipment is acquired, the old equipment having a net book value of $20,000 will be sold for $5,000. The loss of $15,000 on the sale is deductible in computing income tax estimated at 40 percent of income before tax.[1]

The company can reduce its income tax by $6,000 (40% of $15,000 loss) by selling the equipment. The total benefit to be derived from selling this equipment amounts to $11,000—the $5,000 proceeds from the sale plus the income tax reduction of $6,000. The net investment is computed as follows:

Investment in new equipment		$100,000
Less benefit from the sale of old equipment:		
Gross proceeds	$5,000	
Add reduction of income tax (40% of $15,000 loss deduction)	6,000	
Total benefit		11,000
Net investment.......................................		$ 89,000

If a taxable gain results from the sale of property, income tax is increased. The total amount received from the sale of property is reduced by the tax on the gain to determine the net amount retained by the taxpayer. For example, assume that the equipment having a net book value of $20,000 can be sold for

---

[1]The federal tax rate on the ordinary income of an operation above $100,000 is 46 percent. In most instances throughout this text, a 40 percent rate is used to simplify illustrations.

$35,000 and that the gain of $15,000 will be taxed at a rate of 40 percent.[2] The net proceeds from the sale of equipment will amount to $29,000 after subtracting the tax of $6,000 (40 percent of $15,000) from the $35,000 received from the sale of the equipment.

The net investment in the new equipment is computed as follows:

Investment in new equipment		$100,000
Less net benefit from the sale of old equipment:		
Gross proceeds	$35,000	
Less income tax on gain of $15,000 (40% of $15,000)	6,000	
Net benefit		29,000
Net investment		$ 71,000

Often the old equipment will be traded in when new equipment is acquired. There is no income tax on a gain from a trade-in transaction, nor is any loss deduction allowed. Therefore, the net investment is equal to the cost of new equipment minus the trade-in allowance.

INCOME TAX EFFECTS

Before any capital investment decision is finalized, the implication of taxes to the investment should be explored. Understanding the advantages and disadvantages of the tax effect will benefit the decision-making process.

Depreciation

In many investment projects, the firm may acquire assets that are depreciable for income tax purposes. In financial accounting and reporting, depreciation is a process of allocating the cost of a depreciable asset to the accounting periods, such as years, over which the asset is used. This is part of the process of matching costs with revenues to calculate the period net income. For example, if the firm acquires a $100,000 machine with an estimated useful life of five years, and if the salvage value of the machine in five years is estimated to be zero, an annual depreciation cost of $20,000 would be recognized under a straight-line depreciation method. For capital investment analysis, this annual cost is not recognized, since it does not involve a cash outflow. The cash outflow takes place at the time the asset is purchased. However, when income tax effects are considered, depreciation will affect cash flows, because it is deductible as a cost for tax purposes and will reduce the income tax that would otherwise have to be paid. This reduction in income tax does affect cash flows associated with an investment project, and it should be part of the process of evaluating capital investments.

---

[2]The gain on the sale of an asset might be taxed as a capital gain rather than ordinary income. If so, the tax rate might be lower. However, the tax laws are quite restrictive. Hence, it is assumed in this text that such gains are taxed as ordinary income.

For example, assume that the $100,000 machine investment will automate a production process and that the annual cash labor and materials cost savings are estimated at $45,000 per year for five years before any consideration of depreciation or income tax. Also, assume that the firm is subject to a 40 percent corporate tax rate. The after-tax savings, assuming that straight-line depreciation on the machine is a tax deduction, can be calculated as follows:

(1) Calculate the Income Tax on the Cost Savings:

Year	Increase in Taxable Income due to Cost Savings	Less Additional Depreciation Deduction for Tax Purposes	Taxable Increase in Income	Additional Income Tax at 40%
1	$45,000	$20,000	$25,000	$10,000
2	45,000	20,000	25,000	10,000
3	45,000	20,000	25,000	10,000
4	45,000	20,000	25,000	10,000
5	45,000	20,000	25,000	10,000

(2) Calculate the After-Tax Cash Cost Savings:

Year	Annual Cost Savings before Tax (from above)	Additional Income Tax (from above)	Cost Saving After Tax
1	$45,000	$10,000	$35,000
2	45,000	10,000	35,000
3	45,000	10,000	35,000
4	45,000	10,000	35,000
5	45,000	10,000	35,000

These calculations are more detailed than required, but they are done to illustrate some key points. First, the depreciation deduction for tax purposes is sometimes referred to as the depreciation tax shield. As is evident in the first calculation, the depreciation deduction "shields" $20,000 of the cash cost savings from income tax. The value of such a tax shield at a 40 percent tax rate is $8,000 per year, which is the reduction in income tax due to the depreciation deduction. That is, annual income tax without the depreciation would be $18,000 (40% × $45,000), while the income tax with a depreciation deduction (as shown in Calculation #1) is $10,000 per year. Hence, the depreciation deduction, while not a cash flow itself, does increase cash flows by $8,000 per year through reduced income tax.

The second point to emphasize is that depreciation is not a cash flow. Cash flows are affected by the $45,000 cost savings, the $100,000 investment, and the $10,000 additional income tax that must be paid. Hence, the annual cash flows are emphasized in Calculation (2).

Alternative calculations could be made to achieve the same result:

(1) Calculation of After-Tax Cost Savings:

Annual cost savings before tax	$45,000
Less depreciation	20,000
Cost savings subject to tax	$25,000
Less tax at 40%	10,000
Total	$15,000
Add back depreciation which is not a cash flow	20,000
After tax cost savings	$35,000

(2) Calculation of After-Tax Cost Savings:

Annual cost savings before tax		$45,000
Tax effects:		
Tax on cost saving at 40%	$18,000	
Less depreciation tax shield (.4 × $20,000)	8,000	
Net income tax		10,000
After-tax cost savings		$35,000

As can be seen, either of these two methods will give the same result.

To complete the decision, the after-tax rate of return can be calculated as follows:

$$\frac{\$100,000 \text{ investment}}{\$35,000 \text{ after tax cost savings}} = 2.86 \text{ Table II, 5 year factor}$$

From Table II, 5 year row: 2.86 gives 22% after tax rate of return on investment

If 22 percent is an acceptable after-tax rate of return on investment, the investment should be made; otherwise, it should be rejected.

Tax Advantage of Accelerated Depreciation.

Forms of depreciation more accelerated than straight-line (SL) have been allowed for income tax purposes. This has been done by Congress as a means of stimulating business investment in long-term assets. In 1981, the Economic Recovery Tax Act was passed. This act made significant changes in the tax depreciation rules in an attempt to stimulate business investment in productive assets. Before the new depreciation rules are explained, let us examine why business investment might be stimulated by allowing for acceleration of depreciation tax deductions.

One form of accelerated depreciation that was allowed prior to the 1981 tax act was the sum-of-the-years-digits (SYD) depreciation. In this method, the years digits in the useful life were summed to provide the denominator. For a five-year asset, the sum of the years digits would be $1+2+3+4+5 = 15$. The first year's depreciation would be 5/15 of the asset cost, the second year would be assigned 4/15 of the cost and so forth. For a 5-year, $600,000 asset with no salvage value, the SL depreciation and SYD depreciation are as follows:

Year	SYD Depreciation	SL Depreciation
1	5/15 × $600,000 = $200,000	1/5 × $600,000 = $120,000
2	4/15 × 600,000 = 160,000	1/5 × 600,000 = 120,000
3	3/15 × 600,000 = 120,000	1/5 × 600,000 = 120,000
4	2/15 × 600,000 = 80,000	1/5 × 600,000 = 120,000
5	1/15 × 600,000 = 40,000	1/5 × 600,000 = 120,000
	$600,000	$600,000

In either case the total depreciation over the five years is the same ($600,000), so any tax advantage depends on the time value of money—the cost of capital being used as the discount rate. The more the acceleration, the higher the tax rate, and the higher the cost of capital, the greater the tax advantage of accelerated depreciation. Assuming taxes are paid at the end of each year, the net advantage of SYD depreciation over SL depreciation, assuming a 40 percent tax rate and discount rates of 10 percent and 20 percent are shown in the following table. To make the point even stronger, we have included in the calculation a rather extreme acceleration in the form of a tax deduction of the entire asset cost in the first year.

1. Present value (PV) at 10% and 20% of tax deduction in the 1st year (assume taxes paid at the end of year).

$$PV(10\%) = \$600,000 \times .40 \times .909 = \$218,160$$

$$PV(20\%) = \$600,000 \times .40 \times .833 = \$199,920$$

2. Present value at 10% and 20% of tax deduction using SYD depreciation:

Year	SYD Depreciation	Tax Reduction at 40%	10%	Present Value $	20%	$
1	$200,000	$ 80,000	.909	$ 72,720	.833	$ 66,640
2	160,000	64,000	.826	52,864	.694	44,416
3	120,000	48,000	.751	36,048	.579	27,792
4	80,000	32,000	.683	21,856	.482	15,424
5	40,000	16,000	.621	9,936	.402	6,432
	$600,000	$240,000		$193,424		$160,704

3. Present value at 10% and 20% of tax deduction using SL depreciation:

$$PV(10\%) = \left(\frac{\$600,000}{5}\right) \times .4 \times 3.791 = \$181,968$$

$$PV(20\%) = \left(\frac{\$600,000}{5}\right) \times .4 \times 2.991 = \$143,568$$

4. Comparison of present values:

	10%	Difference	20%	Difference
Deduction in 1st year	$218,160	$24,736	$199,920	$39,216
SYD depreciation	193,424	11,456	160,704	17,136
SL depreciation	181,968		143,568	
Difference between deduction in first year and SL		$36,192		$56,352

As is evident from the above calculations and comparison, the total depreciation deducted for tax purposes over the five year period is the same $600,000. It is only the timing of the deduction that differs. However, the present value advantage of accelerated forms of deductibility is apparent, and the greater the time preference for money, the greater the difference. At 20 percent, a deduction in Year 1 enjoys a $56,352 present value advantage over SL depreciation, while at 10 percent, the deduction in Year 1 enjoys an advantage of $36,192. If a decision maker had no time preference, the discount rate would be zero, and there would, of course, be no advantage to accelerated depreciation tax deductions. This is an unlikely situation, but the analysis of an extreme situation may serve to make the point more clearly. Since present values from investments are increased and, therefore, rates of return on investments are increased, it is apparent why accelerated depreciation deductions as allowed by the tax laws can serve as a stimulus to capital investment by tax-paying firms.

Depreciation Deductions Under the Current Tax Law

The Economic Recovery Tax Act of 1981 as modified by the Tax Equity and Fiscal Responsibility Act of 1982 made some sweeping changes in the provisions for depreciation deductions. Some of the important features are reviewed here to show the impact of taxes on capital investment analysis and decisions.

Prior to the 1981 Act, tax depreciation deductions were generally based on the useful life of the asset acquired from the investment and various depreciation methods were acceptable. A firm could elect SL depreciation or any one of the more accelerated methods. The choice of a useful life of a major asset investment might have been negotiated with the Internal Revenue Service (IRS). The IRS published guidelines to aid firms in the choice of a useful life for purposes of taxation.

The 1981 Act did away with the concept of useful life depreciation systems and substituted the Accelerated Cost Recovery System (ACRS). The emphasis is on "capital recovery" deductions for tax purposes, and periods for capital recovery are established for various types of assets. For example, four capital recovery periods are established—three years, five years, ten years, and fifteen years. As an aside, the new ACRS systems is sometimes referred to as the "10-5-3" system! All eligible property, i.e., assets depreciable for tax purposes, is assigned to one of the classes, and capital recovery percentages for each year within each class are specified. The following are some of the depreciable assets associated with the various classes.

> 3-year class — Included are automobiles, light-duty trucks, and equipment used for research and development experimentation.
>
> 5-year class — Included is tangible property not specifically included in the 3-, 10-, or 15-year classes, and this includes most machinery, equipment, and furniture.
>
> 10-year class — Public utility property with a useful life of 18 to 25 years and, for example, railroad tank cars.
>
> 15-year class — Real property not specifically included in the 5- or 10-year classes or public utility classes, and public utility property with a useful life of longer than 25 years.

For each of these classes of assets, then, the capital recovery rates are specified. The current recovery schedule is as follows:

ACRS Schedule
Property Placed in Service After 12/31/80

Ownership Year	Class of Investment			
	3-Year	5-Year	10-Year	15-Year Utility Property
	%	%	%	%
1	25	15	8	5
2	38	22	14	10
3	37	21	12	9
4		21	10	8
5		21	10	7
6			10	7
7			9	6
8			9	6
9			9	6
10			9	6
11				6
12				6
13				6
14				6
15				6
	100	100	100	100

In reviewing the preceding schedule, a question might be raised as to the acceleration of capital recovery. For example, the percent for year one in the three-year class is 25 percent. A straight line rate would give 33-1/3 percent deduction for an asset with a three year useful life. It is necessary to keep in mind, however, that a reduction in the capital recovery period is also a form of acceleration in the tax deduction and that is, of course, fundamental to the ACRS schedule. This is apparent in the 10 and 15 year classes when, for example, utility property with a useful life of 18 to 25 years is given a 10 year capital recovery period.

Acceleration of capital recovery for tax purposes may not be advantageous to some firms as, for example, those firms that are incurring losses and pay no taxes. It is still possible for a firm to elect straight-line depreciation for each class of assets over longer periods. The SL recovery periods allowed for each class are shown as follows:

ACRS Class	Straight-Line Recovery Periods Available
3-year property	3, 5, or 12 years
5-year property	5, 12, or 25 years
10-year property	10, 25, or 35 years
15-year real property	15, 35, or 45 years
15-year public utility property	15, 35, or 45 years

Hence, a firm that wishes to lengthen the capital recovery period can still do so by using SL depreciation according to the preceding schedule. However, for a tax-paying firm, the economic incentives to choose the regular capital recovery rate schedule are strong; the time value of money offers the explanation.

The Investment Tax Credit

Since the Revenue Act of 1962, an investment tax credit (ITC) has been a feature of tax law, and this provision has an impact on capital investment analysis and decisions. Currently a tax credit of 10 percent is allowed on investments in assets which fall in the 5-, 10-, and 15-year classes and 6 percent for assets in the 3-year class. However, the asset must be reduced for depreciation purposes by 50 percent of the tax credit if this option is elected. The taxpayer has the option of electing an 8 percent tax credit for assets in the 5-, 10-, or 15-year classes and a 4 percent tax credit for assets in the 3-year class. With this option, the asset does not have to be reduced by any portion of the tax credit.[3]

Immediate Expensing of Assets

Another feature of the Economic Recovery Tax Act of 1981 is to allow immediate expensing for tax purposes of a limited amount of the cost of assets acquired that would otherwise be subject to capital recovery deductions according to the ACRS schedule. The maximum amount currently allowed is $7,500, and this goes to $10,000 for 1986 and subsequent years. Although the

---

[3]Under either alternative, the maximum investment tax credit may not exceed $25,000 plus 85 percent of that year's tax liability in excess of $25,000. Unused investment tax credits may be carried back three years and forward fifteen years.

firm has the advantage of this immediate tax deduction, it gives up the ITC on the amount expensed, and the basis of the asset that is allowed for capital recovery deductions is also reduced.

Tax Options

The taxpayer must decide which combination of options is best in the taxpayer's particular situation.[4]

1. Elect 10 percent investment tax credit for 5-, 10-, or 15-year classes (6% for 3 years) and reduce depreciation base by half the amount of the investment credit.
2. Elect 8 percent investment tax credit for 5-, 10-, or 15-year classes (4% for 3 years) with no reduction in asset base.
3. Take immediate expense of $7,500 ($10,000 after 1985) but give up that amount as base for investment tax credit and depreciation charges.

A tax credit has much more impact than a tax deduction. For example, assume that a company with an income tax of $50,000 has the option of taking a tax credit of $5,000 or can deduct $5,000 in depreciation. The income tax rate is 46 percent.

	Tax Credit—$5,000	Tax Deduction—$5,000
Income tax	$50,000	$50,000
Tax credit	5,000	
Tax of 46% on $5,000 depreciation deduction		2,300
Net income tax	$45,000	$47,700

The tax credit is a direct reduction against the tax, but the tax deduction only reduces the tax by the tax rate multiplied by the deduction.

In making a decision, the taxpayer in a higher income tax bracket with a relatively high cost of capital will generally select options that will emphasize immediate benefits over later benefits. With a high discount rate, later returns have a much smaller present value relative to the more immediate returns. This effect is not as pronounced with low discount rates. Hence, the taxpayer with a high tax rate and a relatively-high rate-of-return situation will tend to prefer the investment tax credit at the maximum rate combined with immediate expensing. The amounts of future capital recoveries will have less significance.

Illustration—Tax Options

Assume that a company is considering the purchase of equipment costing $100,000 with an estimated useful life of five years. The income tax rate is 46 percent, and the minimum acceptable rate of return on investments has been established at 20 percent.

---

[4]Hobbs, James B., "Selecting the Optimum Tax Recovery Method for Depreciable Property," *The Journal of Taxation*, Vol. 59, No. 1 (July, 1983), pp. 48-51.

Option A

Immediate expense of $7,500 and investment tax credit of 10 percent
with reduction of asset base by 50 percent of tax credit

Computation of depreciation base

Cost of equipment...	$100,000
Less immediate expense..	7,500
	$ 92,500
Investment tax credit as reduction of base:	
Tax credit (10% of $92,500) $9,250	
50% of tax credit (50% of $9,250)	4,625
Depreciation base	$ 87,875

Computation of depreciation

Years	Depreciation Base	ACRS Rates	Depreciation
1	$87,875	.15	$13,181
2	87,875	.22	19,332
3	87,875	.21	18,454
4	87,875	.21	18,454
5	87,875	.21	18,454

Income tax reductions

Years	Immediate Expense	Tax Credit	Depreciation	Tax Rate	Income Tax Reduction
1		$9,250		—	$ 9,250
1	$7,500			.46	3,450
1			$13,181	.46	6.063
2			19,332	.46	8,893
3			18,454	.46	8,489
4			18,454	.46	8,489
5			18,454	.46	8,489
Total tax reductions					$53,123

Option B
No immediate expense and investment tax
credit of 8 percent with no reduction of asset base

Depreciation base $100,000

Computation of depreciation

Years	Depreciation base	ACRS rates	Depreciation
1	$100,000	.15	$15,000
2	100,000	.22	22,000
3	100,000	.21	21,000
4	100,000	.21	21,000
5	100,000	.21	21,000

(continued on next page)

Income tax reductions

Years	Tax credit	Depreciation	Tax Rate	Income Tax Reduction
1	$8,000		—	$ 8,000
1		$15,000	.46	6,900
2		22,000	.46	10,120
3		21,000	.46	9,660
4		21,000	.46	9,660
5		21,000	.46	9,660
Total tax reductions..				$54,000

The present value of the tax reductions is computed using a discount rate of 20 percent.

Present value of tax reductions

	Tax Reductions		Present Value Factors	Present Value of Tax Reductions	
Years	Option A	Option B	20%	Option A	Option B
1*	$18,763	$14,900	.833	$15,629	$12,412
2	8,893	10,120	.694	6,172	7,023
3	8,489	9,660	.579	4,915	5,593
4	8,489	9,660	.482	4,092	4,656
5	8,489	9,660	.402	3,413	3,883
Present value of tax reductions				$34,221	$33,567

*Sum of the tax reductions computed for the first year.

With a discount rate of 20 percent, Option A is the better alternative. The present value of the tax reductions is somewhat higher for Option A. If the present value of the tax decreases (reductions) is larger, the present value of the returns from the investment after income taxes will also be larger.

In the illustration, the present value was better for Option A, because with a high discount rate, the large reduction in the first year has more impact.

Assume now that the company has a discount rate of only 6 percent. The present value of the tax reductions for Option A and Option B are computed as follows:

Present value of tax reductions

	Tax Reductions		Present Value Factors	Present Value of Tax Reductions	
Years	Option A	Option B	6%	Option A	Option B
1*	$18,763	$14,900	.943	$17,694	$14,051
2	8,893	10,120	.890	7,915	9,007
3	8,489	9,660	.840	7,131	8,114
4	8,489	9,660	.792	6,723	7,651
5	8,489	9,660	.747	6,341	7,216
Present value of tax reductions				$45,804	$46,039

*Sum of the tax reductions computed for the first year.

With a relatively low discount rate, the situation changes, and Option B is better. Note that with a lower discount rate the present value factors for later years do not decrease as rapidly as they do with higher rates. Hence, not as much emphasis is placed upon more immediate returns when the discount rate is lower. In any situation, management must decide which combination of options will be better after considering discount rates and income tax rates.

INCREMENTAL RETURNS

Up to this point, most of the illustrations have assumed that a single investment alternative existed, so the firm must decide whether or not to invest in that single project. In actuality, a firm may have an opportunity to invest in more than one project but may still have to select only one of the projects. In such a case, care must be exercised in using the discounted rate of return method because the project with the highest discounted rate of return may not be the most desirable. This can happen in those cases where the dollar investment is not the same in, for example, two investment alternatives. The dollar amount of the return from a larger investment, in many cases, will exceed the dollar return from a smaller investment having a better rate of discounted return.

Assume that Globe Transit Company has an opportunity to invest in one of two projects. Each project has an estimated life of five years with annual returns as follows:

	Project I	Project II
Net investment	$75,000	$100,000
Annual return for each of 5 years	30,000	38,000

Investments are expected to yield a discounted rate of return of at least 15 percent.

The discounted rate of return is computed on each alternative:

	Project I	Project II	Incremental
Net investment	$75,000	$100,000	$25,000
Annual return	$30,000	$ 38,000	$ 8,000
Ratio of net investment to annual return	2.5	2.632	3.125
Present value factor from 5-year line of Table II that most nearly corresponds with ratio of net investment to annual return	2.532	2.635	3.127
Rate of return from Table II	28%	26%	18%

It appears that Project I should be selected because the discounted rate of return is higher. However, the key to the problem is the incremental investment and the incremental returns. If the rate of return on the incremental investment is greater than the cutoff rate of return, the additional investment should be made. In this example, an additional $8,000 a year is returned on an additional investment of $25,000. The rate of return on the incremental investment is 18 percent, and the cutoff rate is 15 percent.

A solution by the net present value method follows:

	Project I	Project II
Present value of returns at 15%:		
$30,000 × 3.352	$100,560	
$38,000 × 3.352		$127,376
Investment	75,000	100,000
Excess present value of returns	$ 25,560	$ 27,376

Project II should be selected. It yields greater excess returns on a net present value basis.

The concept of incremental investment applies even though the initial investments are the same. The returns are reinvested and may be viewed as potential investments in the future. If one alternative produces larger returns than another in the early years, while the other alternative produces better returns in later years, the problem of incremental investment arises. Should the company forego the more immediate returns for even larger returns in the future? The answer will depend upon the rate at which future returns can be invested and the amount of the future returns as compared with the sacrifice of immediate returns. A solution to the problem is to discount at the lowest acceptable rate of return.

Sometimes the investment problem can be understood better when the returns are depicted on a graph. The returns from each alternative are discounted at various discount rates. The investment is subtracted from the discounted returns, and the excess or negative discounted returns are plotted on a graph.

Conceptually, the following graph is not unlike the P/V graph used in break-even analysis. Positive discounted returns are given on a vertical scale above a zero line, and negative discounted returns are shown below the line.

Data from the previous illustration are depicted on the graph on page 366.

Computations at the 10 percent rate are given in the following table to illustrate the procedure employed:

	Project I	Project II
Present value of returns	$113,730	$144,058
Less present value of investment	75,000	100,000
Net positive discounted returns	$ 38,730	$ 44,058

Note that Project II is a better investment candidate when the lowest acceptable rate of return is less than 18 percent. If the company can reinvest returns at more than 18 percent, Project I is better. The discounted rate of return for each alternative is at the point where the present value line crosses the zero axis on the chart. The cost of the investment is balanced by the discounted returns at the rate indicated at the point of crossover.

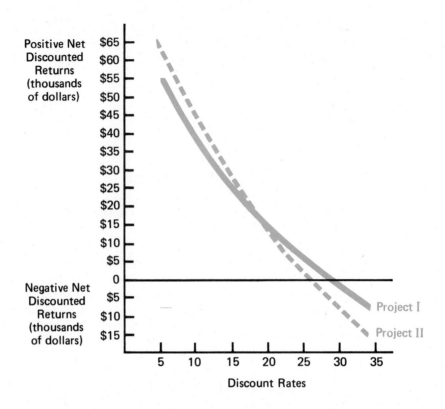

THE EVALUATION PROCESS

The task of ranking investment alternatives is usually not as difficult as the task of collecting reliable data that can be used in making the evaluation. Even with experience, it is not easy to make predictions of future returns and the rates that should be used in discounting.

Generally, certain policies and procedures are followed in the acquisition of investments of various types. For example, requests for new equipment or for special projects are reviewed by the engineering department or may even be initiated by that department as a result of studies made. The technological aspects are evaluated, and competing pieces of equipment are compared as to performance. Revenue, cost, and saving are identified with each alternative through the combined efforts of the engineers and the accountants.

Ordinarily, special forms are used to record data with respect to the cost of the investment and the anticipated returns. When the evaluation reports have been completed, they are submitted to a screening committee for critical review. Some of the investment expenditures are approved by this committee and recommended to the project or equipment planning committee of the board of directors who gives final approval or disapproval.

Sometimes the discounted return approach is rejected as an analytical tool because of the difficulty in making estimates. But the problem of estimation cannot be avoided under any method that may be used to evaluate investment alternatives. Giving recognition to time adjustments for monetary amounts does not add uncertainty. Even in a simple payback calculation, the investor must make the same estimates.

Anticipation of Change

In making any decision, particularly a decision that will have a long-range effect, there is always the risk that the predictions will be wrong because of changes in the company, the industry, or the general economic environment. While it is not possible to anticipate all changes, the problem can be approached by examining what-if type questions.

For example, assume that a firm can invest $100,000 for additional production capacity, and it is predicted that 10,000 units per year can be sold at a net contribution of $3 per unit or $30,000 per year (ignore income tax). Suppose that the minimum acceptable rate of return is 10 percent. With a five-year useful life, the rate of return would be:

$100,000 ÷ $30,000 = 3.33 which converts (using Table II) to a rate of return of slightly in excess of 15%

Based on the prediction, the firm should invest.

However, suppose that there is uncertainty about the annual sale prediction of 10,000 units. Sensitivity analysis might be used to see how sensitive the decision is to the uncertainty of the sales prediction. Analyzing what-if type questions is a form of sensitivity analysis. For example, the firm might analyze the question of what happens if the actual quantity of sales units is 20 percent lower than predicted, or 8,000 units per year. The rate of return under such conditions would be:

$100,000 ÷ $24,000 (i.e., 8,000 units @ $3) = 4.16 which converts to a rate of return of 6% to 8%

As can be seen, if the prediction is 20 percent off, the project is not favorable, but what about a 10 percent decline in sales? Actually, it is possible to calculate the rate of annual sales required to earn the minimum acceptable rate of return of 10 percent. The relevant equation is as follows:

$100,000 = $3 × 3.791 × unit sales

That is, the annual unit sales required to earn 10 percent is that number of units which when multiplied by $3 (the selling price) and the present value at 10 percent of $1 received annually for five years (3.791) is equal to the required investment, $100,000.

The solution is as follows:

$$\text{Unit sales} = \$100,000 \div 11.373$$
$$= 8,793 \text{ Units}$$

At annual sales of 8,793 units or greater, the investment will earn 10 percent or more; at annual sales less than 8,793 units, the return will be less than 10 percent. This analysis does not solve the problem, but it should help management make the decision because it shows how sensitive the decision is to the uncertain sales prediction.

The Post Audit

After a piece of equipment has been acquired, or after a project has been started, it is watched closely. Its performance, both from a technical and an economic point of view, is audited or reviewed at the end of its "shakedown period." During this period, it may be found that certain corrections have to be made if the equipment or project is going to realize its potential. At the end of the period, an audit or review shows whether or not the investment met expectations and may indicate ways in which the operation can be improved.

The audit referred to is not an audit in the true sense of the word. It is in reality a general review and, like the original evaluation, may contain errors of estimation. The review may also be limited by the accounting information that is available. On a special project, the operating results may be shown separately in the accounting records. But on an individual piece of equipment, which is only one among many items, there may be no separate accounting. In fact, it would be difficult to identify the operating results with any one piece of equipment. Whether or not additional effort should be exerted to have separate accountability depends upon the relative importance of the investment and the cost incurred to get the additional information.

The post audit is a means by which errors of operation can be detected and corrected. The audit may also serve as a control in that employees may tend to be more careful if they realize that the equipment is under surveillance. Furthermore, project evaluations may be more thoroughly made if these evaluations are to be given a performance test at some later date. And, of course, the audit may reveal information that can be applied in future investment planning.

Terminology Review

Scarce factor (344)
Production (344)
Time value of money (345)
Capital budgeting (345)
Net investment (346)
Net return (347)
Discounted rate of return on the
    investment (348)
Net present value (350)

Investment (351)
Depreciation (354)
Straight line depreciation (354)
Sum-of-the-years-digits
    depreciation (356)
Accelerated Cost Recovery
    System (358)
Tax credit (360)

QUESTIONS FOR REVIEW

1. How does a capital investment differ from other investments?

2. Is a long-term investment in the capital stock of another company a capital investment?

3. Why are capital investment decisions so important?

4. What three factors are related in the evaluation of capital investment alternatives?

5. What is the net investment from a decision-making point of view?

6. Can a capital investment be made when there is no outflow of resources? Explain.

7. Are the returns from an investment the same as the accounting profit? Explain.

8. The return from an investment is not always in the form of a net inflow of net working capital. Explain.

9. Explain the difference between the discounted rate of return method and the net present value method in the evaluation of investment alternatives.

10. What is the net present value of an investment alternative costing $175,000 with the expected annual return of $60,000 for a period of 5 years when the minimum acceptable rate of return is 22%?

11. The net present value of a certain investment is zero. Does this mean the investment earns no profit? Explain.

12. What is an avoidable cost? Why is the avoidable cost reduced by the income tax effect?

13. In a replacement situation, how are the proceeds from the sale of old equipment used in computing the net investment?

14. In computing the net investment in a replacement situation, what is the effect of selling old equipment at a loss? At a gain?

15. Cash, accounts receivable, and inventory are classified as current assets. How can they be considered part of a capital investment in the decision-making process?

16. Why is depreciation an important factor in the computation of the annual net returns?

17. What is the advantage of accelerated depreciation in capital investment analysis?

18. The investment alternative yielding the highest discounted rate of return is the most acceptable. Will this always be true? Explain.

EXERCISES

1. Net Investment. The management of Worth Machine Company plans to replace a sorting machine that was acquired several years ago at a cost of $50,000. The machine has been depreciated to its salvage value of $5,000. A new sorter can be purchased for

$70,000. The dealer will grant a trade-in allowance of $6,000 on the old machine. If a new machine is not purchased, Worth Machine Company will spend $25,000 to repair the old machine. Gains and losses on trade-in transactions are not subject to income tax. The cost to repair the old machine can be deducted in the first year for computing income tax. Income tax is estimated at 40% of the income subject to tax.

Required: Compute the net investment in the new machine for decision-making purposes.

2. Net Returns and Discounted Rate of Return. The Pepper Company is considering a new production method that can reduce materials cost by an estimated $45,000 a year. The new method is also expected to result in annual savings in labor and overhead cost of $55,000. The new equipment required for this method will cost $400,000 and will be depreciated on a straight-line basis for tax purposes. There will be no residual value at the end of 10 years, the estimated life of the equipment. Income tax is estimated at 40% of income before income tax.

Required:
(1) Determine the annual net return for the proposed investment.
(2) Will the investment earn a 20% after-tax rate of return?

3. Sales Offer as Investment. The owner of a mini storage unit has just received an offer of $400,000 for the storage buildings. The owner is interested in another investment opportunity that can probably yield an annual discounted return of 18% after income tax. The storage unit is expected to continue to yield an annual cash flow, before income tax, of $100,000 for a period of 10 years. The book value of the storage buildings is $500,000 and straight-line depreciation is used for tax purposes. The remaining life is 10 years, so the depreciation is $50,000 per year. Zero salvage value is predicted.

Required: If income tax is 40%, should the offer for the sale of the storage unit be accepted or refused?

4. Net Investment and Discounted Rate of Return. A unit of equipment used in stamping out plastic parts can be acquired from an equipment manufacturer at a cost of $200,000. If this equipment is acquired, an old unit of equipment that is fully depreciated will be sold for $20,000.

Annual returns from the new equipment before deducting depreciation or income tax have been estimated at $80,000 for a period of 5 years. Depreciation of $40,000 is to be deducted each year, and the new equipment is expected to have no salvage value at the end of the 5 years. Income tax is at the rate of 40% on ordinary income and at the rate of 30% on any gain from the sale of equipment.

Required:
(1) Determine the net investment in the new equipment.
(2) What is the net annual return on the investment?
(3) Will this investment be acceptable if the minimum rate of return has been established at 20%?

5. Incremental Investment and Discounted Rate of Return. A manufacturer of equipment quotes a price of $130,000 for a unit of equipment that is being considered by Tan Products Inc. This equipment should be able to produce net returns of $41,000 each year for 5 years. Another equipment manufacturer offers a unit of equipment at a price of

$180,000. This unit of equipment is expected to yield $55,000 in net returns each year for 5 years. These are mutually exclusive investment alternatives. An investment of this type is expected to yield a discounted rate of return of no less than 12%. Ignore income tax.

Required:

    (1) Which investment alternative is more attractive if a discounted rate of return of 12% is expected? Show computations.

    (2) What is the discounted rate of return on each investment alternative?

    (3) What is the discounted rate of return on the incremental investment?

6. Net Present Value and Discounted Rate of Return. Two competing investment alternatives are being considered by the Mills Company. One alternative costs $170,000 with estimated annual returns after income tax of $50,000 each year for a period of 5 years. The other alternative costs $130,000 with estimated annual returns after income tax of $40,000 each year for a period of 5 years. An investment of this type is expected to earn a discounted rate of return of at least 15%.

Required:

    (1) Determine the more desirable alternative by the net present value method. (Discount the returns at 15% and compare the discounted returns with the investment.)

    (2) What is the discounted rate of return on each investment alternative?

7. Investment in Another Company. The management of Burch Enterprises Inc. is considering the investment of $10,000,000 to acquire the assets of Ener-Tec Company, a small company that has developed a more economical means of using electrical energy. Last year Ener-Tec reported net sales of $18,000,000 and operating expenses of $16,000,000. Included in the operating expenses is depreciation of assets in the amount of $800,000. This level of earnings is expected to continue for 5 years, after which the technology will be outdated and the assets will have no value.

Required: Ignoring income tax, what approximate rate of return would be earned by the investment?

8. Investment Returns and Sales Volume. Plastic Products Inc. is considering an investment of $2,000,000 in a new product line. Depreciation of $200,000 is to be deducted in each of the next 10 years (salvage value is estimated at zero). A selling price of $60 per unit is decided upon; unit variable cost is $30. The sales division believes that a sales estimate of 50,000 units per year is realistic. The controller states that there is a solid market for only 20,000 units a year. Projects must meet a minimum rate-of-return requirement of 12%. Income tax is estimated at 40% of income before tax.

Required: Evaluate the project using each of the sales volume alternatives given. Use the net present value method.

9. Effect of Accelerated Depreciation. The molding department of Hayes Inc. has been investigating the possibility of acquiring a new unit of equipment at a cost of $60,000. Cash savings before income tax from the use of this equipment have been estimated at $20,000 per year for a period of 5 years. At the end of 5 years, the equipment will have no salvage value. The rate to be used in evaluating investments is 10% after income tax of 40%.

Required: Calculate the net present value if straight-line depreciation is used for tax purposes and if the sum-of-the-years-digits is used as the depreciation method for tax purposes. (Round all amounts to nearest dollar.)

10. Effect of Accelerated Depreciation. At a 40% tax rate and a 20% discount rate, how much greater is the economic present value of the sum-of-the-years-digits method as compared with straight-line depreciation on a 5-year asset (no salvage value) costing $150,000? How much greater is the economic value at a 10% discount rate?

11. Mutually Exclusive Alternatives. The Jason Company has $50,000 to invest in either of two alternatives. Investment I yields $12,000 a year in after-tax annual cash flows for 10 years. Investment II yields a one-time after-tax return of $180,000 at the end of 10 years.

Required:

(1) Using Tables I and II, find the present value for all interest columns from 4% through 24%, using the 10-year row.

(2) If the minimum rate of return is in the range of 4% to approximately 9%, which investment is preferred?

(3) Over which range of minimum interest rates is Investment I preferable to Investment II?

(4) At which minimum interest rate is neither Investment I nor Investment II preferred?

12. Investment in Securities. Sumio Enami has $10,000 available for investment in one of 3 stocks to cover a period of 5 years. The stocks and their cash flows are as follows:

Company K stock yields dividends annually of $3,000 but is not expected to appreciate in price over 5 years.

Company L stock yields dividends of $1,000 and its price should double so that Enami can sell it for $20,000 at the end of 5 years.

Company M stock will not yield any dividends but its price will increase 2½ times in 5 years, allowing Enami to sell the stock for $25,000.

Required: Which stock should Enami invest in, assuming his minimum rate is 15%? Ignore income taxes.

PROBLEMS

12-1. Net Investment and Returns. The management of the Ohio Company has rejected an opportunity to buy new machinery costing $110,000. Although it would probably yield cash savings after income tax, including the effect of depreciation on income tax, of $30,000 each year for 5 years, it would not meet the rate-of-return objective of at least 18%.

The assistant manager believes that the investment could have met the standard if other factors had been considered. For example, if this equipment had been purchased, old equipment with a net book value of zero could have been sold for $30,000. The income tax rate for the year on the sale of equipment is 40%.

Required. Use the net present value method to determine whether or not the assistant manager is correct in the analysis.

12-2. Payback and Discounted Returns. The manager of Creek Inc. uses a simple payback method in selecting investment alternatives. She states that if she can recover the investment in 3 years, she is virtually in the same position as another investor who requires a discounted rate of return of 18% on a 5-year investment. In her business, the investment produces uniform returns over a 5-year period and has no residual salvage value. Three investment alternatives are outlined as follows:

	Alternatives		
	1	2	3
Investment	$90,000	$24,000	$44,000
Annual return for each of 5 years	$30,000	$7,500	$11,000

Required:

(1) Which, if any, of the investment alternatives meets the 3-year payback criterion? Ignore tax effect.

(2) Evaluate the three alternatives by using the net present value method with a minimum rate of return of 18% and compare the results arrived at in (1). Ignore tax effect.

12-3. Depreciation and Rate of Return. The president of Tipton Company has been considering an investment of $600,000 in equipment that should have a useful life of 3 years with a salvage value of zero. This type of investment is expected to yield a discounted rate of return of 12%.

An estimate indicates that the cash flow before income tax from this investment will probably amount to $300,000 a year. Straight-line depreciation is normally used and income tax is 40%.

The president has been informed that depreciation may be deducted by the SYD method and that this method would make the investment more favorable than if straight-line depreciation is used. He does not understand how a "bookkeeping method," as he calls it, can help to improve the investment.

Required:

(1) Compute the net present value of the investment with straight-line depreciation.

(2) Compute the net present value of the investment with SYD depreciation.

(3) Explain to the president how a "bookkeeping method" can help to improve the investment.

12-4. Improving Investment Returns. For many years Emilio Perez has been a successful manufacturer in the garment industry. Recently he has learned of an opportunity to purchase a two-story brick building for $750,000. He believes that he can operate successfully by using only one of the two floors. At the present time, he is operating in an older building where he uses both floors. This is inconvenient, he admits, but he has become accustomed to the situation.

Furthermore, he estimates that the annual returns from his business after income tax will amount to $150,000 over the next 20 years. With the prospect of more inflation and high interest rates, he would hesitate to invest unless he could obtain a discounted rate of return of at least 20%. This investment opportunity does not appear that good to him, and he is inclined to continue to operate as he has before.

His daughter, who has recently graduated from medical school, disagrees with his position:

"You forget that this area is growing. We have no professional building; and I know of several doctors, dentists, and lawyers who would be happy to have offices on the second floor if you did some remodeling. I have already obtained estimates and find that you can have the second floor remodeled for $100,000. The offices should yield annual rentals after income tax of $40,000.''

Required: From the information given, does it appear that the investment can meet a minimum rate-of-return requirement of 20%? (Use the net present value method.)

12-5. Change in the Value of Money. Lauretta Donnelly, manager of the Town Company, states that she used to accept investment opportunities that yielded discounted returns (after income tax) at a rate of 18%. With a slightly decreasing cost of capital, she now expects a 16% discounted rate of return.

Two competing investment proposals are now waiting for her evaluation, and the data are presented as follows:

	Alternatives	
	1	*2*
Estimated life	5 yrs.	5 yrs.
Net investment	$170,000	$190,000
Estimated annual return before depreciation and income tax	65,000	90,000

Depreciation is to be deducted by the straight-line method, and there is no estimated salvage value at the end of the estimated life of the investment proposal.

Income tax is estimated at 40% of income before tax.

Required:

    (1) Does either or both of the alternatives meet a requirement of 18%? (Use the net present value method and round all amounts to nearest dollar.)

    (2) Does either or both of the alternatives meet a requirement of 16%? (Use the net present value method and round all amounts to nearest dollar.)

12-6. Sell or Use Equipment. An offer of $130,000 has been made for a unit of equipment that Herrera Products has been using to make parts for one of its divisions. The equipment is fully depreciated but can be used for 5 more years. At the end of 5 years, it is expected to have little, if any, value.

The variable cost of producing the parts is $10 per unit. A total of 10,000 units are to be manufactured each year. If the parts are not manufactured, the company must buy them from an outside supplier at a cost of $15 per unit. Also, if the parts are not produced, the space occupied by the equipment can be rented for $12,000 per year. Income tax is estimated at 40% of the income before tax. The company expects a discounted rate of return of 16% on this type of investment.

Required: Should the offer for the sale of the equipment be accepted, or should the parts be manufactured? (Use the net present value method.)

12-7. Alternative Project Requiring Additional Investment in Current Assets. An interesting project is being considered by Bunn Company. The project will require an investment of $300,000 in equipment that is expected to have a useful life of 10 years with no salvage value. Cash, accounts receivable, and inventory will be required in the amount of $100,000 and will be released at the end of 10 years. Annual cash flow returns before income tax from this project have been estimated at $100,000.

Depreciation is to be deducted by the straight-line method. Income tax is estimated at 40% of income before income tax.

A minimum rate of return objective has been established at 14%.

Required. Does the investment alternative meet the rate-of-return objective? (Use the net present value method.)

12-8. Incremental Investment and Returns. Tom Eaton has an average-rate-of-return objective of 16% for acceptable capital investment projects and a rate of return of 18% on incremental investments. In the evaluation process, he prefers to use straight-line depreciation.

At the present time, he is interested in the acquisition of equipment for producing a product line which can be sold for $30 per unit with a unit variable cost of $19. His sales manager believes that there is a market for 30,000 units each year. The equipment has an installed cost of $800,000 and should have a useful life of 5 years with no salvage value.

A representative of the equipment manufacturer has gone over the cost estimates that Eaton has prepared and stated that the variable cost per unit of product can be cut to $15 with an equipment modification costing an additional $250,000. This modification will not extend the useful life of the equipment or change the salvage value.

Required:

(1) Evaluate each of the alternatives by the net present value method with straight-line depreciation, using the 16% average-rate-of-return objective. Which alternative is better? (Use a 40% income tax rate.)

(2) Evaluate the incremental investment to see if the higher investment meets the rate-of-return objective of 18%.

12-9. Changes in Economic Environment. Four years ago Bolin Properties Inc. invested $10,000,000 in a venture in another country. The investment was estimated to have a 10-year life and was expected to produce a cash flow of $2,500,000 each year before income tax. It did exactly this for 4 years. Conditions are less favorable now, and the revised estimate indicates that the cash flow will be only $1,500,000 but will last for 7 years. (Because this is a foreign investment, it has a special tax status and is not subject to income tax.)

The investment can now be sold for $5,400,000. At the present time, an investment can be justified only if the discounted rate of return is expected to be no less than 18%.

Required: Should the investment be sold for $5,400,000 or continued in operation? Show computations by the net present value method and by calculating the rate of return.

12-10. Break-Even Volume and Investment. For several years, Lomax Company has used a combination of its own equipment and equipment rented from others to handle standard materials. The company has enough of its own equipment to handle routine work but sometimes must rent equipment during periods of peak activity. The cost to rent equipment from others has been estimated to average $4,000 a year.

An evaluation of the operation indicates that the company can save $.10 per unit of material by using its own equipment instead of rented equipment.

An equipment manufacturer offers the necessary additional equipment at a cost of $45,000. The equipment will probably have a useful life of 5 years with no salvage value at the end of the 5 years.

There is some uncertainty with respect to how much work will be required from the new equipment if it is purchased. Estimates of the number of units that might possibly be handled in each of the 5 years are 80,000 units, 100,000 units, and 120,000 units.

On this type of investment, a 15% discounted return is considered to be appropriate (ignore taxes).

Required:

(1) Can the investment meet the minimum rate-of-return requirement if 80,000 units are handled? If 100,000 units are handled? If 120,000 units are handled?

(2) Determine the break-even volume, that is, the number of units at which the investment can just meet the 15% return requirement. (Round all amounts to nearest dollar.)

12-11. Acquisition of Additional Units of Equipment. A new product line is being considered by the Ingram Company. A survey has been made in an attempt to estimate the potential demand for this product. A special type of equipment will be required for the manufacturing process, and one or more units of this equipment will be acquired if the project is accepted.

Data with respect to the production and sale of this product follow:

Number of Equipment Units	Product Unit Capacity
1	60,000
2	120,000
3	160,000
4	200,000

The new product line will increase out-of-pocket annual fixed cost (excluding depreciation) by $100,000. It is estimated that this increase can be expected regardless of the number of product units manufactured. The variable cost of producing a unit has been estimated at $6 and the selling price at $10. The company has the physical space to install up to 5 units of equipment. The machine sells at $300,000 per unit and the useful life is estimated at 5 years with no salvage value.

Required: Using straight-line depreciation, a 40% tax rate, a 15% discount rate, and the net present value method, determine how many machines, if any, should be purchased. Assume that the company can sell all units that can be produced under the conditions stated. Show calculations.

12-12. Timing the Investment. The capital investment committee of the board of directors of Massey Inc. is considering the acquisition of a unit of equipment costing $80,000. Shipping and installation costs are estimated at an additional $9,000. The equipment is expected to have a useful life of 6 years with a salvage value of $5,000 at the end of 6 years. Before considering the effect of depreciation, the annual cash flow returns after income tax from the use of this equipment are estimated at $20,000.

One member of the committee believes that the equipment now in service for this production can be used for another year, yielding after-tax cash flow and depreciation of $10,000. A new and improved model is expected in another year that can be acquired at a cost of $91,000. Shipping and installation costs are also estimated at

$4,000, and the estimated salvage value at the end of the expected 5-year life is $5,000. Annual cash flow returns after income tax but before considering the effect of depreciation are estimated at $25,000.

The company has set a minimum rate-of-return objective of 18%. Depreciation is to be deducted by the sum-of-the-years-digits method. The income tax rate is 40%.

Required: Does it appear that the equipment should be purchased now, or should the company wait a year for the new model? Use the net present value method and show computations.

12-13. Purchase Versus Lease Decision. Cottin Farms is considering replacing a technologically obsolete tractor currently used in farming operations. The tractor in use is in good working order and will last, physically, for at least 5 years. However, the proposed tractor is so much more efficient that Cottin Farms predicts cost savings of $15,000 a year if the new tractor is acquired. The tractor's delivered cost is $40,000. Its technological useful life is 5 years, although the physical useful life is 15 years. The salvage value of the tractor is $10,000 in 5 years and zero in 15 years. The sum-of-the years-digits method of depreciation will be used on the new tractor. If the new tractor is acquired, Cottin Farms can sell the old tractor at a capital gain of $5,000.

Cottin Farms requires a minimum of 15% after-tax return on all investments. The income tax rates are 30% for capital gains and 50% for ordinary income.

If Cottin Farms decides to acquire the new tractor, it has the option of purchasing or leasing the tractor. The distributor will sell the tractor outright for $40,000 delivered cost or will lease the tractor at $12,000 per year for 5 years. Under the lease, the first payment of $12,000 is due now and at the end of 5 years the tractor reverts back to the distributor.

Required:
(1) Should Cottin Farms acquire the new tractor?
(2) If Cottin Farms should acquire the new tractor, would the company prefer an outright purchase or a lease?

12-14. Investment Tax Credit Decision. Jean Morales and Melissa Soto have been investigating an investment opportunity for Metro Electronic Company. An investment in automated equipment is being considered at a cost of $200,000. The equipment is expected to have a useful life of 10 years with no residual value at the end of the 10 years. Annual returns of $40,000 before income tax are expected for each of the 10 years.

Both of them agree that the estimated returns will not meet the minimum-rate-of-return requirement of 12% if depreciation is deducted by the straight-line method over 10 years with no investment tax credit or immediate expensing.

However, Morales recommends that the project be accepted if a 10% investment tax credit is taken, $7,500 of the cost is immediately expensed, and ACRS depreciation is deducted over an allowable class life of 5 years. She states that the investment should be recommended to the board of directors on this basis.

Soto believes that with a relatively low discount rate of 12% the investment should be recommended with an 8% investment tax credit, no immediate expensing, and ACRS depreciation over 5 years. If the discount rate were 18 or 20%, her decision would be different, she explains.

The income tax rate is 46%.

The ACRS percentages for each year for the 5-year class are as follows:

Year	ACRS Percentages
1	15
2	22
3	21
4	21
5	21

Required:

(1) Evaluate the investment using straight-line depreciation over 10 years with no investment credit or immediate expensing. Does the investment meet the minimum-rate-of-return requirement?

(2) Determine the net present value of the investment under the option recommended by Morales and under the option recommended by Soto.

(3) In this situation, which option (if either) should be recommended? Comment.

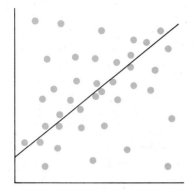

13

MANAGERIAL CONTROL AND DECISION MAKING IN DECENTRALIZED OPERATIONS

Chapter Objectives

This chapter will enable you to:

1. Discuss the basic criteria needed for a control system.
2. Define the components of division net income, division direct profit, division controllable profit, and division contribution margin.
3. Evaluate a division's performance using a profit index and residual income.
4. Define a transfer price and identify the major bases for determining such a price.
5. Discuss the influence on a transfer price of the existence of an intermediate market and the lack of an intermediate market.

One of the most striking characteristics of business operation and organization during the past two decades has been the tendency toward decentralized operations. This movement has been accelerating at the same time that the number of business combinations and mergers has been increasing. Many companies are simultaneously seeking the advantages of bigness through combinations and of smallness through decentralizing the management of the combined operations.

In general, a decentralized company is one in which operating divisions are created. Each division is staffed with a management that has some authority

379

for making decisions and thus becomes responsible for a segment of the company's profit. Even though the amount of decision-making authority granted to division management varies among companies, the spirit of decentralization is quite clear—to divide a company into relatively self-contained divisions and allow these divisions to operate in an autonomous fashion.

Decisions as to capital investment are sometimes centrally controlled; but decisions as to selling price and quantity and method of production are frequently delegated to the division management.

Two of the alleged advantages of decentralized organization are:

1. It provides a systematic means of delegating a portion of the decision-making responsibility to managers below top management.
2. It motivates managers in charge of certain company activities by involving them more closely with the company's profit objectives.

Top management wants to know whether the advantages mentioned above are being realized, thus necessitating the question of how best to control and evaluate division management. Division control and evaluation is usually more complex than controlling a single activity within a company. For example, in a centralized company a problem of control may exist with respect to certain production activities. A cost center may be established and reports may be generated to assure top management that the product is being produced at the lowest possible level of cost. The problem is usually one of cost control. In decentralized divisions, the division management may have authority over selling prices of the finished product, make or buy decisions, some investment decisions, and so forth. The problem here is mainly one of profit control, which is much broader and often more complex than a problem of cost control. The fact that the division manager usually has more freedom than a production supervisor in making decisions usually means that a simple cost index is not an adequate control device. Control over cost does not indicate how efficient the division manager is as a price-maker for the finished products.

THE CRITERIA NEEDED FOR A CONTROL SYSTEM

In general, in order to control anything, it is necessary to have:

1. An index (measure) of overall actual performance.
2. A standard with which to compare the actual performance.

A comparison of actual performance with standard performance produces variance information that forms a basis for corrective action.

The selection of an evaluation index is rarely an easy matter. The index chosen must encompass as many of the operating variables as possible. The operating variables that are important are those over which the supervisor or manager has control. Rarely can one single index of performance be established that encompasses all of the factors that are considered important in evaluating an operation.

In evaluating a production operation, cost is usually considered to be a good evaluation index. The cost figure that should be used is the controllable cost. However, this index, although useful, may not be sufficient for performance measurement. The cost in a certain activity may be high because the supervisor spends much time developing personnel. If this supervision helps to provide a good training ground for future managers, perhaps the supervisor is being more efficient than the cost performance indicates. From a long-run viewpoint, this situation may be quite desirable.

In a decentralized operation, the selection of the index used to evaluate division performance is usually more complex because a division manager has quite broad decision-making authority and thus has direct control over many decision factors. Consequently, a greater burden is placed on the evaluation index. Cost as an index is usually not broad enough for evaluating division operation.

Profit as a measure of division performance may also be inadequate. This index is broader than cost because it includes revenue considerations, thus reflecting the price-making authority of the division manager in the index. However, the ability of the division manager to build good customer relations, to secure employee loyalty, and to provide a good training ground for future management prospects may not be adequately reflected in the short-run profit figure. Furthermore, the ability of the division manager to produce a given level of profit with a minimum capital investment is not evident by looking at profit alone. Capital investment should be assigned to the division and a rate-of-return index should be computed by relating profit to investment. This rate-of-return index, which is broader than profit alone, may be especially useful if the division manager has some control over increases or decreases in the amount of capital invested in the division.

The problem of selecting an appropriate index is further complicated when one division furnishes goods and services to another division; hence, the divisions are not completely autonomous. In order to use division profit as an index where goods or services are transferred between divisions, it is necessary to develop a solution to the intra-company or transfer pricing problem. For example, if a warehouse division furnishes services to an operating division, a decision must be made as to the price at which the services are to be transferred for purposes of determining the warehouse division's revenue and the operating division's cost.

The overall problem is even more complex because division profit, rates of return, and transfer prices are frequently used as an aid in making decisions as well as in evaluating performance. A transfer price that is satisfactory for performance evaluation may be poorly suited for decision making.

When the index has been chosen, it is then necessary to settle on a standard against which to measure or compare the actual performance. The standard can be based on last year's results or the results of similar divisions within the company. Such standards presume that the respective operations are performing at efficiency. A better solution may be to choose independently determined standards such as a budgeted profit for the division or a budgeted rate of return. If the profit is budgeted, it is possible to consider the capital invested in the division in establishing the budget. Hence, it may be that the investment can be effectively considered without actually budgeting a rate of return.

Having described an overall system of control for division operations, the remainder of this chapter is devoted to a discussion of the following specific points:

1. The selection of a profit index.
2. The problems encountered in using division controllable profit as an evaluation index.
3. The problems encountered in determining division investment.
4. The intracompany pricing (transfer pricing) problem.
5. The possible conflicts that may arise in using transfer prices for both performance evaluation and decision making.
6. The selection of the standard against which to compare the actual performance.

THE PROFIT INDEX

The choice of the profit index is not simple. However, there really is no question of whether a performance index is needed. It is rather a question of how to construct the best one, and several different profit concepts can be used. These concepts can best be illustrated by an example. It is possible for a division to be assigned the following profit and loss data:

Revenue from division sales	$1,000
Direct division costs:	
Variable cost of goods sold and other operating costs	700
Fixed division overhead that is controllable at the division level, such as the cost of certain indirect labor and operating supplies	100
Fixed division overhead that is noncontrollable at the division level, such as the division manager's salary	50
Indirect division costs:	
Allocated (fixed) general office overhead, such as the division's share of the cost of the president's office	60

These data make it possible to select several different profit calculations. The following summary calculation presents some of the commonly suggested alternatives.

	Division Contribution Margin	Division Controllable Profit	Division Direct Profit	Division Net Profit
Revenue	$1,000	$1,000	$1,000	$1,000
Direct cost:				
Variable cost	$ 700	$ 700	$ 700	$ 700
	$ 300			
Fixed controllable cost........................		100	100	100
		$ 200		
Fixed noncontrollable cost....................................			50	50
			$ 150	
Indirect cost: Allocated home office overhead..........................				60
				$ 90

The four profit calculations are not the only possible ones, but they are the most reasonable. The names or titles assigned to each are descriptive of each calculation, but the terminology in this area has not been standardized. The important point is to recognize what is included and excluded in each calculation.

Division Net Profit

It may appear that the best profit calculation to use in measuring division performance is the division net profit. However, net profit is usually calculated by deducting some pro rata share of the home office overhead. An example of this cost would be the cost of operating the president's office. Although each division benefits from the incurrence of such a cost, it is not controllable at the division level. Although benefit received is the main criterion used to allocate cost for income reporting to outside investors, there is a real question as to whether this criterion is the proper one for performance evaluation purposes. If controllability is accepted as the main criterion in assigning cost for evaluation purposes, then net profit is a poor measure of performance.

The main argument for using net profit, which implies an allocation of home office costs, is that it makes the division manager aware of the full cost of operating the division. Even though part of this full cost is not controllable at the division level, by reporting the full cost the division manager may work harder to control the costs which are controllable. This argument rests largely on how the division manager is motivated. Perhaps a better approach would be to assign only controllable costs to the division and then to establish a rigorous standard in hopes that the manager will be highly motivated to meet the standard. As a result, the manager will be concentrating on those costs that can be controlled at the division level.

The other difficulty in using division net profit is that some method of allocation must be found for assigning the home office cost to divisions. Whatever method is chosen is likely to be arbitrary and open to question by the division managers. In order for the allocation procedure to have the desired motivational results, it is necessary to find an allocation procedure for the home office cost that is acceptable to the division managers. If this is not done, a division manager may spend much time attempting to reduce cost by getting top management to change the allocation procedure.

Division Direct Profit

Division direct profit is defined as the total division revenue less the direct cost of the division. This concept avoids the main difficulty of division net profit in that the home office cost is not allocated. However, as can be noted from the calculation summary given on page 383, there may still be some direct costs included in the calculation that are not controllable at the division level; that is, some costs that can be traced directly to the division may not be controllable. Costs such as the division manager's salary are controllable only at the top management level. Also, some division overhead, such as insurance, taxes, and depreciation on fixed assets, is due to past investment decisions that were made by top management. If costs are to be assigned to the division on the basis of controllability, then these previously-mentioned costs should be excluded from the profit calculation. If this is not done, the division profit used for performance evaluation may be increased or decreased by actions of someone outside the division.

Division Controllable Profit

Division controllable profit is defined as the total division revenue less all costs that are directly traceable to the division and that are controllable by the division management. It appears that this calculation is best for performance measurement, because it reflects the results of the division manager's ability to carry out the assigned responsibility. Changes in the profit figure from year to year should be a reflection of how management responsibility is being carried out at the division level. Provided the standard used for the comparison is valid, any variances between actual and standard can be explained in terms of factors over which the division manager has control. Some of these factors may be difficult for the division manager to influence; for example, the prices of materials may be increasing. If the standard (budget) is not revised each year, unfavorable price variances will result. Even though the price cannot be influenced, perhaps alternate materials can be used or alternate sources of supply can be found. Problems of this nature may be difficult to solve, but they are part of the division management's responsibility. Failure to solve such problems is different from being unable to take action because of a lack of authority.

In calculating controllable profit, some fixed costs are included. A cost may be controllable even though it is fixed. "Fixed" does not mean fixed in amount, but rather fixed with respect to changes in volume. The division manager may be able to reduce the level of supervisory salaries by reorganizing .

division operations. The new cost level achieved is still fixed with respect to volume changes, but profit will increase because the total dollar amount of supervisory salaries has decreased. If the fixed controllable cost is not included, important spending variances may be overlooked.

Division Contribution Margin

The contribution margin or **marginal income** of the division is defined as the total revenue less the variable costs. Although contribution margin is useful in decision making, for performance evaluation its defect is obvious; namely, there are some controllable items of fixed cost that are excluded from the calculation. As a performance evaluation index, therefore, division contribution margin is incomplete.

The fact that controllable profit is used in overall performance evaluation should not be taken as an indication that contribution margin has to be abandoned as a decision-making technique. The report that follows, indicates both the contribution margin and the controllable profit.

Division A
Profit Report

Revenue	$1,000
Variable cost	700
Contribution margin	$ 300
Fixed controllable cost	100
Controllable profit	$ 200

In this report, both the contribution margin and the controllable profit are available as a management tool, and there is no need to choose one or the other. Furthermore, the controllable profit may be the best guide for some decisions. If a particular decision will change the level of fixed cost, then this cost should be considered. For example, if the division manager decides to eliminate a department, it may be possible to reduce supervisory salaries that are included in fixed controllable cost; thus, the entire profit statement should be used as a basis for the decision.

SOME PROBLEMS IN USING DIVISION CONTROLLABLE PROFIT AS AN EVALUATION INDEX

There are several accounting problems that must be solved in order for controllable division profit to be a good index for evaluating performance. The most important of these problems are discussed in the following paragraphs.

There are several ways in which the division manager can increase the short-run profit of the division to the detriment of the company as a whole. For example, it may be possible to delay the maintenance cost. Such an action will inflate profit, but the long-run profitability of the division and the company may be affected adversely. Expenditures that engender employee loyalty such as division social gatherings may be eliminated. By reducing supervision cost, the division manager may not develop long-run top management personnel. In short, a solution must be found to the problem of the division manager's potential to create division profit that may cause a long-run decline in company profit.

Other accounting problems may arise if profit comparisons are made between similar operating divisions. For such comparisons to be valid, all profit calculations should rest on the same inventory and depreciation procedures. A problem also arises with respect to cost items that sometimes are inventoried (and written off as used) and other times are expensed directly. For example, the purchase of indirect operating supplies may create a problem in interpreting profit differences between divisions as well as profit differences between accounting periods for the same division. If potential inventory items such as indirect production supplies are expensed when purchased, it may be that an increase in a division's profit for a period was due merely to a large purchase of supplies in the previous period. Likewise, differences in profit between divisions during a given period may be caused by a difference in the timing of purchases and the failure to reflect inventories. If these differences are significant, the profit figure will be distorted and may be difficult to interpret correctly.

Problems of revenue recognition may require attention before the division profit can be used effectively in evaluating performance. When the sale is only a matter of delivery, as can be the case for some precious metals and agricultural products that have an unlimited market at a predetermined price, for example, the ability of the division manager to influence the amount of profit and the profit pattern by choosing the time of sale may destroy comparisons between years and between divisions.

If controllable profit is to be used as an evaluation index, it is necessary to be able to define and measure controllable cost. Whether a cost is controllable depends on the level of management under consideration. The cost of owning a building may only be controllable at the top management level; the division manager may have little influence over such cost.

Controllability also has a time dimension. If the time horizon is very long, some costs may be controllable which would not be controllable in the short run. For example, the cost of owning a machine may be controllable by a department manager if the time horizon is at least as long as the life of the machine. Conversely, if the time horizon for the profit calculation is one year, perhaps only the cost of operating the machine is controllable. All costs are controllable at some level in the organization if the time horizon is sufficiently long. However, this does not resolve the problem since profit reporting periods may be as short as one month or one quarter of a year. In distinguishing controllable from noncontrollable costs, it is necessary to consider the time period as well as the level of management for whom the profit report is prepared. This applies not only to cost and revenue items but to investment items as well.

DETERMINING DIVISION INVESTMENT

If divisions are to be evaluated on the basis of rate of return on investment, it is necessary to determine the investment base to be used. There are many problems associated with this determination.

The Investment Base

The first problem is to decide which assets to assign to the division. Many assets can be traced directly to the division. For example, a division may handle its own receivables and inventory and may even have jurisdiction over its own cash balance. Also, much of the physical property used may be traceable to a particular division. Sometimes traceable assets such as receivables, inventories, and cash are centrally administered and controlled. However, by proper account coding it is usually possible to trace receivables and inventories to the division operation even though these assets are administered centrally. If cash is centrally administered, it is usually very difficult to trace to division operations.

There is usually some investment that is common to several divisions. In such a case, no amount of coding, sorting, or classifying will provide a basis for directly tracing this investment to a division. If this type of investment is to be assigned to the division, a basis of allocation must be found. An example of common investment would be the investment in building, furniture and fixtures, and so forth, used by the central corporate administration. Any basis of allocation used to assign this type of investment must be an arbitrary one. If such an assignment is made, the division investment is no longer the traceable investment but is the traceable investment plus some allocated share of common investment.

The relevant investment base for division evaluation might be thought of as the amount of investment uniquely devoted to the support of the particular division operation. If this criterion is applied to common investment, the amount of the common investment allocated to a division would be that part of the total common investment which could be avoided if the division did not exist. This is a difficult concept to apply, but its application can be approached by seeking relationships between the level of common investment and the level of certain division activities. For example, perhaps a relationship can be established between the level of common investment in a personnel department and the number of employees in each division.

If this procedure cannot be applied, it is difficult to justify the allocation of common investment. At best, the procedure used is likely to be quite arbitrary.

If divisions are compared with one another, this comparison will probably be affected by the basis of allocation chosen. In fact, the basis of allocation could well determine the ranking of each division. In an earlier section of the chapter, it was stated that the best profit calculation for performance evaluation is the one based only on factors under the control of the division management. If this same criterion is used in determining investment, the common investment should not be allocated. Traceable investment is a better measure of controllable investment than traceable investment plus some allocated share of common investment.

Once the method of assigning investment to divisions has been determined, it is necessary to decide the amount at which the plant assets will be stated. One might argue that replacement cost or perhaps original cost adjusted for changes in the price level should be used. It may seem that, if rate of return is to be used as a measure of division efficiency, the investment should be stated on some current value basis rather than on a historical cost basis. The obvious difficulty is the measurement problem. How would replacement costs be approximated? What happens when the specific plant or equipment asset is not replaced? If a common-dollar base is desirable, which price-level index should be used? It is easier to raise questions than to give answers in this problem area.

Up to this point, return on investment has been discussed in terms of the calculation being made in ratio form, that is, the division profit divided by the division investment. Return on investment may create problems simply because of the ratio nature of the calculation. For example, suppose that one division of a company is currently earning 30 percent on investment. The division manager may be reluctant to make additional investments at, perhaps, 20 percent because the average return of the division would be lowered. However, if investment offerings in other divisions of the company yield only 15 percent, company management may prefer that the additional investment with a yield of 20 percent be accepted. The division manager may still be reluctant to lower the past average return on investment from 30 percent even though the company management has set a standard for comparison of 15 percent. That is, the manager may choose to maximize the favorable variance between the standard and the actual; and this cannot be done if the past average return is lowered by selecting additional investments with returns of 20 percent. Thus, the use of return on investment as a ratio might restrict additional investment at the expense of company-wide profitability.

Residual Income

The use of residual income has been proposed as an alternative to the ratio form of determining return on investment. Residual income focuses the attention of the division manager on a dollar amount instead of a ratio. The maximization of the dollar amount will tend to be in the best interest of both the division manager and the company as a whole, thus the incongruence of goals experienced when return on investment is viewed as a ratio can be eliminated. The discussion which follows illustrates the residual income method.

In general, the residual income is defined as the operating profit of a division less an imputed charge for the operating capital used by the division. The problems involved in selecting the profit index and the investment base still apply to the residual income alternative. That is, a decision must still be made to determine what concept of profit and investment is to be used. For purposes of illustration, assume that division controllable profit is to be used and that a similar choice has been made for the determination of the investment base. Assume further that the current controllable profit (before any imputed capital charge) is $300,000 and the relevant investment is $1,000,000. The return on investment, then, is 30 percent; that is, $300,000 ÷ $1,000,000. Suppose top management wants the division management to accept incremental investments so long as the return is greater than 15 percent.

This percentage is then used as the imputed charge for division investment, and the residual income would be calculated as follows:

Division controllable profit (before imputed capital charge)................	$300,000
Less imputed capital charge (15% × $1,000,000)	150,000
Division residual income	$150,000

The advantage of this evaluation index is that the division manager is concerned with increasing a dollar amount (in this case, the $150,000) and is more likely to accept incremental investments which have a yield of over 15 percent (in this example). Even if a budget standard for judging residual income is used and the division manager focuses on the variance between the budget and the actual, there would still be a tendency to select additional investments with a yield in excess of 15 percent since such investments maximize the dollar residual income and reduce an unfavorable variance or increase a favorable variance. Division management behavior under a residual income concept, then, should be more congruous with company-wide objectives.

THE INTRACOMPANY OR TRANSFER PRICING PROBLEM

In calculating division profit, problems arise when the divisions are not completely independent. If one division furnishes goods or services to another division, a transfer price must be established in order to determine the buying division's cost and the selling division's revenue. Both revenue and cost are necessary to calculate profit. There is a possible conflict in establishing transfer prices because the data may be used in making decisions as well as in calculating a profit index for performance evaluation. In this section of the chapter, the use of transfer prices for performance evaluation is emphasized. In the next section, the use of transfer prices for decision making will be discussed, and some of the possible conflicts that can arise will be explored.

The most common transfer prices are as follows:

1. Market price.
2. Negotiated or bargained market price.
3. Transfer price based on a cost calculation such as full cost or marginal (variable) cost.
4. Dual transfer prices.

Market Price

There may be real difficulty in determining a market price. The use of a market price assumes that a market exists at the transfer point. Even if this is the case, the appropriate market price may be difficult to establish. Frequently, the list or catalog price is only vaguely related to the effective market price. Often the market price is a fluctuating one. The selling division may incur less cost in selling to the buying division than would be incurred if the product were sold to outsiders. This occurs when the buying division is a captive market. In such an instance, if the market price is not adjusted downward, the selling division will get the entire benefit of the savings in shipping and marketing costs.

A more difficult problem exists where there is no real market at the transfer point. If the selling division furnishes repair, research, or storage services to the buying division, for example, it is difficult to establish a satisfactory market price for such services.

Despite the problem of arriving at market price, there is general agreement that if a market price can be determined, it is probably the best price for use in performance evaluation because the use of a decentralized organization structure is largely motivated by a desire to create smaller, autonomous operating divisions that conduct their business as separate entities. The use of a market transfer price, where possible, creates the actual market conditions under which these divisions would operate if they were separate companies rather than divisions of one organization. To the extent that market prices can be established on the basis of outside forces, they form an excellent performance indicator, because they cannot be manipulated by the individuals who have an interest in the resulting profit calculation.

For purposes of illustrating the preceding comments, assume that a company has two divisions, a producing division and a marketing division. The operation might be a corporate farm. The producing division is to produce a bushel of grain, which can be sold as soon as it is produced or transferred to the marketing division where the decision will be made as to the future date of sale. This situation is diagrammed as follows:

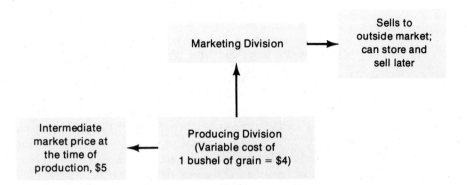

If management desires to evaluate each division manager, the $5 market price should be used as a transfer price. This price compared with the $4 variable production cost results in a $1 profit. This profit is dependent on the efficiency of the production operation. It also depends on the ability to produce the proper grain crop (wheat, corn, etc.) at the right time. These decisions are within the jurisdiction of the producing division manager. The marketing division should buy from the producing division only if it is felt that the grain can be stored and sold at some later date at a profit. These decisions are the responsibility of the marketing division. If the marketing division buys the bushel of grain and sells it six months later at $5.50, having incurred interest and storage costs of 30 cents, the profit resulting from this operation is 20 cents. A summary calculation is as follows:

	Producing Division	Marketing Division
Sales	$5	$5.50
Cost	4	($5 + 30¢) 5.30
Profit	$1	$ .20

The total profit for the company is $1.20; but by using a market transfer price, the total profit is divided into a producing and a marketing profit. These individual profit figures serve as the basis for evaluating each division's operation.

Negotiated or Bargained Market Price

The use of negotiated or bargained prices has often been suggested as a refinement of market-based transfer pricing. There may be real advantages in allowing the two division managers, who must have complete freedom to buy and sell outside, to arrive at the transfer price through arms-length bargaining. The selfish interest of the division managers in the division profit and related bonuses serves the company objectives as long as:

1. All transfer prices are determined by negotiation between the buyer and the seller.
2. Negotiators have all the data on alternative sources, markets, and market prices.
3. Both the buyer and seller are free to buy and sell outside the company.

A negotiated market price may solve some of the problems encountered in trying to base the market transfer price on a list price, which may have no meaning, or on a market price, which is really not applicable because the cost of selling to the division is much less than that of selling outside the firm. Furthermore, much of the friction and bad feeling that may arise from a centrally controlled market transfer price may be eliminated without incurring any misallocation of resources. Much of the division managers' time may be consumed in negotiating the transfer prices. If this is undesirable, a possible remedy is to negotiate these prices for a certain time period instead of for each transfer that takes place.

Many of the problems that arise in transfer pricing are created because the buying division is a captive customer and is unable to bargain effectively with the selling division. Real competition can be injected into the situation by encouraging the division managers to buy and sell outside and by praising them when their results are favorable.

Bargained or negotiated price may solve some of the problems encountered in transfer pricing, but such a method will probably not eliminate all of them. If the buying division can obtain a lower price by purchasing outside, it is true that the buying division's profit will be increased. However, the selling division's decrease in profit because of a loss in volume may more than offset this profit increase. In such an instance, the total company may suffer. In the long run, the selling division manager would probably lower the price so as not to create large losses because of unused capacity. If this happens, the freedom to negotiate market price is certainly superior to a centrally administered market price from which the division managers cannot depart.

Transfer Price Based on Cost

For performance evaluation, it is difficult to justify transfer prices based on either full cost or variable cost. A transfer price based on variable cost is useful in decision making; but for performance evaluation, such a figure may well result in no profit or even a loss for the selling division. In such an instance, there is little or no motivation for the selling division to supply the goods or services. Where no intermediate market exists or where there are significant imperfections in the intermediate market, there may be little choice on transfer prices and some cost measure may be the only real possibility. It is possible, of course, for management to centralize by combining the buying and selling divisions where no intermediate market exists for some of the major products or product lines; but that would undermine the decentralized nature of the organization.

The use of full cost or full cost plus a profit percentage can also create problems. If either of these measures is higher than the price from an outside vendor, the buying division would be motivated to buy outside the company and thus create excess capacity in the internal selling division. That is, the variable cost of the selling division plus some of the allocated fixed cost (full cost) might be higher than the price from an outside vendor; but if the outside price is higher than the variable cost alone, the company (overall) would be better off to have the selling division produce the good or service in question, especially if there is excess capacity in that division. This problem is discussed in more depth in the next section of the chapter.

Another difficulty in using full cost (or full cost plus a profit percentage) is that it may give rise to arguments over how full cost should be determined — essentially cost-allocation arguments. Such arguments may consume managerial time that could be better spent on other matters. On the positive side, however, using full cost or full cost plus a profit percentage can motivate the internal supplying division to accommodate the order of the buying division. Even the use of full cost as a transfer price would increase the selling division's profit so long as the full cost is greater than the variable cost and there is excess capacity. That is, the difference between the selling division's full cost and variable cost is a contribution to fixed cost (contribution margin) which increases profit.

Dual Transfer Prices

The use of dual transfer prices has been suggested as a means of creating a profit, and thus a positive motivation, in the selling division while transferring the goods or service to the buying division at variable cost. Variable cost is probably the best figure to guide the decisions of the buying division manager. If the transfer price is higher than variable cost, there is always the risk that the buying division manager will buy outside the company (because the internal price to be paid may be higher than the outside market price) and by so doing create more excess capacity in the selling division. If there is already excess capacity in the selling division, the buying division should buy from the inside division so long as the variable cost is less than the outside price.

Using variable cost as the single transfer price creates no motivation for the selling division manager to sell, since there would be no increase in the profit of the selling division. A dual system allows the selling division to "sell" at what might be considered a synthetic market price (such as variable cost plus a profit percentage or full cost plus a profit percentage), yet the transfer price to the buying division is the variable cost. Thus, the selling division manager is motivated to sell because profit will be increased and the buying division manager will buy internally unless the outside price is less than variable cost. Hence, the main purpose of the dual system is to motivate both the buying and selling division managers to make decisions that are consistent with the interests of the company as a whole.

Such a system, however, does create a problem which may or may not be important. If a dual system is used, it is not possible to add the division profits to arrive at the total company profit. That is, since both the buying and selling divisions are recognizing some of the same profits, eliminations have to be made before the total company profit can be determined. Such a problem does not seem to be especially serious, but it is sometimes cited as an argument against the dual pricing system. The example which follows illustrates the dual transfer price system and the nature of the double counting problem.

Assume that Division X (the buying division) has an order from a customer for 1,000 units of Product A at a price of $20 per unit. To fill the order, Division X must buy 1,000 units of a particular part or subassembly which can be purchased from Division Y (the selling division) or can be purchased outside the company. In addition, Division X must incur a variable cost of $10 per unit to assemble Product A. The variable cost of producing the part or subassembly in Division Y is $4 per unit, and there is capacity to produce 1,000 units of the part. Instead of using a single transfer price of $4, the company allows the buying division to buy at the variable cost of $4 and allows the selling division to sell at variable cost plus a profit percentage of 50 percent of variable cost — in this case, $2 per unit. If the intracompany transaction is completed, the partial income statements for the divisions will appear as follows:

Division X
Partial Income Statement

Sales (1,000 units @ $20)	$20,000
Variable cost:	
Cost of parts from Division Y (1,000 units @ $4)	$ 4,000
Cost incurred in Division X (1,000 units @ $10)	10,000
Total variable cost	$14,000
Contribution margin	$ 6,000

Division Y
Partial Income Statement

Sales (1,000 units @ $6)	$ 6,000
Variable cost (1,000 units @ $4)	4,000
Contribution margin	$ 2,000

Although the total contribution margin for the company as a whole appears to be $8,000 ($6,000 + $2,000), it is actually only $6,000 ($20 unit selling price of the final product — $14 total unit variable cost incurred in both Divisions X and Y = $6 unit contribution margin; $6 unit contribution margin × 1,000 units = \$6,000 total contribution margin). In this example, the full contribution is reflected in the statement of Division X. The additional contribution of \$2,000 reflected in Division Y's income statement occurred because Division Y was allowed to "sell" at a profit percentage of variable cost. However, this transaction was not a source of outside income.

The advantages of the dual transfer price system are illustrated by the above example. On the one hand, it is desirable for Division X to use Division Y's variable cost in deciding whether to buy internally or externally. Since there is unused capacity in Division Y, the part should be purchased from that division so long as the outside price is higher than the variable cost of \$4 per unit. On the other hand, motivation is provided by allowing Division Y to "sell" at variable cost plus a 50 percent profit percentage. Thus, the dual system is a way of providing the buying division with the proper information while at the same time allowing the selling division the possibility of a profit. Such a system maximizes the congruence of divisional goals with the company-wide goals.

TRANSFER PRICES FOR DECISION MAKING – A SYSTEM OF INFORMATION AND COMMUNICATION

As was indicated earlier, one of the basic reasons for decentralization is that it makes possible the delegation of decision-making authority throughout the firm. If one person or a small group can efficiently make all decisions for the firm, then much, if not all, of the impetus for decentralization will disappear. Hence, one of the basic assumptions in decentralization is that the firm-wide decision process is too complex for a few persons to effectively control.

If delegation of decision-making authority is to be effective, a communication system must be established throughout the firm. The need for a system of communication on which decisions can be based usually varies directly with the degree of decentralization involved. If all decisions are made centrally, the only need for communication is so that the subordinate managers can implement the decisions. Conversely, if the subordinate managers make and implement decisions, the need for a system of communication is enhanced.

In a decentralized operation, if the divisions are interdependent, a system of transfer prices can provide a communication system or a set of signals which the submanagers can use as a basis for their decisions. In such a setting, the system of internal prices serves the same purpose in facilitating internal transactions as the external price system does in facilitating transactions between the firm and outsiders.

To develop this point, consider the role of the external price system in providing information and communication for facilitating transactions between firms. If a make or buy decision is to be made by Firm A, the first step in the decision is to compare the inside prices of labor and materials (and other factors of production) with the outside price of the part. The decision depends primarily on how these costs compare with each other. Note that the external price system furnishes the information which guides the actions of the decision maker. Note also how much more difficult it would be to make a decision if the information on cost was not available in the form of external prices. It is in this sense that a system of prices is a powerfully efficient information system.

In a decentralized operation where divisions are interdependent, the manager of a division needs information to decide when to deal with another division and when to deal with an outside firm. For example, assume that Division B can buy a component part from Division S or from an outside firm. This problem is just another version of the make or buy situation discussed in the preceding paragraph. The decision depends primarily on a comparison of the internal transfer price (Division S's price) and the external price (the outside firm's price). If the internal transfer price is higher than the external price, the manager of Division B has a signal to buy outside the firm, and vice versa. It is, therefore, important that the transfer prices give the right signals; otherwise the decision process will not be carried out efficiently.

The following discussion of the problems and difficulties in using transfer prices is offered with the hope that a clear understanding of these problems will lead to better internal price systems and practices. It is difficult to anticipate all potential problems, but it is possible to describe some of the general problems of which management should be aware. Two distinct cases are distinguished: they are (1) a situation in which a market exists at the transfer point and (2) a situation in which a market does not exist at the transfer point.

The Intermediate Market Case

In the case of division operation, two general types of decisions may be called for: (1) how to produce and (2) how much to produce, including the decision as to both price and quantity. Assume that Division A is the selling division and Division B is the buying division. One decision B must make is whether or not to buy from A. B is encouraged to buy from A as long as the price quoted by A compares favorably with the outside market price.

In a perfectly competitive market, it makes little difference in the overall profit picture whether B buys inside or outside. A should be able to sell all of its output on the outside market; hence, B's decision to buy outside should not cause A to have any idle capacity. Furthermore, if the market is perfectly competitive, the selling costs of selling outside are likely to be about the same as the cost of selling to B.

When the market is not perfectly competitive, the situation changes somewhat. If market price is used as the transfer price, it would be undesirable for the price to be so inflexible that B might go outside to find a lower price and not buy from A without A's being allowed to lower its price. Such an action might cause A to have idle capacity, and the overall company profit would be lower than if A reduced the price to encourage B to buy internally.

Actually, B should buy inside so long as A's variable cost is below the outside market price. In such a situation, a possible conflict arises. As discussed earlier, it is possible to use a dual price system; that is, the transfer price to A could be the market price and the transfer price to B could be A's variable cost. However, such a practice may destroy some of the advantages of decentralization. By using a dual standard, the competitive atmosphere may be destroyed. A negotiated market price may be preferable. A would probably not allow idle capacity to persist in the long run. Rather, the market price to B would probably be negotiated at a low enough price so that B would not continue buying outside.

For most decisions of how to produce, even where there is capital investment involved, the proper calculation is the variable cost. This is so because, from the viewpoint of the entire company, the how-to-produce decision should be made so as to achieve the minimum cost possible. Cost that changes with volume is the relevant cost, and this cost is the variable cost. Any time a market transfer price is used, there is a potential conflict that may arise in connection with how-to-produce problems. In some cases a negotiated market price may accommodate the situation, as in the example; but, in any case, the safest transfer price for the decision is the variable cost. Such a transfer price, however, is generally a poor one for performance evaluation.

In pricing and output decisions for the end product, again it is the variable cost that is relevant. This is particularly true when the intermediate market is not perfectly competitive. If the intermediate market is perfectly competitive, the market price will suffice. For example, assume that Division A produces unprocessed meat and that Division B can buy from Division A and sell the meat processed. In order to justify processing, the variable cost of processing in Division B plus the opportunity market price as determined by the intermediate (unprocessed) market must be less than the selling price of processed meat. Hence, market price will accommodate a sell-or-process-more decision in a competitive market.

In terms of economic theory, the market price and the marginal cost in a perfectly competitive market should be equal; that is, to maximize profit, the division manager should produce and sell until marginal cost and marginal revenue are equal. In a perfectly competitive market, the demand curve is horizontal, because the division can sell any output at the market price. Hence, marginal revenue and market price are equal. If production is expanded until marginal cost and marginal revenue are equated, marginal cost will equal the market price. Marginal revenue is the additional revenue from selling one additional unit. Likewise, marginal cost is the additional cost of producing and selling one more unit. If marginal cost is constant, it is the same as the variable cost per unit. Variable cost can be viewed as an accounting measurement of marginal cost.

In the case of an imperfect intermediate market, the following decisions must be made with respect to output:

1. What price should be charged for the final product?
2. What price should be charged for the intermediate product?
3. How much of the intermediate product should be produced for sale on the outside market and how much for sale to Division B?

All of these decisions should be made on the basis of a marginal cost and a marginal revenue schedule for the several products involved. Neither market price nor a transfer price based on full cost will suffice in making these decisions. Therefore, a conflict is bound to arise between choosing a transfer price for performance evaluation and one for decision making.

The following example illustrates the imperfect market situation. Assume that Division A sells to Division B. The output of Division A is Product X_1, which can be sold at the intermediate market stage or can be transferred to Division B and processed and sold as Product X_2. The marginal revenue and variable cost information is as shown in the following table:

	Division A		Division B		
Number of Units	X_1 Marginal Revenue	X_1 Variable Cost	X_2 Marginal Revenue	X_2 Variable Cost	X_2 Marginal Revenue Less X_2 Variable Cost
11	$ .25	$1.50	$ .50	$1.00	$—.50
10	.25	1.50	.50	1.00	—.50
9	.50	1.50	1.00	1.00	—0—
8	.75	1.50	1.50	1.00	.50
7	1.00	1.50	2.00	1.00	1.00
6	1.25	1.50	2.50	1.00	1.50
5	1.50	1.50	3.00	1.00	2.00
4	1.75	1.50	3.50	1.00	2.50
3	2.00	1.50	4.00	1.00	3.00
2	2.25	1.50	4.50	1.00	3.50
1	2.50	1.50	5.00	1.00	4.00

This example is simplified by using a constant variable cost as a measure of marginal cost. In comparing the marginal costs and revenues, it can be seen that six units of X_2 can be sold in the final market before the net marginal revenue equals the variable cost of X_1 of $1.50; therefore, six units of X_1 should be sold to Division B for processing into X_2 and sale in the final market. But five units of X_1 can also be sold in the intermediate market before the marginal revenue equals the variable cost of $1.50. Hence, 11 units X_1 should be produced.

Note that this output decision has been made by using the marginal revenue of Product X_1 and the net marginal revenue of Product X_2. A unit of X_1 has a marginal variable production cost of $1.50, and it should be sold in that market where the profit is the highest. In the case of the intermediate market, no further processing is necessary. The production cost of $1.50 represents the total additional cost to be incurred in selling Product X_1 in the intermediate market. However, if X_1 is processed and sold as X_2, the additional processing cost is $1 per unit; and this amount should be deducted from the marginal revenue of X_2 to arrive at the net amount of additional revenue that will eventually accrue to the company.

In the above example, the total production schedule calls for 11 units of X_1 to be produced by Division A. It is assumed that the capacity of Division A is such that at least 11 units of X_1 can be produced. This may or may not be the case. Suppose, for example, that the capacity of Division A is limited to less than 11 units. A priority schedule must be developed to decide which units of X_1 should be sold to the intermediate market and which units should be sold to Division B for further processing and sale in the final market.

This priority schedule can be determined by comparing the marginal revenue schedule of Division A and the net marginal schedule (marginal revenue less X_2 variable cost) of Division B. For example, the first three units of X_1 should be transferred to Division B, since the net marginal revenue of this division is greater than the marginal revenue of Division A. On the 4th and 5th units, the marginal revenue of X_1 in either the final or the intermediate market is $2.50; so there is a point of indifference. The 6th unit should be allocated to the intermediate market, the 7th and 8th units have equal value in either market, the 9th unit should stay in Division A, and the 10th and 11th units have equal value in either market. The 12th unit should not be produced, since the marginal revenue in either market is lower than the marginal cost of $1.50. The following schedule, where the unit numbers are in parentheses, summarizes the priority for each unit. If for some reason the productive capacity of Division A is restricted to less than 11 units, this priority schedule should be used.

Units of Product $_1$	Marginal Revenue If X_1 Is Sold in the Intermediate Market	Net Marginal Revenue If X_1 Is Sold to Division B for Sale in the Final Market
1	$ 2.50 (4 or 5)	$4.00 (1)
2	2.25 (6)	3.50 (2)
3	2.00 (7 or 8)	3.00 (3)
4	1.75 (9)	2.50 (4 or 5)
5	1.50 (10 or 11)	2.00 (7 or 8)
6	1.25	1.50 (10 or 11)
7	1.00	1.00
8	.75	.50
9	.50	–0–
10	.25	–.50
11	.25	–.50

As can be seen from the example, the allocation problem in an imperfect market situation requires variable cost transfer prices. A market transfer price may cause Division B to restrict production. This restriction could cause

Division A to stop short of the most profitable level of production. Yet a variable cost transfer price is inadequate for performance evaluation. In the imperfect market situation, therefore, a conflict will undoubtedly arise where the data must also be used for pricing and output decisions.

The No Intermediate Market Case

If no intermediate market exists for the product of Division A, then Division A is really not a profit center. Such a division may still be set up as a decentralized independent operating unit, but it is more like a cost center within a centralized firm. To treat such a division as a profit center requires the determination of a transfer price that may be quite arbitrary. Furthermore, there is no real possibility for negotiation between Divisions A and B since Division A has no outside market alternative.

For decision problems, the proper transfer price for Product X_1 would be its marginal or variable cost. Since no market price exists, the main alternative is likely to be the full cost. The full cost may be an acceptable transfer price for performance evaluation; but such a figure will undoubtedly lead to poor decisions, because the buying division will be more likely to buy outside and in doing so may create excess capacity in the selling division. It is probably better to recognize Division A as a cost center and to evaluate it on the basis of a controllable cost budget or standard. The variable or marginal cost should be used as the transfer price to Division B. This figure can be used for evaluating Division B on a profit basis and it also is useful to Division B in making output and production decisions.

THE EVALUATION CRITERION OR STANDARD

The main indexes of division performance discussed earlier in this chapter were (1) division profit and (2) division return on investment with residual income as an alterative to using return on investment as a ratio. Where no intermediate market exists, it may be difficult to calculate profit, and cost may be the best performance index. Standards for cost control have been discussed in earlier chapters and will not be reviewed here.

If profit alone is used as an evaluation of division performance, the standard for measurement will probably be a profit budget for the division. This budget can be constructed by referring to other similar division operations within or outside the company. If this is done, the factors that are unique to the operations of a particular division should be considered. If the market is temporarily depressed and if this factor is not controllable by the division manager, it should receive proper consideration in establishing the budget. A detailed division profit budget should show, after a comparison with the actual performance, the parts of the division operation that are the weakest and on which a concentrated managerial effort is justified. Only the factors that are controllable by the division manager should be included in the profit budget.

The use of a profit index has been criticized on the grounds that a charge for investment controllable at the division level may not be included in the profit calculation. This criticism has probably been the main reason for the use of return on investment or its variation, residual income, as a performance index. A return on investment calculation relates profit to investment, and the resulting ratio becomes the performance index. In the residual income method, the performance index is an absolute dollar amount (rather than a ratio) calculated by deducting a capital charge from the operating profit. In either case, management must decide on an appropriate return on investment rate to use in the evaluation of a division. This return on investment rate becomes the standard for comparison if a return on investment (ratio) method is used; it becomes the capital charge if residual income is used as the performance index.

The choice of the appropriate return on investment standard is not without its problems. It is probably a mistake to compare a division's rate of return with the overall average rate desired by the top management. It may be that the division can never measure up to the desired overall average rate of return. Just because management desires 20 percent rate of return, there is no guarantee that a particular division can ever hope to earn this rate. Also, a division that earns 15 percent should not necessarily be liquidated. Even if other parts of the company can earn 20 percent on additional investment, the 15 percent division should not be liquidated unless the division investment is based on liquidation value and unless the 15 percent division can be liquidated without affecting the other operating divisions of the company. To the extent that the 15 percent return is based on historical investment, it is probably a poor guide for capital budgeting decisions; and depending on the standard used, it may be a poor index of performance.

Another problem in using a return on investment standard for judging performance can arise when the division manager does not have control over investment decisions. If the capital budget is administered centrally, it is more effective to control division investment by making the division manager's new projects compete for funds by using as a standard the best projects that exist elsewhere within the company. In this respect, the division rate of return budgeted for performance evaluation may be an extremely poor guide for additional investment because the money may find a better use elsewhere.

Even though the division manager may not have complete control over division investment in fixed assets, a good deal of control may be exercised over the working capital requirements of the division. The performance index should allow for this aspect of division operation. However, instead of calculating a rate of return on working capital investment, it is probably easier and more effective to include a charge for this investment in establishing the profit budget. This charge may be based on the rate that could be earned on working capital investment elsewhere in the company. If such a procedure is followed, the division manager will be reluctant to demand excess working capital. Furthermore, top management can also tell whether a particular division's use of working capital is as profitable as that of other divisions.

The problem of controlling and evaluating division operations in a decentralized company is exceedingly complex. Yet, top management really has no choice as to whether or not control is needed; it is rather a question of finding the most effective control device. Every manager must have some means of answering the question, "Where are the problems and the weak spots in the overall operation?" In a decentralized operation, the contact with the various parts of the operation is likely to be quite impersonal. Usually some reporting system must be used. Accounting concepts are useful because they can facilitate management by exception. If a good standard is established and if a good index of actual performance is calculated, the two can be compared and the exceptional case demanding management's attention can be found. However, since the control problem is a difficult but an important one, it behooves the manager to be very familiar with the strong features of a particular system as well as the troublesome problems that will undoubtedly be encountered in using accounting information.

Terminology Review

Decentralized company	(379)	Division controllable profit	(384)
Cost control	(380)	Contribution margin	(385)
Profit control	(380)	Investment base	(387)
Index	(380)	Return on investment	(388)
Standard	(380)	Residual income	(389)
Division direct profit	(384)	How-to-produce decision	(397)

QUESTIONS FOR REVIEW

1. What are the advantages of decentralization?

2. What criteria are needed for a control system?

3. Why is cost not a good control index in evaluating a division manager who has decision power on prices and combination of products?

4. What are some of the disadvantages of using division profit as an evaluation index?

5. Briefly state the difference between division controllable profit and division direct profit.

6. If the management of a company wanted to evaluate whether a particular division is a worthwhile economic investment, which concept of profit would it use?

7. Should investment which is common to several divisions be allocated to those divisions for the purpose of calculating a rate of return?

8. How is residual income defined? What is the major advantage of using residual income in performance evaluation?

9. What is a transfer price? Under what conditions are transfer prices necessary?

10. If a market transfer price can be determined, why is such a price usually considered the best one to use?

11. Briefly describe a dual transfer pricing system.

12. If the intermediate market is perfectly competitive, will a market-based transfer price ever lead to excess capacity in a producing division?

13. What is the disadvantage of using negotiated transfer prices when there is no intermediate market in which the producing division can sell its products?

EXERCISES

1. Profit Indexes. The following data are given for a division of a company:

Revenue from sales	$20,000
Division variable cost	9,500
Allocated home office overhead	1,600
Fixed overhead traceable to division ($3,000 is controllable, and $5,000 is not controllable)	8,000

Required: Calculate division contribution margin, division controllable profit, division direct profit, and division net profit.

2. Comparison of Return on Investment and Residual Income. A division of the Shaw Company has been reporting operating income of $1,800,000 per year based on an investment of $8,000,000. The company is considering the use of return on investment (ratio form) or residual income as an evaluation measure. At the present time, the division manager is faced with a decision on an incremental investment of $4,000,000 which will increase annual operating income by $700,000 per year.

Required: Provide a calculation which shows the difference between the 2 performance measures and explain the possible advantage of using residual income assuming that a 15% return on investment standard is considered acceptable.

3. Return on Investment and Residual Income. Provide the missing data as follows:

	Divisions			
	A	B	C	D
Net income	?	$500,000	?	$ 300,000
Investment base	$1,500,000	?	$2,000,000	$3,000,000
Return on investment	?	20%	12.5%	?
Imputed rate	6%	18%	?	?
Residual income	$ 15,000	?	$ (50,000)	-0-

4. Transfer Price Based on Full Cost. The Owen Company has a division which produces a single product that sells for $22 per unit in the external market. The full cost of the product is $16, calculated as follows:

> Variable materials and labor cost per unit $12
> Fixed cost per unit 4*
> $16
>
> *Total fixed cost of $400,000 divided by current production and sales of 100,000 units.

Another division has offered to buy 20,000 units at the full cost of $16. The producing division has excess capacity, and the 20,000 units can be produced without interfering with the current external sales volume of 100,000 units. The total fixed cost of the producing division will not change as a result of the order. However, the division manager of the producing division is inclined to reject the order, feeling that the division's profit position will not be improved.

Required: Explain to the division manager (by means of a calculation) why transferring 20,000 units at the full cost of $16 per unit will result in an increase in the profit of the producing division.

5. Transfer Pricing Problem. The Nash Company has a producing division which is currently producing 100,000 units but has a capacity of 150,000 units. The variable cost of the product is $20 per unit, and the total fixed cost is $600,000 or $6 per unit based on current production.

A selling division of the Nash Company offers to buy 50,000 units from the producing division at $19 per unit. The producing division manager refuses the order because the price is below variable cost. The selling division manager argues that the order should be accepted since by taking the order the producing division manager can lower the fixed cost per unit from $6 to $4 (output will increase to 150,000 units). This decrease of $2 in fixed cost per unit will more than offset the $1 difference between the variable cost and the transfer price.

Required:

(1) If you were the producing division manager, would you accept the selling division manager's argument? Why or why not? (Assume that the 100,000 units currently being produced sell for $30 per unit in the external market.)

(2) From the viewpoint of the overall company, should the order be accepted if the manager of the selling division intends to sell each unit in the outside market for $22 after incurring an additional processing cost of $2.25 per unit?

6. Dual Transfer Price System. The Crawford Company has two divisions, A and B. Division B produces a product at a variable cost of $8 per unit and sells 50,000 units to the external market at $12 per unit and 40,000 units to Division A at variable cost plus 50%. However, under the dual transfer price system in use, Division A pays only the variable cost per unit. The fixed cost of Division B is $160,000 per year.

   Division A sells 40,000 units of its finished product in the external market at $25 per unit and has a variable cost of $6 per unit in addition to the cost of the subassembly purchased from Division B at variable cost. The annual fixed cost of Division A is $120,000.

Required: Show the income statements for the two divisions and the income statement for the company as a whole (assuming the company consists of only the two divisions). Explain why, under the dual transfer price system, the income for the company is less than the sum of the profit figures shown on the income statements for the two divisions.

7. Market Value Transfer Price. Company X has two divisions, M and S. Division M manufactures a product and Division S sells it. The intermediate market is perfectly competitive, but the product can be stored and sold later or processed and sold in the final processed market. Once the product is manufactured, some of it is sold by Division M and some is transferred to Division S which decides whether to hold or process and sell the product. The following information pertains to the current year.

Manufacturing cost incurred by Division M in producing 1,000,000 units	$6,000,000
Of the 1,000,000 units produced:	
500,000 sold by M in intermediate market	5,000,000
200,000 held by S for sale later (no additional processing work done on	
these units in Division S)	2,000,000
300,000 processed by S and sold	5,400,000
Sales value of 500,000 units at the time they were transferred to S	5,000,000
Total additional processing cost of S	1,200,000

There were no beginning inventories.

Required:
   (1) Prepare an income statement for the whole firm.
   (2) Prepare a separate income statement for each division using a market value transfer price.

8. Choosing an Appropriate Transfer Price. The Walker Oil Company has just decentralized its Refining and Marketing divisions. Refining is allowed to sell to outside wholesalers while Marketing is permitted to buy from other refiners. Walker Oil produces only unleaded gasoline at a variable refinery cost of $.30 per gallon and a fixed refining cost of $140,000 per month for a capacity of 400,000 gallons. The market price in the intermediate market is $1 per gallon. Marketing sells the fuel to independent service stations at $1.20 per gallon and incurs transportation costs of $.10 per gallon.

Required: Show the impact on profits of Refining, Marketing, and Walker Oil Company of using each of the following transfer prices, assuming all refined gallons are sold to Marketing: (a) variable cost, (b) market price, and (c) full cost. What conclusion can you draw?

9. Decision Making in Decentralized Operation. The Quinn Company is going to build an office building for itself. The company has a construction division which builds all buildings and equipment for the entire company. The construction division has requested bids on the elevators for the building from two companies. The O Company gives a bid of $5,000,000, and the U Company bids $4,000,000. However, the O Company would buy materials for the elevators from a fabricating division of the Quinn Company. This order would result in the fabricating division earning $1,500,000 after covering all costs. Since the Quinn Company is decentralized, the construction division is not aware of this possibility.

Required: Which bid would you expect the construction division to take? Which bid would the Quinn Company prefer to have the construction division accept?

10. Transfer Pricing Problem. The tailor shop in a men's clothing store is set up as an autonomous unit. The transfer price for tailoring services is based on the variable cost which is estimated at $8 per hour. The store manager feels that the suit and sport coat department is currently using too much tailor time and that this department could cut down on hours used by taking more care in fitting the garments. The manager has decided to double the hourly tailor rate even though this new rate will be no reflection of the real variable cost. The idea is simply to provide an incentive to the suit and sport coat department to conserve on tailor time.

Required: What possible disadvantages do you see in the store manager's action? Do you agree or disagree with this means of stressing the need to conserve tailor time? Would it make any difference if the various selling departments were required to use the tailor shop and were not allowed to take their tailor work to some outside tailor shop?

11. Allocation of Central Corporate Office Cost. The Horton Company has several operating divisions which are largely autonomous as far as decision making is concerned. The central corporate office consists mainly of the president and immediate staff. The annual cost is $8,750,000, and this cost is fixed. In calculating division profit, this cost is allocated to divisions on the basis of sales. The current allocation rate is $.35 per sales dollar based on the company-wide normal sales volume of $25,000,000 per year. The company controller does not consider this to be a transfer price because he feels that the divisions are not really buying anything. In the controller's view, the charge is a method of allocating cost which should be absorbed by the divisions when they calculate their annual net income.

Required: Do you agree with the controller? In what sense is the charge a transfer price? Could the charge affect the decision of a division manager considering the introduction of a new product with a variable cost of $5.50 and a selling price of $8? Explain.

12. Transfer Pricing Problem. Divison 1 produces 100,000 units of a product with a variable cost of $5 per unit and a fixed cost of $3 (based on $300,000 fixed cost allocated to 100,000 units of production). These units can be sold in an intermediate market for $1,000,000 ($10 per unit) or transferred to Division 2 for additional processing and sold in a processed market. The selling price processed is $14 per unit and the additional processing cost in Division 2 is $1.50 per unit. The fixed cost in the Division 2 processing unit is $100,000. At this time, there will be excess capacity in the Division 2 processing unit if the units are not transferred.

Required: Should the 100,000 units be sold by Division 1 or by Division 2? Would a transfer price based on either market price or variable cost be likely to lead to the right decision? Which price would you favor if Division 1 can always sell at least 100,000 units at $10 per unit in the intermediate market and Division 2 could buy under similar conditions?

PROBLEMS

13-1. Transfer Price Based on Full Cost. Division P of the Freddie Company produces a large metal frame which is sold to Division S of the company. Division S uses these frames in constructing metal lathes which are sold to machine tool manufacturers. In Division P, the frames are produced in a stamping process and are then run through a finishing process in which they are trimmed and polished before being shipped to Division S.

The current estimate of the variable cost of materials and labor to produce a frame in the stamping process is $125 per frame. The fixed overhead associated with this process in Division P is $640,000 per year. Current production is 40,000 frames, and this is full capacity for both the stamping and the trimming-polishing processes.

The variable cost of labor in the trimming-polishing process (no additional materials are required) is $12 per frame since labor in this process is paid on a piece-rate basis. The fixed overhead in this process is $280,000 per year, and this amount is largely due to equipment depreciation and related costs. The machines have no salvage value to speak of since they are fairly specialized equipment.

The transfer price to Division S is a full-cost transfer price, and the fixed cost per unit is calculated by prorating the current fixed cost in each process over the 40,000 frames being produced. The price is quoted for each process, and the calculation presented to the manager of Division S by the manager of Division P is as follows:

Stamping process:	
Materials and labor cost per unit.....................................	$125
Fixed overhead cost per unit ($640,000 ÷ 40,000 units)	16
	$141
Trimming-polishing process:	
Labor cost per unit	$ 12
Fixed overhead cost per unit ($280,000 ÷ 40,000 units)	7
	$ 19
Total cost per unit	$160

An outside company has offered to rent to Division S machinery which would perform the trimming and polishing part of the frame manufacturing. The rental cost of the machinery is $200,000 per year. With the new machinery, the labor cost per frame would remain at $12. The Division S manager sees the possibility of obtaining the frames from Division P for $141 by eliminating the $19 cost of trimming and polishing and performing these processes in Division S. An analysis is given as follows:

New Process:

Machine rental cost per year	$200,000
Labor cost ($12 × 40,000 units)	480,000
	680,000
Current process (40,000 units @ $19 per unit, portion of Division P transfer price attributable to trimming-polishing process)	$760,000

The manager of Division S has approached the company vice-president of operations for approval to acquire the new machinery.

Required:

(1) As the vice-president, how would you advise the manager of Division S?

(2) Could the transfer pricing system be modified; and, if so, how?

13-2. Allocation of Central Office Overhead. The Wiley Company has several departments which operate quite autonomously as far as decision making is concerned. The company allocates central office overhead to all these operating departments based on the total labor dollars incurred by each division. The central office overhead budget and the allocation rate are as follows:

Executive offices	$190,000
Legal	60,000
Advertising	50,000
Personnel	90,000
Accounting	60,000
Total	$450,000
Total estimated payroll in operating departments	$600,000

Allocation rate—$450,000 ÷ $600,000 = $.75 per labor dollar

The central office overhead of $450,000 is considered to be a fixed cost. Also, once the rate is established, it is not changed for one year.

The engineering research department conducts research on certain engineering problems related to the company's products and issues reports to clients who request this service. The manager of this department is faced with a need to hire two more technical assistants because of an increased work load. If the manager works through the company's personnel department, these positions can be filled at a cost of $1,000 per month for each employee. However, the usual $.75 per dollar of payroll will also be charged against the research department's budget for central office overhead. The manager discovers that it is possible to hire the technical services of an outside engineering firm which will furnish two technical assistants for as long as they are required, and the cost will be considered a consulting cost and not part of the division's payroll. The cost will be $1,500 per month for each assistant.

Required

(1) Is the central office overhead charge a transfer price? Explain.

(2) What is the manager of the engineering research department likely to do? Show your calculations.

(3) If the Wiley Company wants to continue to allocate central office overhead, advise the president how this might be done so as not to affect the hiring decisions of the various department managers.

13-3. *Decision Making in Decentralized Operation.* The Main Company has several divisions. Division S produces (among other products) a metal container which is sold to customers who use it for shipping liquid chemicals. The main material used in manufacturing these containers is a metal which can be purchased from Division M, one of the other divisions of the company, or from several outside sources. Division S has received a customer order for 100 containers at $400 each. It will require two tons of materials to produce the 100 containers. The manager of Division S requests bids for the materials required to produce the containers from Division M and from two outside companies. Division M, bidding a transfer price based on full cost, bids a price of $8,000 per ton on the materials order. Division M's variable cost is only $4,500 per ton, and there is excess capacity. However, Division M regularly bases price bids on full cost whether the order is from another division or from an outside customer.

The two outside companies bid $6,000 and $6,500 per ton. However, Company A, which bid $6,500, would buy the manufacturing supplies necessary to produce the materials from Division P, another division of the Main Company. The supplies would amount to $1,500 per ton of materials required, and the profit to Division P would be about 60% of the selling price.

Required:

(1) What would you expect Division S to do?

(2) Will Division S accept the right outside bid?

(3) Should Division M's transfer pricing policy be changed? If so, how?

13-4. *Transfer Pricing Problem.* The Cook Company has a central computer facility which is used by several operating departments for data processing and problem-solving purposes. The center's budget for the current year is given as follows:

Rentals.	$1,200,000
Payroll, operators	250,000
Payroll, programmers	150,000
Payroll, supervision and secretarial.	90,000
Miscellaneous supplies	150,000
Utilities	250,000
Total	$2,090,000

It is estimated that 10,000 computer time units will be available.

All of the costs shown in the budget are considered to be fixed, except for utilities and miscellaneous supplies, which are variable.

During the past 5 years, the computer facility has not been operated at full capacity. The percentage of capacity has increased from 40% in the first year of operation to about 70% of capacity estimated for the current year.

A transfer price policy has been established which calls for the use of a full cost per unit of time. Thus, an operating department that needs one half of a time unit would be charged at the rate of $104.50 [1/2 × ($2,090,000 ÷ 10,000 time units)]. All operating departments do most of their own programming. The central staff has four programmers who are used to solve special problems as they arise in the center.

The associate director of the center has approached the director to revise the transfer price policy to include only the variable costs. His argument is that the operating departments would thereby be encouraged to make greater use of the facility. The director's response is that she sees no reason why this should be so.

"After all," she points out, "the operating departments need only so much time anyway; and besides, the various managers cannot buy computer time outside the company. So how could the transfer price affect their behavior?"

The associate director's response is that he knows of several instances where the operating departments have secured additional outside-the-company programming services so that the program submitted would require less running time.

"In fact," he says, "I know of one case where the operating manager spent $300 on additional programming to save an estimated 2 time units of running time."

The director's response is, "He should have—after all, it cost us $209 per time unit to run the program!"

Required:

(1) Do you agree with the associate director or the director? Explain.

(2) Was the behavior of the operating manager (as described by the associate director) optimal as far as the whole company is concerned?

(3) Assuming that the additional programming effort could not have been done inside the company, what is the maximum price that the operating manager should have paid?

13-5. Preparation of Divisional Income Statements. The Wyatt Packing Company has two divisions. Division 1 is responsible for slaughtering and cutting the unprocessed meat. Division 2 processes meat such as hams, bacon, etc. Division 2 can buy meat from Division 1 or from outside suppliers. Division 1 can sell at the market price all the unprocessed meat that it can produce. The current year's income statement for the company appears as follows:

The Wyatt Packing Company
Income Statement
For the Current Year

Sales			$2,400,000
Cost of goods sold:			
Beginning inventory		—0—	
Manufacturing costs:			
Materials, Division 1	$ 600,000		
Labor, Division 1	400,000		
Overhead, Division 1	500,000		
Processing Supplies, Division 2	200,000		
Labor, Division 2	300,000		
Overhead, Division 2	100,000		
Cost of goods available for sale	$2,100,000		
Less ending inventory cost:			
Division 1		—0—	
Division 2	$150,000	150,000	1,950,000
Gross margin			$ 450,000
Operating expenses:			
Sales and administrative, Division 1	$ 120,000		
Sales and administrative, Division 2	100,000		
Central office overhead	100,000	320,000	
Income before income tax			$ 130,000

The ending inventory of $150,000 is at the cost of production incurred in Division 1. This inventory is as yet unprocessed. The market value unprocessed is $200,000. The sales for the year can be broken down as follows:

Division 1	$ 500,000
Division 2	1,900,000
	$2,400,000

The market value of the unprocessed meat actually transferred from Division 1 to Division 2 (exclusive of the ending inventory) was $1,600,000.

Required:

(1) Prepare division income statements that might be used to evaluate the performance of the two division managers.

(2) Explain the transfer pricing policy you have used in preparing the statements.

(3) Can you see any conflict in the policy you have used if this same transfer price is to be used for decision making?

13-6. Preparation of Divisional Income Statements. A large farming company has 2 divisions; one produces grain, and the other sells the grain. As soon as the grain is produced, it is transferred to the selling division where it is stored in anticipation of future sales at a higher price.

During the year, 3 grain crops of 1,500,000 bushels each were produced. All 3 have now been sold although some were held in inventory for various periods of time. The market price at production time was $5 per bushel for the first crop, $6 per bushel for the second, and $3 per bushel for the third. There were no beginning inventories.

The annual income statement for the entire company appears as follows:

Revenue:	
Sales (4,500,000 bushels)	$22,500,000
Cost:	
Producing division labor and materials	$10,000,000
Selling division labor	1,250,000
Producing division overhead	8,000,000
Selling division overhead	750,000
	$20,000,000
Net income	$ 2,500,000

Required: The company president is very pleased with the total profit but wants to determine whether the price speculation activities of the selling division are earning a profit. You are requested to prepare divisional income statements for the producing division and the selling division. Decide what type of transfer price, market or cost, to use. Explain which transfer price is better. Are the division income statements useful? Explain.

13-7. Evaluation of a Division Using Return on Investment. A company has a division which manufactures and sells furniture. The income statement of this division is as follows:

Furniture Division
Income Statement
For the Current Year

Sales		$15,000,000
Division costs:		
Variable cost	$10,000,000	
Fixed cost	4,000,000	14,000,000
		$ 1,000,000
Allocated central office overhead.............................		500,000
Net income		$ 500,000

Investment allocated to division—$5,000,000
Return on investment—10%

The management is disturbed at the low return on investment. The corporate treasurer indicates that the company can earn at least 20% on additional investment in any number of other projects. Furthermore, the treasurer points out that the investment is actually understated because the plant and facility carried at cost of $5,000,000 could be disposed of for twice that amount.

An investigation reveals that the division fixed cost of $4,000,000 cannot be eliminated even if the division is sold. The allocated central office overhead is a pro rata share of operating the corporate offices, and sale of the division would not affect this cost either.

Required:

(1) Assuming that an expenditure of $1,000,000 annually would maintain the facility in good operating condition for at least 10 years, should the division be sold?

(2) If not, is there a better way of reporting the return on investment that would alert the management to consider selling if volume begins to decline?

13-8. Internal or External Sales. Wendover Company has the capacity to manufacture 700 units of a part used in machine tool production. This part is manufactured in batch lots of 100 units each. Division A makes this part at a uniform variable cost of $5 per unit. The manufactured batches can be sold either to outside customers or to Division B where the parts are used in machine tool assembly.

Data with respect to prices per batch from outside sales are given along with prices charged to outsiders after further processing in Division B.

Batch No.	Division A Price to Outside Customers	Division B Price to Outside Customers After Additional Processing
1	$15	$35
2	14	32
3	12	30
4	9	25
5	9	22
6	9	20
7	8	20

The additional processing cost of Division B for each unit of the first 3 batches is $10. The next 3 batches cost $12 per unit to process. The seventh batch costs $13 per unit to process.

Required: Decide which batches should be sold after production in Division A and which batches should be transferred to Division B for further processing. Show computations.

13-9. Transfer Pricing Problem. The Leisure Company has a producing division (Division 1) that supplies several parts to another producing division (Division 2) which produces the main product. These component parts are listed as follows with relevant cost information:

Component No.	Variable Cost per Unit	Quantity Produced
1	$ 9	20,000
2	13	30,000
3	5	10,000
4	3	10,000

The out-of-pocket fixed cost of Division 1 amounts to $270,000. This cost consists of the salary of the division management, indirect labor, payroll, and the like. In addition, the fixed cost which is not out-of-pocket (consisting mainly of depreciation on machinery) amounts to $80,000 per period.

In calculating unit cost, the total fixed cost of $350,000 is allocated to units to arrive at a full cost. This calculation is shown in the following table:

Component No.	Variable Cost per Unit	Fixed Cost per Unit	Full Cost per Unit
1	$ 9	$ 5	$14
2	13	5	18
3	5	5	10
4	3	5	8

In establishing transfer prices, the full cost is used. In Division 2, which uses the 4 components, the manager has authority to buy inside the company or to buy from an outside supplier. The outside prices vary somewhat throughout the year. At the present time, the outside prices are as follows:

Component No.	Outside Price
1	$14.50
2	19.20
3	9.40
4	8.10

The manager of Division 2 notices that the outside purchase price of Component 3 is $.60 lower than the transfer price and places an order with an outside supplier. Division 1 stops producing Component 3, reallocates the fixed cost to the remaining units, and adjusts the full cost transfer prices.

Required:

(1) Reallocate the fixed cost and determine the adjusted transfer prices based on full cost. If there is no communication between the two divisions, what action will the manager of Division 2 be likely to take?

(2) Comment on the deficiencies of the full cost transfer price system.

(3) Devise a method of assigning the fixed cost of Division 1 to Division 2 that will not cause Division 2 to buy outside when the components should be produced by Division 1. Consider the possibility of charging Division 2 a flat rate, regardless of the volume purchased, plus a charge per unit for the number of units purchased.

13-10. Evaluation of Alternative Transfer Pricing Systems. The Stratton Company has a division that manufactures shafts, some of which are used by other divisions and some of which are sold in the outside market. This division is organized in two sections which are described as follows:

> *Section 1—Machining and Grinding.* This highly mechanized section has much heavy equipment that is used to give shape to the shafts and to perform grinding operations on shafts with special requirements.

> *Section 2—Cleaning and Packing.* This section consists primarily of workers who clean and pack all shafts.

The costing system used by the company charges materials, direct labor, and overhead to each unit of product. The labor and the materials are considered to be variable costs, but the overhead is fixed. The overhead is allocated on the basis of the labor cost required to produce each product. Furthermore, the rate is a division rate and not a section overhead rate. This rate is developed from the following information.

	Direct Labor Payroll	Overhead
Section 1	$200,000	$ 800,000
Section 2	600,000	240,000
Total	$800,000	$1,040,000

Overhead rate: $\dfrac{\$1,040,000}{\$800,000}$ = $1.30 per dollar of labor cost

The average wage for Section 1 is $6 per hour; for Section 2, $3 per hour.

A full cost transfer price is used for selling shafts to other producing divisions. If an order is placed by another producing division that calls for $40 of materials and 2 hours of labor time in each section, the price that is quoted would be arrived at as follows:

	Hours	Total
Labor:		
Section 1	2	$12.00
Section 2	2	6.00
		$18.00
Overhead ($1.30 × $18)		23.40
Materials		40.00
Transfer price		$81.40

The assistant to the controller has been considering a change in the costing system whereby an overhead rate would be developed for each section. It is believed that such a system would give a more equitable price for the work done for other divisions and would be a better basis for determining the profit from sales to outsiders. Since the shaft sold on the outside market is standardized, the price is determined by the customers of the industry; and the primary decision that must be made is whether to accept or reject orders at a given price. At times the division is near enough to capacity that outside work must be stopped if inside work is to be done.

At the moment two outside orders are being considered. These orders are from another division that can buy either inside or outside the company. The details on the two orders are as follows:

	Order 1	Order 2
Materials	$50	$20
Labor:		
Section 1	3 hours	6 hours
Section 2	3 hours	1 hour

Required:
(1) Calculate the transfer prices for the two orders under the present system.
(2) Calculate the transfer prices under the proposed system.
(3) Explain the differences in the prices.
(4) Recalculate the transfer prices for the two orders based on variable cost only.
(5) Which of the three systems do you prefer? Why?

13-11. Transfer Price Decision. The Elkton Division of Nordic Instruments Inc. manufactures small printed circuit boards and has the capacity to make 100,000 units of a given model each year. At the present time, only 75,000 units are being made each year and sold to an outside customer for $6.50 a unit.

Fixed manufacturing costs are applied on the basis of an annual production of 100,000 units each year. Total fixed cost for the year is $150,000. The total unit cost of each circuit board is $5.80

The Reeves Division of Nordic Instruments Inc. has been purchasing this type of circuit board from an outside supplier at a price of $6.50 per unit. The president of the company requests that the Elkton Division deliver 25,000 circuit boards to the Reeves Division at a price equal to the variable cost.

The superintendent of Elkton states that the division gains no advantage by selling at variable cost. No contribution is made to the recovery of the fixed cost. Furthermore, the superintendent states that the company gains nothing. The fixed cost of Elkton must be recovered and Reeves should pay the full price of $6.50 as it would by buying outside.

Required:
(1) Is the argument of the superintendent valid? Explain.
(2) What is the variable cost of manufacturing each circuit board?
(3) Describe a pricing system that should benefit the company and be acceptable to each division.

13-12. Internal Pricing Decision. Mark Dolan is the manager of the Burling Division of Ace Machine Company. This division manufactures spring assemblies that are sold to various outside customers at a price of $30 per unit.

Recently the division has been operating below normal capacity at 500,000 direct labor hours. Normal capacity has been defined at 600,000 direct labor hours and is approximately equal to the practical capacity.

Each assembly requires 15 minutes of direct labor time. The direct materials and direct labor cost per assembly is $16.20, and overhead varies at the rate of $8.40 per direct labor hour. The total fixed overhead for the year is $3,420,000.

Dolan's division has just been awarded a contract for the sale of 400,000 units in another country at a unit price of $24. This contract will not interfere with the regular sales at a price of $30, and it is anticipated that this contract can be renewed in future years.

The Judd Division of the company has started production of a product line that will required 400,000 units of the type of assembly made by the Burling Division. The president of the company states that the assemblies should be transferred between the divisions at the variable cost to the Burling Division. If Burling Division does not furnish the units, the Judd Division will be forced to purchase the assemblies on the outside market at $30 apiece. With higher costs, Judd will have lower profits on the sale of the end products.

Required:

(1) Determine the variable cost to produce each spring assembly.

(2) Under the circumstances, should the Burling Division supply the Judd Division?

(3) What price should be used for the internal transfer, assuming a transfer should be made?

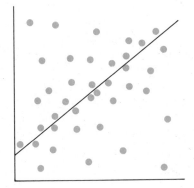

14

THE BUDGET PROCESS

Chapter Objectives

This chapter will enable you to:
1. Describe how the budget process begins with an estimation of the factor that will limit sales and production.
2. Describe the importance of sales forecasting in the preparation of budgets.
3. Evaluate models of future expectations that can be built using probabilities.
4. Describe how sales budgets in units of product are translated into sales revenue budgets.
5. Discuss how sales and production budgets are closely interlocked.
6. Discuss how inventory planning becomes a part of the budget process.

As stated in the first chapter, a budget is a plan showing how resources are to be acquired and used over a specified time interval. Before anyone can properly understand how a budget is prepared and how the various parts of the operation interlock, it is necessary to understand cost behavior and the ways in which revenues and costs are brought together in profit planning.

An operating budget is usually for a year, with the year divided further into quarters and months. All persons in the organization working in a managerial capacity will be involved in the budgeting process, contributing budget data and modifying it as necessary to fit into the overall plan for the company.

SALES FORECASTING

The budgeting operation begins with a recognition of the limits that are imposed upon the company either by external or by internal factors. For example, if a shortage of available materials will limit production to 40,000 units of product for the year, then plans must be built around this limit even if 70,000 units could be sold to customers. Or, in another situation, if plant capacity limits production to 50,000 units, then the company must plan accordingly even if it were possible to sell more units than could be provided by past inventories and maximum current production.

In most cases, sales volume is the limiting factor, and the budget plan begins with a forecast of sales volume for the year. All other budgets, such as the production budget and the selling and administrative budget, will depend directly or indirectly upon the sales forecast, which in turn is translated into a sales budget.

Wide Variety of Factors Affecting Sales

The sales forecast is based upon a variety of interlocking factors, such as price policy, the general economic outlook, conditions within the industry, governmental policies, and the position of the company in the economy. In relatively large companies, an economic forecasting department or a division of the controller's department devotes its full time to economic forecasting, with forecasts prepared not only for the immediate future, but for ten to twenty years ahead.

Methods used in forecasting sales vary widely. Each industry and company has distinctive characteristics which in themselves tend to create differences in outlook. In general, the sales forecast is based upon an analysis of past sales and an estimate of future economic prospects.

Basis for Sales Forecasts

Sales from past years can be broken down by product lines, regions, and salespeople to provide a basis for estimating possible future sales. The regional sales managers and salespeople prepare sales estimates for the coming year in light of their knowledge of the past and their expectations for the future. Higher echelons of management who are better informed with respect to the total economic picture review these estimates and fit them into a composite forecast for the company, making adjustments wherever necessary.

A sales forecast is sometimes made on a more scientific basis by fitting the business activity of the company to published indexes and reports on the economy at large. A given company may find that its activity tends to follow the Federal Reserve Board's Index, statistics on bank deposits, national income, population trends, and so forth. It is possible to predict future sales trends from established relationships.

Many factors operate to complicate sales forecasting. A company may appear to fit into a particular industry grouping, yet upon closer examination it may be found that the company handles many different lines of products and in reality has the attributes of several industries. In addition, products may be sold through various channels in different territories or even in different countries. Some products, such as food staples and clothing, are produced for sale to the consumer, while other products are indirectly related to consumer demand. For example, basic products such as glass, steel, and aluminum are not sold to the consumer directly but are used in the manufacture of other products. The demand for basic products that are used in making other products is said to be a derived demand. Sales forecasts for these products depend upon forecasts and data prepared for other industries. The demand for paint and lumber, for example, is influenced to a large extent by the number of new housing starts planned. If products are sold to automobile manufacturers, then the demand is derived from forecasts of new car sales.

Sometimes a computer is used in forecasting. The computer is a means by which diverse information can be brought together in various combinations and tested for validity. A watch manufacturer, for example, knows that watches are often purchased as graduation gifts and that sales bear a relationship to the number of graduates in a given year. But the manufacturer may not know how high a correlation there is between watch sales and the number of students graduating. Various factors that have a bearing on watch sales can be brought together in weighted formulas and can be tested on the computer. Experimentation and testing reveal whether or not the weights used in any of the formulas are valid. If a reasonable degree of correlation is found to exist in any formula tested, the formula may be used in estimating the sales potential.

A forecast of sales on an industry-wide basis must be broken down so that it applies to a particular company. Each company looks at its position relative to the total market and calculates its share of the market. In some areas and in certain product lines, one company may dominate; while in other areas and in other product lines, the sales may be divided in different proportions. Market studies show customer preference by locality and may reveal why one brand sells better than another. Market surveys are not made so that they can be used in budgeting, but data taken from surveys can often be applied in budget preparation.

MODELS FOR PLANNING

Models may be built that incorporate various assumptions with respect to economic conditions, volume of sales, prices and costs. By means of a computer, the models may be tested in simulation studies to determine what can be expected if certain assumptions are made and probability estimates are applied. The probabilities reflect the likelihood that a certain business condition will occur. Information can be derived for realistic budgeting, and at the same time the effect of a particular change in any factor can be determined. In other words, the sensitivity of profits to changes in factors such as sales volume and prices can be tested; thus providing management with not only budget data, but also data that can help to identify areas of the operation that will require close attention.

A simple illustration is given to show how probabilities can be applied in determining the expected value (the average or mean) of sales, costs, and profits. Assume, for example, that a company plans to sell one product line next year at a price of $20 a unit. Probability estimates have been made for sales volume and variable costs per unit. The variable costs per unit do not vary with changes in the expected sales volume levels.

Sales Volume (Number of Units)	Probabilities
150,000	.20
200,000	.70
250,000	.10
	1.00

Variable Unit Costs	Probabilities
$15	.80
10	.20
	1.00

In this illustration, the relationship of the individual probabilities to their respective sales volume and variable unit costs is the basis for understanding the total expected value of the contribution margin and the expected value of the profit plan.

Fixed costs are estimated at $500,000 for the next year, and income taxes are estimated at 40 percent of income before income tax.

The expected value of the contribution margin for the next year is computed as shown at the top of the next page.

Similarly, the total expected value of sales and variable cost can be determined as shown:

Sales Volume	Probabilities	Expected Value (units)
150,000	.20	30,000
200,000	.70	140,000
250,000	.10	25,000
Total expected value (units)		195,000

Sales revenue (195,000 units × $20) **$3,900,000**

Unit Variable Costs	Probabilities	Expected Value
$15	.80	$12
10	.20	2
Total expected value		$14

Total variable costs expected (195,000 units × $14)......$2,730,000

Contribution Margin
(In thousands of dollars)

Events	Sales Revenue	Variable Cost	Contribution Margin	Probabilities Sales	Probabilities Variable Cost	Probabilities Joint	Expected Value
20% probability, sales of 150,000 units							
Unit variable costs:							
$15	$3,000	$2,250	$ 750	.20	.80	.16	$ 120
10	3,000	1,500	1,500	.20	.20	.04	60
70% probability, sales of 200,000 units							
Unit variable cost:							
$15	4,000	3,000	1,000	.70	.80	.56	560
10	4,000	2,000	2,000	.70	.20	.14	280
10% probability, sales of 250,000 units							
Unit variable cost:							
$15	5,000	3,750	1,250	.10	.80	.08	100
10	5,000	2,500	2,500	.10	.20	.02	50
Total expected value, contribution margin.........							$1,170

The expected value of the profit plan is given as follows:

Sales	$3,900,000
Variable costs	2,730,000
Contribution margin	$1,170,000
Fixed costs	500,000
Income before income tax.....................	$ 670,000
Income tax (40%)	268,000
Net income	$ 402,000

The probabilistic approach to budgeting can provide a general guideline to the possible outcome of a combination of different factors under conditions of uncertainty. Past experience coupled with a careful analysis of the future can serve as a basis for establishing probability estimates. Admittedly, probability estimates will not be precise, but they should be more accurate than rough approximations or intuitive judgments.

In each particular circumstance, the profit will vary according to the combination of conditions. The expected value, however, results from assigning weights to the various conditions in combination and is a weighted value.

A SALES BUDGET ILLUSTRATION

The Donovan Company has made a careful estimate of sales volume for 1985 by product line and by calendar quarters. During 1985, the company expects to sell the following quantities of each product:

Donovan Company
Sales Budget—Units of Product
For the Year Ended December 31, 1985

	Total	First Quarter	Second Quarter	Third Quarter	Fourth Quarter
Product 1	300,000	100,000	60,000	60,000	80,000
Product 2	200,000	10,000	60,000	90,000	40,000

Each of these products is sold on a seasonal basis. Product 1 tends to sell better in winter months, while Product 2 sells better during the summer.

By handling product lines that sell better in different seasons, the Donovan Company hopes to be able to even out production over the year. The extent to which the company can realize its goal of balanced production will depend upon the time required to manufacture a unit of one product as compared with another, the sales volume of each product line, the labor and facilities required in manufacturing, and other factors related to the peculiarities of the products themselves.

To produce a sales revenue budget, prices established for the various product lines are applied to the sales budget in units of product. If price changes are expected during the year, then the budget should be altered accordingly. The Donovan Company plans to sell its products at uniform prices throughout the year: Product 1 at $30 a unit and Product 2 at $20 a unit. The prices are attached to the physical units and the budget of sales revenue is prepared.

Donovan Company
Gross Sales Revenue Budget
For the Year Ended December 31,1985
(In thousands of dollars)

	Total	First Quarter	Second Quarter	Third Quarter	Fourth Quarter
Product 1	$ 9,000	$3,000	$1,800	$1,800	$2,400
Product 2	4,000	200	1,200	1,800	800
Total sales revenue	$13,000	$3,200	$3,000	$3,600	$3,200

The gross sales as budgeted will not be realized even if the actual sales are made according to plan. Some of the customers will return products or will expect allowances for one reason or another. Still other customers will fail to pay what they owe, and their accounts will have to be written off as uncollectible. Management will be reluctant to admit that accounts cannot be collected or that allowances of any consequence will be granted. Nevertheless, if the budget is to be realistic, provision must be made for deductions from gross sales revenue.

A study of past experience shows that the Donovan Company has lost about five percent of its billed revenue each year because of returns, allowances, and uncollectible accounts. The returns and allowances have averaged about 3 percent of gross sales, while uncollectible accounts have averaged about 2 percent. From all indications, future revenues will be reduced in approximately the same proportions, and the following budget has been prepared on that basis.

Donovan Company
Sales Revenue Budget
Net of Returns, Allowances, and Uncollectibles
For the Year Ended December 31, 1985
(In thousands of dollars)

	Total	First Quarter	Second Quarter	Third Quarter	Fourth Quarter
Gross sales	$13,000	$3,200	$3,000	$3,600	$3,200
Returns and allowances..............	$ 390	$ 96	$ 90	$ 108	$ 96
Uncollectible accounts	260	64	60	72	64
Total deductions	$ 650	$ 160	$ 150	$ 180	$ 160
Net sales.........................	$12,350	$3,040	$2,850	$3,420	$3,040

SALES AND PRODUCTION

The sales budget is the foundation for the production budget. From an estimate of sales, it is possible to draw up plans for the manufacture of the products that will be needed. In making its plans, the manufacturing division will schedule production so that deliveries can be made to customers promptly. Therefore, the plans for production will have to be synchronized with the sales budget.

Also, the sales division will be limited in its planning by the capabilities and the capacity of the manufacturing division. It may be possible to sell a particular product, but perhaps it cannot be manfactured at a reasonable cost. The company will then have to abandon prospects for the sale of the product or find a way to cut the costs. When products are required to meet exacting standards and specifications, the sales division and the manufacturing division will have to join forces in working with the customers. The sales potential exists, but the company will not get the order if the manufacturing division cannot meet the stringent standards imposed. Sales estimates must also be tied in with manufacturing capacity. It is possible, of course, to sell more than the factory can normally produce by depleting inventories, by subletting the work, or by producing at overcapacity. At some point a limit will be reached, and the company will be forced to add its productive capacity if it expects to increase its sales volume.

Sales and production must be coordinated closely. Neither function can be planned in isolation. The sales division depends upon the plant for its products, and the manufacturing division will be guided by sales estimates.

INVENTORIES AND PRODUCTION

Assuming that a workable sales budget has been agreed upon, plans can be drawn up to produce the quantities of products specified. If the products are relatively perishable or if they cannot be stored, they will have to be manufactured at about the time that they are to be sold. On the other hand, if the products can be stored, the production schedule can be more flexible.

Given a choice, a company may choose to operate at a fairly uniform level throughout the year; or, conversely, it may prefer to manufacture products as they are needed. With variations in sales volume throughout the year, inventories will increase or decrease if production is held at a constant level. When production is tied in closely with sales, the inventories will not vary to any extent, but production will go up or down with sales. Each approach to the production problem has its cost advantages and disadvantages, and the decision will generally be made on a least cost basis.

When production is stabilized at a certain level, the manufacturing costs tend to be more uniformly distributed throughout the year. In all likelihood the manufacturing costs will also be lower. Plant facilities will not be overworked in some months only to remain idle at some later time. By employing workers steadily throughout the year, the company can retain good employees and avoid the cost and the nuisance of hiring and laying off temporary personnel. Probably the company will attract a better type of employee, who will be more satisfied with a steady job and, as a result, will be more productive.

However, other problems arise when production is stabilized. Inventories of finished product will be built up when sales volume is low and will be liquidated during the busy season. The variations in inventory will create a storage problem and will add to carrying costs. Funds may be invested in inventories when they could be used elsewhere to better advantage. The interest cost of this nonproductive investment must be taken into account. Furthermore, there is the risk that the inventories will deteriorate in storage, will become obsolete, or will not sell in the quantities anticipated. This general type of problem is also encountered in planning raw materials inventories.

Some compromise should be made. If sales volume is irregular, it will not be possible to schedule production evenly throughout the year and to maintain a constant level of inventory at the same time. A middle position can be reached at which costs and inconvenience will be at a minimum. The plant should be operated at a fairly even rate throughout the year without allowing the inventories to pile up beyond reason. Peaks and valleys in the operating cycle can be leveled out to some extent by selecting product lines that will sell heavily in different seasons.

If at all possible, a flexible position is usually taken. Moderate inventory reserves may be held so that unexpected increases in demand can be filled. In planning how plant facilities and other productive factors are to be used, some leeway should be allowed so that production can be increased or decreased within limits while using the existing labor and facilities. In order to have flexibility, the flow of work must be carefully planned by cost centers. A bottleneck in one department can hold up production for the entire plant, thereby creating rigidity.

THE PRODUCTION BUDGET ILLUSTRATED

The production budget stems from the sales budget, but, as explained in the preceding paragraphs, there is some degree of latitude. Inventories may be built up or liquidated, depending upon the policy adopted by management and the outlook for future sales. The sales budget, on a unit basis related to the desired inventory level, can be converted into a budget of units to be manufactured.

In the budget for the Donovan Company, given in the following table, sales and production for the year are equal, although there are variations within the year. If sales volume is expected to increase in the first quarter of the following year, some increase in inventory would be likely in the fourth quarter of the budget year. Production varies with sales volume for the most part with some differences in inventory. However, with seasonal products that complement each other, the plant may still be used rather evenly throughout the year.

Donovan Company
Production Budget—Units of Product
For the Year Ended December 31, 1985
(In thousands of units)

	Total	First Quarter	Second Quarter	Third Quarter	Fourth Quarter
Product 1:					
Units to be sold	300	100	60	60	80
Less inventory planned at beginning of quarter	40	40	20	20	40
Total	260	60	40	40	40
Add inventory planned at end of quarter .	50	20	20	40	50
Units to be produced	**310**	**80**	**60**	**80**	**90**
Product 2:					
Units to be sold	200	10	60	90	40
Less inventory planned at beginning of quarter	5	5	15	25	10
Total	195	5	45	65	30
Add inventory planned at end of quarter .	10	15	25	10	10
Units to be produced	**205**	**20**	**70**	**75**	**40**

Terminology Review

Budget (417)   Models (419)
Sales forecast (418)   Expected value (420)
Derived demand (419)

QUESTIONS FOR REVIEW

1. In most cases, what is the limiting factor in budget preparation?

2. What is derived demand?

3. What part does derived demand play in budgeting?

4. How can simulation studies be used in planning budgets?

5. When probabilities are estimated for various possible contribution margins, what is meant by the term, *expected value of the contribution margin*?

6. What steps can be taken to even out production throughout the year when a product line sells more heavily in one season than at other times in the year?

7. Explain how a budget of sales expressed in units of product is converted to a budget of net sales in dollars.

8. What limits are placed upon the sales division by the manufacturing division?

9. What are the advantages of stabilizing production throughout the year?

10. What are the disadvantages of stabilizing production throughout the year?

11. Explain how a production budget is prepared from a budget of sales.

EXERCISES

1. Budget Limits. Caldwell Parts Company has the capacity to manufacture 400,000 units of a certain product line each year. Each unit of product requires 2 pounds of a metal that is difficult to obtain. The sales department estimates that 300,000 units of product can be sold next year, and the purchasing department states that 40,000 pounds of the metal are on hand at the beginning of the year and that only 280,000 pounds can be purchased on the market next year.

Required:
(1) What is the limiting factor in budgeting next year?
(2) How many units of the product can be produced and sold next year?

2. Budget Limits. The Christopher Company can manufacture a maximum of 500,000 units of product a year. At the end of the current year, an inventory of 70,000 units of product is on hand. An arrangement has been made to obtain 150,000 units from another manufacturer if necessary. Sales for the next year have been budgeted at 850,000 units.

Required:
(1) What is the limiting factor in budgeting next year?
(2) How many units of product will be available for sale next year?

3. Expected Value of Profit. The vice-president of sales states that the company should be able to sell 250,000 units of product next year. The selling price, however, will depend upon the price established by overseas competitors. There is a 70% probability that the price will be $6 per unit and a 30% probability that the price will be at $5 per unit. The president of the company states that the variable cost per unit should be $3 in any case and that the fixed costs should be $280,000.

Required: Compute the expected value of income before income tax next year.

4. Expected Value of Profit. The supervisor of the economic forecasting department has estimated that there is a 60% probability that sales volume for next year will be 400,000 units of product if the selling price is established at $6 per unit. There is a 40% probability that sales will be 250,000 units if the selling price is established at $8 per unit. Variable cost per unit is estimated at $4 with a probability of 80% and at $5 a unit with a probability of 20%. Fixed costs for the next year have been estimated at $220,000.

Required: Compute the expected value of income before income tax next year.

5. A Sales Budget. Two product lines are manufactured and sold by Garner Company. It is estimated that 150,000 units of Product 1 will be sold next year and that 240,000 units of Product 2 will be sold. Product 1 will be sold at $8 per unit, and Product 2 will be sold at $10 per unit. Product 1 is expected to sell more heavily during the first half of the year with 80% of sales being in the first 6 months, evenly spread over the 2 quarters. During the third quarter, it is estimated that 20,000 units will be sold with the balance being sold in the last quarter. Sales for Product 2 will be evenly distributed over the year.

Required: Prepare a budget of sales in units and dollars by product line for each quarter of the year.

6. Net Sales Budget. Emsworth Machine Company has prepared a sales budget for next year for the major product line. The estimated units to be sold are as follows:

Quarters	Number of Units
1	10,000
2	15,000
3	25,000
4	10,000

The selling price for the first half of the year has been estimated at $500 per unit and will be increased to $700 a unit for the last half of the year.

Judging from past experience, 1% of sales will be deducted for allowances and returns. Also, it is likely that 2% of sales will prove to be uncollectible.

Required: Prepare a budget of gross and net sales revenue by quarters.

7. Net Sales Budget. Country Trails Inc. has estimated sales volume for the next year as follows:

Quarters	Products 1	2	3
1	30,000	60,000	70,000
2	25,000	50,000	90,000
3	15,000	40,000	120,000
4	15,000	20,000	140,000
Totals	85,000	170,000	420,000

Product 1 is expected to sell at $4 per unit, Product 2 at $6 per unit, and Product 3 at $2 per unit.

Sales returns and allowances are estimated at 3% of sales revenue, and uncollectible accounts are estimated at 2% of sales revenue.

Required: Prepare a budget of gross and net sales revenue by quarter and by product line.

8. Production Budget. Swiss Chalet Company manufactures a line of product that tends to sell better in the fall and winter months. Estimates of sales volume for each of the last six calendar months are as follows:

Months	Units
July	8,000
August	7,000
September	10,000
October	12,000
November	17,000
December	19,000

Production must be scheduled so that all units are available by the first of the month in which the sales occur. Units cannot be stored for more than a month. The company expects to sell 20,000 units in the following January.

Required. Prepare a schedule of units to be produced each of the last six months of the year. There was an inventory of 8,000 finished units on hand at July 1 ready for delivery to customers. No inventories beyond the sales requirements are to be held at the end of any month.

9. Production and Inventories. Ventura Company has irregular sales volume during the year, and management is planning to produce at a uniform rate with inventories increasing or decreasing throughout the year.

A sales budget in product units is given for the first six months of 1985.

Months	Units
January	30,000
February	25,000
March	45,000
April	15,000
May	40,000
June	25,000

The production cycle is short and units can be produced during the month of sale. An inventory of 10,000 units was on hand at January 1, and the same amount of inventory is planned at June 30.

Required: Prepare a production schedule that will be uniform, giving the expected inventories at the end of each month.

10. Production and Inventories. The production manager of Gillen Company plans to have an inventory on hand at the end of each month that will be equal to one half the sales of the next month. This requirement was met at the end of June.

A sales budget for the last six months of the year is as follows:

Months	Units
July	40,000
August	40,000
September	50,000
October	50,000
November	60,000
December	70,000

In January of the following year, it is estimated that 80,000 units will be sold.

Required: Prepare a production budget for the last six months of the year.

11. Sales Loss Estimates. A fire at Powell Appliances Inc. on August 12, 1984, not only damaged property but also caused a loss of potential sales by disrupting normal production. Fortunately, the company has insurance protection for profits lost as a result of the fire. An inventory of 4,200 completed units of product was stored in a separate location and was not damaged by the fire. In August only 19,000 units were manufactured. In September production was restored to 50% of normal capacity, and in October production was up to 70% of normal capacity. In subsequent months, the company was able to produce 60,000 units a month, its normal capacity. At the time of the fire, the company had orders for the sale and delivery of 50,000 units in August. New orders for 40,000 units were received in August for September delivery, and in September orders for 60,000 units were received for October delivery. Customers will not accept delivery after the scheduled month for delivery. Each unit of product sells for $25.

Required: You have been asked to furnish information to the insurance company showing the loss of sales in units and in dollars by not being able to fill customer orders. This is to be part of the loss claim filed with the insurance company.

12. Revised Production Budget. By the middle of September, the sales manager of Frank Supplies Inc. realized that the original forecast for the fourth quarter would have to be revised. The original forecast showed that 160,000 units would be sold in October, 220,000 units would be sold in November, 270,000 units would be sold in December, and 300,000 units would be sold in January.

It now appears that sales will be as follows:

	Units
October	150,000
November	200,000
December	230,000
January	250,000

Normally, 200 units of this product can be produced in one hour. An inventory equal to 20% of the estimated sales for the next month is to be on hand at the end of each month, and the company plans to have 30,000 units in the inventory on September 30.

Required:
(1) Prepare a revised production budget for each of the three months of the fourth quarter of the year.
(2) How many hours of production can be released each month for other work in this department by the expected reduction in sales? (Assume that the inventory is to be 30,000 units on September 30 in either case.)

15

A Master Budget Plan

This chapter should enable you to:
1. Explain how the individual budgets interlock.
2. Describe the process by which a production budget is broken down by the three cost elements and ultimately becomes a part of the cash payments budget.
3. Discuss how all of the expense budgets are brought together in the cash budgeting process.
4. Understand how planning the flow of cash receipts and disbursements is essential in financial planning for loans and their repayment.
5. Describe how budgets are brought together in the preparation of pro forma financial statements.
6. Explain how the budgeting process in itself helps management learn more about operations.

A realistic sales budget serves as a keystone for the master budget. All other budgets are related to the sales budget either directly or indirectly. The individual budgets and their relationship to one another are set forth in the following diagram:

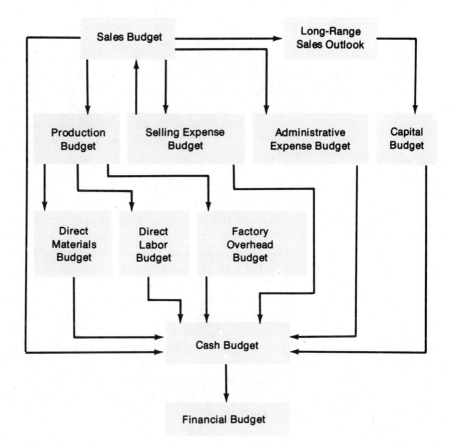

Since the activities and the budgets for all phases of the business operation are influenced by sales, plant production is geared to the expected demands of customers as set forth in a sales budget; and the cost of selling the product and administering the business is also planned in relation to sales activity. Selling expenses such as advertising, travel, and entertainment are not only dependent upon sales activity but also help to create it. There is a certain degree of interdependence. Capital expenditures, on the other hand, are only indirectly related to the sales of any one year. Ordinarily, long-range plans for asset acquisitions are not curtailed because of estimates of reduced sales in any given year. The plans, however, may be postponed or revised if there is little prospect for sales recovery over the long run.

The detailed budgets underlying the budgets of production, selling expenses, administrative expenses, and capital expenditures are prepared from the summary budgets to which they are related. Finally, the various budgets are drawn together in the cash budget. For example, a budget of materials to be used can be prepared only after a decision has been reached as to what types and quantities of products are to be made. The budget of products to be made is, of course, derived in turn from the sales budget. The materials consumption budget is then translated into a purchases budget by estimating materials inventory levels and relating them to budgeted consumption. The purchases budget is then converted to dollars. Plans are made to pay for the materials purchased, and these plans are a part of the cash budget for the year. Thus, the budgeting process that begins with sales is tied in eventually with the cash budget.

The cash receipts and disbursements from all sources are estimated according to time period, and these estimates constitute the cash budget. There will be times when cash receipts exceed disbursements, or times when disbursements exceed receipts. In a given month, for example, an insurance policy may come up for renewal or an extraordinarily large tax payment may fall due. During this month, cash outflows may exceed cash inflows.

Variations in the flow of cash during the year can be evened out by making use of short-term credit. A line of credit is drawn upon during the months in which cash outflows are heavy. Loans are then repaid with interest at a later date when the cash inflow exceeds the outflow. Planning short-term credit is a part of the financial budgeting operation.

The financial budget is based upon estimates of the cash flow, which in turn depend upon anticipated revenue and expected cost. Long-term debt is planned in the same manner, with projections being extended into the future. In the final analysis, this budget, like all the others, is based upon sales in the immediate or distant future.

THE MANUFACTURING COST BUDGET

The sales budget, as stated earlier, is the keystone for the master budget; and the production budget is the keystone for the manufacturing cost budget. After decisions have been reached as to what quantities of products are to be manufactured, the manufacturing cost can be estimated. Manufacturing cost is budgeted in the same way that it is accounted for, by cost element. The manufacturing cost budget is nothing more than the summary of the direct materials budget, the direct labor budget, and the factory overhead budget.

The Direct Materials Budget

The quantities of materials that are required for manufacturing the products are estimated, with the estimate being translated into a budget of purchases for the year. Purchases, like production, are planned in relation to the inventories. If materials can be stored, the purchasing department has a certain amount of leeway and is not forced to follow the fluctuations of the production cycle. Perhaps materials can be purchased in advance at a particularly favorable price, or savings may be obtained by purchasing in large quantity lots. The purchasing department, however, cannot be permitted to operate without restraint. Savings that are obtained by purchasing under favorable conditions can be more than offset by the cost of carrying excessive quantities in inventory. Ordinarily a company tries to seek a compromise position, one in which neither the cost of purchasing nor the cost of storing an inventory is excessive.

The materials inventories are balanced so that there is not an excess of one item and a lack of another. If inventory control is inadequate, quantities of one type of material may be built up beyond any reasonable need while some other material may be in short supply. The investment in aggregate inventory may be large, yet production may have to be curtailed because some essential part is not available.

Inventories should be planned so that they vary only within maximum and minimum limits. These limits are set for each item of material by estimating how much is needed during a procurement period. There is no point in carrying a supply that is greatly in excess of current need. Conversely, inventory balances can be trimmed to a point where there is a real risk that shipments will not be received in time for factory use.

Careful estimates must be made of how many units of different types of materials are needed to make the various products. If standards have been established, they can be used and adjusted as necessary in reaching a reasonable estimate of how much material will probably be used. The materials requirements are then translated into a budget of materials to be purchased by subtracting the estimated beginning inventory and by adding the desired ending inventory.

The Purchases Budget

The purchases budget is derived from the production budget. Unit costs are estimated and used in converting the purchases budget to a dollar basis. The budget expressed in dollar amounts aids the treasurer in the planning of future cash disbursements and also is a step in the collection of the manufacturing costs that eventually appear on the estimated income statement and balance sheet. The purchasing department is in the best position to furnish data with respect to estimated cost. It maintains contact with suppliers and knows what prices are offered by competing firms. Even so, the task of estimating future prices is difficult. To a certain extent, past records of materials consumption can be used in planning a materials requirement budget, but historical prices will not necessarily hold in the future. Published price schedules and announcements of effective dates for price changes help in immediate planning, but beyond this point estimates have to be based on a forecast of market conditions.

In addition to the cost of the materials, there are other costs that should be included as a part of the materials cost. Freight on incoming materials and the cost of purchasing, receiving, handling, and storing materials are a part of materials cost. Usually it is difficult to relate these costs to any specific item of material purchased; as a matter of expediency, they are often budgeted as a part of factory overhead.

The purchases budget for the Donovan Company, introduced in Chapter 14, is given in the following table in physical units and is then converted to dollars. Assume that two units of Material A and one unit of Material B are used for each unit of Product 1 and that one unit of Material A and one unit of Material B are used for each unit of Product 2. The cost of a unit of Material A has been estimated at $6, and the cost of a unit of Material B has been estimated at $3. Also assume that costs, such as freight, handling, and other costs related to materials, have been estimated and are included as a part of the materials cost.

The Donovan Company
Purchases Budget - Units
For the Year Ended December 31, 1985
(In thousands of units)

	Total	First Quarter	Second Quarter	Third Quarter	Fourth Quarter
Materials A:					
Production requirement:					
Product 1	620	160	120	160	180
Product 2	205	20	70	75	40
Total	825	180	190	235	220
Less estimated inventory, beginning of period	30	30	40	50	60
	795	150	150	185	160
Add desired inventory, end of period	50	40	50	60	50
Units to be purchased	845	190	200	245	210
Materials B:					
Production requirement:					
Product 1	310	80	60	80	90
Product 2	205	20	70	75	40
Total	515	100	130	155	130
Less estimated inventory, beginning of period	20	20	30	40	30
	495	80	100	115	100
Add desired inventory, end of period	30	30	40	30	30
Units to be purchased	525	110	140	145	130

The units of materials needed to meet the production requirement were determined by multiplying the product units to be made, as given in Chapter

14, by the units of materials required for each unit of product. The desired levels of inventory during the year have been assumed.

The Donovan Company
Purchases Budget - Dollars
For the Year Ended December 31, 1985
(In thousands of dollars)

	Total	First Quarter	Second Quarter	Third Quarter	Fourth Quarter
Materials A:					
Materials for production	$4,950	$1,080	$1,140	$1,410	$1,320
Less estimated inventory, beginning of period	180	180	240	300	360
	$4,770	$ 900	$ 900	$1,110	$ 960
Add desired inventory, end of period . . .	300	240	300	360	300
Estimated purchases cost	$5,070	$1,140	$1,200	$1,470	$1,260
Materials B:					
Materials for production	$1,545	$ 300	$ 390	$ 465	$ 390
Less estimated inventory, beginning of period	60	60	90	120	90
	$1,485	$ 240	$ 300	$ 345	$ 300
Add desired inventory, end of period . . .	90	90	120	90	90
Estimated purchases cost	$1,575	$ 330	$ 420	$ 435	$ 390
Total estimated purchases cost	$6,645	$1,470	$1,620	$1,905	$1,650

The Direct Labor Budget

The direct labor budget is estimated first on a physical quantity basis. Production quotas are translated into labor requirements. There is no inventory planning problem as such, but there are many other similar problems. Workers meeting the qualifications set by the production division are hired by the personnel department. The new employees may have to be trained, in which case they must be hired in advance of the time when they begin on the production line. Hiring plans should be coordinated closely with production plans. An ill-conceived employment policy can be costly. With improper timing, there is a risk that trained workers will not be available when needed or, conversely, that they will be ready before they can be utilized. If too many employees are hired or if anticipated increases in production are not permanent, some workers may have to be terminated. This represents the loss of an investment in training cost and may help to boost unemployment tax rates, not to mention the damage to reputation that a company suffers in the labor market by hiring and laying off workers repeatedly.

The labor time required to manufacture the products can be estimated from standards or from records of past performance. In either event, adjustments most likely have to be made. New production methods may bring about savings in labor time, thus making past records of performance obsolete. Some allowance also has to be made for idle time, setup time, and other expected variations from the standards in setting up a budget of total labor hours.

Labor hours are broken down by pay classifications, with estimated rates being applied in the calculation of a labor cost budget. Rates are often specified by jobs in labor contracts, with provisions being made for adjustment in pay under given circumstances. Estimates are more difficult to make if a contract change is anticipated during the year or if cost-of-living increases and other indefinite factors play a part in the determination of wage rates. Various fringe benefits, such as pensions, group insurance, and vacations, add to labor cost and may create uncertainties in budgeting. Labor cost is sometimes projected from average standard rates used in product costing, with the rates being adjusted as necessary.

A direct labor budget in hours has been assembled for the Donovan Company on the basis of 15 minutes of labor time required for each unit of either product line. Labor cost has been established at the rate of $8 per hour. The direct labor budget is as follows:

Donovan Company
Direct Labor Budget
For the Year Ended December 31, 1985
(In thousands of dollars)

	Total	First Quarter	Second Quarter	Third Quarter	Fourth Quarter
Units to be produced:					
Product 1	310	80	60	80	90
Product 2	205	20	70	75	40
Combined units....................	515	100	130	155	130
Labor hours (25% of units).............	128.75	25	32.5	38.75	32.5
Labor rate per hour	$ 8	$ 8	$ 8	$ 8	$ 8
Estimated labor cost	$1,030	$200	$260	$310	$260

The Factory Overhead Budget

Factory overhead cost deserves considerable attention. Individual cost classifications are examined closely to see how the cost reacts to changes in volume or in relation to other factors. Past records may show that a cost generally follows a certain pattern of increase or decrease in response to a change in some other cost or activity. One company may find that certain overhead costs are influenced by indirect labor hours, while another company bases estimates of overhead on direct labor hours or even on materials cost or machine hours.

For many companies, the best opportunity for cost savings lies in the factory overhead area. Direct materials cost and direct labor cost are often determined by factors that are beyond the control of management. For example, materials of a specified quality may be required and may be obtainable only at set prices, or labor contracts may prescribe what rates have to be paid for various types of work. Whenever possible, of course, management searches for ways to save materials, to substitute cheaper materials, or to reduce labor cost by improving methods of production. In addition, there probably will be opportunities to trim overhead cost. An apparently insignificant saving on a unit basis can be surprisingly large when the total effect is appraised. A small waste in the use of some lubricant, for example, is unimportant if only one machine is considered, but when this waste is multiplied by all machines in the plant, the loss may be substantial. By paying attention to details, management can control overhead cost and thereby increase profit.

The forecast budget of factory overhead, unlike the budget used to cost products or to control cost in the plant departments, is an estimate of the cost that can be expected during the next year. Products, however, are usually costed with overhead budget at the normal capacity level even if it is reasonably certain that the plant will not operate at that level in the coming year. Relatively tight budgets that can be used for controlling plant costs should be adhered to in practice if the company is to achieve its aims. Yet, if it appears that variances will develop in spite of all efforts, the variances should be included in a forecast budget so that all costs can be anticipated before they arise. A falsely optimistic budget can create difficulties in other areas of planning. For instance, the cash disbursements budget and the financial budget for the year are incorrect to the extent that cash requirements have been understated.

The forecast budget of factory overhead for the Donovan Company for the next year appears in the table on page 440. Factory overhead is applied to production at the rate of $4 per direct labor hour with normal capacity for the year defined at 130,000 direct labor hours.

The overhead cost anticipated for the year is distributed to each quarter on an accrual basis and is rounded to the nearest thousand dollars. At this point, no relationship between the costs and the cash disbursements has been established. For example, taxes and insurance cost of $20,000 is spread over the year with $5,000 being apportioned to each quarter. Payments for insurance protection may not follow this pattern. The entire cost may be prepaid at one time, or payments in varying amounts may be made throughout the life of the policies. The budget only reveals that the taxes and insurance expense for the year will probably amount to $20,000. There is no indication as to whether the cost is to be paid or whether it is a reasonable cost.

The Donovan Company
Factory Overhead Budget
For the Year Ended December 31, 1985
(In thousands of dollars)

	Total	First Quarter	Second Quarter	Third Quarter	Fourth Quarter
Variable:					
Supplies	$129	$ 25	$ 33	$ 39	$ 33
Heat and light	52	10	13	16	12
Repairs and maintenance	78	15	19	23	20
Total variable overhead	$259	$ 50	$ 65	$ 78	$ 65
Fixed:					
Supervision	$ 72	$ 18	$ 18	$ 18	$ 18
Indirect labor	88	22	22	22	22
Taxes and insurance	20	5	5	5	5
Heat and light	44	11	11	11	11
Repairs and maintenance	12	3	3	3	3
Depreciation	24	6	6	6	6
Total fixed overhead	$260	$ 65	$ 65	$ 65	$ 65
Total factory overhead	$519	$115	$130	$143	$130

THE SELLING EXPENSE BUDGET

The cost of promoting, selling, and distributing the products is budgeted by combining the costs into a selling expense budget. Although the selling cost is not included as a part of product cost, it is frequently broken down by product lines, sales regions, customers, salespersons, or some other significant unit basis. Analysis may reveal that it costs too much to sell a certain product or that the company would do better by concentrating on a particular customer group. Perhaps the cost of operating a retail unit is not justified by the return, in which case it may be better to close the unit or to seek more profitable sales outlets. Cost analysis can be applied in planning sales activity, revealing what it probably costs to sell different quantities and combinations of products. Furthermore, if cost is budgeted and accumulated on a unit of responsibility basis, it is possible to detect differences by sales region, salesperson, customer group, and so forth. Thus the selling cost, like the manufacturing cost, can be identified by area of responsibility and can be used as a means for control.

It is not as easy to budget selling expenses for the year as it might appear. Some of the expenses, of course, can be estimated with little or no difficulty. For example, the relatively fixed cost of operating a sales office, such as rent, sales salaries, heat and light, and depreciation of equipment, presents little or no problem. Similarly, sales commissions based upon a stipulated percentage of net sales can be calculated directly from a budget of net sales. Many of the selling expenses, however, bear no direct relationship to sales and may be arbitrarily determined by managerial policy.

Promotional expenses and shipping expenses, for example, are dependent upon sales, but they are also influenced by other factors. Promotional expenses such as advertising, travel, and entertainment not only are governed by sales but also help to determine sales. Shipping expenses vary according to the destination of the products and agreements reached with customers.

Budgets for sales promotion and advertising are often made on an appropriation basis, with the amount to be spent left to the general discretion of management. The amount to be spent depends upon the sales objectives, studies of past results, and estimates of how much must be spent to attain the objectives. Sometimes promotional expenses are budgeted at a certain percentage of sales, but this policy is not generally recommended. With a decline in sales, there would be a reduction in sales promotion. This could lead to further decreases in sales, aggravating a condition that is already unsatisfactory. Perhaps even greater expenditures for promotion can be justified when sales are declining.

Selling expenses for the Donovan Company are estimated and summarized in the budget given as follows:

Donovan Company
Selling Expense Budget
For the Year Ended December 31, 1982
(In thousands of dollars)

	Total	First Quarter	Second Quarter	Third Quarter	Fourth Quarter
Variable:					
Sales supplies	$ 250	$ 55	$ 60	$ 75	$ 60
Telephone	100	22	24	30	24
Shipping and delivery	150	33	36	45	36
Total variable expense	$ 500	$110	$120	$150	$120
Fixed:					
Sales salaries	$ 360	$ 90	$ 90	$ 90	$ 90
Advertising	336	84	84	84	84
Travel and entertainment	80	20	20	20	20
Sales office rent	64	16	16	16	16
Utilities	48	12	12	12	12
Depreciation	32	8	8	8	8
Total fixed expense	$ 920	$230	$230	$230	$230
Total selling expense	$1,420	$340	$350	$380	$350

THE GENERAL AND ADMINISTRATIVE EXPENSE BUDGET

The cost of administration and the cost of maintaining a corporate form of business are frequently combined into a general and administrative expense budget. While these fixed costs are less directly related to sales, they are nevertheless dependent upon sales volume in the long run. With minor variations in business activity, the cost of operating the administrative offices remains relatively fixed. However, during prolonged periods of inactivity, this cost is reduced. Office personnel are laid off, officers' salaries are cut, and various economy measures are instituted during a business slump. In relatively prosperous times, costs tend to creep upward and excesses may be overlooked. The result is that changes in administrative costs tend to lag behind changes in business conditions.

Administrative cost, like manufacturing and selling costs, is broken down for use in control. Budgets of costs chargeable to individual administrative supervisors provide controls against which actual costs can be compared. By following the general principles of cost accounting, it is possible to set standards of work performance for various activities and to establish cost standards. For example, the cost to process specific accounting data or the cost to assemble data for reports can be calculated by using techniques similar to those employed in job order manufacturing operations. The cost is either directly or indirectly identified with the activity, and the actual cost is then compared with a predetermined budget. If variations are unfavorable and material in amount, the necessary remedial steps should be taken.

A budget of estimated general and administrative expenses for the Donovan Company follows. This budget, along with the budget of manufacturing cost and the budget of selling expenses, is used in planning cash disbursements and in the preparation of an estimated income statement.

Donovan Company
General and Administrative Expense Budget
For the Year Ended December 31, 1985
(In thousands of dollars)

	Total	First Quarter	Second Quarter	Third Quarter	Fourth Quarter
Variable:					
Supplies used	$ 200	$ 44	$ 48	$ 60	$ 48
Heat and light	160	35	38	48	38
Telephone	40	9	10	12	10
Total variable expense	$ 400	$ 88	$ 96	$120	$ 96
Fixed:					
Officers' salaries	$ 472	$118	$118	$118	$118
Office salaries	240	60	60	60	60
Corporate taxes	60	15	15	15	15
Rent	60	15	15	15	15
Heat and light	16	4	4	4	4
Depreciation	12	3	3	3	3
Total fixed expense	$ 860	$215	$215	$215	$215
Total general and administrative expense	$1,260	$303	$311	$335	$311

THE CAPITAL BUDGET

A plan for the acquisition of various properties such as buildings, machinery, equipment, and other long-term investment is sometimes referred to as a capital budget or as a **capital expenditure budget**. For purposes of this discussion, assume that plans for the acquisition of capital assets have been approved by top management, and that these plans are ready to be interlocked with the budget plans for the year. Each year a provision must be made in the current annual budget for the portion of the plan to be carried out that year. Expenditures for minor additions and replacements are not planned far in advance nor do they require the approval of top management. Ordinarily, supervisors at the lower levels are granted appropriations that can be used in acquiring properties whose costs lie within prescribed limits.

Although properties that are used in operations for long periods of time are not acquired on the basis of current sales estimates, the prospects for immediate sales have some influence. If the outlook for sales is not promising, projects that have been planned for the current year may be postponed or cut back, or the original schedule may be followed so that the company is ready to capture opportunities when conditions are favorable. Replacements and minor additions are more likely to be influenced by the current sales picture.

During the coming year, the Donovan Company expects to acquire new equipment at a cost of $500,000. Part of the cost is to be refinanced by the issue of $400,000 in equipment notes.

The capital budget is as follows:

Donovan Company
Capital Budget
For the Year Ended December 31, 1985
(In thousands of dollars)

New machinery (to be acquired in December, 1985)	$500
Less cost to be financed by notes	400
Current cash expenditure	$100

THE CASH RECEIPTS BUDGET

Sales activity and redemption of investments are brought together in a cash receipts budget. Normally, sales activity is expected to produce the bulk of the cash receipts. If sales are made on a credit basis, accounts receivable are eventually translated into cash as customers pay their accounts. The time required to collect outstanding accounts has to be estimated, and provisions must be made for discounts, returns, allowances granted, and uncollectible accounts. From a study of past records and recent experience in the rate of collections, it should be possible to predict approximate receipts on account. The collection pattern for the Donovan Company is as follows:

70% of the net sales for the quarter is collected during that quarter.
20% of the net sales for the quarter is collected during the following quarter.
10% of the net sales for the quarter is collected during the second subsequent quarter.

Returns and allowances and uncollectible accounts cannot be determined exactly in the quarter in which the goods are sold. As stated in Chapter 14, though, the Donovan Company estimates that about 3 percent of gross sales for any quarter are returned or reduced by allowances granted, and 2 percent of gross sales will be uncollectible. Net sales for the third quarter of 1984 were $2,800,000 and are estimated to be $3,000,000 for the last quarter of 1984, the period in which the budget for 1985 is being completed.

A partial budget of cash receipts is prepared by applying the collection percentages to the appropriate net sales for each quarter. Additionally, accounts receivable balances are estimated as they will probably appear at the end of each quarter net of returns, allowances, and uncollectibles. The accounts receivable collection schedule for the Donovan Company is as follows:

Donovan Company
Schedule of Estimated Collections on Accounts Receivable
and Computation of Net Receivable Balances
For the Year Ended December 31, 1985
(In thousands of dollars)

	Total	First Quarter	Second Quarter	Third Quarter	Fourth Quarter
Net accounts receivable, beginning of quarter	$ 1,050	$1,050	$1,082	$1,029	$1,181
Net sales	12,350	3,040	2,850	3,420	3,040
Total	$13,400	$4,090	$3,932	$4,449	$4,221
Collections:					
70% of net sales for the quarter	$ 8,645	$2,128	$1,995	$2,394	$2,128
20% of the net sales of the preceding quarter	2,462	600	608	570	684
10% of the net sales of the second preceding quarter	1,169	280	300	304	285
Total collections and reduction of receivables	$12,276	$3,008	$2,903	$3,268	$3,097
Net accounts receivable, end of quarter	$ 1,124	$1,082	$1,029	$1,181	$1,124

During the last quarter of 1985, the Donovan Company plans to receive $80,000 from the redemption of marketable securities. Included in this amount is interest of $10,000. Bank loans are to be made as needed, but cash receipts from this source are planned after both receipts and disbursements have been budgeted. The total cash receipts budget is as follows:

Donovan Company
Summary of Cash Receipts
For the Year Ended December 31, 1985
(In thousands of dollars)

	Total	First Quarter	Second Quarter	Third Quarter	Fourth Quarter
Collections on accounts receivable	$12,276	$3,008	$2,903	$3,268	$3,097
Redemption of marketable securities.....	70	—	—	—	70
Interest received	10	—	—	—	10
Total cash receipts	$12,356	$3,008	$2,903	$3,268	$3,177

THE CASH PAYMENTS BUDGET

The various cost budgets for capital acquisitions, commitments for the discharge of debt, and plans for dividend payments are brought together in a cash payments budget. If at all possible, payments are scheduled at convenient times, that is, when cash balances are expected to be sufficiently high. Frequently the demand for cash is not spread evenly throughout the year. Several large payments may become due in one particular month, in which case the company must either plan to retain cash for these payments or to borrow if cash receipts in that month are not expected to be sufficient.

Disbursements are not always made at the same time that cost is incurred or materials and services are used. Advertising, insurance, and rent, for example, are often paid in advance with the cost being absorbed against future operations. Payments for materials, labor, supplies, and other costs of operation frequently follow acquisition and use. A budget of cash disbursements is made by scheduling payments that must be made for materials, labor, other operating costs, dividends, debt service, and so forth.

Freedom in planning is restricted somewhat by customary practice and by commitments that have already been made. Ordinarily, employees have to be paid at periodic intervals, and rents usually are paid on a monthly or on an annual basis. Some payments, however, may be prepaid or deferred as desired. If discounts are allowed on certain purchases, however, payments should be made within the discount period.

The cash payment schedule for the Donovan Company is given on page 446.

The schedule indicates that disbursements are relatively large during the last two quarters of the year. Anticipating this situation, management has built up the cash position early in the year. At a later date, if necessary, the company could obtain one large bank loan under more favorable terms than it could get with a series of small loans. Also, the debt will not be outstanding for a longer period than necessary.

Donovan Company
Schedule of Cash Payments
For the Year Ended December 31, 1985
(In thousands of dollars)

	Total	First Quarter	Second Quarter	Third Quarter	Fourth Quarter
Materials purchases	$ 6,740	$1,360	$1,580	$2,100	$1,700
Direct labor	1,030	200	260	310	260
Factory overhead	485	100	115	146	124
Selling expense	1,389	330	340	375	344
General and administrative expense . . .	1,246	295	305	336	310
Plant asset acquisition	100	—	—	—	100
Income tax payments	732	168	188	156	220
Dividends	480	120	120	120	120
Total payments scheduled	$12,202	$2,573	$2,908	$3,543	$3,178

FINANCIAL PLANNING

Budgeted cash receipts and disbursements are brought together to form a summary cash budget. From this summary of estimated cash flows, it is possible to anticipate future cash balances. In some months, receipts may not be large enough to cover disbursements, in which case the cash balance is reduced. If the outflow of cash is too great, plans have to be made to borrow funds. In other months when receipts are greater than disbursements, loans can be repaid, investments can be made in marketable securities, and cash balances can be built up.

Financial plans are made so that a minimum balance of cash is available at all times. The amount to be held depends upon estimated future cash flows and the financial policy adopted. In general, the cash balance should be large enough to enable the company to meet its payrolls and to pay its operating cost for the next month with some allowance being made for contingencies and miscalculations in planning. By holding adequate cash balances, management is able to cope with small adversities and is not forced to borrow under unfavorable conditions. While cash reserves are being used, management can make alternate plans and can secure additional cash from other sources to meet future needs.

Opinions differ as to what amount of cash should be held. Some companies maintain fairly substantial cash balances and have a secondary reserve consisting of marketable securities that can easily be converted into cash. Many other companies, however, prefer to operate with smaller cash reserves, relying upon bank credit when cash is needed. Often a line of credit is established at a bank. Cash up to a certain limit can be borrowed when needed, with arrangement made for repayment.

The management of the Donovan Company believes that it can compete more successfully and can obtain larger orders with the increased volume of output expected from the new machinery. With a larger volume of business the company needs more cash. Anticipating the need for a larger cash balance, management plans to increase the balance by at least $200,000 by the end of the year. Based upon budget projections, no short-term bank loans should be needed in 1985.

Compare the following summary cash budget given with the estimated income statement on page 449. Note that the net income for each quarter does not correspond with the increase or decrease in the cash balance, because the accrual concept used for measuring net income ignores the timing of the cash receipts and disbursements.

The Donovan Company
Summary Cash Budget
For the Year Ended December 31, 1985
(In thousands of dollars)

	Total	First Quarter	Second Quarter	Third Quarter	Fourth Quarter
Cash balance, beginning	$ 216	$ 216	$ 651	$ 646	$ 371
Budgeted receipts	12,356	3,008	2,903	3,268	3,177
	$12,572	$3,224	$3,554	$3,914	$3,548
Budgeted disbursements	12,202	2,573	2,908	3,543	3,178
Cash balance, ending	$ 370	$ 651	$ 646	$ 371	$ 370

A plan showing how cash flows in and out of the business is dependent upon the other budgets and is in itself important enough to justify much of the effort expended in budget preparation. Preliminary estimates may reveal that disbursements are lumped together and that, with more careful planning, payments can be spread out more evenly throughout the year. As a result, less bank credit is needed and interest cost is lower. Banks and other credit-granting institutions are more inclined to grant loans with favorable terms if the loan request is supported by a methodical cash plan which provides reasonable assurance that the loans can be repaid on schedule.

THE ESTIMATED INCOME STATEMENT

An estimated income statement can be prepared from the budget data for the year. The estimated or **pro forma** income statement is a summary of the expected results and shows whether or not profit plans as reflected in the budgets can be realized. It brings together the various revenue and expense budgets, making it easier to evaluate the overall operation. Management can compare its actual income statement with the estimated statement both during the year and at the end of the year. If budgeted profit is to be realized, adjustments may have to be made as operations progress. Perhaps the budget itself requires revision. At the end of the year, a comparison of actual results with the budget may indicate areas of operation that deserve more attention in the future; or a comparison may reveal ways to prepare more realistic budgets.

In practice, an estimated income statement is broken down by quarters and by months. In addition, it is subdivided according to product lines, sales regions, and customer groupings. From an analysis of the statements, management can determine which products, regions, or customers groups are likely to be the most profitable. Plans for the year may be revised if it appears that better alternatives are available, and actual operations may be conducted so that profits are maximized.

The estimated income statement for the Donovan Company has been prepared from the revenue and cost budgets. The products were costed at standard costs by the absorption costing method. The standard costs per unit of product are given as follows:

	Product Lines	
	1	2
Direct materials:		
Material A:		
2 units @ $6	$12	
1 unit @ $6		$ 6
Material B: 1 unit @ $3	3	3
Standard materials cost	$15	$ 9
Direct labor: ¼ hour @ $8	2	2
Factory overhead: ¼ hour @ $4	1	1
Total standard cost per product cost	$18	$12

The total fixed factory overhead is budgeted at $260,000 for the year. The direct labor hours at normal capacity are budgeted at 130,000. Hence, the fixed factory overhead rate is $2 per hour. If four units of product are to be produced each hour, the fixed overhead rate per product unit is $.50. In this illustration, the variable overhead is also $.50 per unit of product. The total factory overhead per unit of product is then $1.

An estimated income statement for the Donovan Company is given on page 449.

The company plans to operate close to the standard cost during the year and anticipates no significant variances aside from the capacity or volume variance. The 130,000 normal hours for the year amount to 32,500 each quarter. In the first quarter, the company plans to operate at 25,000 direct labor hours, or 7,500 hours below normal. In the third quarter, plans have been made to operate at 38,750 direct labor hours, or 6,250 hours over normal capacity. In the other two quarters, the company should operate at normal capacity. The capacity variance for the first quarter is unfavorable by $15,000 (7,500 hours × $2 per hour) and is favorable by $12,000 in the third quarter (6,250 hours × $2 per hour, rounded to $12,000).

The Donovan Company
Estimated Income Statement
For the Year Ended December 31, 1985
(In thousands of dollars)

	Total	First Quarter	Second Quarter	Third Quarter	Fourth Quarter
Net sales..........................	$12,350	$3,040	$2,850	$3,420	$3,040
Cost of goods sold:					
Beginning inventory	$ 780	$ 780	$ 540	$ 660	$ 840
Current production	8,040	1,680	1,920	2,340	2,100
Total.........................	$ 8,820	$2,460	$2,460	$3,000	$2,940
Less ending inventory	1,020	540	660	840	1,020
Cost of goods sold at standard.......	$ 7,800	$1,920	$1,800	$2,160	$1,920
Capacity variance	3	15	—	(12)	—
Total cost of goods sold	$ 7,803	$1,935	$1,800	$2,148	$1,920
Gross margin	$ 4,547	$1,105	$1,050	$1,272	$1,120
Selling expense	$ 1,420	$ 340	$ 350	$ 380	$ 350
General and administrative expense ...	1,260	303	311	335	311
Total operating expenses.........	$ 2,680	$ 643	$ 661	$ 715	$ 661
Operating income	$ 1,867	$ 462	$ 389	$ 557	$ 459
Interest earned	$ 10	—	—	—	$ 10
Income before income tax............	$ 1,877	$ 462	$ 389	$ 557	$ 469
Income tax	747	188	156	220	183
Net income.......................	$ 1,130	$ 274	$ 233	$ 337	$ 286

The selling expenses and the administrative expenses shown on the budgeted income statement are taken directly from the expense budgets. The income tax is estimated at approximately 40 percent of the income before income tax.

THE ESTIMATED BALANCE SHEET

The estimated or **pro forma** balance sheet indicates budgeted financial position for some later date. Like the estimated income statement, it is a summary budget statement that depends upon the various individual budgets which have been prepared. It can be compared with historical statements to show how the assets and the equities are affected by operations during the budget year. Balance sheets from past years may reveal unfavorable trends. Perhaps debt has been increasing beyond a safe limit. These trends should have been recognized in the preparation of the budget for the year, and any remedial action taken should be reflected in the estimated balance sheet for the end of the budget year.

The estimated balance sheet also serves as a point of reference during the year. Interim statements prepared at various dates can be compared with corresponding budget statements. It may be possible to detect some unfavorable variation that should be corrected during the year, or the budget itself may require revision.

A comparison of the budget statements with the actual statements can be utilized in the preparation of future budgets. Knowledge gained by experience can be applied in making better estimates and in controlling operations more effectively so that they tend to conform to the budget.

The differences noted in a comparison between budget and actual statements reveal that the company cannot earn the profit it hopes to or have the financial position it wants without paying close attention to the budget throughout the year. These statements clearly indicate that the desired profit and financial position can be achieved only by making careful plans that are implemented by all members of the organization.

The estimated balance sheet for the Donovan Company is given as follows:

Donovan Company
Estimated Balance Sheets
(To the nearest thousand dollars)

	January 1, 1985	March 31, 1985	June 30, 1985	September 30, 1985	December 31, 1985
Assets					
Current assets:					
Cash	$ 216	$ 651	$ 646	$ 371	$ 370
Marketable securities	100	100	100	100	30
Accounts receivable, net	1,050	1,082	1,029	1,181	1,124
Inventories:					
Finished goods	780	540	660	840	1,020
Materials	240	330	420	450	390
Total current assets	$2,386	$2,703	$2,855	$2,942	$2,934
Plant and equipment, net of accumulated depreciation	1,530	1,513	1,496	1,479	1,962
Total assets	$3,916	$4,216	$4,351	$4,421	$4,896
Equities					
Current liabilities:					
Accounts payable	$1,280	$1,406	$1,460	$1,249	$1,195
Estimated income tax payable	168	188	156	220	183
Total current liabilities	$1,448	$1,594	$1,616	$1,469	$1,378
Notes payable, equipment	–	–	–	–	400
Total liabilities	$1,448	$1,594	$1,616	$1,469	$1,778
Stockholders' equity:					
Capital stock, $1 par value	1,500	1,500	1,500	1,500	1,500
Retained earnings	968	1,122	1,235	1,452	1,618
Total equities	$3,916	$4,216	$4,351	$4,421	$4,896

WORK SHEET

Financial statements for the budget year can be prepared directly from the budgets, but it may be easier to gather all of the data on a budget work sheet before attempting to prepare the statements. The following work sheet summarizes the transactions for the budget year for the Donovan Company. By following the same general methods of summarization, interim statements can be prepared for a six-month period or for a calendar quarter.

The transactions for the year are taken from the budgets indicated as follows and are shown on the work sheet opposite the numbers given in parentheses:

1. Accounts Receivable 12,350
    Sales 12,350
        Composite entry for net sales.
2. Materials.. 150
    Finished Goods 240
    Cost of Goods Sold 7,803
        Accounts Payable... 8,169
        Accumulated Depreciation 24
        Composite entry for cost of goods sold. Combine direct materials used direct labor, and factory overhead for charge to cost of goods sold. Debit inventory accounts for planned inventory increases.
3. Selling Expense 1,420
    General and Administrative Expense 1,260
        Accounts Payable... 2,636
        Accumulated Depreciation 44
        Composite entry for selling and administrative expenses.
4. Cash 12,356
        Accounts Receivable 12,276
        Marketable Securities 70
        Interest Earned 10
        Composite entry from cash receipts and summary cash budget.
5. Accounts Payable... 10,890
    Plant and Equipment 100
    Estimated Income Tax Payable 732
    Retained Earnings 480
        Cash 12,202
        Composite entry from cash payments budget. Combine purchases and cost and expense items for charge to accounts payable. Direct charge to retained earnings for dividends.
6. Plant and Equipment 400
        Notes Payable, Equipment 400
        Portion of machinery financed, taken from capital budget.
7. Income Tax 747
        Estimated Income Tax Payable 747
        Computed from income statement data.
8. Net Income 1,130
        Retained Earnings 1,130
        Closing computed net income to Retained Earnings.

Donovan Company
Budget Work Sheet
For the Year Ended December 31, 1985
(In thousands of dollars)

Accounts	Balance Sheet January 1, 1985		Budgeted Transactions		Estimated Results December 31, 1985	
	Dr.	Cr.	Dr.	Cr.	Dr.	Cr.
Cash	216		(4) 12,356	(5) 12,202	370	
Marketable securities	100			(4) 70	30	
Accounts receivable, net	1,050		(1) 12,350	(4) 12,276	1,124	
Inventories:						
Finished goods	780		(2) 240		1,020	
Materials	240		(2) 150		390	
Plant and equipment, net	1,530		(5) 100	(2) 24	1,962	
			(6) 400	(3) 44		
Accounts payable		1,280	(5) 10,890	(2) 8,169		1,195
				(3) 2,636		
Estimated income tax payable		168	(5) 732	(7) 747		183
Notes payable, equpment				(6) 400		400
Capital stock		1,500				1,500
Retained earnings		968	(5) 480	(8) 1,130		1,618
Sales				(1) 12,350		
Cost of goods sold			(2) 7,803			
Selling expense			(3) 1,420			
General and administrative expense ...			(3) 1,260			
Interest earned				(4) 10		
Income tax			(7) 747			
Net income			(8) 1,130			
	3,916	3,916	50,058	50,058	4,896	4,896

THE USE OF BUDGETS

It may appear from the illustrations given that budgets can be drawn up quite accurately and brought together into financial statements. Unfortunately, this is not always so. The mechanical process of bringing the data together on work sheets can be carried out exactly, but all of the data used has been taken from estimates that may or may not prove to be correct. Thus, the budget summaries and the statements are only as good as the estimates upon which they rest.

By preparing a budget, management learns more about its operations and with experience can improve the accuracy of its estimates. Management learns how cost varies with the volume of sales and production and observes how certain peculiarities in some aspect of the operation influence cost. With continued practice, it is possible to avoid errors and to arrive at budget estimates.

Budgets are used as a guide in conducting operations, and when actual operations are compared with the budget, discrepancies reveal the need for further attention in the areas where material discrepancies occur. Usually reports are prepared showing actual data in one column and budget data in an adjoining column. Differences are then computed and shown in still another column. Often the variations are also expressed as percentages. If variations are material, they are traced to determine underlying causes. Attention to only those items that exhibit significant variation from budgeted amounts is known as management by exception.

Sometimes outside factors beyond the control of the company are responsible for budget variations, in which case the budget may have to be revised. Conversely, it may be found that the budget is in error due to poor estimation under existing circumstances, or it may be that budgeted operations were not properly implemented.

Terminology Review

Manufacturing cost budget   (434)

Direct labor budget   (437)

Selling expense budget   (440)

General and administrative expense
   budget   (441)

Capital budget   (443)

Cash receipts budget   (443)

Cash payments budget   (445)

Summary cash budget   (446)

Estimated income statement   (447)

Estimated balance sheet   (449)

Budget work sheet   (451)

Management by exception   (453)

QUESTIONS FOR REVIEW

1. What is the usual limiting factor in the preparation of a budget for a commercial or industrial firm?

2. What limiting factor may be imposed on a not-for-profit entity in budget preparation?

3. Why is the sales budget considered to be the keystone for the total budget?

4. What steps can be taken to even out the effect of differences in the flow of cash over the year?

5. Is it possible to have an excessive inventory investment while running the risk of inventory shortages? Explain.

6. Name three major budgets that are combined to form the manufacturing cost budget.

7. How is a direct materials budget translated into a purchase budget?

8. In labor planning, what problems are similar to inventory planning for materials?

9. What are labor fringe benefits?

10. Why are relatively small cost savings on a unit basis important?

11. Is the factory overhead budget equivalent to a budget of cash disbursements for factory overhead? Explain.

12. Which of the costs normally included in a factory overhead budget would require no cash disbursement?

13. Why may selling cost be broken down by product lines, sales regions, customers, salespeople, and so forth?

14. Why is it a poor policy to budget promotional expenses at a certain percentage of sales?

15. General and administrative expenses are usually considered to be fixed in amount and to be influenced very little by changes in sales activity. Explain.

16. What is a capital budget?

17. How are long-range plans for the acquisition of plant assets included in current budgets?

18. Explain why cash receipts from customers may not fall in the same fiscal period as sales revenue.

19. What budgets are combined in planning a cash disbursements budget?

20. What are the advantages and disadvantages in holding large cash reserves?

21. How is a cash budget used in planning short-term bank loans?

22. What type of costing method is used when fixed factory overhead is included as a part of product cost?

23. Why would profit tend to be higher under absorption costing when inventories are being increased?

24. How can management benefit from the experience gained in the preparation of a budget?

EXERCISES

1. Production Cost Budget. A budget of the number of product units to be manufactured next year was prepared by Crane Metals Company and is given as follows:

First quarter	48,000
Second quarter...........................	56,000
Third quarter	64,000
Fourth quarter...........................	60,000

The direct materials cost per unit is estimated at $6. Direct labor cost is budgeted at $4 per unit, and factory overhead is to be applied at 50% of direct labor cost; 80% of the production for the quarter is to be sold in the quarter, and 20% of the production is to be sold in the following quarter. An inventory of 9,600 units on hand at the beginning of the budget year is to be sold in the first quarter.

Required:

(1) Prepare a production cost budget for each quarter and for the year.

(2) Compute estimated cost of goods sold for each quarter and for the year.

2. Materials Cost. Kessler Products Inc. plans to produce the following quantities of product in each of the months given.

	Units
October	15,000
November	25,000
December	30,000
January	35,000

Materials are to be purchased in the month before they are needed in production. This requirement was met on October 1. Three units of Material A, each unit of material costing $3, is required for a unit of product. Two units of Material B, each unit of material costing $5, is required for a unit of product.

Required:

(1) How many units of each material should be purchased in October, November, and December?

(2) Prepare a purchases cost budget for October, November, and December.

3. Purchases and Cash Payments. A production budget by fiscal quarter for Galveston Company is given as follows:

	Units
First quarter	24,000
Second quarter	30,000
Third quarter	32,000
Fourth quarter	42,000

Four units of materials are used in producing each unit of product. Each unit costs $.60. The materials inventory is to be equal to 25% of production requirements for the next quarter. This requirement was met at the beginning of the year. Production for the first quarter following the budget year is estimated at 28,000 units.

Accounts payable for materials purchased are estimated at $38,400 at the beginning of the current budget year. It is estimated that accounts payable at the end of the quarter for materials purchased will be equal to 40% of the purchases during the quarter.

Required:

(1) Determine the number of units of materials to be purchased each quarter.

(2) Determine the cost of materials to be purchased by quarters.

(3) Estimate the payments to be made each quarter for materials.

4. Direct Materials Cost and Purchases. The Dodson Company prepared a production budget for the first quarter of 1985 as follows:

	Units
January	18,000
February	16,000
March	20,000

Two units of Material 03 are required for each unit of product. Each unit of material costs $1.50. One unit of Material 08 is required for each unit of product. Each unit of material costs $5.

All materials must be purchased in the month preceding production. Half of the materials cost is paid during the month of purchase and the other half is paid in the following month. Production for April is estimated at 24,000 units. Accounts payable at the beginning of January for materials purchases is estimated at $64,000.

Required:

(1) Determine the number of units to be purchased each month.

(2) Determine the cost of purchases by months.

(3) Determine the cost of direct materials in production cost each month.

(4) Prepare a budget of cash payments for materials by month.

5. Supplies and Labor Cost. The Chee Health Clinic serves as an outpatient clinic for the citizens in the Brant City area. Medicines, drugs, and various medical supplies must be obtained, and cost estimates must be made for each month. In addition to physicians who are available on a contract basis at a cost of $50,000 a month, there are nurses on a salary basis at $40,000 a month. Other employees are engaged on a part-time basis at a cost of $8 per hour. Past experience shows that one part-time person is required for each 50 patients served in a month. The typical part-time employee works 100 hours in a month.

The cost of medicines and various supplies varies at the rate of $5 per patient served, and there is a fixed cost of $15,000 for medicines and supplies each month.

An estimate was made of patients to be served in the last quarter of the year:

	Number of Patients
October	800
November	1,200
December	1,800

Required:

(1) Estimate the cost of the medicines and other supplies for each month.

(2) Prepare a budget of the cost of the medicines and supplies, contract services, and part-time labor cost for each month.

(3) According to the estimates, how many part-time persons will be needed each month?

6. Labor Cost Budget. Budget plans of Mayford Supply Company are being revised for the last two quarters of 1985. Two product lines are manufactured. Under the revised plan, production in units of product is estimated as follows:

	Product Lines	
	_1_	_2_
Third quarter	12,000	15,000
Fourth quarter	16,000	18,000

The labor rate per hour is to be $9 during the third quarter and $10 during the fourth quarter. Standards indicate that 15 minutes are required to produce each unit of Product 1 and that 20 minutes are required to produce each unit of Product 2.

In preparation of the budget, provision is to be made for the fringe benefit costs such as pensions and medical health insurance. The total fringe benefit cost is to be estimated at 20% of the total labor cost.

Required:

(1) Prepare a budget of direct labor cost for each product line for each quarter.

(2) Prepare a budget of fringe benefit cost in total for each quarter.

7. Labor Cost Budget. Adilaz Cartons Inc. manufactures two basic lines of product—Sturdee and Rain-Proof. Past experience has shown that 6 units of Sturdee can be produced each labor hour and that 5 units of Rain-Proof can be produced each labor hour. Direct labor is paid at the rate of $9 per hour, and each employee works approximately 300 hours each fiscal quarter of a year. Production has been estimated for 1985 as follows:

	Units	
	Sturdee	*Rain-Proof*
First quarter	12,600	12,000
Second quarter	16,200	9,000
Third quarter	14,400	15,000
Fourth quarter	14,400	18,000

Required:

(1) Compute the total direct labor hours needed each quarter to meet the production requirements.

(2) Compute the direct labor cost budget each quarter.

(3) How many employees will be needed each quarter?

8. Factory Overhead Budget. The Trail Blazer Company is planning a factory overhead cost budget for the next year. Fixed overhead for each quarter of the year is budgeted at $68,000. Overhead that varies with the number of units produced is estimated to vary at the rate of $4 per unit. Overhead that varies with direct labor hours is estimated to vary at the rate of $2 per labor hour.

Production for the next year is estimated as follows:

	Units of Product
First quarter	30,000
Second quarter..........................	44,000
Third quarter	42,000
Fourth quarter..........................	38,000

Standards indicate that 1½ hours are required to manufacture each unit of a product line.

Required: Prepare a budget of factory overhead for each quarter of the next year.

9. Factory Overhead Budget. An overhead cost budget for the next year is being prepared by Hannibal Supply Company. Past studies indicate that costs have followed behavior patterns as shown in the following table:

	Variable Cost per Direct Labor Hour
Indirect materials and supplies.................	$ .77
Heat, light, and power	1.50
Repairs and maintenance......................	5.00
Lubrication	.65

In addition, management estimated fixed factory overhead costs as follows:

Supervision......................................	$ 86,000
Indirect labor	72,000
Heat, light, and power	21,000
Repairs and maintenance.........................	23,000
Taxes and insurance.............................	17,000
Depreciation	29,000
Total......................................	$248,000

A fixed overhead rate of $3.10 per direct labor hour has been established for costing the fixed overhead to the products.

During the next year, the company plans to manufacture 280,000 units of product. Products are manufactured at the rate of 4 units per hour.

Required:

(1) Prepare a factory overhead budget showing variable and fixed costs separately.

(2) Compute the variable and fixed overhead to be applied to each unit of product.

(3) Determine the capacity variance, if any.

10. Cash Collections—Receivables. Past experience has demonstrated that 60% of the net sales billed in a month by Cantor Company are collected during the month, 30% are collected in the following month, and 10% are collected in the second following month.

A record of estimated net sales by month is given in the following table.

1984	November	$450,000
	December	460,000
1985	January	480,000
	February	420,000
	March	500,000
	April	550,000
	May	600,000
	June	700,000

On January 1, 1985, the net accounts receivable balance is planned at $183,000.

Required: Prepare a schedule of expected collections on accounts receivable for each of the first six months of 1985 and show the estimated balance of net accounts receivable at the end of each month.

11. Cash Budget. The Olson Company has planned a cash budget for the first six months of 1985. Estimates show that $60,000 should be collected in March and June for dividends received on investments in the stock of other companies. Each month, fixed operating expenses for wages, rent, heat, and light, etc., must be paid in the amount of $220,000.

Collections on accounts receivable are estimated as follows:

50% collected in month of sale
30% collected in month following sale
20% collected in second month following sale

Payments for merchandise purchased are scheduled so that 60% of the payments are made in the month of purchase with the balance paid in the following month. The cash balance is estimated at $175,000 for January 1, 1985.

Estimated net sales and purchases by month are estimated as follows:

		Net Sales	Purchases
1984	November	$560,000	$320,000
	December	550,000	380,000
1985	January	640,000	420,000
	February	700,000	400,000
	March	650,000	350,000
	April	580,000	280,000
	May	460,000	260,000
	June	520,000	260,000

An income tax payment of $100,000 is to be made in February, and a payment of $150,000 is to be made in June. A loan repayment of $80,000 will be made in February with interest added at $12,000.

Required: Prepare a budget of cash receipts and payments for each month. If a minimum cash balance of $150,000 will be available at the end of each month, identify the months, if any, when short-term loans will be required and the amounts of the loans. Also, indicate months, if any, when short-term loans can be repaid.

12. Cash Budget. Judy Cochran is preparing a budget of cash receipts and disbursements for Food Services Inc. Some of the sales are cash sales, and some of the sales are on a contract basis and are billed.

Sales and collection data for April to August, 1985, are as follows:

	Cash Sales	Billed Sales	Total
April	$65,000	$40,000	$105,000
May	72,000	46,000	118,000
June	84,000	68,000	152,000
July	88,000	72,000	160,000
August	86,000	70,000	156,000

Half of the billed sales are collected during the month of sale, and the other half are collected in the following month.

Food costs amounting to 70% of sales must be paid during the month. Operating costs of $24,000 must be paid each month. Food costs will increase to 80% of sales in June. The cash balance at May 1 amounted to $8,000. If the cash balance is over $20,000 on August 31, Judy and the other stockholders will receive the excess as dividends.

Required:

(1) Prepare a budget of cash receipts and disbursements for each month, May to August, inclusive.

(2) Compute the amount, if any, that can be paid in dividends at the end of August.

13. Estimated Income Statement. The management of Ramsey Parts Inc. prepared a budget for each quarter of 1985. Data taken from the budgets are as follows:

	Net Sales	Cost of Production	Finished Goods First of Month
First quarter	$850,000	$600,000	$35,000
Second quarter	900,000	650,000	40,000
Third quarter	960,000	685,000	50,000
Fourth quarter	880,000	620,000	40,000
First quarter, 1986	—	—	30,000

Payments for selling and administrative expenses are made at about the time the items are expensed. The payments are as follows:

First quarter	$128,000
Second quarter	142,000
Third quarter	146,000
Fourth quarter	142,000
Total	$558,000

Depreciation on fixtures used for selling and administration amounts to $16,000 each quarter.

Required: Prepare an estimated income statement showing income before income tax for each quarter and for the year.

14. Estimated Income Statement. Buckhorn Appliances Inc. prepared a budget for 1985 by quarters. Data from the budget appear as follows:

	Materials Purchased	Materials Inventory, First of Month
First quarter	$280,000	$60,000
Second quarter	360,000	75,000
Third quarter	400,000	50,000
Fourth quarter	300,000	40,000
First quarter, 1986	—	40,000

Direct labor is budgeted at $140,000 each quarter with factory overhead estimated at 60% of direct labor cost. Selling and administrative expenses are budgeted at $115,000 each quarter. Net sales are budgeted by quarters as follows:

First quarter	$660,000
Second quarter........................	740,000
Third quarter..........................	800,000
Fourth quarter........................	760,000

The amount of finished goods is estimated to be $120,000 at the beginning of the year. It is expected to increase to $150,000 by the end of the first quarter and will remain at that level until the end of the year when it will be reduced to $120,000.

Required: Prepare an estimated income statement for each quarter and for the year. Income tax is estimated at 40% of income before income tax.

15. Estimated Balance Sheet. You have been asked to prepare an estimated balance sheet at June 30, 1985, for Hormel Stores Inc. A balance sheet at December 31, 1984, as follows:

Assets

Cash	$ 82,000
Accounts receivable.....................................	112,000
Inventory	136,000
Building and fixtures, net...............................	358,000
Total assets	$688,000

Equities

Accounts payable.......................................	$ 62,000
Capital stock	300,000
Retained earnings.......................................	326,000
Total equities....................................	$688,000

Cash receipts for the year are collections on accounts receivable amounting to $846,000. Cash payments are budgeted at $838,000. Included in those payments are payments of $126,000 for various expenses that do not flow through accounts payable. Credits to accounts payable for the year, estimated at $715,000, all result from merchandise purchased. Cash payments are all for expenses or purchases. Depreciation expense is estimated at $75,000. Net sales are estimated at $930,000. The inventory of merchandise is expected to increase to $147,000 by the end of the year.

Required:

(1) From the information given, prepare an estimated balance sheet at December 31, 1985.

(2) Prove the retained earnings balance by computing the net income. Income tax is estimated at 40% of income before income tax.

PROBLEMS

15-1. Purchases Budget. In the production of a line of product, Wiggins Supply Company uses 4 units of Material R and 2 units of Material S. All materials are purchased in the month before they are to be used in production. The production cycle takes about a month, and all units of product are sold in the month following production.

The cost per unit of materials is estimated as follows:

Material R — $3
Material S — $5

A production schedule for June 1985 to January 1986, inclusive, is as follows:

1985	Units of Product
June	42,000
July	45,000
August	48,000
September	47,000
October	50,000
November	55,000
December	60,000
1986	
January	65,000

Required:

    (1) Prepare a budget for each of the last six months of 1985 in units of each material to be purchased.

    (2) Convert the budget or purchases in units to a total purchases dollar budget.

    (3) Compute the cost of materials in cost of goods sold for October, November, and December.

15-2. Purchases Budget. The Seeloff Processing Company has prepared production estimates for the two product lines that it manufactures as shown in the following table:

	Units of Product	
	Product 1	Product 2
1985		
June	2,000	3,500
July	2,600	3,200
August	4,200	2,400
September	5,800	2,200
October	6,000	2,000
November	3,200	3,500
December	2,500	4,600
1986		
January	2,000	5,000

The purchasing department buys materials in the month before they are to be used in production. Materials requirements per unit of product and prices are as follows:

Materials Code	Product Line	Requirements per Unit of Product	Materials Unit Price
225	1	3	$5
420	2	4	3

The purchasing department has located a new supplier for Material 225 who can furnish the material in the desired quality and quantity at a cost of $4 per unit. The present contract for delivery expires on September 30, 1985, and a contract with the new supplier will be made for deliveries after that date.

Required:

    (1) Prepare a purchases budget in units of materials and in dollars for each month from July to December, inclusive.

    (2) Compute the total cost saving in the cost of materials purchased that can be expected by dealing with the new supplier.

15-3. Sales Budget from Incomplete Data. You have been working on the budget for 1985 for WLT Company. The president of the company plans to leave for a tour of overseas plants within two hours, and you have been asked to have a sales budget in units of product prepared for the main plant at Atlanta so that this can be made available to the overseas producers. (The information can be typed with copies made after the president arrives at the overseas plants.)

You have certain data on your desk but nothing about units to be sold. Available information reveals that 5 units of direct materials are required for each unit of product manufactured. An inventory of 150,000 units of materials is to be on hand at the beginning of the year. This inventory level is to be maintained until the end of the third quarter, when it will be increased to 200,000 units.

Materials can be used in production during the quarter acquired.

Purchases for the year have been planned as follows:

	Units of Materials
First quarter	1,200,000
Second quarter	1,500,000
Third quarter	2,000,000
Fourth quarter	2,500,000

Each unit of materials purchased costs $2.

The inventory of finished goods is 25,000 units at the beginning of the year. At the end of the second quarter, it is to be 30,000 units; at the end of the third quarter, it is to be 40,000 units; and at the end of the year it is to be 50,000 units.

Required:

(1) Prepare a budget of sales by quarters in units of product.

(2) Prepare a budget of sales in dollars assuming a selling price per unit of product of $60.

(3) You have made up the requested sales budget well ahead of schedule, and you now decide to convert the purchases budget in units to dollars and to determine the cost of materials in cost of goods sold.

15-4. Direct Labor Cost Budget. Sonora Hacienda Inc. manufactures three basic implements: a machete, a shovel, and an electric trimmer. There are 15 qualified employees at the present time, and new employees will be engaged as production increases. Each employee works approximately 150 hours a month and is paid at the rate of $9.60 per hour.

Production budgets in units of product are given as follows:

	Product Lines		
	Machetes	Shovels	Trimmers
1985			
March	6,000	3,000	1,000
April	9,000	3,000	1,000
May	12,000	6,000	2,000
June	15,000	7,500	2,000
July	12,000	6,000	3,000
August	9,000	3,000	1,000

The direct labor time required for one person to produce each unit of product has been estimated as follows:

Machete	10 minutes
Shovel	20 minutes
Trimmer	30 minutes

Required:

(1) Prepare a budget of direct labor hours for each month and convert it into a budget of direct labor cost.

(2) How many employees will be needed for production each month?

15-5. Payments for Materials. Duren Mills Inc. is hard-pressed for cash to meet scheduled payments for materials and other costs.

A month is required for production, and materials are purchased as production progresses. All production is sold during the following month.

In the production operation, there is a natural loss of materials so that the final output is equal to only 80% of the input.

Sales by month have been budgeted as follows:

	Units
June	200,000
July	240,000
August	320,000
September	280,000
October	300,000

Each unit is sold for $6. Half of the amount billed is collected during the month sold with the other half being collected during the next month.

The materials used in production cost $.60 a unit, and 4 units of materials are in each completed unit of product.

Costs of operation, other than materials cost, amount to $500,000 each month and must be paid during the month.

Purchases are paid for during the month following purchases.

Required:

(1) Determine the cost of purchases for July, August, and September.

(2) Compute the expected cash inflow from customers and subtract estimated disbursements for July, August, and September.

(3) Can the company meet the demands for cash each month?

15-6. Budgeted Savings—Materials and Labor. James Vogler is concerned about losses of materials in production and is especially concerned because of anticipated increases in the prices of materials.

Data with respect to materials for one of the major product lines are given as follows:

	Quantity in Final Product Unit	Materials Price Per Pound
Materials A	24 pounds	$.12
Materials B	12 pounds	.08
Materials C	12 pounds	.08

The product yield is 75% of the input for all three materials.

During the next fiscal quarter, the company plans to produce and sell 1,800,000 units of this product at a price of $12 per unit.

The labor rate is $9.60 an hour, and 12 units of product are to be made each hour. Overhead varies at $1.20 per unit of product. The fixed overhead is budgeted at $3,000,000 for the fiscal quarter. The company costs only the variable costs to the product.

Vogler believes that the yield from materials should be increased to 80% of input for all materials. Also, with some changes in production methods, 15 units of product should be made each hour. No other changes are anticipated.

Required:

(1) Prepare a budgeted income statement for the manufacturing operation under present conditions without savings in materials or labor time.

(2) Prepare a budgeted income statement for the manufacturing operation with the planned savings in materials and labor time.

(3) How much will the combined materials and labor saving contribute to manufacturing profits?

15-7. Product Cost Budget. The Arno Metals Company plans to manufacture 600,000 units of its basic product line next year. Direct materials that cost $8 per unit of product will be used to produce 400,000 product units. Materials prices are expected to increase during the year, and it is estimated that 200,000 units will be produced at a unit materials cost of $10.

Direct labor cost for part of the year will be at a rate of $12 an hour, and 5 units are to be produced each hour. The cost per hour will likely increase to $15 an hour after 300,000 units of product are made with no change expected in productivity per hour.

The factory overhead is fixed and is budgeted at $1,200,000 for the year. The company plans to operate at a normal capacity of 120,000 direct labor hours next year.

Required:

(1) Compute the estimated cost of production next year by cost element.

(2) Determine the average estimated cost per unit of product next year.

15-8. Product Cost Budget. The management of Dalton Glass Products Inc. has become aware of increased competition in the industry and has taken steps to increase cost control. Product costs for last year are given as follows on a unit-of-product basis.

	Product Lines		
	1	*2*	*3*
Direct materials	$ 6.00	$3.00	$ 5.00
Direct labor	3.00	2.00	3.00
Applied factory overhead	3.00	2.00	3.00
Total unit cost.....................................	$12.00	$7.00	$11.00

The direct materials are manufactured by another division of the company and next year can be delivered to the fabricating division at a lower cost. As a result, the direct materials cost per unit of product will be 10% lower.

Direct labor cost will remain at $12 an hour, but increases in productivity are planned. Fixed overhead cost will be increased by $30,000 a year, but the revision of the production process will make it possible to manufacture 6 units of Product 1 in one hour and 10 units of Product 3 in one hour. Product 2 will not be affected.

Last year the company operated at a normal capacity of 200,000 direct labor hours with budgeted and actual factory overhead cost of $2,400,000. Next year, normal capacity is to be redefined at 124,000 direct labor hours with factory overhead (including the fixed overhead increase of $30,000) amounting to $1,860,000.

Last year the company manufactured the following quantities of products:

Product Lines	Number of Units
1	300,000
2	240,000
3	340,000

The same quantities are to be manufactured next year.

Required:

(1) Determine the cost of production next year in total and on a unit-of-product basis.

(2) Compute the expected cost saving in total compared with last year.

15-9. Expenses and Cash Disbursements. Sharon Ruhf, the treasurer of Cummings Ancient Studies Association, is planning an expense budget for 1985. Rent for the office is expected to amount to $6,000 for the year and will be paid in lump sum during December of 1985.

Insurance costing $840 for the year is to be prepaid in January for the entire year.

Salaries for the employees have been budgeted at $72,000 for the year and will be paid at about the time that the services are rendered. Salaries are evenly distributed throughout the year.

An outside service has been engaged to obtain speakers and to schedule outside archaeological digs during the year. The entire cost for the year, estimated at $36,000, must be paid during September. It is estimated that the services will be distributed throughout the year as follows:

First quarter	$ 3,000
Second quarter	12,000
Third quarter	15,000
Fourth quarter	6,000

Telephone and postage have been budgeted at $600 each quarter with payment being made during the quarter.

Travel expenses of $6,000 for the year will be paid during the second quarter with the cost being equally divided between the second and third quarters of the year.

Depreciation on office furniture and various implements has been estimated at $600 for the year.

Supplies costing $300 are to be used each quarter with payment for the entire year being budgeted for February.

Required:

(1) Prepare an expense budget for Sharon Ruhf for 1985 by quarters.

(2) Convert the expense budget into a cash payments budget for 1985 by quarters.

15-10. Cash Receipts and Sales. Alfred Beamer, a member of the board of directors of Handee Markets Inc., is concerned about the ability of the company to repay a loan in the amount of $250,000 that matures on June 30, 1985. In addition to the principal of the loan, the company must pay interest of $50,000.

The cash balance at January 1, 1985, is $82,000. Sales for December 1984 to June 30, 1985, have been budgeted as follows:

		Net Sales
1984 December	....	$236,000
1985 January	....	137,000
February	....	142,000
March	....	182,000
April	....	170,000
May	....	156,000
June	....	148,000

Cash sales each month are equal to approximately 30% of net sales. Collections on accounts receivable are expected as follows:

60% collected during the month of sale
40% collected in the following month

Total cash disbursements are estimated at $115,000 each month.

Required:

(1) Prepare a cash budget for each month and for the first six months of 1985 in total.
(2) Will the company be able to pay the loan with interest of June 30 and still maintain a cash balance of no less than $60,000 on June 30?

15-11. Cash Budget and Revisions. Andrea Cortellini, as a consultant to Hartman and Moss Inc., has advised management that collections on accounts receivable will likely be slower than in the past. If at all possible the company should try to reduce operating costs.

A budget of revenue for each month from November 1984, to June 1985, is as follows:

		Revenue
1984 November	....	$450,000
December	....	430,000
1985 January	....	420,000
February	....	400,000
March	....	350,000
April	....	330,000
May	....	280,000
June	....	250,000

During the first 3 months of 1985, collections on account are expected as follows:

70% collected in the month of billing
20% collected in the following month
10% collected in the second following month

Beginning with April billings, the collection pattern may be as follows:

50% collected in the month of billing
20% collected in the following month
10% collected in the second following month

The remaining percentage owed may not be collectible.

Various costs of operation that must be paid are estimated at $300,000 per month. In addition, the company has had a tradition of paying dividends of $80,000 in March and $80,000 in June.

The cash balance on January 1, 1985, was $93,000.

Required:

(1) Prepare a cash budget for each month from January to June, inclusive.

(2) Do you believe that Cortellini's concern is justified? Explain.

15-12. Cash and Short-Term Loans. Every year Beaver Lake Inc. has operated at about the same level but sales vary substantially by season. As a result, the company needs short-term credit that is to be paid when the cash position improves.

Sales revenue for December 1984, and for each of the first six months of 1985 has been budgeted as follows:

	Revenue
1984 December	$540,000
1985 January	620,000
February	580,000
March	360,000
April	270,000
May	130,000
June	120,000

Sixty percent of the revenue is to be collected in the month billed with 40% collected in the following month.

Cash payments have been budgeted at a steady rate of $400,000 per month.

The cash balance at January 1, 1985, is $120,000 and is to be maintained at approximately that level throughout the year. Cash in excess of that amount is to be invested in U.S. Treasury Bills, and loans are to be made as necessary.

Required: Prepare a cash budget for the first six months of 1985, indicating how much excess cash is invested and how much cash must be borrowed. For purposes of the problem, ignore interest earned and interest expense.

15-13. Estimated Financial Statements. Alabama Fasteners Inc. has budgeted operations for each quarter of 1985. Budget data are given as follows:

	Net Sales	Production Cost	Operating Expenses
First quarter	$750,000	$480,000	$145,000
Second quarter	800,000	500,000	160,000
Third quarter	850,000	520,000	170,000
Fourth quarter	900,000	500,000	175,000
1986, first quarter	800,000	520,000	170,000

Finished goods inventory has been planned as follows:

January 1, 1985.........................	$120,000
April 1, 1985	135,000
July 1, 1985	130,000
October 1, 1985	140,000
December 31, 1985	125,000

Included in production cost each quarter is $120,000 in depreciation, and depreciation of $30,000 is included in each quarter in operating expenses.

All production cost and operating expenses with the exception of depreciation are to be paid during the quarter.

Collections on sales are planned at 60% during the quarter of sale and 40% during the quarter following sale. The balance of collections on net sales for the fourth quarter of 1984 has been estimated at $280,000 to be included in total receipts for the first quarter of 1985.

Materials are purchased as needed in production and are not held in inventory.

Income tax is estimated at 40% of income before income tax and is paid during the subsequent quarter.

Dividends of $100,000 are to be paid in June and again in December if covered by sufficient profits. No dividends will be paid if the profits for the year are less than $300,000.

A summary balance sheet at December 31, 1984, is given as follows:

Alabama Fasteners Inc.
Balance Sheet
December 31, 1984

Assets

Cash..	$ 115,000
Accounts receivable	280,000
Inventory...	120,000
Plant and equipment net of accumulated depreciation	1,450,000
Total assets	$1,965,000

Equities

Estimated income tax payable	$ 55,000
Capital stock	1,500,000
Retained earnings	410,000
Total equities	$1,965,000

Required:

(1) Prepare an estimated income statement for each quarter and for the year.

(2) Prepare a balance sheet at the end of each quarter of 1985.

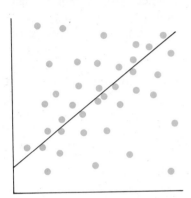

16

THE PRICE-LEVEL PROBLEM

Chapter Objectives

This chapter will enable you to:

1. Explain how changes in the level of prices can cause financial and accounting problems.
2. Explain how the lifo inventory method and accelerated depreciation methods can result in matching more current costs against revenue.
3. Distinguish between monetary and nonmonetary items.
4. Determine purchasing power gains or losses from holding net monetary items.
5. Distinguish between the concepts of constant dollar and current costs.
6. Explain how measurements in mixed dollars can distort financial statement relationships.
7. Describe how amounts equal to price-adjusted depreciation must be reinvested in order to maintain the company's investment.
8. Discuss how dividends in some situations may in reality be a distribution of invested capital.
9. Distinguish between real potential holding gains and increases that are necessary to maintain purchasing power.

Monetary units such as the dollar, the franc, and the pound are standards of measurement in finance and accounting; they measure a given amount of purchasing power at any particular time. However, this purchasing power does not remain constant over the years. In contrast, the physical units of measurement, such as the meter, kilometer, and kilogram, do remain constant as standards of measurement. This peculiarity of monetary units makes it difficult to evaluate financial data. In the physical sciences it would be similar to having a meter that measured one distance in 1979 and a different distance in 1984. When historical financial data are combined with current financial data, the result is a measurement in monetary units of mixed value.

Because of the relatively rapid increases in prices during the late 1970s, the price-level problem has received increasing attention. Several approaches have been recommended for reporting financial data when there are changes in the purchasing power of the dollar. Four of the most commonly recommended methods are:

1. Use selected accounting methods which have the effect of matching more recently incurred costs against revenue in income determination.
2. Restate historical financial data in constant dollars of purchasing power by using an index series designed to measure changes in the general price level.
3. Express financial data in terms of current costs (or current values) that pertain to the specific assets and liabilities held by the company. This approach may involve the use of specific, rather than general, price indexes related to the company's operations.
4. Combine the concepts of constant dollar restatement with current value or current cost measurements.

Constant dollars are dollars of uniform purchasing power as measured by an index series developed for the general economy. A generally recognized series such as the Consumer Price Index has often been selected to produce constant dollar measurements. The Gross National Product Implicit Price Deflator is another index that has been used by the Department of Commerce to measure changes in the gross national product. This index may be favored by some because it is more comprehensive.

It is extremely difficult, if possible at all, to measure the effect of price changes on each individual or business entity. Each person or entity purchases different goods or services in various quantities at various times and will be affected in different ways. The constant dollar approach measures the impact of price changes by means of an average of prices for goods and services that are most commonly used.

Current costs are the prices that an entity would currently pay to replace or reproduce assets sold or used during the year or on hand at the end of the year. Current costs are often favored over constant dollars because the amounts are specific to the company rather than to the population at large.

THE CHARACTER OF ASSETS AND EQUITIES

When prices go up in general, there is inflation. Conversely, when prices go down, there is deflation. However, all goods and services are not affected in the same way. The prices of some goods and services may be relatively stable while the prices of others will change substantially.

During a period of inflation, the holder of cash or assets expressed in a specific quantity of dollars loses purchasing power. For example, a person may have earned and saved $6,000 at a time when a medium-sized automobile could be purchased for that amount. At a later date, the $6,000 will not even be enough to purchase a subcompact automobile. There has been a loss of purchasing power.

A borrower, on the other hand, may gain by inflation. A loan of $5,000 may have been taken when the price level was lower. When the loan is repaid at a higher price level, the $5,000 may be equivalent to $2,500 in purchasing power when the loan was made. Hence, the borrower gained purchasing power.

Not all assets and equities respond to changes in the price level in the same way. Some assets tend to adjust themselves, increasing or decreasing in price in rough correspondence with the general price level. Tangible assets such as inventories and plant assets generally go up and down in price. Cash and claims to cash remain at stated fixed amounts without regard to shifts in the price level.

Monetary Items

Cash and claims to cash, as well as liabilities stated in a fixed number of dollars, are called monetary items. The monetary items at any given time are always stated in purchasing power at that time without adjustment.

An individual who has $100 in cash today, regardless of when received, has $100 in purchasing power today. If the $100 was received when prices were at an index of 100 and today the index is at 120, $20 in purchasing power is lost by holding the $100, but the purchasing power is $100.

Dollars needed today to equal purchasing power when index was 100

$$\$100 \times \frac{120}{100} = \$120$$

Actual dollars held	100
Loss in purchasing power	$ 20

Conversely, a debt of $100 incurred at an index of 100 would result in a gain in purchasing power if the index increased to 120.

Dollars in debt today to equal purchasing power borrowed when index was 100

$$\$100 \times \frac{120}{100} = \$120$$

Actual debt	100
Gain in purchasing power	$ 20

Nonmonetary Items

Assets and equities that cannot be stated in fixed monetary amounts are referred to as nonmonetary items. Tangible items, such as buildings, machinery, and inventories of materials or products awaiting resale, tend to sell at higher or lower dollar amounts at different times.

A residence, for example, may have cost $30,000 when the price index was at 100. At a later date, when the price index is at 150, the fair market value of the house is $65,000. On a constant dollar basis, the house would be restated at $45,000.

$$\$30,000 \times \frac{150}{100} = \$45,000$$

A further restatement at current value would show the house at $65,000. The difference between the current value of the house ($65,000) and the constant dollar amount to keep up with the price level ($45,000) is the holding gain. If the house were sold, there would be a real gain of $20,000. The increment from $30,000 to $45,000, or $15,000, is necessary to keep up with general price-level changes and is not a gain at all.

Investments in stocks or bonds may have the characteristics of fixed monetary claims, or they may be similar to tangible properties. Bonds usually are a claim to a fixed quantity of dollars and would, therefore, be similar to cash. An investment in common stock, however, is not a stated claim to any given quantity of dollars, but it is an ownership claim to the assets of a business and would be somewhat similar to an investment in tangible property.

The stockholders' equity, with the exception of preferred stock that may be callable in a fixed number of dollars, is a nonmonetary item. The common stock and the retained earnings are not fixed in dollar amounts but will vary as a result of many factors, including price-level changes.

MORE RECENT COSTS MATCHED AGAINST REVENUES

This approach to the price-level problem does not deal with the problem directly. Instead, it is an attempt to get around the problem. The objective is to minimize the effect of price-level changes by matching the most recent costs against revenues. The argument for this procedure is that net income is more accurately determined if both the revenues and costs are on the same dollar basis. Furthermore, there can be no objection that the historical cost principle has been violated. Actual incurred costs are accounted for. However, with recent costs reported on the income statement, the older costs will remain on the balance sheet and distort the already mixed dollar relationship even more.

Lifo Inventory

The matching of the most current cost against revenue is implicit in the lifo inventory method. With lifo, the cost of the most recent purchases is matched against revenue as cost of goods sold, and the older cost remains on the balance sheet as inventory. In some circumstances, the lifo inventory method may not result in matching current cost against revenue. If the quantity sold, for example, is in excess of the current quantity purchased, the older cost will be mixed with current cost in the cost of goods sold.

The fifo inventory method operates in the opposite way and matches older cost against current revenue and thus may be less desirable from the income statement point of view when prices are rising. On the other hand, the current cost is shown as inventory on the balance sheet.

The general effect of the two inventory methods is illustrated in the following table. Assume that an inventory of 10,000 units costing $3 each was on hand at the beginning of the year, that 10,000 units each costing $5 were purchased during the year, and that 10,000 units were sold for $8 each.

	Fifo	Lifo
Income statement:		
Sales	$80,000	$80,000
Cost of goods sold:		
Older cost (beginning inventory—10,000 × $3)	30,000	
More recent cost (purchase—10,000 × $5)		50,000
Gross margin	$50,000	$30,000
Balance sheet:		
Inventory end of year:		
More recent cost	$50,000	
Older cost		$30,000

The lifo method, by matching more recent cost against revenue, results in better income measurement but in doing so leaves the older costs on the balance sheet.

Accelerated Depreciation

Accelerated depreciation methods are usually favored because of the income tax advantage, but they may also be favored as a means of matching current costs against revenues. If a large part of the cost of a plant asset can be written off as depreciation during a few years, it is hoped that the bulk of the cost can be matched against revenue before the price level has changed to any appreciable extent. Whether or not this will work in practice depends upon how rapidly the price level changes.

The income tax advantage from accelerated depreciation arises because depreciation deductions in the early years of the life of a plant asset are larger than they are under the straight-line method. During these years, the net income and the income tax for each year are lower than they would be under the straight-line method of depreciation. With a lower income tax, the company is able to use more resources for a longer period because the tax payment is delayed. In later years, the depreciation deductions are smaller, and the net income and the income taxes will be larger under accelerated depreciation. In the meantime, the company has additional resources available that can be reinvested to earn a return. Perhaps, losses because of a change in the price level can be avoided or at least held to a minimum.

The advantage of accelerated depreciation is illustrated by assuming that Company A and Company B each earned $500,000 before deducting depreciation and income tax. Company A used accelerated depreciation and deducted $200,000 in depreciation on equipment that it had purchased at the beginning of the year. Company B purchased equipment having the same cost at the same time but took depreciation of $100,000 on a straight-line basis.

	Company A Accelerated Depreciation	Company B Straight-Line Depreciation
Income before depreciation and income tax	$500,000	$500,000
Less depreciation	200,000	100,000
Income before income tax................................	$300,000	$400,000
Income tax, 40%	120,000	160,000
Net income..	$180,000	$240,000
Add depreciation	200,000	100,000
Net inflow of current resources from operations	$380,000	$340,000

Depreciation, unlike many operating expenses such as wages or heat and light, does not reduce current resources. Depreciation expense is deducted on the income statement with a corresponding credit to accumulated depreciation to reduce the plant asset. Current assets and current liabilities are not affected.

Note that Company A paid $40,000 less in income tax than Company B as a result of deducting $100,000 more in depreciation. The depreciation deduction operated as a tax shield. Company A, with a smaller income tax, has additional resources of $40,000 to employ as it wishes. Furthermore, by deducting relatively large amounts of depreciation in the early years, Company A may be able to recover most of the cost of the plant asset before the price level changes appreciably.

ILLUSTRATION—HISTORICAL COST/CONSTANT DOLLAR STATEMENTS

The following financial statements for Fife Company are given in historical dollars. The balance sheet at December 31, 19X0 is in uniform dollars of purchasing power at a price index of 100, and the costs of inventory and plant assets are current. The company uses the lifo inventory method, and the plant and equipment were acquired at the end of 19X0. Straight-line depreciation is to be deducted over four years with no provision for a residual salvage value.

Fife Company
Balance Sheet
December 31, 19X1 and 19X0
Historical Dollars
(In thousands of dollars)

	19X1	19X0
Monetary assets:		
Cash and accounts receivable	$400	$280
Nonmonetary assets:		
Inventory	60	60
Plant and equipment, net of depreciation	225	300
Total assets	$685	$640
Monetary equities:		
Accounts and notes payable	$200	$200
Nonmonetary equities:		
Stockholders' equity	485	440
Total equities	$685	$640

Fife Company
Income Statement
For the Year Ended December 31, 19X1
Historical Dollars
(In thousands of dollars)

Sales	$500
Cost of goods sold...	$300
Operating expenses, excluding depreciation	50
Depreciation	75
	$425
Income before income tax...	$ 75
Income tax, 40%	30
Net income..	$ 45

The price index was at an average of 110 during 19X1 and was at 110 on December 31, 19X1.

The objective is to convert the statements for 19X1 to constant dollars of purchasing power.

First, the net monetary balance at the beginning of the year was computed by subtracting the accounts and notes payable of $200,000 from the cash and accounts receivable of $280,000 given on the balance sheet at the end of 19X0.

Second, the transactions for the year that affect net monetary items were added or subtracted to obtain the net monetary items at the end of the year.

Note that purchases are included inasmuch as they affect accounts payable, a monetary item. Cost of goods sold is not included, because costs of goods sold reduces inventory, a nonmonetary item. In this example, the inventory did not increase or decrease in 19X1. Under the lifo method, the purchases for the year for 19X1 were equal to cost of goods sold.

Third, the purchasing power gain or loss from holding net monetary items is computed. The conversion is made by using a multiplier. The numerator is the current index, in this case 110. The denominator is the index at the time the asset or equity was acquired.

$$\text{Multiplier} = \frac{\text{Current index}}{\text{Index at acquisition date}}$$

In the illustration, it has been assumed that both sales and purchases were made during the year at two different price levels. One level was at the price index of 100, the other was at the price index of 110. All of the operating expenses were at the price index of 100, and the income tax was at the index of 110.

The computation of the purchasing power loss for 19X1 is given as follows:

Purchasing Power Gains or Losses
Net Monetary Items
For the Year Ended December 31, 19X1
(In thousands of dollars)

	Unadjusted	Multiplier	Adjusted
Net monetary balance, beginning of year	$ 80	110/100	$ 88
Add sales	300	110/100	300
	200	110/110	200
	$ 580		$618
Less: Purchases	$ 200	110/100	$220
	100	110/110	100
Operating expenses	50	110/100	55
Income tax	30	110/110	30
	$ 380		$405
Net monetary balance, end of 19X1	$ 200		$213
Purchasing power loss	13		
	$ 213		$213

In order to avoid a purchasing power loss in 19X1, the company should have had $213,000 in net monetary items at the end of 19X1. Instead, net monetary items were only $200,000. There was a purchasing power loss of $13,000.

The income statement for 19X1 is converted to constant dollars at an index of 110.

Fife Company
Income Statement
For the Year Ended December 31, 19X1
Constant Dollars—19X1
(In thousands of dollars)

	Unadjusted	Multiplier	Adjusted
	$300	110/100	$330
Sales	200	110/110	200
	$500		$530
	$200	110/100	$220
Cost of goods sold.............................	100	110/110	100
Operating expenses, excluding depreciation	50	110/100	55
Depreciation	75	110/100	82
Income before income tax.......................	$425		$457
Income before income tax.......................	$ 75		$ 73
Income tax, 40%	30		30
Net income......................................	$ 45		$ 43
Purchasing power loss............................			(13)
Net income and purchasing power loss.............			$ 30

Note that the income tax is not at 40 percent of the price-adjusted income but is based on the legally determined income on a historical cost basis of $75,000. With inflation, income tax may, in some cases, be partially a tax on capital or at least at a higher rate than stated when constant dollars are considered.

The balance sheet at December 31, 19X1, is converted to constant dollars at an index of 110.

Fife Company
Balance Sheet
December 31, 19X1
Constant Dollars—19X1
(In thousands of dollars)

	Unadjusted	Multiplier	Adjusted
Monetary assets:			
Cash and accounts receivable	$400	—	$400
Nonmonetary assets:			
Inventory.....................................	60	110/100	66
Plant and equipment, net	225	110/100	248
Total assets	$685		$714
Monetary equities:			
Accounts and notes payable	$200	—	$200
Nonmonetary equities:			
Stockholders' equity.........................		(see	
	485	computation)	514
Total equities	$685		$714

The adjusted stockholders' equity was computed as follows:

Balance, beginning of 19X1 ($440,000 × 110/100)	$484,000
Add net income at 110 index	43,000
	$527,000
Less purchasing power loss on net monetary items	13,000
Adjusted balance, end of 19X1	$514,000

The monetary assets and equities on the balance sheet were not adjusted for the change in the index. Monetary items are automatically expressed in current purchasing power. The purchasing power loss from holding net monetary items has already been computed.

The price-index-adjusted statements reveal that the net income as computed in constant dollars was not so large as the net income computed in mixed dollars of purchasing power. The statements also reveal the purchasing power loss by holding net monetary items.

In an industry that requires a relatively large investment in plant and equipment, a company may find that depreciation charges, even on an accelerated basis, will not be sufficient to recover the price-adjusted cost of the plant and equipment. The temptation is to borrow heavily and to rely on purchasing power gains from holding debt to compensate. However, if profits do not increase at the same rate as the price level, the company may find itself short of cash to meet debt obligations and may find it hard to replace plant assets.

ILLUSTRATION—HISTORICAL COST/CURRENT COST STATEMENTS

Another approach to the price-level problem is to show a conversion of historical cost to current cost. Assets such as inventories and plant assets that tend to go up or down in value as measured by quantities of dollars are restated at current cost to replace, and the cost of goods sold and depreciation are also restated at current cost.

Holding gains or losses are measured as the difference between the current cost and the historical cost. The holding gains or losses on inventories and plant assets are unrealized holding gains or losses. However, the holding gains or losses on cost of goods sold and depreciation are realized holding gains or losses because the current cost of goods sold and depreciation have been deducted on the adjusted income statement.

Current dollars have been assumed as follows for 19X1.

Cost of goods sold	$349,000
Depreciation	90,000
Inventory	72,000
Plant and equipment, gross	360,000

The realized holding gains are computed as follows:

	(In thousands of dollars)		
	Historical Dollars	Current Costs	Holding Gains
Cost of goods sold	$300	$349	$49
Depreciation	75	90	15
Total	$375	$439	$64

Note that if the plant and equipment, gross has a current value of $360,000, the depreciation on current cost for one year with a four-year life estimate is one fourth of $360,000, or $90,000.

The unrealized holding gains are computed as follows:

	(In thousands of dollars)		
	Historical Dollars	Current Costs	Holding Gains
Inventory	$ 60	$ 72	$12
Plant assets, net	225	270	45
Total	$285	$342	$57

The adjusted financial statements are given as follows:

Fife Company
Income Statement
For the Year Ended December 31, 19X1
Current Cost/Historical Dollars
(In thousands of dollars)

Sales	$500
Cost of goods sold	$349
Operating expenses, excluding depreciation	50
Depreciation	90
	$489
Income before income tax	$ 11
Income tax	30
Loss on operations	$(19)
Holding gains:	
Realized:	
Cost of goods sold	49
Depreciation	15
Unrealized:	
Inventory	12
Plant and equipment	45
Net loss and holding gains	$102

Fife Company
Balance Sheet
December 31, 19X1
Current Cost/Historical Dollars
(In thousands of dollars)

Assets
Cash and accounts receivable	$400
Inventory	72
Plant and equipment, net of depreciation	270
Total assets	$742

Equities
Accounts and notes payable	$200
Stockholders' equity	542
Total equities	$742

The stockholders' equity in historical dollars at the beginning of 19X1 of $440,000 is increased by the net loss and holding gains for 19X1 of $102,000 to arrive at the stockholders' equity at the end of 19X1 of $542,000.

ILLUSTRATION—CURRENT COST/CONSTANT DOLLAR STATEMENTS

The current cost concept can be combined with the constant dollar concept. The financial statements will then show both the purchasing power gain or loss, as computed under constant dollar accounting, and the holding gains or losses.

The real holding gains or losses are computed differently than the nominal holding gains or losses under the historical cost/current cost method. Two steps are taken:

1. The historical costs are converted to constant dollars.
2. The current cost amounts are converted to constant dollars at the end of the year by using a multiplier equal to the end-of-year index over the average index for the year.

The net holding gain or loss is equal to the difference between the two computations.

Computations for this illustration are as follows:

Step 1 (same as computations made for constant dollar example.)

	(In thousands of dollars)		
	Historical Cost	Multiplier	Constant Dollars
Realized:			
Cost of goods sold	$200	110/100	$220
	100	110/110	100
Depreciation	75	110/100	82
Total	$375		$402
Unrealized:			
Inventory	$ 60	110/100	$ 66
Plant assets, net....................................	225	110/100	248
Total	$285		$314

The average price index for the year is assumed to be 105.

Step 2

	(In thousands of dollars)		
	Current Cost	Multiplier	Adjusted Current Cost
Realized:			
Cost of goods sold	$349	110/105	$366
Depreciation	90	110/105	94
Total	$439		$460
Unrealized:			
Inventory	$ 72	110/105	$ 75
Plant assets, net....................................	270	110/105	283
Total	$342		$358

The real holding gains are computed as follows:

	(In thousands of dollars)		
	Adjusted Historical Costs	Adjusted Current Costs	Real Holding Gains
Realized:			
Cost of goods sold	$320	$366	$46
Depreciation	82	94	12
Total	$402	$460	$58
Unrealized:			
Inventory	$ 66	$ 75	$ 9
Plant assets, net....................................	248	283	35
Totals	$314	$358	$44

Fife Company
Income Statement
For the Year Ended December 31, 19X1
Current Cost/Constant Dollars
(In thousands of dollars)

Sales	$530
Cost of goods sold	$366
Operating expenses, excluding depreciation	55
Depreciation	94
	$515
Income before income tax	$ 15
Income tax	30
Net loss	$(15)
Purchasing power loss	(13)
Holding gains:	
Realized:	
Cost of goods sold	46
Depreciation	12
Unrealized:	
Inventory	9
Plant and equipment, net	35
Net loss, purchasing power loss, and holding gains	$ 74

Fife Company
Balance Sheet
December 31, 19X1
Current Cost/Constant Dollars
(In thousands of dollars)

Assets	
Cash and accounts receivable	$400
Inventory	75
Plant assets, net	283
Total assets	$758

Equities	
Accounts and notes payable	$200
Stockholders' equity	558
Total equities	$758

The stockholders' equity at the beginning of the year of $440,000 in historical dollars is converted to constant dollars of $484,000 ($440,000 × 110/100). The net income, including the purchasing power loss and the holding gains, amounts to $74,000 and is added to the adjusted beginning balance of $484,000 to arrive at the adjusted ending balance of $558,000.

The financial reporting methods described in this chapter are summarized in the following diagram:

	Historical Cost Valuation	Current Cost Valuation
Nominal Dollars	Historical Cost/ Nominal Dollar	Current Cost/ Nominal Dollar
Constant Dollars	Historical Cost/ Constant Dollar	Current Cost/ Constant Dollar

The upper left-hand cell is the conventional historical cost system. The lower left-hand cell was the first method described, with historical cost being converted to constant dollars. Then, the current cost method was described— shown in the upper right-hand cell. Current cost was then converted to constant dollars, as shown in the lower right-hand cell.

Management may find constant dollars, current dollars, or a combination of the two more appropriate in understanding how changes in prices have affected the company. When possible, management will want to take steps to cope with the problem of changing prices and will base its actions on an assessment of price trends in the future.

MANAGERIAL POLICY AND PRICE LEVEL

During periods of anticipated inflation, management will tend to invest more in assets such as plant and equipment that will tend to go up and down in price in rough correspondence with the price level. Management will also tend to hold less in cash or other monetary assets and will be inclined to borrow more heavily. Conversely, with deflation, management will want a stronger cash position and less debt.

Mixed dollar statements are misleading, and during periods of increasing prices, it may appear that profits are increasing. This results from matching older cost against current revenues. When the statements are placed on a constant or current dollar basis, the profits may be greatly reduced with income tax at a higher rate than the legally stated rate.

Plant Asset Replacement

Presumably, a company with a heavy investment in plant assets can keep up with inflation by reinvesting in plant assets each year an amount equal to the price-adjusted depreciation charge. This may be true if the company can earn enough on the assets to keep up with the rate of inflation. Some companies have not been able to keep their earnings up to the rate of inflation and are falling behind even though they are investing amounts equal to the price-adjusted depreciation.

Dividend Policy

The net income reported for the year is only one element, although an important one, in the formation of dividend policy. A company may appear to have sufficient net income for dividends, but a measurement of net income on a constant or current dollar basis may reveal that the dividends are in excess of net income. In reality, the company may be distributing dividends that are partly a distribution of present and past earnings and partly a distribution of capital. In short, the company is gradually liquidating.

In the example given in the following table, the company intended to pay half of the net income to stockholders as dividends, and the income tax based on net income computed in mixed dollars of purchasing power was at the rate of 40 percent.

	Mixed Dollars	Constant Dollars
Income before income tax	$500,000	$300,000
Income tax	200,000	200,000
Net income	$300,000	$100,000
Dividends	150,000	150,000
Earnings reinvested	$150,000	$(50,000)

On a constant dollar basis, the income tax is in reality equal to two thirds of income before tax. Dividends were not equal to 50 percent of net income. In fact, all of the current net income was distributed plus $50,000 of either past earnings or invested capital. Often management is aware of this situation but feels obligated to maintain the dividends to stockholders.

Holding Gains and Losses

A gain from holding a plant asset is not a realized gain. It is an indication that the current value of the asset is higher than the constant dollar cost, but the gain is not realized until the asset is sold. If anything, the holding gain puts pressure on management to prepare for asset replacement at a higher cost if the business is to continue operating as it has in the past.

In situations where plant assets or other nonmonetary assets are sold, adjustments for price level reveal how much of a gain is real and how much of a so-called gain is merely an adjustment to keep up with the general price level. The following example illustrates how gains or losses can be measured more realistically.

Reston Company has a tract of land that was acquired at a cost of $150,000 when the price index was at 100. The company has been offered $350,000 for this land when the price index was 200. Income tax on the gain is at a 25 percent rate.

Sales price	$350,000
Cost	150,000
Gain	$200,000
Tax on gain, 25%	50,000
Gain after tax	$150,000

The computation is in mixed dollars of purchasing power. The real gain is much less than the computed gain. A computation is given in the following table to match constant dollar cost against the expected proceeds from sale.

Sales price	$350,000
Cost in constant dollars ($150,000 × $\frac{200}{100}$)	300,000
Gain	$ 50,000
Tax on gain	50,000
Gain after tax	-0-

When the cost is adjusted to constant dollars, it can be seen that the sale will result in a recovery of cost after tax, but there is no real gain after income tax. The company is only maintaining its position.

Terminology Review

Constant dollars (472)
Current costs (472)
Monetary items (473)
Nonmonetary items (474)
Purchasing power gain or loss (478)

Multiplier (478)
Unrealized holding gains or
    losses (480)
Realized holding gains or losses (480)

QUESTIONS FOR REVIEW

1. Explain how the standard of measurement in finance and accounting differs from the standard used for physical measurements.

2. What approaches have been recommended for dealing with the problem of changes in the purchasing power of the dollar?

3. How does the lifo inventory method operate to provide a better matching of revenues and costs?

4. How can accelerated depreciation methods reduce the impact of price-level changes?

5. During a period when prices are increasing, does an individual or business benefit by holding cash? Explain.

6. How does a borrower benefit during a period of increasing prices?

7. What is meant by the term *constant dollars of purchasing power*?

8. Name two index series that may be used to measure changes in the general price level.

9. Distinguish between monetary items and nonmonetary items.

10. Explain how a monetary asset as stated is always at current purchasing power.

11. Dollar amounts from the past are brought up to date by the application of an index number multiplier. What index number is used as the numerator of the multiplier fraction? The denominator of the multiplier?

12. How is the purchasing power loss on a monetary asset computed?

13. What is meant by the term *current dollars of purchasing power*?

14. What is a holding gain or loss?

15. Is a holding gain or loss a realized gain or loss?

16. If you were a lender, would you prefer to have the debt paid in a fixed number of dollars or in dollars adjusted for changes in the price level as measured by a selected index?

17. Assume that you own a tract of land or other nonmonetary asset. How might you distinguish between a reported gain from sale and a real gain or loss?

18. If a company invests an amount each year equal to depreciation on historic cost, will it be able to maintain plant investment?

19. If a company invests an amount each year equal to constant dollar depreciation, will it be able to maintain plant investment?

20. Explain how a board of directors can unintentionally distribute more than the amount of current earnings as dividends.

EXERCISES

1. **Lifo Inventory.** Williams Inc. uses the Lifo inventory method. At the beginning of 1985, the company had 50,000 units in inventory at a cost of $12 per unit. During the year, prices went up sharply, and it cost $2,400,000 to purchase 120,000 units. The company does not keep a perpetual inventory record. The company sold 110,000 units during the year.

Required:

> **(1)** Were current costs matched against revenue? Compute cost of goods sold.
>
> **(2)** Assume that the company sold 150,000 units during the year. Were current costs matched against revenue? Compute cost of goods sold.

2. Lifo and Fifo Inventory. The president of Haber Company asks you to prepare partial income statements to illustrate how the results would appear under Lifo inventory and then under Fifo. Perpetual inventory records are not kept, and there was no inventory on hand at the beginning of the year. Sales were $1,400,000. Early in the year, 80,000 units were purchased at $5 each, and later in the year 60,000 units were purchased at a cost of $8 each. The company sold 100,000 units during the year.

Required:

> **(1)** Prepare a partial income statement with inventory maintained on a lifo basis.
>
> **(2)** Prepare a partial income statement with inventory maintained on a fifo basis.

3. Debt and Price Levels. Miliken Company incurred a debt of $60,000 when the price index was at 120. One year later when the debt was still outstanding, the price index was at 150.

Required: Compute the gain or loss in purchasing power during the year.

4. Purchasing Power and Monetary Items. At the beginning of the year, Sidrow Inc. held cash and receivables of $150,000 and had accounts payable of $50,000. The price index at the beginning of the year was 100. During the year, sales of $300,000 were made at an index of 120. Merchandise costing $120,000 was purchased at an index of 120. Expenses of $60,000 were paid at an index of 150, and dividends of $40,000 and income tax of $60,000 were paid at an index of 150. The index at the end of the year was 150. Accounts payable remained at $50,000.

Required: Compute the purchasing power gain or loss from holding net monetary items during the year.

5. Depreciation and Price Level. Montgomery Smith Inc. invested $2,000,000 in equipment estimated to have a useful life of 4 years with no residual salvage value at the end of the 4 years. The equipment was purchased when the price index was 100. The price indexes during and at the end of each of the next 4 years are as follows:

Years	
1	110
2	121
3	133
4	146

An amount equal to straight-line depreciation has been reinvested at the end of each year at an earnings rate of 6%.

Required: Assuming that the replacement cost of new equipment has increased with the price index, will the company have retained enough resources to replace the equipment through its depreciation and reinvestment policy? Show computations.

6. Accelerated Depreciation. Mesa Frame Company purchased equipment at a cost of $750,000. The equipment was estimated to have a 5-year life with no residual salvage value at the end of the 5 years. Three years later, the plant manager finds that this equipment can be traded in on new equipment costing $950,000. The dealer will grant a trade-in allowance on the old equipment of $300,000, an amount equal to its fair market value at the time. The company reinvested an amount equal to the straight-line depreciation at the end of each year, the amount reinvested earning a 10% return.

Required:
> **(1)** Was the company able to acquire the new equipment with reinvested funds, or was it necessary to borrow? Show computations.
> **(2)** Would the company have been able to acquire the new equipment with reinvested funds if SYD depreciation had been deducted? Show computations.

7. Investments and Deflation. Chester Rabold invested $120,000 in land at a time when the price index was 120, anticipating that the price level and land values would continue to increase. However, in the past 5 years, inflation was brought under control and the general price index decreased to 100. The market for land was depressed, and he found that he could get only $80,000 for this land.

Required:
> **(1)** What amount at an index of 100 would be equal to the amount Rabold invested in land 5 years ago?
> **(2)** If Rabold were to sell the land, what would the reported loss be? What would the real loss be? Do not consider the income tax effect.

8. Purchasing Power Gain or Loss. The Alabama Freight Company issued 5-year notes payable in the amount of $3,000,000 when the price index was at 150. At the end of the 5 years, the price index was at 240.

Required: Compute the purchasing power gain or loss over the time that the notes payable were outstanding.

9. Purchasing Power Gain or Loss. Nadine Santana asks you to compute the purchasing power gain or loss on net monetary items for Santana Trading Company for the year. At the beginning of the year when the price index was at 100, net monetary items were $180,000. Sales were made during the year in the amount of $600,000 when the index was at 120.

Merchandise costing $300,000 was purchased at an index of 150. Cash of $45,000 was paid for equipment purchased when the index was at 150. Various operating expenses of $90,000 were paid when the index was 180. The index at the end of the year was 180.

Required: Compute the purchasing power gain or loss for Nadine Santana.

10. Income Statement—Constant Dollars. Data pertaining to the operations of Harkness Supply Company are given for the year.

Sales of $450,000 were made at a price index of 150. Cost of goods sold of $300,000 was at a price index of 100 as was depreciation expense of $60,000. Other operating expenses of $40,000 were incurred at a price index of 250. Income tax was at 40% of income before income tax and was at the 250 index. The price index at the end of the year was 250.

Required:

(1) Prepare an income statement for the year in mixed dollars of purchasing power.

(2) Prepare an income statement in constant dollars of purchasing power at an index of 250.

11. Balance Sheet—Constant Dollars. A balance sheet for Conroy Motors Inc. in mixed dollars of purchasing power at June 30, 19X1, shows cash and receivables of $140,000 and plant and equipment net of accumulated depreciation at $90,000. Accounts payable were $30,000 and stockholders' equity was $200,000. The plant and equipment were acquired at a price index of 100, and the price index at June 30, 19X1, was 150.

Required:

Prepare a balance sheet in constant dollars of purchasing power at June 30, 19X1, at an index of 150.

12. Fixed Income and Retirement. Clyde Dover retired 10 years ago on an annual pension of $24,000. At that time the price index was 120. At the present time the index is at 200. Dover is finding it more difficult to live on his pension than he did at the time he retired.

Required:

(1) Show Dover how his pension shrank in purchasing power. Convert the present pension of $24,000 to dollars of purchasing power 10 years ago.

(2) How many dollars should Dover now receive to maintain the purchasing power of $24,000 that he received 10 years ago.

13. Computation of Real Gains. Margaret Hamilton purchased a tract of land 15 years ago at a cost of $160,000 when the price index was at 100. Recently, she has been offered $400,000 for this tract. The price index is now at 240, and a gain from the sale is taxable at a rate of 20%.

Required:

(1) If Hamilton sells the land, will she recover the purchasing power invested 15 years ago? Show computations.

(2) What real gain can be expected from the sale of the land?

14. Paper Gains and Real Gains. Hong Lee, the president of Hillsborough Products, admits that the firm has earned relatively low profits in recent years. However, he states that the firm is rich in assets. Plant and equipment, net of accumulated depreciation, is shown on the records at $2,000,000. The plant and equipment were acquired at a price index of 100. Today the price index is 250. Lee states that the plant and equipment in its present state could be sold for $5,200,000. Hence, if the plant and equipment were sold, the company would have more than a 150% return on the investment.

Required:

(1) How much should be received from the sale of the plant assets to maintain the purchasing power invested?

(2) Compute the real gain that could be realized from the sale of the plant assets.

15. Current Dollars—Balance Sheet. The Waner Company adjusted financial statements to a constant dollar basis at an index of 150 on June 30, 19X1.

A balance sheet on a constant dollar basis at June 30, 19X1, is given as follows in summary form:

The Waner Company
Balance Sheet
Constant Dollars—150
June 4, 19X1

Monetary assets:	
Cash and receivables	$300,000
Nonmonetary assets:	
Inventory	160,000
Plant and equipment, net	400,000
Total assets	$860,000
Monetary equities:	
Accounts payable and long-term notes payable	$460,000
Nonmonetary equities:	
Stockholders' equity	400,000
Total equities...	$860,000

The current cost to replace inventory is $240,000, and the current cost to replace the plant and equipment in its present state is $650,000.

Required: Prepare a balance sheet in current cost dollars at June 30, 19X1.

PROBLEMS

16-1. Adjusted Billing. Weltmeir Metals Company manufactures a product that includes one ounce of a metal that moves up and down in price over relatively short intervals. When the metal cost $200 an ounce, the customers were billed as follows:

Cost of metal...	$200
Labor and overhead	100
	$300
Profit of 20%..	60
Selling price of product.................................	$360

Prices for the metal are given over a period of 2 years.

19X1	Cost per Ounce
January to June	$250
July to December	360
19X2	
January to June	420
July to December	530

In light of the volatility of the metal prices, the company has announced that prices will be adjusted up or down as the price of the metal changes. The $60 markup for profit will not be adjusted on a percentage basis but will be held at $60.

Required: Determine prices for the product during each of the 6-month periods given. Assume no change in labor and overhead costs or in the dollar amount of the markup for profit.

16-2. Index-Adjusted Loan. Bayside Finance Company, in an attempt to reduce potential losses in purchasing power while loans are outstanding, decided to hold interest rates down to 10%, but to adjust the amount of the loan to be repaid by using an index series. Assume that a loan was made when the index was 150. The loan with interest on the unadjusted loan balance was to be repaid a year later when the index was 180. The original loan was for $525,000.

Required:

(1) How much should Bayside Finance Company receive at the end of the year? Identify interest as a separate item.

(2) As a customer under the conditions outlined, would you rather repay the loan as adjusted with interest at 10% for the year on the unadjusted balance, or would you rather have a straight loan with the annual interest rate at 15%?

16-3. Lifo or Fifo Inventory. Ellis Pattern Company recorded sales of $4,500,000 in 1985. Inventory at the beginning of the year, consisting of 200,000 units, cost $1,200,000. During the year, 400,000 units were purchased at a cost of $4,000,000. Operating expenses amounted to $800,000, and income tax was at 40% of income before income tax. The company sold 300,000 units in 1985.

Required:

(1) Prepare summary income statements for 1985 using the fifo inventory method for one statement and the lifo inventory method for the other.

(2) How much of the profit reported under the fifo method must be used to replace inventories at the most recent cost?

16-4. Purchasing Power and Monetary Items. The Posner Company had cash and accounts receivable of $180,000 at January 1, 19X1. The inventory at that date cost $235,000, and accounts payable were $72,000. The inventory was acquired at an index of 80. The price index on January 1, 19X1, was 120.

Transactions for the year 19X1 are summarized as follows:

	Unadjusted Amount	Index
Sales	$960,000	120 (average)
Purchases:		
January to June	240,000	120 (average)
July to December	360,000	150 (average)
Expenses paid	80,000	160
Down payment on equipment purchased..................	54,000	180
Dividends paid.......................................	30,000	200

At the end of the year, accounts payable were $90,000, and the price index was at 200.

Required: Compute the gain or loss in purchasing power by holding net monetary items.

16-5. Purchasing Power and Monetary Items. Chris Wenzel had $350,000 in U.S. Treasury Bills on January 1, 19X1, when the price index was at 100. On the same date, loans of $80,000 were outstanding. Cash received from earnings in 19X1, when the price index was at 140, amounted to $280,000. Various expenses amounting to $60,000 were paid at an index of 150. Land was purchased at a cost of $75,000 when the index was at 150. Cash of $50,000 was paid for the land and a loan was taken for the balance owed.

Required: Compute the purchasing power gain or loss on net monetary items at December 31, 19X1, when the index was at 200.

16-6. Income Statement in Constant Dollars. Harry Natter, president of Natter Industries Inc. announced that the company earned record profits in 19X1. An income statement for the year follows:

Natter Industries Inc.
Income Statement
For the Year Ended December 31, 19X1
(In thousands of dollars)

Net sales	$5,860
Cost of goods sold	2,300
Gross margin	$3,560
Operating expenses	900
Income before income tax	$2,660
Income tax, 40%	1,064
Net income	$1,596

The board of directors, in light of the good news for 19X1, declared a dividend of $400,000.

Further examination shows that all sales were made at the most recent price index of 250. Cost of goods sold, however, was on a price index basis of 200. Depreciation, included in operating expenses at $300,000, was based on plant assets acquired at an index of 100. All other expenses and the dividends were at the most recent price index of 250.

Required:

(1) Prepare an income statement in constant dollars at an index of 250 for 19X1.
(2) What was the percentage of income tax to constant dollars in 19X1?
(3) How much of the constant dollar net income was retained for reinvestment after deducting the dividends?

16-7. Income Statement and Current Dollars. Celia Connors, the chief executive officer for Portsmouth Supply Company, states that the company appears to be earning profits, but it seems that additional loans must always be made to replace inventories and equipment. Also, she explains that the dividends are very modest.

An income statement for 19X1 is given as follows:

Portsmouth Supply Company
Income Statement
For the Year Ended December 31, 19X1
(In thousands of dollars)

Net sales	$8,500
Cost of goods sold	$4,800
Operating expenses, excluding depreciation	500
Depreciation expense	800
Interest expense	300
	$6,400
Income before income tax	$2,100
Income tax, 40%	840
Net income	$1,260

After some investigation, she has found that the current cost to replace the goods sold amounted to $7,400,000 and that the depreciation on the replacement cost of the plant assets was $1,600,000.

Required: From the information furnished, prepare a revised income statement on a current dollar basis. Sales, other operating expenses, interest, and income tax are stated in current dollars.

16-8. Income Statement and Current Dollars. The president of Walnut Creek Windings Inc., Wade Graham, is disappointed to find that the net income of $750,000 that he expected from operations for 19X1 becomes a net loss of $160,000 when the income statement is restated on a current dollar basis.

"Anyway," he said, "we did make a nice purchasing power gain from net outstanding debt and holding gains from inventories and plant assets."

The executive vice president replied that the company is doing well because it is so deeply in debt. Also, the holding gains can't be realized unless the property is sold and the company goes out of business. To stay in business the plant assets must be replaced at much higher costs than the amount originally invested.

The last part of the income statement under discussion is given as follows:

Net loss from operations on a current dollar basis	$(160,000)
Gain in purchasing power from net outstanding debt	340,000
Holding gains on inventories and net plant assets.........................	475,000
Net income, purchasing power gain and holding gains included............	$ 655,000

Required:

(1) Comment on the validity of the point made by the executive vice-president.

(2) Assume that income tax at a 40% rate was $500,000 on income measured in mixed dollars of purchasing power. Would the company have reported a profit on operations if the income tax were based on a current dollar measurement of income?

16-9. Income Statement and Constant Dollars. The following income statement for Wolfe and Moran Inc. for the year ended June 30, 19X2, is given in mixed dollars of purchasing power.

Wolfe And Moran Inc.
Income Statement
For the Year Ended June 30, 19X2

Net sales	$1,720,000
Cost of goods sold	$ 750,000
Operating expenses, excluding depreciation	140,000
Depreciation	300,000
Total expenses	$1,190,000
Income before income tax	$ 530,000
Income tax, 40%	212,000
Net income	$ 318,000

Sales of $520,000 were made at a price index of 130. The balance of sales was at the index at June 30, 19X2, of 200.

Cost of goods sold was at an index of 150. Operating expenses, excluding depreciation, and income tax were at the 200 index. Depreciation was recorded on assets recorded at an index of 100.

The president of the company believes that the company would have earned a much lower net income if measurements had been made in uniform dollars of purchasing power. Before recommending dividends, he would like to see what the results would have been if all dollars were restated at the index of 200 at June 30, 19X2.

Required:

(1) Prepare an income statement on a uniform dollar basis at an index of 200.

(2) Is there a basis for the president's concern? Explain.

16-10. Gains and Losses on Investments. Craig Sellers has been uncertain about the direction in which the economy would move. Hence, he has tried to balance his investments so that he would have some investments that would be successful during periods of inflation and others that would be successful during periods of deflation.

A list of his investments is given as follows:

	Cost	Price Index at Time of Investment
Municipal bonds	$ 90,000	150
Money market fund	120,000	120
Land	200,000	100
Coins	60,000	120
Total cost	$470,000	

On September 30, 19X2, he had his assets appraised. The general price index at September 30, 19X2, was 200. The municipal bonds declined in quality and were valued at $70,000. The money market fund could be redeemed at $130,000. The land was appraised at $500,000. The coins have numismatic value and have been appraised at $100,000.

Required:

(1) Determine the price-index adjusted basis of Sellers' investments at an index of 200.

(2) Compute any real holding gains based on an index of 200.

(3) Assume that the price index decreased to 100. With no market quotations given, what would be the constant dollar value of the investments?

16-11. Investment Policy and Price Level. Rosa Torres chairman of the board of directors of Reed Industries Inc., has been concerned about the effects of inflation for several years. As a result, she has advocated a policy of operating with a minimum of monetary assets and has reinvested profits in modern equipment that not only is more efficient but also tends to increase in value as the price level increases. To a large extent, she has financed acquisitions by long-term loans.

A balance sheet at June 30, 19X2, is given as follows:

Reed Industries Inc.
Balance Sheet
June 30, 19X2

Cash	$ 46,000
Accounts receivable	77,000
Inventory	100,000
Land	200,000
Buildings, net of accumulated depreciation	840,000
Equipment, net of accumulated depreciation	580,000
Total assets	$1,843,000
Accounts payable	$ 68,000
Short-term loans	80,000
Long-term loans	560,000
Capital stock	400,000
Retained earnings	735,000
Total equities	$1,843,000

The price index at June 30, 19X2, was 280. Inventory was acquired at a price index of 250. Land costing $200,000 was acquired at an index of 200. The buildings were purchased at an index of 140. Equipment having a net book value of $300,000 was purchased at an index of 150, and additional equipment having a net book value of $280,000 was acquired at an index of 250. Capital stock was issued at an index of 100.

Required:

(1) Prepare a balance sheet on a uniform dollar basis at an index of 280.

(2) Assume that the price index decreased to 100. Prepare a balance sheet at an index of 100.

(3) Point out the risks that Torres assumes in following her policy.

16-12. Land Investment. Puller and White Inc. has plans to locate plants in various parts of the country and has saved funds for that purpose. The president of the company believes that it is more appropriate to invest in various land sites now rather than to hold funds in the form of securities or to take chances on the conditions of a future capital market for later borrowing or capital stock issues. Some later financing will be necessary, but management would like to keep the amount as low as possible.

The president believes that land will always go up in value because they are not making any more of it.

If the land is not needed, the plan is to sell unused portions at a gain.

Investments in land were made as follows:

	Cost	Price Index
Tract 1	$ 42,000	120
Tract 2	130,000	200
Tract 3	110,000	220
Tract 4	180,000	240

Five years later the price index was at 300. The tracts of land were appraised as follows:

	Current Value
Tract 1	$125,000
Tract 2	215,000
Tract 3	130,000
Tract 4	190,000

Required:

(1) Prepare a report to show the original cost, the index-adjusted cost, the current values of the tracts, and the holding gains and losses.

(2) Point out possible fallacies in the position taken by the president.

16-13. Balance Sheet—Constant and Current Dollars. A balance sheet for Cecil Supply Company is given below in mixed dollars of purchasing power as of December 31, 19X2.

Cecil Supply Company
Balance Sheet
December 31, 19X2

Assets

Cash	$135,000
Accounts receivable	82,000
Inventory	60,000
Equipment, net of accumulated depreciation	86,000
Total assets	$363,000

Equities

Accounts payable	$ 70,000
Capital stock	200,000
Retained earnings	93,000
Total equities	$363,000

Rita Quinn, a financial analyst, asks you to prepare a balance sheet in constant dollars of purchasing power and a balance sheet in current dollars of purchasing power. The inventory was acquired when the general price index was 120, the equipment was acquired at an index of 100, and capital stock was issued at an index of 100.

The general price index at December 31, 19X2, was 250.

It was also found on December 31, 19X2, that the inventory could be replaced at a cost of $140,000, and that the equipment in its present condition net of accumulated depreciation could be replaced for $235,000. Capital stock should be shown at $200,000.

Required: Prepare the balance sheet as requested by Rita Quinn.

16-14. Comprehensive Price Index Problem. The balance sheet for Orben Metals Company at June 30, 19X2, is given. All items are stated on a uniform dollar basis at an index of 100.

Orben Metals Company
Balance Sheet
June 30, 19X2
(Uniform dollars at index of 100)

Assets

Cash		$115,000
Accounts receivable		55,000
Inventory		96,000
Plant assets, net of accumulated depreciation		152,000
Total assets		$418,000

Equities

Accounts payable		$ 48,000
Capital stock		150,000
Retained earnings:		
Operations	$250,000	
Accumulated purchasing power losses	30,000	220,000
Total equities		$418,000

Transactions for the fiscal year ended June 30, 19X3, are summarized as follows:

(1) Sales:

At index of 150 . . . . $225,000

At index of 180 540,000

(2) Purchases:

At index of 120 180,000

At index of 180 270,000

(3) Cost of goods sold was $500,000. The lifo inventory method was used, and the inventory at June 30, 19X3, of $46,000 was at an index of 100.

(4) Operating expenses for the fiscal year, excluding depreciation, were $72,000. They were incurred at an index of 180.

(5) Accounts payable at the end of the fiscal year were $48,000, as they were at the beginning of the fiscal year.

(6) Accounts receivable at the end of the fiscal year amounted to $153,000.

(7) Depreciation of $20,000 for the fiscal year was on assets acquired at an index of 100.

(8) Income tax of $70,000 was computed and paid at an index of 200.

(9) The index at June 30, 19X3, was 200.

(10) The cash balance at June 30, 19X3, was $190,000.

Required:

(1) Compute the purchasing power gain or loss for the fiscal year from holding net monetary assets.

(2) Prepare an income statement for the year in mixed dollars and convert the statement to uniform dollars of purchasing power at an index of 200.

(3) Prepare a balance sheet in mixed dollars of purchasing power at June 30, 19X3.

(4) Prepare a balance sheet in uniform dollars of purchasing power at an index of 200 for June 30, 19X3.

16-15. Dividends and Price Level. The board of directors is reluctant to declare dividends on the basis of the income statement for 19X1, prepared on a mixed dollar basis. Before making a decision, the board asks you to present them with an income statement in constant dollars of purchasing power. Past practice has been to pay dividends of $1 per share each year on 100,000 shares of stock outstanding. If the net income on a constant dollar basis is sufficient, the practice will be continued.

An income statement in mixed purchasing power dollars is as follows:

Findley Supply Company

Income Statement

For the Year Ended December 31, 19X1

(In thousands of dollars)

Net sales	$930
Cost of goods sold	$280
Operating expenses, excluding depreciation	140
Depreciation expense	150
	$570
Income before income tax	$360
Income tax, 40%	144
Net income	$216

The price index at December 31, 19X1, was 300. Sales of $600,000 were made at the price index of 250 with the balance being at the current index. All of the cost of goods sold was at the index of 200. Depreciation expense was at an index of 100. All other items on the income statement were at the current index of 300.

Required:

(1) Prepare the income statement requested in constant dollars of purchasing power at an index of 300.

(2) If net income cannot cover a dividend of $1 a share, can a dividend of $.50 a share be covered?

(3) How would you explain to the stockholders that dividends must be reduced or eliminated when they have an income statement showing full coverage of the dividend?

16-16. Current Cost/Constant Dollar Statements. The president of Klingman Company, upon examining the financial statements for the year ended June 30, 19X1, questions how realistic the statements are when the level of prices has changed substantially as it did last year. You have been asked to prepare the financial statements on a current cost/ constant dollar basis.

The following balance sheet is at the beginning of the fiscal year, June 30, 19X0. All data are on the basis of an index of 100, and current costs are approximately equal to the dollar amounts shown.

Klingman Company
Balance Sheet
June 30, 19X0

Assets

Cash	$ 50,000
Accounts receivable	40,000
Inventory	54,000
Plant assets, net	120,000
Total assets	$264,000

Equities

Accounts payable	$ 30,000
Stockholders' equity:	
Capital stock	20,000
Retained earnings	229,000
Accumulated purchasing power loss	(15,000)
Total equities	$264,000

An income statement in historical dollars is given as follows:

Klingman Company
Income Statement
For the Year Ended June 30, 19X1

Sales...	$450,000
Cost of goods sold...	$300,000
Operating expenses, excluding depreciation	60,000
Depreciation	30,000
	$390,000
Income before income tax	$ 60,000
Income tax..	24,000
Net income	$ 36,000

A balance sheet in historical dollars is given as follows:

Klingman Company
Balance Sheet
June 30, 19X1

Assets

Cash	$ 60,000
Accounts receivable..	76,000
Inventory	84,000
Plant assets, net..	90,000
Total assets	$310,000

Equities

Accounts payable...	$ 40,000
Stockholders' equity:	
Capital stock..	20,000
Retained earnings..	265,000
Accumulated purchasing power loss	(15,000)
Total equities..	$310,000

Price indexes when various transactions took place are given as follows:

	Index
Sales	180
Cost of goods sold..	150
Depreciation	100
Operating expenses, excluding depreciation	150
Income taxes	200

The average price index for the year was 140 and was 200 at June 30, 19X1.

Purchases in the amount of $330,000 were made during the year at a price index of 150. Inventory at June 30, 19X1, with a cost of $54,000 was acquired when the price index was 100. The balance of inventory costing $30,000 was acquired at a price index of 150.

Current costs have been determined as follows:

Cost of goods sold	$420,000
Depreciation	70,000
Inventory	140,000
Plant assets, net	210,000

Required: Prepare an income statement for the year ended June 30, 19X1, and a balance sheet at June 30, 19X1, on a current cost/constant dollar basis.

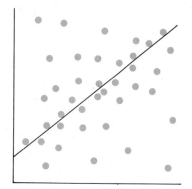

17

ANALYSIS OF FINANCIAL STATEMENTS

Chapter Objectives:

This chapter will enable you to:
1. Describe the relationships between data on financial statements.
2. Evaluate the data used in analysis and explain how the data must be stated in dollars that can be compared properly.
3. Explain the relationship between rate of return on sales, rate of return on assets, and leverage.
4. Explain some of the risks of analysis when data are not truly comparable.
5. Describe profitability and its relationship to liquidity and safety.

Information derived from financial statements and interrelationships of financial data can be most helpful in the evaluation of the profitability of an enterprise and safety of investment. Financial analysts, stockholders, creditors, employees, prospective investors, and the public at large judge a company, in part at least, by financial measurements that are revealed through statement analysis. Business management, recognizing that the statements are a report on the company and on managerial skill, see statement analysis as a means of self-evaluation. Knowledge derived from analysis can be combined with other information in planning and controlling various aspects of the business. Also, statement analysis reveals how closely financial data are interlocked. No one piece of financial information is isolated; and financial statement analysis is important because it can give the reader a better understanding of business operations and the related financial effects.

It is very important that the data selected for analysis be comparable. With changes in the level of prices, it is easy to make the mistake of comparing current dollars of purchasing power with out-of-date dollars of purchasing power. Analysis with incorrect data is misleading and is worse than no information at all. For example, in computing a rate of return, a net income unadjusted for current dollars of depreciation and cost of goods sold may be computed as a percentage of assets stated at older costs.

$$\frac{\$150,000 \text{ net income}}{\$600,000 \text{ assets}} = 25\% \text{ rate of return at historical cost}$$

This rate of return may appear to be attractive. However, net income, after allowing for higher current depreciation charges and cost of goods sold, may amount to only $90,000. The assets restated at current values may be $1,500,000.

$$\frac{\$90,000 \text{ net income}}{\$1,500,000 \text{ assets}} = 6\% \text{ rate of return at current value}$$

The true rate of return is only 6 percent, not at all attractive.

Statement analysis furnishes general answers to the following questions:

1. Does the company earn adequate profit?
2. Can the company pay its bills promptly? In other words, does it have sufficient liquidity?
3. Is an investment in the company a safe investment?

Exact answers cannot be given to these questions; the answers depend upon what will happen in an uncertain future. But statement analysis can reveal what has taken place in the past and give some indication of what can be expected.

RATE-OF-RETURN CONCEPT

The rate-of-return concept is employed to evaluate the earning power of a company. The percentage of net income to sales is the rate of return on sales, the percentage of net income to assets is the rate of return on assets, and the percentage of net income to owners' equity is the rate of return on the owners' equity. These respective percentages, or rates of return, reveal the relationships between the net earnings and the sales revenue, the net earnings and the assets employed, and the net earnings and the owners' interest in the business.

Rate of Return — Assets

The rate of return on assets is one of the most important measurements obtained from an analysis of financial statements. This rate of return is computed as follows:

$$\frac{\text{Net income}}{\text{Assets}} = \text{Rate of return on assets}$$

Both the net income and the assets must be defined carefully in order to obtain a rate of return that is appropriate for a given purpose.

Net Income

For purposes of financial statement analysis, the income statement should be adjusted to remove items that are of an unusual nature and that are not expected to recur with regularity. For example, a loss from a fire should not be included in the computation of net income. If the loss is not removed, the rate of return may be distorted. Furthermore, if unusual items are allowed to remain in the income statement, comparisons cannot be made, with other years. In effect, "net income" becomes synonymous with income from continuing operation, thus excluding extraordinary items, disposals of segments of a business, and the cumulative effect of changes in accounting principle.

The dividends and the interest earned on investments are included in net income if the investments are also included in the asset base, but the dividends and the interest should be excluded if the investments have been removed from the assets category.

The income before the deduction of interest expense and income tax is used if the intention is to measure operational performance. A manager may be responsible for how an asset is used but may have had nothing to do with the acquisition of the asset. Resources are often borrowed to finance the purchase of assets; and interest expense, the cost of borrowing resources, should not be charged to personnel who have had no part in making these financial arrangements. Furthermore, comparisons between companies may be distorted by differences in financing. To test the effectiveness of operation as opposed to financing, interest expense should not be deducted from income.

Top management, on the other hand, is responsible not only for how the assets are used but also for how they are acquired. Therefore, it is proper to use the income after the deduction of interest to evaluate the total managerial effort. The rate of return is then a rate of return to the owners on the total asset investment since the income has already been reduced for amounts due to other equity holders. In other words, income has already been reduced by the interest on the debt.

Likewise, income tax may or may not be deducted depending upon circumstances. Management at the operating level has no control over the computation of income tax or the tax planning activities; consequently, income before the income tax deduction would be a more appropriate measurement of its efficiency. From the owners' viewpoint, however, there can be no return until all expenses, including income tax, have been deducted. The income tax is as much an expense of doing business as any other expense and should be considered as such in rating the total business performance.

The Asset Base

Assets as shown on the balance sheet may also have to be adjusted in making rate-of-return computations. The nature of the adjustments depends upon the definition of the rate of return. Since assets increase or decrease during the year, a rate-of-return measurement may be more meaningful if the assets are averaged. When reference is made in this chapter to total assets or to total owners' equity, it is assumed that the data have been properly averaged or are representative data for rate-of-return computations.

Assets that are not available for productive use should be excluded from the asset base in the calculation of a rate of return on assets that are actively employed in profit-making activity. The cost of idle facilities, for example, and the cost of construction in process produce nothing in the way of current profit. Presumably these assets are expected to yield profit at a later date. At the present time, however, there is no profit yield, and the cost should be subtracted from the asset base so that the return will be related to the assets that produced it. An additional rate of return calculation may be made with the cost of standby and idle facilities included in the asset base. This rate of return can be compared with the rate of return on the productive assets and may reveal that management is retaining more nonproductive assets than is warranted.

If management at the operating level is to be evaluated, investments in the securities of other companies should also be eliminated. Operating management cannot take credit for the dividends or interest earned on investments, nor can it be held responsible for the cost of the investments.

Asset Turnover and Rate of Return

In seeking a given rate of return, management recognizes that various factors interlock. These factors are:

1. The rate of profit on the sales dollar.
2. The volume of sales
3. The investment in assets.
4. The ratio of sales to the asset investment (asset turnover).

The rate of return on total assets depends upon the ratio of net income to sales and the ratio of sales to total assets (asset turnover). Often these relationships are expressed in equation form as follows:

$$\text{Rate of return on sales} = \frac{\text{Net income}}{\text{Sales}}$$

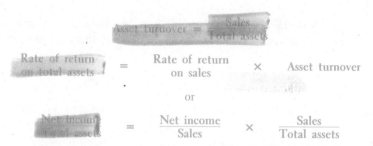

$$\text{Asset turnover} = \frac{\text{Sales}}{\text{Total assets}}$$

$$\text{Rate of return on total assets} = \text{Rate of return on sales} \times \text{Asset turnover}$$

or

$$\frac{\text{Net income}}{\text{Total assets}} = \frac{\text{Net income}}{\text{Sales}} \times \frac{\text{Sales}}{\text{Total assets}}$$

Assume that two companies each with assets of $500,000 earn a 20 percent return on assets, or $100,000 in net income. Company A is a manufacturer and turns its assets over only once but earns a 20 percent return on sales. Company B is a retailer and turns its assets over ten times but earns only 2 percent on the sales dollar.

Rate of Return on Assets

	Company A	Company B
Net sales	$500,000	$5,000,000
Total assets	$500,000	$500,000
Net income	$100,000	$100,000
Percentage of net income to net sales (rate of return on sales)	20%	2%
Asset turnover	1	10
Rate of return on total assets	20%	20%

Company A relies upon its profit margin to obtain a 20 percent return on assets, while Company B depends upon turnover. By doubling asset turnover, Company A can double the rate of return on assets with the same volume of sales and profit percentage. If Company B can increase its profit margin to 4 percent of net sales, it can also double the rate of return on assets with the same sales volume and turnover.

Various combinations of turnovers and profit percentages can be computed to arrive at a combination that most likely will be realized in seeking a certain rate of return. By examining these relationships, management can in certain industries, however, impose limitations. For example, a company that manufactures heavy equipment generally requires a large asset investment. It may be difficult to improve asset turnover to any extent, and an improved rate of return on assets may depend largely upon an increased rate of return on sales.

The Management of Assets

Different types of assets or resources must be available and be employed in balanced proportions to achieve an optimum rate of return. Cash, accounts receivable, inventory, various plant assets, and a supply of labor are all necessary in the production of goods and services for sale to customers.

With a surplus of assets, the company is in a good position to meet emergency situations and does not have to plan operating activity with much precision. But there is a price for this luxury. The rate of return on assets tends to be depressed with a large asset base; and the cost to hold large inventories or reserve plant facilities, for example, may be beyond reason. Creditors and stockholders furnish resources at a cost, and efforts must be made to minimize that cost. Conversely, if the investment in assets is too small, the company may not be able to meet production schedules promptly and may lose sales and customers.

A balanced asset structure is essential. It is possible to have an excess investment in one asset category with a shortage in another. For example, more plant and equipment may be available than is necessary for the production of one line of product while there is a shortage of facilities in another area. Inventories may be stockpiled beyond reasonable need when there is a shortage of cash to meet obligations to creditors, or collection policy may be lax, resulting in large accounts receivable balances that should be realized in cash.

The Combination of Assets

In conducting operations, resources may be combined in various ways. To some extent, one factor of production may be substituted for another. For example, it may be possible to use more automated equipment and less labor. A shift of this sort has both advantages and disadvantages that must be evaluated. Some of the cost and problems associated with labor are avoided, but cost and problems associated with the maintenance and operation of sophisticated equipment are added.

In a manufacturing operation, three cost elements are combined to form the finished product:

1. Direct materials.
2. Direct labor.
3. Factory overhead.

Direct Materials. Within limits it may be possible to substitute one type of material for another or to reduce the quantity of materials used. A shift to a less expensive material or a saving in quantity may reduce cost of production and reduce the investment in inventory. As a result, the rate of return on assets is improved.

Direct Labor. As stated earlier, there may be an opportunity to substitute equipment for labor or vice versa. Before making any changes, management should evaluate the effect on the rate of return. With labor or equipment management, there is the question of how much time is needed for production. In evaluating alternative combinations of labor and equipment, cost and time must be considered together. Overhead cost that varies with labor or machine hours is influenced by labor time or machine time and must also be recognized in any evaluation of alternatives.

Factory Overhead. With the different types of overhead, the rate of return can be improved by paying attention to the need for certain costs. Both the variable and fixed overhead should be examined for possible savings. There is often a tendency to authorize additions to fixed overhead without adequately evaluating potential needs. Fixed overhead thus becomes institutionalized as an established "necessity." For example, does an annual training program at a national training center produce results that justify travel and lodging costs? Could the same or even better results be obtained via training programs at local offices?

Rate of Return by Segment

In examining the various aspects of rate of return such as revenue, cost, and supporting assets, it is important to determine not only the rate of return for the company as a unit but also the rates of return for segments of the company such as divisions or product lines. Attempts to compute rates of return by segments are complicated when assets are shared by two or more segments. How much of the asset base should be assigned to one segment as compared with another? Attempts to allocate the supporting assets can become quite arbitrary.

Perhaps the best approach is to consider only the assets that can be directly identified with a segment. It may be recognized that each segment receives benefits from assets shared in common with other segments. However, in determining the profitability of a segment, it may be better not to make allocations that are questionable.

Assume that Heiser and Wolfe Inc. operates with three product line divisions. Data with respect to operations for 1985 are given as follows:

	Product Line Divisions			
	1	*2*	*3*	*Total*
Sales	$250,000	$320,000	$400,000	$ 970,000
Direct cost of division	180,000	230,000	300,000	710,000
(1) Margin over direct cost of division	$ 70,000	$ 90,000	$100,000	$ 260,000
Cost common to total operation				140,000
(2) Net income				$ 120,000
(3) Assets identified directly with division	$350,000	$540,000	$250,000	$1,140,000
Assets common to total operation				360,000
(4) Total assets				$1,500,000
Rate of return on segment assets [(1) ÷ (3)]	20%	16.7%	40%	
Rate of return, overall [(2) ÷ (4)]				8%

Note that the rates of return for the segments are computed by excluding expenses that are not directly identified with the segments. It is true that these rates do not reflect the support furnished at the top corporate level. However, the rates are useful in that they indicate which divisions are more profitable in relation to the assets that they employ. In still another way, they reveal whether or not top corporate management is operating efficiently. In the example given, the cost common to the overall operation is relatively high. This depresses the total net income substantially and, when considered along with the addition of the assets used in common, significantly reduces the rate of return. Perhaps the cost of top administration should be examined more closely.

Depreciable Assets

In working with rates of return in total or by segments, the question arises as to how depreciable assets should be handled. Should depreciable assets be shown at the gross amount or at the net amount after the deduction for accumulated depreciation?

Assume that a net income of $50,000 has been earned for the year and that most of the assets employed were depreciable assets. Total assets with no reduction for accumulated depreciation had a cost of $500,000. A rate of return on assets is computed as follows:

Without Accumulated Depreciation

$$\frac{\$50,000 \text{ net income}}{\$500,000 \text{ total assets}} = 10\% \text{ rate of return on assets}$$

Suppose that the accumulated depreciation was $200,000. Then the asset base would be $300,000 ($500,000 − $200,000) if assets are to be included net of accumulated depreciation.

With Accumulated Depreciation

$$\frac{\$50,000 \text{ net income}}{\$300,000 \text{ total assets}} = 16.7\% \text{ rate of return on assets}$$

The rate of return, of course, is higher when computed on a lower asset base. Furthermore, assuming no other changes the rate of return tends to increase in the future as the asset base is reduced even more by depreciation.

Instead of being concerned about the effect of depreciation on the asset base, it may be more to the point to determine if the net income and the asset base are stated in comparable dollars of purchasing power. In Chapter 16, it was pointed out that comparisons cannot be made properly with mixed dollars of purchasing power.

A more realistic rate of return may be measured on a current value basis. For example, assume that the net income would be $40,000 rather than $50,000 if the income statement is on a current value basis. The depreciable assets and other assets have a combined current value of $600,000. The rate of return on assets should then be recomputed as follows:

$$\frac{\$40,000 \text{ net income (current value)}}{\$600,000 \text{ total assets (current value)}} = 6.7\% \text{ return on assets}$$

The result is significantly different. The rate of return is much lower when both the net income and the assets are stated on a comparable current dollar basis.

In management situations, one can be deceived by an artificially high rate of return and retain an unsatisfactory investment. The high rate of return may result from the use of an outdated asset base. For example, one may boast of an investment that has been yielding a 30 percent return. A number of years ago the investment cost $60,000 and now earns $18,000 a year with a present market value of $300,000. It is incorrectly reasoned that the current rate of return is 30 percent:

$$\frac{\$18,000 \text{ net income}}{\$60,000 \text{ original cost of investment}} = 30\% \text{ rate of return on investment}$$

The current rate of return is only 6 percent:

$$\frac{\$\ 18,000 \text{ net income}}{\$300,000 \text{ value of investment}} = 6\% \text{ rate of return on investment}$$

The investment should be evaluated on the basis of current value, not historical cost. There is an opportunity cost of $300,000 attached to the decision to hold the investment; that is, the real question is whether or not $300,000 could be employed elsewhere to earn more than a 6 percent return.

Leverage

The rate of return on assets is important, but it is also important to go a step further and determine the rate of return on the owners' equity. This rate of return depends upon decisions made with respect to the financial structure and also upon profit that in turn depends upon the effective employment of available resources.

Resources or capital may be furnished directly by the owners through the sale of capital stock if the business is incorporated or may be furnished indirectly by the owners through the reinvestment of profit that has been retained. Capital may also be furnished by outsiders either in the form of short-term credit or long-term credit. Ordinarily a business employs resources that have been furnished by both owners and outsiders in a ratio relative to management's philosophy toward risk taking.

The equity of the common stockholders is the residual equity, i.e., the equity remaining after provision has been made for the claims of all other equity holders. The stockholders' equity, for example, is reduced by the liquidation value of preferred stock. Similarly, net income must be reduced by the dividend claims of preferred stockholders.

The rate of return on the common stockholders' equity is computed as follows:

$$\frac{\text{Net income less dividend requirements on preferred stock}}{\text{Average common stockholders' equity}} = \text{Rate of return on common stockholders' equity}$$

If there is only one class of stock outstanding, the rate of return is net income as a percentage of the average stockholders' equity, with the average being computed as a simple average of the balances at the beginning and at the end of the year or, if desired, an average of monthly balances.

Management sometimes tries to increase the rate of return on the owners' equity by using resources furnished by outsiders. If borrowed assets can be put to work to earn a return in excess of the interest cost, the owners will benefit. Suppose that $100,000 can be borrowed at 9 percent and put to work to earn 20 percent. The owners receive a net return after interest cost of $11,000 without any investment on their part. Using borrowed assets to enhance the return to the owners is called leverage or **trading on the equity.**

Leverage is frequently employed by finance companies, savings and loan institutions, and public utilities. The finance company, for example, many lend money at 9 percent interest. Without a fresh source of funds, a finance company would have to wait until payments were made on the loans before it could make additional loans. Instead of doing this, the company borrows money at, perhaps, 7 percent interest and pledges loans as security. The money obtained at 7 percent interest cost is loaned at 9 percent with the owners of the finance company receiving the advantage of the interest differential.

The effect of leverage is illustrated by the following example. Company A and Company B each possesses assets in the total amount of $1,000,000. Each company has current liabilities of $100,000. Company A has no long-term debt and has a stockholders' equity of $900,000. Company B, on the other hand, has $500,000 of 8 percent bonds payable and a stockholders' equity of $400,000. Summary balance sheet data as of December 31, 1985, are given as follows:

	Company A	Company B
Total assets	$1,000,000	$1,000,000
Equities:		
Current liabilities	$ 100,000	$ 100,000
Bonds payable, 8%	—0—	500,000
Stockholders' equity	900,000	400,000
Total equities...................................	$1,000,000	$1,000,000

Each company earns income before interest and income tax of $200,000, or, in other words, earns a 20 percent return on the assets before interest and income tax.

Summary income statement data for the two companies for 1985 are given as follows:

	Company A	Company B
Income before interest and income tax.............	$ 200,000	$ 200,000
Interest (8% of $500,000)........................	—0—	40,000
Income before income tax	$ 200,000	$ 160,000
Income tax (40%)	80,000	64,000
Net income	$ 120,000	$ 96,000
Total assets	$1,000,000	$1,000,000
Stockholders' equity	$ 900,000	$ 400,000
Rate of return on total assets....................	12%	9.6%
Rate of return on stockholders' equity	13.33%	24%

The rates of return on total assets and on stockholders' equity have been computed for each company after deducting both interest and income tax from income. The rate of return of 13.33 percent on the stockholders' equity of Company A is only slightly higher than the rate of return of 12 percent on the total assets. The leverage from the current liabilities accounts for this differential.

Company B earns a lower rate of return on total assets than Company A because of the interest on the bonds. But the rate of return on the stockholders' equity is much higher. The stockholders' investment in Company B is $500,000 less than in Company A; and the resources obtained from the bond issue earn more than the interest cost, as shown in the following computation:

Earnings on $500,000 furnished by the bondholders:		
Income before interest and income tax (20% of $500,000)		$100,000
Less income tax (40%)..		40,000
Income before interest, after income tax		$ 60,000
Cost of $500,000 furnished by the bondholder:		
Interest (8% of $500,000).....................................	$40,000	
Less income taxes (40%)......................................	16,000	
Interest after income tax		24,000
Net return for the stockholders		$ 36,000

The rate of return on the stockholders' equity is, of course, higher. The investment base is lower, and the bonds earn $36,000 for the owners net of interest and income tax.

Without Bond Leverage—Company A

$$\frac{\$120,000 \text{ net income}}{\$900,000 \text{ stockholders' equity}} = 13.33\% \text{ rate of return on stockholders' equity}$$

With Bond Leverage—Company B

$$\frac{\$\ 96,000 \text{ net income}}{\$400,000 \text{ stockholders' equity}} = 24\% \text{ rate of return on stockholders' equity}$$

Although there are advantages to leverage, there are also disadvantages. With leverage there is greater risk. Possibly the borrowed assets will not even earn the interest cost or may earn so little that the additional expected return is not worth the risk. When conditions are unfavorable, the owners of the leveraged company do not benefit from debt and in extreme cases may even have to relinquish control to the creditors.

Earnings and Market Value of Stock

The rate of return on stockholders' equity depends upon the earnings in relation to the total investment and the ways in which the total investment is financed. This rate of return as computed from data appearing on past financial statements may not necessarily be in agreement with the rate of return used by investors to determine the market price of the stock.

The market price of a stock depends upon many factors; one of the most important is anticipated future earnings. The market price of a stock should be approximately equal to the present value of the expected future earnings per share. The rate used to discount the future earnings is the rate desired by investors as determined by market conditions and conditions with the industry and within the company itself. Past earnings may serve as a guide as to what may be expected in the future, but the value of a stock depends upon future earnings rather than earnings in the past.

The net income for any one year may be stated on a unit basis as the earnings per share of outstanding stock. For example, a company with 1,000,000 shares of common stock outstanding may report a net income for the year of $2,500,000. Assuming that there is no dividend requirement on preferred stock, the earnings per common share are $2.50 ($2,500,000 net income ÷ 1,000,000 shares outstanding).

The price of a stock is sensitive to the prospects for future earnings, and investors establish the price on the basis of their estimates of the future and the rate of return that they expect on investments. The rate of return in the market may be considerably different than the rate of return computed from data appearing on the financial statements. This difference can be readily understood when it is recognized that the stockholders' equity on the balance sheet has resulted from past investments by the stockholders and reinvested earnings. The market rate of return, on the other hand, is not determined as a relationship between the net earnings of the past year and the stockholders' equity as it appears in the accounting records. Rather, it is a relationship between expected future earnings and the market value of the stock.

Sometimes a book value per share of stock is computed. The book value per share of stock is equal to the stockholders' equity identified with that class of stock divided by the number of shares outstanding. Assume that a company with one class of stock outstanding has a stockholders' equity of $35,000,000 with 1,000,000 shares of stock outstanding. The book value per share is then $35.

$$\frac{\text{Stockholders' equity}}{\substack{\text{Number of shares} \\ \text{outstanding}}} = \frac{\$35,000,000}{1,000,000} = \$35 \text{ book value per share}$$

The book value per share and the market price per share may differ widely, as would be expected, considering that the market price is determined by future anticipations while book value is determined by amounts recorded in the past. Normally the stock of a company with prospects for growth sells for a price that is considerably higher than book value. On the other hand, a company in a declining industry may sell for a price that is even less than book value.

COMPREHENSIVE ANALYSIS

The analysis of financial statements extends beyond the concept of earning power and encompasses both the income statement and the balance sheet. Data from both the income statement and the balance sheet may be brought together in the form of ratios to reveal important relationships. In short, statement analysis calls attention to the significant relationships that would otherwise be buried in a maze of detail.

Furthermore, the ratios pertaining to any given year cannot stand alone. There should be a basis for comparison between years and between companies. Ordinarily the statements and the ratios for the current year are presented along with the statements and the ratios for one or two preceding years so that improvements or deteriorations can be detected. Comparisons are made not only with the company's own past performance but also with the average performance of the industry.

SOME HAZARDS OF ANALYSIS

There are many pitfalls to be avoided in analysis; and, at best, statement analysis can be used as a rough approximation. However, it serves as a general guide, pointing to areas that need further management study and investigation.

A Mixture of Valuations

One of the most serious defects of analysis results from a mixture of dollar valuations on the financial statements. In Chapter 16 it was pointed out that dollars do not have the same purchasing power at all times and that, as a result, financial statements may include a mixture of dollar valuations. Relationships can be distorted if dollars of current purchasing power are compared with dollars having some other purchasing power. Data should be adjusted to a common purchasing power basis if relationships are to be meaningful.

Differences Between Companies

In comparing companies, inherent differences must be considered. A relationship that may indicate great risk for one company may be quite reasonable for another. For example, a company in a cyclical industry has a less certain profit and should have a smaller proportion of debt in its equity structure than an electric power company. The electric power company has a relatively stable market and can safely operate with a high proportion of debt. Therefore, there is little basis for comparison between two such companies.

Variations in Accounting Methods and Estimates

A comparison between companies is even more difficult when differences in methods of accounting are considered. Significant variations between companies are often caused by the methods of matching cost against revenue. One company, for example, may capitalize a cost and write it off against revenue in future years while another company elects to write off a similar cost in the year that it is incurred. Estimation also varies. One company may depreciate a unit of equipment over 10 years while another company depreciates a similar unit over 12 years. Both companies may be justified by differences in how the equipment is used in operations.

An Average Concept

There is always the risk that the data do not truly represent what has taken place throughout the year. To overcome this problem, data may be averaged either by taking an average of the beginning and ending balances or by obtaining monthly averages. For example, a relationship between outstanding balances due from customers and credit sales may show how rapidly collections are being made from customers. The amount shown for accounts receivable at the end of the year, however, may be abnormally high or low because of seasonality. A better measurement can be made by selecting an average balance that would be more typical of the situation throughout the year.

ILLUSTRATION OF ANALYSIS

Financial statements are given in thousands of dollars for Durban Products Inc. as shown below and on the next page.

Durban Products Inc.
Balance Sheet
December 31, 1985, 1984 and 1983
(In thousands of dollars)

	1985	1984	1983
Assets			
Current assets:			
Cash	$ 488	$ 523	$ 384
Accounts receivable, net of uncollectibles	2,130	1,145	520
Inventories:			
Finished goods	1,033	617	426
Materials	1,157	738	282
Prepaid expenses	14	37	23
Total current assets	$ 4,822	$3,060	$1,635
Plant assets, net of accumulated depreciation	8,418	6,748	3,427
Total assets	$13,240	$9,808	$5,062
Equities			
Current liabilities:			
Accounts payable	$ 1,951	$ 637	$ 215
Notes payable	100	80	50
Other current liablities	1,044	523	158
Total current liabilities	$ 3,095	$1,240	$ 423
Long-term notes payable	4,000	3,500	—0—
Stockholders' equity:			
Capital stock, $1 par value	300	300	300
Paid-in capital in excess of par value	1,250	1,250	1,250
Retained earnings	4,595	3,518	3,089
Total equities	$13,240	$9,808	$5,062

In the following income statement, the percentage of increase or decrease of each item over the base year 1983 is given beside the dollar amounts. The trend percentages are helpful in that they call attention to large proportionate changes, but they can be misleading if used improperly. The percentages of increase computed on a small base may be large, but the dollar amount involved may be relatively insignificant. For example, an increase from $20 to $60 is an increase of 200 percent; but the absolute amount of increase is only $40. On the other hand an increase of $100,000 measured from a base of

Durban Products Inc.
Income Statement
For the Years Ended December 31, 1985, 1984 and 1983
(In thousands of dollars)

				Percentages— Increase or (Decrease)	
				1985 over	1984 over
	1985	1984	1983	1983	1983
Net sales..................	$15,240	$5,811	$3,140	385.4%	85.1%
Cost of goods sold.........	11,787	3,933	1,632	622.2%	141.0%
Gross margin	$ 3,453	$1,878	$1,508	129.0%	24.5%
Operating expenses	1,127	915	739	52.5%	23.8%
Operating income	$ 2,326	$ 963	$ 769	202.5%	25.2%
Interest expense	430	148	5	8500.0%	2860.0%
Income before income tax...	$ 1,896	$ 815	$ 764	148.2%	6.7%
Provision for income tax	759	326	306	148.0%	6.5%
Net income	$ 1,137	$ 489	$ 458	148.3%	6.8%
Depreciation included in cost of goods sold and operating expenses.......	$ 486	$ 317	$ 184	164.1%	72.3%

$400,000 is stated as an increase of only 25%. Thus, one must consider the dollar amount of increase or decrease as well as the percentage.

A common base year should be used consistently in making the computations. Comparison is more difficult if base years are changed. For Durban Products Inc. 1983 was used as the base year, and the results for 1984 and 1985 were both related to that year. Normally the earliest year in a series is used as a base. A percentage of change can be computed only if there is a positive amount for the base year.

A Review of Earning Power

For purposes of illustration, it is assumed that the average amounts of the assets and the equities for the year are equivalent to the balances at the end of the year. It is also assumed that the dollar amounts are on the same price-level basis and that they can be compared in other respects. Dividends of 20 cents a share, a total amount of $60,000, were declared and paid in each of the three years.

In absolute terms, net sales and net income have increased; yet, as shown in the following table, the percentage of net income to net sales has decreased, indicating that cost in total has increased at a faster rate than revenue. Operating expenses, however, have decreased as a percentage of net sales while the cost of goods sold has increased relative to sales as shown by the much lower gross margin rate. The substantial reduction in gross margin percentage indicates that perhaps the mix of products sold may have changed, with a greater proportion of less profitable lines being sold. The cost of the merchandise also may have increased relative to selling prices. Various factors may account for changes in the rate of gross margin, and investigation may reveal possibilities for corrections.

Earning Power Relationships

Percentages, Net Income, and Dividends per Share	1985	1984	1983
(1) Net income to net sales*	7.5%	8.4%	14.6%
(2) Gross margin rate	22.7%	32.3%	48.0%
(3) Percentage of oeparting expense to net sales	7.4%	15.7%	23.5%
(4) Net income to total assets*	8.6%	5.0%	9.0%
(5) Net income to stockholders' equity*	18.5%	9.6%	9.9%
(6) Net income per share	$3.79	$1.63	$1.53
(7) Dividends per share	$.20	$.20	$.20
(8) Net income	$1,137,000	$489,000	$458,000
(9) Total assets	$13,240,000	$9,808,000	$5,062,000
(10) Total stockholders' equity.................	$6,145,000	$5,068,000	$4,639,000
(11) Number of shares of stock outstanding	300,000	300,000	300,000

*Also referred to as rate of return on sales (1), total assets (4), or stockholders' equity (5).

The rate of return on total assets decreased in 1984 but returned to almost the 1983 level in 1985. This percentage in 1985 was somewhat higher than the percentage of net income to net sales, indicating that the assets turned over more than once during the year.

$$\frac{\text{Net sales}}{\text{Total assets}} = \frac{\$15,240,000}{\$13,240,000} = 1.15 \text{ asset turnover}$$

The rate of return on total assets is then equal to 1.15 times the rate of return on net sales. The calculation is made as follows:

7.5% return on net sales × 1.15 turnover = 8.6% return on total assets

The rate of return on the stockholders' equity each year is greater than the rate of return on the total assets, and the difference in 1985 is much greater than it was in 1983. This means that the company is making more use of leverage. On the basis of the information given, no judgment can be made as to whether or not leverage is justified. If the company is in a cyclical industry, debt can be a handicap. If business declines, it may become difficult to pay the interest and to retire the debt according to schedule. It appears, however, that Durban Products Inc. may have sacrificed some safety for potentially greater growth. The net income per share has increased from year to year, and the dividends are well covered. Management has tried to finance a part of the growth by a retention of earnings. The expansion in plant assets, however, has been financed to a large extent by long-term debt. Further evaluation depends upon a more complete analysis of the company as viewed against the backdrop of the industry.

The Management of Working Capital

The current assets of a business are put to active use in conducting operations and are sometimes called working capital. The term "working capital" is also applied to the excess of the current assets over the current liabilities. To avoid any misunderstanding, the excess of current assets over current liabilities will be referred to in this text as net working capital

There is a very close relationship between the income statement and the current assets and current liabilities on the balance sheet. For example, materials and services may be purchased on credit terms with the liability being shown as a current liability. Costs identified with the products appear under the inventories caption in the current asset classification. When the inventories are sold to customers, the accounts receivable is increased by the amounts billed, and the inventory cost is reduced by the cost of the goods delivered. Ultimately, cash is realized from the accounts receivable and applied to the reduction of the current liabilities arising out of operating transactions. If the business is successful, it should generate more cash than it uses in operations. This cash may be used to acquire plant assets or investments, to retire long-term debt, to increase net working capital, or to make payments of dividends to the stockholders.

Within certain limits, the operating cycle should be repeated as frequently as possible. The inventories should be converted rapidly into accounts receivable and cash, current obigations should be paid, and the cycle should be started again. Limitations are imposed, however, by the nature of the business and by the investment required to support business volume. In some lines of business, rapid turnover cannot be expected. In the shipbuilding industry, for example, materials cannot be converted quickly into a finished product. The nature of the product, the time required for its production, and the demand for the product according to the season have an effect upon the rapidity of the conversion of current assets.

A company that earns a relatively low return on sales may be able to maintain a satisfactory rate of return on its investment by a rapid turnover of that investment. On the other hand, if the return on sales is fairly high, the rate earned on the investment can be maintained with a lower turnover.

Current Asset Turnover

Sometimes the ratio of cost of goods sold and expenses to current assets, the current asset turnover, is computed. In computing current asset turnover, depreciation should be eliminated from the cost of goods sold and expenses because the depreciation charge for the year is not dependent upon current assets.

A rapid turnover of current assets generally indicates that the current assets are more liquid. Inventories are probably not being built up needlessly if the ratio of cost of goods sold and expenses to current assets is fairly high, considering the nature of the industry. Other things being equal, increased turnover should result in a better rate of return on current assets and on total assets. This is true, however, only if the profit per turnover can be maintained.

Turnover in itself does not give the complete answer. Turnover may increase, but if the rate of return per turnover decreases, there may be a smaller rate of return on total assets. In fact, an increase in the current asset turnover may indicate that the company is trying to support too large a volume of business on its current investment.

The current asset turnover analysis for Durban Products Inc. follows:

Current Asset Turnover and Rate of Return

	1985	1984	1983
Cost of goods sold and operating expenses, less depreciation	$12,428,000	$4,531,000	$2,187,000
Current assets	$ 4,822,000	$3,060,000	$1,635,000
Net income	$ 1,137,000	$ 489,000	$ 458,000
Current asset turnover	2.58 times	1.48 times	1.34 times
Rate of return on current assets	23.6%	16.0%	28.0%
Rate of return per turnover (Rate of return ÷ Number of turnovers)	9.1%	10.8%	20.9%

The turnover has increased since 1983. Both rate of return on current assets and the rate of return per turnover were lower in 1985 than in 1983. This indicates that the current assets are being worked harder but that they are earning less.

Current and Acid-Test Ratios

The general ability of a company to meet its short-term indebtedness is measured by the current ratio. The current ratio is the ratio of current assets to current liabilities. Although a ratio of 2 to 1 has often been singled out as desirable, this rule of thumb is not necessarily valid. Ratios will vary in different industries. In fact, some companies may operate quite satisfactorily with ratios of only slightly more than 1 to 1.

The current ratio for Durban Products Inc. was more than 3 to 1 at the end of 1983 but has decreased to less than 2 to 1 at the end of 1985. The current assets have increased, but the current liabilities have increased by an even greater rate.

Current Ratio

	1985	1984	1983
Current assets	$4,822,000	$3,060,000	$1,635,000
Current liabilities	$3,095,000	$1,240,000	$423,000
Current ratio	1.56	2.47	3.87

A more rigorous measurement of the company's ability to service short-term debt is made by excluding inventories and prepaid expenses from current assets in computing the ratio. The so-called quick assets consisting of cash, marketable securities, and accounts receivable are divided by the current liabilities in the computation of the acid-test ratio. It is generally considered that dollar in quick assets should lie behind each dollar of current debt.

Acid-Test Ratio

	1985	1984	1983
Quick assets	$2,618,000	$1,668,000	$904,000
Current liabilities	$3,095,000	$1,240,000	$423,000
Acid-test ratio	.85	1.35	2.14

The substantial decrease of the acid-test ratio since 1983 indicates that the company is much less liquid at the end of 1985 than it was at the end of 1983.

Accounts Receivable Turnover

Analysis of the working capital can be extended further to determine how long it takes for inventories and accounts receivable to be converted into cash.

When the customers accounts are collected promptly with little loss or collection expense, it is much easier to meet obligations when they become due. But if there is a severe time lag in the collection of accounts receivable, this may have an adverse effect upon a company's ability to pay its debts. Conversely, higher turnovers may offset a lower current ratio. An approximation of the average time required to collect accounts receivable can be calculated by dividing the net credit sales by the average balances of accounts receivable that are outstanding. The turnover, referred to as the accounts receivable turnover, can be converted into the number of days that sales are in accounts receivable by dividing the turnover into 360 (or 365) days.

It is assumed that Durban Products Inc. made all of its sales on credit and that the ending accounts receivable can be considered to be typical of the balances throughout the year. The following accounts receivable turnover computations show that Durban Products Inc. has increased turnover, thereby reducing the collection period.

Accounts Receivable Turnover

	1985	1984	1983
Net credit sales	$15,240,000	$5,811,000	$3,140,000
Accounts receivable	$2,130,000	$1,145,000	$ 520,000
Accounts receivable turnover	7.15 times	5.08 times	6.04 times
Number of days sales in accounts receivable (360 days ÷ Number of turnovers)	50 days	71 days	60 days

Inventory Turnovers

Turnovers can also be computed for the inventory investments. A turnover of the average investment in materials is calculated by dividing the cost of materials used during the year by the average investment in materials. Too high a ratio may indicate that the inventory balance is too low. Orders then have to be placed more frequently, and there is a risk of production slowdowns because of insufficient materials. Conversely, a low ratio may call attention to an investment that is too high in relation to the production requirements. Funds may be needlessly tied up in materials inventory.

An inventory turnover of finished goods is calculated by dividing the cost of goods sold by the average finished goods inventory. The average number of days that sales are in inventory can also be calculated. In addition, the gross margin per inventory turnover may be computed as an indication of profitability in relation to inventory movement. These computations for Durban Products Inc. are shown as follows:

Finished Goods Turnover

	1985	1984	1983
Cost of goods sold	$11,787,000	$3,933,000	$1,632,000
Average inventory of finished goods.........	$1,033,000	$617,000	$426,000
Inventory turnover.......................	11.4 times	6.4 times	3.8 times
Number of days' sales in inventory (360 days ÷ Number of turnovers)	32 days	56 days	95 days
Gross margin	$3,453,000	$1,878,000	$1,508,000
Gross margin per turnover (Gross margin ÷ Number of turnovers) ...	$302,895	$293,438	$396,842

The ratios show that Durban has not increased its investment in finished goods in relation to sales. Inventory turnover has improved.

The inventory turnover is significant, but it is also important to find out how much is being earned per turnover. A company may be moving its inventories more rapidly and be more liquid, but the amount earned for each turnover or even the total earned may be less. Durban Products Inc. increased its turnover of inventory but earned less per turnover in 1985 than in 1983. The company earned a larger total gross margin in 1985 by more rapid inventory turnover. However, the company earned less in proportion to inventory investment.

The Equity Relationships

Ordinarily, as a company progresses, the owners' proportionate share in the total equity should increase or at least should be maintained at some established level. When the relative interest of outsiders is increased, there is an advantage to the owners in that they get the benefit of a return on assets furnished by others; yet in gaining this advantage there is increased risk. The relative interests of the various equity holders in Durban Products Inc. are given at the end of each of the three years:

	1985	1984	1983
Current liabilities	23.4%	12.6%	8.4%
Long-term liabilities	30.2	35.7	−0−
Stockholders' equity	46.4	51.7	91.6
	100.0%	100.0%	100.0%

The proportionate interest of the owners has declined substantially since 1983. However, in 1983 the company had very little debt in its equity structure and was not getting much benefit from leverage. On the other hand, there may be too much debt in the equity structure at the end of 1985. Justification of greater risk depends on the level and stability of future earnings.

Net Income and Fixed Charges

Risk has many aspects, but one important aspect concerns the fixed charges imposed against earnings. Resources obtained from outsiders can be used to produce increased profit for the stockholders. However, a fixed charge is imposed for the use of these resources. For example, rental payments must be made for leased equipment, interest must be paid on debt, and dividends must be paid on preferred stock. If the level of revenue drops enough, the company may not be able to meet its fixed charge obligations; thus both the outsiders who have furnished resources and the stockholders may suffer losses.

A computation may be made of the number of times that fixed charges are covered by earnings. This computation is made by dividing the income before the charges are deducted by the fixed charges. Durban Products Inc. had no fixed charges aside from interest, and the computations for the company are given as follows:

Times Interest Earned

	1985	1984	1983
Operating income	$2,326,000	$963,000	$769,000
Interest	$430,000	$148,000	$5,000
Times interest earned	5.4 times	6.5 times	153.8 times

The interest charges are well covered, but the trend indicates increasing risk.

An Evaluation of the Company

One particular percentage or relationship may not be too significant in itself. Taken together, however, the results of analysis help to point out areas that require attention.

Durban Products Inc. has grown considerably since 1983, and there are many favorable points. Sales volume has increased; and even with a reduced gross margin rate, the rate of return on assets in 1985 is about equal to the rate of return in 1983. Operating expenses appear to be under control and are not increasing proportionately. Inventories appear to be turning over well, and collections on accounts receivable are proceeding at a faster rate.

However, there are also some weak spots. It appears that the company may have been too conservative in 1983 but has gone to the other extreme in 1985. With an increased proportion of debt in the equity structure in 1985, the company is under more strain financially. Obligations will be more difficult to meet, and the question may be raised as to whether or not there is sufficient net working capital to support the larger scale of operation.

The equity structure should be balanced by the issuance of more capital stock. This gives the stockholders a larger proportionate interest in the firm, thereby reducing the risk and providing net working capital to support the expanded scale of operation.

Terminology Review

Rate of return (505)
Income from continuing
    operation (506)
Asset turnover (507)
Leverage (513)
Earnings per share (515)
Book value per share (516)
Working capital (521)

Net working capital (521)
Current asset turnover (521)
Current ratio (522)
Quick assets (523)
Acid test ratio (523)
Accounts receivable turnover (523)
Inventory turnover (524)
Fixed charge (525)

QUESTIONS FOR REVIEW

1. What three basic questions can be answered by statement analysis?

2. How is rate of return on sales computed? On assets? On owners' equity?

3. What is asset turnover? What effect does a higher asset turnover tend to have on the rate of return on assets? Give a logical explanation for this effect on the rate of return on assets.

4. If management is unable to increase asset turnover, what other alternatives may be used to improve the rate of return on assets?

5. If rate of return is to be used to evaluate management at the operating level, what adjustments should be made to net income and to the assets?

6. How can there be a disadvantage in having more assets than are needed?

7. Is it possible to substitute one factor of production for another? Explain.

8. Explain how the asset base is determined in computing the rate of return for a segment of a business.

9. Explain how the rate of return for the total business may be considerably lower than the rate of return for any of the segments.

10. The rate of return will tend to increase as the asset base is reduced by depreciation. Explain how this effect can be avoided through a more accurate computation of the rate of return.

11. What is leverage? Explain how it works.

12. Explain the difference between the market value of a share of stock and its book value.

13. List some of the pitfalls to be avoided in the analysis of financial statements.

14. What is indicated by an increased current asset turnover with a lower rate of return per turnover?

15. In general, what is being measured by the current ratio and by the acid-test ratio? What is the difference between the two ratios?

16. If net credit sales for the year are $15,000,000 and the average accounts receivable are $3,000,000, how many days does it take to collect accounts receivable on the average?

17. If the cost of goods sold is $7,200,000 and the average inventory of merchandise is $600,000, how many days does it take to convert inventory to sales on the average?

18. If it has been determined that accounts receivable should be collected in 40 days and that inventory turns over every 30 days, how long is the operating cycle?

19. Why is a computation made to determine how many times fixed charges are earned?

20. What may be indicated by an evaluation that shows a sharp increase in the current ratio and a rate of return on stockholders' equity that is approaching the rate of return on assets?

EXERCISES

1. Rate of Return. Colorado Bindery Inc. earned $620,000 on net sales of $12,400,000 during 1985. The average investment in assets during the year was $3,100,000.

Required:

    (1) Compute the rate of return on net sales.

    (2) Compute the rate of return on the average asset investment.

    (3) Compute the asset turnover.

2. Changing the Rate of Return Relationships. For several years Gator Supply Company has earned 5% on net sales with an asset turnover of 3.2 each year. With new product lines, net sales are estimated at $8,000,000 next year with the rate of return on net sales increasing to 10%. The average investment in assets is estimated at $2,000,000 for next year.

Required:

    (1) Compute the former rate of return on assets.

    (2) Compute the new asset turnover.

    (3) What is the new expected rate of return on assets?

3. Comparability of Data. Judy Kargle boasts that she has been earning 30% on her investment in Pride Metals each year. The net income has averaged at $450,000 each year, and the assets invested cost $1,500,000. You have examined the data and find that the depreciation charges should have been on a current dollar basis and that net income was really only $300,000. The assets when revised to current values should be shown at $2,400,000.

Required:

    (1) Show how Kargle computed the 30% rate of return on assets.

    (2) Compute the correct rate of return on assets.

4. Changing Rate of Return Relationships. Last year Wessex Company reported a net income of $720,000 on net sales of $24,000,000. The average investment in assets for the year was $4,000,000. This year the company has changed some of its product lines and plans to earn a net income of $1,080,000 on net sales of $18,000,000. The average investment in assets for the year can be reduced to $3,000,000 because of the reduced requirement for inventories for the new product lines.

Required:

    (1) Compute the rate of return on net sales, the asset turnover, and the rate of return on average assets for last year.

    (2) Compute the rate of return on net sales, the asset turnover, and the rate of return on average assets for the year.

    (3) Comment on the changes that are expected to yield a better rate of return on average assets this year.

5. Turnover and Rate of Return Relationships. In the following situations outlined, compute the rate of return on net sales, the asset turnover, or the net sales as requested.

    (1) What is the rate of return on net sales if the asset turnover is 3.5 and 14% is earned on the assets?

    (2) Sales for the year were $15,000,000 and the average asset investment was $6,000,000. Determine the asset turnover.

(3) Assets are turned over 2.2 times in earning 6% on net sales. What is the rate of return on the assets?

(4) With an asset turnover of 3.6, what must the rate of return be on net sales if the rate of return on the assets is to be 18%?

(5) The return on the assets has been computed at 15%. The net income was $600,000, and the asset turnover was 1.5. You do not have the net sales figure but you have been asked to give the amount of net sales and the rate of return on the sales dollar.

(6) If the total cost of operation excluding income tax amounts to $2,700,000, compute net sales if the net income is 6% of net sales. The income tax has been computed at $120,000.

(7) The rate of return on net sales has remained at 4% for the past two years. The asset turnover in the first year was 4.5 and declined to 3.8 in the second year. Compute the rate of return on assets for each of the two years.

(8) Net sales for the year were $7,200,000. Assets turned over 1.8 times during the year. Cost of goods sold and operating expenses including income tax amounted to $6,552,000. Compute the rate of return on net sales and on total assets.

6. Revised Rate of Return Computations. Ben Clymonds has computed the rate of return on assets for Stone Hill Company at 15% with an asset turnover of 2.5 and a return of 6% on the sales dollar. Net sales for the year were $5,000,000 with a net income of $300,000 and an average investment in assets of $2,000,000.

You have found that depreciation after income tax should be increased by $100,000 to place it on a current dollar basis. Also, the current cost to replace the average investment in assets would be $4,000,000.

Required: Make revised computations for:

(1) the rate of return on net sales.

(2) the rate of return on the average assets, and

(3) the asset turnover.

7. Asset Base and Rate of Return. The president of Meckley Patterns Company has tried to handle a large volume of sales on a small asset base. For example, last year the company earned 4% on net sales of $6,000,000. The average asset base for the year was $1,200,000. This year the company planned to increase sales volume even more but through inability to meet delivery schedules to customers promptly, had net sales of only $5,000,000. The rate of return on net sales was the same, and the asset base still averaged at $1,200,000.

Required:

(1) Compute the asset turnover and the rate of return on assets for last year.

(2) Compute the asset turnover and the rate of return on assets for the current year.

(3) Explain why the company may have been in a poor position to sustain sales volume.

8. Depreciation and Rate of Return. Herd and Porter Inc. has a plant and equipment in operation at June 30, 1985, with a cost of $1,600,000. Accumulated depreciation of

$1,200,000 has been deducted. If the plant and equipment were replaced at June 30, 1985, the cost of replacement would be $4,000,000. Estimated accumulated depreciation on replacement cost is $2,800,000. During the year ended June 30, 1985, the company reported a net income of $120,000. based on replacement cost, the depreciation for the fiscal year would be higher, and the resulting net income would be only $20,000.

Required: (1) Compute the rate of return on the plant and equipment, using the original cost net of accumulated depreciation.

(2) Compute the rate of return using replacement cost net of accumulated depreciation on the replacement cost.

9. Depreciation and Rate of Return. The management of Donahue Company is concerned that the rate of return is inflated by computing the return with net income computed in mixed dollars of purchasing power and plant assets at original cost net of accumulated depreciation. For example, the rate of return on net plant assets last year was 28.6% computed with a net income of $200,000 and net plant assets of $700,000. The current value of the plant assets in their present condition is estimated at $1,500,000, and net income, revised to show current dollar revenue and expense, has been recomputed at $60,000.

Required: Compute the revised rate of return on the plant assets.

10. Segment Rate of Return. Tarheel Chemical Company produces and sells three major product lines, each line being produced in a separate division. The president of the company wants to know what the rate of return is for each division and for the company in total.

Data pertaining to the operation for last year are as follows:

	Net Income	Average Assets
Division 1	$20,000	$2,000,000
Division 2	60,000	480,000
Division 3	60,000	1,800,000

The average assets are the assets directly identifiable with the divisions. In addition, there are corporate assets (averaged) of $720,000 that are not directly identifiable with any division. Expenses, after deducting the effect of income taxes that are common to the total operation, have been allocated to the three divisions in computation of net income. These corporate expenses were $300,000 in total and were allocated 40:20:40.

Required: Compute the rate of return on average assets for each division and for the company in total. (Carry to three decimal places.)

11. Segment Rate of Return. A rate of return on assets has been computed for Wade and Hartzell Inc. Wade and Hartzell has a metals division and a plastics division.

	Metals Division	Plastics Division	Total
Sales...	$700,000	$500,000	$1,200,000
Cost of goods sold	$400,000	$200,000	$ 600,000
Direct expenses of division	100,000	50,000	150,000
Indirect expenses of division........................	50,000	100,000	150,000
Total	$550,000	$350,000	$ 900,000
Income from operations	$150,000	$150,000	$ 300,000
Average assets directly identified with division	$600,000	$750,000	$1,350,000
Average assets allocated to divisions	150,000	150,000	300,000
Total assets	$750,000	$900,000	$1,650,000
Rate of return on assets	20%	16.7%	18.2%

Required: Compute a revised rate of return for each of the two divisions.

12. Leverage and Rate of Return. Jay Hummer plans to invest his time and resources in a firm that will provide video equipment and small computers for the household market. Hummer can invest personally $500,000 and plans to borrow another $500,000 with interest at the rate of 12% per year.

At the very least, he estimates net sales for the year at $1,500,000 with a gross margin of 40% percent. Operating expenses have been budgeted at a fixed amount of $280,000 for the year. There is a reasonable prospect that net sales for the year could amount to $2,000,000 with the same gross margin rate and operating expenses. Income tax is estimated at 40% of income before income tax.

Hummer can earn a rate of return of 20% on other investment situations and wants to earn at least 25% on this business to compensate for the additional risk.

Required:

(1) Does it appear that Hummer's investment will yield the required return objective on net sales of $1,500,000? On net sales of $2,000,000? Show computations.

(2) Compute the estimated rate of return on total assets under both sales estimates.

13. Leverage and Rate of Return. In 1983 Dendros Supply Company reported income before interest and income tax of $1,600,000. Total liabilities and stockholders' equity at the end of that year were as follows:

Current liabilities, excluding short-term notes	$ 1,000,000
Short-term notes payable, interest at 12% per annum	2,500,000
Long-term notes payable, 10% interest per annum	4,500,000
Stockholders' equity	4,000,000
Total equities..	$12,000,000

The president stated that the use of debt in financing has helped to improve the rate of return for the stockholders.

In 1984 the equity structure of the firm was approximately the same as it was the year before. However, the rate of interest on short-term notes increased to 18% and long-term debt was refinanced at 16%. Income before interest and income tax decreased to $1,200,000. Income tax is computed at 40% of income before income tax.

Required:

(1) Is the president correct in stating that the use of financing has helped to improve the rate of return for the stockholders? Explain.

(2) Compute the rate of return after interest and income tax on the total assets and on the owners' equity for 1983. (Assume that the equities are the average equities for the year.)

(3) Compute the rate of return after interest and income tax on the total assets and on the owners' equity for 1984. (Assume that the equities are the average equities for the year.)

14. Current Asset Turnover. The Bio-Chemical Company has grown rapidly, increasing net income from $180,000 in 1984 to $650,000 in 1985. Cost of goods sold and operating expenses excluding depreciation amounted to $560,000 in 1984 and $2,700,000 in 1985. The average investment in current assets was $840,000 in 1984 and $900,000 in 1985. The company had some difficulties in meeting delivery schedules in 1985 and in making payments to creditors.

Required:

(1) Compute the rate of return on current assets each year.
(2) Compute the current asset turnover for each year.
(3) What was the rate of return per turnover each year?
(4) Can you explain why the company may be having trouble in meeting delivery schedules and in making payments to creditors?

15. Inventory Turnovers. Pam Adams, the president of Illinois Stores Inc. has been concerned about the relatively slow turnover of inventory and the gross margin. Some new product lines that require less investment in inventory and yield better gross margins were substituted for older lines in 1985.

Data for 1984 and 1985 are given as follows:

	1984	1985
Net sales	$3,600,000	$4,000,000
Cost of goods sold	2,700,000	2,600,000
Average inventory	900,000	650,000

Required:

(1) Compute the inventory turnovers for 1984 and 1985.
(2) Determine the gross margin for each year.
(3) What was the gross margin per turnover.
(4) Has the inventory and gross margin situation improved in 1985?

16. Accounts Receivable Turnovers. The credit and collection department of Oberlin Mills has been concerned about the slower rate of collections on credit sales. This slowdown in collections has made it necessary for the company to obtain more short-term credit to finance operations. A summary of sales and collection data are given as follows:

	1984	1983	1982
Cash sales	$535,000	$576,000	$640,000
Credit sales	567,000	612,000	680,000
Accounts receivable, beginning of year	72,000	64,000	72,000
Accounts receivable, end of year	90,000	72,000	64,000

The president of the company believes that decreased sales volume and general economic conditions are largely responsible for the problem.

Required:

(1) Compute the accounts receivable turnovers for each of the three years.

(2) Compute the number of days per turnover.

(3) Comment on the belief of the president.

17. Improving the Ratios. A new management started with Odenweiler Mills Inc. on July 1, 1984. A review of the operations shows that a large proportion of the assets are not being utilized and could be retired.

Data from the financial statements on July 1, 1984, appear as follows:

Current assets	$ 600,000
Plant and equipment, net of accumulated depreciation	2,400,000
Total assets	$3,000,000
Current liabilities	$ 400,000
Long-term debt	800,000
Stockholders' equity	1,800,000
Total equities	$3,000,000

The company plans to sell equipment having a net book value of $500,000 with no gain or loss on the transaction. Proceeds from the sale will be held as current assets with the current liabilities being reduced to $200,000 by June 30, 1985.

Net income is estimated at $240,000 for the fiscal year ended June 30, 1985. Depreciation of $100,000 after income tax will be deducted during the fiscal year ended June 30, 1985. No dividends are to be paid.

Required:

(1) Compute the following ratios and percentages at July 1, 1984:

(a) Current ratio.

(b) Percentage of stockholders' equity to total equity.

(2) Compute the following ratios and percentages for the fiscal year ended June 30, 1985:

(a) Current ratio.

(b) Rate of return on total assets at June 30, 1985.

(c) Rate of return on stockholders' equity at June 30, 1985.

(d) Percentage of stockholders' equity to total equity at June 30, 1985.

(3) Comment as to whether or not the company improved its position with respect to liquidity and safety.

18. Net Income and Fixed Charges. Starke Supply Company must make substantial payments each year on equipment it leases from others. In addition, there is interest to be paid on debt each year. Both the company and its creditors are concerned about whether or not the company can meet these obligations each year inasmuch as sales volume has been decreasing.

A condensed income statement is given for each of the past three years.

	1985	1984	1983
Net sales	$1,260,000	$1,580,000	$1,740,000
Cost of goods sold	$ 695,000	$ 870,000	$ 975,000
Operating expenses excluding rent	210,000	230,000	245,000
Rent expense	130,000	130,000	155,000
Interest expense	125,000	125,000	125,000
Income tax	40,000	90,000	100,000
Total expenses	$1,200,000	$1,445,000	$1,600,000
Net income	$ 60,000	$ 135,000	$ 140,000

Required:

(1) Determine how many times the fixed charges were earned for each of the three years.

(2) Does it appear that the coverage of fixed charges is sufficient? Has it improved over the years?

PROBLEMS

17-1. Rate of Return Relationships. David Wright, as manager of product development, has introduced a new line of product that is expected to yield a gross margin of 40%. Sales of this product line have been estimated at $900,000 for the coming year. All earlier product lines are to be discontinued.

Last year the company had sales of $900,000 with a gross profit rate of 20%. Operating expenses were $120,000 last year and are expected to remain at this level next year.

The average investment in assets last year and for the next year is expected to be $250,000.

Income tax is 40% of income before income tax.

Required:

    (1) Compute the rate of return on sales for each year.

    (2) Compute the rate of return on average assets for each year.

17-2. Rate of Return Relationships. Ellinger Foods Inc. earns a small rate of return on the sales dollar but is able to turn assets over quickly and earn a better rate of return on the assets. Data for 1984 are given as follows:

RRA = 15

Net sales...	$4,600,000
Net income	138,000
Average assets	920,000
Average stockholders' equity	690,000

    The Caffrey Manufacturing Company earns a relatively large rate of return on the sales dollar but is not able to turn assets over quickly and, as a result, earns a lower rate of return on average assets. Data for 1984 are given as follows:

RRA = 500

Net sales...	$5,200,000
Net income	1,040,000
Average assets	6,500,000
Average stockholders' equity	5,200,000

Required:

    (1) Compute the rate of return on sales for both companies, the asset turnover, the rate of return on average assets, and the rate of return on average stockholders' equity.

    (2) Which company has the better rate of return on average assets? On average stockholders' equity?

17-3. Comparison of Rates of Return. Stable Products Company earns a relatively low profit margin on sales while Recreation Industries handles much less volume but earns a much better return on the sales dollar. Summarized financial statements for the two companies are given for 1984.

Income Statement

For the Year Ended December 31, 1984

	Stable Products Company	Recreation Industries
Net sales	$8,700,000	$3,160,000
Cost of goods sold and expenses	8,178,000	2,370,000
Net income	$ 522,000	$ 790,000

Balance Sheet
December 31, 1984

	Stable Products Company	Recreation Industries
Assets		
Current assets	$2,100,000	$1,650,000
Plant assets	3,700,000	2,300,000
Total assets	$5,800,000	$3,950,000
Equities		
Current liabilities	$ 450,000	$ 790,000
Long-term debt	1,000,000	—0—
Stockholders' equity	4,350,000	3,160,000
Total equities	$5,800,000	$3,950,000

Required:

(1) Compare the two companies by computing the following percentages and ratios.
    (a) Rate of return on sales.
    (b) Rate of return on assets.
    (c) Rate of return on stockholders' equity.
    (d) Asset turnover.

(2) Which company earns a better rate of return for the stockholders? Point out factors that help to enhance the rate of return for the stockholders.

17-4. Adjustments for Rate of Return. Karen Silfies is responsible for evaluating investment candidates for a mutual fund. Silfies is presently examining Aster Company that reported a rate of return of 30% on assets last year.

Data drawn from the financial statements of Aster Company last year are as follows:

Net sales	$12,000,000
Net income	1,800,000
Average assets	6,000,000

Further investigation shows that on a current cost basis, cost of goods sold after considering the effect of income tax would have been higher by $300,000, and that depreciation on a current cost basis after allowing for the income tax effect should have been higher by $500,000.

Also, on a current cost basis, the average assets should be stated at $8,000,000.

Required:

(1) Compute the rate of return on sales, the asset turnover, and the rate of return on average assets from the unadjusted data.

(2) Compute the rate of return on sales, the asset turnover, and the rate of return on average assets for Silfies from the adjusted data.

17-5. Rates of Return by Segments. The president of Javelin Parts Company has been going over financial data for 1984 and is concerned that one of the operating divisions is not doing as well as the others. The company manufactures three different lines of product in three separate operating divisions. Financial data from 1984 are given as follows:

	Product Divisions		
	1	*2*	*3*
Net sales	$800,000	$ 920,000	$ 760,000
Cost of goods sold	$430,000	$ 515,000	$ 320,000
Operating expenses...............................	180,000	230,000	140,000
Total expenses	$610,000	$ 745,000	$ 460,000
Net income	$190,000	$ 175,000	$ 300,000
Supporting asset investment	$950,000	$1,750,000	$1,200,000
Rate of return on assets	20%	10%	25%

Closer examination reveals that some of the operating expenses are common to the total operation and have been allocated to the divisions as follows:

Divisions	Allocated Expenses
1	$ 30,000
2	100,000
3	20,000

Also included in the assets are amounts pertaining to the total operation but not identifiable with any particular division. The amounts that have been allocated to the divisions are given as follows:

Divisions	Allocated Assets
1	$ 50,000
2	550,000
3	200,000

Required:

(1) From the information given, recompute the rate of return for each division and for the total operation. Carry answers to the third decimal place.

(2) Why was the rate of return for Division 2, as originally computed, relatively low?

17-6. Comparative Relationships. Betty Stevens is president of a company that she and a group of associates acquired three years ago. New product lines have been substituted in order to improve profitability. While Stevens knows that some progress has been made, you are asked, as the accountant, to examine the financial statements and to compute some important relationships. Summarized income statements are given as follows:

Income Statements
(In thousands of dollars)

	1985	1984	1983
Net sales	$2,160	$1,080	$850
Cost of goods sold and operating expenses excluding depreciation . .	$1,528	$ 772	$683
Depreciation	200	200	150
Total	$1,728	$ 972	$833
Net income	$ 432	$ 108	$ 17

A balance sheet in summarized form is given at the end of 1982, when the company was acquired. Balance sheets are also given at the end of each of the subsequent years.

Balance Sheets
December 31
(In thousands of dollars)

	1985	1984	1983	1982
Assets				
Current assets	$ 957	$ 525	$ 417	$ 250
Plant assets, net of accumulated depreciation	1,000	1,200	1,400	1,550
Total assets	$1,957	$1,725	$1,817	$1,800
Equities				
Current liabilities	$ 300	$ 300	$ 300	$ 300
Long-term notes payable	800	1,000	1,200	1,200
Stockholders' equity	857	425	317	300
Total equities	$1,957	$1,725	$1,817	$1,800

Required:

(1) Compute the rate of return on sales, total assets, and the stockholders' equity for each of the three years. (Round to the third decimal place and use year-end amounts.)

(2) Determine the current asset turnover for each of the three years.

(3) Compare the percentage of stockholders' equity to total equities at the end of 1982 with 1985.

17-7. Explanation for Income Improvement. The president of Flynn Products Inc., Henry Cahill, stated in the annual report that the net income is more than 30% higher in 1985 than in 1983 even though the growth of sales was relatively modest. Data taken from the annual reports are given as follows:

	1985	1984	1983
Sales	$5,400,000	$5,200,000	$5,000,000
Cost of goods sold*	$2,860,000	$2,850,000	$2,820,000
Operating expenses*	830,000	840,000	860,000·
Income tax	670,000	600,000	530,000
	$4,360,000	$4,290,000	$4,210,000
Net income	$1,040,000	$ 910,000	$ 790,000

*Total depreciation of $640,000 each year is divided between cost of goods sold and operating expenses.

Detail of Cost of Goods Sold

	1985	1984	1983
Inventory, beginning of year	$1,470,000	$ 930,000	$ 870,000
Current production	3,500,000	3,390,000	2,880,000
	$4,970,000	$4,320,000	$3,750,000
Less inventory, end of year	2,110,000	1,470,000	930,000
Cost of goods sold	$2,860,000	$2,850,000	$2,820,000

Average investment in current assets:

1985	$3,280,000
1984	2,670,000
1983	2,140,000

Required: From the information given, determine relationships that may explain, at least in part, the increase in net income from year to year. Point out favorable or unfavorable factors.

17-8. Evaluation of Revised Management Policy. Ted Mayberry and his associates have acquired a controlling interest in Jarvis Home Products Inc. Mayberry has stated that the company did not reach its potential and was too conservatively managed. With some imagination and courageous leadership, Mayberry believes that sales volume can be improved, and the rate of return on sales and the rate of return for the stockholders can be improved. Accordingly, the company has invested substantially in modern equipment and has agressively promoted additional sales volume.

Summarized data from the last annual report under the old management are given as follows:

Current assets	$1,280,000
Plant assets, net of accumulated depreciation	670,000
Total assets	$1,950,000
Current liabilities	$ 370,000
Mortgage payable	150,000
Capital stock	500,000
Retained earnings	930,000
Total equities	$1,950,000
Net sales	$3,220,000
Net income	$ 174,000

Summarized data from an annual report after the new management had been in control for three years are as follows:

Current assets	$ 1,860,000
Plant assets, net of accumulated depreciation	3,880,000
Total assets	$ 5,740,000
Current liabilities	$ 1,247,000
Long-term notes payable	2,000,000
Mortgage payable	500,000
Capital stock	500,000
Retained earnings	1,493,000
Total equities	$ 5,740,000
Net sales	$11,240,000
Cost of goods sold and operating expenses	$ 9,380,000
Interest expense	250,000
Income tax	644,000
	$10,274,000
Net income	$ 966,000

As an outside consultant, you have been asked by Mayberry to make a comparison between conditions now and conditions as they were under the old management. Your comparison will either support or not support a request for additional loans.

Required: On the basis of the information given, make your recommendations to Mayberry. Support your conclusions by computing the following relationships from both sets of data.

(1) Rate of return on net sales.
(2) Rate of return on assets.
(3) Rate of return on stockholders' equity.
(4) Current ratio.
(5) Percentage of debt in equity structure.

17-9. Review of Company Policy. The board of directors of Coulter Equipment Company authorized the addition of new product lines and an increase in plant and equipment. In light of increasing prices, it was recommended that inventories be increased before prices increase even more. Also, with an anticipated increase in sales, a larger inventory will be needed to serve the customers.

Financial statements in summary form for the last three years are given in thousands of dollars:

Income Statements

	1986	1985	1984
Sales	$7,370	$6,684	$6,140
Cost of sales	$4,542	$4,125	$3,650
Operating expenses	1,434	1,310	1,162
Interest expense	295	270	20
Income tax	495	410	588
	$6,766	$6,115	$5,420
Net income	$ 604	$ 569	$ 720
Depreciation included in cost of sales	$ 375	$ 340	$ 168
Depreciation included in operating expenses	$ 45	$ 55	$ 26

Balance Sheets

	1986	1985	1984
Assets			
Current assets:			
Cash	$1,011	$1,446	$1,088
Accounts receivable	1,527	1,372	1,115
Inventories	2,784	2,145	1,586
Total current assets	$5,322	$4,963	$3,789
Plant assets, net of accumulated depreciation	4,530	4,070	2,150
Total assets	$9,852	$9,033	$5,939
Equities			
Current liabilities:			
Accounts payable	$1,620	$1,530	$1,280
Bank loans	770	480	150
Accrued expenses	665	630	485
Total current liabilities	$3,055	$2,640	$1,915
Long-term notes payable	2,000	2,000	–0–
Stockholders' equity:			
Capital stock, $10 par	$2,000	$2,000	$2,000
Retained earnings	2,797	2,393	2,024
Total equities	$9,852	$9,033	$5,939

Dividends of $1 per share were paid in 1985 and in 1986 on the 200,000 shares outstanding.

Required:

(1) Compute the current ratio and the acid test ratio for each of the three years.

(2) Determine the percentage of the stockholders' equity to the total equity for each of the three years.

(3) Compute the current asset turnover for each of the three years.

(4) Determine the following rates of return for each of the three years:

    (a) Rate of return on sales.

    (b) Rate of return on assets.

    (c) Rate of return on stockholders' equity.

(5) Comment on the trends with respect to earning power and liquidity. Also, comment on the policy with respect to the inventories. Use balance sheet data at the end of the year without averaging.

17-10. Rate of Return Relationships. Summarized financial statements are given as follows for Janoski Windings Company.

Income Statement
For the Years Ended December 31, 19C, 19B, 19A
(In thousands of dollars)

	19C	19B	19A
Net sales	$6,824	$6,275	$5,843
Cost of goods sold	$5,459	$5,020	$4,558
Operating expenses, excluding depreciation	751	690	584
Depreciation	350	350	350
	$6,560	$6,060	$5,492
Net income	$ 264	$ 215	$ 351

Balance Sheet
December 31, 19C, 19B, 19A
(In thousands of dollars)

	19C	19B	19A
Assets			
Current assets	$4,305	$3,835	$3,340
Property, plant, and equipment net of accumulated depreciation	2,190	2,190	2,540
Total assets	$6,495	$6,025	$5,880
Equities			
Liabilities	$2,896	$2,490	$2,360
Stockholders' equity	3,599	3,535	3,520
Total equities	$6,495	$6,025	$5,880

The company has maintained dividends at $200,000 each year in spite of decreased earnings in 19B and 19C. In 19B, no additional plant assets were acquired, but at the end of 19C, an amount equal to the depreciation expense was invested in new equipment.

The cost to replace the plant and equipment in their present condition at the end of each year has been computed by using a specially developed index series for the industry. All plant and equipment listed on the balance sheet at December 31, 19A, were acquired at an index of 100. The index was at 150 at the end of 19A, 160 at the end of 19B, and 180 at the end of 19C.

Even with increases in sales volume, the president of the company is concerned with the inability of the company to increase prices in a highly competitive market. Yet, in spite of all cost control measures, the costs have been increasing.

With pressure on earnings, the company has attempted to maintain the rate of return on the stockholders' equity by improving asset turnover and making use of leverage.

Required:

(1) For each year, determine the percentage of each expense item to net sales.

(2) Compute the rate of return on net sales, the rate of return on total assets, and the rate of return on stockholders' equity. Use the balance sheet at the end of the year for your computations.

(3) Redraft the income statements each year with depreciation being restated on the basis of replacement cost information. Use dollars current for the year in question.

(4) Point out the risks inherent in the present policy of depreciation and the reinvestment in plant assets.

(5) Compute the rates of return on total assets using the income statements as adjusted in (3) and the assets adjusted to replacement costs. Use dollars current for the year in question.

17-11. Measures of Liquidity. Rachel Bock, a member of the board of directors of Hermosa Creations Inc., expresses concern about the trend in liquidity. Samuel Watters, the president of the company, assures Bock that the company has become more profitable and that the increased volume of business can be handled properly with a smaller investment in inventory—a large portion of the current asset investment.

Financial data for the past three years are summarized as follows:

	1985	1984	1983
Current assets:			
Cash	$ 821,000	$ 756,000	$ 690,000
Accounts receivable	2,412,000	1,752,00	1,090,000
Inventories	2,045,000	2,316,000	2,855,000
Total current assets	$5,278,000	$4,824,000	$4,635,000
Total current liabilities	$2,973,000	$2,560,000	$2,280,000
Net sales (credit sales)	$9,646,000	$8,763,000	$6,542,000
Cost of goods sold	$5,256,000	$5,035,000	$4,890,000
Operating expenses excluding depreciation	933,000	893,000	746,000
Depreciation	500,000	500,000	350,000
Income tax	1,180,000	930,000	220,000
Totals	$7,869,000	$7,358,000	$6,206,000
Net income	$1,777,000	$1,405,000	$ 336,000

Required:

(1) Compute the relationships that will give an indication of the trend in liquidity and point out various factors that should be considered. (Do not average data.)

(2) How long should it take each year to convert inventories to accounts receivable and to cash.

(3) Is Bock's concern justified?

17-12. Inventory and Accounts Receivable Turnovers. On March 1, the creditors of Doyle and Anderson extended until July 1 the terms for payment of amounts due them and requested that cash of $1,500,000 be raised by that time.

The company had an inventory of materials on hand at March 1 costing $750,000 and an inventory of finished goods costing $420,000. There was no work in process on that date.

Data from past operations indicate that it takes 75 days to convert materials into finished products. Combined labor and overhead required for conversion are equal to 80% of the materials cost, and cash is available for the required labor and overhead payments. The manufactured cost of the product is equal to 75% of the selling price.

Last year the company reported net credit sales of $7,200,000 and had an average accounts receivable balance of $900,000. The rate of collectibility on accounts receivable is expected to be the same as it was last year. After the product is manufactured, it takes about 15 days to deliver the product to customers.

There were no accounts receivable outstanding on March 1, and all cash had been paid over to creditors to reduce past indebtedness with the exception of the cash needed to pay labor and overhead cost for processing inventory and the cash needed for operating expenses until July 1.

Required: From the information given, does it appear that the creditors' terms can be met by July 1? Show computations and comment on the situation as you see it. (Use a 360-day year.)

17-13. Evaluation of Policy Changes. During the past two years, Hahn and Brown Inc. have had liquidity problems. In late 1984, a new management group assumed control and has been trying to improve the rate of profitability and to solve the liquidity problem. You have been asked to examine the financial statements for 1984 and 1985 and to evaluate any progress that has been made.

Summarized financial statements for 1984 and 1985 are given as follows:

Hahn and Brown Inc.
Income Statement
For the Years Ended December 31, 1984 and 1985
(In thousands of dollars)

	1985	1984
Net sales	$6,560	$4,330
Cost of goods sold	$3,870	$3,110
Operating expenses	610	530
	$4,480	$3,640
Income from operations	$2,080	$ 690
Interest expense	140	330
Income before income tax	$1,940	$ 360
Income tax	780	140
Net income	$1,160	220

Hahn and Brown Inc.
Balance Sheet
December 31, 1985 and 1984
(In thousands of dollars)

	1985	1984
Assets		
Current assets:		
Cash	$1,490	$ 430
Accounts receivable	660	540
Inventories	650	1,190
Total current assets	$2,800	$2,160
Plant and machinery, net of accumulated depreciation	2,760	2,580
Total assets	$5,560	$4,740
Equities		
Current liabilities:		
Accounts payable	$ 960	$1,270
Other amounts currently due	650	780
Total current liabilities	$1,610	$2,050
Notes payable, 10%, due June 30, 1995	600	1,000
Capital stock, $10 par value	1,200	800
Paid-in capital in excess of par	300	200
Retained earnings	1,850	690
Total equities	$5,560	$4,740

Required:

(1) Evaluate the changes made in 1985 by computing the following amounts, ratios, and percentages for both years. Assume all sales are on credit. (Use asset and equity amounts without averaging. Round to the third decimal place.)
   (a) Operating rate of return on net sales.
   (b) Net income as a percentage of total assets.
   (c) Net income as a percentage of stockholders' equity.
   (d) Current ratio and acid test ratio.
   (e) Turnover of accounts receivable and inventory.
   (f) Earnings per share.
   (g) Book value per share.

(2) From your analysis, does it appear that the management has taken steps to bring the company into a more secure position?

17-14. Comprehensive Analysis. Edward Parry, chief executive officer of Murphy Parts Company, has been concerned about conditions in the general economy and the impact of these conditions on the company. He stated that the company sold more during the past year, but doesn't seem to be making much progress in earning larger profits.

You are to prepare a report for Parry that will reveal relationships with respect to profitability and safety.

Income statements for 1985 and 1984 are given in summary form as follows:

Murphy Parts Company
Income Statement
For the Years Ended September 30, 1985 and 1984
(In thousands of dollars)

	1985	1984
Net sales	$3,050	$1,820
Cost of sales	$1,830	$1,270
Operating expenses and interest	530	240
Income tax	280	125
	$2,640	$1,635
Net income	$ 410	$ 185

Murphy Parts Company
Balance Sheet
September 30, 1985 and 1984
(In thousands of dollars)

	1985	1984
Assets		
Current assets:		
Cash	$ 920	$ 560
Accounts receivable, net of uncollectibles	300	300
Inventories	150	200
Total current assets	$1,370	$1,060
Plant and equipment, net of accumulated depreciation	580	860
Total assets	$1,950	$1,920
Equities		
Current liabilities:		
Accounts payable and accrued expenses	$ 480	$ 650
Long-term notes payable	400	400
Stockholders'equity:		
Capital stock	500	500
Retained earnings	570	370
Total equities	$1,950	$1,920

Required:

(1) Compute the following relationships. (Use data from the year without averaging.) Round answers to the third decimal place.

(a) Percentage of each income statement classification to net sales.

(b) Rate of return on assets and stockholders' equity.

(c) Accounts receivable turnover each year.

        (d) Inventory turnover each year.

        (e) Current ratio each year.

        (f) Percentage of total current assets and plant and equipment to total assets each year.

        (g) Percentage of stockholders' equity to total equity each year.

    (2) Comment on the relationships that you have computed.

18

TRACING THE FLOW OF NET WORKING CAPITAL AND CASH

Chapter Objectives

This chapter will enable you to:

1. Distinguish between the situations where net working capital flow can be appropriate and where cash flow can be appropriate.
2. Determine why profits are important and also why liquidity is so important.
3. Explain how net working capital is obtained and used.
4. Describe how cash flow is related to the income statement.
5. Explain how cash flow can be derived as an extension of net working capital flow analysis.
6. Describe how cash flow analysis can be important in planning and liquidity management.

The focus of attention in this chapter is directed to three important flow statements that can help management to plan and control the inflow and outflow of the current resources that are vital to company operation. These statements are:

1. The statement of sources and uses of net working capital — Measures the inflows and outflows of net working capital that result from any type of activity.
2. The statement of cash receipts and disbursements — Measures the inflows and outflows of cash that result from any type of activity.
3. The statement of changes in financial position — Measures the inflows and outflows of net working capital and includes the changes in noncurrent assets and equities that do not pass through net working capital.

DESCRIPTION AND EVALUATION OF THE STATEMENTS

The three statements are very similar, differing only with respect to the detail provided. The statement of sources and uses of net working capital gives a broad perspective, showing how the total current assets minus the total current liabilities have flowed in and out of the business during the fiscal period. This statement is more useful for longer-term planning, periods of six months to a year or more, when broad approximations are acceptable. In contrast, the statement of cash receipts and disbursements deals specifically with the inflow and outflow of cash and is more appropriate for short-term planning from month to month.

For long-range planning, the information furnished by a statement of sources and uses of net working capital is sufficient. For example, management may want to know if enough net working capital will be available two years from now to make a payment on long-term debt. It may not be possible or even necessary to make an exact projection of the cash flow for two years. Current resources can generally be converted into cash for repayment in a relatively short time, and an estimate of net working capital will serve the purpose for a longer range forecast.

In contrast, a statement of cash receipts and disbursements tends to be more useful in short-run analysis. Reliable projections of cash receipts and disbursements can generally be made for the immediate future but not for years in advance. The treasurer of a company, for example, may project cash collections expected from accounts receivable over the month. During periods when the cash outflow for purchases and operating expenses is expected to exceed the cash inflow, arrangements may be made to borrow on short-term notes. In periods when the cash receipts are substantially larger than cash disbursements, plans may be made to liquidate the short-term notes and to invest any excess cash in temporary investments.

Sometimes the statement of sources and uses of net working capital is extended to include shifts within the noncurrent balance sheet categories. For example, capital stock may be issued in exchange for plant and equipment. Net working capital is not affected by this type of transaction, but there is a significant change in the financial structure. This extended statement is called a *statement of changes in financial position.* The American Institute of Certified Public Accountants recommends that a statement of changes in financial position be presented as a basic financial statement for each period in which an income statement is presented.[1] This recommendation governs financial reporting but does not bind management in the preparation of reports and other data that are to be used exclusively for internal purposes.

---

[1] *Opinions of the Accounting Principles Board, No. 19,* "Reporting Changes in Financial Positon" (New York: American Institute of Certified Public Accountants, 1971), par. 7.

THE SIGNIFICANCE OF NET WORKING CAPITAL FLOWS

An analysis of how net working capital is provided and used can be applied in many ways. Some of the more important applications are listed as follows:

1. It may suggest ways in which the net working capital position can be improved.
2. It focuses attention on what resources are available for the acquisition of plant assets or other investments.
3. It can help in the selection of the best investment alternative.
4. It can be used in deciding how to finance the acquisition of plant assets and other long-term investments.
5. It can be used in planning for the retirement of long-term debt.
6. It can also serve in the planning of a sound dividend policy.

A statement of the sources and uses of net working capital tells management where net working capital was obtained in the past and how it was put to use. With this background, management can then make plans for the future. Estimates can be made of future net working capital flows that can be applied to the retirement of long-term debt, to the expansion or replacement of plant facilities, or to the payment of dividends.

Profit is very important, but there are other elements to be considered in a successful business operation. For example, a company may earn an adequate return on investment, but at the same time the net working capital position may deteriorate, resulting in serious liquidity problems. With a large proportion of the resources frozen in the form of plant assets or other long-term investments, the company may have to increase its debt excessively to obtain liquid resources.

Often a company that is growing rapidly is faced with a shortage of net working capital. Profit may be increasing, but the company may not have the liquid resources that are required to expand plant facilities to meet increased sales demand. To obtain liquid resources, the company may borrow heavily. As a result, the interest of the owners is proportionately smaller with increased risk in the event of business reverses.

Also, large and well established companies may experience severe liquidity problems when sales volume drops substantially. Net working capital that was once provided by operations with higher sales volume is no longer available. Hence, obligations cannot be paid as scheduled, and new loans may have to be made under unfavorable terms with higher interest rates. Management, recognizing the importance of net working capital and cash flow, is most interested in projections of probable future net working capital and cash flows.

NET WORKING CAPITAL FLOWS

A statement of sources and uses of net working capital indicates how net working capital is acquired and used. A company in the normal course of events has transactions that change net working capital and others that have no effect on net working capital. The transactions may be classified in the following manner:

1. Transactions that result in an increase or decrease in the net current balance sheet accounts:
   (a) Certain income statement transactions.
   (b) Transactions that affect both current and noncurrent balance sheet accounts.
2. Transactions that do not increase or decrease the net current balance sheet accounts:
   (a) Shifts within the current balance sheet structure that have no effect on the net balance.
   (b) Transactions that affect only the noncurrent balance sheet accounts.

The transactions classified under (1) change net working capital and are explained in a statement of sources and uses of net working capital. For example, sales normally increase cash or accounts receivable while expenses such as salaries, rent, insurance, and taxes either decrease cash or increase accounts payable. Hence, such income statement transactions either increase or reduce net working capital.

Transactions affecting both current and noncurrent balance sheet accounts also change net working capital. Cash (part of net working capital) is increased by borrowing on a long-term note (noncurrent balance sheet account). Conversely, net working capital is reduced by the retirement of long-term debt or by the acquisition of the company's own stock (treasury stock).

The transactions in classification (2) do not affect net working capital. For example, cash may be collected on accounts receivable, or accounts payable may be converted to short-term notes payable. Transactions such as these causes shifts within the net working capital structure but do not increase or decrease the net balance.

There are transactions that affect only the noncurrent balance sheet accounts. Depreciation expense, for example, reduces plant assets. Net working capital is neither increased nor decreased. Hence, in determining the net inflow of net working capital from operations, depreciation expense is added to net income to reverse the effect of the depreciation deduction.

Shifts may also occur in the noncurrent area. Long-term notes payable may be exchanged for capital stock, or a long-term investment may be acquired by issuing capital stock. These transactions do not increase or decrease net working capital. As stated earlier, the effect of these transactions must be reported on a statement of changes in financial position, but not on a statement of sources and uses of net working capital.

Sources of Net Working Capital

Some of the most common sources of net working capital are:

1. Operations.
2. Investment by the owners.

3. Issuance of long-term debt.
4. Sale of long-term investments.
5. Sale of plant assets.

Changes in all noncurrent balance sheet accounts are analyzed to determine their effect on the net working capital balance. Net working capital is normally increased as a result of transactions that (1) decrease noncurrent assets or (2) increase noncurrent equities. For example, long-term investments or plant assets can be sold to provide additional net working capital. Net working capital can also be increased by long-term borrowing or by issuing additional shares of stock in return for cash, other current assets, or in return for cancellation of short-term debt. In any given fiscal period, a company obtains its net working capital from many different sources.

Ordinarily, profitable operation is expected to be the main source of net working capital. In the long run a successful business acquires plant assets and investments, pays long-term debt, and distributes dividends to the stockholders from the net working capital generated as a result of rendering goods and services to customers.

The following summary shows the effect of certain income statement items on net working capital.

Income Statement Item	Changes in Assets and Liabilities	Effect on Net Working Capital
Sales	Increases accounts receivable or cash	Increases net working capital
Gain on sale of plant assets	Part of increase of net working capital arising from sale of plant assets	Excluded from net working capital received from operations. (The *total* amount received from the sale is reported separately.)
Cost of goods sold	Decreases inventory	Decreases net working capital
Wages, rent, repairs, and other operating expenses that are currently paid	Decreases cash or prepayments or increases current liabilities	Decreases net working capital
Depreciation, depletion, and amortization	Decreases plant assets or intangibles	Does not affect net working capital

The net income is restated to reflect a flow of net working capital from operations by adding or deducting items that do not affect the net working capital flow from operations.

Net income	$XXX
Add depreciation	XXX
	$XXX
Less gain on sale of plant assets	XXX
Net working capital flow from operations	$XXX

Depreciation, for example, is offset against revenue in the determination of net income or loss but is in no way related to net working capital. Net income is closed to the owners' equity at the end of the fiscal period and is lower than it would have been if depreciation had not been deducted. Therefore, depreciation has reduced a noncurrent equity (the owners' equity) and has reduced a noncurrent asset (the plant asset) with no effect on net working capital.

Sometimes it is said that depreciation provides net working capital that may be used for expansion or for the replacement of plant assets. This is not true. The net working capital is provided by the revenue from sales, not from depreciation. Depreciation, unlike many operating expenses, does not require the use of net working capital. The net increase or decrease in net working capital from operations is generally computed by adding depreciation and other expenses not requiring the use of net working capital to the net income or subtracting them from the net loss.

Uses of Net Working Capital

Some of the more common ways in which net working capital is put to use are:

1. Acquisition of investments, plant assets, or other noncurrent assets.
2. The retirement of long-term debt or the redemption of an issue of capital stock.
3. The acquisition of treasury stock.
4. The payment of dividends.
5. Involuntary losses on operations.

Net working capital is normally decreased as a result of transactions that (1) increase noncurrent assets or (2) decrease noncurrent equities. For example, if cash is used to purchase plant assets, the noncurrent asset is increased and net working capital is decreased. If long-term debt is retired by using available cash, net working capital is also reduced.

Operations are not always profitable. In fact, an operating loss may be of such magnitude that there may even be a decrease in net working capital from operating activity after the depreciation and other items that have no effect on net working capital have been applied in computing the net working capital flow from operations. A short example is given as follows:

Net loss on operations	$(115,000)
Add depreciation	21,000
Net working capital reduction from operations	$(94,000)

In still other circumstances a net loss may be reported; yet when depreciation or other charges not requiring net working capital are considered, there may be a net inflow of net working capital from operations as shown in the following table:

Net loss on operations	$ (8,000)
Add depreciation	21,000
Net working capital provided by operations	$ 13,000

A COMPREHENSIVE ILLUSTRATION – SOURCES AND USES OF NET WORKING CAPITAL

A statement of sources and uses of net working capital can often be prepared quite easily from comparative balance sheets, income statement data for the period, and supplementary data. The sources and uses of net working capital analysis can be made in a three-step procedure as follows:

1. Compute the increase or decrease in net working capital.
2. Determine the net working capital provided by operations.
3. Analyze the changes in the noncurrent assets and equities for the effect of the changes on net working capital.

Step 1 computes the increase or decrease in net working capital, and Steps 2 and 3 explain how this increase or decrease is obtained.

A comparative balance sheet as of December 31, 1984 and 1985, and an income statement for 1985 are given for Myron Products Inc. on page 554.

Additional data are given as follows:

(a) Myron Products Inc. paid $26,000 in 1985 for an investment in the stock of Haven Inc.

(b) Details on the plant assets follow:

	1985	1984
Plant assets......................................	$96,000	$76,000
Accumulated depreciation	14,000	12,000
Plant assets, net of accumulated depreciation.......	$82,000	$64,000

During the year equipment costing $12,000 with accumulated depreciation of $5,000 was sold.

(c) No payments were made on the long-term notes in 1985.

(d) The bonds payable were converted to capital stock.

(e) Additional shares of stock were issued to the shareholders in 1985 as a dividend. The stock dividend amounted to $10,000. Cash dividends amounting to $21,600 were also declared.

(f) A statement of changes in retained earnings is summarized as follows:

Balance of retained earnings, beginning of 1985		$ 67,300
Net income, 1985..		61,900
		$129,200
Less: Stock dividends....................................	$ 10,000	
Cash dividends	21,600	
		$ 31,600
Balance of retained earnings, end of 1985		$ 97,600

Myron Products Inc.
Comparative Balance Sheet
December 31, 1985 and 1984

	1985	1984	Changes Debit	Changes Credit
Current assets:				
Cash....................................	$ 22,100	$ 18,300		
Marketable securities	14,000	15,000		
Accounts receivable	43,200	44,900		
Inventories	76,200	67,100		
Total current assets	$155,500	$145,300		
Current liabilities:				
Accounts payable	$ 10,300	$ 11,500		
Wages payable	8,500	8,100		
Estimated income tax payable	56,100	52,400		
Dividends payable.........................	6,000	5,000		
Total current liabilities	$ 80,900	$ 77,000		
Net working capital	$ 74,600	$ 68,300	$ 6,300	
Investment in Haven Inc.....................	26,000	–0–	26,000	
Plant assets, net of depreciation	82,000	64,000	18,000	
	$182,600	$132,300		
Less: Long-term notes.......................	$ 25,000	$ 15,000		$10,000
Bonds payable	–0–	35,000	35,000	
	$ 25,000	$ 50,000		
Stockholders' equity.........................	$157,600	$ 82,300		
Detail of stockholders' equity:				
Capital received from stockholders	$ 60,000	$ 15,000		45,000
Retained earnings	97,600	67,300		30,300
Total stockholders' equity	$157,600	$ 82,300	$85,300	$85,300

Myron Products Inc.
Income Statement
For the Year Ended December 31, 1981

Sales and other income:		
Net sales...		$326,400
Gain on sale of equipment		3,200
		$329,600
Costs and expenses:		
Cost of goods sold...		$149,800
Operating expenses, including depreciation of $7,000		57,800
Interest expense		4,000
Income tax		56,100
		$267,700
Net income		$ 61,900

Step One — Schedule of Changes in Net Working Capital

The first step in preparing a statement of sources and uses of net working capital is to determine the increase or decrease in net working capital. If detail with respect to the specific account changes within the net working capital category is desired, a schedule of changes in net working capital can be prepared as follows:

Myron Products Inc.
Schedule of Changes in Net Working Capital
For the Year Ended December 31, 1985

	December 31 1985	December 31 1984	Net Working Capital Increase	Net Working Capital Decrease
Current assets:				
Cash..................................	$ 22,100	$ 18,300	$ 3,800	
Marketable securities	14,000	15,000		$ 1,000
Accounts receivable	43,200	44,900		1,700
Inventories	76,200	67,100	9,100	
Total current assets	$155,500	$145,300		
Current liabilities:				
Accounts payable	$ 10,300	$ 11,500	1,200	
Wages payable	8,500	8,100		400
Estimated income tax payable	56,100	52,400		3,700
Dividends payable.....................	6,000	5,000		1,000
Total current liabilities	$ 80,900	$ 77,000		
Net working capital	$ 74,600	$ 68,300		
Increase in net working capital				6,300
Total.................................			$14,100	$14,100

Net working capital is increased by increases in the current assets and is decreased by decreases in the current assets. The opposite is true for changes in current liabilities. The current liabilities are a negative factor in the computation of net working capital. Therefore, an increase in a current liability decreases net working capital, and a decrease in a current liability increases net working capital. In this illustration, net working capital has increased by $6,300. The next two steps of the analysis explain how net working capital was provided and used to bring about the net increase of $6,300.

Step Two — Net Working Capital from Operations

Net income and net working capital from operations normally are not the same figure. As explained earlier, there are transactions that affect net income that do not affect net working capital. The net income for 1985 of $61,900 includes the effect of a depreciation deduction of $7,000. Since depreciation does not reduce net working capital, the effect of the deduction is removed by adding it back to net income.

The gain on the sale of equipment does represent an inflow of net working capital, but it is deducted from net income in the computation of the net inflow of net working capital from operations. The total amount received from the sale of the equipment (the recovery of the net book value of the asset and the gain) is reported as one item on the sources and uses of net working capital statement. If the gain were included in both the net working capital flow from operations and the net working capital received from the sale of the asset, double-counting would occur. The double-counting is avoided by deducting the gain in computing the flow of net working capital from operations.

Net income	$61,900
Add depreciation	7,000
	$68,900
Less gain on sale of equipment	3,200
Net working capital flow from operations	$65,700

If there is a loss on the sale of a noncurrent asset, the loss is added to net income in calculating the flow of the net working capital from operations. Although the loss is a deduction in computing net income, it does not reduce net working capital. The total amount received from the sale of the asset is reported as one item on the statement of sources and uses of net working capital.

Step Three — Analysis of Noncurrent Items

The final step in the analysis is to explain the effect of the changes in the noncurrent balance sheet items.

1. Investment in Haven Inc. +$26,000.
   The investment was increased by $26,000; and, with no information to the contrary, it can be assumed that net working capital of $26,000 was used to acquire this investment.

2. Plant assets (gross), +$20,000.
   The detail on the plant assets shows that the plant assets before deducting accumulated depreciation increased by $20,000 ($96,000 − $76,000). It is stated that equipment costing $12,000 was sold. This decreased plant assets, yet the assets increased by a net amount of $20,000. Apparently plant assets costing $32,000 were acquired.

Cost of assets acquired	$32,000
Less cost of assets sold	12,000
Net increase in assets	$20,000

In short, add the $12,000 deduction resulting from the sale to the net increase to obtain the cost of acquisition, $32,000. The net book value of the equipment sold was $7,000 ($12,000 cost — $5,000 accumulated depreciation). The equipment was sold at a gain of $3,200. Hence, $10,200 was the net amount received from the sale of equipment.

Assume that the detail on plant assets is not given. The increase in net plant assets of $18,000 ($82,000 — $64,000) can be converted to a gross increase of $20,000 by analysis of the changes in accumulated depreciation. Then analysis for the net working capital effect can proceed as usual. Changes in accumulated depreciation can be accounted for as follows:

Depreciation expense (increases accumulated depreciation)	$ 7,000
Less accumulated depreciation removed by sale of equipment ..	5,000
Net increase in accumulated depreciation	$ 2,000

With a net increase of $2,000 in accumulated depreciation, the net plant asset increase of $18,000 is $2,000 less than the gross increase of $20,000.

3. Long-term notes, +$10,000.
   No payments were made during the year, and the increase of $10,000 indicates that this amount was provided by long-term borrowing.

4. Bonds payable, —$35,000.
   The bonds payable were converted to capital stock with no effect on net working capital. There has been a change in the financial structure, and this will be revealed on a statement of changes in financial position.

5. Capital stock, +$45,000.
   The conversion   bonds payable in the amount of $35,000 and the stock dividend of $10,000 account for the increase of $45,000. There is no effect on net working capital. The stock dividend is not viewed as a substantive change in financial structure and does not have to be reported on a statement of changes in financial position. However, the conversion of bonds to stock should be reported on such a statement.

6. Retained earnings, +$30,300.
   The statement of changes in retained earnings shows that cash dividends of $21,600 were declared. These dividends reduced net working capital.

Statement of Sources and Uses of Net Working Capital

The results of the analysis are incorporated in the following statement:

Myron Products Inc.
Statement of Sources and Uses of Net Working Capital
For the Year Ended December 31, 1985

Sources of net working capital:		
Operating activity:		
Net income	$61,900	
Add depreciation	7,000	
	$68,900	
Less gain on sale of equipment	3,200	
Net working capital from operations		$65,700
Sale of equipment		10,200
Issuance of long-term notes		10,000
Total sources		$85,900
Uses of net working capital:		
Acquisition of investment in Haven Inc.		$26,000
Acquisition of plant assets		32,000
Dividends payable in cash		21,600
Total uses		$79,600
Net increase in net working capital		$ 6,300

Statement of Changes in Financial Position

The statement of sources and uses of net working capital can be expanded to a statement of changes in financial position, shown on page 559, by including the changes in noncurrent assets and equities that do not pass through net working capital. In this illustration bonds payable of $35,000 were converted to capital stock. Net working capital was not affected, but there was an overall change in the financial structure. For the sake of convenience this transaction can be described and labeled both as a source and a use since it balances out with no effect on net working capital. It is treated as if two separate transactions occurred; that is, net working capital was increased by the issuance of stock, the funds from which were used to redeem the bonds payable.

THE DEMAND FOR NET WORKING CAPITAL

The techniques of net working capital analysis can also be applied in the preparation of estimates of future sources and uses of net working capital. Planning net working capital flow is an important part of budgeting and is applied in making decisions as to whether or not certain investments should be

Myron Products Inc
Statement of Changes in Financial Position
For the Year Ended December 31, 1985

Sources of funds:		
Operating activity:		
Net income	$61,900	
Add depreciation	7,000	
	$68,900	
Less gain on sale of equipment	3,200	
Net working capital from operations		$ 65,700
Sale of equipment		10,200
Issuance of long-term notes		10,000
Capital stock issued (direct issue in exchange for bonds payable retired)		35,000
Total sources		$120,900
Uses of funds:		
Acquisition of investment in Haven Inc.		$ 26,000
Acquisition of plant assets		32,000
Dividends payable in cash		21,600
Bonds payable redeemed (by issue of capital stock)		35,000
Total uses		$114,600
Net increase in funds		$ 6,300

made. A statement of estimated flow of net working capital can be prepared for future years and rearranged to show how much net working capital should be available after all required commitments have been met.

Assume, for example, the The Webb Company has estimated a net income of $1,350,000 for the year ending June 30, 1985. Depreciation and other charges not requiring the use of net working capital are estimated at $240,000 and are added back to obtain the expected flow of net working capital from operations of $1,590,000. Plans for dividends, the proceeds from the sale of plant assets, payment on debt, and a planned increase in net working capital are added or deducted to yield net working capital of $1,210,000 which is available for approved projects, projects under consideration, or projects still to be considered. The planned increase of net working capital for the year of $200,000 is treated as if it were a use on the estimated statement and is deducted to arrive at the net working capital of $1,210,000 that may be applied for other purposes. An estimated statement is shown as on page 560.

CASH FLOW

In making plans for the more immediate future, management wants to know how much cash will be available to meet obligations to trade creditors, to pay bank loans, to pay dividends to stockholders, and to make payments on

The Webb Company
Statement of Estimated Sources and Uses of
Net Working Capital
For the Year Ending June 30, 1985

Net income	$1,350,000
Add depreciation and other charges not requiring the use of net working capital	240,000
	$1,590,000
Less dividends	160,000
Estimated net working capital to be provided from operations after dividends .	$1,430,000
Add proceeds from sale of plant assets	80,000
	$1,510,000
Less payment on debt	100,000
	$1,410,000
Planned increase (decrease) in net working capital	200,000
Net working capital available	$1,210,000
Demand for net working capital:	
Approved projects	$ 800,000
Unapproved projects	300,000
Amount still available	110,000
Total demand for net working capital	$1,210,000

the currently maturing portion of long-term debt. With careful planning, there should be enough cash available for the payment of obligations on schedule; but the cash balance should not be excessive. Cash in itself is not productive and, if not immediately needed, should be employed to earn a return. Ordinarily excess cash will be invested in short-term securities that can be easily liquidated.

A statement of the flow of cash, known as a statement of cash receipts and disbursements, can be prepared by extending the steps used in the analysis of sources and uses of net working capital. Recall that changes in noncurrent assets and equities are analyzed for the effect on net working capital. These relationships are summarized in T-account form:

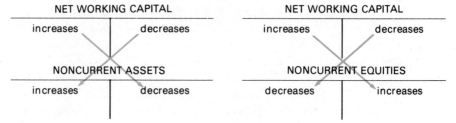

Net Working Capital Flow

NET WORKING CAPITAL		NET WORKING CAPITAL	
increases	decreases	increases	decreases
NONCURRENT ASSETS		NONCURRENT EQUITIES	
increases	decreases	decreases	increases

To determine cash changes, the noncurrent assets and noncurrent equities are analyzed as before, and changes in current assets other than cash and changes in current liabilities are also analyzed. The following T-account summary illustrates how the changes in cash can be related to the changes in other balance sheet classifications.

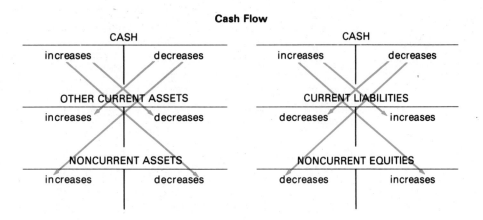

Cash Flow

Cash and Operations

There is a close relationship between the revenues and expenses and the current assets and liabilities. The relationships are summarized as follows:

Current Assets	Related To
Cash	Sales
Accounts receivable	
Inventory	Cost of goods sold
Prepaid expenses	Operating and other expenses, excluding depreciation and the amortization of other noncurrent items
Current Liabilities	
Accounts payable	Cost of goods sold
Operating costs payable	Operating and other expenses, excluding depreciation and the amortization of other noncurrent items

In analysis, an income statement can be restated in terms of cash received and disbursed for each item:

(1) In the illustration given for Myron Products Inc. accounts receivable decreased by $1,700. This indicates that collections on account were greater than sales revenue.

Sales	$326,400
Add decrease in accounts receivable	1,700
Collections from sales activity	$328,100

If accounts receivable had increased, the increase would be deducted from the current period sales to obtain the cash inflow.

In more complicated situations, increases or decreases in accounts receivable may arise not only from cash collection activity but also as a result of the write-off of uncollectible accounts. Assume that an accounts receivable account appears as follows:

Accounts Receivable

Beginning balance	50,000	Write-off uncollectible	
Sales.........................	1,000,000	accounts.....................	20,000
		Cash collections (a).............	930,000
		Ending balance	100,000
	1,050,000		1,050,000

Cash

Cash collections (a).............	930,000

Superficial analysis would indicate that the $50,000 increase in accounts receivable should be deducted from sales of $1,000,000 to obtain cash collections of $950,000. However, the write-off of uncollectible accounts reduced accounts receivable with no corresponding cash flow. The analysis should be made as shown in the following table:

Accounts receivable, beginning balance		$ 50,000
Sales...		1,000,000
Potential cash collections		$1,050,000
Less:		
Write-off uncollectible accounts	$ 20,000	
Ending balance of accounts receivable (to be collected)	100,000	120,000
Current collections..................................		$ 930,000

If there is estimated uncollectible accounts expense, it is recorded with a credit being made to the allowance for doubtful accounts. The net accounts receivable is reduced as a result of this entry, but there is no effect on the flow of cash. The estimated uncollectible accounts expense, like depreciation, is not deducted in computing the net inflow of cash from operations.

(2) The cash paid for merchandise is computed from cost of goods sold in two steps:

1. Purchases during the year are computed by relating cost of goods sold to the change in the inventory.
2. Cash payments for merchandise are computed by relating purchases to the change in the accounts payable.

In the illustration given for Myron Products Inc. inventory has increased by $9,100. This means that purchases were in excess of the cost of goods sold.

Cost of goods sold	$149,800
Add inventory increase	9,100
Cost of purchases	$158,900

If inventory had decreased, purchases would be less than cost of goods sold by the amount of the decrease.

In the next step, cash payments are calculated by relating the purchases to the changes in the accounts payable. The accounts payable decreased by $1,200 because payments were greater than purchases.

Cost of purchases	$158,900
Add accounts payable decrease	1,200
Cash payments for merchandise	$160,100

The analysis is repeated in T-account form:

Cash

	Cash payments (c) 160,100

Accounts Payable

Cash payments (c)	160,100	Beginning balance	11,500
Ending balance	10,300	Purchases (b)	158,900
	170,400		170,400

Inventory

Beginning balance	67,100	Cost of goods sold (a)	149,800
Purchases (b)	158,900	Ending balance	76,200
	226,000		226,000

Cost of Goods Sold

Cost of goods sold (a)	149,800	

(3) Cash was also disbursed to pay operating and other expenses. These payments can be computed by relating the expenses to prepayment accounts and accrued liabilities. Prepayment accounts are similar to inventory accounts. Assume, for example, that there was prepaid rent of $1,500 at the beginning of the year, rent expense of $6,000, and $2,300 of prepaid rent at the end of the year. The "inventory" of prepaid rent increased because cash payments for insurance premiums exceeded the rent expense by the amount of the increase.

Cash

	Payments (b) 6,800

Prepaid Rent

Beginning balance	1,500	Expense (a)	6,000
Payments (b)	6,800	Ending balance	2,300
	8,300		8,300

Rent Expense

Expense (a)	6,000	

Conversely, a decrease in the prepayment would mean that cash payments were less than the expense by the amount of the decrease.

(4) Accrued liabilities are like accounts payable. If the liability is decreased, payments are more than expenses. When debts are reduced, more goods and services are being paid for than are being used. Conversely, when debts increase, expenses are greater than payments.

In the example for Myron Products Inc. wages payable increased from $8,100 to $8,500. Payments for wages were less than the expense by the amount of the increase of $400. Also, the income tax liability increased by $3,700. Income tax expense of $56,100, when reduced by the $3,700 liability increase, yields the payments of $52,400. In this particular case, the company paid the entire amount that was owed at the beginning of the year and at the end of the year owed the current tax expense.

	Cash	
	Payments (b).....................	52,400

Estimated Income Tax Payable			
Payments (b).....................	52,400	Beginning balance	52,400
Ending balance	56,100	Expense (a).....................	56,100
	108,500		108,500

Income Tax Expenses	
Expense (a).....................	56,100

(5) Depreciation and uncollectible accounts expense are operating expenses not requiring a cash disbursement and are subtracted to compute the cash disbursed for operating and other expenses.

(6) Receipts from the sale of plant assets are added in their entirety on the statement of cash receipts and disbursements. To avoid double-counting, the gains or losses on such sales are deducted or added back in determining cash flows from operations.

A schedule of the cash flow from operations for Myron Products Inc. is given below. Explanations of the amounts appearing in the cash effect columns immediately follow the schedule.

	Income Statement		Cash Effect Increase		Decrease	Cash Flow
Net sales	$326,400	(a)	$1,700			$328,100
Gain on sales of equipment.........	3,200			(g)	$3,200	–0–
	$329,600					$328,100
Cost of goods sold	$149,800	(b)	9,100			$160,100
		(c)	1,200			
Operating expenses...............	57,800			(d)	7,000	50,400
				(e)	400	
Interest expense..................	4,000					4,000
Income tax.......................	56,100			(f)	3,700	52,400
	$267,700					$266,900
Net income	$ 61,900					
Net cash flow from operations						$ 61,200

(a) Add decrease in accounts receivable.
(b) Add increase in inventory
(c) Add decrease in accounts payable.
(d) Eliminate depreciation.
(e) Subtract increase in wages payable.
(f) Subtract increase in estimated income tax payable.
(g) Eliminate gain on sale of equipment.

Analysis of Other Current Items

Certain current assets and liabilities are not related to income statement classifications. Changes in these categories are analyzed separately. In the illustration, marketable securities decreased by $1,000; with no information to the contrary, this indicates that cash was increased by a corresponding amount. The increase of $1,000 in dividends payable is subtracted from the cash dividends of $21,600 to obtain cash payment of dividends in the amount of $20,600.

A Statement of Cash Flow

The remainder of the analysis for cash flow is the same as it was for sources and uses of net working capital—an analysis of changes in noncurrent balance sheet items. Cash flow analysis extends net working capital analysis by examining the cash effect of changes in the accounts that comprise net working capital. Most of these accounts are related to the income statement items and are so related in the analysis. A statement of cash receipts and disbursements for Myron Products Inc. is given as follows:

Myron Products Inc.
Statement of Cash Receipts and Disbursements
For the Year Ended December 31, 1985

Cash balance, January 1, 1985.....................................		$ 18,300
Add:		
Net cash flow from operations	$61,200	
Receipts from sale of marketable securities.....................	1,000	
Receipts from sale of equipment.............................	10,200	
Receipts from long-term notes................................	10,000	82,400
		$100,700
Less:		
Disbursements for dividends...................................	$20,600	
Disbursements for investment in Haven Inc......................	26,000	
Disbursements for plant assets	32,000	78,600
Cash balance, December 31, 1985		$ 22,100

Simplified Cash Flow from Operations

The cash flow from operating activity can be computed more simply if detail with respect to the income statement classifications is not desired. The effect of cash flow increases or decreases in current asset or current liability items can be added or deducted from net income. In the example just given for Myron Products Inc. the cash flow from operating activity could have been computed as follows:

Net income	$ 61,900
Add:	
Decrease in accounts receivable	1,700
Depreciation	7,000
Increase in wages payable	400
Increase in income tax payable	3,700
	$ 74,700
Deduct:	
Increase in inventory	$ 9,100
Decrease in accounts payable	1,200
Gain on sale of equipment	3,200
	$ 13,500
Net cash flow from operations	$ 61,200

Terminology Review

Statement of sources and uses of net working capital (547, 549)

Statement of cash receipts and disbursements (547, 560)

Statement of changes in financial position (547, 558)

Schedule of changes in net working capital (555)

QUESTIONS

1. Identify two important flow statements that are helpful in the measurement of liquidity.

2. What is the net working capital?

3. How can a statement of sources and uses of net working capital be used by management?

4. When can a statement of cash receipts and disbursements be more helpful in planning?

5. There are many transactions that result in an increase or a decrease in the net current balance sheet accounts. Give two general types of transactions that fit in this category.

6. Explain in general how net working capital is increased or decreased by income statement transactions.

7. Is net working capital increased or decreased by transactions that affect only the noncurrent balance sheet accounts? Explain.

8. Name some major sources of net working capital.

9. Does depreciation provide net working capital for a business? Explain.

10. List some ways in which net working capital may be used.

11. Is it possible for a business to have net losses from operations and yet increase its net working capital? Explain.

12. Give the three steps that must be taken to prepare a statement of sources and uses of net working capital.

13. What additional information is provided to convert a statement of sources and uses of net working capital into a statement of changes in financial position?

14. What additional analysis is required in the preparation of a statement of cash receipts and disbursements?

15. Explain the logic of why a decrease in a liability account indicates that the cash disbursement was larger than the amount of the related expense on the income statement.

16. If prepaid rent has increased during the year, does this indicate that more or less cash was disbursed than the amount shown as rent expense?

17. Kelly Company reported a net loss of $38,000 for 1985. Depreciation of $95,000 was deducted in computing the net loss. Compute the increase or decrease in net working capital from operations.

18. The manager of Bast Fixtures Company states that cash dividends in the amount of $85,000 were declared but not paid during the year. Inasmuch as the dividends were not paid, the manager insists that there was no effect on net working capital. Explain.

19. A mowing unit was sold by Valley Country Club last year at a gain of $250. The mowing unit was shown on the records of the country club at a net book value of $650 at the date of the sale. Determine the proceeds from the sale of the mowing unit.

20. Marketable securities costing $1,600 were sold for $2,300. Would this be shown on a statement of sources and uses of net working capital? Explain.

EXERCISES

1. Sale of Equipment. Equipment that had an original cost of $84,000 to Yoder Company was sold at a loss of $3,000. At the date of sale, accumulated depreciation on the equipment amounted to $47,000.

Required: Determine the inflow of net working capital from sale of the equipment.

2. Acquisition of Equipment. At the beginning of the year, Norfolk Company had equipment net of accumulated depreciation of $115,000. No equipment was sold during the year. Depreciation of $23,000 was deducted for the year. At the end of the year, equipment net of accumulated depreciation was $136,000.

Required: Determine the amount of net working capital used to buy equipment.

3. Schedule of Changes in Net Working Capital. Lester Cole has asked you to prepare a schedule of changes in net working capital for Georgia Parts Company for the fiscal year ended June 30, 1985. Cole has been assured by the controller that the ledger was in balance at the end of each fiscal year. The account balances are as follows:

	June 30	
	1985	*1984*
Wages payable	$ 3,480	$ 3,240
Inventory	14,060	14,230
Plant and equipment, net of accumulated depreciation	43,400	46,800
Cash	26,450	22,360
Accounts payable	12,350	15,440
Notes payable, due on August 1, 1992	35,000	40,000
Investment in Pelham Co.	65,000	65,000
Accounts receivable	17,320	16,920
Capital stock	75,000	75,000
Unexpired insurance	2,170	2,040
Estimated income tax payable	18,960	17,250
Retained earnings	23,610	16,420

Required: Prepare a schedule of changes in net working capital for the fiscal year ended June 30, 1985.

4. Net Working Capital from Operations. Hackett Brown Company reported net income of $131,000 for the fiscal year ended April 1985. Included on the income statement was a deduction for depreciation expense of $27,500 and amortization of patents of $4,700. A loss of $6,000 on the sale of machinery was also deducted.

Required: How much net working capital was received during the fiscal year from operations?

5. Net Working Capital Flow. Data are summarized from Hattiesburg Forms Company at June 30, 1984 and 1985.

	June 30	
	1985	*1984*
Current assets	$ 86,000	$ 73,000
Investment in Greenville Company	30,000	–0–
Plant and equipment, net of accumulated depreciation	74,000	68,000
Total assets	$190,000	$141,000
Current liabilities	$ 37,000	$ 36,000
Long-term notes payable	25,000	40,000
Capital stock...	60,000	50,000
Retained earnings.....................................	68,000	15,000
Total equities......................................	$190,000	$141,000

There was no sale of plant and equipment during the fiscal year.

Net income for the fiscal year was $65,000. Depreciation of $8,000 was deducted on the income statement.

Dividends in the amount of $12,000 were declared during the fiscal year.

Required: Prepare a statement of sources and uses of net working capital for the fiscal year ended June 30, 1985.

6. Net Working Capital Flow. Noncurrent assets and equities of Edelman Products Company at December 31, 1984 and 1985, are as follows:

	December 31	
	1985	*1984*
Investment in Collins Company......................	$ 138,000	$ 76,000
Land	65,000	30,000
Building, net of accumulated depreciation	542,000	558,000
Equipment, net of accumulated depreciation	237,000	216,000
Total	$ 982,000	$ 880,000
Bonds payable	$ 150,000	$ 170,000
Capital stock......................................	500,000	450,000
Retained earnings...................................	464,000	415,000
Total	$1,114,000	$1,035,000

The company reported a net income of $136,000 in 1985 and paid dividends of $87,000. Depreciation on the building and equipment for the year was $46,000. A gain of $6,000 was shown on the sale of equipment.

There was no addition or reduction of the building account during the year. The reduction in the building net of accumulated depreciation resulted from depreciation.

Equipment costing $78,000 was acquired.

Required: Prepare a statement of sources and uses of net working capital for the year 1985.

7. Incomplete Data and Net Working Capital. From incomplete data given for Terry Company, you have been asked to prepare a statement of sources and uses of net working capital for 1985.

Noncurrent balance sheet account balances are given as follows:

	December 31	
	1985	*1984*
Plant assets, net of depreciation	$181,000	$186,000
Long-term debt.......................................	—0—	45,000
Capital stock	150,000	125,000
Retained earnings....................................	216,000	168,000

Dividends of $34,000 were paid during the year. Depreciation of $19,000 was deducted on the income statement.

Equipment having a net book value of $48,000 was sold. A gain of $3,000 on the sale was included on the income statement.

Required: Prepare a statement of sources and uses of net working capital for 1985.

8. Net Loss and Net Working Capital Flow. Julie Foster is concerned that operations will not provide additional net working capital for further exploration of Northern Creek Mines. The following estimated income statement for the next year shows a substantial net loss.

Net sales	$1,754,000
Cost of goods sold, excluding depletion and depreciation	$ 878,000
Operating expenses, excluding depletion and depreciation	426,000
Depletion	383,000
Depreciation	262,000
Total expenses	$1,949,000
Net income (loss)......................................	$ (195,000)

Required:

(1) Compute the amount of net working capital provided by operations.

(2) Explain to Foster how there can be a positive flow of net working capital from operations in spite of the net loss.

9. Estimated Net Working Capital Flow. By a year from now, the president of Delisa Services Inc. hopes that the net working capital can be increased by $350,000 to help in financing some improvements to the building.

Sales for the next year have been budgeted at $1,700,000. Cost of goods sold and expenses of operation, including income taxes, have been estimated at $1,450,000. Depreciation of $80,000 is included in operating expenses.

Equipment is to be sold during the year, and it is estimated that $50,000 should be received from the sale of the equipment.

An installment of $30,000 becomes due on long-term notes payable.

Required:

(1) From the information furnished, prepare a statement of estimated sources and uses of net working capital for next year.

(2) According to the estimates, does it appear that net working capital can be increased by $350,000?

10. Cash Flow from Operations. Current assets and current liabilities of Yucatan Supply Company at June 30, 1984 and 1985, are as follows:

	June 30	
	1984	*1985*
Current assets:		
Cash	$ 37,250	$ 54,100
Accounts receivable.................................	26,220	25,870
Inventory	21,360	22,590
Prepaid insurance...................................	3,250	2,880
Total current assets...............................	$ 88,080	$105,440
Current liabilities:		
Accounts payable...................................	$ 17,540	$ 19,630
Accrued wages payable	5,270	4,720
Estimated income taxes payable.....................	21,520	20,340
Total current liabilities............................	$ 44,330	$ 44,690

Net income for the fiscal year ended June 30, 1985, was $14,000. Depreciation of $3,000 was deducted in the computation of the net income.

Required: Compute the cash flow from operations for the fiscal year ended June 30, 1985.

11. Cash Flow Effect of Sales and Cost of Goods Sold. Kappel Inc. reported net sales of $845,000 for the year. Accounts receivable decreased by $38,500 during the year. Part of the decrease was caused by the write-off of uncollectible accounts to the allowance account in the amount of $5,800.

The merchandise purchased during the year cost $624,000. Inventory at the beginning of the year was $17,700 and was $24,200 at the end of the year.

The accounts payable increased by $6,700 during the year.

Required: Determine the cash inflow from sales activity and the cash outflow resulting from merchandise acquisitions.

12. Cash Flow for the Year. The following income statement is for Santa Ana Company for 1985.

Santa Ana Company
Income Statement
For the Year Ended December 31, 1985

Net sales	$946,000
Cost of goods sold	$634,000
Operating expenses, including depreciation of $17,000	116,000
	$750,000
Income before income tax	$196,000
Income tax	78,000
Net income	$118,000

A statement of sources and uses of net working capital for 1985 is as follows:

Santa Ana Company
Statement of Sources and Uses of Net Working Capital
For the Year Ended December 31, 1985

Sources:		
Operations:		
Net income	$118,000	
Add depreciation	17,000	$135,000
Proceeds from the issue of long-term notes payable		150,000
Total sources		$285,000
Uses:		
Dividends declared		$ 45,000
Acquisition of machinery		175,000
		$220,000
Increase in net working capital		$ 65,000

Current assets and current liabilities at the end of 1984 and 1985 are as follows:

	1984	1985
Current assets:		
Cash	$ 48,000	$113,000
Marketable securities	50,000	20,000
Accounts receivable	54,000	86,000
Inventory	82,000	95,000
Total current assets	$234,000	$314,000
Current liabilities:		
Accounts payable	$ 17,000	$ 28,000
Accrued operating expenses payable	7,000	5,000
Income taxes payable	36,000	30,000
Dividends payable	3,000	15,000
Total current liabilities	$ 63,000	$ 78,000

The marketable securities were sold at the book value of $30,000.
Dividends of $45,000 were declared during the year.

Required: Prepare a statement of cash receipts and disbursements for the year. Convert each item on the income statement to a cash basis.

13. Estimated Cash Flow from Operations. An estimated income statement for Mickley Crossings Company for October, 1984, follows:

Net sales	$284,600
Cost of goods sold	167,200
Gross margin	$117,400
Supplies used	$ 7,800
Wages and salaries	34,100
Taxes and insurance	4,700
Advertising	3,500
Rent	6,000
Amortization of patents	500
Depreciation expense	2,600
Total expenses	$ 59,200
Net income	$ 58,200

Changes in current assets and liabilities have been estimated as follows:

Increases:

Accounts receivable	$ 11,300
Accounts payable	6,100
Prepaid taxes and insurance	800
Accrued wages and salaries payable	1,700

Decreases:

Accrued rent payable	600
Prepaid advertising	300
Inventory	9,700
Supplies	400

Required: Convert each item on the income statement to a cash flow basis by relating it to the increases or decreases in corresponding current assets or liabilities.

14. Net Working Capital and Cash Flow. Data from the financial statements of Cavern Equipment Company are given for 1985:

	Balances	
	December 31, 1985	January 1, 1985
Cash	$ 80,000	$ 65,000
Accounts receivable	81,000	78,000
Inventory	76,000	73,000
Current assets	$237,000	$216,000
Accounts payable	$ 29,000	$ 67,000

The income statement for the year shows net sales of $382,000, cost of goods sold of $213,000, and operating expenses of $121,000. Included in operating expenses is depreciation of $18,000. A loss of $4,000 is reported from the sale of equipment.

Equipment costing $75,000 was acquired, and the equipment sold had a net book value of $27,000 at date of sale. The company borrowed $45,000 on a long-term note payable.

Required:

(1) From the information given, prepare a statement of sources and uses of net working capital.

(2) Also prepare a statement of cash receipts and disbursements for the year.

15. Planning Debt Retirement. The president of Emerald Packing Company is concerned about the prospect of paying off long-term notes of $500,000 that become due for payment in three years. You have been asked to assemble data to indicate whether or not the debt can be retired without issuing new notes or capital stock.

(a) The net income next year has been estimated at $70,000 and is expected to increase to $90,000 in the year after next. In the third year, net income should be $120,000.

(b) Goodwill in the amount of $10,000 is to be amortized in each of the next three years, and this has been included in the estimates of net income.

(c) Depreciation of $35,000 is to be deducted each year and has been included in the estimates of net income.

(d) During the second year, the company plans to retire old equipment and estimates that $40,000 should be realized from the retirement. No gain or loss is expected from the transaction.

(e) Dividends of $15,000 are to be paid to the stockholders for each of the three years.

Required: Prepare a statement of estimated sources and uses of net working capital for the three years to show whether or not the long-term notes can be paid as planned. (Combine the three years.)

16. Planning Acquisitions. Condor Heights Inc. plans the acquisition of the stock of other companies, and the chairman of the board of directors estimates that this objective can be accomplished if additional net working capital of $8,000,000 can be provided within three years.

Estimates of net income and depreciation for each of the next three years are as follows:

Year	Net Income	Depreciation
1	$1,650,000	$320,000
2	2,160,000	370,000
3	2,820,000	560,000

In the second year, equipment having a net book value of $420,000 is to be retired. It is estimated that $600,000 can be realized from the retirement. The gain on the retirement has been included in the computation of the net income estimate for the second year.

Additional net working capital of $1,500,000 is to be raised from the issuance of capital stock in the first year.

Dividends of $250,000 are to be paid each year.

Required: According to the estimates, does it appear that Condor Heights Inc. can increase the net working capital by $8,000,000 in three years? (Combine the three years.)

PROBLEMS

18-1. Net Working Capital Flow. Roland Tyre asks you to prepare a statement that will show how net working capital increased by $165,000 during 1984.

The following are summarized financial statements.

Tyre Industries Inc.
Income Statement
For the Year Ended December 31, 1984

Net sales	$2,642,000
Cost of goods sold	$1,288,000
Operating expenses, including depreciation of $156,000	730,000
	$2,018,000
Income before income tax	$ 624,000
Income tax	250,000
Net income	$ 374,000

Tyre Industries Inc.
Balance Sheet
December 31, 1985 and 1984

	1985	1984
Current assets	$ 863,000	$ 684,000
Plant and equipment, net of accumulated depreciation	554,000	370,000
Total assets	$1,417,000	$1,054,000
Current liabilities	$ 356,000	$ 342,000
Long-term notes payable	100,000	—0—
Capital stock	500,000	500,000
Retained earnings	461,000	212,000
Total equities	$1,417,000	$1,054,000

Additional data:

(a) There were no sales or retirements of plant and equipment during the year.
(b) Dividends of $125,000 were paid.

Required: Prepare a statement of sources and uses of net working capital for Roland Tyre.

18-2. Decrease in Net Working Capital. Peter Garcia cannot understand why net working capital decreased by $26,000 during the last fiscal quarter when the net income for the quarter was $31,000. He had expected that the net working capital would increase by the amount of the net income. Depreciation of $4,000 was deducted on the income statement.

Noncurrent balance sheet items from the statements at the beginning and at the end of the quarter follow:

	Beginning of Quarter	End of Quarter
Plant and equipment, net of accumulated depreciation	$118,000	$143,000
Long-term debt	80,000	60,000
Retained earnings	106,000	125,000

Required: Prepare a statement of sources and uses of net working capital that will show why Garcia's expectations were not realized.

18-3. Net Working Capital and Acquisitions. The president of Stevenson Appliances has been looking at the financial statements of a competitor, Denny Appliances. The president observes that the company invested $8,500,000 in new plant and equipment in 1984 and did not finance it by the issuance of debt or capital stock. Furthermore, dividend payments to stockholders were not reduced. The president asks you to determine how the competitor was able to finance these additions without borrowing or issuing stock.

In 1983, equipment having a net book value of $2,364,000 was sold at a gain of $375,000, net of income tax. No other plant assets were sold.

Financial data from the statements for Denny Appliances for the past three years are:

	Year Ended December 31 (In thousands of dollars)		
	1984	*1983*	*1982*
Net income*	$1,807	$1,692	$1,286
Depreciation deducted for the year......................	912	985	985
Dividends declared and paid............................	250	250	250

*Excludes effect of gain on sale of equipment.

Required:

(1) Explain to the president how net working capital was acquired for the plant additions made by Denny Appliances.

(2) Prepare statements for 1982, 1983, and 1984 that will show how net working capital was obtained and put to use.

18-4. Cash Flow from Operations. "Net income is fine," the president of Oliver Parts Company exclaims, "but what I want to know is how much cash is coming in to keep us solvent."

An income statement for 1984 is given for Oliver Parts Company.

Oliver Parts Company
Income Statement
For the Year Ended December 31, 1984

Net sales	$7,215,000
Cost of goods sold	$4,126,000
Operating expenses......................................	973,000
Income tax...	846,000
	$5,945,000
Net income	$1,270,000

Depreciation of $176,000 is included in operating expenses.

Current assets and current liabilities are given as of December 31, 1983 and 1984.

	December 31	
	1984	*1983*
Current assets		
Cash	$ 932,000	$1,340,000
Accounts receivable...................................	921,000	746,000
Inventory	1,464,000	872,000
Prepaid expenses.....................................	26,000	28,000
Total current assets.................................	$3,343,000	$2,986,000
Current liabilities		
Accounts payable.....................................	$ 632,000	$ 924,000
Accrued operating expenses payable	82,000	97,000
Income taxes payable	157,000	324,000
Dividends payable	70,000	85,000
Total current liabilities..............................	$ 941,000	$1,430,000

Dividends of $600,000 were declared in 1984.

Aside from depreciation, net income, and dividends, no transactions affected noncurrent assets or equities.

Required:

(1) Prepare a statement of the flow of cash. Show the cash flow effect of each item on the income statement.

(2) Is the president justified in being concerned about the cash position? Explain.

18-5. Operational Flow of Net Working Capital and Cash. Jennifer Mayleth operates a stationery and office supply store. Next year Mayleth hopes to increase the cash balance of the business by $15,000. Net income for the year has been estimated at $82,000, and Mayleth plans to withdraw $50,000 for personal use. She states that depreciation will provide enough cash for the acquisition of new store fixtures.

An estimated income statement follows:

Rainbow Stationery
Estimated Income Statement
For the Year Ended June 30, 1985

Net sales	$916,000
Cost of goods sold	$709,000
Operating expenses, including depreciation of $18,000	125,000
	$834,000
Net income	$ 82,000

During the coming fiscal year, fixtures costing $31,000 are to be acquired.

Current assets and liabilities at June 30, 1984, and estimated current assets and liabilities at June 30, 1985, follow:

	Estimated Balances June 30, 1985	Actual Balances June 30, 1984
Current assets:		
Cash	$ 65,000	$ 62,000
Accounts receivable......	38,000	43,000
Inventories	123,000	112,000
Prepaid expenses..........................	15,000	9,000
Total current assets.......................	$241,000	$226,000
Current liabilities:		
Accounts payable..........................	$ 48,000	$ 25,000
Bank loans................................	35,000	60,000
Accrued operating expenses	21,000	23,000
Total current liabilities...................	$104,000	$108,000
Net working capital	$137,000	$118,000

Required:

   (1) Is Mayleth correct in stating that depreciation can provide cash for the acquisition of store fixtures? Explain.
   (2) Prepare a statement of estimated sources and uses of net working capital.
   (3) Prepare a statement of estimated cash receipts and disbursements. Convert each item on the income statement to a cash basis.
   (4) Explain why the cash balance did not increase by $15,000 as anticipated.

18-6. Planning Net Working Capital With Debt Retirement. The management of Stapleton Industries Inc. is faced with increasing costs and a resistance to higher prices for the products sold. Credit is difficult to obtain, and the holders of the long-term notes request that the company reduce the debt in the equity structure. On February 1, 1986, long-term notes of $900,000 become due.

   A balance sheet at December 31, 1984, along with an estimated balance sheet at December 31, 1985, follow.

Stapleton Industries Inc.
Balance Sheet
December 31, 1984 and 1985
(In thousands of dollars)

Assets	1985	1984
Cash	$ 949	$ 377
Accounts receivable	337	295
Inventories	563	612
Prepaid expenses	37	46
Plant and equipment, net of accumulated depreciation	2,152	2,557
Total assets	$4,038	$3,887

Equities	1985	1984
Accounts payable	$ 127	$ 115
Accrued operating expenses	92	87
Short-term bank loans	180	250
Current installment, long-term notes payable	900	–0–
Long-term notes payable	500	1,400
Capital stock	500	500
Paid-in capital in excess of par	900	900
Retained earnings	839	635
Total equities	$4,038	$3,887

An estimated income statement for the year ended December 31, 1985, follows.

Stapleton Industries Inc.
Estimated Income Statement
For the Year Ended December 31, 1985
(In thousands of dollars)

Net sales	$2,742
Cost of goods sold, including depreciation of $124,000	$1,780
Selling and administrative expenses, including depreciation of $34,000.	527
Interest expense.	158
Gain on sale of equipment	(63)
	$2,402
Income before income tax	$ 340
Income tax.	136
Net income	$ 204

Additional data:

(a) Equipment costing $33,000 is to be purchased during the year ending December 31, 1985.

(b) The company management hopes to have a net working capital balance of at least $500,000 after payment of the current installment of the long-term notes.

Required:

(1) Does it appear that the company will have a net working capital balance of at least $500,000 after retirement of $900,000 in long-term notes payable?

(2) Prepare an estimated statement of sources and uses of net working capital for the year ended December 31, 1985.

18-7. Net Working Capital and Cash Flow—Incomplete Data. From incomplete information, you are trying to reconstruct how the net working capital and cash changed for Warm Springs Container Company during the year ended June 30, 1985.

Data from the balance sheets at June 30, 1984 and 1985, are as follows.

	June 30	
	1985	*1984*
Noncurrent assets:		
Investment in Cole Fasteners	$1,386,000	$1,146,000
Land	171,000	133,000
Buildings, net of accumulated depreciation	935,000	680,000
Equipment, net of accumulated depreciation	1,077,000	950,000
	$3,569,000	$2,909,000
Noncurrent equities:		
Long-term notes payable	$1,500,000	$1,000,000
Capital stock.	1,160,000	1,060,000
Paid-in capital in excess of par	1,670,000	1,530,000
Retained earnings.	1,512,000	1,274,000
	$5,842,000	$4,864,000

You have been given the following information with respect to increases and decreases in current assets and current liabilities.

	Increases	Decreases
Accounts receivable	$94,000	
Inventory	68,000	
Prepaid expenses		$11,000
Accounts payable		56,000
Accrued expenses payable	16,000	
Dividends payable	75,000	

Net income for the fiscal year ended June 30, 1985, was $538,000. Included on the income statement was total depreciation expense of $175,000 and a loss of $32,000 on equipment sold during the fiscal year.

The equipment sold had an original cost of $155,000 and accumulated depreciation of $46,000 to date of sale.

No buildings were retired during the fiscal year. Depreciation of $55,000 was taken on the buildings during the fiscal year.

Capital stock was issued in exchange for the stock of Cole Fasteners.

Required:

(1) Prepare a statement of changes in financial position for the year ended June 30, 1985.

(2) Prepare a statement showing the net increase or decrease in the cash balance for the year ended June 30, 1985.

18-8. Net Working Capital Plan. Hobart Products Inc. is planning to construct a new building and to make some major changes in operations.

In anticipation of construction, the company has conserved net working capital and has not paid dividends during the past year.

Estimates show that the building will probably cost $18,000,000 and that furnishings and equipment may cost another $4,000,000.

Other actions that have been planned for the next year, 1986, are:

(a) The company plans to issue 50,000 additional shares of capital stock at an average price of $21 per share.

(b) Old plant assets having a net book value of $1,910,000 are to be retired. It is estimated that $3,170,000 will be received from their sale. Costs of $60,000 will be incurred for advertising and for the sale of the assets. Income tax on the gain will be at the rate of 25%.

(c) The investment in Barnes Tool Company will be sold for $3,550,000 with a 25% tax on the gain.

(d) The company plans to have a minimum of $3,000,000 in net working capital by the end of the next year.

(e) The building can be partially financed by a long-term loan of $10,000,000, with interest at the rate of 15% being deducted to leave net proceeds of $8,500,000. In later years, interest of $1,500,000 is to be paid each year until the loan becomes due. Management would prefer not to finance this much but will do so if necessary.

The following are estimated income statement data for the next year.

Net sales are estimated at $36,000,000 with cost of goods sold and operating expenses combined at $26,370,000. Included in cost of goods sold and operating expenses is depreciation of $1,230,000. Interest expense (including $1,500,000 interest on the proposed long-term loan) has been estimated at $1,550,000. Income tax is at the rate of 50%.

Balance sheet data as of December 31, 1985, are:

Assets

Cash	$ 1,086,000
Temporary investments	3,500,000
Accounts receivable.	1,631,000
Inventories	2,463,000
Investment in Barnes Tool Co.	1,550,000
Plant and equipment, net of accumulated depreciation	7,340,000
Total assets	$17,570,000

Equities

Accounts payable.	$ 1,033,000
Short-term bank loans	400,000
Accrued operating expenses payable	720,000
Interest payable	35,000
Capital stock, $10 par value, 300,000 shares issued and outstanding	3,000,000
Premium on stock	6,240,000
Retained earnings.	6,142,000
Total equities.	$17,570,000

Required:

(1) Prepare a statement of estimated sources and uses of net working capital for 1986. (Assume that new building and furnishings will require net working outlay in 1986.)

(2) Will the company need all or part of the long-term loan?

18-9. Planning Net Working Capital Flow. The board of directors of Pinnacle Systems Inc. is reviewing a plan for the acquisition of new machinery and equipment. The cost of this project has been estimated at $25,000,000.

Next year, old equipment with a cost of $3,800,000 and accumulated depreciation of $2,200,000 is to be sold.

There has been some dissatisfaction expressed with respect to the preferred stock. For a number of years, 8% preferred stock with a par value of $100 per share has been outstanding. The 10,000 shares of this stock can be retired at a cost of $120 per share, and the board of directors has voted to do this next year.

Ordinarily, a dividend of $2 per share is paid each year on the 600,000 shares of outstanding common stock; and this policy is to be followed next year.

One of the board members states that the common stockholders are becoming disturbed with dividends of $2 per share when the earnings per share have been much higher. The stockholders report indicates that earnings have been intentionally held for capital improvements. However, the board member warns that a more liberal dividend policy must be taken in future years.

An estimated income statement is given for the next year.

(In thousands of dollars)

Net sales	$31,560
Cost of goods sold	$16,450
Variable operating expenses	2,760
	$19,210
Contribution margin	$12,350
Fixed cost, including depreciation on manufacturing facilities of $1,050,000 and $700,000 on selling and administrative facilities	4,650
Operating income	$ 7,700
Interest expense	500
Gain on sale of equipment	(1,300)
Income before income tax	$ 8,500
Income tax	3,400
Net income	$ 5,100
Dividend requirement on preferred stock	80
Net income for common stock	$ 5,020

The dividends on the preferred stock must be paid before the stock can be retired.

Before going ahead with the new equipment acquisition, the board of directors recognizes that net working capital accumulated from the past can be reduced by $8,000,000 and still leave a substantial backlog to support an increased volume of sales in the future. Even so, the board does not want to seek more than $10,000,000 in new capital—debt or stock—if possible.

Required: Prepare an estimate of the sources and uses of net working capital next year. Arrange the statement so that new capital required will appear as the final item. Will the board need more than $10,000,000 in new capital?

18-10. Cash Flow and Dividends. Business for McElroy Windings Company is expected to be slow during the next quarter but should pick up later in the year. If possible, the board of directors would like to continue the policy of paying a $.60 dividend per share of stock each quarter. There are 750,000 shares of common stock outstanding, and the board will not vote for the dividend if it will reduce the cash balance at the beginning of the quarter by more than $75,000.

The following is an estimated income statement for the next quarter.

McElroy Windings Company
Estimated Income Statement
For the Next Quarter

Net sales	$1,213,000
Cost of goods sold, including depreciation of $87,000	$ 604,000
Selling and administrative expense, including depreciation of $38,000	209,000
Income tax	184,000
Total expenses	$ 997,000
Net income	$ 216,000

Estimates indicate that accounts receivable should be reduced during the quarter by $32,000 as a result of a stricter policy on collections. However, inventories must be increased by $45,000 in anticipation of future sales. Payments on the accounts payable will be delayed, causing accounts payable to increase by $27,000. The liability for selling and administrative expenses is to be increased by $16,000. An income tax payment of $120,000 will be made during the quarter.

Required: From the information given, does it appear that the dividend of $.60 a share can be paid under the terms given? Support your conclusion with a statement of estimated cash flow for the quarter. (Show estimated receipts and subtract estimated disbursements to solve for the expected increase or decrease in cash.)

18-11. Net Working Capital and Cash Flow. Donald Bowers, the president of Metairie-Delta Company, noted that net working capital increased by $1,361,000 during 1984, but he is concerned to see that the cash balance increased by only $337,000.

You have been asked to prepare statements that will show how net working capital increased by $1,361,000 and how cash increased by $337,000.

An income statement for 1984 is given below.

Metairie-Delta Company
Income Statement
For the Year Ended December 31, 1984
(In Thousands of Dollars)

Net sales		$16,427
Cost of goods sold, including depreciation of $2,173		11,083
Gross margin		$ 5,344
Operating expenses:		
Wages and salaries	$724	
Insurance expense	33	
Advertising..	46	
Property taxes	221	
Depreciation	278	
Amortization of patents.......................................	35	
Amortization of goodwill	50	
Other operating expenses	168	1,555
Operating income		$ 3,789
Other deductions:		
Interest expense..	$512	
Loss on sale of marketable securities..........................	37	
Loss on sale of equipment	126	675
Income before income tax		$ 3,114
Income tax..		1,244
Net income		$ 1,870

Balance sheets at December 31, 1983 and 1984, follow.

Metairie-Delta Company
Balance Sheet
December 31, 1984 and 1983
(In thousands of dollars)

Assets

	1984	1983
Current assets:		
Cash	$ 1,683	$ 1,346
Marketable securities	1,500	1,700
Accounts receivable, net of estimated uncollectibles	1,481	1,264
Inventories	2,579	1,587
Prepaid insurance	71	66
Total current assets	$ 7,314	$ 5,963
Property, plant, and equipment, net of accumulated depreciation	8,388	9,846
Intangible assets:		
Goodwill	250	300
Patents	240	275
Total assets	$16,192	$16,384

Equities

	1984	1983
Current liabilities:		
Accounts payable	$ 1,746	$ 1,621
Wages payable	52	87
Other accrued operating expenses	123	134
Bank loans payable	160	360
Dividends payable	118	94
Income taxes payable	347	386
Total current liabilities	$ 2,546	$ 2,682
Long-term debt payable	2,500	3,626
Stockholders' equity:		
Capital stock	3,000	3,000
Paid-in capital in excess of par	2,816	2,816
Retained earnings	5,330	4,260
Total equities	$16,192	$16,384

Additional data:

(a) No marketable securities were purchased. The marketable securities sold were shown on the records at $200,000.

(b) Uncollectible accounts expense of $21,000 was included in other operating expenses.

(c) Uncollectible accounts in the amount of $14,000 were written off against the allowance for uncollectibles.

(d) Equipment sold during the year had a net book value of $487,000 at date of sale.

Required:

(1) Prepare a statement of sources and uses of net working capital for the year.

(2) Prepare a statement of cash receipts and disbursements. (Show the detail of cash receipts and disbursements from operations.)

18-12. Net Working Capital Flow. The following financial statements are given for Rapp Machine Company.

Rapp Machine Company
Income Statement
For the Year Ended April 30, 1985

Net sales	$4,163,500
Cost of goods sold	2,376,700*
Gross margin	$1,786,800
Operating expenses	691,300*
Operating income	$1,095,500
Interest expense	126,000
Gain on sale of equipment	(82,000)
Income before income tax	$1,051,500
Income tax	420,000
Net income	$ 631,500

*Included in cost of goods sold and operating expenses is depreciation expense of $172,000.

Rapp Machine Company
Comparative Balance Sheet
April 30, 1985 and 1984

Assets	1985	1984
Current assets:		
Cash	$ 226,000	$ 273,300
Accounts receivable	217,200	196,500
Inventories	530,000	314,800
Total current assets	$ 973,200	$ 784,600
Investment in Gregg Equipment Inc.	$ 350,000	-0-
Property, plant, and equipment		
Land	$ 56,000	$ 40,000
Buildings, net of accumulated depreciation	524,000	562,000
Equipment, net of accumulated depreciation	583,00	677,000
Total property, plant, and equipment	$1,163,000	$1,279,000
Total assets	$2,486,200	$2,063,600
Equities		
Current liabilities:		
Accounts payable	$ 317,800	$ 287,600
Wages and salaries payable	158,400	143,100
Other accrued liabilities	166,000	151,200
Total current liabilities	$ 642,200	$ 581,900
Notes payable, due October 1, 1992	$ 250,000	$ 400,000
Stockholders' equity:		
Capital stock, $10 par value	$ 400,000	$ 300,000
Premium on capital stock	724,000	563,000
Retained earnings	470,000	218,700
Total stockholders' equity	$1,594,000	$1,081,700
Total equities	$2,486,200	$2,063,600

Additional data:

(a) Buildings were neither acquired nor retired during the year.

(b) Equipment costing $235,000 was purchased during the year.

(c) The company declared and paid dividends of $380,200 in April, 1985.

Required: Prepare a statement of sources and uses of net working capital for the fiscal year ended April 30, 1985.

18-13. Reduced Net Working Capital. Mary DeWalt, chairman of the board of directors of Bedford Fabricating Company, is distressed to find that net working capital has decreased and that the company is having so much difficulty with debt management.

The president of the company, while concerned, stated that high interest rates have created a problem and that additional capital cannot be raised under present conditions. However, last year the company had to have new equipment to stay in business. In the president's opinion, the reduced sales volume has created problems that can be resolved when economic conditions improve. The company is still profitable and able to pay dividends, the president states, and the situation is not critical.

The following are the financial statements for the company.

Bedford Fabricating Company
Balance Sheet
December 31, 1985 and 1984

Assets	1985	1984
Current assets:		
Cash	$ 73,000	$ 116,000
Accounts receivable.	168,000	173,000
Inventories	217,000	226,000
Total current assets.	$ 458,000	$ 515,000
Property, plant, and equipment, net of accumulated		
depreciation	982,000	859,000
Total assets	$1,440,000	$1,374,000

Equities		
Current liabilities:		
Accounts payable	$ 116,000	$ 108,000
Bank loans.	215,000	206,000
Accrued expenses payable	71,000	64,000
Total current liabilities	$ 402,000	$ 378,000
Notes payable, due May 1, 1988	810,000	810,000
Stockholders' equity:		
Capital stock	150,000	150,000
Retained earnings.	78,000	36,000
Total equities.	$1,440,000	$1,374,000

Bedford Fabricating Company
Income Statement
For the Year Ended December 31, 1985

Net sales	$1,324,000
Cost of goods sold	$ 752,000
Operating expenses, including depreciation of $77,000	317,000
Interest expense	141,000
	$1,210,000
Income before income tax	$ 114,000
Income tax	42,000
Net income	$ 72,000

Dividends of $30,000 were declared and paid during the year.

On September 1, 1985, the company purchased equipment at a cost of $200,000. No equipment was sold during the year.

Required:

(1) Prepare a statement of sources and uses of net working capital for 1985.

(2) How was the company able to finance the acquisition of the new equipment without additional long-term loans or without issuing capital stock?

(3) Do you believe that the net working capital situation is serious? Comment.

18-14. Statement of Changes in Financial Position. As a financial analyst, you have been asked to make a report on Herron Products Company. Financial statements are as follows:

Herron Products Company
Income Statement
For the Year Ended December 31, 1985
(In thousands of dollars)

Net sales	$6,137
Cost of goods sold, including depreciation of $215,000	$3,019
Operating expenses, including depreciation of $126,000	1,140
Interest expense	219
Loss on sale of equipment	28
Loss from flood of May 14	96
Income tax	654
Total expenses	$5,156
Net income	$ 981

Herron Products Company
Comparative Balance Sheet
December 31, 1985 and 1984
(In thousands of dollars)

	1985	1984
Assets		
Current assets:		
Cash	$ 1,543	$ 1,062
Temporary investments	1,030	1,015
Accounts receivable	2,175	2,073
Inventories	2,320	1,940
Prepaid expenses	137	146
Total current assets	$ 7,205	$ 6,236
Investment in Pearson Designs Inc.	1,600	–0–
Property, plant, and equipment:		
Land	1,218	936
Buildings, net of accumulated depreciation	4,657	4,627
Equipment, net of accumulated depreciation	7,466	7,462
Total assets	$22,146	$19,261
Equities		
Current liabilities:		
Accounts payable	$ 1,218	$ 1,327
Bank loans payable	1,100	1,000
Accrued operating expenses	373	386
Income tax payable	287	261
Total current liabilities	$ 2,978	$ 2,974
Bonds payable	3,300	1,700
Stockholders' equity:		
Capital stock, $10 par value	6,000	5,800
Paid-in capital in excess of par	5,800	5,200
Retained earnings	4,068	3,587
Total equities	$22,146	$19,261

Further examination has provided you with the following information.

(a) Bonds were issued in exchange for the capital stock of Pearson Designs Inc.

(b) A flood caused damage to the buildings and equipment. Buildings having a net book value of $173,000 at the date of the flood were destroyed along with equipment having a net book value of $580,000. The insurance recovery from the loss was $657,000.

(c) Buildings were not retired during the year. Replacements and renovations, however, cost $386,000.

(d) Depreciation on the buildings, included in total depreciation expense, was $183,000.

(e) The net book value of equipment sold was $194,000.

(f) The company issued 20,000 shares of capital stock selling at a price of $40 per share for equipment. Additional equipment was acquired for cash.

(g) Dividends of $500,000 were paid during the year.

Required: From the information furnished, prepare a statement of changes in financial position.

18-15. Cash Flow Plan. In 1985, Gifford Company plans to acquire new equipment costing $2,500,000. Plans have been made to finance $900,000 of the cost with long-term notes payable. The balance is to be paid when the equipment is acquired.

James Gifford, the president of the company, hopes that the cash flow will be enough to meet the required payment for equipment without reducing the cash balance below $450,000 needed for normal operations.

Actual balances of current assets and liabilities are given at December 31, 1984, along with estimated balances at December 31, 1985.

| | December 31 | |
	1985	1984
Current assets:		
Cash	?	$ 626,000
Marketable securities	$ 80,000	230,000
Accounts receivable net of uncollectibles	372,000	418,000
Inventories	336,000	387,000
Total	$788,000	$1,661,000
Current liabilities:		
Accounts payable	$273,000	$208,000
Notes payable	200,000	50,000
Accrued expenses payable	143,000	126,000
Total	$616,000	$384,000

Gifford is not sure what the cash balance may be at December 31, 1985, considering the plan for equipment acquisition.

An estimated income statement for 1985 follows.

Gifford Company
Estimated Income Statement
For the Year Ended December 31, 1985

Net sales	$2,032,000
Cost of goods sold	1,423,000
Gross margin	$ 609,000
Operating expenses:	
Wages and salaries	$ 95,000
Advertising	38,000
Taxes and insurance	27,000
Heat and light	20,000
Uncollectible accounts expense	32,000
Depreciation expense	186,000
Other operating expense	47,000
Total	$ 445,000
Operating income	$ 164,000
Add interest earned	22,000
Deduct: Interest expense	(29,000)
Loss on sale of marketable securities	(11,000)
Total	$ (18,000)
Income before income tax	$ 146,000
Income tax	58,000
Net income	$ 88,000

During the year, marketable securities shown on the records at $150,000 are to be sold.

Accounts receivable in the amount of $45,000 are to be written off against the allowance for uncollectibles as uncollectible.

Required:

(1) Based upon the information furnished, prepare an estimated statement of cash receipts and disbursements.

(2) Can Gifford accomplish his objective?

18-16. Estimated Cash Receipts and Disbursements. Redden and Evans Inc. has expanded operations without sufficient net working capital to support the expanded operation. At the end of 1984, the company is faced with an acute cash shortage.

Short-term bank loans have been increased to pay for current operating costs. The bank refuses to extend more credit until the company shows that it has taken steps to improve its cash position.

The current assets and current liabilities as of December 31, 1984, are as follows:

Current assets:	
Cash	$ 214,600
Accounts receivable, net of uncollectibles	1,384,200
Inventories	2,037,600
Supplies inventory	233,000
Unexpired insurance	17,000
Total current assets	$3,886,400
Current liabilities:	
Accounts payable	$2,387,500
Bank loans payable	2,000,000
Rent payable	54,000
Wages and payroll taxes payable	39,000
Estimated income tax payable	72,400
Total current liabilities	$4,552,900

The loan officer at the bank recommends that the accounts payable be reduced next year to $1,800,000 and that the bank loans payable be reduced to $1,500,000 by June 30, 1985.

The president of the company plans some emergency measures to meet the goals of the loan officer. The inventory is to be reduced by $150,000 by selling many of the slower-moving items at lower prices. A more rigorous collection policy will be undertaken to reduce accounts receivable, net of allowance for uncollectibles, to $1,150,000 by June 30, 1985.

Other current asset and current liability balances, with the exception of cash, have been estimated as follows:

Unexpired insurance	$ 12,000
Supplies inventory	215,000
Rent payable	24,000
Wages and payroll taxes payable	42,000
Estimated income tax payable	68,200

During the six months ended June 30, 1985, the company plans to sell long-term investments that have been recorded in the accounts at $480,000.

The following is an estimated income statement for the six months ended June 30, 1985.

Redden and Evans, Inc.
Estimated Income Statement
For the Six Months Ended June 30, 1985

Net sales	$7,163,000
Cost of goods sold*	5,842,000
Gross margin	$1,321,000
Operating expenses:	
Supplies used	$ 227,000
Wages and payroll taxes	443,000
Depreciation	115,000
Estimated uncollectible accounts expense	46,000
Rent expense	30,000
Amortization of goodwill	15,000
Insurance expense	5,000
Total operating expenses	$ 881,000
Operating income	$ 440,000
Interest expense	$ 165,000
Loss of sale of investments	55,000
Total	$ 220,000
Income before income tax	$ 220,000
Income tax	88,000
Net income	$ 132,000

*Includes depreciation of $110,000.

Required:

(1) On the basis of the estimates, prepare a statement of cash receipts and disbursements for the six months ended June 30, 1985.

(2) Can the objectives be met without reducing the cash balance below the amount at June 30, 1984?

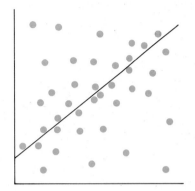

Appendix A

AN OVERVIEW OF THE ACCOUNTING PROCESS

The American Institute of Certified Public Accountants has defined accounting as follows:

> Accounting is the art of recording, classifying, and summarizing in a significant manner and in terms of money, transactions and events which are, in part at least, of a financial character, and interpreting the results thereof.[1]

THE ACCOUNTING CYCLE

In this appendix the recording, classifying, and summarizing aspects of accounting — that is, the accounting cycle — will be described and illustrated.

Duality

The properties of an entity and the rights in those properties are accounted for as they enter or leave the business, as they circulate within the business, or as they stand at any point in time. The properties are called assets, and the rights in the properties are called equities. The rights or equities of outsiders are called liabilities, and the rights of the owners are called the owners' equity. Some typical assets are described as follows:

---

[1] *Accounting Research and Terminology Bulletins — Final Edition,* "Accounting Terminology Bulletins, No. 1, Review and Résumé" (New York: American Institute of Certified Public Accountants, 1961), par. 9.

Cash — cash on hand or on deposit in banks.

Accounts receivable — amounts owed by customers of the business.

Inventory — materials to be used in manufacturing products and finished or partly finished products and merchandise to be sold to customers.

Land — real estate owned and used by the business.

Building — building owned and used in conducting business activities.

Equipment — equipment owned and used in conducting business activities.

Some typical equities are described below:

Accounts payable — amounts owed to trade creditors of the business.

Notes payable — promissory notes owed to the bank or to other outsiders.

Mortgage payable — debt owed and secured by a mortgage on business property.

John Adams, capital — designation of the interest in a business of an owner named John Adams.

Both the assets and the equities are accounted for simultaneously. A business transaction does not affect just one item alone. There are at least two items to be considered in each transaction. It would not be possible, for example, for a business to have a transaction that resulted only in the increase of the asset cash. There must be some explanation as to why cash increased. Cash may have been received in exchange for some other asset that left the business, or the cash may have entered the business as a result of a loan made by some outsider or as a result of investment by the owner.

The dual aspect of each transaction forms the basis underlying what is called double-entry accounting. In double-entry accounting, it is recognized that no asset can exist without someone having a claim or a right to it. Therefore, both the specific assets and the equities are accounted for at the time that transactions are recorded. The assets of a business can be increased by:

1. Donations.
2. Investments by the owners.
3. The service performed by the business.
4. Loans or credit furnished by outsiders.

Assets obtained through loans or credit result in an increase in liabilities. In all the other situations listed above, the owners' equity is increased. Both the increase in the assets and the increase in the rights to the assets are recorded. The total assets of a business can be decreased by:

1. Losses such as fire or theft.
2. Withdrawal of assets by owners, such as dividend payments.
3. The use of assets, such as inventory, to conduct operations.
4. Donations to others.
5. The settlement of the claims (liabilities) of outsiders.

The use of assets to settle the claims of outsiders results in a reduction in liabilities. In all the other situations listed, the owners' equity is decreased. The decrease in the asset and the decrease in the equity are both recorded.

One asset may be exchanged for another, or one type of equity may be converted to another form. For example, an account receivable from a customer in the amount of $2,000 may be collected. Total assets remain unchanged in amount. There has only been a change in the composition of the assets: cash has increased by $2,000, and the account receivable from the customer has been reduced by $2,000. The holder of a note against the company may be issued stock in exchange for rights as a creditor; that is, the liability for the note payable is eliminated and is replaced with an addition to the owners' equity. The total equity in the firm is the same in amount as it was before, but the form of the equity has changed.

The Accounting Equation and Transactions

The relationship between the properties called assets and the rights in the properties called equities can be expressed in the form of an equation, as follows:

$$\textbf{Assets} = \textbf{Equities}$$

The rights of outsiders called liabilities and the rights of the owners called owners' equity or capital are recognized and expressed as a relationship, which is known as the accounting equation:

$$\text{Assets} = \text{Liabilities} + \text{Capital}$$

A business transaction is an event or condition that requires an entry in the accounting records. Business transactions can be expressed in terms of their effect on the accounting equation. The effect of changes on the three basic elements can be illustrated by examining the accounting equation and some typical transactions. The amounts are numbered so that they can be identified with the transactions.

(1) Karen Weaver begins business on October 1 by investing $75,000 in cash. After this transaction, the business has cash as an asset in the amount of $75,000; and the owner's equity, that is the claim of Weaver on the assets, is $75,000.

(2) Weaver pays $900 for the rental of a store for three months. The asset cash is traded for the asset prepaid rent, representing the right to occupy the store for three months.

(3) New equipment costing $30,000 is purchased for the store on account. An asset is increased in exchange for an increase in a liability.

(4) Payments of $28,000 were made to the creditors from whom equipment was purchased. The asset cash is reduced by $28,000, and the liability accounts payable is reduced by $28,000.

	Assets			= Liabilities +	Capital
		Prepaid		Accounts	Karen Weaver
	Cash	+ Rent	+ Equipment =	Payable +	Capital
(1)	+75,000				+75,000
(2)	−900	+900			
(3)			+30,000	+30,000	
(4)	−28,000			−28,000	

The Accounting Equation and Revenue and Expense

In the previous illustration, no transactions were included which required the recognition of revenue or expense. Assets are increased by revenue received for services performed by a business. Revenue can be defined as the consideration received by the business for rendering goods and services to its customers. Terms used for particular types of revenue, such as sales, indicate how the revenue was earned. Revenue is treated as an increase in capital. Expense can be defined as a measure of the decrease in assets incurred in the process of producing revenue. Terms used for particular types of expenses, such as *rent*, indicate how the asset was used. Expense is treated as a reduction in capital.

The relationship between assets, liabilities, capital, revenue, and expense can be expressed with the accounting equation as follows:

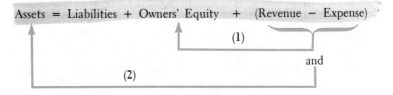

$$Assets = Liabilities + Owners'\ Equity + (Revenue - Expense)$$

(1)

and

(2)

(1) (Revenue − Expense) — measurement of *net* increase or decrease in owners' equity from rendering goods or services to customers during an accounting period.

(2) (Revenue − Expense) — measurement of *net* inflow or outflow of assets as a result of rendering goods or services to customers during an accounting period.

The equation as presented above is somewhat oversimplified, but it is essentially true. Revenue and expense accounts measure aggregate increases or decreases in assets, but no specific assets are identified. More precisely, it may be stated that net assets (assets − liabilities) are increased or decreased when revenue and expense are recognized. Sometimes assets are received with a corresponding liability being recorded until goods or services are delivered. When the goods or services are delivered, the liability is reduced and revenue is recorded. For example, a cash deposit may be received from a customer with a liability being recorded for the obligation to deliver goods or services in the future. Eventually, when the goods or services are delivered, the liability is removed and revenue is recognized.

Often the relationship between the assets and the revenue and expenses is direct. For example, assets such as cash or accounts receivable are usually increased when sales revenue is recorded. At the same time, cost of goods sold is recorded as an expense and the inventory (asset) is reduced.

Source Documents

A business transaction is ordinarily supported by some form or source document which serves as evidence or proof of the transaction and gives information about what has happened. It may be received from an outsider, or it may originate within the business unit. A bill or an invoice received from a supplier of materials supports an entry to record an increase in the materials inventory asset and the accounts payable liability. Sometimes materials are transferred within the company. A document is usually prepared to support the transfer and to give the essential facts of the transaction. The materials inventory of one division is increased, while the materials inventory of the other division is decreased. Forms originating within the enterprise are also sent to outsiders. Bills or invoices are mailed to customers when sales are made, and checks are sent to creditors in payment of amounts owed.

Accounts

The method of accumulating data should be designed so that information can be collected easily.

Data can be collected by classification in accounts. In essence, accounts are pages or cards divided into two halves by a vertical line and may appear somewhat as follows.

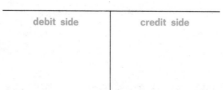

There is an account for each asset, liability, owner's equity, revenue, and expense. The left side of the account is called the debit side of the account, and the right side of the account is called the credit side. Debit and credit are the terms used for left and right in accounting. A book of accounts or a file of account cards is referred to as a ledger.

Increases in accounts are recorded on one side of the account, and decreases are recorded on the other side. The balance of the account is the difference between the sum of the items on each side of the account. There is a debit balance if the amounts on the left side are greater, and there is a credit balance if the amounts on the right side are greater.

Increases and Decreases in Accounts.

Special rules for recording increases and decreases are employed for each basic type of account: asset, liability, owners' equity, revenue, and expense. The accounting equation is given once more to show the rules of increase and decrease:

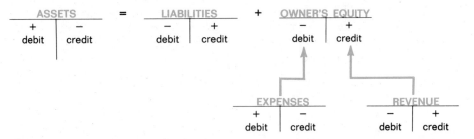

The increases and decreases are arranged so that each transaction can be recorded and classified properly while maintaining an equality of debits and credits. If the recording process is carried out properly in the mechanical sense, the sum of the accounts with debit balances will equal the sum of the accounts with credit balances.

Note that the equation itself can be stated as follows:

$$\text{Assets} = \text{Liabilities} + \text{Owners' Equity} + (\text{Revenue} - \text{Expenses})$$

This merely says that assets are equal to the claims that individuals or other entities have in those assets. Revenue and expenses measure how assets enter or leave the business in performing services for customers, and the net result is eventually added to the owners' equity.

The rules to be followed for debiting and crediting accounts are arbitrarily defined but are logically consistent. For example, a debit means an increase in any asset, but a debit will also decrease any liability or owners' equity account. The rules of debit and credit have been set up so that the accounting equation will hold true and so that debits will always be equaled by credits. Therefore, assets will always equal equities; and the sum of the amounts shown as debits will always agree with the sum of the amounts shown as credits. Note that a revenue account is credited to increase it. This is logical inasmuch as an increase in revenue is an increase in the owners' equity; and, therefore, an increase in revenue is handled in the same way as a direct increase in owners' equity. Similarly, increases in expenses reduce owners' equity and, like direct reductions in owners' equity, are recorded by debits.

Use of Accounts.

The transactions previously given for Weaver have been expanded and are listed and numbered as follows:

(1) Karen Weaver invested $75,000 in cash to begin business operations.
(2) A $900 prepayment was made for rent of a store for three months.
(3) Equipment was purchased on account at a cost of $30,000.
(4) Cash of $28,000 was paid to the creditors from whom equipment was purchased.
(5) Merchandise costing $50,000 was purchased on credit terms.
(6) Merchandise was sold to customers on account for $48,000.
(7) Paid wages of $800 in cash for two weeks.
(8) Received a promissory note for $8,000 from a customer on account.
(9) Paid cash of $200 for heat and light for one month.

The ledger accounts with the transactions analyzed and entered according to the rules of increase and decrease shown by the accounting equation are given below. The entries are numbered so that they can be identified with the transactions.

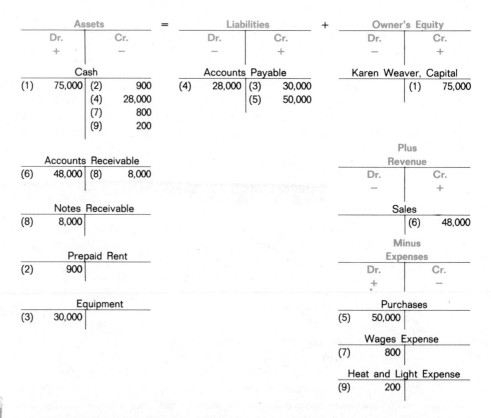

The Journal

The direct recording of transactions in the ledger accounts is inconvenient and errors are difficult to find. It takes time to leaf through the ledger pages or cards; and if there are many transactions, there is no time to enter each transaction in the ledger cards as it takes place. Furthermore, there should be some chronological record of the transactions with the entire transaction being shown in one place. Errors can then be located with less difficulty by tracing transactions from the chronological record to the ledger accounts.

A preliminary analysis of transactions is made in a book of original entry called a journal In its simplest form, the journal consists of a book with a column for dates at the left, a wide Description column for account titles and explanations, and two columns for entering monetary amounts. The first of the two monetary columns is called the Debit column, and the second is called the Credit column. A simple journal of this type is usually called a general journal The preliminary record entered in the journal is called a journal entry

Each transaction is analyzed to identify the accounts that are to be debited and credited. The transaction is then recorded as follows:

1. The date is entered in the Date column.
2. The name of the account to be debited is entered in the Description column, and the dollar amount is entered in the Debit money column.
3. The name of the account to be credited is entered in the Description column on the next line in an indented position, and the dollar amount is entered in the Credit money column.
4. A brief explanation of the transaction is written beneath the account titles.

The general journal entries for Weaver's transactions would appear as follows:

GENERAL JOURNAL   Page 1

Date		Description	Post. Ref.	Debit	Credit
19-- Oct.	1	Cash		75,000	
		Karen Weaver, Capital			75,000
		Investment of $75,000 by Karen Weaver.			
	1	Prepaid Rent.....................................		900	
		Cash			900
		Rent paid in advance for 3 months.			
	2	Equipment		30,000	
		Accounts Payable............................			30,000
		Equipment bought on account.			
	6	Accounts Payable...............................		28,000	
		Cash			28,000
		Creditors paid on account.			
	9	Purchases		50,000	
		Accounts Payable............................			50,000
		Merchandise purchased on account.			
	12	Accounts Receivable		48,000	
		Sales.......................................			48,000
		Merchandise sold on account.			
	15	Wages Expense		800	
		Cash			800
		Wages paid for two weeks.			
	15	Notes Receivable		8,000	
		Accounts Receivable			8,000
		Note received from customer on account.			
	30	Heat and Light Expense.........................		200	
		Cash			200
		Utilities paid for October.			

Posting

The number and the kind of accounts kept in the ledger depend upon the information desired or required. It is advisable to keep separate accounts for each type of asset, liability, revenue, and expense. An owner's equity or capital account should be kept for information relative to the owners' equity in the business. Generally, a list of accounts, called a chart of accounts, is prepared and each account is assigned a number. After the transactions have been recorded in the journal, the information is transferred to the ledger accounts through a process called posting. When information is posted from the journal to the ledger, the date and amount of each transaction and the page number of the journal are entered in the account. The narrow column headed "Post. Ref." in the journal is a cross-reference column called the posting reference column. The number of the ledger account is entered in the "Post. Ref." column so that a transaction can be easily traced to the ledger accounts if that should become necessary at a later date. Space is also provided in the ledger accounts for page numbers of the journal where the transactions were first entered. Thus a transaction can easily be traced from the journal to the ledger or from the ledger back to the journal.

Posting is a process of organizing data according to account classifications from the chronological record contained in the journal. After the data have been classified in the accounts and summarized, they can be used in the preparation of financial statements and reports.

While the two-column journal does provide a chronological record of transactions with both parts of the transaction in one place, it is not very helpful as a labor-saving device. In fact, there is more accounting work because the transaction must be entered first in the journal and then it must be posted to the ledger accounts. Weaver would have to make a journal entry for each transaction, then post the information from the journal to the ledger accounts before the ledger would contain the debits and the credits shown on page 598.

Special Journals

Often business transactions of a certain type are repeated time and again. There are likely to be many purchases of merchandise, sales to customers, cash receipts, and cash disbursements. To record each transaction separately in a two-column journal as an increase or as a decrease to a given account is unduly burdensome. Transactions of a similar type should be classified together, summarized for a period such as a month, and posted as one aggregate transaction for the month.

There are several types of journals, each type being designed to serve a special purpose. For example, all sales transactions could be entered in a sales journal. Similarly, purchases, cash receipts, and cash disbursements are entered respectively in a purchases journal, a cash receipts journal, and a cash disbursements journal. Other specialized journals can be used if transactions occur frequently enough to warrant their use. A manufacturing company, for example, may use a special journal to record materials withdrawn and transferred to production. Miscellaneous transactions that do not occur often enough to merit the use of a special journal are entered in the two-column general journal referred to earlier.

The special journals have columns so that similar transactions can be conveniently added together and posted as one transaction. For example, sales for the month may be shown in a sales journal designed as follows:

SALES JOURNAL						Page 4
Date		Account Debited	Post. Ref.	Cash Dr.	Accounts Receivable Dr.	Sales Cr.
1984 Oct.	4	Customer A		500		500
	11	Customer B			2,300	2,300
	18	Customer A		800		800
	25	Customer E			1,500	1,500
				1,300	3,800	5,100

This design indicates that sales are often made on both cash and credit terms, since the sales journal has a column for cash debits, a column for accounts receivable debits, and a column for sales credits. At the end of the month, the sum of the two debit columns should be equal to the sum of the credit column.

It should not be inferred from the example given that all sales journals are designed with three columns. Journals are designed to fit the needs of the user, and special columns are provided for frequently used accounts.

Trial Balance

After posting from the journal to the ledger accounts, the balances of the accounts are determined and are listed on a trial balance. This listing shows whether or not the debit balances are equal to the credit balances. Mechanical accuracy is verified if the total of the debit balances and the credit balances is equal. However, this does not prove that all amounts have been recorded in the proper accounts.

A balance for the cash account, for example, is computed by subtracting the sum of the credit entries of $29,900 from the sum of the debit entries of $75,000 to obtain a debit balance of $45,100. Other account balances are similarly computed, and all balances are listed to form the following trial balance.

Karen Weaver
Trial Balance
October 31, 19—

	Dr.	Cr.
Cash	45,100	
Accounts Receivable	40,000	
Notes Receivable	8,000	
Prepaid Rent	900	
Equipment	30,000	
Accounts Payable		52,000
Karen Weaver, Capital		75,000
Sales		48,000
Purchases	50,000	
Wages Expense	800	
Heat and Light Expense	200	
	175,000	175,000

ADJUSTING PROCESS

Business transactions are accumulated over an interval of time designated as an accounting period or a fiscal period. The period of time may be a month, a quarter of a year, a year, or any other significant time interval. Ordinarily, financial measurements are made over a period of a year, with the year being divided into months or quarters. During the course of a fiscal period, a company records purchases, sales, cash receipts, cash disbursements, returns of merchandise from customers, payrolls, transfers of materials and labor into production, and other events that arise in the normal course of its operations. Other important information may not be recorded at all, or the information may be recorded but with the passage of time may require adjustment. The adjustments are made after the transactions for the fiscal period have been recorded and after a trial balance has been prepared. To illustrate the adjusting procedure, adjustment data are given along with ledger accounts.

Adjustment data:

(1) Wages in the amount of $700 have been earned by the employees at October 31 but have not been paid or recorded.
(2) The note receivable has been outstanding for half of the month and yields interest at 12%. The total interest earned is $40 [$8,000 × 12%) ÷ (12 × ½)].
(3) Rent of $900 was prepaid for three months beginning October 1.
(4) The equipment was acquired at a cost of $30,000. Depreciation of the equipment has been estimated at $250.
(5) The inventory of merchandise on hand was counted and assigned a cost of $10,000.
(6) It has been estimated that sales in the amount of $1,500 are not collectible.

Usually, the adjustments for a company can be classified under the following three general headings:

1. The accrual adjustment
2. The prepayment adjustment
3. The valuation adjustment

Accrual Adjustments

Often wages, rent, interest, and the various costs of business operations are recorded only at the time they are paid. However, some costs grow or **accrue** with the passage of time. For example, wages are earned by the employees each working day even though they are paid at designated times.

Since the last payroll, wages of $700 have been earned. The additional expense and the liability are computed and the effect of the adjusting entry is illustrated in the following T accounts.

Wages Expense		Wages Payable	
800			700
700			

Looking at accruals in another way, assets and revenue also grow or accrue. Weaver has earned a total of $40 on the note receivable. The ledger accounts after posting the adjusting entry would appear as follows:

Interest Receivable		Interest Earned	
40			40

The need for accrual adjustments arises when all of the data pertaining to the fiscal period have not been recorded. Expenses that increase with the passage of time must be recorded, whether paid or not; and the liability for unpaid expenses must also be recognized. Similarly, revenue that increases with the passage of time must be recorded, whether collected or not; and the asset representing the amount due must be recognized.

In the following accounting period, when the $40 interest receivable is collected in cash, the collection is viewed as a conversion of assets; that is, the asset cash is increased and the asset interest receivable is decreased. The revenue was recognized in the prior accounting period even though the cash was not received until the subsequent period. Revenue is viewed as being the result of the earning process. The cash collection may or may not take place at the same time that the revenue is actually recognized (recorded).

Prepayment Adjustments

Business events should be properly analyzed and recorded as they occur. For example, an asset may be recorded at the time it is acquired for cash, or a liability may be recorded when an advance collection is received from a customer. By the end of the fiscal period, however, the situation may have changed. An adjustment may be required to show the part of the asset that was used in profit-making activity. The expense will be recorded, and the asset previously entered will be reduced. Likewise, deliveries of products may have been made against advance collections received from customers. The liability initially entered in the records will be reduced, and the portion earned will be recorded as revenue. Adjustments made to separate expenses from assets and revenue from liabilities are referred to as prepayment adjustments.

Karen Weaver, for example, has prepaid rent of $900 at the beginning of October. At the end of the month, one third of the prepaid rent has expired. The adjusting entry to record the rent expense and the reduction of the asset will bring the accounts up to date as follows:

Prepaid Rent		Rent Expense	
900	300	300	

The Depreciation Adjustment

To conduct business operations, a company normally requires the use of buildings, fixtures, machinery, and equipment. Assets of this type have a relatively long useful life and are classified under the general heading of plant assets or fixed assets. The expense resulting from the use of these assets is designated as depreciation expense. Depreciation represents an estimate of the physical wear and tear as well as any obsolescence relative to the use of the asset.

Plant assets are somewhat like prepaid expenses. The cost of a plant asset, like the cost of an insurance policy, for example, is allocated over its useful life. Ordinarily the plant asset has a longer life than the prepaid expense, but the adjustment procedure is somewhat similar. Unlike the prepayment, however, the plant asset may not be paid for at the time it is acquired. Debt may have been incurred to finance the cost of the asset. But the way in which it is financed has no effect upon the allocation of its cost to operations. The cost is allocated or assigned to time periods according to the flow of benefits received from the use of the asset over its useful life.

An asset such as a building or a piece of equipment has a limited useful life; it does not yield benefits indefinitely. It eventually wears out, becomes outmoded with the passage of time and changes in technology, or becomes inadequate as the company grows and requires the use of larger assets or assets with greater productive capacity. Over the total period of time the asset is in use, its cost is allocated to the various fiscal periods as depreciation expense.

Generally the cost of a plant asset is substantial, and the asset may be in service for a number of years. Often detailed underlying records are maintained to show the original cost of the asset, the name of the company from which the asset was purchased, the history of maintenance and repair service, the depreciation that has been recorded each year, and other pertinent details with respect to the asset and its operation. Ordinarily the plant asset account itself is not credited directly when depreciation adjustments are made. Instead, a special asset reduction account called "Accumulated Depreciation" or "Allowance for Depreciation" is credited. The original cost is then preserved in the plant asset account, and the reductions because of depreciation are shown in a separate offsetting account. The remaining cost to be charged against future operations, or the net book value of the asset, as it is called, is equal to the balance shown in the plant asset account minus the balance shown in the accumulated depreciation account. The accumulated depreciation account has a credit balance and is frequently referred to as a contra asset account.

Assume that Weaver has estimated the useful life of the equipment at 10 years with no provision for salvage value. Each month depreciation of $250 [($30,000 ÷ 10) ÷ 12] is to be deducted. When an equal amount of cost is assigned to each accounting period, the company is said to be recording depreciation according to the straight-line method.

After the adjusting entry is posted, the ledger accounts appear as:

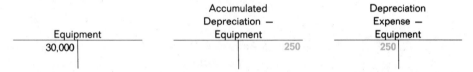

Equipment	Accumulated Depreciation — Equipment	Depreciation Expense — Equipment
30,000	250	250

There is no necessary connection between the net book value of a plant asset and its market value. At the end of the first accounting period Weaver might be able to sell the equipment for more or less than the net book value of $29,750. Depreciation policy is not intended as a device for the valuation of plant assets. It is merely a means of allocating the cost to the fiscal periods during which the assets are in service. The allocation of cost is made to facilitate the determination of net income for the period.

The depreciation procedure in accounting is an estimating process and is filled with uncertainty. An estimate of the useful life and the salvage value is required, and a judgment on how to assign the cost must be made. As a result, accounting data are not as precise as they may appear. Estimates and human judgments enter into the processing operation, depreciation policy being a good example. The user of accounting information must be aware of these underlying judgments and estimates. The student of accounting should be constantly on the alert for other areas in the accounting process where estimates and judgments are filled with uncertainty.

The Inventory Adjustment

Some companies maintain perpetual inventory records, recording purchases as additions to inventory and withdrawals or sales as deductions from inventory and as increases in cost of goods sold. The inventory records should then show the proper balances on hand at all times. At the end of the fiscal year, a physical count may reveal errors in the book record that should be corrected. However, if the accounting system is operating properly and if there is proper control over the physical inventories, the corrections should not be substantial in amount.

Many companies do not keep a perpetual record of inventories. The purchases are recorded, but there is no record of the cost of items withdrawn or sold. As a general rule, it is impractical to record the cost of items sold if merchandise is sold to customers over the counter in relatively small lots. At the end of the fiscal year, the physical quantity remaining in inventory can be determined by count. Cost is then identified with the inventory according to the particular costing method that is employed. The cost of goods sold during the year is then computed indirectly as the sum of the beginning inventory and purchases minus the inventory at the end of the year. This method of arriving at inventory cost and the cost of goods sold is called the periodic inventory method.

A variety of practices may be employed in making the periodic inventory adjustment. The essential point is that the cost of goods sold should be determined as accurately as possible and that the inventory at the end of the year should be valued properly.

The inventory adjustment may be made by setting up a new account entitled "Cost of Goods Sold." The balance of inventory at the beginning of the year and the purchases for the year are closed out by credits, with the debit being entered in the cost of goods sold account. At this point, the cost of goods sold account has a balance representing the cost of goods available for sale. It is converted to cost of goods sold by removing the cost attached to the inventory remaining at the end of the year. This is accomplished by a debit to the merchandise inventory account in an amount equal to the cost of the inventory at the end of the year and by a credit to the cost of goods sold account.

To illustrate: (a) The inventory at the beginning of the month (no inventory existed at the beginning of the month) and the purchases of $50,000 are transferred (closed) to Cost of Goods Sold. (b) At the end of the month, a count of the inventory reveals that the merchandise on hand cost $10,000. After the adjustments are recorded, the affected ledger accounts are shown as follows:

Merchandise Inventory		Purchases		Cost of Goods Sold	
(b) 10,000		50,000 (a) 50,000		(a) 50,000 (b) 10,000	

Valuation Adjustments

There is another type of adjustment that may be looked upon as being a valuation adjustment. Certain assets, such as marketable securities, accounts receivable from customers, and inventories are to be realized in cash in the normal course of events. But the assets may not be realized at the amounts shown in the ledger accounts.

Accounts receivable, for example, show the amounts due from the customers; but not all of the customers will pay their accounts. There will be uncollectible accounts. At the end of the year, there is no way of knowing which customers will default. Yet, sales should be charged with the estimated uncollectible accounts arising out of sales operations for the year. An adjusting entry is made to record the estimated uncollectible accounts chargeable to the year, and the credit is made not to accounts receivable but to an account that may be entitled "Allowance for Doubtful Accounts."

Of the total accounts receivable of $40,000, Weaver estimates that $1,500 will not be collected. When the estimate is made, no specific accounts receivable have been identified as uncollectible. Therefore, the credit is made to an allowance account. The affected ledger accounts after posting the adjusting entry are given below.

Accounts Receivable		Allowance for Doubtful Accounts		Uncollectible Accounts Expense	
40,000			1,500	1,500	

In the next accounting period, as specific accounts are identified as being uncollectible, they will be written off against the allowance for doubtful accounts. Assume that one of the customers defaults during the next accounting period in the amount of $400. After recording the default, the affected ledger accounts would appear as follows:

Accounts Receivable		Allowance for Doubtful Accounts	
40,000	400	400	1,500

The estimating procedure previously illustrated is subject to errors in judgment but nevertheless tends to produce more useful data than would be the case if the estimate were not made. There is no logical reason why losses on customers' accounts should be matched against revenue of the fiscal period in which the losses are detected. The losses should be matched against the revenue recorded when the initial transaction took place. Unfortunately, no exact determination of the losses can be made at that point. It should be possible, however, to make reasonable estimates based on past experience. Hence, this device is a method for recognizing the uncollectible accounts expense in the period in which the sale was made and not in a subsequent period when the account receivable is actually judged to be uncollectible.

Marketable securities and inventories are also subject to valuation adjustments. It is customary to value marketable securities and inventories at the lower of cost or market. If market values are lower than cost, an adjustment may be made to charge a loss to the year in which the market decline occurred. The offsetting credit may be made directly to the asset account or to an adjunct allowance account similar in concept to the allowance account used with accounts receivable.

Adjusted Trial Balance

After the adjusting entries are posted, an adjusted trial balance is prepared as follows:

Karen Weaver
Adjusted Trial Balance
October 31, 19—

	Dr.	Cr.
Cash	45,100	
Accounts Receivable	40,000	
Allowance for Doubtful Accounts		1,500
Notes Receivable	8,000	
Interest Receivable	40	
Merchandise Inventory, October 31	10,000	
Prepaid Rent	600	
Equipment	30,000	
Accumulated Depreciation — Equipment		250
Accounts Payable		52,000
Wages Payable		700
Karen Weaver, Capital		75,000
Sales		48,000
Cost of Goods Sold	40,000	
Wages Expense	1,500	
Uncollectible Accounts Expense	1,500	
Rent Expense	300	
Depreciation Expense — Equipment	250	
Heat and Light Expense	200	
Interest Earned		40
	177,490	177,490

Financial Statements

From an adjusted trial balance, the financial statements can be prepared. A statement of revenue and expenses is called an income statement. Expenses are deducted from revenue. If revenue exceeds expenses, the difference is called net income. If expenses exceed revenue, the difference is called net loss. The income statement shows the net changes in owners' equity that result from operating at a profit or at a loss. The income statement is used to measure revenue and expenses for a given accounting period or a fiscal period. An income statement for Karen Weaver is given as follows:

Karen Weaver
Income Statement
For Month Ended October 31, 19—

Sales		$48,000
Cost of goods sold		40,000
Gross margin		$ 8,000
Operating expenses:		
Wages	$1,500	
Uncollectible accounts	1,500	
Rent	300	
Depreciation	250	
Heat and light	200	3,750
Operating income		$ 4,250
Add interest earned		40
Net income		$ 4,290

A balance sheet is essentially a formal classified listing of assets and equities at one particular time. As time pases and as other transactions take place, the balance sheet becomes out of date; but as of the balance sheet date, it is a statement of the financial position of the enterprise. The following is a balance sheet for Karen Weaver on October 31.

Karen Weaver
Balance Sheet
October 31, 19—

Assets

Cash		$ 45,100
Accounts receivable	$40,000	
Less allowance for doubtful accounts	1,500	38,500
Notes receivable		8,000
Interest receivable		40
Merchandise inventory		10,000
Prepaid rent		600
Equipment	$30,000	
Less accumulated depreciation	250	29,750
Total assets		$131,990

Equities

Liabilities:		
Accounts payable		$ 52,000
Wages payable		700
Total liabilities		$ 52,700
Owner's equity:		
Karen Weaver, capital		79,290
Total equities		$131,990

Note that the owner's equity is $4,290 more than the owner's equity shown on the adjusted trial balance. The net income of $4,290 has been added to the $75,000 on the adjusted trial balance to yield an owner's equity of $79,290 at the end of the month.

THE CLOSING PROCEDURE

At the end of the accounting period, the revenue, expense, and cost of goods sold accounts have served their purpose. Measurements of the extent of the net increase or decrease in net assets resulting from profit-making activity during the accounting period have been taken. Now the income statement accounts can be closed; that is, the balances can be reduced to zero so that new measurements can be made in the following year. Revenue and expense classifications are like meters that measure the flow of liquids or gases for an interval of time. When the time interval has lapsed, the dials on the meters are set back to zero so that new measurements can be made for the next period of time. The closing entry for Karen Weaver on October 31 would be made as follows:

Sales	48,000	
Interest Earned	40	
Cost of Goods Sold		40,000
Wages Expense		1,500
Uncollectible Accounts Expense		1,500
Rent Expense		300
Depreciation Expense — Equipment		250
Heat and Light Expense		200
Karen Weaver, Capital		4,290
Entry to close revenue and expense accounts for the year and to close net income to Karen Weaver's capital account.		

After the revenue and expense accounts are closed, only the asset, liability, and owner's equity accounts have balances to be carried forward to the next accounting period and to serve as a cumulative record. The balances after closing are listed on a post-closing trial balance. The purpose of this final trial balance is to prove that the general ledger is in balance before transactions are entered for the new year. The ledger is now ready to receive entries for the next fiscal year, and the cycle of processing accounting data is repeated again.

The post-closing trial balance for Karen Weaver on October 31, 19--, is given at the top of the next page.

Karen Weaver
Post-Closing Trial Balance
October 31, 19--

	Dr.	Cr.
Cash	45,100	
Accounts Receivable	40,000	
Allowance for Doubtful Accounts		1,500
Notes Receivable	8,000	
Interest Receivable	40	
Merchandise Inventory, December 31	10,000	
Prepaid Rent	600	
Equipment	30,000	
Accumulated Depreciation — Equipment		250
Accounts Payable		52,000
Wages Payable		700
Karen Weaver, Capital		79,290
	133,740	133,740

FORMS OF BUSINESS OWNERSHIP

Up to this point in the discussion of the accounting cycle, it has been assumed that one person owned the business, that is, the business was a proprietorship. With a proprietorship, the owner's equity is simply shown in one account and designated by the name of the owner, for example, Karen Weaver, Capital or Karen Weaver, Proprietorship.

Actually, there are various legal forms of business ownership. The most important forms are:

1. The proprietorship
2. The partnership.
3. The corporation.

A business that is owned jointly by two or more individuals or entities who share ownership is designated as a partnership. Each partner's interest is identified by his or her name and is designated as his or her capital.

A business may also be incorporated; that is, the business is given an existence apart from its owners through a charter issued by a state. The corporation is like a person at law, being able to transact business in its own right and having the legal rights and responsibilities of individuals in the commercial field.

The owners' equity in a corporation is not identified according to the persons who have ownership rights; that is, the stockholders. Instead, the owners' equity is shown under two broad general classifications:

1. The investment of the owners, which under ordinary circumstances will remain as a permanent investment.
2. The accumulated retained earnings of the business. In general, the accumulated retained earnings will be the total of all profits reduced by losses and by cash dividend payments.

In the formation of a corporation, the organizers agree that a certain stated amount shall be invested for each share issued. This original investment constitutes a permanent investment, assuming, of course, that there is no reorganization or other drastic change in the corporate structure. The amount of this stipulated investment is designated as capital stock if only one class of stock is issued. If more than one class of stock is issued, the stated amount for each class is shown separately and is appropriately designated as preferred stock or as common stock, as the case may be.

Often a corporation will receive more than the legal minimum investment per share. For example, it may be agreed that for each share issued there will be $1 invested and credited to capital stock. The shares are issued, however, for $5 each. The amount of the investment in excess of the stated value, in this case $4 per share, is credited to Paid-In Capital in Excess of Stated Value. Ordinarily, the amount credited to this account cannot be withdrawn and is looked upon as a part of the permanent investment.

The accumulated net earnings of the corporation as reduced by net losses, distributions to the owners, or transfers to paid-in capital are called retained earnings. Barring restrictions that may be imposed by law or by contractual agreement, the retained earnings establish the amounts that may be withdrawn by the owners as dividends.

SOME BASIC CONCEPTS

The mechanical features of processing accounting data have been discussed, but there is much more involved in the preparation of data for presentation in the financial statements. Certain fundamental concepts are observed, some of which are discussed at this point.

The Going Concern

In accounting, the assumption is made that a business will continue to operate in the future and that it will not cease doing business, sell its assets, and make final payments to creditors and owners. Therefore, it is said that accounting is carried out on a going concern basis. The plant assets, for example, are not normally adjusted to liquidation values. Presumably the plant assets will not be sold but will be used in future business operations. On the balance sheet given for Tobinton Products, Inc., on page 620, the building and equipment, for example, are shown at a net amount of $254,500. This does not mean that they can be sold for that amount. The valuation of $254,500 is the undepreciated cost to be carried forward to future years. As the building and equipment are used in conducting operations, a cost of using them will be recognized in the determination of net income or net loss.

There are, of course, circumstances in which the going concern assumption would not apply. If a business is to be discontinued, a different type of statement could be prepared and assets could be revalued at amounts that would possibly be realized upon their sale. However, this would be a special case, and the business would not be a going concern but would be a "quit concern."

Cost

Cost is conventionally used as the basis for accountability. Assets when acquired under normal circumstances are recorded at the price arrived at by negotiation between two independent parties dealing at arm's length. Simply stated, the cost of an asset to the purchaser is the price that must be paid now or later to obtain it. The fair value of the asset is not relevant in recording the transaction. A purchaser may acquire an asset at a cost that is greater or less than the fair value determined in the marketplace. If so, the asset is accounted for at the purchaser's cost, value notwithstanding.

Accounting for cost is an extremely complex process. In conducting business operations, some assets lose their original identity, that is, they are converted into some other form. For example, materials used in a chemical process often cannot be identified as such in the end product. Costs are traced through operations, wherever possible, as the assets are transferred or converted in the course of operations.

One of the principal objectives in accounting for cost is the measurement of profit and loss. The cost attached to the products or services sold is matched against the consideration received from the customers in the determination of profit or loss. This is not always easy to do. For example, several product lines may be produced together, with one particular cost common to all lines. The assignment of the cost to any one line is difficult at best, with further complexities being introduced when attempts are made to apportion the cost attached to any one line between the cost of the goods or services sold and the cost remaining on hand as inventory.

The Realization Concept

The profit and loss of a business is measured as the difference between the consideration received from customers and the cost attached to the products or services given in exchange. In conventional accounting, profit is not recognized unless it is realized. For the most part, realization depends upon an agreement with a customer to pay a stipulated amount for the product.

The point at which the revenue is realized will vary depending upon circumstances. The amount of the consideration received from the customer is frequently looked upon as being realized when title to the items sold is vested in the customer. At that point there is an enforceable claim against the customer. It is not necessary that the consideration be in the form of cash; the promise of the customer to make eventual payment is sufficient. In some cases, profit realization and cash realization go together. For example, a barber will realize the amount to be received from the customer when the service is given the customer, and the consideration will be realized in cash immediately after the service has been given. For all practical purposes, it can be said that the barber would be entitled to measure profit as cash is realized. On the other hand, when merchandise is delivered to customers on installment sales, there may be considerable doubt as to whether or not the promise of the customer to make eventual payment will be fulfilled. Profit on installment sales may be looked upon as realized when cash is collected.

In some cases, profit is realized before delivery is made to the customer and before cash is collected. For example, a shipbuilder may build a vessel on government contract. As the work progresses, profit may be realized by matching cost for the percentage of work completed against a corresponding percentage of the amount of the consideration to be received. This method of accounting for profit, known as the percentage-of-completion method, is sometimes used by contractors who build highways, buildings, bridges, and other structures and properties that are completed over a relatively long period of time.

Periodicity

The income statement has already been described as a statement pertaining to a given period of time only. Ideally, no measurement of net income or net loss should be made while a business is still actively conducting operations. A more accurate measurement of the net income or the net loss could be made after a company had ceased doing business and had sold all of its assets and had paid off all of its liabilities. The net income or loss would then be the difference between the amount ultimately realized by the owners and their initial investment. As a practical matter, however, measurements must be made while the business is in progress and the results must be reported periodically.

Ordinarily revenue and expense are measured over a period of one year. This year does not necessarily correspond with the calendar year but instead may correspond with the natural cycle of business activity. Logically, a fiscal year should end with the close of a cycle of business activity, that is, when inventories and accounts receivable are at a minimum but before new inventory is acquired for another cycle of sales and subsequent collections. For example, a department store may choose a year extending from March 1 of one year to February 28 (or 29) of the next calendar year. The Christmas sales and the January sales for the same season will then fall within the same year, and the inventories and the amounts receivable will generally be low just before merchandise is purchased for spring and summer sales. The year chosen for financial measurements is called the fiscal year or fiscal period.

Although a year is generally the longest period of time used in making measurements, it is possible to take measurements over shorter time intervals, such as a quarter of a year or a month. During the year, an income statement may be prepared for both a given month and for the year to date, or for a quarter of a year and the year to date. Sometimes the data for a corresponding period in the previous year is presented along with the current data, thus making comparison possible.

Matching

A reasonably accurate measurement of the net income or the net loss for a fiscal period depends upon the matching of expenses against related revenue. The matching of revenue and expense is difficult. With a going concern there is always the possibility that a revenue or an expense should have been recognized in a previous fiscal period or that it should have been deferred until some future period. If expenses have not been properly offset against revenue, the resulting net income or net loss for the fiscal period will be reported incorrectly.

The revenue and the expense pertaining to a fiscal period may have to be estimated. A company might sell a product under an agreement to guarantee against defects and furnish future maintenance and repair services. Not only must the estimated liability to the customer be recognized, but the expense of giving this service should be estimated and offset against the revenue resulting from the initial sales transaction. The cost of giving this service to the customer is related to the sales transaction; therefore, the estimated expense and liability should be recorded during the period in which the sale was made.

When a company purchases a piece of equipment, the cost of the equipment should be matched against the revenue of the future fiscal periods that will benefit from its use. The portion of the cost which should be deferred and matched against the revenue of any given year depends upon the estimation of the useful life and salvage value of the equipment. There are many similar situations in which matching must be done on an estimated basis. Estimates have to be made on a judgmental basis using information available.

Consistency

Not only are the results of an accounting system dependent in many cases upon estimates, but also they are influenced by the choice of an accounting method and the consistency with which it is applied. For example, inventories may be accounted for on a first-in, first-out basis, a last-in, first-out basis, or by some other means.

The first-in, first-out (fifo) method of costing inventories occurs when the older cost is traced through to the cost of goods sold while the more recent cost is identified with the inventories at the end of the period. On the other hand, the more recent cost may be traced through to the cost of goods sold, with the older cost being held as inventories at the end of the period. This method of costing is called the last-in, first-out (lifo) method. Inventory cost may also be averaged, with the cost of goods sold and the inventories at the end of the period stated on an average cost basis according to the particular averaging technique employed. The distinction between the cost to be matched against revenue as cost of goods sold and the cost to be held as inventories is highly important in the income determination process. One method of accounting for the flow of cost cannot be labeled as the correct method to the exclusion of all others. Yet, the choice of a particular method and the way in which it is carried out over the years has an influence on the profit reported as well as on the inventory cost for the balance sheet.

Assume, for example, that a company keeping its inventory records on a fifo basis computed its cost of goods sold for a year as shown below:

Inventory, January 1 (50,000 units @ $2)	$ 100,000
Purchases:	
January to June (150,000 units @ $3)	450,000
July to December (200,000 units @ $4)	800,000
Cost of goods available	$ 1,350,000
Less inventory, December 31 (40,000 units @ $4)	160,000
Cost of goods sold	$1,190,000

If the company had decided for some valid reason to change its method of accounting for inventories to the lifo method at the beginning of the year, it would compute a different cost of goods sold and a different inventory cost at the end of the year. The results might have appeared as follows:

Inventory, January 1 (50,000 units @ $2)	$ 100,000
Purchases:	
January to June (150,000 units @ $3)	450,000
July to December (200,000 units @ $4)	800,000
Cost of goods available	$ 1,350,000
Less inventory, December 31 (40,000 units @ $2)	80,000
Cost of goods sold	$1,270,000

The cost of goods sold is higher by $80,000 than it would have been without the change. Unless this is pointed out, the reader of the financial statements in making a comparison with the previous years might reach an inaccurate conclusion as to why the cost of goods sold had increased.

An accounting method or procedure once chosen should be followed consistently from year to year. Consistency in accounting is not advocated just for the sake of consistency, but rather to avoid the confusion that would result if profit or loss were to be calculated on a different basis each year. Desirable changes should be made, of course; but when changes are made, the effect of such changes upon the financial statements should be fully disclosed.

The Accrual Principle

Revenue and expense are accounted for on the accrual basis. Revenue is defined as the consideration (measured in monetary terms) received for rendering goods and services. Revenue is usually recognized when the following conditions are satisfied:

1. The amount of revenue must be capable of objective measurement.
2. The earning process must be reasonably complete or complete enough so that the cost of completion can be determined.
3. The revenue must be realized.

Revenue is not necessarily recognized at the time cash is collected. For example, goods and services are often sold on credit terms. At some later date collections will be made from the customers, but collections of cash are not a realization of revenue. Instead, the collections are a realization in cash of the asset, accounts receivable, which was increased at the time revenue was recorded, that is, at the date when goods or services were delivered and billed.

Occasionally customers will pay in advance for goods and services that will be delivered later. The advance payments have not been earned and cannot be recorded as revenue. The company, in accepting these advance payments, is obligated to the customers until it makes delivery. As deliveries are made, the liability is reduced and revenue is earned. If the accounting records have not been kept up to date during the fiscal period, adjusting entries will be made at the end of the period so that the portion of the advance earned is shown as revenue with the portion still owed to the customers being shown as a liability.

When merchandise is sold on the installment plan, there may be some question as to whether or not revenue should be recognized when deliveries are made to the customers. The collections may not be made according to plan, and the merchandise may have to be repossessed. Under the circumstances, there may be a justification for the recognition of revenue as collections are made. At that time there is no question about the realization of the revenue.

Reductions in revenue should be offset against the corresponding revenue recorded. Cash discounts and allowances granted to customers should be estimated and deducted from the related revenue. The loss is related to the revenue and not to the period of time in which the discount or the allowance is finally granted.

Similarly, expenses are carefully matched against related revenue and are not necessarily recognized when cash payments are made for goods and services.

An expense occurs when the asset leaves the business as a result of revenue-producing activity and not when cash payments are made to creditors. The cost of the asset becomes expense in the fiscal period that benefits from the use of the asset. For example, supplies may be purchased on credit terms. At the time of purchase the supplies are recorded as an asset, and a liability to the creditor is recorded. When payment is made for the supplies, the liability to the creditor is reduced. But the payment is not related to the use of the supplies. As the supplies are used in earning revenue, the cost of the portion used should be recorded as expense with the supplies asset account being reduced by a corresponding amount.

Often expenses will have to be estimated. Goods and services may be delivered with an agreement that defects will be corrected or that future services will be given without charge. The costs to correct the defects and to furnish the additional services should be estimated and deducted as expenses in the same period in which the related revenue is recorded.

The problem of matching expenses against revenue in the income determination process is a challenging problem. The identification of revenue with a given interval of time is not an exact process, nor is it a simple matter to identify expenses with the resulting revenue. Judgments and estimates will have to be made in many cases, using the best information that is available to management.

Conservatism

Usually the accountant takes a conservative position. Revenue is generally not recognized by recording value increases that may take place on unsold products or merchandise, even if it can be demonstrated that the items in question can be sold at the current market prices in excess of their cost. The principles of valuing assets at cost and recognizing revenue only when the sale is made go hand in hand. If market increments were recorded, assets would be reflected at market value and not at cost.

On the other hand, losses may be recorded when the market price declines below cost. This inconsistency in the application of accounting principles has been justified on the basis of conservatism. As a rule the accountant is skeptical of claims that assets are worth more than cost but will be more inclined to accept evidence that assets may be realized at even less than cost. Conservatism can be carried too far, however. It has merit in that the readers of the balance sheets are not led to expect that marketable securities, for example, can be realized at cost when in reality the current market prices are below cost. But excessive undervaluation can make the business appear to be in poor financial condition when such is not the case. Investment may be discouraged if a business appears to be less valuable than it is. The accountant must recognize that persons can be injured by understatements as well as by overstatement.

Valuation

The reader of the balance sheet should be acquainted with the principles of valuation that are commonly applied in arriving at the dollar amounts shown for the various assets and equities. Sometimes the basis of valuation is indicated in the body of the statement or in accompanying footnotes. In many cases, however, the basis of valuation is not given, it being assumed that the reader is familiar with conventional practices. Recently the conventional practices of valuation have been criticized. Questions have been raised as to whether or not assets should be valued at cost on the balance sheet when there is evidence that the assets are worth considerably more or less than cost.[2] Or is the profit for a fiscal period properly measured when historical cost is matched against revenue as expense in the period of sale? The valuation problem cannot be separated from the problem of income determination. With rapid inflation in the past few years, the problem of financial measurement has been receiving increasing attention not only from accountants but from various business groups and the average consumer.

BALANCE SHEET CLASSIFICATIONS

A classified balance sheet for Tobinton Products Inc. as of April 30, 1984, is illustrated on page 620.

Both the assets and the equities are usually listed separately and are not reduced by offsetting one against the other. This holds true even though specific assets may be pledged to secure the payment of a debt such as notes payable or bonds payable. Ordinarily the debt holder will receive payment in cash and will lay claim to the assets pledged only if the debtor defaults. The equity holders are said to have an undivided interest in the total assets. Thus, the equities are looked upon as a measurement of the extent of the rights of any individual or entity to the total assets but not to any particular asset. In the statement given for Tobinton Products Inc. the holders of the long-term notes payable do not have a $75,000 interest in cash, accounts receivable, inventories, or any other specific asset. They do, however, have a $75,000 claim against the assets in total.

On the balance sheet the assets and the equities are listed under classifications according to their general characteristics. Similar assets or similar equities are listed together, so that it is a relatively simple matter to make a comparison of one classification with another or to make comparisons within a classification. Some of the most commonly used classifications are:

---

[2]See Robert T. Sprouse and Maurice Moonitz, *A Tentative Set of Broad Accounting Principles for Business Enterprises,* Accounting Research Study No. 3 (New York: American Institute of Certified Public Accountants, 1962).

ASSETS	EQUITIES
Current assets	Current liabilities
Investments	Long-term liabilities
Plant assets	Deferred revenue
Intangible assets	Other liabilities
Other assets	Owners' equity

Tobinton Products Inc.
Balance Sheet
April 30, 1984

Assets

Current assets:			
Cash		$ 41,370	
Marketable securities at cost (market value, $38,250)		36,430	
Notes receivable		3,000	
Accounts receivable	$ 68,490		
Less allowance for discounts, returns, allowances, and			
doubtful accounts	2,640	65,850	
Inventories		86,420	
Prepaid insurance		1,770	$234,840
Investment in stock of Rabold Mills, Inc.			165,000
Plant assets:			
Land		$ 14,600	
Building and equipment	$292,700		
Less accumulated depreciation	38,200	254,500	269,100
Intangible assets:			
Organization expense		$ 4,900	
Goodwill		28,000	32,900
Other assets:			
Advances to company officers			8,500
Total assets			$710,340

Equities

Current liabilities:			
Bank loans		$ 18,000	
Accounts payable		41,350	
Accrued payroll and other expenses		19,540	
Estimated income tax payable		28,400	$107,290
Long-term notes, due August 31, 1988			75,000
Deferred rental revenue			2,700
Stockholders' equity:			
Capital stock, $10 par value, 5,000 shares issued and outstanding.		$ 50,000	
Premium on stock		82,500	
Retained earnings		392,850	525,350
Total equities			$710,340

Current Assets

The current assets include cash and other assets that in the normal course of events are converted into cash within the operating cycle. A manufacturing enterprise, for example, will use cash to acquire inventories of materials that are converted into finished products and sold to customers. Cash is collected from the customers, and the circle from cash back to cash is called an operating cycle. In a merchandising business, one part of the cycle is eliminated. Materials are not purchased for conversion into finished products. Instead, the finished products are purchased and are sold directly to the customers.

Several operating cycles may be completed in a year, or it may take more than a year to complete one operating cycle. The time required to complete an operating cycle depends upon the nature of the business.

It is conceivable that virtually all of the assets of a business can be converted into cash within the time required to complete an operating cycle. But a current asset is an asset that is converted into cash within an operating cycle *in the normal course of events.* Assets such as buildings, machinery, and equipment that are used in conducting the business are not converted into cash in the normal course of operations. They are held because they provide useful services for the business; they are excluded from the current asset classification.

On the other hand, a manufacturer or a dealer who holds assets such as buildings, machinery, and equipment for resale to customers in the regular course of the business includes these items in the inventory under the classification of current assets. The manufacturer or dealer does not hold these assets for use in the business but holds them as an inventory of product in the expectation that the assets will be converted into cash in the normal course of operations. An automobile dealer, for example, has company cars that are not to be sold but are to be used in operating the business. These cars are not included in the inventory. But the cars that are held for resale to customers are an inventory of product that should be listed under the current assets.

In many cases, the operating cycle does not extend beyond a year. However, there are exceptions. An inventory of liquor in the distilling industry must be aged, for example, and may be shown as a current asset even though it will not be converted into cash within the next year. It qualifies as a current asset inasmuch as it is converted into cash in the normal course of events within the operating cycle of the business.

Investments

Investments are funds in cash or security form held for a designated purpose or for an indefinite period of time. This classification includes investment in the stocks or bonds of another company, real estate or mortgages held for income-producing purposes, and investments held for a pension or other special fund.

Plant Assets

The assets such as land, buildings, machinery, and equipment that are to be used in business operations over a relatively long period of time are often classified as fixed assets or more specifically as plant assets or as plant and equipment. It is not expected that these assets will be sold and converted into cash as are inventories. Plant assets produce income indirectly through their use in operations.

On the balance sheet for Tobinton Products Inc. the land is shown separately at $14,600; the building and the equipment are shown at both the gross amount and at the net amount after deducting accumulated depreciation. Land does not have a limited useful life and is not reduced by depreciation. However, the cost of buildings, equipment, and other plant assets having a limited useful life is matched against revenue during the fiscal periods in which they are used.

Adjustments are usually not made in conventional accounting practice to restate plant assets at current replacement cost or at net realizable value. Plant assets, unlike the inventories, are not to be sold in the normal course of operations. Instead, they are used in performing the work of the business enterprise. The investment in plant assets should be recovered gradually as the assets are used in producing profit, but it is not expected that the investment will be recovered by direct sale as is the case with inventory.

In accounting for profit, the replacement cost of a plant asset and its net realizable value are not generally considered; yet in special decision-making situations these valuations can be applied. When equipment is to be replaced, for example, management considers the current replacement cost and the amount that should be realized upon the sale or trade-in of the present equipment. During the course of operations, recognition may also be given to the possibility that new equipment may cost more in the future. Profit that would otherwise be distributed to the stockholders as dividends may be retained to the extent of the anticipated increase in replacement cost. By following this policy, the company hopes to be able to retain the purchasing power of its initial investment.

Intangible Assets

Other fixed assets that lack physical substance are often referred to as intangible assets The intangible assets consist of valuable rights, privileges, or advantages. Although the intangibles lack physical substance, they have value. Sometimes the rights, privileges, and advantages of a business are worth more than all of the other assets combined.

Typical items included as intangible assets are patents, franchises, organization expense, and goodwill. Patents give the business an exclusive privilege of using a certan process in manufacturing. Franchises permit a company to handle a given product or to operate within a given territory or along a certain route. To become incorporated, a company must incur certain costs, such as the initial incorporation fee to the state and the cost of legal services in connection with the formation of the corporation. These costs are the costs of the privilege of having a corporation and are designated as organization expense A company is said to possess goodwill if it can earn a higher-than-normal rate of return upon invested resources. The higher rate of return may be caused by various factors such as managerial skill, popular acceptance of the products, or some other favorable circumstance. In setting a selling price for a prosperous business, it is recognized that the business as such may be worth more than the fair market value of the properties listed on the balance sheet as reduced by the liabilities. In other words, a value is placed on the anticipated earnings above an established normal level.

Goodwill is recorded only when it is purchased or sold. Frequently goodwill is recorded when a profitable business is acquired or when there is a change in the form of ownership. In the balance sheet given for Tobinton Products Inc., goodwill is shown at $28,000. Perhaps the business was at one time a sole proprietorship and developed goodwill. When the business was incorporated, stockholders purchased ownership interests and in doing so recognized and paid for goodwill. Or Tobinton Products Inc. may have purchased some other business, paying in excess of the values of the listed properties transferred less the liabilities assumed. This additional payment was made for anticipated future earnings above a normal level or, in short, was a payment for goodwill.

The cost of an intangible asset should be written off on the income statements over the fiscal periods during which it is estimated that the asset will yield benefits. For example, a franchise may enable a company to operate over a given route for only a stipulated period of time. The cost of the franchise should then be written off during the estimated fiscal periods that will benefit.

Other Assets

There are other assets that cannot be classified as current assets, investments, plant assets, or intangible assets. These assets are listed as other assets. Frequently the other assets consist of advances made to company officers, cost of buildings in the process of construction, and miscellaneous funds held for special purposes.

Current Liabilities

On the equity side of the balance sheet, as on the asset side, a distinction is made between current and long-term items. The current liabilities are obligations that are to be discharged within the normal operating cycle of the business and in most circumstances are liabilities that are to be paid within the next year by using the assets now classified as current. The amounts owed under current liabilities often arise as a result of acquiring current assets, such as inventory, or acquiring services that will be used in current operations. The amounts owed to trade creditors arising out of the purchase of materials or merchandise are shown as accounts payable. If the company is obligated under promissory notes that support bank loans or other amounts owed, the liability is shown as notes payable. Other current liabilities may include the estimated amount payable for income tax and the various amounts owed for wages and salaries of employees, utility bills, payroll taxes, local property tax, and other services.

Long-Term Liabilities

Debts not falling due until more than a year from the balance sheet date are generally classified as long-term liabilities. Notes, bonds, and mortgages are often listed under this heading. If a portion of the long-term debt is to become due within the next year and is to be paid, it should be removed from the long-term debt classification and shown under current liabilities with a caption such as "current installment of long-term debt payable." This reclassification will not be necessary, however, if the debt is to be refunded. Tobinton Products Inc. has a long-term debt of $75,000 evidenced by notes that will not become due until August 31, 1988. No portion of this debt is to be paid during the next fiscal year; therefore, the entire amount is shown separately and is excluded from the current liability classification.

Other Liabilities

Liabilities, like assets, cannot always be classified as being either current or long-term. In some cases the creditors will not expect to receive payment either in the near or the distant future.

Deferred Revenue

Customers may make advance payments for merchandise or services. The obligation to the customers will, as a general rule, be settled by delivery of the products or services and not by cash payment. Advance collections received from customers are usually classified as deferred revenue, pending delivery of the products or services. On the balance sheet given for Tobinton Products Inc., rent has been collected in advance from the tenants who have leased space in the building. When Tobinton Products Inc. gives rental service to the tenants, the obligation will be removed from the balance sheet. The rentals will then be realized and shown on the income statement.

Owners' Equity

The owners' equity in a corporation, often called stockholders' equity, is subdivided:

1. One portion represents the amount invested by the owners directly, plus any portion of retained earnings converted into paid-in capital.

2. The other portion represents the retention of net earnings in the business.

This rigid distinction is necessary because of the nature of a corporation. Ordinarily the owners of a corporation, that is, the stockholders, are not personally liable for the debts contracted by the company. A stockholder may lose the amount invested, but creditors usually cannot look to the stockholder's personal assets for satisfaction of their claims. Under normal circumstances, the owners may withdraw as cash dividends an amount measured by the corporate earnings. This rule gives the creditors some assurance that a certain portion of the assets equivalent to the stockholders' investment cannot be arbitrarily withdrawn. Of course, this portion could be depleted because of operating losses.

The investment by the stockholders or the paid-in capital may also be divided into two portions. One portion of the investment is the legal minimum that must be invested according to the corporate charter as approved by the state. Each share of stock may be assigned a par value such as $1, $5, or $10 per share. For each share issued, the stipulated value is to be received by the corporation. This minimum investment is generally labeled as capital stock. Any amount invested in the corporation that is in excess of par value is shown separately and is labeled as premium on stock or as paid-in capital in excess of par value.

Sometimes shares are not assigned a par value. The state may require that the entire amount received from the sale of no-par stock be held as the legal minimum investment, in which case the total amount received would be credited to capital stock. In some states, however, no-par shares are virtually equivalent to par-value shares for accounting purposes in that they are assigned a stated value per share. Any amount received in excess of the stated value can be classified as paid-in capital in excess of stated value.

Ordinarily, the premium on stock or the paid-in capital in excess of stated value is not reduced as a result of dividend distributions. Many states, however, allow dividends to be charged against this portion of the stockholders' investment, but some states require that the source of such dividends be revealed to the stockholders.

If stock is issued at less than its par value or its stated value, it is issued at a discount. Some states do not permit the issuance of stock at a discount, while other states hold the stockholders liable to creditors to the extent of the stock discount if the corporation cannot meet the claims of its creditors.

The accumulated net earnings of a corporation are shown under a separate heading such as retained earnings or reinvested earnings. As a general rule, this portion of the stockholders' equity may be voluntarily reduced by the distribution of dividends to the stockholders and, of course, involuntarily by losses. Net losses in excess of retained earnings are shown as a deduction in the stockholders' equity section and are labeled as a deficit.

The owners' equity in an unincorporated business is shown more simply. The interest of each owner is given in total, usually with no distinction being made between the portion invested and the accumulated net earnings. The creditors are not concerned about the amount invested because, if necessary, they can attach the personal assets of the owners. The owners' equity in a partnership may appear as follows:

Owners' equity:
Craig Bergman, Capital $161,000
Lucy Sutton, Capital 53,000
Total owners' equity $214,000

INCOME STATEMENT CLASSIFICATIONS

The income statement, like the balance sheet, is a classified statement. An income statement for Tobinton Products Inc. for the fiscal year ended April 30, 1985, is illustrated as follows:

Tobinton Products Inc.
Income Statement
For the Year Ended April 30, 1985

Net sales...		$1,283,480
Cost of goods sold...		756,560
Gross margin		$ 526,920
Selling expenses:		
Sales salaries	$79,940	
Advertising	31,870	
Travel and entertainment..................................	6,460	
Freight and delivery	4,850	
Depreciation	6,140	$ 129,260
General and administrative expenses:		
Officers' salaries	$53,180	
Office salaries	38,870	
Taxes	7,610	
Insurance..	1,740	
Utilities	6,480	
Uncollectible accounts expense	6,760	
Amortization of organization expense	2,450	
Amortization of goodwill	4,000	
Depreciation	1,050	122,140
Total operating expenses.....................................		$ 251,400
Operating income		$ 275,520
Other revenue and expense:		
Interest and dividends earned	$ 5,320	
Rent revenue	8,600	
	$13,920	
Less interest expense	9,340	4,580
Income before income tax....................................		$ 280,100
Estimated income tax		139,600
Income before extraordinary loss		$ 140,500
Loss on fire at Woodward plant (net of tax saving of $19,000)		21,000
Net income..		$ 119,500
Earnings per share of stock		$ 23.90

Operating Revenue

The revenue resulting from the predominant activities of the business is listed first and is called the operating revenue. The gross operating revenue is often reduced by customer returns and allowances and cash discounts in arriving at net operating revenue. Tobinton Products Inc. earns gross operating revenue by making sales to customers; and this revenue has been reduced by returns and allowances and cash discounts in arriving at the net sales of $1,283,480.

Cost of Goods Sold

If a company is engaged in selling goods, the cost of goods sold is computed and is deducted from the net sales to obtain the gross margin. The cost of goods sold can be computed quite easily in two steps as follows:

| (1) Finished goods available at the begining of the fiscal period | + | Cost of goods manufactured or purchased during the fiscal period | = | Cost of goods available for sale during the fiscal period |
| (2) Cost of goods available for sale during the fiscal period | − | Finished goods available at the end of the fiscal period | = | Cost of goods sold |

Gross Margin

The gross margin of $526,920 is equal to the net sales of $1,283,480 reduced by the cost of goods sold of $756,560. Gross margin measures the difference between the net revenue realized from the sale of goods and their cost. No final profit has been earned at this point, of course, because there are operating expenses and other revenue and expenses that must be considered. However, the gross margin is significant. The relationship between the gross margin and net sales may be expressed as a percentage. A comparison of gross margin percentages between years may reveal that selling prices are increasing or decreasing relative to the cost of goods sold. Or it may reveal a change in a mix of products sold. Under certain conditions, gross margin percentages can also be used to estimate the amount of inventory that should be available.

If an inventory has been destroyed or stolen, an insurance claim can be established by using the typical gross margin percentage to estimate the amount of the inventory loss. The cost of the goods sold up to the time of the loss is estimated to be equal to the complement of the gross margin percentage multiplied by net sales. The estimated cost of goods sold is then subtracted from the cost of the goods that were available for sale to arrive at an estimated cost of the inventory at the time of the loss. The cost of the goods available for sale is equal to the cost of the inventory at the beginning of the fiscal period plus the cost of purchases or goods manufactured to the point of the loss.

Operating Expenses

The expenses of operating the business are then classified according to functional purpose and are deducted from the gross margin to arrive at the operating income. Expenses of promoting, selling, and distributing products are classified as selling expenses and include such items as advertising, sales commissions, delivery expense, sales supplies used, travel and entertainment, and sales office rent. The general expenses of business administration are classified as general and administrative expenses and include such items as officers' salaries, office salaries, office supplies used, taxes, insurance and uncollectible accounts expense.

Other Revenue and Expense

Various incidental or miscellaneous revenue and expenses not related to the main operating purpose of the business are combined with the operating income in the computation of income before income tax. In this example, interest, dividends, and rents were earned, and interest expense was incurred.

Income Tax

Corporate federal income tax is as much an expense for an incorporated business as any other operating expense. Yet it is usually shown separately near the bottom of the statement because (1) it is based upon the taxable income or loss for the period, and (2) it is usually a significant amount.

Extraordinary Gains and Losses

Unusual gains and losses that are not expected to recur are shown as extraordinary gains and losses. The Accounting Principles Board has defined extraordinary items strictly.[3] In order to qualify as an extraordinary item, a transaction or event must be both unusual in nature and infrequent in occur-

---

[3]See *Opinions of the Accounting Principles Board, No. 30*, "Reporting the Results of Operations" (New York: American Institute of Certified Public Accountants, 1973), pars. 19-24.

rence; and the amount must be material. The definition of "unusual" depends upon the nature of the business and the environment in which it operates. For example, the gain or loss from the retirement of plant assets would not be considered unusual in most circumstances and, hence, should not be reported as an extraordinary gain or loss. On the other hand, a fire loss or a loss from some type of natural disaster, if material in amount and both unusual in nature and infrequent in occurrence, would be classified as extraordinary on the income statement. Extraordinary items are shown on the income statement net of the related income tax. Note, for example, that the fire loss on page 530 would have been $40,000 before tax.

Net Income

The final result on the income statement is labeled net income if the revenue and gains exceed the expenses and losses. Otherwise, the net result is labeled a net loss.

Earnings per Share

Those who read financial reports look for the earnings per share of stock. If there is only one class of stock outstanding with no complexities in the equity structure, the computation can be made quite easily by dividing the number of shares of outstanding stock into the net income. In the illustration given for Tobinton Products Inc., the earnings per share were computed at $23.90 ($119,500 net income ÷ 5,000 outstanding shares). With two or more classes of stock outstanding or with senior securities (bonds or preferred stock) that may be converted to common stock, the computation becomes more complicated. The rights to earnings by security holders other than the common stockholders must be considered before computing the earnings per share of common stock.

BALANCE SHEET, END OF FISCAL YEAR

A balance sheet for Tobinton Products Inc. at the end of the fiscal year April 30, 1985, is given on the next page.

A STATEMENT OF CHANGES IN RETAINED EARNINGS

The statement of changes in retained earnings connects the stockholders' equity in retained earnings as shown on the balance sheet with the results as shown on the income statement. Other additions or deductions are also shown in the computation of retained earnings at the end of the fiscal period.

A statement of changes in retained earnings for Tobinton Products Inc. is given on the succeeding page. The dividends are a distribution of earnings to the stockholders and are not an expense of doing business. Hence, they are deducted on the statement of changes in retained earnings.

Tobinton Products Inc.
Balance Sheet
April 30, 1985

Assets

Current assets:			
Cash		$ 40,680	
Marketable securities at cost (market value, $74,200)		71,740	
Notes receivable		14,000	
Accounts receivable	$ 94,380		
Less allowances for discounts, returns, allowances, and doubtful accounts	2,870	91,510	
Inventories		96,400	
Prepaid insurance		2,080	$316,410
Investment in bonds of Konrad Inc.			50,000
Plant assets:			
Land		$ 14,600	
Building and equipment	$381,150		
Less accumulated depreciation	45,390	335,760	350,360
Intangible assets:			
Organization expense		$ 2,450	
Goodwill		24,000	26,450
Other assets:			
Advances to company officers			8,500
Total assets			$751,720

Equities

Current liabilities:			
Bank loans		$ 10,000	
Accounts payable		31,250	
Accrued payroll and other expenses		25,420	
Estimated income tax payable		46,500	$113,170
Long-term notes, due August 31, 1988			75,000
Deferred rental revenue			2,700
Stockholders' equity:			
Capital stock, $10 par value, 5,000 shares issued and outstanding.		$ 50,000	
Premium on stock		82,500	
Retained earnings		428,350	560,850
Total equities			$751,720

Tobinton Products Inc.
Statement of Changes in Retained Earnings
For the Year Ended April 30, 1985

Balance of retained earnings, April 30, 1984	$392,850
Add net income for the year	119,500
	$512,350
Less dividends	84,000
Balance of retained earnings, April 30, 1985	$428,350

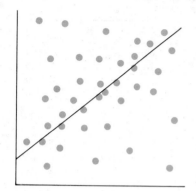

Appendix B

THE ACCOUNTING CYCLE: PRACTICE PROBLEMS

B-1. Recording Directly to Ledger Accounts. Frank Mussio began business on September 1, 19--, at a store on College Avenue. He sells jackets, shirts, and various novelties that are embossed with the university or fraternity insignia. Mussio deposited $4,600 in a separate bank account for store operations. A check for $1,700 was written for store fixtures and counters. Rent of $250 was paid by check for use of the store in September. Merchandise costing $3,300 was purchased on credit terms. During the month, cash sales of $5,900 were recorded on the cash register and deposited in the bank account for the store. A check in the amount of $280 was issued for supplies that were used during the month, and a check for $320 was for wages paid to a student who worked in the store during the evenings. A check for $2,100 was mailed to the supplier from whom the merchandise was purchased. At the end of the month, merchandise costing $800 was on hand. Depreciation on the counters and fixtures for the month has been estimated at $20.

Required:

(1) Record the transactions for the month of September directly directly in the ledger accounts. Use the ledger account titles given below:

Cash	Sales
Merchandise Inventory	Purchases
Store Fixtures	Cost of Goods Sold
Accumulated Depreciation	Wages Expense
— Store Fixtures	Rent Expense
Accounts Payable	Supplies Expense
Frank Mussio, Capital	Depreciation Expense
	— Store Fixtures

(2) Prepare an adjusted trial balance as of September 30, 19--.

(3) Prepare an income statement for month of September.

(4) Prepare a balance sheet as of September 30, 19--.

B-2. Journal Entries, Ledger, and Trial Balance. Eleanor Keefer owns and operates Western Record Store. A post-closing trial balance at June 30, 19--, is as follows:

Western Record Store
Post-Closing Trial Balance
June 30, 19--

	Dr.	Cr.
Cash	3,450	
Accounts Receivable	1,730	
Merchandise Inventory	2,340	
Accounts Payable		2,170
Eleanor Keefer, Capital		5,350
	7,520	7,520

Transactions for the month of July are summarized below. (Add ledger accounts as needed.)

(a) Merchandise costing $6,180 was purchased on credit terms.

(b) Rent for the store and equipment in the amount of $250 was paid for the month of July.

(c) Merchandise was sold to customers on credit terms in the amount of $8,740.

(d) Payment of wages for the month was made in the amount of $980.

(e) A payment of $90 was made for electric service in July.

(f) Cash of $9,300 was collected on accounts receivable.

(g) Keefer withdrew $1,500 during the month for personal use.

Required:

(1) Prepare journal entries to record the transactions.

(2) Record the balances at June 30 in ledger accounts. Post the journal entries to the ledger accounts.

(3) Prepare a trial balance at July 31.

B-3. Adjusting Entries and Adjusted Trial Balance. Transactions for the month of August 19--, have been recorded by journal entry and posted to the ledger accounts of Magill Furnishings. A trial balance at August 31, 19--, appears on page 634.

Data to be used for making adjustments are given below:

(a) Advertising used for the month amounted to $760, but only $680 of this amount was paid and recorded.

(b) Some of the equipment was rented to another store during the month at an agreed rental of $200 for the month. Magill did not collect any of the rent during the month.

(c) Customers paid $800 in advance for merchandise to be delivered at a later date. The collection was recorded as a credit to Advances from Customers. During August, deliveries of $650 were made against the advances.

Magill Furnishings
Trial Balance
August 31, 19--

	Dr.	Cr.
Cash	4,370	
Accounts Receivable	8,260	
Allowance for Doubtful Accounts		320
Merchandise Inventory, August 1	4,190	
Prepaid Insurance	330	
Equipment	11,400	
Accumulated Depreciation — Equipment.....................		1,500
Accounts Payable..		3,270
Advances from Customers.................................		800
Thomas Magill, Capital		12,920
Sales		43,700
Purchases	31,200	
Wages Expense	1,750	
Advertising Expense	680	
Utilities Expense...	330	
	62,510	62,510

(d) The prepaid insurance of $330 provides insurance coverage for 11 months.

(e) Depreciation for the month of August has been estimated at $50.

(f) It has been estimated that sales during August in the amount of $600 will not be collectible.

(g) Inventory at the end of August has been counted and assigned a cost of $3,840.

Required: Prepare a form with six columns and label the column headings as follows:

Accounts	Trial Balance		Adjustments		Adjusted Trial Balance	
	Dr.	Cr.	Dr.	Cr.	Dr.	Cr.

Copy the trial balance in the first pair of columns. Enter adjustment information as debits and credits in the second pair of columns opposite the appropriate accounts. Add account titles as necessary. Combine the data in the trial balance and adjustment columns and extend final amounts to the adjusted trial balance columns.

B-4. **Adjusting Entries by Type.** Information with respect to adjustment situations is given below for Castor Company:

(a) A building costing $850,000 was acquired on July 1, 19--. Estimates indicate that the building should have a useful life of 20 years with a salvage value of $50,000 at the end of the 20 years. The difference between the cost of the building and the salvage value is to be written off over the 20 years in equal annual amounts.

(b) Utility bills were paid in advance in the amount of $4,000 on January 1, 19--. During the year, the company used $3,720 of the utility service.

(c) Wages amounting to $47,800 were paid during the year. The employees earned an additional $630 that was not recorded or paid by December 31.

(d) A portion of a warehouse has been rented to Herd Company at an agreed monthly rental of $700. On October 1, Castor Company collected rent for the period extending from October 1 to February 28 of the following year and recorded the collection as a credit to Rent Collected in Advance.

(e) The inventory at January 1 was $15,800. Purchases during the year amounted to $106,000. At the end of the year, inventory was counted and given a cost of $14,900.

(f) Castor Company estimates that 2% of the credit sales of $195,000 will prove to be uncollectible.

Required: Prepare adjusting journal entries for each situation given. Identify each situation by type as a prepaid, accrual, valuation, or inventory adjustment.

B-5. Adjusting Entries and Statements. A trial balance is given for Selden Company at March 31, 19--. Financial statements and closing entries were last made on December 31 of the previous year.

COS = BI + Pur - END

Selden Company
Trial Balance
March 31, 19--

	Dr.	Cr.
Cash	14,300	
Accounts Receivable	17,600	
Merchandise Inventory	19,400	
Prepaid Rent	4,800	
Equipment	47,000	
Accumulated Depreciation — Equipment		8,000
Accounts Payable		15,300
Capital Stock		20,000
Retained Earnings		34,100
Sales		135,000
Purchases ....*CCS*	84,600	
Wages Expense	16,700	
Taxes and Insurance	4,300	
Heat and Light	3,700	
	212,400	212,400

Adjustment data are as follows:

(a) Rent has been prepaid for the entire year, beginning January 1.

(b) Total wages earned by employees amounted to $18,600 in the first quarter. A large portion of this amount has been paid and recorded.

(c) Depreciation of equipment for the quarter has been estimated at $500.

(d) The inventory at the end of March has been counted and assigned a cost of $20,800.

Required:

(1) Set up ledger accounts from the trial balance and enter balances at March 31.

(2) Enter adjustment data directly in the ledger accounts. Open up new ledger accounts as needed.

(3) Prepare an adjusted trial balance, an income statement for the first quarter of the year, and a balance sheet at March 31, 19--.

(4) Enter closing entries directly in the ledger accounts.

(5) Prepare a post-closing trial balance at March 31, 19--.

B-6. Financial Statements. An adjusted trial balance is given for Van Kirk Company with the accounts in random sequence.

Van Kirk Company
Adjusted Trial Balance
September 30, 19--

	Dr.	Cr.
Cost of Goods Sold	146,300	
Wages Expense	18,400	
Wages Payable		1,200
Accounts Payable		32,500
Notes Payable (long-term)		50,000
Land	6,000	
Accounts Receivable	19,200	
Cash	31,800	
Building and Equipment	145,000	
Sales		220,000
Advertising Expense	1,600	
Prepaid Rent	3,000	
Capital Stock, $1 par value		40,000
Rent Expense	1,200	
Depreciation Expense — Building and Equipment	3,000	
Merchandise Inventory, September 30	24,300	
Estimated Income Tax Payable		7,000
Accumulated Depreciation — Building and Equipment		18,000
Heat and Light Expense	2,600	
Taxes and Insurance Expense	3,400	
Income Tax Expense	17,000	
Dividends	10,000	
Retained Earnings		65,100
Interest Expense	1,000	
	433,800	433,800

Required: Prepare an income statement for the fiscal quarter ended September 30, and prepare a classified balance sheet for September 30.

B-7. Ledger-Adjusting and Closing. At the top of the next page, ledger accounts for Tri-City Appliance, Inc., are given after all transactions for the quarter ended June 30, 19--, have been recorded.

Adjustment data are given as follows:

(a) The insurance recorded as prepaid insurance provides protection from April 1 to December 31, 19--.

(b) Wages of $600 were earned by the employees at June 20 but were not paid or recorded by that date.

(c) Estimates indicate that 1% of the sales for the quarter will probably be uncollectible.

(d) Depreciation is recorded on the equipment at the rate of $300 per month.

(e) The inventory at June 30 has been counted and has been given a cost of $18,400.

Cash			Capital Stock		
15,000					20,000

Accounts Receivable			Retained Earnings		
21,000					43,400

Allowance for Doubtful Accounts			Sales		
		500			70,000

Merchandise Inventory			Purchases		
17,000			45,000		

Prepaid Insurance			Cost of Goods Sold		
900					

Equipment			Wages Expense		
40,000			7,000		

Accumulated Depreciation — Equipment			Rent Expense		
		4,500	300		

Accounts Payable			Insurance Expense		
		8,200			

Wages Payable			Depreciation Expense		

			Other Expenses		
			400		

Required:

(1) Copy the ledger accounts with the balances at June 30. Record adjusting entries directly in the ledger accounts. Add any additional accounts needed.

(2) Prepare an income statement for the quarter ended June 30, 19--, and a balance sheet at June 30, 19--.

(3) Record closing entries directly in the ledger accounts.

(4) Prepare a post-closing trial balance.

B-8. The Accounting Cycle. A post-closing trial balance for Angela Burns Inc. at June 30, 19-- is as follows:

Angela Burns Inc.
Post-Closing Trial Balance
June 30, 19--

	Dr.	Cr.
Cash..	14,100	
Accounts Receivable	36,500	
Allowance for Doubtful Accounts		600
Merchandise Inventory, June 30, 19--.............................	14,800	
Prepaid Rent	2,400	
Equipment..	56,000	
Accumulated Depreciation — Equipment		12,000
Accounts Payable		6,500
Notes Payable		30,000
Capital Stock		25,000
Retained Earnings		49,700
	123,800	123,800

Transactions for the following quarter ended September 30 are summarized:

(1) Sales to customers on credit terms amounted to $104,000.
(2) An accounts receivable in the amount of $200 was written off as uncollectible.
(3) Merchandise costing $58,000 was purchased on account.
(4) Wages of $8,100 were paid during the quarter for wages earned by employees.
(5) Cash of $93,700 was collected on the accounts receivable.
(6) Cash of $12,000 was paid to acquire new equipment.
(7) Advertising was used and paid for in the amount of $3,800.
(8) Heat and light expense for the quarter was paid for in the amount of $4,700.
(9) Income tax for the quarter has been estimated at $10,000.
(10) Payments on accounts payable during the quarter amounted to $61,000.
(11) Dividends of $4,000 were paid during the quarter. Record in an account entitled Dividends.

Adjustment data are given below.

(a) It has been estimated that sales in the amount of $1,000 will be uncollectible.
(b) The inventory at September 30 has been counted and assigned a cost of $15,600.
(c) Prepaid rent at June 30 consisted of rent for the last six months of the year.
(d) Depreciation on the equipment has been estimated at $1,400 for the quarter.
(e) Interest on the notes payable is at the annual rate of 8%.

Required:

(1) Prepare journal entries to record the transactions for the quarter ended September 30.
(2) Post the journal entries to ledger accounts. Set up ledger accounts as needed with beginning balances when appropriate.

(3) Prepare journal entries to record the adjustments for the quarter ended September 30.

(4) Post the journal entries to ledger accounts.

(5) Prepare an adjusted trial balance.

(6) Prepare an income statement for the quarter and a balance sheet at September 30, 19--.

(7) Prepare closing journal entries and post the entries to the ledger accounts.

(8) Prepare a post-closing trial balance at September 30, 19--.

Appendix C

THE PRESENT VALUE CONCEPT

TABLE I
Present Value of $1

Years Hence	4%	5%	6%	8%	10%	12%	14%	15%	16%	18%	20%	22%	24%	25%	26%	28%	30%	35%	40%
1	0.962	0.952	0.943	0.926	0.909	0.893	0.877	0.870	0.862	0.847	0.833	0.820	0.806	0.800	0.794	0.781	0.769	0.741	0.714
2	0.925	0.907	0.890	0.857	0.826	0.797	0.769	0.756	0.743	0.718	0.694	0.672	0.650	0.640	0.630	0.610	0.592	0.549	0.510
3	0.889	0.864	0.840	0.794	0.751	0.712	0.675	0.658	0.641	0.609	0.579	0.551	0.524	0.512	0.500	0.477	0.455	0.406	0.364
4	0.855	0.823	0.792	0.735	0.683	0.636	0.592	0.572	0.552	0.516	0.482	0.451	0.423	0.410	0.397	0.373	0.350	0.301	0.260
5	0.822	0.784	0.747	0.681	0.621	0.567	0.519	0.497	0.476	0.437	0.402	0.370	0.341	0.328	0.315	0.291	0.269	0.223	0.186
6	0.790	0.746	0.705	0.630	0.564	0.507	0.456	0.432	0.410	0.370	0.335	0.303	0.275	0.262	0.250	0.227	0.207	0.165	0.133
7	0.760	0.711	0.665	0.583	0.513	0.452	0.400	0.376	0.354	0.314	0.279	0.249	0.222	0.210	0.198	0.178	0.159	0.122	0.095
8	0.731	0.677	0.627	0.540	0.467	0.404	0.351	0.327	0.305	0.266	0.233	0.204	0.179	0.168	0.157	0.139	0.123	0.091	0.068
9	0.703	0.645	0.592	0.500	0.424	0.361	0.308	0.284	0.263	0.225	0.194	0.167	0.144	0.134	0.125	0.108	0.094	0.067	0.048
10	0.676	0.614	0.558	0.463	0.386	0.322	0.270	0.247	0.227	0.191	0.162	0.137	0.116	0.107	0.099	0.085	0.073	0.050	0.035
11	0.650	0.585	0.527	0.429	0.350	0.287	0.237	0.215	0.195	0.162	0.135	0.112	0.094	0.086	0.079	0.066	0.056	0.037	0.025
12	0.625	0.557	0.497	0.397	0.319	0.257	0.208	0.187	0.168	0.137	0.112	0.092	0.076	0.069	0.062	0.052	0.043	0.027	0.018
13	0.601	0.530	0.469	0.368	0.290	0.229	0.182	0.163	0.145	0.116	0.093	0.075	0.061	0.055	0.050	0.040	0.033	0.020	0.013
14	0.577	0.505	0.442	0.340	0.263	0.205	0.160	0.141	0.125	0.099	0.078	0.062	0.049	0.044	0.039	0.032	0.025	0.015	0.009
15	0.555	0.481	0.417	0.315	0.239	0.183	0.140	0.123	0.108	0.084	0.065	0.051	0.040	0.035	0.031	0.025	0.020	0.011	0.006
16	0.534	0.458	0.394	0.292	0.218	0.163	0.123	0.107	0.093	0.071	0.054	0.042	0.032	0.028	0.025	0.019	0.015	0.008	0.005
17	0.513	0.436	0.371	0.270	0.198	0.146	0.108	0.093	0.080	0.060	0.045	0.034	0.026	0.023	0.020	0.015	0.012	0.006	0.003
18	0.494	0.416	0.350	0.250	0.180	0.130	0.095	0.081	0.069	0.051	0.038	0.028	0.021	0.018	0.016	0.012	0.009	0.005	0.002
19	0.475	0.396	0.331	0.232	0.164	0.116	0.083	0.070	0.060	0.043	0.031	0.023	0.017	0.014	0.012	0.009	0.007	0.003	0.002
20	0.456	0.377	0.312	0.215	0.149	0.104	0.073	0.061	0.051	0.037	0.026	0.019	0.014	0.012	0.010	0.007	0.005	0.002	0.001
21	0.439	0.359	0.294	0.199	0.135	0.093	0.064	0.053	0.044	0.031	0.022	0.015	0.011	0.009	0.008	0.006	0.004	0.002	0.001
22	0.422	0.342	0.278	0.184	0.123	0.083	0.056	0.046	0.038	0.026	0.018	0.013	0.009	0.007	0.006	0.004	0.003	0.001	0.001
23	0.406	0.326	0.262	0.170	0.112	0.074	0.049	0.040	0.033	0.022	0.015	0.010	0.007	0.006	0.005	0.003	0.002	0.001	—
24	0.390	0.310	0.247	0.158	0.102	0.066	0.043	0.035	0.028	0.019	0.013	0.008	0.006	0.005	0.004	0.003	0.002	0.001	—
25	0.375	0.295	0.233	0.146	0.092	0.059	0.038	0.030	0.024	0.016	0.010	0.007	0.005	0.004	0.003	0.002	0.001	0.001	—
26	0.361	0.281	0.220	0.135	0.084	0.053	0.033	0.026	0.021	0.014	0.009	0.006	0.004	0.003	0.002	0.002	0.001	—	—
27	0.347	0.268	0.207	0.125	0.076	0.047	0.029	0.023	0.018	0.011	0.007	0.005	0.003	0.002	0.002	0.001	0.001	—	—
28	0.333	0.255	0.196	0.116	0.069	0.042	0.026	0.020	0.016	0.010	0.006	0.004	0.002	0.002	0.001	0.001	0.001	—	—
29	0.321	0.243	0.185	0.107	0.063	0.037	0.022	0.017	0.014	0.008	0.005	0.003	0.002	0.002	0.001	0.001	0.001	—	—
30	0.308	0.231	0.174	0.099	0.057	0.033	0.020	0.015	0.012	0.007	0.004	0.003	0.002	0.001	0.001	0.001	—	—	—
35	0.253	0.181	0.130	0.068	0.036	0.019	0.010	0.008	0.006	0.003	0.002	0.001	0.001	—	—	—	—	—	—
40	0.208	0.142	0.097	0.046	0.022	0.011	0.005	0.004	0.003	0.001	0.001	—	—	—	—	—	—	—	—
45	0.171	0.111	0.073	0.031	0.014	0.006	0.003	0.002	0.001	0.001	—	—	—	—	—	—	—	—	—
50	0.141	0.087	0.054	0.021	0.009	0.003	0.001	0.001	0.001	—	—	—	—	—	—	—	—	—	—

TABLE II

Present Value of $1 Received Annually for N Years

Years (N)	4%	5%	6%	8%	10%	12%	14%	15%	16%	18%	20%	22%	24%	25%	26%	28%	30%	35%	40%
1	0.962	0.952	0.943	0.926	0.909	0.893	0.877	0.870	0.862	0.847	0.833	0.820	0.806	0.800	0.794	0.781	0.769	0.741	0.714
2	1.886	1.859	1.833	1.783	1.736	1.690	1.647	1.626	1.605	1.566	1.528	1.492	1.457	1.440	1.424	1.392	1.361	1.289	1.224
3	2.775	2.723	2.673	2.577	2.487	2.402	2.322	2.283	2.246	2.174	2.106	2.042	1.981	1.952	1.923	1.868	1.816	1.696	1.589
4	3.630	3.546	3.465	3.312	3.170	3.037	2.914	2.855	2.798	2.690	2.589	2.494	2.404	2.362	2.320	2.241	2.166	1.997	1.849
5	4.452	4.330	4.212	3.993	3.791	3.605	3.433	3.352	3.274	3.127	2.991	2.864	2.745	2.689	2.635	2.532	2.436	2.220	2.035
6	5.242	5.076	4.917	4.623	4.355	4.111	3.889	3.784	3.685	3.498	3.326	3.167	3.020	2.951	2.885	2.759	2.643	2.385	2.168
7	6.002	5.786	5.582	5.206	4.868	4.564	4.288	4.160	4.039	3.812	3.605	3.416	3.242	3.161	3.083	2.937	2.802	2.508	2.263
8	6.733	6.463	6.210	5.747	5.335	4.968	4.639	4.487	4.344	4.078	3.837	3.619	3.421	3.329	3.241	3.076	2.925	2.598	2.331
9	7.435	7.108	6.802	6.247	5.759	5.328	4.946	4.772	4.607	4.303	4.031	3.786	3.566	3.463	3.366	3.184	3.019	2.665	2.379
10	8.111	7.722	7.360	6.710	6.145	5.650	5.216	5.019	4.833	4.494	4.192	3.923	3.682	3.571	3.465	3.269	3.092	2.715	2.414
11	8.760	8.306	7.887	7.139	6.495	5.938	5.453	5.234	5.029	4.656	4.327	4.035	3.776	3.656	3.544	3.335	3.147	2.752	2.438
12	9.385	8.863	8.384	7.536	6.814	6.194	5.660	5.421	5.197	4.793	4.439	4.127	3.851	3.725	3.606	3.387	3.190	2.779	2.456
13	9.986	9.394	8.853	7.904	7.103	6.424	5.842	5.583	5.342	4.910	4.533	4.203	3.912	3.780	3.656	3.427	3.223	2.799	2.468
14	10.563	9.899	9.295	8.244	7.367	6.628	6.002	5.724	5.468	5.008	4.611	4.265	3.962	3.824	3.695	3.459	3.249	2.814	2.477
15	11.118	10.380	9.712	8.559	7.606	6.811	6.142	5.847	5.575	5.092	4.675	4.315	4.001	3.859	3.726	3.483	3.268	2.825	2.484
16	11.652	10.838	10.106	8.851	7.824	6.974	6.265	5.954	5.669	5.162	4.730	4.357	4.033	3.887	3.751	3.503	3.283	2.834	2.489
17	12.166	11.274	10.477	9.122	8.022	7.120	6.373	6.047	5.749	5.222	4.775	4.391	4.059	3.910	3.771	3.518	3.295	2.840	2.492
18	12.659	11.690	10.828	9.372	8.201	7.250	6.467	6.128	5.818	5.273	4.812	4.419	4.080	3.928	3.786	3.529	3.304	2.844	2.494
19	13.134	12.085	11.158	9.604	8.365	7.366	6.550	6.198	5.877	5.316	4.844	4.442	4.097	3.942	3.799	3.539	3.311	2.848	2.496
20	13.590	12.462	11.470	9.818	8.514	7.469	6.623	6.259	5.929	5.353	4.870	4.460	4.110	3.954	3.808	3.546	3.316	2.850	2.497
21	14.029	12.821	11.764	10.017	8.649	7.562	6.687	6.312	5.973	5.384	4.891	4.476	4.121	3.963	3.816	3.551	3.320	2.852	2.498
22	14.451	13.163	12.042	10.201	8.772	7.645	6.743	6.359	6.011	5.410	4.909	4.488	4.130	3.970	3.822	3.556	3.323	2.853	2.498
23	14.857	13.489	12.303	10.371	8.883	7.718	6.792	6.399	6.044	5.432	4.925	4.499	4.137	3.976	3.827	3.559	3.325	2.854	2.499
24	15.247	13.799	12.550	10.529	8.985	7.784	6.835	6.434	6.073	5.451	4.937	4.507	4.143	3.981	3.831	3.562	3.327	2.855	2.499
25	15.622	14.094	12.783	10.675	9.077	7.843	6.873	6.464	6.097	5.467	4.948	4.514	4.147	3.985	3.834	3.564	3.329	2.856	2.499
26	15.983	14.375	13.003	10.810	9.161	7.896	6.906	6.491	6.118	5.480	4.956	4.520	4.151	3.988	3.837	3.566	3.330	2.856	2.500
27	16.330	14.643	13.211	10.935	9.237	7.943	6.935	6.514	6.136	5.492	4.964	4.524	4.154	3.990	3.839	3.567	3.331	2.856	2.500
28	16.663	14.898	13.406	11.051	9.307	7.984	6.961	6.534	6.152	5.502	4.970	4.528	4.157	3.992	3.840	3.568	3.331	2.857	2.500
29	16.984	15.141	13.591	11.158	9.370	8.022	6.983	6.551	6.166	5.510	4.975	4.531	4.159	3.994	3.841	3.569	3.332	2.857	2.500
30	17.292	15.373	13.765	11.258	9.427	8.055	7.003	6.566	6.177	5.517	4.979	4.534	4.160	3.995	3.842	3.569	3.332	2.857	2.500
35	18.665	16.374	14.498	11.655	9.644	8.176	7.070	6.617	6.215	5.539	4.992	4.541	4.164	3.998	3.845	3.571	3.333	2.857	2.500
40	19.793	17.159	15.046	11.925	9.779	8.244	7.105	6.642	6.234	5.548	4.997	4.544	4.166	3.999	3.846	3.571	3.333	2.857	2.500
45	20.720	17.774	15.456	12.108	9.863	8.283	7.123	6.654	6.242	5.552	4.999	4.545	4.166	3.999	3.846	3.571	3.333	2.857	2.500
50	21.482	18.256	15.762	12.234	9.915	8.304	7.133	6.661	6.246	5.554	4.999	4.545	4.167	4.000	3.846	3.571	3.333	2.857	2.500

INDEX

A

Absorption costing, 235, defined, 236
  and variable costing compared, 237
  income statement, 249
Accelerated cost recovery, 358
Accelerated depreciation, 475
  tax advantage of, 356
Account, contra asset, 605
Accountant, contribution of, 9
  illus., 10
Accounting, defined, 592
  double entry, 593
  regulation of, 2
  responsibility, 13, 19, defined, 33
  some difficulties with, 36
Accounting cycle, 592
Accounting data, use of, 19
  and prediction, 269
Accounting equation, 594
  and transactions, 595
Accounting, financial, 1
  managerial, 1
Accounting methods and estimates,
    variations in, 517
Accounting period, 602
Accounting procedures, payroll, 107
Accounts, 596
  chart of, 600

increases and decreases in, 597
use of, 597
Accounts receivable turnover, 523
Accrual adjustments, 603
Accrual principle, 617
Accrue, defined, 603
Acid-test and current ratios, 522
Adjusted trial balance, 608
Adjusting process, 602
Adjustments, accrual, 603
  depreciation, 604
  inventory, 605
  prepayment, 603, defined, 604
  valuation, 606
Administrative and general expense budget,
    441
  illus., 442
Administrative expenses, 628
Allocation, basis of, 304
Allocation problem, 304
Allocations, cost, 30
  illus., 31
Alternatives, available, 266
  choosing best, 267
  evaluating, 267, 270
  identification of, 267
Alternatives and problem, 268
Analysis, break-even, 277, defined, 200
  an alternative form of, 204

comprehensive, 516
cost-volume-profit, 200
form of, 277
some hazards of, 516
total vs. incremental, 278
Analysis of noncurrent items, 556
Analysis of other current items, 565
Anticipation of change, 367
Asset account, contra, 605
Asset base, 507
Asset replacement, plant, 485
Asset turnover, current, 521
Asset turnover and rate of return, 507
Asset valuation, 619
Assets, 592, 594
    combination of, 509
    current, 620
    depreciable, 511
    fixed, 604, 621
    immediate expensing of, 360
    intangible, 622
    management of, 508
    net, 595
    other, 623
    plant, 604, 621
    rate of return, 505
Assets and equities, character of, 473
Attainable standards, 97
Audit, post, 368
Average, 169
Average concept, 517
Avoidable costs, 275, 300, 351

B

Balance, trial, 601
Balance of sales and production, 239
Balance sheet, *illus.*, 609
    comparative, 554
    end of fiscal year, 629
    estimated, 449
    illus., 450
    pro forma, 449
Balance sheet analysis, *illus.*, 518
    Balance sheet classifications, 619

illus., 620
Balancing order and storage costs, 111
Bargained or negotiated market price, 391
Base year, 519
Basic concepts, 612
Basic standards, 98
Benefits, fringe, 108
Book value, net, 605
    per share, 516
Bogies, 98
Break-even analysis, an alternative form of, 204
    defined, 200
    use of, 277
Break-even chart, 201
    cost detail on the, 201, *illus.*, 202
    illus., 203
Break-even point, defined, 200, 247
Budget, 6, 24
    capital expenditure, 443
    capital investment, defined, 13
    cash payments, 445, *illus.*, 446
    cash receipts, 443, *illus.*, 445
    control, 10, 12
    defined, 11, 417
    direct labor, 347
    direct materials, 434
    factory overhead, 438
    general and administrative expense, 441, *illus.*, 442
    manufacturing cost, defined, 434
    master plan, 14
    personal attitudes, 13
    preparation of, 15
    product, 12
    production, 425
    progressive, 15
    project, 12
    purchases, 435
    responsibility, defined, 12
    rolling, 15
    sales, 422
    selling expense, 440
    summary cash, 446
Budget, flexible, 65, *illus.*, 66
    and variances, 134

summarized, *illus.*, 134
Budgetary control, defined, 11
Budgeting, scope of, 12
Budgeting by computer, 14
Budgeting process, *illus.*, 11
Budget period, 14
Budget rate, 65
Budgets, advantages of, 11
    use of, 452
Budget slack, 13
Budget variances and variable costing, 248
Budget work sheet, 451
    illus., 452
Bulletin standards, 98
Business transaction, 594

C

Calculating order and storage costs, 112
Capacity, normal, 71, 139
    practical, 71
    practical plant, defined, 139
Capacity and control, plant, 138
Capacity variance, 69, 137, 237
Capital, 594
    sources of net working, 550
Capital budget, defined, 443
Capital budgeting, defined, 331
Capital budgeting process, defined, 345
Capital flows, significance of net working, 579
    working, 549
Capital investment, 334
Capital investment budget, 13
Capital investment decision, 322
Capital investment decisions, comparison of with decisions not involving capital investment, 344
Capital investments in not-for-profit organizations, 335
Capital stock, 612, 625
Cash and operations, 561
Cash budget, summary, 446
Cash flow, 559
    statement of, 565

Cash flow from operations, 566
Cash payments budget, 445
    illus., 446
Cash receipts and disbursements, statement of, 547, 560
Cash receipts budget, 443
    illus., 445
Change, anticipation of, 367
Changes in financial position, statement of, 547, 558
    illus., 559
Chart of accounts, 600
Classification, natural, defined, 41
Classification by function, defined, 41
Closing procedure, 610
Coefficient of determination, 179
Combination decisions, 10
Commercial enterprise, 5
Committed costs, defined, 44
Common stock, 612
Companies, differences between, 517
Company evaluation, 525
Compound amount, 324
Comprehensive analysis, 516
Conservatism, 618
Consistency, 615
Constant dollar, current cost statements, 482, *illus.*, 484
    historical cost, statements, 476, *illus.*, 477
Constant dollars, 472
Continuing operation, income from, 506
Contra asset account, 605
Contribution margin, 238
    division, 385
Control, 18
    cost, 380
    costs and, 28
    labor standards, 105
    plant, 138
    profit, 380
Control and planning decisions, 6
Control budget, 12
Control features, 37
Controllable costs, defined, 32
Controllable profit, division, 384
Controllable variance, 135, 136

Controller, defined, 3
  organization under, *illus.*, 4
Control limits, 172
Control of factory overhead, 67
Control standards, 99
Control system, criteria needed for, 380
Corporation, 611
Cost, decremental, defined, 25
  defined, 24, 613
  differential, defined, *illus.*, 18, 25
  direct, 237, defined, 30
  fixed, 25
  full, defined, 17, 301
  incremental, defined, 25
  indirect, defined, 30
  job order, 61, 71
  opportunity, 275, 293, defined, *illus.*, 27
  period, defined, 41
  product, defined, 41
  relevant, 272
  standard, *illus.*, 141
  sunk, 275, defined, *illus.*, 26
  transfer price based on, 392
  uncontrollable, defined, 32
  variable, defined, 25
  see also Costs
Cost accounting beyond the manufacturing
    area, 41
Cost allocations, 30
  illus., 31
Cost behavior options, 167
Cost-benefit, 146
Cost budget, manufacturing, defined, 434
Cost concepts, 24
Cost control, 380
Cost elements, 42, 79
Cost estimates of production order, *illus.*,
    68
Cost flow, process, 75
Costing, absorption, 235, defined, 236
  direct, 237
  full, defined, 236
  variable, 237
Costing direct labor, 61
Costing direct materials, 61
Costing factory overhead, 64

Costing fixed overhead, *illus.*, 69
Costing procedure, *illus.*, 43
Cost of goods sold, 627
Cost overrun, 64
Cost pricing, variable, 305
Cost problem, fixed, 301
Cost reports, *illus.*, 34, 35
Cost responsibility, defined, 33
Costs, avoidable, 275, 300, 351
  balancing of order and storage, 111
  calculating order and storage, 112
  committed, defined, 44
  controllable, defined, 32
  decision making, *illus.*, 27
  differential, 272
  discretionary, 44
  fixed, 166, defined, 44
  human elements of, 38
  managed, 44
  noncontrollable, 32
  nonmanufacturing, 144
  opportunity, 26
  semivariable, 167, defined, 44
  standard, 94
  sunk, 26
  unavoidable, 300
  variable, 166, 208, defined, 44, *illus.*, 209
  see also Cost
Costs and charges, responsibility of, 38
Costs and control, 28
Cost segregation, 167
Costs for planning, 24
Costs matched against revenues, 474
Cost standard, defined, 29
Cost system, process, 75
Credit, 596
Criterion, evaluation, 400
Current and acid-test ratios, 522
Current assets, 620
  additional investment in, 352
Current asset turnover, 521
Current cost, constant dollar statements,
    482, *illus.*, 484
  historical cost statements, 480, *illus.*, 481
Current costs, 472
Current items, analysis of, 565

Current liabilities, defined, 623
Current ratio, defined, 522
Curvature of revenue and cost lines, *illus.*, 204
Curve, learning, 117
   illus., 118
Cycle, operating, 621

D

Data, relevant, defined, 270
Debit, 596
Decentralized company, 379
Decision, how-to-produce, 397
   pricing, 301
   product combination, 294
   variable or fixed cost, 214
Decision making, an overview, 266
   alternatives available, 266
   choosing best alternative, 267
   consequences of actions, 267
   evaluating alternatives, 267
   problem, 266
   transfer prices for, 395
   variable costing in planning, 247
Decision making costs, *illus.*, 27
Decision rule, 266, 294
Decisions, classified by function and time element, 8
   combination, 10
   planning and control, 6
   specialized, 17
Decreases in accounts, 597
Decremental cost, defined, 25
Deductions, depreciation under current tax law, 358
Deferred revenue, 624
Deficit, 625
Demand, derived, defined, 419
Demand for net working capital, 558
Departmental production report, 75
Depreciable assets, 511
Depreciation, 604
   accelerated, 475
   defined, 354

   straight line, 354
   sum-of-the-years-digits, 356
   tax advantage of accelerated, 356
Depreciation adjustment, 604
Depreciation deductions under the current tax law, 358
Depreciation expense, 604
Derived demand, defined, 419
Description and evaluation of statements, 548
Differences between companies, 517
Differential cost, defined, 18, 25
   illus., 18, 25
Differential costs, 25, 272
   review of other cost concepts useful for predicting, 274
Differential revenue, defined, 18
   illus., 18
Direct cost, 237
   defined, 30
Direct costing, 237
Direct labor, 42, 61, 509
   costing, 61
Direct labor budget, 437
Direct labor cost, *illus.*, 64
Direct labor hours, *illus.*, 64
Direct materials, 42, 61, 509
   costing, 61
   illus., 63
Direct profit, division, 384
Discounted rate of return method, 348
Discounting, defined, 327
Discount rate, 327
Discretionary costs, 44
Distress pricing, 305
Distribution, normal, defined, 170
   illus., 173
Dividend policy, 486
Division contribution margin, 385
Division controllable profit, 384
Division controllable profit as an evaluation index, 385
Division direct profit, 384
Division investment, determining, 387
Division net profit, 383
Document, source, 596

Dollar discount, defined, 327
Double-entry accounting, 593
Duality, 592
Dual transfer prices, 393
Dumping, 306

E

Earning power, 519
Earnings, reinvested, 625
    retained, 612, 625
Earnings and market value of stock, 515
Earnings per share, 515, 629
Efficiency variance, 105, 136
    labor, defined, 106
Entry, journal, 599
Equation, accounting, 594
Equities, 592, 594
Equities and assets, character of, 473
Equity, owners', 624
    stockholders', 624
Equity relationships, 524
Equivalent unit, 78
Estimated balance sheet, 449
    illus., 450
Estimated conditional standard deviation,
    defined, 173
    illus., 174
Estimated income statement, 447
    illus., 449
Evaluation and description of statements,
    548
Evaluation criterion or standard, 400
Evaluation index, division controllable
    profit, 385
Evaluation of company, 525
Evaluation process, 366
Exception, management by, defined, 453
Expense, defined, 595
    depreciation, 604
    organization, 623
Expense budget, general and administrative,
    441
    illus., 442
    selling, 440

Expenses, general and administrative, 628
    operating, 628
    selling, 628
Expensing of assets, immediate, 360
Extraordinary gains and losses, 628

F

Factory overhead, 510
    control of, 67
    costing, 64
Factory overhead budget, 438
Favorable variance, 70, 99
Fifo, defined, 40
    first-in, first-out, 616
Finance, 3
Financial accounting, 1, 2
Financial decision examples, 331
Financial planning, 446
Financial position, statement of changes in,
    547, 558
    illus., 559
Financial statements, 608
Firm, organization of, 2
Firm organization, illus., 3
First-in, first-out (fifo), 616
First-in, first-out inventory method (fifo),
    defined, 40
Fiscal period, 602, 615
Fiscal year, 615
Fixed assets, 604, 621
Fixed charges and net income, 525
Fixed cost problem, 301
Fixed costs, 25, 166, 213
    defined, 44
    troublesome, 45
Fixed or variable cost decision, 214
Fixed overhead, costing, illus., 69
Flexible budget, 65
Flexible budget and variances, 134
Flow, cash, 559
Forecasting, sales, 417
Franchises, 622
Fringe benefits, 108
Full cost, defined, 17, 301

price based on, 301
Full costing method, defined, 236
Function, classification by, defined, 41
Future cash flows, present value of, 328
Future value and present value,
    comparison, series of cash flows, 330
Future value of money, 324

G

Gains and losses, extraordinary, 628
  holding, 486
General and administrative expense budget,
  441
  illus., 442
General and administrative expenses, 628
General journal, 599
Going concern, 612
Goods sold, cost of, 627
Goodwill, 623
Governmental and not-for-profit entities,
  146
Governmental unit, 5
Gross margin, 627

H

High-low point method, 170
Historical cost, constant dollar statements,
  476
  illus., 477
Historical cost, current cost statements, 480
  illus., 481
Holding gains and losses, 486
How-to-produce decision, 397
Human elements of costs, 38

I

Incentives, 109
Income, net, 608, 629
  residual, defined, 389
Income from continuing operation, 506

Income measurement, 39
Income statement, 608
  estimated, 447, *illus.*, 449
  pro forma, 447
Income statement classifications, 626
Income tax, 628
Income tax effects, 354
Incorporated, 611
Increases in accounts, 597
Incremental cost, defined, 25
Incremental returns, 364
Incremental vs. total analysis, 278
Index, profit, 382
Indirect cost, defined, 30
Indirect labor, 42
Indirect materials, 42
Intangible assets, 622
Interest, undivided, 619
Interest rate, approximation of, 334
Intermediate market case, 396
Internal rate of return, defined, 334
Intracompany or transfer pricing, 389
Inventories and production, 424
Inventory, lifo, 475
  periodic, 606
  perpetual, 605
  units, *illus.*, 114
Inventory adjustment, 605
Inventory and profits, 244
Inventory flow, manufacturing, *illus.*, 40
  merchandise, *illus.*, 39
Inventory level, 103
Inventory method, (fifo), defined, 40
Inventory method, (lifo), defined, 40
Inventory turnover, defined, 524
Investment, net, defined, 346
  refining the, 351
  return on, 388
Investment alternatives, rating, 347
Investment base, defined, 387
Investment capital budget, 13
Investment decision, capital, 322
  noncapital, 322
Investment in additional current assets, 352
Investments, 621
Investment tax credit, 360

J

Job order, 61
Job order cost, 61, 71
Journal, 598
  general, 599
  special, 600
Journal entry, 599

L

Labor, 116
  direct, 42, 61, 509
  indirect, 42
Labor budget, direct, 437
Labor cost, additions to, 108
  direct, *illus.*, 64
Labor efficiency variance, defined, 106
Labor hours, direct, *illus.*, 64
Labor rate variance, defined, 105
Labor standards and control, 105
Last-in, first-out inventory method (lifo),
    defined, 40
Last-in, first-out (lifo), 616
Lead time, 114
Learning curve, 117
  illus., 118
Learning phase, 117
Least-cost decisions, 271
Least squares method, 170
Levels of management, 6
Leverage, 512
  or trading on the equity, 513
Liabilities, 592, 594
  current, defined, 623
  long term, 624
  other, 624
Lifo, defined, 40
  last-in, first-out, 616
Lifo inventory, 475
Line of regression, 168, 170
Long term liabilities, 624
Long term plans, 219
Loose standards, 97
Loss, net, 608

Losses and gains, extraordinary, 628
  holding, 486
Lowest acceptable rate of return, 347

M

Managed costs, 44
Management, levels of, 6
  objective of, 5
Management by exception, 95
  defined, 453
Management planning and control, *illus.*, 7
Managerial accounting, 1
  defined, 4
  scope of, 4
Managerial policy and price level, 485
Manufacturing cost budget, defined, 434
Manufacturing inventory flow, *illus.*, 40
Manufacturing margin, 238
Margin, division contribution, 385
  gross, 627
Market case, intermediate, 396
Market demand curve, 271
Market demand function, 271
Market price, 390
  negotiated or bargained, 391
Market value of stock and earnings, 515
Markup pricing method, 301
Matching, 615
Materials, 111
  direct, 42, 61, 509
  illus., 63
Materials acquisition, 103
Materials budget, direct, 434
Materials, indirect, 42
Materials price variance, 99
Materials quantity variance, 101
Materials standards, 99
Materials standards control, 99
Materials usage, 101
Merchandise inventory flow, *illus.*, 39
Merchandising and service entities, 145
Mixture of valuations, 517
Models for planning, 419
Monetary items, 473

Money, present value of, 326
    time value of, 323, 345
Multiple regression, 183

                    N

Natural classification, defined, 41
Negotiated or bargained market price, 391
Net assets, 595
Net book value, 605
Net income, 608, 629
Net income and fixed charges, 525
Net investment, defined, 346
Net loss, 608
Net proceeds from the sale of other
    properties, 353
Net profit, division, 383
Net return, defined, 347
Net working capital, defined, 521
    demand for, 558
    schedule of changes in, *illus.*, 555
    sources and uses of, 553
    sources of, 550
    statement of sources and uses of, 547,
        558
    uses of, 552
Net working capital flows, significance of,
    549
Net working capital from operations, 555
Noncapital investment decision, 322
Noncontrollable costs, 32
Noncurrent items, analysis of, 556
Nonmanufacturing costs, 144
Nonmonetary items, defined, 474
Normal capacity, 71, 139
Normal distribution, defined, 170
    illus., 173
Normal volume, 303
Not-for-profit and governmental entities,
    146
Not-for-profit entity, 335
Not-for-profit organizations, capital
    investments in, 335

                    O

Objective of management, 5
On-line, real-time system, defined, 96
Operating cycle, 621
Operating expenses, 628
Operating revenue, 627
Operations, cash flow from, 566
Operations and cash, 561
Opportunity cost, 275, 293
    defined, 27
    illus., 27
Opportunity costs, 26
Order, time to, 113
Order and storage costs, balancing of, 111
    calculating, 112
Organization expense, 623
Organization of firm, 2
Other assets, 623
Other liabilities, 624
Other revenue and expense, 628
Overabsorbed variance, 70
Overapplied variance, 70
Overhead, control of factory, 67
    costing fixed, *illus.*, 69
    factory, 42, 438, 510
Overhead costing, factory, 64
Overhead rate, 65
Overhead variance, disposition of, 69
Overhead variances, 135
    summary of, 140
Owners' equity, 592, 594, 624

                    P

Paid-in capital in excess of par value, 625
Paid-in capital in excess of stated value,
    625
Partnership, 611
Patents, 622
Payback method, 347
Payroll accounting procedures, 107
Percentage-of-completion, 614
Period, accounting, 602
    fiscal, 602, 615

Period cost, defined, 41
Periodic inventory, 606
Periodicity, 614
Perpetual inventory, 605
Planning, 10
   costs for, 24
   financial, 446
   models for, 419
   variable costing in decision making, 247
Planning and control decisions, 6
Plant asset replacement, 485
Plant assets, 604, 621
Plant capacity, 138
   practical, 139
Plant control, 138
Point of indifference, defined, 215
Policy, price, 210
Post audit, 368
Posting, 600
Posting reference column, 600
Practical capacity, 71
Practical plant capacity, 139
Prediction, importance of, 269
Prediction and accounting data, 269
Preferred stock, 612
Premium on stock, 625
Preparation of budgets, 15
Prepayment adjustments, 603
   defined, 604
Present value, net, 350
Present value analysis applied, 331
Present value and future value, comparison, series of cash flows, 330
Present value of a future amount, 326
Present value of a series of future cash flows, 328
Present value of money, 326
Price, market, 390
Price, outside influences on, 309
Price, transfer, based on cost, 392
Price based on full cost, 301
Price level and managerial policy, 485
Price policy, 210
Prices, dual transfer, 393
   transfer, for decision making, 395
Price variance, 99

materials, 99
Pricing, distress and special order, 305
   intracompany or transfer, 389
   markup method, 301
   variable cost, 305
Pricing decision, 301
Problem and alternatives, 268
Process, adjusting, 602
Process cost flow, 75
Process cost system, 75
Process or sell, 293
Procurement period, defined, 104
Product budget, 12
Product combination decision, 294
Product combinations, 294
   illus., 297, 298
Product cost, defined, 41
Production, 344
Production and inventories, 424
Production and sales, 423
   balance of, 239
   out of balance, 241
Production budget, 425
Production order, 61
   cost estimates of, illus., 68
   illus., 62, 73
Production or sales, 245
Production report, 75
   departmental, 75
Product line, elimination of, 300
Products, regular, 308
Profit, division controllable, 384
   division direct, 384
Profit control, 380
Profit index, 382
Profits and inventory, 244
Profit-volume graph, 206
   illus., 207, 209, 212, 213, 218, 219
Pro forma balance sheet, 449
Pro forma income statement, 447
Progressive budget, 15
Project budget, 12
Proprietorship, 611
Purchase budget, 435
Purchasing power gain or loss, 478

Q

Quality of standards, 96
Quantity variance, 99
  accounting for, 102
  materials, 101
Quick assets, 523

R

r^2 test, 179
Rate of return, assets, 505
  discounted method, 348
  lowest acceptable, 347
Rate of return and asset turnover, 507
Rate of return by segment, 510
Rate-of-return concept, 505
Rate variance, 105
  labor, defined, 105
Realization concept, 613
Reference column, posting, 600
Refining the investment, 351
Regression, line of, 168, 170
  illus., 169, 173
  multiple, 183
Regular products, 308
Regulation of accounting, 2
Reinvested earnings, 625
Relevant cost, 272
  illus., 34, 35
Relevant data, defined, 270
Relevant revenues, 271
Residual income, defined, 389
Responsibility accounting, 13, 19
  defined, 33
  some difficulties with, 36
Responsibility, cost, defined, 33
Responsibility budget, 12
Retained earnings, 612, 625
  statement of changes in, 629
Return on investment, 388
Revenue, 617
  deferred, 624
  defined, 595
  differential, defined, 18

illus., 18
  operating, 627
Revenues, recent costs matched against, 474
Revenues, relevant, 271
Revising standards, 98
Rolling budget, 15

S

Sale of other properties, net proceeds from, 353
Sales, 595
  wide variety of factors affecting, 418
Sales and production, 423
  balance of, 239
  out of balance, 241
Sales budget, 422
Sales forecasting, 417
Sales forecasts, basis for, 418
Sales mix, changes in, 216
Sales or production, 245
Sales volume, 207
Scarce factor, 344
Selling expense budget, 440
Selling expenses, 628
Sell or process, 293
Semivariable costs, 167
  defined, 44
Service and merchandising entities, 145
Share, earnings per, 629
Shipping routes, 115
Short-term plans, 219
Source document, 596
Sources and uses of net working capital,
  comprehensive illus., 553
  statement of, 547, 558
Sources of net working capital, 550
Special journals, 600
Special order pricing, 305
Spending variance, 135
Standard, 93
  cost, defined, 29
  evaluation, 400
Standard cost, *illus.*, 141
Standard cost accounting, advantages, 95

Standard costs, 94
  control of, 95
  variations of, 95
Standard deviation, defined, 173
  estimated conditional, defined, 173
  illus., 174
Standards, attainable, 97
  basic, 98
  bulletin, 98
  control, 99
  loose, 97
  materials, 99
  quality of, 96
  revising, 98
  strict, 96
  use of, 94
Standards and control, labor, 105
Stated value, paid-in capital in excess of,
  625
Statement, income, 608
Statement of cash flow, 565
Statement of cash receipts and
  disbursements, 547
Statement of changes in financial position,
  547, 558
  illus., 559
Statement of changes in retained earnings,
  629
Statement of sources and uses of net
  working capital, 547, 558
Statements, description and evaluation of,
  548
  financial, 608
Static phase, 117
Stock, capital, 612, 625
  common, 612
  preferred, 612
  premium on, 625
Stockholders' equity, 624
Storage and order costs, balancing of, 111
  calculating, 112
Straight line depreciation, 354
Straight-line method, 605
Strict standards, 96
Summary cash budget, 446
Summary of overhead variances, 140

Summary of variances, 110
Sum-of-the-years-digits (SYD) depreciation,
  356
Sunk cost, 26, 275
  defined, 26
  illus., 26

                           T

Tax, income, 628
Tax advantage of accelerated depreciation,
  356
Tax credit, investment, 360
Tax law, depreciation deductions under the
  current, 358
Tax options, 361
Time scale, *illus.*, 114
Time value of money, 323, 345
Timing concept, 15
Total vs. incremental analysis, 278
Trading on the equity or leverage, 513
Transaction, accounting, 594
  business, 594
Transfer or intracompany pricing, 389
Transfer price based on cost, 392
Transfer prices, dual, 393
Transfer prices for decision making, 95
Transportation model, 116
Treasurer, defined, 3
Trial balance, 601
  adjusted, 608
Turnover, accounts receivable, 523
  current asset, 521
  inventory, defined, 524

                           U

Unavoidable costs, 300
Uncontrollable cost, defined, 32
Underabsorbed variance, 70
Underapplied variance, 70
Undivided interest, 619
Unfavorable variance, 70, 99
Units, inventory, *illus.*, 114

Usage, materials, 101
Use of accounts, 597
Use of budgets, 452
Uses and sources of net working capital,
    statement of, 547
Uses of net working capital, 552

V

Valuation, 619
Valuation adjustments, 606
Valuations, mixture of, 517
Value, net book, 605
Variable and absorption costing compared,
    237
Variable costing, 237
    advantages of, 245
    disadvantages of, 246
Variable costing and budget variances, 248
Variable costing in planning and decision
    making, 247
Variable cost per unit, defined, 25
Variable cost pricing, 305
Variable costs, 166, 208
    defined, 44
    illus., 209
Variable or fixed cost decision, 214
Variance, accounting for quantity, 102
    capacity, 69, 137, 237
    controllable, 135, 136
    efficiency, 105, 136
    favorable, 70, 99
    labor efficiency, defined, 106
    labor rate, 105
    materials price, 99
    materials quantity, 101

    overabsorbed, 70
    overapplied, 70
    price, 99
    quantity, 99
    rate, 105
    spending, 135
    underabsorbed, 70
    underapplied, 70
    unfavorable, 70, 99
    volume, 69, 137
Variances, overhead, 135
    summary of, 110
    summary of overhead, 140
Variances and flexible budget, 134
Variations, 93
Visual fit, 168
Volume, normal, 303
    sales, 207
Volume variance, 69, 137

W

Working capital, defined, 521
    management of, 521
    net, defined, 521
    sources of net, 550
    use of net, 552
Working capital flows, 549
    significance of net, 549
Work sheet, budget, 451
    illus., 452

Y

Year, fiscal, 615